HANDLOADING

HANDLOADING

By Wm. C. Davis, Jr.

Published by the
National Rifle Association of America
Washington, D.C.

NRA BOOKS — Bill Askins, *Director;* Ted Bryant, *Editor;* Mike Fay, *Production Chief;*
Angel Guzman, *Art Director;* Gerald B. Howard, Jr., *Copy Editor;* Cover photo by Gary Putnam
Copyright © 1981 by the National Rifle Association of America
All rights reserved including the right to reproduce this
book or portions thereof in any form.
Library of Congress Catalog Card Number 79-93175.
Published January 1981.
ISBN 0-935998-34-9
Printed in the United States of America.

CONTENTS

CONTENTS

CONTENTS

CONTENTS

CONTENTS

CONTENTS

CONTENTS

CONTENTS

FOREWORD

When the NRA Book Service was rejuvenated in mid-1978, the first project considered was a rewrite of the old standard of the reloading field, the *NRA Handloader's Guide*.

I blithely projected publication in less than a year and dragooned my esteemed technical colleague, Bill Davis, into writing new text, revising the old and generally charged him with producing the finest book of its sort, one that NRA and the shooting fraternity could use for many years as the standard reference on handloading.

Bill Davis was clearly the best person to undertake this massive endeavor. He is a professional engineer and handloader with more than 30 years experience. He has contributed to the *American Rifleman* since 1949 and has served as a contributing editor since 1974. His text is in language that handloaders understand, but written from the authoritative viewpoint of a professional engineer who has long experience in the principal ballistics laboratories of the government and the research-and-development departments of the firearms industry.

Publication of this new handloading book developed into a massive project, took much longer than anticipated, and is a real labor of love on the part of all of us. Kudos must go to Bill Davis for his thoroughness, the tech staff for their review, and Ted Bryant for the massive editing job.

So here it is with the best wishes of the NRA Book Service. We know you'll enjoy it.

Bill Askins

Bill Askins

WARNING

The loads listed throughout this book are believed to be safe and satisfactory loads when properly assembled, and fired in sound firearms of the appropriate types, in good mechanical condition. All technical data conveyed in this book reflect the experience of persons using specific equipment and components under specific circumstances. However, because of unavoidable variations in handloading components used in various combinations, and the firearms in which the handloaded ammunition may be fired, neither the National Rifle Association of America, or any of the manufacturers whose products are listed, or publishers whose data are quoted from original sources, can assume any responsibility for any consequence of using the information in the following pages or data tables. The data are furnished for the information and use of handloaders, entirely at the user's own risk, initiative and responsibility.

PREFACE

Handloaders in America today are certainly the most fortunate in the world. Handloading here has not been subjected to the strangling interference of government restrictions that have virtually eliminated it in some other countries of the world, owing largely to the vigilance of you, the shooters, the NRA, and other organizations who defend our right to enjoy the shooting sports. American handloaders certainly have more firms catering to their requirements than have the handloaders anywhere else in the world. Three giant industrial firms in the U.S. produce and market no less than 31 types of powder specifically for handloading. In addition, domestic, foreign and military surplus powders marketed by other U.S. firms supply 28 more types especially for handloading. The major ammunition producers, once committed to discouraging the practice of handloading, now produce primers, cases and bullets for practically every reasonably common cartridge, and now actively support handloading. Bullet manufacturers supply hundreds of different types of bullets, suitable for practically any conceivable purpose, available especially for handloaders. The manufacturers of handloading equipment supply a huge variety of tools, from simple and inexpensive ones to highly sophisticated ones, at very reasonable prices. Finally, the manufacturers of reloading components and equipment supply extensive literature on reloading, and specific data for literally thousands of different loads, carefully developed at great expense, and made available free or at very moderate cost.

This book is not presented as a book to be owned *instead* of any of the other excellent reloading handbooks and manuals, but *in addition* to them. It is, in fact, only through the generous cooperation of the other publishers of handloading data that publication of this book, in its present form, has been possible.

This book is in two parts. The first is a series of articles on handloading and related subjects, that we believe will be interesting and useful to handloaders, from beginners to those of long experience. This material is original with the NRA, consisting of the most useful and still timely articles from the previous *NRA Handloader's Guide* (updated for present conditions), articles previously published in *The American Rifleman*, and a considerable amount of new material that has not previously been published. This material has been selected on the basis of essentiality to the safe and enjoyable practice of handloading, and on reader interest as we perceive it from the thousands of handloading questions received each year by the Dope Bag information service, provided to NRA members through *The American Rifleman*. We hope you will enjoy these articles, and find them useful.

The second part of this book consists of specific loading data, and it is for this part that we are deeply grateful to the other sources for their generous cooperation. When this book was conceived, it was recognized that the laboratory resources of the NRA were not sufficient for the development of loading data on even a representative sample of the hundreds of different components now available to handloaders. Indeed, it seemed wasteful and unnecessary to duplicate the effort of thousands of man-hours that have been devoted to developing excellent data by all the producers of reloading components, equipment, and other books on handloading. Accordingly, the NRA sought the assistance of these other producers, in a cooperative effort to produce a new NRA reloading book, to replace the *NRA Handloader's Guide* that had been issued during the 1960's. Almost without exception, they agreed. They did not perceive the NRA as a competitor in the publication of handbooks, but as an organization who shared their goal of providing the American handloader with the best possible information. We are deeply gratified by their attitude, because that is exactly how we perceive ourselves.

Some of the data contained in the second part of this book were developed in the NRA laboratory, where the equipment and practices are in conformity with those of the ammunition industry and/or the Government ballistic laboratories. The great preponderance of the data were developed in the laboratories of other organizations, and are given here by their generous consent. The loads listed here are only a small part of the data available from those other sources. There are thousands of other good loads not included, because one book of practicable size could not contain them all. The sources of data are identified in the loading tables of this book. The reader is encouraged to obtain the other publications, from which these data were selected, and thereby avail himself of a much greater variety of loads than we could possibly include. These are the firms who have graciously allowed us to include their loading data, in alphabetical order:

DBI Books/Frank C. Barnes, Publisher/Author of *Cartridges of the World*
DuPont, *Handloader's Guide for Smokeless Powders*
Hercules Inc., *Reloaders' Guide for Hercules Smokeless Powders*
Hodgdon Powder Company, *Hodgdon's Data Manual Number 23*
Hornady Manufacturing Co./Pacific Tool Co., *Hornady Handbook of Cartridge Reloading, Rifle-Pistol, Volume II*
Norma-Precision, *Loading Data for Norma Powder*
Nosler/Leupold, *Nosler Reloading Manual Number One*
Sierra Bullets Inc., *Sierra Bullets Reloading Manual (2nd Edition)*
Speer/CCI/RCBS (Omark Industries), *Speer Reloading Manual Number 9 and 10*
Winchester-Western, *Winchester-Western Ball Powder Loading Data*

Wm C Davis, Jr

WM. C. DAVIS, JR.

INTRODUCTION

It is usually concluded that the handloader assembles his cartridge for reasons of economy. But this is only partly true. The facts are he authors his round more from an urge to fire a cartridge which best fits his needs. It is tailored to his rifle, to his shooting scheme, and to his notion of what he wants most.

Happily there is a wide choice of cases, powders, bullets, primers and firearms which afford an almost endless variety of change. The selection provokes experimentation, and serves as an invitation to test each loading.

The shooter who puts together his own cartridges solely for the purpose of economy misses the best and richest aspect of the game.

Quite apart from the versatility inherent in the handloaded round is another virtue which emphasizes the quality of the product. The dedicated reloader produces a more accurate round than the factory through meticulous attention to detail, smaller output, and the opportunity to test-fire each of his creations.

The benchrest marksman, the world's most precise shooter, is an example of this. His phenomenal performance can be ascribed, in major part, to the quality of his hand-assembled cartridge.

The dedicated shooter would indeed be seriously handicapped if he was compelled to fire only factory cartridges. These offer only a few bullet weights, powder charges and velocities. The dedicated handloader can put together squib loads for grouse or full-charge loads for elk, in the same afternoon. Handgunners can fire a gallery charge in the .38 and then switch to full-service loads, all in the same handgun and all the product of their ingenuity.

After assembling a handload peculiarly my own, then journeying to a hunting ground halfway around the world, the greatest gut feeling of all comes from the realization that the success of the hunting venture came not from the journey or the shot but from my hand-tailored cartridge. My own.

I commend to you this handloading manual which is, in my opinion, the most complete treatment of the science of handloading cartridges ever written. Its completeness, its thoroughness, its lucidity, and its timeliness places it in the unique position of *best*.

Colonel Charles Askins

HANDLOADING TECHNIQUES, COMPONENTS, & BALLISTICS

SMALL ARMS AMMUNITION

An explanation of terms used in describing the classifications and nomenclature of small arms ammunition.

By M. D. WAITE

THERE are many technical terms relevant to the classification and nomenclature of small-arms ammunition. A knowledge of these is necessary in differentiating between the various types of ammunition, obsolete and modern.

The term 'small arms' is not subject to precise definition, but is generally considered to embrace projectile firearms of small caliber, including rifles, handguns, shotguns, submachine guns, and machine guns.

There are numerous cartridge-firing (powder actuated) devices, both industrial and military, which are not classed as small arms because they were not designed and made to function as weapons. In this category are stud drivers, oil well casing perforators, engine starters, gun chargers, kiln guns, and cable splicers.

Early cartridges

The earliest small-arms cartridge consisted of a pre-measured charge of powder wrapped in paper. The word 'cartridge' is derived from *charta,* the Latin word for paper. The use of the paper-wrapped powder charge speeded the loading of military weapons, avoided waste of powder from spillage, and provided a uniform charge from shot to shot. In time, the bullet was either attached to or wrapped with the powder charge to make loading faster and more convenient. In some forms of the paper cartridge the cap or primer was attached to the cartridge, but was detached before the powder and bullet were loaded into the gun bore.

The paper cartridge remained standard for muzzle-loading military arms through the middle of the 19th century.

The combustible cartridge was an outgrowth of the paper cartridge. It was employed in muzzle-loading arms, revolving chamber arms, and in several early breech-loading arms. The casing enclosing the powder charge was made from nitrated paper, collodion, cloth, animal intestine, or some other material which would not leave a burning residue in the chamber or barrel.

The combustible cartridges for the Prussian needle-gun and French Chassepot breech-loading rifles were of self-contained type. That is, the means of ignition (primer) was a part of the cartridge. These early self-contained (self-primed) cartridges were not self-obturating (self-sealing). Sealing of the breech against rearward escape of gas usually depended on a close mechanical fit between component parts of the breech mechanism. Accumulated powder fouling and erosion made it difficult to maintain effective mechanical obturation, and for those reasons these arms were only partially successful.

Early breech-loading arms using rigid non-expanding metal or metal-base cartridges or 'loaded-ball' ammunition were likewise of minor importance only, and for the same reasons.

Truly successful breech-loading small arms were not possible until the development of efficient self-obturating cartridges which occurred around the middle of the 19th century.

Classifications

The self-contained small-arms cartridge, or 'round', combines all of the components necessary to fire a weapon once. Based upon type of ignition, currently available self-contained small-arms cartridges are classed as pin-fire, rimfire, or center-fire.

Pin-fire cartridges are made in a few types only, and are essentially obsolete. No modern guns are adapted for pin-fire ammunition.

In the conventional externally-primed center-fire cartridge, the primer or means of ignition is seated in a small pocket in the center of the case head. A vent or flashhole in the bottom of the primer pocket communicates with the powder chamber within the case. Most forms of externally-primed center-fire cartridges are reloadable.

In the rimfire cartridge the priming mixture is spun centrifugally into the internal rimfold at the base of the case. The rim locates the cartridge in the gun chamber and also serves as a means of extracting the loaded cartridge or fired case from the chamber. The reloading of rimfire ammunition is not practicable.

Percussion primers

Percussion primers are standard in most forms of small-arms ammunition, but some types of military ammunition have electrically-fired primers.

The American, or Boxer, primer is standard in American-made commercial and military small-arms ammunition. The Boxer primer is assembled with an anvil. Center-fire ammunition made in other countries may be primed with the Berdan primer which lacks an anvil. Cartridge cases adapted for the Berdan-type primer have anvils formed in the bottom of their pockets.

Internally-primed center-fire ammunition has been obsolete for many years except for the German-made cal. 4 mm. Uebungsmunition which is still manufactured.

Many small-arms cartridges are designed to function in one class of firearm only, i.e., shotgun, rifle, or handgun. This serves as a general means of grouping cartridges by type. However, there are numerous cartridges which are regularly used in more than one class of firearm.

The term 'metallic' as used in cartridge nomenclature indicates that the cartridge case is of all-metal construction. Most bulleted cartridges fired in rifled firearms have metallic cases although plastic cases have been used.

Some shotgun shells are made with metallic cases, but the more common forms combine a metal base with body of plastic or rolled paper. Some shotgun shells have all-plastic cases.

Many early breech-loading small arms were adapted for self-obturating cartridges which did not contain an integral primer or means of ignition. This form of cartridge is called 'separate primed'. Separate-primed cartridges were fired by percussion cap, disk primer, pill primer, or tape primer.

There have been fairly recent military experiments with combustible or caseless self-primed small-arms cartridges, but none has been successful. The problem of obturating or sealing the breech of the gun against the escape of gas has not been completely solved.

Small-arms cartridges may be classified according to use:

1. Combat or Service
   a. Ball
   b. Armor-piercing
   c. Armor-piercing-Incendiary
   d. Armor-piercing-Incendiary-Tracer
   e. Armor-piercing-Lachrymatory
   f. Incendiary
   g. Tracer
   h. Spotter-Tracer
   i. Observation
   j. Explosive
   k. Grenade launching
   l. Shotgun shell

2. Non-combat and Special
   a. Sporting
   b. Practice
   c. Match
   d. High-pressure test
   e. Blank
   f. Frangible
   g. Dummy (range or functioning)
   h. Flare (signal)
   i. Line throwing
   j. Shotgun shell

Small-arms cartridges may be classified further according to case shape and head form.

There are 3 general shapes of cartridge case: (1) straight, (2) tapered, and (3) bottleneck.

Most modern center-fire rifle cartridge cases are of bottleneck type since this case form provides the greatest powder capacity commensurate with over-all case length. The tapered case form is obsolescent. Cartridges of this type manufactured currently were introduced many years ago. All bulleted rimfire cartridges and most center-fire revolver cartridges now manufactured have straight cases. All conventional shotgun shells have straight cases. Cal. .22 rimfire shotshells have slightly bottlenecked cases.

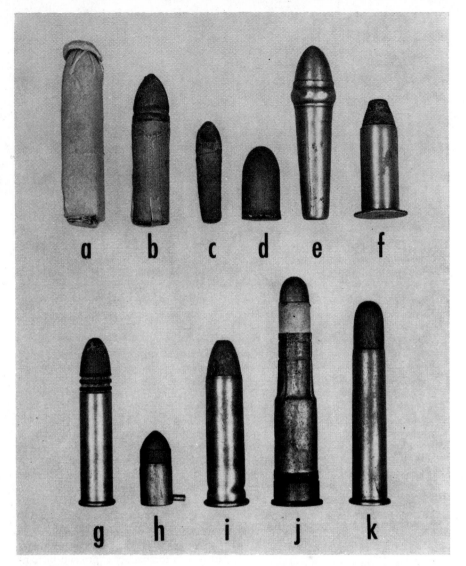

Evolutionary cartridge types

(a) Cal. .58 paper-wrapped cartridge for U. S. Civil War period muzzle-loading rifle-musket. After breaking cartridge, powder charge was poured down barrel and then wadded with paper wrapping. Naked hollow-base Minie bullet was seated on charge with ramrod. Ignition was by external percussion cap or tape primer.
(b) Sharps cal. .52 linen-cased combustible cartridge for Sharps breech-loading rifle and carbine. Cartridge was loaded directly into gun chamber. Knife edge on upper face of breechblock sheared off base of cartridge as action was closed. Ignition was by external percussion cap, disk primer, or tape primer.
(c) Colt cal. .36 combustible cartridge for percussion revolvers. Fragile outer casing of animal intestine was ruptured in ramming cartridge into chamber. Ignition was by external percussion cap. Similar cartridges were made for Colt revolving rifles.
(d) Hunt cal. .54 'loaded ball' cartridge for Jennings rifle. Powder charge was contained in cavity in bullet base. Ignition was by external pill primer.
(e) Burnside cal. .54 metal-cased cartridge for Burnside carbine and rifle. This self-obturating cartridge was loaded into front end of tilting breechblock. Case bulge at base of bullet contained lubricant. Hole in base of cartridge case allowed primer flame to pass into charge. Ignition was by exter-

nal percussion cap.
(f) Maynard cal. .50 metal-cased cartridge for Maynard carbine. Body of case was soldered sleeve which was soldered to disk base. This self-obturating cartridge was reloadable. Ignition was by external percussion cap or tape primer. Primer flame entered charge through hole in base of cartridge case.
(g) Cal. .46 Extra Long rimfire cartridge. Typical copper-cased self-primed rimfire cartridge in which priming mixture was spun centrifugally into internal rim fold. Rimfire cartridge types are now made in small calibers only.
(h) Cal. 11 mm. pin-fire revolver cartridge. In this self-contained cartridge, the internal percussion cap was installed horizontally with base of the case. A pin resting against the cap extends through the case wall so that it can be struck by the hammer of the gun.
(i) U. S. cal. .50-70 center-fire Service cartridge with Benet internal cup primer. This form of folded-head copper-cased cartridge was not reloadable.
(j) British cal. .577/.450 Martini-Henry center-fire Service rifle cartridge with Boxer primer. Body of the case was coiled brass riveted to an iron base.
(k) U. S. cal. .45-70 center-fire Service cartridge with Boxer-type external primer. This solid-head copper-cased cartridge was reloadable.

Typical rimfire cartridge series. (l. to r.) .22 BB cap, .22 CB cap, .22 short, .22 long, .22 long rifle, .22 extra long. Introduced about 1857, the .22 short is oldest metallic cartridge manufactured in the United States today.

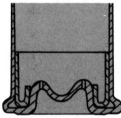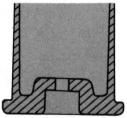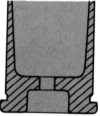

Typical center-fire cartridge cases. Early Sharps folded-head case on left has internal cup reinforcement to strengthen head. Center cartridge is solid-drawn balloon-head (hollow bar head) case developed later. Now almost obsolete, balloon-head case was superseded by stronger solid-drawn solid-head (solid bar head) case at right.

Standard cartridge head forms are:

1. Rimmed (flanged)
2. Semi-rimless
3. Rimless
4. Rebated-rimless (reduced rim)
5. Belted rimless

A few metallic center-fire cartridges have been made without a flange or extractor groove. Most of these have been experimental and are unlikely to be encountered except in collections.

All currently manufactured shotgun shells and metallic rimfire cartridges are of rimmed type.

Solid-head case

The solid-drawn, solid-head case is now standard for most metallic center-fire cartridges. In the solid-head (solid bar head) cartridge case, the interior base is level with the top edge of the vent opening. This method of construction has largely superseded the balloon-head (hollow bar head) case which is not as strong. In the balloon-head case the base portion or web is relatively thin and the primer pocket extends up into the powder chamber.

The folded-head center-fire cartridge case became obsolete with the introduction of smokeless powder. Center-fire metallic cartridges with soldered or riveted-on heads also became obsolete at that time.

Naming Systems—Several systems have been devised for naming metallic cartridges. Under the American system the designations for rimfire cartridges begin with the caliber expressed in hundredths of an inch. The relative case length may be given where more than one case length exists in a specific caliber. A typical series would be the .32 extra short, .32 short, .32 long, and .32 extra long rimfire cartridges. The name of the originating firm, country of issue, designer, or weapon for which it is adapted, may be included in the designations. The .44 Henry, .41 Swiss, .58 Roberts, and .58 Musket are typical.

The weight of the powder charge in grains (and occasionally the weight of the bullet) was often given in the designations of early American rimfire cartridges. The .52-70 Sharps and .25-10-67 Stevens are representative. The first number indicates the caliber, the second the powder charge, and the third the weight of the bullet.

The obsolete series of Spencer rimfire cartridges, adapted to Spencer lever-action rifles and carbines, were named under a system peculiar to the Spencer firm. The basic Spencer cartridge was the No. 56 or .56-.56. This cartridge had a straight case and its nominal caliber was .56. The Spencer .56-.50, .56-.52, and .56-.46 cartridges were derived from the parent .56-.56 case. The Spencer cartridges were the exception to the

general rule in that the nominal caliber was expressed by the second number, not by the first.

American and foreign ammunition catalogs have always listed rimfire and center-fire cartridges separately. This was essential to avoid confusion between rimfire and center-fire cartridges which were designated similarly. Several early metallic cartridges were made in both rimfire and center-fire form. They were not interchangeable, but some rifles were made with a convertible firing pin to permit optional use of either type cartridge.

Uncomplicated system

The system for naming American center-fire blackpowder cartridges was uncomplicated. The full designation gave the nominal caliber in hundredths of an inch, weight of powder charge, weight of bullet, and basic name, in that order. For example, the Service cartridge for the Springfield Model 1873 Service rifle was designated .45-70-500 Government. It was loaded with 70 grs. of blackpowder and a 500-gr. bullet.

The length of the case in inches and the general form of the cartridge case (straight or bottleneck) were sometimes included in the designation to distinguish between similar cartridges which were not interchangeable.

The blackpowder nomenclature system was employed in naming some of the early American smokeless powder cartridges including the .30-30 W.C.F. (Winchester Center-Fire) and .30-40 Krag (.30 U. S. Army). The second number in these designations represented the standard charge weights of the smokeless powders first used in loading these cartridges. These charge weights were soon changed with the development of more efficient smokeless powders, but the original designations were retained.

Powder capacities

Powder capacities of several early center-fire blackpowder cartridges were reduced in the transition from the folded head to the stronger solid-head case construction, but the original charge designations were retained.

The year of adoption is a part of the designations of several U. S. Service small-arms cartridges. One so named was the U. S. Cartridge, Cal. .30, Model of 1903 (.30-'03 Govt.). On adoption of the 150-gr. Model 1906 pointed bullet, the cartridge case was shortened slightly. It was then redesignated U. S. Cartridge, Cal. .30, Model of 1906 (.30-'06 Govt.). The Model 1906 cartridge with Model 1906 bullet remained standard until 1925 when the Model 1906 bullet was superseded by the 172-gr. M1 boattail bullet. The U. S. Service rifle cartridge was then redesignated Cartridge, Ball, Cal. .30 M1. In 1944 this cartridge was superseded by the Cartridge, Ball, Cal. .30 M2 assembled with 152-gr. M2 pointed bullet. The latter cartridge had been standard for ground use since 1939.

NATO cartridge adopted

On Dec. 15, 1953, the Cartridge, 7.62 mm. NATO was adopted as the standard rifle and machine gun cartridge for member nations of the NATO. It was the second U. S. Service rifle and machine gun cartridge to be designated under the metric system, the first being the 6 mm. Lee of 1895.

The U. S. Cartridge, Ball, Cal. .45, Model of 1911 (M1911) is another official U. S. Service cartridge in which the year of adoption was included in the designation. This practice was dropped for new items with introduction of the M system of Ordnance designations (M1, M2, etc.) in 1925.

The advertised muzzle velocity was made a part of the designation for the Savage .250-3000 center-fire cartridge designed by Charles Newton for the Savage Model 1899 lever-action rifle. No other American factory-loaded cartridge has been named in this manner.

The calibers of some of the earliest American smokeless powder cartridges were expressed in thousandths of an inch. The .303 Savage and .236 U.S.N. were among the first in this group. The Service designation for the .236 U.S.N. cartridge was 6 mm. Lee.

Some American cartridges have been given a variety of names which conceals the fact that they are interchangeable insofar as cartridge case dimensions are concerned. The following cartridges have different designations, but are interchangeable:

.25-20 Winchester, Marlin, Remington
.25-20 Winchester & Marlin
.25-20 W.C.F.
.25-20 Winchester
.25-20 Winchester High Velocity
.25-20 Marlin

Information on cartridge interchangeability will be found in most factory ammunition catalogs.

It is not always possible to determine the actual caliber of a cartridge from its factory designation. For example, the .38 S&W Special cartridge is not a true cal. .38 since its nominal bullet diameter is .357″. The groove diameter of barrels made for this cartridge will vary from .352″ up to .358″ and larger, depending on the manufacturer. A similar

Boxer primer and case (l.) and Berdan primer and case. Boxer primer contains its own anvil. Anvil is integral in primer pocket of Berdan case.

situation exists with .22 center-fire rifle cartridges. The .218 Bee, .219 Zipper, .220 Swift, .221 Remington, .222 Remington, and .223 Remington cartridges are all loaded with .224″ diameter bullets. Cartridge designations often reflect the whims of their designers or manufacturers. They may indicate the nominal bore or groove diameter of the firearm to which they are adapted, or differ from any of these dimensions.

The term 'magnum'

The term 'magnum' as applied to small-arms cartridges is of British origin. Magnum cartridges are generally larger and more powerful than the usual cartridges in any given caliber.

The term 'express' is also of British origin. Express cartridges are generally loaded with lighter than usual bullets and heavy powder charges to provide the highest possible velocity levels.

The German or European system of naming center-fire metallic cartridges is based on the metric system. The cartridge designation gives both the caliber and the case length in millimeters. The suffix "R" is added to the designation if the cartridge is of rimmed construction. The name of the designer, originating firm, or date of adoption for a military cartridge, may supplement the dimensional data. The caliber designations may not be precise, but are usually based on the nominal barrel groove or bore diameters.

In 1904 the German Government adopted a 154-gr. pointed rifle bullet to replace the original 227-gr. round-nose bullet which had been adopted in 1888. The nominal diameter of the M1888 bullet was .318″; that of the new bullet was increased to .323″. The adoption of the larger *Spitzgeschoss* or S-bore bullet

necessitated a change in rifling specifications. The original German Service cartridge had been designated 8x57J, but the new cartridge was designated 8x57JS to distinguish it from the earlier round. The letter "J" in these designations is the abbreviation for Infanterie, or Infantry. The letter "J" is often used for "I" in the German language. Under current West German military practice, the 9 mm. Parabellum (Luger) cartridge is designated 9 mm.x19. The 7.62 mm. NATO cartridge is designated 7.62 mm.x51.

Some German sporting rifle cartridges in cal. 8 mm. are optionally available with .318″ or .323″ S-bore bullets. The letter "S" is always present in the catalog designation when the cartridge is loaded with the .323″-diameter S-bore bullet.

American-designed metallic center-fire cartridges manufactured by European firms are often given metric designations. The following are typical:

7.62x63	.30-'06
7.62x51	.308 Winchester (7.62 mm. NATO)
7.62x51R	.30-30 Winchester
6.5x52R	.25-35 Winchester
5.6x35R	.22 Hornet
5.6x52R	.22 Savage Hi-Power

English System—The modern English system of cartridge nomenclature is similar to the American. The cartridge caliber is nearly always expressed in thousandths of an inch. The terms 'Nitro' or 'Blackpowder' may be included in the designation to indicate the propellant loaded in the cartridge.

The designations of some English rifle cartridges contain 2 sets of numbers, i.e., .400/.375 Holland & Holland. This form of identification always indicates that the cartridge is of bottleneck type.

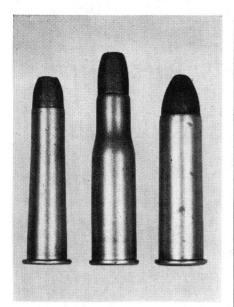

Cartridge case shapes. (l. to r.) tapered, bottleneck, straight. Tapered case form is obsolescent.

The smaller number on the right represents the actual caliber of the cartridge. The number on the left is the nominal caliber of the parent cartridge from which it was derived.

Shotgun Gauges—The English system of shotgun gauges is essentially standard throughout the world. The shotgun gauge indicates the nominal diameter of the hole through the barrel. A 10-ga. gun has a bore diameter equal to the diameter of a lead sphere weighing 1/10 lb. The bore diameters of other gauges (with the exception of the .410-bore) were derived similarly. The following are the current sizes:

10-ga.	.775"
12-ga.	.729"
16-ga.	.662"
20-ga.	.615"
28-ga.	.550"
.410-bore	.410"

The designations for shotshells include the length of the *fired* shell in inches and fractions thereof. The following are the basic shotshells now manufactured in the United States:

10-ga.—2⅞", 3½" Magnum
12-ga.—2¾", 2¾" Magnum, 3" Magnum
16-ga.—2¾", 2¾" Magnum
20-ga.—2¾", 2¾" Magnum, 3" Magnum
28-ga.—2¾"
.410-bore—2½", 3"

In Great Britain the 12-ga. shell is also loaded in 2" and in 3¼" Magnum lengths. A few small shotgun ('garden gun') shells of Central European origin were given metric designations, but all are now obsolescent or obsolete. ∎

NONCORROSIVE PRIMERS IN FOREIGN MILITARY AMMUNITION

Q. *I have the information published by the NRA on corrosive and noncorrosive primers in U.S. military ammunition, but is any comparable information available on military ammuniton of foreign manufacture?*

A. The late Col. B. R. Lewis, a former Contributing Editor to THE AMERICAN RIFLEMAN, investigated this question for the NRA in the late 1960's, and published his findings in THE AMERICAN RIFLEMAN of April 1969 (pp. 34-35). His information was from first-hand sources in the respective countries of manufacture, and is believed to be reliable, but supporting documentation comparable to that on U.S. military ammunition is unavailable, and possible exceptions exist. The following information is extracted from the aforementioned article.

Belgium: Fabrique Nationale d'Armes de Guerre has been a major ammunition producer for years. Its typical marking is FN and date. Fabrique Nationale changed to noncorrosive priming exclusively on December 6, 1957. Thus all dated 1958 and later is noncorrosive. This includes all types in both U.S. and foreign military calibers. Most production before 1958 had primers that were both mercuric and corrosive.

Canada: Information is available only on .30-06 ammunition made on contract for the U.S. Valcartier Industries made one lot, in its Verdun Arsenal (Lot 42000), which was headstamped VC 45, and contained noncorrosive primers. Dominion Arsenal made one lot (Lot 44000), headstamped DAQ 45, and it contained nonmercuric but corrosive primers. Previous information on this DAQ 45 ammunition, indicating it had noncorrosive primers, was published both by the NRA and official Government sources, but subsequently was found incorrect. All other ammunition made by Dominion Arsenal prior to 1951 contained primers that were both mercuric and corrosive.

Germany: Rheinisch-Westfaelische Sprengstoff Actien Geselleschaft of Nuernburg, a subsidiary of Dynamit Nobel, uses the RWS headstamp, usually with the date. Though some RWS ammunition used noncorrosive primers several years before World War II, some corrosive primers were used during World War II, and there is no way to distinguish the corrosive from noncorrosive lots. Since World War II, all RWS ammunition has contained noncorrosive primers having the RWS composition tradenamed Sinoxid.

Great Britain: Imperial Metal Industries (Kynoch) Ltd. produced cartridges in several plants, marked Kynoch or K, with the date. Changeover from corrosive to noncorrosive primers was made gradually over a number of years, and dates are not available. As a general rule, their brass primers are nonmercuric and noncorrosive, and copper primers are corrosive and mercuric. This rule is not entirely reliable, however, as a few lots having brass primers contained corrosive composition.

Israel: All ammunition loaded by the Israeli Arsenal at Tel Aviv contains noncorrosive primers. The ammunition is marked Tel Aviv in Hebrew characters, with the date in Arabic numerals.

Since Col. Lewis' compilation was made in the late 1960's, great quantities of foreign military ammunition have been imported, from many countries. There is no systematic compilation of data on all that ammunition. The best source of information is the importer, whose name may be available from the dealer who sold the ammunition in the U.S. If there is any doubt about the corrosiveness, the user is well advised to clean his gun as prescribed for corrosive ammunition, or make tests of his own.

A fairly reliable test can be made by firing an empty primed case against a thoroughly cleaned bare steel surface held about one inch from the gun muzzle. For comparison, fire a primer known to be noncorrosive on another piece of steel. Put the pieces of steel in a humid place for 24 hours. A corrosive primer should show markedly more rusting than the noncorrosive one.

WCD, JR.

CARTRIDGE MEASUREMENTS

Dimensions of metallic cartridges that are of interest to shooters and collectors.

By Col. B. R. LEWIS

A knowledge of cartridge dimensions is sometimes necessary to the shooter, as well as the collector, for identification of ammunition.

Following are principal dimensions of the metallic cartridges which appear likely to be of significance to shooters and collectors.

Cartridge dimensions shown are taken from typical single specimens, to the nearest .001″. Modern manufacturing tolerances may give several thousandths more or less. Though dimensions are now reasonably well standardized in the United States, they used to vary greatly between factories, and sometimes still do abroad.

Bullet diameter has been measured at the case mouth. Many bullets are somewhat larger inside the case. Base-to-shoulder measurements should be considered approximate, because of the rounded intersection of shoulder and body of case.

Many cartridges have been designated by more than one name at various times. The name given here is that in most common use, except when otherwise required for accuracy in identification.

In matching an unidentified cartridge to these tables, it is suggested that the combination of bullet diameter and case length measurements will give the clue best, followed by comparison of head diameters.

The illustrations on pages 61 and 62 should be used to locate the measurements given in the tables for the particular type of case to be identified.

AMERICAN CALIBERS

Rimmed Straight Case

Caliber	DIAMETER (IN.) A–Rim	B–Head	C–Mouth	D–Bullet	LENGTH (INS.) a–Case	b–Over-all
.25–25 Stevens	.376	.300	.278	.246	2.369	2.624
.32 Colt New Police	.375	.337	.335	.312	.925	1.250
.32 Long Colt	.380	.316	.316	.292	.913	1.219
.32 Short Colt	.368	.318	.318	.316	.631	.993
.32 S&W	.370	.334	.334	.313	.600	.918
.32 S&W Long	.373	.338	.335	.314	.914	1.283
.32–40 Winchester	.494	.410	.340	.310	2.125	2.495
.32–44 S&W Target*	.409	.348	.348	—	.979	1.012
.357 Mag.	.435	.379	.375	.352	1.283	1.560
.38 Long Colt	.435	.375	.373	.347	1.028	1.367
.38 Short Colt (Long Case)	.440	.378	.378	.378	.760	1.193
.38 Short Colt (Short Case)	.433	.378	.375	.379	.679	1.100
.38 S&W (Colt New Police)	.437	.386	.385	.357	.763	1.176
.38 Special	.434	.372	.372	.357	1.155	1.544
.38–44 S&W Target*	.437	.384	.384	—	1.466	1.466
.375 Winchester	.506	.419	.400	.376	2.020	2.560
.38–55 Winchester	.505	.417	.395	.366	2.127	2.546
.40–60 Winchester	.623	.504	.424	.400	1.874	2.255
.40–72 Winchester	.522	.459	.432	.408	2.583	3.172
.405 Winchester	.544	.457	.432	.409	2.583	3.162
.41 Long Colt	.433	.408	.406	.373	1.127	1.410
.41 Short Colt	.435	.409	.405	.407	.638	1.079
.41 Remington Magnum	.488	.433	.432	.410	1.285	1.580
.44 Bulldog	.503	.454	.445	.442	.552	.941
.44 Colt	.483	.461	.451	.449	1.060	1.514
.44 S&W American	.510	.439	.437	.430	.888	1.420
.44 S&W Russian	.505	.457	.455	.425	.954	1.443
.44 Special	.507	.455	.454	.420	1.151	1.586
.44 Remington Magnum	.507	.455	.453	.429	1.277	1.592
.444 Marlin	.510	.467	.451	.422	2.220	2.559
.45 Auto Rimmed	.511	.473	.472	.439	.897	1.266
.45 Colt	.510	.478	.475	.446	1.266	1.575
.45 S&W Schofield	.520	.478	.478	.445	1.118	1.438
.45–70 Gov't	.608	.503	.479	.448	2.104	2.546
.45–90 Winchester	.607	.500	.476	.448	2.400	2.755
.50 Remington Pistol, Navy (M1867)**	.645	.563	.532	.497	.877	1.215
.50–70 Gov't	.660	.565	.537	.503	1.750	2.230
.50–110 Win. Exp.	.605	.552	.532	.502	2.400	2.741

*Bullet seated completely within case.
**Bullet diameter on some specimens may be as high as .531″.

Rimmed Necked Case

Caliber	DIAMETER (IN.) A–Rim	B–Head	C–Shoulder	D–Mouth	E–Bullet	LENGTH (INS.) a–Base to Shoulder	b–Case	c–Over-all
.218 Bee	.405	.345	.331	.241	.224	.924	1.334	1.670
.219 Zipper	.493	.417	.363	.250	.224	1.361	1.924	2.262
.22 Hornet	.342	.295	.274	.242	.220	.845	1.388	1.712
.22 Jet	.435	.377	.352	.250	.223	.600	1.280	1.641
.22 Savage	.494	.414	.358	.251	.228	1.386	2.042	2.483
.22 WCF	.342	.294	.275	.246	.226	.833	1.400	1.685
.25–20 Single Shot	.376	.317	.301	.272	.250	1.123	1.633	1.883
.25–20 Winchester	.405	.345	.330	.275	.253	.850	1.307	1.583
.25–35 Winchester	.494	.412	.364	.283	.255	1.407	2.036	2.545
.25–36 Marlin	.502	.419	.359	.282	.249	1.491	2.130	2.506
.256 Winchester	.434	.377	.365	.283	.250	.977	1.277	1.550
.30–30 Winchester	.505	.417	.388	.330	.302	1.425	2.045	2.545
.30–40 Krag	.541	.456	.417	.334	.309	1.708	2.309	3.080
.303 Savage	.508	.440	.402	.333	.307	1.352	2.010	2.524
.32 Win. Special	.498	.419	.392	.338	.320	1.466	2.045	2.525
.32–20 WCF	.404	.349	.333	.326	.302	.845	1.300	1.592
.33 Winchester	.600	.495	.434	.359	.335	1.600	2.115	2.777
.348 Winchester	.607	.548	.474	.374	.342	1.667	2.250	2.800
.35 Winchester	.542	.455	.425	.382	.358	2.000	2.411	3.166
.38–40 Winchester	.518	.466	.435	.416	.398	.900	1.303	1.593
.38–56 Winchester	.604	.503	.444	.400	.370	1.268	2.100	2.500
.38–72 Winchester	.521	.459	.427	.397	.377	1.896	2.580	3.174
.40–82 Winchester	.603	.504	.452	.427	.395	1.712	2.393	2.779
.44–40 Winchester	.515	.465	.453	.443	.423	.900	1.300	1.596
.45–75 Winchester	.628	.563	.542	.478	.457	1.040	1.883	2.250
.50 Remington Pistol, Army (M 1871)	.665	.565	.559	.535	.503	.555	.870	1.250
.50–95 Winchester	.625	.560	.550	.533	.493	1.490	1.928	2.270

Semi-Rimmed Straight Case

Caliber	DIAMETER (IN.) A–Rim	B–Head	C–Mouth	D–Bullet	LENGTH (INS.) a–Case	b–Over-all
.25 Auto	.300	.279	.277	.250	.613	.900
.32 ACP	.357	.337	.334	.306	.679	.980
.32 Win. S.L.	.391	.350	.345	.321	1.286	1.984
.35 Win. S.L.	.404	.382	.375	.350	1.147	1.653
.351 Win. S.L.	.408	.377	.377	.353	1.372	1.886
.38 AMU*	.404	.376	.375	—	1.150	1.175
.38 Colt Auto	.405	.384	.383	.355	.894	1.274
.401 Win. S.L.	.459	.431	.429	.408	1.494	2.009

*Bullet seated completely within case.

Semi-Rimmed Necked Case

Caliber	DIAMETER (IN.) A–Rim	B–Head	C–Shoulder	D–Mouth	E–Bullet	LENGTH (INS.) a–Base to Shoulder	b–Case	c–Over-all
.220 Swift	.469	.446	.400	.257	.225	1.702	2.196	2.668
.225 Winchester	.469	.417	.400	.253	.224	1.530	1.924	2.437

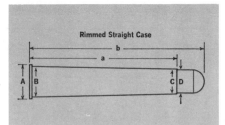
Rimmed Straight Case

Type "A" Head

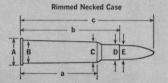
Rimmed Necked Case

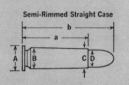
Semi-Rimmed Straight Case

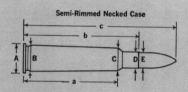
Semi-Rimmed Necked Case

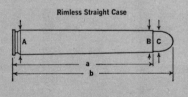
Rimless Straight Case

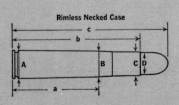
Rimless Necked Case

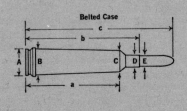
Belted Case

Semi-Rimmed Necked Case

Caliber	DIAMETER (IN.) A–Rim	B–Head	C–Shoulder	D–Mouth	E–Bullet	LENGTH (INS.) a–Base to Shoulder	b–Case	c–Over-all
.280 Ross	.556	.525	.420	.318	.288	2.172	2.600	3.455

Rimless Necked Case

Caliber	DIAMETER (IN.) A–Head	B–Shoulder	C–Mouth	D–Bullet	LENGTH (INS.) a–Base to Shoulder	b–Case	c–Over-all
.242 Nitro	.465	.421	.282	.250	2.006	2.387	3.186
.318	.466	.439	.356	.330	1.959	2.400	3.392
.333	.543	.487	.359	.333	1.754	2.485	3.493
.350 Rigby Mag.	.516	.448	.380	.358	2.333	2.748	3.540
.404 Jeffery	.546	.529	.449	.420	2.009	2.874	3.510
.505 Gibbs	.636	.589	.530	.499	2.433	3.140	3.833

Belted Case

Caliber	DIAMETER (IN.) A–Rim	B–Under Head	C–Shoulder	D–Mouth	E–Bullet	LENGTH (INS.) a–Base to Shoulder	b–Case	c–Over-all
.240 Belted	.476	.455	.401	.276	.244	1.925	2.493	3.210
.244 H&H Mag.	.530	.508	.446	.275	.244	2.312	2.783	3.595
.275 H&H Mag.	.530	.513	.448	.318	.285	2.100	2.494	3.294
.300 H&H Mag.	.524	.508	.446	.335	.310	2.125	2.847	3.574
.375 H&H Mag.	.530	.513	.442	.400	.375	2.380	2.840	3.575

FOREIGN METRIC CALIBERS

Rimmed Straight Case

Caliber (mm.)	DIAMETER (IN.) A–Rim	B–Head	C–Mouth	D–Bullet	LENGTH (INS.) a–Case	b–Over-all
9.3x72R	.480	.429	.383	.369	2.832	3.351

Rimmed Necked Case

Caliber (mm.)	DIAMETER (IN.) A–Rim	B–Head	C–Shoulder	D–Mouth	E–Bullet	LENGTH (INS.) a–Base to Shoulder	b–Case	c–Over-all
6.5x53R Dutch & Roumanian Mannlicher	.528	.448	.418	.294	.263	1.640	2.107	3.054
7x72R	.482	.425	.337	.311	.284	2.000	2.835	3.395
7.62x54R M1891 Russian	.564	.485	.454	.336	.310	1.510	2.100	3.023
8x51R French Lebel	.630	.538	.516/.450	.350	.330	.875/1.452 (dbl. taper)	1.987	2.949
8x57JR	.528	.467	.426	.344	.317	1.817	2.241	3.244
8x58R Danish Krag	.577	.503	.467	.357	.322	1.662	2.277	3.000
8.15x46R	.482	.422	.387	.344	.323	1.150 (slight shoulder)	1.812	2.332
8.2(8)x50R Mannlicher	.552	.492	.475	.355	.323	1.485	1.980	3.000
9.3x74R	.523	.465	.407	.387	.364	2.358	2.935	3.686
11 M1871/84 Mauser	.585*	.515	.507	.465	.433**	1.497	2.363	3.015
11(.43)Spanish Rem.	.630	.518	.507	.459	.433	1.637	2.250	2.831

*Type "A" head. See illustration
**Measured over paper patch

Semi-Rimmed Necked Case

Caliber (mm.)	DIAMETER (IN.) A–Rim	B–Head	C–Shoulder	D–Mouth	E–Bullet	LENGTH (INS.) a–Base to Shoulder	b–Case	c–Over-all
6.5x50 Jap Arisaka	.473	.450	.416	.293	.264	1.528	1.990	2.998

Rimless Straight Case

Caliber (mm.)	DIAMETER (IN.) A–Head	B–Mouth	C–Bullet	LENGTH (INS.) a–Case	b–Over-all
9 mm Makarov	.389	.384	.363	.715	.975
9 Luger	.386	.373	.355	.750	1.150

Rimless Necked Case

Caliber (mm.)	DIAMETER (IN.) A–Head	B–Shoulder	C–Mouth	D–Bullet	LENGTH (INS.) a–Base to Shoulder	b–Case	c–Over-all
5.6x61 vom Hofe	.476	.452	.259	.225	1.730	2.395	3.145
.6.5x52 Italian Carcano	.448	.430	.296	.267	1.628	2.057	2.992
6.5x54 Mannlicher/Sch.	.449	.425	.290	.263	1.645	2.111	3.040
6.5x55 M1894 Norwegian & Swedish	.476	.433	.297	.265	1.696	2.161	3.078
6.5x57 Mauser	.467	.431	.296	.263	1.767	2.227	3.151
7x57 Mauser	.475	.430	.318	.284	1.731	2.240	3.056
7x64 Brenneke	.466	.425	.310	.286	2.025	2.517	3.435
7x66 vom Hofe	.543	.497	.311	.282	2.094	2.596	3.299
7.35x51 Italian Mann-licher/Carcano (Terni)	.450	.424	.325	.300	1.638	2.017	2.894
7.5x54 M1929 French	.485	.444	.338	.309	1.692	2.118	2.985
7.5x54.5 Swiss	.493	.453	.335	.307	1.763	2.182	3.050
7.63 Mauser	.387	.372	.330	.309	.763	.987	1.362
7.65 Luger	.391	.375	.328	.307	.604	.844	1.140
7.65x53 Mauser	.472	.430	.343	.310	1.755	2.101	3.075
7.7x58 Japanese	.472	.434	.339	.310	1.866	2.270	3.139
8 mm Nambu	.413	.408	.388	.338	.596	.865	1.250
8x51 Short Mauser	.469	.437	.345	.318	1.530	1.989	2.768
8x56 Mannlicher/Sch.	.464	.426	.348	.324	1.795	2.220	3.039
8(7.92)x57 JS	.467	.430	.351	.324	1.820	2.238	3.162
8x57J M1888	.470	.430	.343	.318	1.830	2.238	3.245
8x60S	.472	.428	.354	.322	1.920	2.355	3.155
9x56 Mannlicher/Sch.	.464	.420	.378	.354	1.830	2.215	3.056
9x57 Mauser	.469	.429	.385	.359	1.804	2.218	3.182
9.3x57	.470	.430	.389	.366	1.816	2.214	3.104
9.3x62	.469	.442	.385	.363	2.046	2.436	3.288
9.5x57 Mannlicher/Sch.	.467	.452	.400	.373	1.817	2.235	2.972
10.75x68 Mauser	.498	.473	.450	.424	2.069	2.674	3.179

Belted Case

Caliber (mm.)	DIAMETER (IN.) A–Rim	B–Under Head	C–Shoulder	D–Mouth	E–Bullet	LENGTH (INS.) a–Base to Shoulder	b–Case	c–Over-all
7x61 S&H	.532	.512	.463	.316	.285	1.975	2.392	3.258
7x73 vom Hofe	.535	.527	.490	.315	.280	2.110	2.871	3.701 ■

Cartridge Measurements (continued)

Rimless Straight Case

Caliber	DIAMETER (IN.) A–Head	B–Mouth	C–Bullet	LENGTH (INS.) a–Case	b–Over-all
·30 M1 Carbine	.356	.332	.307	1.285	1.681
.35 S&W Pistol	.348	.347	.310	.670	.961
.380 ACP	.373	.373	.355	.675	.980
9 mm Winchester Magnum	.392	.379	.355	1.160	1.545
.45 ACP	.473	.473	.449	.886	1.265
.45 Winchester Magnum	.477	.475	.449	1.198	1.545

Rimless Necked Case

Caliber	DIAMETER (IN.) A–Head	B–Shoulder	C–Mouth	D–Bullet	LENGTH (INS.) a–Base to Shoulder	b–Case	c–Over-all
.17 Remington	.374	.355	.198	.172	1.351	1.796	1.865
.22-.250 Remington	.465	.405	.250	.224	1.517	1.905	2.335
.221 Remington	.374	.356	.250	.223	1.075	1.392	1.810
.222 Remington	.374	.354	.243	.225	1.285	1.696	2.122
.222 Remington Mag.	.373	.353	.247	.223	1.464	1.828	2.270
.223 Remington (5.56 mm.)	.375	.350	.247	.224	1.440	1.752	2.171
.243 Winchester	.467	.447	.275	.244	1.539	2.039	2.669
.244 Remington	.465	.425	.274	.244	1.739	2.229	2.739
6 mm. Remington	.467	.423	.273	.243	1.735	2.225	2.815
6 mm. Navy Lee	.444	.397	.274	.245	1.722	2.353	3.115
.25 Remington	.420	.395	.282	.257	1.497	2.049	2.516
.250 Savage	.466	.413	.282	.254	1.513	1.910	2.444
.256 Newton	.471	.430	.288	.263	1.889	2.245	3.286
.257 Roberts	.469	.428	.289	.259	1.739	2.230	2.708
.25-06 Remington	.470	.441	.290	.257	1.948	2.494	3.005
.270 Winchester	.469	.431	.305	.272	1.967	2.535	3.273
7 mm-08 Remington	.470	.454	.315	.284	1.559	2.035	2.805
.280 Remington	.467	.436	.311	.282	2.000	2.538	3.313
7 mm Express Remington	.470	.442	.315	.284	1.999	2.540	3.320
.284 Winchester (rebated rim .473)	.498	.474	.320	.284	1.774	2.170	2.275
.30 Newton	.525	.495	.342	.308	2.005	2.517	3.378
.30 Remington	.420	.400	.330	.303	1.499	2.050	2.516
.30-'06 Springfield	.470	.435	.334	.309	1.955	2.489	3.332
.300 Savage	.466	.444	.331	.309	1.555	1.862	2.596
.308 Winchester (7.62 NATO)	.470	.450	.336	.309	1.570	2.004	2.742
.32 Remington	.419	.394	.343	.318	1.485	2.047	2.516
.35 Newton	.525	.500	.384	.358	2.005	2.518	3.325
.35 Remington	.457	.423	.383	.354	1.518	1.914	2.512
.35 Whelen	.468	.440	.380	.358	1.975	2.481	3.302
.358 Winchester	.470	.450	.383	.359	1.571	2.003	2.772

Belted Case

Caliber	DIAMETER (IN.) A–Rim	B–Under Head	C–Shoulder	D–Mouth	E–Bullet	LENGTH (INS.) a–Base to Shoulder	b–Case	c–Over-all
.224 Weatherby Mag.	.426	.414	.390	.249	.224	1.505	1.915	2.415
.240 Weatherby Mag.	.469	.449	.425	.269	.244	2.010	2.490	3.060
.257 Weatherby Mag.	.531	.510	.485	.284	.259	2.030	2.540	3.165
6.5 mm. Rem Mag.	.525	.508	.489	.293	.263	1.700	2.160	2.778
.264 Win. Mag.	.531	.508	.487	.294	.261	2.030	2.492	3.307
.270 Weatherby Mag.	.530	.508	.483	.305	.277	2.040	2.542	3.218
7 mm. Rem. Mag.	.527	.509	.484	.312	.282	2.034	2.496	3.276
7 mm. Weatherby Mag.	.530	.510	.485	.310	.282	2.045	2.538	3.274
.300 Winchester Magnum	.532	.513	.489	.339	.308	2.196	2.620	3.305
.300 Weatherby Mag.	.532	.515	.490	.335	.308	2.338	2.809	3.498
.308 Norma Mag.	.528	.508	.488	.337	.309	2.083	2.547	3.246
8 mm Remington Magnum	.532	.512	.487	.351	.323	2.389	2.850	3.598
.338 Win. Mag.	.530	.510	.485	.364	.338	2.038	2.491	3.309
.340 Weatherby Mag.	.529	.509	.485	.365	.334	2.312	2.820	3.560
.350 Remington Mag.	.525	.509	.490	.382	.358	1.695	2.162	2.750
.358 Norma Mag.	.528	.509	.487	.386	.359	2.075	2.508	3.236
.375 Weatherby Mag.	.530	.511	.484	.401	.371	2.374	2.855	3.515
.378 Weatherby Mag.	.578	.580	.550	.400	.370	2.360	2.906	3.643
.458 Win. Mag.	.531	.510	—	.480	.450	—	2.504	3.312
.460 Weatherby Mag.	.578	.581	.555	.484	.457	2.375	2.909	3.773

BRITISH CALIBERS

Rimmed Straight Case

Caliber	DIAMETER (IN.) A–Rim	B–Head	C–Mouth	D–Bullet	LENGTH (INS.) a–Case	b–Over-all
.380 Revolver (Mk I, II)	.433	.384	.384	.359	.759	1.236
.44 Webley (.442 Revolver)	.500	.457	.446	.430	.708	1.154
.450 Nitro Exp.	.617	.545	.478	.452	3.247	3.853
.455 Revolver (Mk II)	.529	.474	.472	.442	.757	1.261
.500 Nitro Exp. 3″	.650	.570	.531	.509	2.989	3.746
.577 Nitro Exp. 3″	.739	.659	.604	.582	2.991	3.619
.577 Snider (coiled brass case)	.741	.657	.614	.564	1.942	2.434

Rimmed Necked Case

Caliber	DIAMETER (IN.) A–Rim	B–Head	C–Shoulder	D–Mouth	E–Bullet	LENGTH (INS.) a–Base to Shoulder	b–Case	c–Over-all
.303 British	.533	.455	.395	.339	.312	1.799	2.204	3.033
.375 Flanged Mag.	.563	.513	.440	.400	.375	2.400	2.921	3.794
.450/400-3¼″ Nitro Exp.	.615	.543	.485	.434	.409	2.008	3.241	3.850
.577/450 Martini-Henry*	.745	.660	.614	.482	.450	1.400	2.355	3.064
.465 Nitro Exp.	.643	.572	.529	.489	.467	2.165	3.239	3.833
.470 Nitro Exp.	.646	.571	.525	.502	.471	2.400	3.242	3.864
.475 No. 2 Jeffery	.669	.580	.540	.506	.481	2.760	3.492	4.313
.577 Snider (drawn brass case)**	.750	.661	.622	.599	.565	1.125	1.610	2.140

*May be drawn brass case or coiled brass case.   **Dominion Cartridge Co., other manufacturers' case length up to 2.000″.

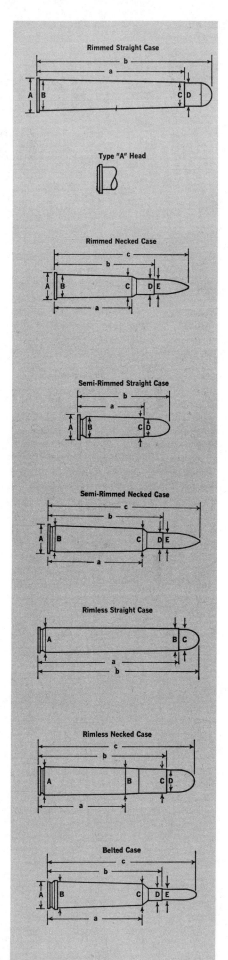

Rimmed Straight Case

Type "A" Head

Rimmed Necked Case

Semi-Rimmed Straight Case

Semi-Rimmed Necked Case

Rimless Straight Case

Rimless Necked Case

Belted Case

MODERN SPORTING RIFLE BULLETS

By M. D. WAITE

MODERN metal-jacketed sporting rifle bullets may be classified into 4 general groups—expanding, non-expanding, fragmenting, and partially fragmenting. The choice of bullet by caliber, weight, and type is related to the animal against which it is to be used.

The outer jacket or envelope can be steel, nickel silver (copper-zinc-nickel alloy), cupro-nickel (copper-nickel alloy), gilding metal (copper-zinc alloy), or Lubaloy (copper-zinc-tin alloy). The steel jacket may be sheathed with thin layers of these alloys, or electroplated with tin, nickel, or copper. These coverings prevent rusting of the jacket and reduce friction between the bullet and the rifle bore.

The expanding bullet

The expanding bullet is designed for use against thin-skinned big game. The significant feature in its construction is that the nose portion is made weak so that it will rupture and upset after impact. The degree and speed of nose disruption can be controlled to some extent by the design of the bullet. Other factors affecting performance of the expanding bullet are its velocity at impact and the density of the tissues struck.

The body, or base portion, of the typical expanding bullet is strengthened so that it will hold together after impact and thus assure adequately deep penetration. The expansion of the nose portion increases the diameter of the wound channel, and particles of the jacket and core torn from the bullet can become effective secondary missiles adding materially to its wounding power. A large wound channel is more conducive to hemorrhaging than a small one, and the probability of an adequate blood trail from wounded game is enhanced.

The increase in the cross-sectional area of the bullet by expansion of the nose retards its passage through tissue and insures maximum energy transmission to the animal.

The simplest and oldest form of expanding bullet is the so-called mushroom or soft-point which has a portion of the soft lead core exposed at the tip. The metal jacket encloses the base and side of the bullet. Other means employed to weaken the noses of expanding bullets are: (1) Slitting the jacket longitudinally, (2) rolling or cutting annular grooves in the jacket, (3) thinning the jacket toward the nose, (4) nicking the jacket annularly, (5) providing an internal cavity in the nose portion, (6) hollow-pointing the nose, (7) providing a hard metal wedge to rupture the nose on impact, (8) making a double jacket, the outer jacket covering the base of the bullet only.

Some expanding bullets are made with a pointed nose cap of thin metal. The cap enhances the flight performance of the bullet by acting as a windshield. It also insures proper feeding of the cartridge in box-magazine rifles. The properly-designed metal-capped expanding bullet is not liable to blunting from impact against the front wall of the magazine box. Bullets with a pointed metal wedge in the nose also have all these advantages.

The non-expanding bullet

Non-expanding sporting bullets, called 'solids' by the British, have one-piece metal jackets covering the nose and body portions. The hardened lead core is usually exposed at the base.

Non-expanding bullets are designed primarily for taking large and often dangerous Asiatic and African game having very tough and thick hides and whose vital organs may be protected by thick layers of bone or muscle. These bullets almost always have round noses. This nose shape is least liable to deflection or tipping when striking bone or muscle. This assures deepest penetration.

Non-expanding jacketed bullets of small caliber are sometimes used in taking valuable fur-bearing game or edible small game such as turkey. Here the purpose is to kill the animal humanely and with minimum damage to pelt or meat. Tissue destruction can be reduced materially by handloading such special-purpose ammunition to reduced velocity levels. Ammunition of this type is not regularly manufactured.

Non-expanding big-game bullets, regardless of caliber or weight, may be upset or deformed on striking bone or dense tissue. This occurs because of weakness in construction and not by intent of the designer or manufacturer.

The fragmenting bullet

The fragmenting bullet is designed to give maximum blow-up effect when driven at high velocity. Fragmenting bullets are made in small and medium calibers only, usually not larger than cal. .30. Fragmenting bullets are made for hunting smaller, varmint-class animals, usually considered inedible. They are highly destructive to tissue, but lack the penetrating ability of expanding and non-expanding big-game bullets. For these reasons, fragmenting bullets are not suitable for taking big game.

Fragmenting bullets fall generally in the lightweight category in each caliber, and are invariably of soft-point or open hollow-point construction. The core is soft lead and the jacket is made thin to insure maximum disintegration of the entire bullet. Disintegration of the fragmenting bullet may not occur reliably at low-velocity levels, although its nose portion may expand appreciably.

The partially fragmenting bullet

The partially fragmenting bullet used in hunting thin-skinned big game has performance characteristics common to both expanding and fragmenting bullets. The nose portion of this bullet form, including lead core and jacket structure, is designed to shatter into numerous random-size fragments which then range outward from the wound channel. These fragments, often sharp and jagged, become effective secondary missiles. Following disruption of the nose portion, the base of the bullet may continue to break down and throw off fragments until it penetrates the animal completely, or is stopped by resistance of tissue or bone. The highest energy yield is obtained when all of the bullet remains in the animal. This holds true for any type.

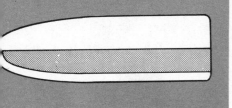

Full-jacketed non-expanding or solid sporting bullet. Also called full-patched, full-mantled, and full metal cased. One-piece jacket is open at base end only. Many early full-jacketed military bullets were of this type

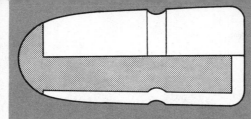

Round-nose soft-point expanding or mushroom bullet with large area of lead exposed at tip. One-piece metal jacket covers base and side of bullet. Rolled cannelure (groove) is provided for crimping cartridge case neck into side of bullet. Rolled cannelure aids in retaining core in jacket. This was first form of expanding bullet

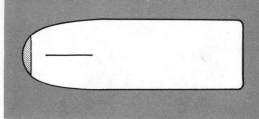

Round-nose soft-point expanding bullet with lead core exposed at tip (British). One-piece jacket covers base and side of bullet. Longitudinal slits in fore-part of jacket provided to weaken nose portion of bullet. One of the first attempts to better expansion qualities of conventional soft-point bullet

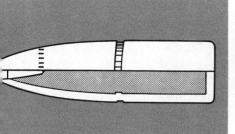

Open hollow-point expanding bullet. Base and side of bullet are enclosed by one-piece jacket. Jacket has been intentionally weakened by annular knurling or nicking near end of nose portion. Knurled cannelure around body of bullet is case crimping groove. Hollow-point fragmenting bullet is constructed similarly, but jacket is thinned to insure maximum blow-up effect in animal

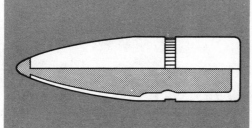

Hornady pointed soft-point expanding bullet. Lead core exposed at tip. One-piece jacket covers base and side of bullet. Note pronounced thinning of jacket in nose section. Rolled cannelure is for case crimping, but also aids in retaining core in base of bullet. Fragmenting soft-point bullets are of similar appearance, but jacket is thinned to insure maximum blow-up effect in animal

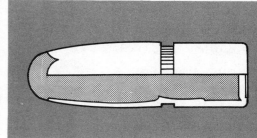

Remington round-nose soft-point Core-Lokt bullet. Mouth of jacket has deeply notched, scalloped edge to insure uniform rupturing of jacket. Similar effect is obtained in Winchester Power-Point bullet by cutting V-shaped notches in jacket mouth. Note how base of Core-Lokt bullet has been reinforced by thickening jacket opposite crimping cannelure. This construction aids in retaining core in base of bullet

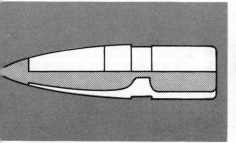

Nosler Partition pointed soft-point expanding bullet. Jacket open at both ends to expose core. Inner partition reinforces base portion of bullet. Note gradual reduction in jacket thickness towards point. Belt-like groove in jacket opposite partition is provided to lower bore pressure

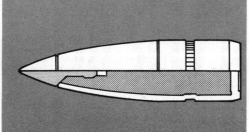

Remington Bronze Point expanding bullet. Wedge-like bronze point located in bullet nose is driven to rear on impact, rupturing jacket and expanding fore-part of the bullet

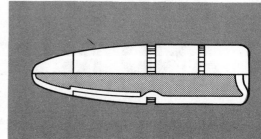

Winchester Silvertip pointed expanding bullet. Outer copper jacket covers base and side of bullet. Lead core tip is protected by soft, easily crushed aluminum casing which extends back and under outer jacket of bullet

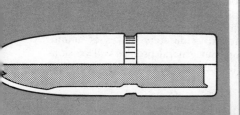

Remington open hollow-point Core-Lokt expanding bullet. Form of open hollow-point bullet with shallow nose cavity to give less rapid expansion or mushrooming. Note how jacket is weakened by abrupt thinning in nose area

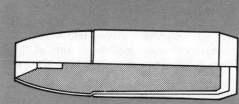

RWS D-Mantle (German) open hollow-point expanding bullet. Unique double jacket construction. Outer jacket enclosing base portion is steel, clad with cupro-nickel alloy. Inner jacket extending to nose is copper

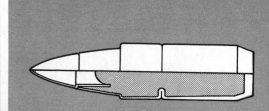

RWS H-Mantle (German) partially fragmenting bullet. Outer jacket is steel, clad with cupro-nickel alloy. Nose cap enclosing internal cavity is copper. Note that jacket is folded inward at mid-point of bullet to divide frangible fore-part from base of bullet ∎

Bullet Forms—The round-nose bullet (1) is the most common form. Most police and military Service ammunition is loaded with this bullet. The wadcutter bullet (2) is loaded primarily in target ammunition, and has been developed over a long period to give fine target accuracy. Abrupt shoulder punches a clean hole in target for easier scoring. Semi-wadcutter (3) has sharp shoulder and nose extending forward of the shoulder.

Truncated-cone bullet (4) typically ends in flat point. Conical (pointed) bullet (5) has a bullet tip which usually ends in a very small flat. The round-nose flat-point bullet (6) is a variation of (1). Hollow-point construction (7) is available in most types of bullets. The function of the hollow point is to aid bullet expansion on striking. The extent of expansion is controlled by varying the size, shape, and depth of cavity.

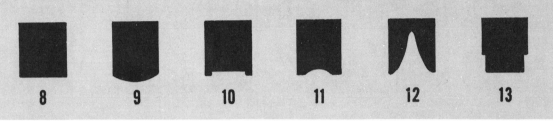

Base Forms—Bullet base forms are named according to their shape: (8) flat, (9) convex, (10) recessed flat, (11) cup, (12) hollow, and (13) heel. Flat base and recessed flat base are the most common forms.

MODERN PISTOL AND REVOLVER BULLETS

By E. W. HETER, JR.

CURRENTLY available commercial pistol and revolver bullets are of 2 basic types according to their construction: solid metal bullets, and composite bullets with some form of a harder metal attachment.

Solid metal bullets are almost always lead, alloyed with tin and/or antimony to make the metal slightly harder. Pure lead is seldom used because it is too soft for most requirements.

The most common form of composite pistol and revolver bullet is a lead slug with outer jacket of harder metal. Semi-automatic pistols larger than cal. .22 commonly use jacketed bullet cartridges because they give more reliable functioning. Jacketed bullets are not easily deformed and give greater penetration than plain lead bullets.

Lead bullets commonly have a forward circumferential groove into which the cartridge case mouth is crimped. There are also one or more grooves be-

hind the crimping groove to hold lubricant. Grooves vary in size, shape, number, and placement. Jacketed bullets sometimes have a crimping groove but seldom have lubricating grooves because metals used in jacketing do not require lubrication.

Factory-made bullets are produced by a cold-forming process called swaging. A lead slug is formed in dies under great pressure to the desired shape and size. Jacketed bullets are formed similarly, with a lead slug inserted into the jacket cup before swaging.

Bullets are also formed by casting, but no major manufacturer now employs this process.

The most significant feature of a pistol or revolver bullet is its nose shape. Those shown in illustration titled "Bullet Forms" are basic types. Variations will be found in different makes of ammunition, but general profiles will be similar to these examples. ∎

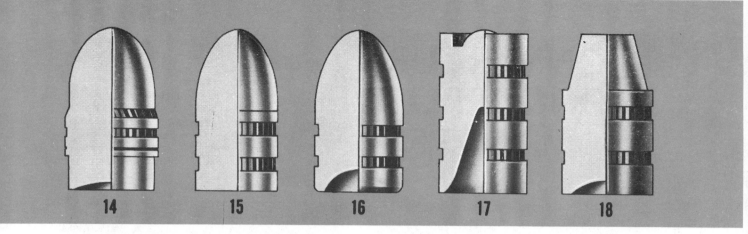

Solid Metal Bullets—Heel-type bullet **(14)** has a short, reduced diameter portion (heel) that seats in cartridge case. Round-nose bullets **(15)** and **(16)** are most common form for revolvers. Hollow-base wadcutter **(17)** gives bullet of desired weight with long bearing surface to grip rifling. Semi-wadcutter **(18)** is loaded for both target and Service use.

A bullet of form **(15)** made of zinc is an exception to the usual lead alloy. It is a metal-penetrating bullet as discussed in illustration titled "Composite Bullets".

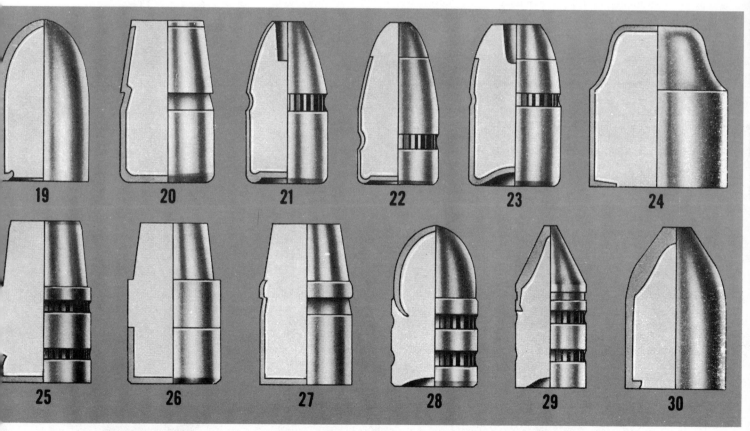

Composite Bullets—Other metals combined with lead in composite bullets may be cupro-nickel (copper and nickel), gilding metal (copper and zinc), nickel, soft steel, or steel coated with the above metals.

Included among the composite types are **(19)** full metal jacketed bullet, the most common type loaded in center-fire auto pistol cartridges; **(20)** truncated-cone nose form with exposed lead tip; **(21)** full metal jacket with hollow point; **(22)** exposed lead tip, permitting bullet expansion; **(23)** exposed tip and hollow point; and **(24)** jacketed target bullet for auto pistols. Short metal cup on **(25)** is a gas check. It provides a better seal against powder gases when used in powerful loads. A base cup about half bullet length describes the half-jacketed bullet **(26)**. A body-jacketed bullet **(27)** has base and full bearing surface covered.

Metal-piercing or metal-penetrating bullets **(28)**, **(29)**, and **(30)** are for special purpose use. They are designed to resist deformation when striking hard objects, and to give maximum penetration. They are used mainly in law-enforcement work to penetrate fleeing automobiles. The point of **(28)** has a heavy gilding-metal covering. Note that the jacket thickens considerably toward the point of bullets **(29)** and **(30)**.

NONMERCURIC, NONCORROSIVE PRIMERS

For many years the primers of small-arms cartridges caused damage to both cartridge cases and rifle barrels. Now the manufacture of such potentially harmful ammunition in this and most other countries is a thing of the past. That which remains in existence, however, is still a problem and will remain so for a long time. Many users wish to know how to recognize and avoid such ammunition, or to minimize its effects.

Two sources of damage

The damage to cartridge cases and barrels is due to 2 quite separate constituents which have been used in primers.

Cartridge cases are ruined by mercury, which is left after the explosion of mercury fulminate. Long known, chemically simple, easy to make, and very sensitive, mercury fulminate was until recent decades the favorite initiator in primers.

In blackpowder days its effect on cartridge brass was minimized by the diluting and sweeping effect of blackpowder fouling. Damage became evident when smokeless powder was introduced in the military cal. .30 cartridge about 1892. Strong primers for the smokeless powder, higher pressures, and the absence of heavy powder residue resulted in depositing much more mercury than before and driving it harder into the brass. Mercury amalgamates with the cartridge brass on firing, making it weak and brittle. The damage cannot be prevented or corrected by any treatment of the case after firing.

In those days the fired cases from military target practice were sent back to the manufacturing arsenal and reloaded. This system was upset when the cases became useless on firing. Investigation by the Ordnance Dept. revealed the cause of case damage to be mercury left by the primer. Mercury fulminate was thereupon discontinued in military primers. This discontinuance was absolute. *There has been no mercury in U. S. military small-arms primers manufactured since about 1898.* It was used to a later date in certain commercial primers.

While mercury fulminate ruined cartridge cases for reloading but was harmless to the gun, another old constituent of primers was harmless to cases but damaging to the gun. This constituent was potassium chlorate. It continued in general use much later than mercury fulminate, and was much the more difficult problem to correct.

Potassium chlorate was added to percussion priming compositions because it was found that such an oxidizer was required, mercury fulminate alone making a poor primer. *So the early smokeless-powder primers were both mercuric and corrosive.* While the mercury was rather soon identified as a cause of trouble and eliminated, the chlorate stayed on because it did its job so well in the primer. Also the barrel damage was not positively traced to it for many years. Even then the knowledge spread very slowly among users. Bore rusting was blamed on the smokeless powder residue, and almost every conceivable type of 'powder solvent' was marketed and used with only indifferent success.

Early non-rusting primers

The Germans began work to develop a non-rusting primer about 1900, and the Swiss Army began use of one about 1911. It was not until 1922, on publication of an investigation by Dr. Wilbert J. Huff of the U. S. Bureau of Mines, that the primer's responsibility for barrel rusting became known in this country. Work then began, based largely on German patents bought by Remington Arms Co., to develop primers without the rust-causing potassium chlorate. Remington Kleanbore priming was put on the market in 1927, and was followed by the other commercial makes.

Though successfully noncorrosive, these primers had the serious defect of often becoming insensitive after only a year or so. The makers had had to reintroduce mercury fulminate to make these primers work, and mercury fulminate mixtures tend to deteriorate in heat and humidity. Also the cases once more were spoiled for reloading by the mercury deposited in them on firing. However, ways were eventually found to make these primers work without mercury fulminate. In the early 1930's all U. S. commercial primers (with a single exception given below) became both nonmercuric and noncorrosive, damaging to neither cartridge cases nor gun bores. Eventually all these primers were made to substantially the same formula, based on a compound called lead styphnate.

U. S. commercial ammunition of noncorrosive or nonmercuric-noncorrosive type is always so marked on the box, and so are primers sold for reloading. There is, in general, nothing to show whether loose commercial cartridges or primers are corrosive or not.

If ammunition containing corrosive primers has been fired, the bore should be cleaned no later than the same day of firing with either U. S. military bore cleaner or water. If water is used, place muzzle in a container of hot soapy water, pump bore full several times with brass brush on cleaning rod, and then wipe bore dry with several snug-fitting patches. After bore is clean and dry, coat it lightly with oil or grease on a patch. Cold water, or saliva on brush and patch, can be used if hot water is not available

The exception to the rule, that U. S. commercial ammunition became both nonmercuric and noncorrosive soon after 1930, was Winchester-Western Super-Match ammunition in cals. .30-'06 and .300 H&H Magnum. This was loaded with a primer (Western 8½ G) which was both corrosive and mildly mercuric, because of a belief that shooting accuracy was improved by such primers. Extensive tests showed the same results could be obtained with existing noncorrosive primers, and in 1960 the 8½ G primer and ammunition loaded with it were dropped. That was so far as known the final U. S. small-arms primer of either mercuric or corrosive type.

The development of noncorrosive primers in U. S. military ammunition took longer because of the more severe military requirements. The erratic ignition and unsatisfactory storage stability of the early commercial noncorrosive primers were unacceptable, as large quantities of small-arms ammunition are stored as a war reserve. This reserve must have unquestioned dependability and long storage life.

Special noncorrosive primer

A special noncorrosive primer was loaded in the 1930 National Match ammunition manufactured at Frankford Arsenal. This was a Berdan primer, since the composition used in it required a larger pellet than could be contained in the regular anvil primer. Trouble was experienced with high pressures during the first few days of use at Camp Perry and, while this may have been due primarily to unusually hot weather at that time, the ammunition was replaced with a lot of conventional loading and not further used.

The tremendous production of U. S. military small-arms ammunition in World War II was (with only 2 exceptions) of nonmercuric but corrosive type. The primer mixture, excellent in every way except its characteristic of rusting gun bores, was that known as FA (Frankford Arsenal) No. 70, and it was used in the FA 26 primer and equivalent primers of the other military ammunition producers. One of the exceptions was a limited quantity of noncorrosive .30-'06 ball ammunition manufactured late in the war in Canada. The other was the entire class of cal. .30 carbine ammunition, all of which was noncorrosive from the beginning.

Frankford Arsenal's work

Since some of the best noncorrosive primer compositions were covered by foreign patents, Frankford Arsenal began study of the problem to find one suitable for standardization as the official Government composition. The search appeared to be ended when the P-4 primer was developed. This had a distinctive composition of red phosphorus and barium nitrate quite unlike that of other noncorrosive primers. It was satisfactory under the severest requirements, and was used for a time in manufacture. However, there was only one source of red phosphorus of adequate quality, that from other sources being not as good in storage life, and this ultimately led to abandoning the P-4 primer. The cup of this primer is zinc-plated to protect it against the action of a constituent of the pellet, and this zinc plating gives a means of identifying the P-4 primer in loaded cartridges.

Ordnance decided in 1950 that the styphnate type was the best available and that further search for new noncorrosive types was not necessary. Interim use of commercial primers was authorized. Meanwhile Frankford Arsenal, with full cooperation from industry, proceeded to develop a military primer of styphnate type. The resulting primer was the FA 36. When adopted in June 1958, this primer was specially made to reproduce the quite 'soft' action of the old FA 26 primer. Later it was found necessary to give it a somewhat stronger action for adequate ignition in extreme cold, and the FA 36 was eventually standardized with an action like the softer commercial types.

As a result of experience and the supply of primers under military procurement, the commercial large rifle primers have become substantially alike in composition and performance, and differences between makes are relatively minor.

Ordnance decision to manufacture all military small-arms ammunition with noncorrosive primers was made in August 1949. Apparently it was hoped that this change could be completed by the beginning of the following year. It actually took much longer, and was fully carried out by different arsenals and manufacturers at different times.

Distinguishing between types

The delayed introduction of non-corrosive primers in military ammunition, and the great quantity of corrosive-type military ammunition still in existence, make it important to be able to distinguish between corrosive and noncorrosive types to prevent unexpected gun damage.

Military primers in boxes labeled "FA 26", or "FA 70" composition, are corrosive. Noncorrosive commercial primers made under military procurement are normally so labeled.

Military ammunition is not marked on the packing to indicate whether it is corrosive or noncorrosive. This can be determined only from the lot or date of manufacture. The following tabulation shows the precise lot number, month, and year of the first all-noncorrosive production by each maker (scattered noncorrosive lots loaded earlier as only a part of production are not considered). The ammunition maker's lot number does not normally appear on packing less than case size. Smaller packings and loose rounds can be determined to be noncorrosive only by the make and year of the cartridge headstamp. Then only ammunition of the next year and later can safely be considered noncorrosive. For example, the Lake City Arsenal went fully over to noncorrosive .30-'06 ball ammunition at its Lot 13700 of June 1951. That and all later lots of .30-'06 ball ammunition by that maker are noncorrosive; all earlier must be considered corrosive. If only the cartridge headstamp information is known, then in ammunition of that make and type only that headstamped "LC 52" and later years can be known to be noncorrosive.

Frankford Arsenal—Headstamp "FA" and last 2 digits of the year. (A single 4 means 1944, a single 5 means 1955.)
.30-'06 ball—Lot 4149, Oct. 1951
.30-'06 AP—Lot 887, October 1951
.45 M1911 ball—Lot 1542, July 1954

Exceptions: 1. .30-'06 ball with zinc-plated primer and headstamped "FA 47" or later is noncorrosive.

2. FA .30-'06 special Match, headstamped "FA 53", "FA 54", or "FA 56" and with red, purple, or green waterproofing around primer, is corrosive.

Federal Cartridge Co. — Headstamp "FCC" and last 2 digits of the year.
.45 M1911 ball—Lot 1801, November 1953

Lake City Arsenal—Headstamp "LC" and last 2 digits of the year.
.30-'06 ball—Lot 13700, June 1951
.30-'06 AP—Lot 13158, April 1952

Remington Arms Co., Inc.—Headstamp "RA" and last 2 digits of the year.
.30-'06 ball—Lot 33853, November 1951
.45 M1911 ball—Lot 5544, September 1952

St. Louis Ordnance Plant—Headstamp "SL" and last 2 digits of the year.
.30-'06 ball—Lot 9420, May 1952
.30-'06 AP—Lot 9467, July 1952

Twin Cities Arsenal—Headstamp "TW" and last 2 digits of the year.
.30-'06 ball—Lot 19362, December 1950
.30-'06 AP—Lot 19776, February 1952

.45 M1911 ball—Lot 18000, August 1953

Western Cartridge Co.—Headstamp "WCC" and last 2 digits of the year.
.30-'06 ball—Lot 6428, June 1951
.45 M1911 ball—Lot 6375, November 1952

Winchester Repeating Arms Co.—Headstamp "WRA" and last 2 digits of the year.
.30-'06 ball—Lot 23201, August 1951
.30-'06 AP—Lot 22007, June 1954
.45 M1911 ball—Lot 22198, November 1951
Steel-case Lots 22000-22007 only, June 1954

Dominion Arsenal, Canada—Headstamp "DAQ" and last 2 digits of the year.
.30-'06 ball—Lot 44000, August 1945 (All by this maker was corrosive)

Verdun Arsenal, Canada—Headstamp "VC" and last 2 digits of the year.
.30-'06 ball—Lot 42000, April 1945 (All by this maker was noncorrosive)

Carbine and 7.62 mm. NATO

All .30 carbine ammunition is noncorrosive. All 7.62 mm. NATO ammunition made in this country is noncorrosive, *except* 1956 International Match ammunition of that caliber made at Frankford Arsenal at the same time as the corrosive .30-'06 International Match ammunition of 1956 tabulated above.

The following establishments manufactured small-arms ammunition during World War II only, and all their production was of corrosive type:

Eau Claire Ordnance Plant—Headstamp "EW" and last 2 digits of the year.

Denver Ordnance Plant—Headstamp "DEN" and last 2 digits of the year.

Des Moines Ordnance Plant—Headstamp "DM" and last 2 digits of the year.

Utah Ordnance Plant—Headstamp "U" or "UT" and last 2 digits of the year.

From time to time ammunition in ordnance storage is repacked as required by condition of the containers. Date of repacking is noted on case-size containers. This is not a remanufacturing operation and does not change the character of the ammunition, which remains corrosive or noncorrosive as it was before repacking.

Many present-day shooters have no clear idea of why corrosive ammunition types rusted gun bores, or how to remove the residue of such ammunition from bores to prevent rusting.

The residue left by the potassium chlorate in corrosive primers was potassium chloride, a compound much like table salt or sea salt but with an even greater affinity for water. As soon as the barrel cooled after firing, water was supplied from the atmospheric moisture which is usually present and the steel, covered with wet salt, rusted.

In blackpowder firearms this was minimized by the weak primers, the diluting and sweeping action of the blackpowder, and the water used after firing to remove the heavy blackpowder fouling. So blackpowder breechloaders sometimes survived unharmed. In smokeless-powder arms the first 2 saving factors were not present, nor was the third except on military ranges where water cleaning was normally enforced. Users elsewhere were reluctant to put water into their guns. The result of this misplaced delicacy was almost invariably bore rusting. In small bores this regularly proceeded to destruction.

Shooters using corrosive ammunition now must know how to remove its residue if they wish to preserve their gun bores. It can be done with the correct cleaning, performed soon enough.

Removing corrosive primer residue

Commercial 'powder solvents' remove smokeless powder residue very well, but in general do not remove potassium chloride directly. Dependence on them after firing corrosive primers usually results in slow roughening of the bore. However, the U. S. military bore cleaner is procured under severe performance specifications which require it to be effective against chlorate primer fouling. It is available from the DCM and sometimes commercially. To clean the gun bore, pour a little of the cleaner on a brass bore brush held upright (do not foul the cleaner by dipping dirty brushes into it), and pass the wet brush several times through the bore. Follow with several cleaning patches wet with the cleaner. Dry the bore, and preserve it by wiping with rust-preventive oil or grease on a patch.

Water, for which potassium chloride has such an affinity, removes it well. Cold water or saliva is effective. Hot water warms the barrel and leaves it easier to wipe dry, and soap or soda relieves the stickiness of the fouling. To clean, stick the rifle muzzle in a can of hot soapsuds, pump the bore full several times with a brass bore brush on the cleaning rod, then dry and grease the bore as already described. To clean the M1 rifle in which the receiver is not open to the rear, turn the rifle sights-down to prevent water running unnecessarily into the gas cylinder, swab bore with soapy water on brass brush and patches, wipe dry, and grease. Barrel of the .45 Service pistol is easily removed for water cleaning. ■

Primer And Bullet Sealer

Some commercial and most military ammunition has a waterproof sealant around the primer and bullet. What are the advantages of this, and is there an easy way for the handloader to do it with common materials?

Answer: Primer and bullet sealants minimize risk of powder or primer contamination by moisture, gun oils, etc. Strong attachment of the bullet is necessary in military ammunition to withstand functioning in automatic weapons. Bullet extraction force is measured in ammunition acceptance tests. In factory loading some pistol and revolver cartridges, such as .38 Spl. or 9 mm Luger with lightweight bullets, increased bullet pull created by a sealant improves ballistic uniformity. Although sealant makes ammunition more resistant to contamination, such risk is not totally eliminated (see *American Rifleman*, Oct., 1976, p. 32).

For many years U.S. military ammunition has employed asphaltic varnish around the bullets. The inside of the case neck is coated with the varnish just before the bullet is seated. One of the primary requirements in such compounds is that they cause no significantly increased bullet extraction force during storage. Substitution of other materials may increase bullet pull undesirably or inhibit proper obturation of the case neck, thereby raising pressures. Asphaltic varnish is not readily available, but can be simulated by thinning asphalt with a non-polymerizing petroleum based solvent such as kerosene or naptha, though such a preparation is messy and difficult to apply by hand.

Satisfactory results are obtained using lacquer around the bullet, as well as the primer. This has been done frequently in European military ammunition. Automotive touch-up lacquer thinned to a watery consistency works well. Lacquer is applied in a narrow band around the joint between the case mouth and bullet, after the bullets have been fully seated. An artists brush works well for application. The lacquer coating must be thin, so that the diameter of the cartridge at the case mouth does not exceed the dimension listed in the appropriate drawing, *after* the lacquer has dried. After the cartridges are placed in boxes, apply a drop of thinned lacquer over each primer with an eye dropper. Cartridges so prepared are adequately sealed for all but the most severe requirements.—R.F.D.

BLACKPOWDER

By E. H. HARRISON

BLACKPOWDER is by far the oldest explosive. Certainly known in Europe by the 13th Century, it was used first in fireworks, then in guns, and finally in mining. It is still made and used.

Blackpowder was the only gun propellant until a century ago. In the United States especially, smokeless powder did not begin to supersede it in sporting arms until 1893. It is still required in muzzle-loading arms and some old breech-loaders for which available smokeless powders appear unsuitable. Its characteristics are therefore still of interest.

Blackpowder (with exceptions which will be mentioned) is made of saltpeter or potassium nitrate, charcoal, and sulphur. The proportions of these have been varied in almost every possible way. The approximate proportions 75% saltpeter, 15% charcoal, and 10% sulphur eventually came to be used in every country. In the United States the proportions are 74%, 15.6%, and 10.4%.

A mechanical mixture

Blackpowder is a mechanical mixture of these ingredients. Its power depends on the intimacy with which they are brought together. It was early found that the ingredients had to be well pulverized and mixed. The powdered mixture was subject to uneven settling of its ingredients when carried, and a very fine powder did not burn regularly. To overcome these troubles a corning, or granulating, procedure was developed after a time, by which the mixture was wetted at the proper stage of its incorporation and pounded or pressed into cake, then broken up into grains. The processes and machinery of blackpowder making have been almost continuously improved even into recent times. The object was usually to improve the thoroughness of mixing and to produce a dense and hard grain, rather than to change the fundamental nature of blackpowder.

Only in the last 125 years has this ancient mixture come to be adequately understood.

The beginning knowledge of modern chemistry in the early 1800's made it possible to purify the ingredients effectively, especially the nitrate. This purification, mainly by removal of chlorides, added greatly to the performance, reliability, and keeping properties of blackpowder. The great American firm of E. I. du Pont de Nemours & Co. had an important part in this work.

Consistent improvement of anything requires the ability to measure it. The velocity given the projectile became measurable when the ballistic pendulum was invented in 1742, and later the electric chronograph of the 1840's. The Rodman pressure gauge in 1861 completed the fundamental instrumentation with which performance at last could be specified.

The pressure gauge revealed how ineffective had been the control of burning by powder granulation up to that time. This was due partly to the grains being somewhat permeable, no matter how dense and smooth they appeared to be, and partly to the lack of any idea as to how large the grains really had to be. With this new knowledge Rodman was led to compress the powder heavily, making it so impermeable that it would burn only on the surface, and to determine grain sizes in true accord with the requirements of the gun. The resulting cannon grains were many times the size of any used before. They made it possible to fire elongated shot of large caliber. Similar work was done in England and Germany.

Brown powder

In pursuance of this line an advantage was found in using underburnt charcoal in the powder. The resulting brown powder, made with help of the instrumentation mentioned, gave performance not very much below that of the later smokeless. It was the highest development of blackpowder. Coming at the end of the blackpowder age, it was superseded by smokeless after little more than a decade, and disappeared after too short a period to make a lasting impression. The blackpowder which has remained in use, principally for small-arms sporting and muzzle-loader ammunition and for mining, is of conventional type.

One important innovation had been made earlier, but since it was restricted to mining powder, only sufficient mention for understanding it will be made.

It consisted in replacing potassium nitrate in the blackpowder formula with sodium nitrate. It was patented by Lammot du Pont in 1857. The object was to use the cheap sodium nitrate then beginning to be mined in Chile (therefore called "Chile saltpeter") in place of the potassium nitrate which at that time was obtained slowly and laboriously, mostly from India.

A second advantage was and still is the lower molecular weight of sodium nitrate which is to that of potassium nitrate as 85 to 101. Because of this a smaller proportion of sodium nitrate can be used and at the same time a more powerful powder is produced. Unfortunately sodium nitrate is markedly more hygroscopic (water-attracting) than potassium nitrate. This characteristic is considered to make sodium nitrate powder unsuitable for most purposes, but mining blackpowder is almost all of this type.

Smoke and fouling

The burning of blackpowder consists in rapid oxidation of its charcoal and sulphur by oxygen supplied by the nitrate. Because of the various compounds which are formed at successive stages, this apparently simple reaction is quite complex. The permanent gases formed are principally carbon dioxide, carbon monoxide, and nitrogen. The solid products are potassium carbonate, potassium sulphate, and potassium mono- and higher sulphides. These, with a little uncombined carbon, make up the smoke and fouling of blackpowder. The solid products total more than half (nearly 56%) the weight of the powder, which obviously is unfavorable.

The solid sulphides and some hydrogen sulphide in the gaseous products account for the stench of blackpowder smoke and fouling. The question arises as to why sulphur should be a constituent of blackpowder at all. Its presence is mostly the result of blind experiment and imitation over a long time. As a fuel, charcoal alone is very good, and it is quite possible to proportion the charcoal and nitrate for a balanced combustion by themselves.

Sulphur turns out to be useful because it lowers the ignition temperature of blackpowder, and also improves the homogeneousness of the mixture. Ease of ignition was not a critical matter in brown cannon powders and the brown charcoal mixed especially well, so these powders were made with as little as 3% sulphur. For the conventional blackpowders which are the ones still in use, the benefits from sulphur are important.

Following are the potassium nitrate blackpowers made in the United States in recent years:

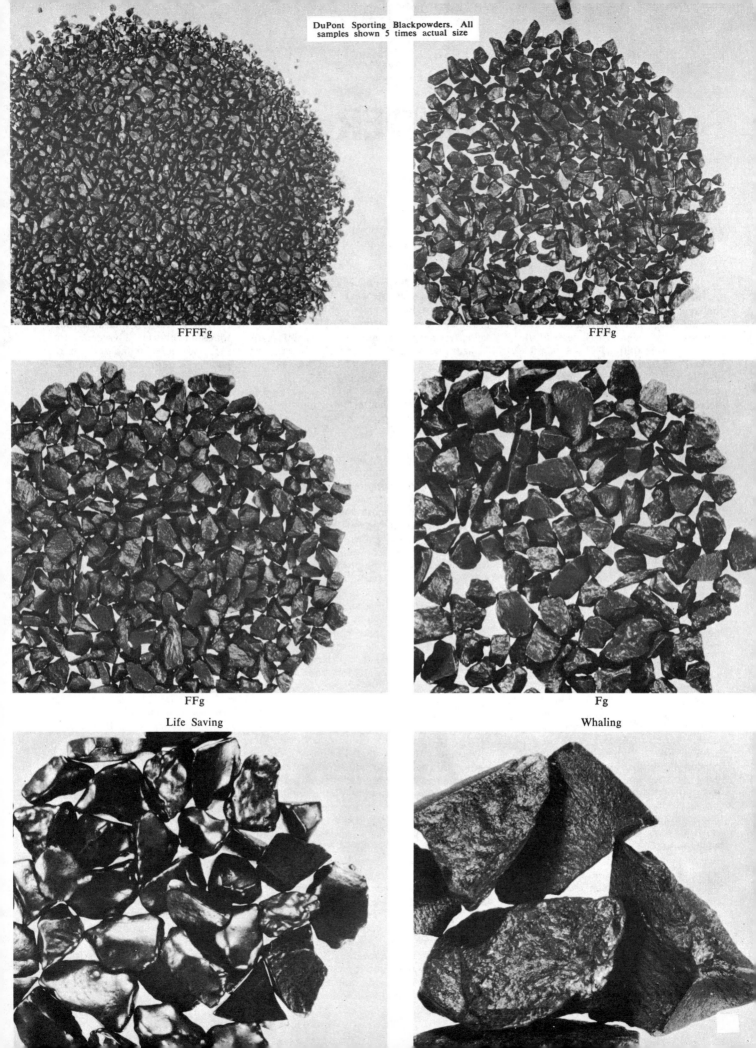

DuPont Sporting Blackpowders. All
samples shown 5 times actual size

FFFFg

FFFg

FFg

Life Saving

Fg

Whaling

| Powder Designation | | | Screen Opening (Square mesh) | |
Army	Navy	DuPont Sporting	Hold	Pass
—	—	Whaling	.441″	.156″
A-1	—	—	.187″	.0937″
—	Cannon	—	.132″	.0661″
—	—	Life Saving	.131″	.065″
—	—	Fg	.0689″	.0582″
A-3	—	—	.0661″	.0469″
—	—	FFg	.0582″	.0376″
—	Musket	—	.0555″	.0280″
—	FFG	—	.0469″	.0232″
A-4	—	—	.0469″	.0165″
—	Shell	—	.0469″	.0117″
—	—	FFFg	.0376″	.0170″
—	FFFG	—	.0331″	.0117″
—	—	FFFFg	.0170″	.0111″
A-5	Fuze	—	.0165″	.0059″
—	FFFFG	—	.0138″	.0041″
—	Meal	—	.0098″	.0029″
A-6,-7	—	—	.0059″	.0041″

For small arms, blackpowder is chosen by granulation according to the size and kind of charge. DuPont Sporting Fg is regularly used for large rifle cartridges, though for cartridges larger than .45-70 a still coarser granulation would be better. FFg is suitable for small rifle and large pistol cartridges, and for medium and heavy shotgun loads. FFFg is used for small pistol cartridges and for light shotgun loads. FFFFg is seldom used in small arms except in the pans of flintlocks.

From the above table it appears at first sight that there is a wide variety of blackpowders. In reality, however, all the powders in the table are of substantially the same composition, and they are all glazed (tumbled with graphite in the final stage of manufacture to give the grains a hard smooth finish) excepting only Army A-5, -6, and -7, and Navy Fuze and Meal, which are unglazed. There is therefore practically no difference between most of these powders except in granulation.

Highest development 1870-1900

Small-arms blackpowders reached their highest development between 1870 and 1900. In that period there were many types made by the several powder makers in the United States, well-known ones being Hazard's Kentucky Rifle and Sea Shooting; Laflin & Rand's Orange Extra, Lightning, and Ducking; DuPont Diamond Grain, Eagle Sporting, Eagle Duck, and Eagle Rifle; Oriental, in various grades; and many others. Some noted English powders were regularly imported such as Curtis & Harvey Diamond Grain and Col. Hawker's Duck Powder, and Pigou, Wilks, and Laurence's powders.

Many of these differed materially in glazing, in hardness and density of grain, and even to a limited extent in composition. It was usual for the careful shooter of either rifle or shotgun to select his powders by brand and type to give the results he preferred in his loadings. Thus, for example, the long-range

rifle shot who loaded his ammunition only a short time before firing and cleaned his rifle barrel after every shot, found it advantageous to select a soft-grained powder quite different from the hard-grained type needed by the hunter whose cartridges might be kept a long time after loading and who often had to fire many shots before cleaning his rifle. Our present powder is of the latter type.

By the beginning of World War I, many complaints were heard from blackpowder users that the powder was not so good as it used to be. Since both materials and manufacturing processes were certainly as good as ever, it was generally considered that these complaints resulted from the contrast between blackpowder and the new smokeless, which made the bad features of blackpowder more annoying than they had been when there was nothing better known. Probably this did account for most of the complaints. But undoubtedly some of them rested on a real worsening of results, following disappearance of the variety of powder types and the possibility of selecting types according to requirements.

Blackpowder advantages

The present-day user of blackpowder needs to understand its peculiar advantages and disadvantages which once were taken as a matter of course but are now less familiar.

Its first advantage is ease of ignition. Obviously this is a necessity in most muzzle-loading guns.

Its second advantage is that the standard charge fills the allotted powder space. This is most evident in breech-loading cartridges, with which consequently it is not possible to make much of a loading mistake; in fact the powder must fill the space to burn at its best. Even in muzzle-loading guns the size of charge cup is in rather obvious relation to requirements.

Its third advantage, the decisive one in most blackpowder loading nowadays, is the low stressing of the gun by blackpowder. Muzzle-loading guns were made for it, based on experience. Very important in this connection is the fact that the blackpowder burning rate is far less sensitive to loading changes than that of any smokeless. Undoubtedly a suitable burning smokeless powder could be found or made for any muzzle-loading gun. But doing so would require a pressure gun of the same dimensions, and the result would be safely applicable to only that very muzzle-loader. Blackpowder, with its peculiar insensitiveness to loading conditions, performs about alike in all.

In breech-loaders, blackpowder is most important for loading ammunition

for Damascus-barrel guns. Fig. 2 shows the pressure for the first 10″ of a 12-ga. barrel with DuPont MX, a dense shotgun smokeless for light and medium loads; DuPont Bulk Shotgun Smokeless, for light and medium loads; FFFg blackpowder; and DuPont Oval, a shotgun smokeless powder for heavy loads. The loads were all 3-1¼-7½ equivalent; that is, they all contained 1¼ oz. No. 7½ shot and a powder charge giving the same velocity as 3 drams blackpowder.

The blackpowder gave this velocity with a peak pressure lower than that of the 2 smokeless powders for light and medium loads and nearly as low as that of the special, slow-burning Oval. This was FFFg blackpowder. With FFg, the normal granulation for this load, the peak pressure would have been markedly lower than that of the slowest smokeless. Most test results have been even more in favor of blackpowder in this respect, and in equivalent shotgun loads the blackpowder peak is expected to average about 60% as high as the allowable smokeless.

Solid products of combustion

The disadvantages of blackpowder in blackpowder arms (there is no occasion to use it in any other) practically all stem from the high solids content of its combustion products.

The smoke nuisance varies with weather, principally humidity. Nothing can be done about it.

Bore fouling is also much affected by humidity, but is always bad. Soon after the introduction of smokeless powders in this country, it was found that a small quantity of bulk smokeless in the blackpowder charge keeps the fouling from accumulating in the bore (it has no effect on the smoke). It is most effective when loaded next the primer, but may be mixed with the charge. In rifles, the smokeless used for this purpose was bulk rifle smokeless, principally DuPont No. 1 and DuPont Schuetzen. Since such powders were made to replace blackpowder bulk-for-bulk in blackpowder cartridge rifles, their use to replace a fraction of the blackpowder charge made no material difference in velocity and pressure.

After disappearance of bulk rifle smokeless powders in the 1920's, the only smokeless of that kind was Du Pont Bulk Shotgun. When used to replace 10% to 15% by volume of the blackpowder charge it prevented heavy fouling. However, Du Pont Bulk Shotgun was dropped from manufacture about 1964, and there is no longer a bulk-for-bulk smokeless powder of any kind.

Some handloaders have used smokeless pistol powders for this purpose, in about 10% of the blackpowder charge by weight. This works, but it is not good since pistol smokeless increases both pressure and energy of the charge. Far better was the same proportion of SR 4759, which was bulkier than pistol powders and burned more slowly, but SR 4759 has also disappeared. Best now available for this purpose appear to be SR 4756 or SR 7625 with medium and heavy blackpowder loads, and PB shotgun with light blackpowder loads. Begin with these in only 5% of the blackpowder charge by weight, and increase as necessary to prevent heavy fouling, but to not more than 10% by weight. Even this much probably raises pressure a little. In a very old and weak gun its use therefore seems inadvisable.

Effect of fouling

Opinion on the effect of blackpowder fouling on the gun has been divided. It certainly rusted many flintlocks, the barrels and locks of which were made of iron and steel of heterogeneous microstructure, and in shapes difficult to clean. (The nipples of percussion muzzle-loaders were rusted by the chloride cap residue).

In breech-loaders, however, only the bores were much fouled (except in revolvers) and the bores were open at both ends for cleaning. Equally important was the fact that the heavy fouling greatly diluted the cartridge primer residue, and the slightly alkaline nature of the fouling probably inhibited corrosion to some extent. Cleaning was best done with water and this disposed of the primer fouling as well. The effectiveness of these factors is shown by the fact that blackpowder breech-loaders of good quality are often found with bores in perfect condition even today, while the bores of early smokeless-powder arms are almost always in poor condition.

Blackpowder fouling must be removed. If the charges contain a small amount of suitable smokeless as described above, the resultant light fouling is easily removed by conventional cleaning. The heavy fouling from straight blackpowder is most practicably removed by pouring water through the bore. Sometimes this requires a funnel with a short rubber tube fixed to the spout. Pour warm water through the bore followed by hot water to make drying easier, wipe the bore dry, and oil or grease.

Brass cartridge cases must be washed soon after firing with blackpowder or the fouling will corrode and ruin them.

Decap, wash with warm water and soap using a bristle brush to dislodge the solid fouling inside the cases, rinse in hot water, and allow to drain and dry. The cases eventually turn black but remain serviceable.

Blackpowder storage rests on considerations quite different from those of smokeless. Blackpowder does not deteriorate with age. It has even been believed that it improved, and partly for this reason some nations have preserved for long periods certain of their powders for such special uses as powder-train fuzes. This improvement may be real, from slow diffusion of the ingredients in the solid state and consequent improvement of the mixture on which blackpowder action depends. Neither is blackpowder harmed by high temperatures, which are very bad for smokeless. The only thing that damages it is water. Blackpowder absorbs moisture to an injurious degree from very humid air and from being even slightly wetted. The damage is irreversible since, while the powder can

be dried easily enough, there is no way to restore the intimate mixture which was destroyed by partial dissolving of the nitrate.

Again unlike smokeless, blackpowder is easily ignited and it explodes even when not confined. It can be fired by flame, spark, or sharp friction or percussion, though it may be added that in general this has occurred only from very bad handling. It should never be spilled underfoot, brought near a flame or spark, or its containers handled with steel tools. Areas contaminated with blackpowder are easily made safe by washing down with water.

The foregoing indicate the simple rules for storage of the handloader's blackpowder. Containers should be kept tightly sealed and stored in a dry place. For safety, the powder should never be exposed to accidental ignition in the possible ways mentioned above. Only small quantities should be kept on hand, and the usual 1-lb. can in which blackpowder is sold for handloading is one of the best containers. ■

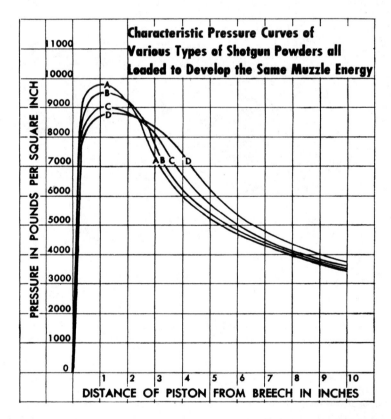

Fig. 2. Powder pressure curves given by 4 different shotgun powders, all in 3-1¼-7½ loading, from test results published by E. I. du Pont de Nemours & Co. A—DuPont MX Smokeless. B—DuPont Bulk Shotgun smokeless. C—FFFg blackpowder. D—DuPont Oval smokeless. Note that FFFg blackpowder, though a fine granulation, gave lower peak pressure than any smokeless except this special underload of DuPont Oval. FFg blackpowder, normal for such a load, would have been still better in this respect

CURRENT POWDERS FOR BLACKPOWDER ARMS

By WM. C. DAVIS, JR.

THE use of blackpowder arms has increased tremendously in recent years, and modern replicas of old blackpowder guns are now widely sold. The continuing supply of blackpowder, which was seriously threatened before the recent revival of interest in blackpowder shooting, now seems assured. There are currently two brands of blackpowder widely available in the United States. One of these is Gearhart-Owen, manufactured by the firm of that name, in Moosic, Pennsylvania. The Gearhart-Owen plant was formerly owned and operated by Du Pont. The other brand commonly available is Curtis & Harvey, distributed by the Hodgdon Powder Company in the United States. Curtis & Harvey powder is made in Scotland, by the venerable and respected Nobel firm.

The Gearhart-Owen and the Curtis & Harvey blackpowders do not produce identical ballistics, in the same charge weights, though both are suitable for use in blackpowder cartridge arms and in muzzle-loaders.

It has often been stated, and correctly so, that smokeless powder should never be used in muzzle-loading guns, or in certain breechloading arms originally designed for blackpowder use. Until about 1975, blackpowder was the only suitable propellant for such weapons. In the early 1970's, however, an inventor named Dan Pawlak developed a propellant that closely reproduced the ballistic performance of blackpowder, but was of entirely different formulation. It is called Pyrodex, and its unique advantage over blackpowder is that it is much less susceptible to accidental ignition. This characteristic substantially reduces the risks in storing and handling it. Possibly even more important, in recognition of its less hazardous nature, the U.S.

Department of Transportation places far less restrictive rules on shipping Pyrodex than on shipping blackpowder. Pyrodex can therefore be made available through channels of distribution in which blackpowder is prohibited, and the shooter of blackpowder arms will benefit from this wider availability. Most unfortunately, the original manufacturing plant for Pyrodex was virtually destroyed on January 27, 1977, by an accident that claimed the life of Dan Pawlak and three other employes. A new plant has been constructed, and production resumed, but availability is still somewhat limited by supply at the present writing. The sole distributor of Pyrodex in the U.S. is the Hodgdon Powder Company, which anticipates that production will soon be increased to meet the demand for this new product.

Pyrodex is neither blackpowder nor smokeless powder, though it shares some characteristics of both. It is called "replica blackpowder" by the manufacturer. The formulation of Pyrodex is considered proprietary information, and has not been divulged by the manufacturer, but there is evidence from other sources that the principal ingredients may be nitrocellulose, graphite and certain oxidizing salts. It is manufactured in various grades, roughly comparable to the different granulations of blackpowder, though not identified in the same way. Pyrodex *RS* grade is intended for muzzle-loading rifles and shotguns, *P* is for use in pistols, *CTG* is especially for use in rifle and shotgun cartridges, and *C* is for use in muzzle-loading cannon. It is designed to be loaded bulk-for-bulk in the same charges as blackpowder. This means that a volumetric measure containing the correct blackpowder charge would also contain the correct charge of Pyrodex.

Because Pyrodex has a lower bulk density than blackpowder, it should **not** be loaded in charges of equal weight. A measure that contains 100 grains of blackpowder, for example, contains only 80 grains of Pyrodex. Handloaders using Pyrodex must clearly understand this relationship, and keep it carefully in mind. The Hodgdon Powder Company, distributor of Pyrodex, furnishes fully tested loading data on request, both for muzzle-loaders and for cartridge arms.

In addition to its safer handling qualities, Pyrodex is claimed to be superior to blackpowder in other ways. The buildup of fouling in the gun bore, a well known nuisance with blackpowder, is said to be much reduced with Pyrodex. This, and possibly other characteristics, are said to contribute to improved shot-to-shot uniformity of pressures and velocities. The desirably low peak pressures of blackpowder loads are retained in comparable loads of Pyrodex, making it safe for use in all guns in which blackpowder loads are safe. Its one disadvantage to blackpowder shooters is that it is not well adapted to the weak ignition system of flintlock arms, but of course that is no disadvantage to handloaders who use it in breech-loading cartridges. The fouling produced by Pyrodex is corrosive, as is the fouling produced by blackpowder, and the same cleaning procedures are required. Handloaders must be aware that special cleaning procedures are required for cartridge cases, as well as for guns, that have been fired with either Pyrodex or blackpowder loads. The corrosive effects of the residue will otherwise soon destroy the cases. Either water or water-base solvents are required to remove the corrosive residue after firing either of these propellants.

Pyrodex RS
(Muzzleloading Rifles, Shotguns)

Pyrodex P
(Pistols)

Pyrodex CTG
(Rifle, Shotgun Cartridges)

All photos are shown five times actual size.

GUNPOWDER DEVELOPMENT

By E. H. HARRISON
and WM. C. DAVIS, JR.

Wʜɪʟᴇ blackpowder has been in use for centuries, and smoklesss powder only since about the end of our Civil War, it is the latter which is of interest to most hand-loaders.

The shortcomings of blackpowder were long felt. It was, however, not until the birth of organic chemistry in the first half of the 19th century that replacement of blackpowder became possible. The historic steps in the development of smokeless powder bring out its characteristics

Nitrocellulose production

The first and basic step was the production of nitrocellulose. While it had been investigated earlier by Pelouze in France, nitrocellulose, in the modern sense, was first prepared by Professor C. F. Schoenbein of the University of Basel, Switzerland, in late 1845, and independently by Professor Bottger in Frankfurt-am-Main, Germany, in 1846. It is made by the action of concentrated nitric acid on cotton or other cellulose fibers, in the presence of sulphuric acid and under carefully controlled conditions. This process, called nitration, adds nitrogen and oxygen to the cellulose molecule. Cellulose nitrate separates explosively, once the reaction has been started, into carbon monoxide and dioxide, nitrogen, hydrogen, and water in the form of steam. All these are gases taking up many times the space of the solid nitrocellulose. The reaction liberates considerable heat, which increases the volume of the gases and adds to the effect.

Nitrocellulose made from cotton (also called guncotton, pyrocellulose, etc., with often a distinction in names to indicate the degree of nitration) differs little in appearance from the original cotton. It is itself unsuitable for a propellant, but it eventually became the principal base of smokeless powders and nitration has remained the basic chemical process for their manufacture.

A number of experimenters, attracted by the cleanliness and power of this new explosive, naively tried to use it directly as a gun propellant. These attempts all ended in failure. The explosion of guncotton is abrupt and violent, damaging the gun when enough is loaded to be effective.

Serious plant explosions at first occurred in England, France, and Austria, the countries where the development was carried on. These resulted in manufacture being stopped for a time. It was resumed after a few years, and led to the development of explosives for military and civil purposes which ultimately became, in many ways, more important than gun propellants. It should be added that long experience, increasing understanding of chemical processes, and conscientious application have put explosives manufacturing in this country near the very top of all manufacturing industries in safety.

Moderation of reaction rates

It was clearly necessary to moderate the reaction rate of nitrates if they were ever to be useful as propellants. This was first successfully done about 1860 by Maj. E. Schultze of the Prussian Artillery. Instead of cotton, he nitrated wood, which had been reduced to suitably small pieces, and impregnated the resulting nitrolignin with barium and potassium nitrates. The structure of the wood, the amount of wood left unnitrated, and the metallic nitrates all helped to slow the explosion. Schultze powder became highly successful in shotguns. It was still, however, too fast for cannon or even for most rifles. A more radical change had to be made in the explosive material.

The means to do so already existed. Only a year after the origination of nitrocellulose, it was found soluble (to an extent depending on the degree of nitration) in a mixture of alcohol and ether, but not in either one alone. This discovery was used at once in the invention of a colloidion coating on photographic plates, an application of great importance, but it was not immediately perceived to be able to control the explosion rate of guncotton.

In 1860 Gen. (then Maj.) Thomas J. Rodman, a U.S. Army Ordnance officer, found that the rate of burning of blackpowder could be controlled by compressing it into grains. Compression restricted burning to the surface much more than is the case with ordinary blackpowder where varying the granulation has only a limited effect. Rate of burning was governed by making the powder into large or small compressed grains, which left relatively small or large surfaces to burn. This is one of the few basic advances made by any American in the field of powders.

The Rodman grains were perforated so the hole or holes increased their surface as the outer surface shrank. This assured that the evolution of gas was not slowed. In the multi-perforated grain, the area of the hole walls increased faster than the outer surface decreased, giving a progressive increase in the rate of gas evolution and making the first progressive-burning powder.

Rodman also invented the copper pressure gauge, providing for the first reliable measurement of pressure in the gun.

The invention of celluloid in 1870, due to an American, showed how to make an impermeable solid of nitrocellulose. Still it was not clearly realized that this state held the secret of smokeless-powder control. An early partial success by Volkmann in Austria in 1870-71 came to nothing, apparently because the Austrian government stopped manufacture of his powder on the grounds it infringed on the government gunpowder monopoly.

Application of processes

Effective application of such processes to make a controlled smokeless powder was accomplished in 1884 by Vieille, a young chemist in the service of the French government. With solvents (ultimately alcohol and ether) he reduced the nitrocellulose to a gelatinous colloid, rolled in into sheets, cut it into flakes, and dried off most of the solvent. The product was dense, with about the strength and elasticity of horn, and it now burned only on the surface. This was the final fundamental step which made smokeless rifle and cannon powders possible.

Successful development of a flake

1 Most smokeless powders burn at the surface only. A powder charge made up of large grains exposes less surface than the same weight in small grains and so burns slower, and burns longer because of the thicker web to be burned through. This gives a means of fitting the rate of gas evolution to requirements of the gun. How far this has been carried is illustrated by this photograph of a grain of 16″ cannon powder, beside a grain of IMR 4350 rifle powder (indicated by arrow)

2 Control by grain size usually is supplemented by making the grains burn slowly at first, then faster. This progressive burning is accomplished in U. S. cannon powders by multiple perforations, the hole surface during burning increasing faster than the outer surface decreases. Such grains have been made with as many as 19 perforations, which proved entirely too progressive burning; a standard of 7 perforations has been settled on for all sizes. The 3 grains above exhibit successive stages in the burning, and show how burning proceeds regularly inward from the surface

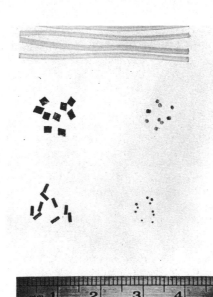

3 Usual forms of small-arms powders— these are too small for multiple perforations. (Top) Cordite M.D.T. (British) tubular rifle powder. (Middle, l. to r.) Rottweil No. 5 (German) flake rifle powder, and Hercules Bullseye (U.S.) flake pistol powder. (Bottom, l. to r.) DuPont IMR 3031 (U.S.) short tubular rifle powder, and Western Ball-Powder (U.S.) spherical-grain rifle powder

4 Burning of small-arms powder grains. The surface area of thin flakes, thin strips, tubes, and short tubes (top row) remains little changed during burning. These forms therefore are called neutral burning. On the other hand, the surface area of strings, spheres, and irregular forms (bottom row) decreases during burning, a generally unfavorable characteristic except in low-pressure or short-barreled guns, and these forms are called degressive burning. However, with development of chemical coatings to slow the early burning it is now possible to make any of these forms as progressive burning as practically necessary

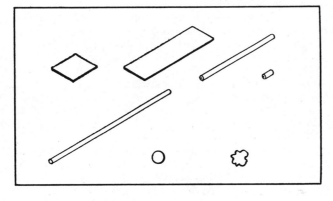

5 Longitudinal section of eroded machine-gun barrel. Under given loading conditions, erosion rate depends on powder flame temperature, and this is determined by the powder composition and coating. Among conditions which affect erosion are powder gas pressure, weight of powder charge, and smallness of the bore through which the powder gases must pass. Rate of fire has a very marked effect

nitrocellulose powder was completed in the same year by Duttenhofer in Rottweil, Germany, with acetic ether as the gelatinizing agent.

In 1887 Alfred Nobel of Sweden, the inventor of dynamite and founder of the Nobel prizes, invented a smokeless powder of somewhat different compositon. Starting with nitrocellulose that was not so highly nitrated as that used for the straight nitrocellulose powder of Vieille, he colloided it with nitroglycerine, then rolled, dried, and cut it into flakes. Solvents were not necessary since nitroglycerine itself is a plasticizer for nitrocellulose of this kind. The nitroglycerine was left in the powder to increase its energy content, a typical composition being 40 per cent nitroglycerine and 60 per cent nitrocellulose. It is a remarkable thing that two such violent high explosives as nitrocellulose and nitroglycerine become a well-controlled propellant when combined in this rather simple way. Nobel named his powder Ballistite.

A powder of nearly similar composition, though made by a different process, is the British Cordite. A highly nitrated nitrocellulose is used, and the nitrocellulose and nitroglycerine are colloided with acetone which is later removed. The mass is extruded in strings or tubes. For most rifle cartridges they are cut to the length of the powder chamber. The advantages in ignition and burning that were expected of this unusual form have not proved important in small arms, though, together with the structural strength of the Cordite bundle, they are useful in large artillery charges.

Cordite was at first made with its basic ingredients in the proportion of 40 per cent nitrocellulose to 60 per cent nitroglycerine. To this was added 5 per cent mineral jelly intended to lubricate the rifle bore. This it entirely failed to do, but it did lessen bore erosion by lowering the temperature of the powder gas and it also improved the storage stability of the powder. The erosion from this Mk I Cordite was so great that in the early 1900's the proportions of the basic ingredients were reversed so that the new powder (called Cordite M.D., or M.D.T. when made tubular) compared with the old as follows:

	Mk I	M. D.
Nitrocellulose	37%	65%
Nitroglycerine	58	30
Mineral jelly	5	5

Other formulations have been used in sporting rifle Cordite, and there are many cannon and rocket Cordites also.

Like other powders, Cordite is made in diameters and webs to suit gun requirements. Cordite M.D. is still highly erosive, but most of its other qualities are favorable. It is, however, slowly going out of use in rifles except in some of the earlier British heavy sporting cartridges of limited powder space, in which it is needed to meet velocity requirements with low pressure at the same time.

Vieille's and Nobel's inventions resulted in smokeless powders so successful that they at once drove out black-powder in military weapons, later in sporting weapons as well.

Characteristics of Two Types

There soon appeared a difference of opinion as to which of the two types was better. The nitrocellulose-nitroglycerine (double-base) powders are simpler to manufacture; they are easy to ignite and burn; their energy content is high which lessens the amount of them that must be used, so they are well suited for maximum performance in chambers of limited volume; and they are resistant to effects of moisture, some double-base powders actually being completely waterproof. On the other hand, the nitrocellulose (single-base) powders burn with a lower flame temperature which causes distinctly less erosion of rifle and cannon barrels, in some loadings very much less. Their performance is also less affected by temperature changes.

Nations have weighed differently the importance of these respective advantages; consequently some have chosen single-base powders for their military weapons and others double-base. The United States, after some difficulty in finding a sufficiently satisfactory powder, standardized in 1909 on a single-base type for most requirements. In sporting ammunition both single-base and double-base powders are in use and there is every indication they will continue to be. Certain features of later smokeless powders have now removed some of the significance from the once hotly-debated differences between these two types.

Deterrent coatings

One important feature is coating. In rifles, with their combiantion of high pressure and very small chamber space, the control of burning rate by grain size was soon brought to its limit by the impracticably large grains required. Rifle grains are much too small for multiple perforations, so some other control had to be found. Nobel patented a progressive-burning powder with grains made in layers of powder types designed to give off gas slowly at first, as large grains would do.

It is now done by chemically treating the grain surface with a deterrent which slows the rate of burning at first. Some deterrents were devised about 1897 by Dr. Walter Volney, a German chemist

working in the United States, and by others a little later. Such treatment made possible the performance of the German military 7.9 mm. "S" cartridge introduced in 1904-5. The flake powder for that cartridge was at first treated with camphor which, however, was volatile and had some other drawbacks. Around 1906, derivatives of urea were developed at the Zentralstelle fuer Wissenschaft-lichtechnische Untersuchungen (Central Office for Scientific-Technical Research) at Neubabelsberg near Berlin, which were far superior to camphor. These compounds were called Centralites from the name of the above organization. The later director of the Rottweil powder factory, Dr. Eble, played an essential role in their development. From 1 to 2 per cent of Centralite I (diethyldiphenylurea) was then used in the powder for the "S" cartridge. Centralities are still the principal coating material for small-arms powders.

Such deterrent coating has been less extensively practiced on double-base powders, since their favorable burning characteristics permit sufficient control in many cases merely by regulation of the grain size. However, it is now applied to both types.

An unexpected effect of surface deterrents has been reduction of rifle bore erosion, due to the lower flame temperature at the beginning of burning.

The graphite in which most finished powders are tumbled has some deterrent effect. However, graphiting is done mainly to improve flow of the powder in measuring, and to carry off electric charges generated by friction of the running grains.

Double-base powders, sold in standard canister types to the handloader in recent times, have almost all been made by the Hercules Powder Co. Most of the current ones were originated before World War I. Single-base canister powders are provided by E. I. Du Pont de Nemours & Co. Du Pont IMR powder was introduced in 1914. Many number-designated types have been made since, but they differ only in granulation and to a limited extent in amount of coating, flash suppressor and preservative added.

Development of Ball powder

Since that time, the only radical commercial step has been the development of Ball powder. This was due to Dr. Fred Olsen, and began in the 1920's when he was employed at the Picatinny Arsenal. His original purpose was to improve the stability of nitrocellulose and to find ways of re-using great quantities of single-base cannon powder left over from World War I. Working alone on these problems, he eventually devised original means of processing

nitrocellulose. Employed by Western Cartridge Co. in 1929, he developed Ball powder, and its manufacture was put on a production basis in 1933.

Both conventional and ball smokeless powders begin with nitrocellulose. In the usual process, necessary removal of acid remaining after nitration is done by pulping, boiling in alkali, and long washing. The nitrocellulose is then freed of water, colloided, extruded or rolled, and cut into the desired grains, and these are dried for removal of most of the solvent.

For Ball powder, the nitrocellulose instead of being colloided is dissolved completely. For many years, the process employed for graining was to agitate the resulting lacquer in a liquid mixture that caused the lacquer to form into small spherical globules or balls. By manipulation of the process, it was possible to control the size of the balls reasonably well for small-arms propellants, though screening was necessary to separate the balls of radically different sizes. During the late 1960's, Olin completed a new powder plant employing a new process of mechanical graining by which the control of the grain size can be much more accurately and precisely maintained. Further control of the "web," or minimum thickness of the grain, is made possible by passing the grains (while in a plastic state) between rollers that are separated by the desired space. This flattens the larger balls more than the smaller ones, so the minimum distance between opposite faces, which is the important "web" dimension for Ball powders, is the same for both. Nitroglycerine is usually added to bring up the energy content. A special deterrent coating, usually dibutylphthalate, is applied to the grains. The spherical grain form is highly degressive because its surface decreases rapidly during burning, and so surface treatment is especially important to this powder's performance.

Ball powder manufacture lends itself to a relatively simple plant, a rapid manufacturing process, and unusual inherent safety since most of the process and transferral steps are done with the material carried in water. These considerations may be especially important in setting up powder manufacture in a new area. In the United States, however, large capacity already exists for making extruded powders, and their manufacture is already carried out with an extraordinary degree of safety.

To the user, therefore, while manufacture of both types is interesting, the suitability of available powders to his requirements is most important. The important characteristics of individual powders are discussed in subsequent articles. ∎

HANDLOADER'S SMOKELESS RIFLE POWDERS

*New propellants
give greater range
for handloading.*

**By E. H. HARRISON
and WM. C. DAVIS, JR.**

WHEN smokeless propellants began to drive out blackpowder in this country in the early 1890's, two kinds of rifles had to be provided for. Those designed for smokeless powder — military rifles at first, then also sporting rifles — were loaded with full charges of the new propellants based on the discoveries of Vieille and Nobel. The many blackpowder rifles in existence required loads of lower power. It was not difficult to make smokeless powders for this use, and it was soon done. Blackpowder velocities were reproduced or exceeded only moderately.

The new powders, however, caused some confusion among handloaders. The universally-practiced handloading of cartridges with blackpowder hardly could be done wrong — one simply filled the cartridge to the base of the bullet. But equivalent charges of dense, high-potential smokeless powders only partly filled the space. The correct charge depended on the kind of powder and loading too much was dangerous.

This led to a demand for smokeless powders filling the blackpowder cartridge case. These were called "bulk" powders because they took up the same room and could be loaded with the same dipper measures as the blackpowder they replaced. Well-known powders of this type were Du Pont Rifle Smokeless No. 1 and Du Pont Schuetzen. They could replace blackpowder bulk for bulk in small rifle cartridges up to about the .38-55. They were eventually replaced with Du Pont Gallery Rifle Powder No. 75 and Du Pont Sporting Rifle Powder No. 80. The latter two were not true bulk powders because they occupied less space than the blackpowder they replaced, but they were better than the earlier bulk smokeless because they were harder-grained and slower to take up moisture from the air. No. 80, last of the group, was manufactured until the beginning of World War II.

Handloaders regretted the disappearance of bulk smokeless rifle powders. There were some attempts to substitute Du Pont Bulk Smokeless Shotgun Powder instead, which was manufactured until a later date. But shotgun pressures are much lower than those of even blackpowder rifles, and firing any rifle cartridge filled with bulk shotgun smokeless gives destructive pressures. So handloaders had to reconcile themselves to losing the bulk smokeless powders. Currently available propellants equal or surpass them in almost every way. From here on, only the now-universal dense types are considered.

Du Pont rifle powders

Development of smokeless propellants was slower in this country than in Europe. Eventual success was of great importance to national defense. It was accomplished principally in long-continued work by E. I. Du Pont de Nemours & Co. The Du Pont powder and process of manufacture eventually were adopted by the United States Army and Navy for all calibers from shoulder rifles to the largest cannon.

The powder was of nitrocellulose or single-base type. The nitrocellulose was of that limited degree of nitration called pyrocellulose, chosen because it is soluble in a mixture of ether and alcohol for the gelatinizing — a fundamental step in manufacture of these powders. An organic chemical called diphenylamine was added as stabilizer, a use originally patented by Nobel. The rifle powder was glazed with 1 per cent of its weight in graphite. This unusually large amount undoubtedly gave some surface deterrent effect, which was not fully appreciated then.

The rifle powder was called Pyro D. G. from its three constituents. It was adopted about 1909, and the United States used it through World War I. Some was later sold through the government office of the Director of Civilian Marksmanship to NRA members for handloading. It was an excellent powder for cartridges of the size and intensity of the .30 M1906 ball cartridge. Other granulations of similar composition, which Du Pont grouped as Military Rifle (MR) powders, filled out the range of smokeless rifle requirements. They were the basis for Du Pont's highly successful Improved Military Rifle (IMR) powders which followed.

Du Pont IMR powder was introduced in 1914. Characteristic features of present IMR types include a coating of dinitrotoluene (DNT) to slow initial burning and make the pressure rise less steep than it otherwise would be; addition of potassium sulphate as a muzzle-flash inhibitor; and addition of diphenylamine as a stablizer. The granules are glazed with graphite to improve flow in powder measures and to carry off electric charges. Since DNT and potassium sulphate are present at the expense of energy content, a part of the basic nitrocellulose is of the insoluble (more highly nitrated) type to bring the energy up to that of the MR powders.

IMR powders appeared too late to be of much importance in World War I, though a quantity of .303 British ammunition was loaded with IMR-16 and gave excellent performance. Beginning about 1920, IMR powders rapidly superseded the MR powders. They were the principal propellants in U.S. small arms ammunition during World War II.

Current IMR powders

Following are the IMR powders of principal interest to riflemen, including some past ones for comparison. The identifying numbers are serials and have no other significance. IMR-3031, the earliest of the current canister powders, dates from 1934 and IMR-4350, the latest until World War II, from 1940. IMR-4895, introduced for cal. .30 use in World War II, became available as military surplus afterward and proved so successful that in 1962 it was added to the list of Du Pont canister powders. IMR-4831, sold as military surplus, was also widely used by handloaders after World War II, and in 1973 it was also added to the Du Pont list of canister powders. It is important to note, however, that the lots of IMR-4831 standardized by Du Pont for canister sales are not identical to the 4831 sold as military surplus. The correct charge weights of Du Pont canister IMR-4831 powder are generally *less* than those of the surplus 4831, for equal pressures, in the same applications. If loading data intended for the surplus 4831 powder are mistakenly used for loading Du Pont canister IMR-4831, *chamber pressures might be increased to hazardous levels.* It is especially important, in the interests of safety, that the handloader understand clearly what type of "4831" powder he is preparing to use, and use it with the loading data appropriate for that particular type. The same is true of other powders bearing the same 4-digit numerical identification as IMR powders, but not made or sold by Du Pont.

Granulation and coating of IMR powders determine performance characteristics. As a guide to these, the table shows the cartridge for which each powder is reported to have been made.

Powder	Diameter- Length	Coating	Cartridge
IMR-16	.030-.084	6% DNT	7.62 Russ.
IMR-16	.030-.084	5% DNT	.303 Brit.
IMR-15	.032-.084	9% DNT	.30-06
IMR-15½	.032-.084	8% DNT	.30-06
IMR-17	.030-.084	7% DNT	.30-06
IMR-17½	.030-.084	8% DNT	.30-06
IMR-18	.031-.046	8% DNT	.30-06
IMR-25	.027-.084	7% DNT	.30-30
IMR-25½	.027-.084	7½% DNT	.30-30
IMR-1147	.034-.042	8% DNT	.30-06
IMR-1185	.032-.084	7% DNT	.30-06
IMR-1186	.029-.042	7% DNT	.30-06
IMR-1204	.025-.021	8% DNT	.25-20
*IMR-3031	.029-.083	7% DNT	.30-06
*IMR-4064	.031-.083	6½% DNT	.30-06
*IMR-4198	.026-.083	4½% DNT	.30-30
*IMR-4227	.024-.023	6½% DNT	.25-20
*IMR-4320	.034-.042	6½% DNT	.30-06
*IMR-4350	.038-.083	5½% DNT	.300 Mag.
IMR-4676	.034-.058	7% DNT	.30-06
*IMR-4831	.038-.083	7% DNT	20 mm. Oerlikon
*IMR-4895	.032-.056	5½% DNT	.30-06

* Indicates current canister powder.

Dimensions are approximate, since grains shrink irregularly on drying.

A ½ after number indicates 2% tin incorporated to reduce metal fouling.

Diphenylamine usually .6%, but 1.1% in IMR 4831.

DNT approximate, may be varied to meet ballistic requirements.

K_2SO_4 in and after IMR-3031 as flash inhibitor, usually 1%.

Du Pont has made selections of IMR powders available to the handloader ever since their introduction. As times passed, these have been obsoleted and replaced by others. The current canister powders are indicated. Because of their essential similarity, they can be considered together.

It should be noted that some distinctly different powders have exactly the same, or nearly the same, grain dimensions. It is therefore impossible for the handloader to distinguish one type from another by inspection, except by the identification on the package. Since a mistake in identification of powder can obviously be dangerous, any powder not positively identified should not be loaded but should be safely destroyed.

The grain of IMR-4320 is only half as long as that of IMR-4198, 3031, 4064, 4350 and 4831, and consequently it measures better than the others. Under some conditions a powder of longer grain has proved more accurate-shooting despite not measuring so uniformly (*Hatcher's Notebook*, page 313). However, handloaders find the performance of IMR-4320 excellent. The grain length of IMR-4895 is about midway between IMR-4320 and the others. IMR-4895 is the most widely adaptable and useful of IMR canister powders, in the experience of many shooters.

Relative Quickness

Du Pont states the relative quickness of its smokeless powders as follows, taking IMR-4350 as 100. The powders above SR-4759 in this list are basically shotgun and pistol powders.

The American Rifleman publishes laboratory-tested loading information including velocities and pressures. This is the only sound basis for loading full

TYPICAL GRAIN FORMS OF SMOKELESS RIFLE POWDERS
Rottweil No. 5 (German) not used in U.S. but shown to indicate form of flake rifle powders. All shown 5 times natural size.

Du Pont IMR-4320

Du Pont IMR-4350

Hercules 2400

WW-748

Du Pont IMR-4227

Rottweil No. 5

Du Pont Powder	Relative Quickness
Hi-Skor 700-X	635
PB	390
SR-7625	340
SR-4756	305
SR-4759	210
IMR-4227	180
IMR-4198	160
IMR-3031	135
IMR-4064	120
IMR-4895	115
IMR-4320	110
IMR-4350	100
IMR-4831	95

charges, however, the preceding table helps to make clear the position of each Du Pont canister powder in the available spectrum.

The Du Pont IMR propellants are the best known and most used among rifle powders for reloading. They continue to give great satisfaction.

Hercules handloading powders

Hercules Powder Co., now Hercules Incorporated, was organized in 1913 to take over some of the Du Pont manufacture of propellants.

Nearly all Du Pont smokeless powders are single-base having only nitrocellulose as their main constituent. In contrast, nearly all Hercules powders are double-base containing an important proportion of nitroglycerine as well as nitrocellulose.

Again unlike Du Pont, the Hercules rifle powders are of several basic compositions and grain forms. In the 1930's these rifle powders were Sharpshooter, Lightning, No. 2400, HiVel 2, HiVel 3, and No. 300 (this last a single-base powder). After World War II and until 1965, the requirements of rifle handloading were covered with only Unique, No. 2400, and HiVel 2. These three powders are quite different so each will be described separately.

Unique was first manufactured about 1898, and was one of the smokeless powders assigned to Hercules in 1913. It is in the form of thin disks, .065" in diameter and .006" thick. It contained originally about 40 per cent nitroglycerine, but some years ago this was reduced to about 20 per cent, and the granulation was changed slightly to maintain burning characteristics similar to those of the original formulation. It is characterized by high energy content, ease of ignition and burning, and excellent waterproofness. For rifles it is offered for midrange or reduced power loading only. In such loads it ignites reliably and burns regularly even though occupying only a small part of the powder space in the cartridge. Unique is widely used in shotgun and pistol handloading.

No. 2400 became available on the market in 1933. It is in the form of disks about .038" in diameter and .013" thick, thus smaller and thicker than Unique. The dimensions make this powder work with great smoothness and regularity

through bench powder measures. No. 2400 is coated, in contrast with both Unique and HiVel 2 which are uncoated. Its nitroglycerine content is 20 per cent. It is designed for full loads in small rifle cartridges, but gives excellent results in reduced loads for military and similar sporting cartridges and has become a much-used powder for heaviest loads in large revolver cartridges.

HiVel 2 was dropped from manufacture about 1964. HiVel was suitable for full charges in nearly all rifle cartridges from .30-30 to .375 Magnum, and also was the favorite for the .30-06 international competition load with match bullets at 2,200-2,300 feet per second (f.p.s.).

Hercules Reloder powders

In January 1965, Hercules introduced Reloder 7, Reloder 11 and Reloder 21 rifle smokeless powders designed especially for handloading. Together they covered and extended the loading range for which HiVel 2 was suitable. The grain dimensions given by Hercules were:

Powder	Diameter	Length
Reloder 7	.034"	.021"
Reloder 11	.030"	.046"
Reloder 21	.039"	.089"

The Reloder powders are specially interesting, because they were developed specifically for handloading and their development was based on advanced technology utilized by Hercules in the development of new propellants for rockets and missile engines. The new powders were made double-base, of slightly lower flame temperature than HiVel 2 but nearly the same high total energy. Additives, proved in special gun and rocket propellants, were used to obtain the performance desired. It is difficult to optimize several variables simultaneously, and four formulas were arrived at differing in type and quantity of additives. A statistical blend of the four was calculated in the same way as used by Hercules in missile propellant programs, and a dye-stuff added to each for identification and control. Each Reloder powder contains these differently formulated granules, though in different proportions.

The Reloder powders contain nitrocellulose, nitroglycerine, salts, additives, and stabilizer. The deterrent grain coating is ethyl centralite, a long-established coating material chosen for its uniform coverage, controlled penetration in manufacture, and non-migratory nature. Easy ignition and burning are favored by the nitroglycerine and additives, and by including a percentage of uncoated grains.

Unfortunately, the Hercules Reloder rifle powders were not immediately received by handloaders with the enthusiasm that their excellent qualities

deserved. Though their popularity increased slowly as handloaders became familiar with them, the market was apparently less than Hercules had originally anticipated, and their manufacture was discontinued in 1972. Benchrest shooters, meanwhile, had found Reloder 7 excellent powder in rifles of the .222 Remington class, and many match winners attributed their success to carefully developed loads using that powder. The increasing demand far exceeded the remaining stocks of Reloder 7 on dealers' shelves and in the hands of handloaders. In response to many requests, Hercules resumed manufacture of Reloder 7 in late 1975, and its popularity continues, especially among benchrest shooters. It is also an excellent powder for reduced loads, especially with cast bullets in calibers such as the .308 Winchester and .30-06. It performs well also in full-charge loads for some of the older blackpowder and low-pressure smokeless cartridges such as the .25-35, .30-30, .32-40, .35 Remington and .45-70. It is the only Hercules powder currently manufactured that is suitable for full-charge loads in rifle cartridges, except 2400, which is limited to relatively small-capacity cases such as the .22 Hornet, .25-20 W.C.F. and .44-40.

Ball powders introduced

At the beginning of 1968 the Winchester-Western Division, Olin Mathieson Chemical Corp., announced seven new handloading Ball powders. Four of them were rifle powders. Winchester-Western published complete loading information at the same time. These were the first rifle Ball powders made available to handloaders by the manufacturer, though military surplus rifle Ball powders came on the market a number of years earlier.

Winchester-Western had begun to offer pistol and shotgun powders for handloading in 1960. The company resisted demands for canister types of Ball powders at that time, preferring to await development of rifle powders that they considered more suitable for handloading, though handloaders had been using military surplus Ball powders successfully for several years.

The shotgun, pistol and rifle powders introduced between 1960 and 1968 gave generally satisfactory results, but all have now been superseded by powders incorporating still further improvements. One of the disadvantages in the earlier rifle Ball powders was that they produced, in certain loads, a stubborn bore fouling that was extremely difficult to remove by normal cleaning methods. It was found in the late 1960's that certain lots of military Ball powder also produced fouling in the gas tube of the M16 rifle, and an intensive investigation was begun to identify the specific cause. By joint efforts of the manufacturer and the Army, it was found that the fouling was caused by excessive quantities of calcium carbonate, a chemical added during manufacture to neutralize any residual acids that might remain in the final product, or might be formed as the powder began to deteriorate in long storage. The investigation revealed that the useful purposes of the calcium carbonate were served by quantities not exceeding 0.25 per cent, and this small quantity did not produce the troublesome fouling, either in the bore or in the gas tube of the M16 rifle. Both the military and commercial Ball powders were accordingly modified to prevent the incorporation of unnecessarily large percentages of calcium carbonate, and the problem of excessive fouling was eliminated. The former commercial rifle powders were identified by the suffix "BR" on the numerical identification, and pistol powders carried the suffix "P". The alphabetical suffixes have been dropped in the later improved powders (though some of them retain the original numerical identifications) and handloaders can distinguish between the older and newer powders by these suffixes. The currently manufactured canister powders offered by Winchester-Western are all Ball powders, and are identified as follows, listed under their principal applications:

Shotgun	Pistol	Rifle
452AA	231	680
473AA	630	748
540	296	760
571		785

Ball powder was developed, at least in part, to use quantities of over-age cannon powder as the material for new propellant, and incidentally to remove nitrating acids completely, thus obtaining an age-resistant product. It was found that Ball powder has certain other advantages in use.

One is smoothness and regularity in volumetric measuring, because of the small rounded grains.

Another is density, which permits loading the maximum amount of propellant in a given volume. The energy content also can be increased if necessary. These characterisitcs have proved important in meeting severe velocity and pressure requirements. They have not been specially significant to handloaders, since the cartridges of general handloading interest can be loaded up to specification with all three basic smokeless powder types. Most of the shotgun and pistol Ball powders are artificially made more bulky so that the charge will not be invonveniently small.

A third distinctive feature is the low rate of bore erosion from Ball powder. This makes it possible to fire more rounds through a rifle barrel, sometimes several times more, than would be possible otherwise. Bore erosion is of no

importance in shotguns and pistols, nor in many rifles. It may be not be a serious consideration even where it occurs. But where it is important, the rifleman by using Ball powder can limit the wear on his barrel.

There are also some disadvantages in Ball powders. Because of their geometrically degressive-burning grain form, it is necessary in most applications to depend upon deterrent coating to provide the desired degree of progressivity in burning. Deterrent coatings tend to inhibit ignition, and each powder must be carefully formulated to meet the ballistic requirements for its specific application. Ball powders perform very well in the loads for which they are designed, but are less flexible in other applications. Two types of canister Ball powder, 785 for rifles and 296 for pistols, are especially inflexible and the manufacturer warns that they should be loaded exactly as specified in Winchester-Western loading data, or other reliable sources of data that have been carefully developed in pressure barrels. Charges of these powders should be neither increased nor reduced from the specified weights and substitution of different brands of primers, cases or bullets is not recommended. The other Ball powders are somewhat more flexible as to charge weight, but are not generally suitable for loads reduced far below the maximum loads listed by the manufacturer, and they should not be used by the experimenter who chooses to work with wildcat cartridges or unusual loads that have not been thoroughly tested. The single exception among the current Ball powders is 630, which performs very well in a variety of medium and heavy handgun loads and in many low-pressure rifle cartridges as well. It has been found to produce excellent results in cast-bullet loads for rifles as different as the .222 Remington and the .45-70.

Since they became available as military surplus after World War II, rifle Ball powders have been widely and successfully handloaded. These new rifle Ball powders increase the choices available.

Norma powders

Smokeless propellants were invented in Europe and first came into use there. Imported European powders were mainstays in the early use of smokeless in this country. The great revival of handloading after World War II caused European powders to be imported once more. At first these were shotgun powders, later rifle powders as well.

Norma rifle powders are supplied by AB Noma Projektilfabrik, Amotfors, Sweden. They are all of extruded type.

Like all responsible suppliers, Norma provides full loading information based on laboratory measurements of velocity

and pressure. All U.S. rifle cartridges, normally handloaded, are included as well as some metric calibers for which loading information is otherwise difficult to obtain.

The Norma powders have proved to perform excellently, and these high-grade propellants are a desirable addition to the components available to handloaders.

Hodgdon powders

All the foregoing powders are offered by their makers. In 1946, however, B. E. Hodgdon of Merriam, Kan., began marketing military surplus rifle powders, a step which had a large and lasting effect on handloading. At that time the manufacturers had not resumed the supply of handloading powders and other components, preferring to apply all they made to the production of finished ammunition. The Hodgdon powders, of excellent quality and moderate price, enabled many individuals to resume handloading and many others to take it up for the first time. Handloaders also met military powders new to them — IMR-4895, IMR-4831 and the rifle Ball powders — finding these highly successful and eventually inducing the powder manufacturers to put similar ones on the market. Demand has more recently caused Hodgdon to add special powders manufactured for himself.

Some of the powders originally available as military surplus are no longer available. To supply the continuing demand for these powders, Hodgdon has arranged with the old and respected firm of Nobel in Scotland to produce new powders that can be used with the same loading data as some of the previously available Hodgdon surplus powders. These are not, in general, of the same chemical formulation as the surplus powders that they replaced, but they are formulated by the manufacturer to produce similar ballistics, in the same cartridges, with the same charge weights. The principal difference in composition is that the powders supplied by Nobel utilize centralite deterrent coatings instead of the dinitrotoluene (DNT) that is most commonly used in Du Pont military rifle powders. Centralite-coated powders have been used with excellent satisfaction in Great Britain for many years, and some military powders in the U.S. have employed centralite coatings as well. The formulation of Hodgdon's powders from Nobel is thus one that has withstood the test of time, and those powders are undoubtedly equal or superior to the surplus powders that they have replaced.

Hodgdon also purchases new powder from some sources in the United States. The prices of these newly manufactured powders are higher than those of surplus powders, as must be expected. Low prices were not the only reason for popularity of the surplus powders, however, as some of them filled certain requirements better than any other available powders, at any price. Handloaders are fortunate that Hodgdon has assured the continuing availability of powders to meet these requirements.

A list of the current 1980 Hodgdon powders, arranged in approximate order of relative quickness, from fast to slow, is as follows:

Powder	Grain Type	Principal Applications
HP-38	Spherical	Target loads in handguns.
Trap 100	Spherical	Target loads in shotguns.
HS-5	Spherical	Field load in shotguns.
HS-6	Spherical	Heavy loads in shotguns.
HS-7	Spherical	Magnum loads in shotguns.
H-110	Spherical	Full-charge loads in .30 Carbine and Magnum revolvers.
H-4227	Tubular	Full-charge loads in .22 Hornet and Magnum revolvers, and cast-bullet loads.
H-4198	Tubular	Full-charge loads in .222 and .223 Remington, reduced loads in larger rifles.
H-322	Tubular	Full-charge loads in .223 Remington, target loads in larger rifles up to .308 Winchester.
BL-C2	Spherical	Excellent for full-charge loads in .308 Winchester and .223 Remington.
H-335	Spherical	Same applications as BL-C2, but surplus powder.
4895	Tubular	Designed for full-charge loads in .30-06, but very versatile.
H-380	Spherical	Full-charge loads in .30-06 and similar cartridges.
H-414	Spherical	Full-charge loads in .270 and .30-06, light bullets in larger cartridges.
H-205	Tubular	Full-charge loads in medium to large-capacity rifle cartridges.
H-450	Spherical	Large-capacity and magnum rifle cartridges.
4831	Tubular	Large-capacity and magnum rifle cartridges.
H-870	Spherical	Very large-capacity, small-bore magnums up to .30 caliber.

Powders in review

It is seen that available smokeless powders date from not later than the 1930's, and in most cases from 1914 or earlier. With few exceptions they are markedly lower in energy than the powder invented by Nobel more than three-quarters of a century ago. However, they have been refined and adapted to the requirements of current cartridges and their performance is a marvel of excellence and reliability.

Consideration of all these powders must impress any thoughful person as to how fortunate the recreation of handloading in this country really is. Three great industrial organizations make propellants especially for it. These powders, of absolutely unsurpassed quality and reliability, are available in styles for every use, and even to permit a choice among types at each step. Surplus military powders are available commercially and high grade handloading powders are imported.

The user, therefore, will wish to protect his investment in such quality items.

Smokeless powders correctly stored have very long life. In the quantities stored and used by handloaders, deterioration, when it does happen, is without material danger. The powder slowly loses its strength. The owner is concerned to store his powder in conditions which will not harm it.

All users have noticed the characteristic odor released when a can of single-base powder is opened. It comes from alcohol and ether intentionally left in the powder in manufacture. The correct proportions of these, together with some water, is required for strength and toughness of the powder grain. If the propellant is dried excessively, the energy normally used to vaporize these substances will serve to increase the burning rate, raising the pressure undesirably. On the other hand, allowing the propellant to absorb additional water from the atmosphere lowers the effective energy of burning and the pressure.

Accordingly, cans of single-base powders should be kept tightly closed to keep the moisture and volatiles at the powder maker's intended level.

Double-base powders have less odor. Less solvent is required in their manufacture, the nitroglycerine performing much of that function, and what solvent is left in the finished powder is held there rather tightly by the nitroglycerine. Double-base powders are affected comparatively little by ordinary storage conditions, some of them not at all, though they are rapidly affected in extremely hot storage.

Preserving powders

Some handloaders, noticing the odor of volatiles and with the idea of preserving the powder, have dumped it into glass jars and sealed it there. Yet the powder can seals amply if its lid screws down well. A glass jar is extremely bad for storing powder because it admits light. On no account should the powder be stored in glass or otherwise exposed to light. It should be left in the factory can.

The main cause of deterioration, however, is heat which drives off the moisture and volatiles necessary to single-base powders. Far more important, heat greatly speeds the chemical changes of aging in any powder, which otherwise proceed very slowly at low temperatures. From time to time reports reach *The American Rifleman* of handloading powder deteriorating and having to be thrown out. Almost always this occurs in hot climates and usually in poorly chosen storage sites. Midday heat in attics and sheds under a summer sun can reach terrific heights.

The handloader's smokeless powder, therefore, should be kept in its original cans, tightly closed, and in the coolest and steadiest temperature available.

Deterioration of smokeless powders

All smokeless powders eventually deteriorate, though some have remained serviceable for more than 50 years and few modern powders have a useful life of less than 20 years unless subjected to very adverse storage conditions. Chemical deterioration causes a decrease in pressure and velocity when the powder is fired, so it is not dangerous to fire aging powder, though the velocity and pressure become more variable as deterioration progresses and performance becomes less satisfactory. Nevertheless, handloaders should be alert to signs of deterioration in old powder, and dispose of it promptly when those signs appear.

The first sign may be a rust-color "dust" on the surface of the powder and among the granules. Metal parts of containers may show signs of corrosion. The characteristic ether-alcohol odor of fresh powder may be replaced by an acrid odor, like that of some acids. These are unmistable signs that the powder has deteriorated beyond serviceability, and should be disposed of. If loaded into cartridges at this stage, the acid products of decomposition may corrode and weaken the cartridge cases, hangfires and misfires may occur in the loaded ammunition, and partial or "squib" ignitions may cause a bullet to become lodged in the bore. It is poor economy to attempt to use up the powder quickly after these signs appear. The process of deterioration is irreversible, and nothing can be done to salvage the powder at this stage.

It is important to dispose of deteriorated powder promptly and safely. The final stages of deterioration produce compounds of nitrogen that are toxic, so the rust-colored "dust" and the fumes from deteriorated powder must not be ingested. Heat is also liberated. If the powder is stored in bulk in large quantities, or in containers from which the heat cannot readily escape, spontaneous combustion is possible, though it is unlikely to occur with handloaders' powders in factory packages.

Small quantities of deteriorated powder can be safely disposed of by scattering it thinly over the ground in an open area, where the deterioration will proceed quickly and harmlessly with exposure to light. Larger quantities can be disposed of by burning, in small piles not exceeding about one pound each, in an open area outdoors. A convenient way is to pour each pile of powder on several sheets of newspaper, twist a corner of the sheets into a "fuze," and ignite the paper with a match before retiring to a safe distance of about 20 feet. The powder will burn vigorously for a few seconds, but will not explode. One should remain upwind of burning powder, however, as burning at atmospheric pressure produces toxic fumes. ■

SMOKELESS SHOTGUN & PISTOL POWDERS

**By E. H. HARRISON
and Wm. C. DAVIS, JR.**

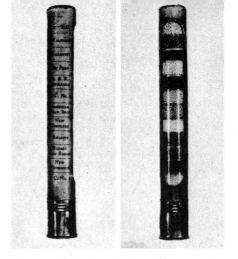

Exhibition shell of Winchester Repeating Arms Co. (2 views), showing samples of standard smokeless shotgun powders regularly loaded before World War I. Others were available also, such as Mullerite, Empire, etc.

SMOKELESS powders were developed for shotguns fully 20 years before any were successful for rifles or cannon. This happened because shotguns, due to their large bore and low pressure, required a comparatively fast-burning propellant and that is what proceeded naturally from the earliest efforts to control the explosion of gun-cotton to permit its use in guns. A powder successful in shotguns could be obtained by only partly modifying the fibrous structure of gun-cotton, but to make it slow enough for rifles required practically destroying this fibrous structure and turning it into a homogeneous solid.

First successful shotgun smokeless

The first successful smokeless shotgun powder was invented by Captain E. Schultze of the Prussian Army. It was patented in 1864 and put on the market in that year. It was almost unique in being made of nitrated wood (nitrolignin) instead of nitrocellulose. To this base material was added barium and potassium nitrate, which provided oxygen during burning to consume residues from the incompletely nitrated wood. At first the original wood was obtained in the desired grains by punching them from thin veneers. Eventually the chemically purified wood fiber was made through chemical manipulation, to gather into lumps of the required size.

Schultze shotgun powder was soon manufactured in England as well as in Germany. A powder called New Schultze was made by Du Pont in the United States for many years.

British manufacture continued to the beginning of World War II. Schultze therefore had a successful history of some 75 years, longer than any other smokeless powder of any kind except Ballistite and Bullseye.

Another well-known smokeless shotgun powder was developed by the Explosives Company in England, and patented in 1882. It was called E. C. from the name of the company. As with Schultze, the manufacture of E. C. spread beyond the country of origin. E. C. was made in the United States by Hercules Powder Co. until the beginning of World War I.

E. C. and most other powders were made of nitrocellulose from cotton. Like Schultze, most of these powders were given additions of barium and potassium nitrate. The grains, formed of little balls of the fiber, were hardened sometimes by a treatment of gum water or, preferably, by partly colloiding the fibers.

Different type

The invention of fully colloided powders produced a quite different type of shotgun powder. Its solid substance made it much denser than either Schultze or E. C. and it possessed more energy in a given weight. Thus arose the distinction between *bulk* and *dense* smokeless shotgun powders.

The obvious difference in loading procedure seems formerly to have been widely understood. Powder type was listed on factory shell boxes, which kept the matter before the shooters. The wide extension of shotshell reloading, beginning a few years after World War II, and the

discontinuance of powder type listings in factory ammunition left new handloaders uninformed about this difference. Resulting loading errors produced poor, sometimes even dangerous, ammunition despite comparatively low pressures of shotgun ammunition and the large factor of safety in modern shotgun construction.

A complicating factor is the drams-equivalent marking on factory shotshells.

Blackpowder shotgun charges were originally specified in drams, a unit of weight equaling 1/16-ounce. The standard 12-gauge blackpowder charge of three drams weighed 82 grains. Since charges of blackpowder normally were measured, the measuring cups were made to deliver three drams of blackpowder, or any other amount desired.

Schultze, E. C., and similar powders, with their fibrous make-up, were much lighter than blackpowder so a much lighter charge was required. Only 42 grains of Schultze in the 12 gauge powders. It was found readily possible to adjust the manufacture of these smokeless powders to make a charge of them fill the same measuring cup as the blackpowder they replaced. The dram marking on the cups then became a measure of volume only. The ammunition maker and the handloader loaded the new powders with the same measures they had used for blackpowder, an obvious convenience and money saver, and everyone accepted this as the most natural thing in the world.

This interchangeability in bulk measure of the then-new smoke-

Hercules Red Dot

Du Pont PB

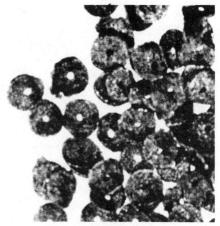

Du Pont Hi-Skor 700-X

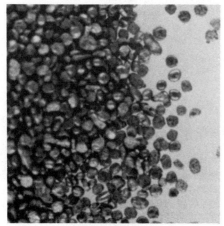

WW-452AA

Hercules Unique

Alcan AL-8

less powders and blackpowder caused them to be called bulk powders. That is the whole meaning of the expression.

Measuring dense powders

The dense smokeless shotgun powders could not, by their nature, be included in this happy interchangeability of measures. For most of the dense powders, the charge giving the same performance as 3 drams of blackpowder weighed between 22 and 33 grains. This small amount of dense material occupied far less space than a 3-dram measure of black or bulk smokeless. Filling such a 3-dram bulk measure with dense powder obviously must result in a gross overcharge. Accordingly, dense powder must be loaded by weight, just as rifle and pistol smokeless powders are — with either scales or a volumetric powder measure adjusted to scales.

The 'drams equivalent' marked on factory shell boxes has nothing to do with this. It is simply a way of indicating the power of the ammunition. The marking 3¾ - 1¼ - 6, for example, means a load of 1¼ ounce No. 6 shot and a charge of any powder giving the performance of 3¾ drams blackpowder.

Multiplication, then simplification

Remarkable as it may appear, factory shotshells were not loaded with smokeless powder in the United States until 1893, 30 years after they appeared successfully in England. Eventually smokeless shotgun powders proliferated here also. There were imported English and German powders, Schultze, E. C., and Ballistite, based on the foreign powders of those names, and ultimately a number of powders of American origin. In those days the powder was named on the shell box and shooters frequently were enthusiastic about one powder or the other. Yet they were all suitable for only light and medium loads and there was no great difference among their results.

To meet shooters' demands actually required about 15,000 separate loads in 1907. World War I provided the opportunity for a radical simplification of the loading list. The process continued until there were only 107 factory shotshell loads in 1953. Since then the number has been increased by new types for which there was a need or demand. The present list, though still numerically short, retains most of the light and medium loads formerly offered (omitting the options in powder and other details) and has heavy and magnum loads of powder beyond anything formerly available.

Developments in smokeless shotgun powders made these powerful loads possible. The number of available powders was increased by our U.S. manufacturers and also by importers, attracted by the great increase of shotshell reloading in this country. Powders are now available for light to medium loads, in which most handloading is still done, and for high velocity and magnum loads.

These numerous powders are, in part, the cause of a great change which has come over the practice of shotshell loading. Even into the 1930's there was only a few powders, substantially only one kind of paper shotshell and of card and filler wadding, and few loads beyond conventional target, light field, and conventional high velocity loads (magnum loads had not yet become important). All shells were assembled in about the same manner and required the user to make a reasonable selection among the limited powder and shot combinations available. But after World War II the practice of handloading experienced a tremendous upswing, mostly for economic reasons. Then new components and materials (plastic cup wads, shot pouches, and shells themselves, as well as new powders) brought within reach a performance level which with the old components, had been possible only with difficulty or not at all. Today such performance is expected.

All this carries, however, a certain penalty. Not only the different powders, but different wads and even various types of plastic shotshells have a striking effect on velocity and pressure. For example, the 3-dram equivalent charge of Red Dot shotgun powder in the 12-gauge with card and filler wadding is about 22 grains. With plastic one-piece wads and shot pouches it is often 19 grains, while with certain combinations of shell and wads the powder manufacturer does not recommend a 3-dram equivalent charge of Red Dot at all. Thus it is no longer possible to state a definite dram equivalent charge of any powder, nor to approach equally simply the other details of shotshell reloading. Its age of innocence has passed.

The shotshell handloader now should load according to specific information for the exact components he is using. Consult the loading directions published by the manufacturers of powder and other components who prepare these (at considerable cost) and make them available for precisely this reason.

Still, many handloaders as a matter of interest like to know something about the components they load. The following describes the smokeless shotgun powders now in successful use, and indicates why they have been successful.

Hercules shotgun powders

Hercules Red Dot is a double-base powder of about 20 per cent nitroglycerine content, introduced in 1932. It is made in round flakes of .065-inch diameter and .004-inch thickness, and a few of the flakes are dyed red to identify the powder. Red Dot is manufactured in a range of burning speeds for factory loading and so may be found in a variety of factory shotshell loads. It is sold to handloaders in only a single canister type, intended for light and standard shotshell loading, including trap and skeet loads. The tremendous scale on which Red Dot is consumed indicates the great satisfaction it has given in use.

Hercules Green Dot, introduced in 1965, is also a double-base powder. Its nitroglycerine content is said to be comparable to Red Dot. It is designed for 12-gauge medium shotshell loads, specifically 3-, 3¼- and 3½-dram-equivalent game, crow, and pigeon loads. Like Red Dot, it is coated and has some special-purpose additives. The round, perforated flakes are .065-inch in diameter and about .005-inch thick, thus being of the same diameter as Red Dot but slightly thicker. A few of the flakes are dyed green to identify the powder. Green Dot is loaded in the same manner as Red Dot and often the same loading tool charge bars can be used, a decided convenience.

Hercules Unique, already mentioned as a rifle powder, is also widely useful in field, high-velocity, and 10-gauge magnum shotgun loads. It is thus perhaps the most adaptable of smokeless shotgun powders. Unique is made in round flakes of .065-inch diameter and .006-inch thickness, therefore of the same diameter as Red and Green Dot, but thicker. Its composition originally was somewhat different, being 40 per cent nitroglycerine, but many years ago the nitroglycerine content was reduced to about 20 per cent, with burning controlled to the desired moderate rate by its granulation.

Hercules Herco is a double-base powder of about 20 per cent nitroglycerine content. It is made in round flakes of .065-inch diameter and .005-inch thickness, thus of the same diameter as Red Dot and Unique but in thickness midway between them.

Hercules Blue Dot is a powder still slower-burning than Herco, and intended for magnum shotshell loads. The flakes are nominally .050-inch in diameter and .010-inch thick, and the nitroglycerine content is nominally 20 per cent. It provides excellent velocity-pressure relationships with heavy shot charges in all magnum loads from the 2¾-inch 28-gauge to the 3½-inch 10-gauge shells.

All of the Hercules shotgun powders also give excellent performance in appropriate handgun loads and data for such loads are furnished by the manufacturer, as well as by other reliable sources. Red Dot and Green Dot are suitable for mild target loads, as are Unique and Herco for medium to heavy loads in practically all handgun cartridges. Blue Dot gives excellent performance in the .357, .41 and .44 Magnum with full-power or slightly reduced loads.

Hercules 2400, though originally designed for small-capacity rifle cartridges such as the .22 Hornet and now frequently used by handloaders in the .357, .41 and .44 Magnum handgun cartridges, finds application also in .410-bore shotshell loads. It is, in fact, the only Hercules powder recommended by the manufacturer for use in the .410-bore shotshell.

Du Pont shotgun powders

Du Pont PB, introduced in 1954, is oldest among the current Du Pont shotgun powders. It is made in perforated disks looking like tiny washers, but their comparatively great thickness of .0095 of an inch makes them work easily and smoothly through powder measures. PB stands for porous base, the grains being made porous by chemical means to assist ignition and burning at the low pressures in shotguns. This procedure, the opposite of coating, has the advantage of allowing a comparatively thick granulation in fast-burning shotgun and pistol powders, with greater convenience in measuring. PB is recommended for medium loads, including 20-gauge and 28-gauge skeet loads. Many users also like it for all 12-gauge target loads, finding its low pressures to be specially easy on shells which are loaded repeatedly. This characteristic and its wide load usefulness have gained for PB an established place.

Du Pont Hi-Skor 700X was introduced in 1964 specifically for target and light field loads. It is remarkable among Du Pont powders in being of double-base type. Du Pont has manufactured relatively few double-base sporting powders since 1913, and Hi-Skor 700X was stated on its introduction to be the first in 10 years. (Du Pont offered also, for a few years after 1962, a single-base shotgun powder designated Hi-Skor, but that has been dropped and the possibility of confusion removed.) Hi-Skor 700X is in the form of black disks with a very small hole in the center. Occasional granules are left in the natural light color to identify the powder. The disks are thick enough to work smoothly through powder measures. Hi-Skor 700X ignites quickly and burns cleanly and has given most excellent results. Notably, it is designed for loading without any pressure on the wads beyond that necessary to force them through a wad guide and seat them on the powder. Thorough tests, however, have shown that any reasonable wad seating force, from zero to 120 pounds, in 12-gauge, can be used without concern for safety or performance. Du Pont now recommends specific loads of Hi-Skor 700X in 12-gauge blanks, an unusual and sometimes valuable use.

Before World War II, the Du Pont powder for heavy and magnum shotshell loads was Oval, a coated single-base powder of composition like the IMR propellants. But Oval was not put back on the market for handloading after the war. For some years there was no Du Pont handloading powder for this requirement. Then several Du Pont powders of the SR series were made available for this purpose.

SR stands for sporting rifle, and it may appear strange that such powders should be loaded primarily in shotshells. However, the designation is used for a class of Du Pont single-base powders intentionally made slightly porous to facilitate low-pressure ignition and burning. (This has been explained for PB powder, which in fact is the only Du Pont handloading propellant of this type which is not called by an SR number.) SR-7625 is now prescribed for 12-gauge high-velocity loads, meaning 3¾ drams equivalent and 1¼ ounce shot. SR-4756 is used specially in magnum loads. These SR powders are also the main propellants in the 10-gauge and enlarged 12-gauge buckshot loads which Du Pont listed in 1968.

None of the aforementioned Du Pont shotgun powders is recommended by the manufacturer for use in .410-bore shotshell loads. For that purpose, Du Pont recommends only IMR-4227, which is primarily a rifle powder that is also used in magnum handgun cartridges. IMR-4227 is also recommended by Du Pont for the heaviest loads in 20-gauge 3-inch magnum shotshells. It is unique among the IMR powders, as the only one recommended for rifles, pistols and shotguns.

Winchester powders

Winchester - Western Division, Olin Mathieson Chemical Corp., has made Ball propellants for its own ammunition since 1930. In 1960, for the first time, it offered some of these to handloaders. The Winchester-Western shotshell powders introduced in 1960 have been improved and the list has been expanded from three original types to the present four types specifically for shotshell loads, and a dual-purpose powder used both in .410-bore shotshells and some metallic cartridges.

The powder used for 12-gauge target loads in Winchester-Western factory ammunition is 452AA, and it is recommended for handloads of the same type. It is a rolled-ball powder, having the grains so flattened that they appear at first glance to be flakes. This reduces the bulk density so that charges of 452AA occupy approximately the same volume in the cartridge as do flake-type powders, a convenience that allows this Ball powder to be loaded with the same shells, wads and shot charges that are used with the flake-type powders commonly used for target loads.

For 20-gauge target loads, Winchester-Western uses 473AA. It is especially recommended for handloads of that type, as well as other applications in both 12-gauge and 16-gauge loads.

Winchester-Western 540 powder is a relatively dense slow-burning type, intended for heavy field loads and some magnum loads in 10, 12, 16 and 20 gauges.

For the heaviest shot charges in magnum shotshell loads, Winchester 571 powder is recommended for 10-gauge to 20-gauge shells. It is specially useful in the long 3-inch cases of 20- and 12-gauge magnum shells, and in the 3½-inch 10-gauge magnum.

Winchester-Western 296 powder is recommended by the manufacturer primarily in full-power loads for the .30 Carbine cartridge, and the 357, .41 and .44 Magnum handgun cartridges, but it is also the only powder recommended by that manufacturer for use in .410-bore shotshell loads.

Winchester-Western supplies detailed loading information developed in its ballistic laboratories for all of these powders.

Hodgdon shotgun powders

The Hodgdon Powder Company distributes a line of spherical-grain shotgun powders comparable to the Ball powders sold for handloading by Winchester-Western. These include Trap 100 for target loads, HS-5 for light to moderate field loads, HS-6 for heavy field loads, and HS-7 for heavy shot charges in magnum shotshell loads. In addition, H-110 is a dual-purpose powder for use in .30 Carbine and magnum handgun loads, as well as the .410-bore shotshell. Though characteristics of Hodgdon spherical-grain powders are similar to those of Winchester-Western powders, it should not be assumed that loading data are interchangeable. The Hodgdon powders should be loaded only as specified by Hodgdon or some other reliable source of pressure-tested loading data.

Imported shotshell powders

For a time after the end of World War II, handloading components of any kind were almost impossible to obtain. At that time the Alcan Co., Inc., Alton, Ill., began importing shotshell reloading components. This put shotshell reloading back on the map, and unquestionably its present practice on a large scale, with components now supplied from many sources, owes much to that early action.

The powders imported by Alcan were originally of great variety, coming from both Sweden and Italy. The Alcan interests were subsequently taken over by the Smith & Wesson Ammunition Company, an element of that firm most famous for its handguns, and the Alcan shotshell powders were reduced to three types that currently remain available. These are AL-5, AL-7 and AL-8, all products of Bofors in Sweden. AL-5 is suitable for light and moderate loads, AL-7 is for heavy field loads, and AL-8 is most useful in magnum loads. All are flake-type powders, of a type that has long been used with satisfaction in Europe. They perform well in recommended loads with U.S. shotshell components. These Alcan shotshell powders also give excellent results in some handgun loads.

Norma Projektilfabrik for some years imported two shotgun powders, 2010 and 2020, for standard and heavy shotshell loads respectively. These powders are no longer imported for sale in the U.S., but some stocks remain on dealers' shelves. Norma is still prepared to furnish laboratory-tested loading data for these powders on request.

Loading small-bore shotshells

It is interesting and important to note that the smallest-bore shotguns require the slowest powders. The only Du Pont propellant recommended for loading the .410 is IMR-4227 and the only Hercules powder is No. 2400, both rifle powders. The .410 and 28-gauge are not much handloaded, partly because those sizes make up only a relatively small fraction of the shotguns in use, and partly because reloading becomes less easy at each step down in size. It is most important in reloading these small gauges to follow loading directions exactly. The handloader has been much helped by recent improvements in shells, wads, and loading tools, and with these plus care and attention he can reload the small sizes with good results.

Pistol powders

As with shotshells, the handloading of pistol and revolver cartridges is practiced on a continually increasing scale. But its development has proceeded on quite different lines. The components of the metallic cartridge have remained largely unchanged, and so have the loads except for some continuation of heavy-load development. Many pistol powders have disappeared from the market. The powder makers however have more than made up for this by publishing handgun loads for a great variety of shotgun and shotgun-pistol powders, providing, in effect, more pistol and revolver powders than handloaders ever had before.

Hercules Bullseye, dating originally from about 1898, is a high-nitroglycerine (about 40 per cent) powder intended for handgun loads of light and moderate power. It is a favorite in .38 Special and .45 ACP target cartridges, which are handloaded more than any other and on which its success speaks for itself. The very thin flakes do not work through all powder measures equally well and clear plastic powder hoppers are attacked, when the powder is left in them for some time, by the plasticizing action of nitroglycerine. These drawbacks are in most cases not serious and the popularity of Bullseye continues unabated.

Winchester-Western until 1980 marketed two pistol powders identified as exclusively for that use. These were 231, suitable for light and moderate loads, and 630, suitable for a wide variety of moderate to heavy loads in handguns. W-W 630 is used for factory loading .45-70 and .38-55 ammunition, and works well for light cast bullet loads in these and similar cartridges, with appropriate light charges. It is no longer available in canister lots for handloading, however, having been recently discontinued. As previously mentioned, Winchester-Western 296 powder is used and recommended by the manufacturer as a powder for .357, .41 and .44 Magnum handgun loads, as well as for .410-bore shotshells.

In addition to these U.S.-made pistol powders, two types are currently imported from Norma in Sweden. Norma R-1 is a relatively fast-burning powder intended for light and moderate handgun loads, and R-123 is a slower-burning powder intended primarily for the magnum handgun cartridges. They are not widely distributed in the U.S. at present, and loading data for them are limited. The manufacturer provides data only for the 9mm Luger, .38 Special, .357 Magnum, .38 Smith & Wesson, and the .44 Magnum, and these only for a limited number of Norma bullets.

The dual-purpose powders that are suitable for use in pistols as well as shotguns and/or rifles have been described previously in connection with those other uses. These include Hercules Red Dot, Green Dot, Unique, Herco, Blue Dot and 2400, covering the complete range of handgun loads, from light target loads and small calibers such as the .25 ACP to heavy loads for the .41 and .44 Magnum cartridges. The same wide range of uses is covered by Du Pont with Hi-Skor 700X, PB, SR-7625, SR-4756 and IMR-4227. Hodgdon supplies HP-38, a spherical-grain powder specially intended for target loads in handguns, and covers the remaining spectrum of handgun loads with the dual-purpose Trap 100, HS-5, HS-6, HS-7, H-110 and H-4227 powders. All of these suppliers furnish loading data for their dual-purpose powders in the pistol calibers for which their uses are appropriate.

The reloader of handgun cartridges has at his disposal four U.S.-made powders and two imported powders specially for handguns, plus 17 dual-purpose powders that are suitable for handgun loads. This selection of 23 different powders is certainly sufficient for any kind of handgun ammunition that the reloader might wish to assemble.

POWDER STORAGE

I have looked thoroughly into the matter of home storage for smokeless powders, primers, ammunition, blackpowder and curio ammunition. Some of this information may be of interest to other NRA Members.

When seeking information from insurance companies, county fire officials, and other sources, be prepared to deal with nervous, ill-informed and perhaps hostile individuals. Some people who are ignorant about shooting, feel anybody who keeps ammunition or propellant powders is a potential anarchist or bomb maker.

It's surprising how many insurance company employees equate propellant powders, or small arms ammunition with other, higher order explosives. Muzzle-loading enthusiasts can expect considerable frustration, because while much information is available on the properties, storage and handling of smokeless powders, to my knowledge there is no similar body of information for blackpowder. Most fire insurance policies permit storage of up to 20 lbs. of flammable solid, propellant powders, but local regulations may not specify whether any quantity of blackpowder may be included in this summation.

Insurance companies seem inclined to modify the terms of their policies to meet local regulations. Many local regulations are based on Department of Transportation regulations and the National Fire Protection Association's pamphlet No. 495, entitled, "Manufacture, Storage, Transportation and Use of Explosive and Blasting Agents."

Recommendations of NFPA-495 are that smokeless propellants for personal use, not to exceed 20 lbs., may be stored in residences; quantities over 20 lbs., but not over 50 lbs., shall be stored in a wooden cabinet or box having walls of at least 1" nominal thickness. Smokeless and black powders must be stored in DOT-approved shipping containers. Do not transfer powder from an approved container, to one which is not.

The above recommendations should be adhered to with blackpowder, with the addition that blackpowder may be stored only in DOT-approved **1-lb.** containers not exceeding a total of 5 lbs., and that blackpowder should not be stored in the same cabinet with percussion caps or primers.

The above recommendations are only suggested procedures. Shooters should check with authorities to insure compliance with local regulations.

Don't be surprised if local authorities or your insurance company are unable to answer your questions. Get as much printed background material on powder storage as you can. This will help you deal with the hysteria which may be encountered. It is wise to recommend answers to your questions be deferred until the party can obtain satisfactory information on which to base a reply. This has resulted in very satisfactory handling of several of my queries.

In general, danger of insurance policy termination is virtually non-existent provided all state and local fire codes are complied with. In my home state of Maryland, for instance, if you store not more than 10,000 primers and percussion caps for small arms; 20 lbs. of smokeless powder (whether any blackpowder can be included in this total is extremely vague), and an unrestricted amount of sporting ammunition, no permit or approved class II magazine is required under the State Fire Code. A class II magazine, smoke detector and an approved fire extinguisher are highly recommended, however.

In closing, I offer the following advise: when dealing with your insurance company or public officials, exhibit courtesy, knowledge of the subject and a great deal of patience.

JAMES E. ROSE

Ed. note, NFPA-495 is available from the National Fire Protection Association, 470 Atlantic Ave., Boston, Mass. 02210, price $2. Information on the properties, storage and handling of smokeless powders is included in most powder manufacturer's loading data and also may be obtained by writing the Sporting Arms and Ammunition Manufacturer's Institute.

Powder Storage

Many shooting books suggest that powder or ammunition be stored "in a cool, dry place." I have a dehumidifier in my basement and keep my reloading tools and handtools down there without rusting. Is this dry enough? Would the attic be better?

Answer: Your basement is a much better place to store powder and ammunition than your attic. If your tools don't rust in your basement, it is dry enough for powder and ammunition storage. While a cool, dry place is ideal for ammunition storage, temperature is much more important than humidity for smokeless powder loads.

Smokeless powder does absorb some excess moisture from humid air, but the only effect is to reduce pressures and velocities slightly. If smokeless powder is removed to a drier place, it loses the excess moisture to the air, and regains its normal ballistic properties, so no permanent change is effected by the damp environment. A hot environment, on the other hand, accelerates chemical deterioration of smokeless powder, and the change is not reversible. For this reason you should avoid storing powder or ammunition in your attic or in the trunk of your car in the summertime since temperatures are likely to exceed 90°F.

For blackpowder, the situation is quite different. Excessive dampness causes permanent changes in blackpowder, whereas it is practically unaffected by storage in a hot environment, as long as it is protected from accidental ignition by static charges or sparks from machinery or electrical equipment.

Your attic is probably a better place to store small quantities of blackpowder than your basement, though if your basement is dry enough that you have no rusting problems with guns or tools, it is dry enough even for blackpowder storage.—W.C.D., JR.

Minute Of Angle Value

I was taught that one minute of angle equals exactly 1" at 100 yds. The American Rifleman *(August, 1978, p. 63) implies that this is not true. What is the exact value of the minute of angle, and how is it determined?*

Answer: One minute of angle equals 1.0472" at 100 yds. This is determined by dividing the number of inches in the circumference of a circle having a radius of 100 yds. (22619.467) by the number of minutes in a circle (21600).

$$7200 \pi = 22619.467 \text{ inches}$$
$$60 \times 360 = 21600 \text{ minutes}$$

$$\frac{22619.467}{21600} = 1.0472''$$

—R.N.S.

Choosing Reloading Equipment

Handloaders have several options when selecting their gear.

BY WILLIAM C. DAVIS, JR.

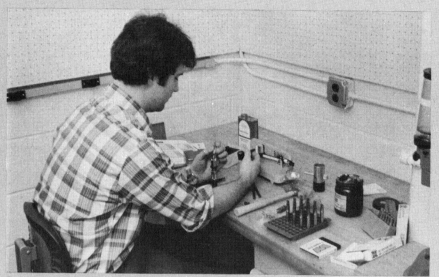

Reloading requires only the simplest of hand tools, like the Lee, shown above, for acceptable results. The average small-volume reloader, however, should use a scale.

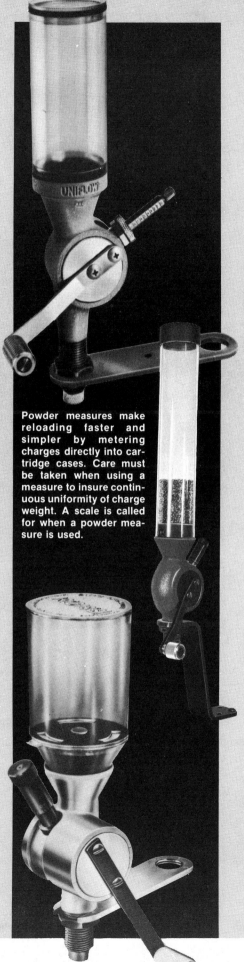

Powder measures make reloading faster and simpler by metering charges directly into cartridge cases. Care must be taken when using a measure to insure continuous uniformity of charge weight. A scale is called for when a powder measure is used.

THE equipment most suitable for a beginning reloader depends on his budget, the space available for his operations, the quantity of ammunition he plans to shoot, and the types of guns for which he plans to reload.

A powder scale is practically a necessity for reloading any type of metallic cartridge. Although it is possible to measure powder using the dipper-type measures furnished with hand-held Lee Loaders, only reduced loads can be safely assembled because of the relatively large variations in powder charges that may occur, and the choice of loads is rather limited. A powder scale is recommended as an accessory, even with the simplest reloading tools.

Weighing charges on a powder scale is the most precise method, but it is relatively slow. Many experienced reloaders use a mechanical powder measure for most of their reloading. The mechanical measure should always be adjusted by check-weighing charges on the powder

scale. When so adjusted, a mechanical measure delivers charges that are acceptably uniform for practically any load. For maximum loads, in which increases of less than about ½ gr. might develop excessive pressures, weighing each charge on an accurate scale is recommended. For specialized rifle loads to be used in long-range competitive shooting, where maximum uniformity of velocity is required for success, weighing each charge is also justified. For all other loads, mechanical powder measures offer the best combination of accuracy and convenience.

Hand-held reloading tools for assembling the cartridges are generally least expensive, and they require no space for installation or mounting. Perfectly acceptable ammunition can be loaded with hand tools, and they are often used by beginning reloaders who want to try handloading before they make a large investment in equipment. There are limitations, however, that should be carefully considered.

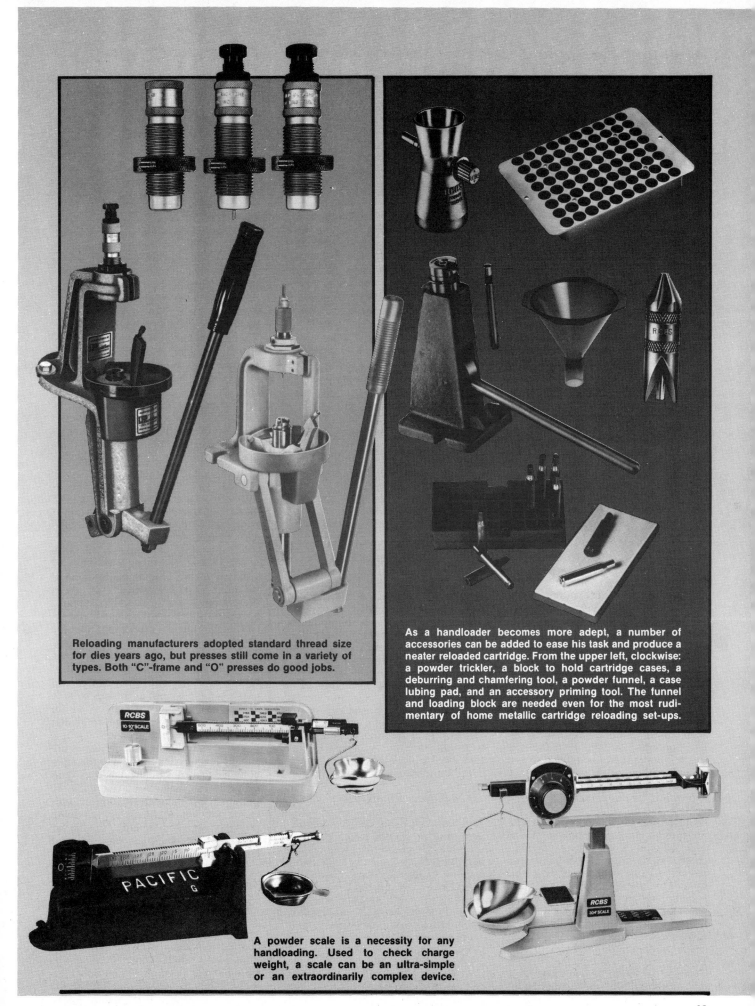

Reloading manufacturers adopted standard thread size for dies years ago, but presses still come in a variety of types. Both "C"-frame and "O" presses do good jobs.

As a handloader becomes more adept, a number of accessories can be added to ease his task and produce a neater reloaded cartridge. From the upper left, clockwise: a powder trickler, a block to hold cartridge cases, a deburring and chamfering tool, a powder funnel, a case lubing pad, and an accessory priming tool. The funnel and loading block are needed even for the most rudimentary of home metallic cartridge reloading set-ups.

A powder scale is a necessity for any handloading. Used to check charge weight, a scale can be an ultra-simple or an extraordinarily complex device.

Reloading Equipment

Probably the most important limitation is that hand-held tools usually are not capable of full-length resizing the cartridge cases. For moderate loads, to be fired in bolt-action or single-shot rifles, or in single-shot pistols, full-length resizing of cases is seldom required, provided the cases are to be reloaded for the same gun in which they were previously fired. For autoloading arms, revolvers, and many lever-action or pump-action rifles, results are often unsatisfactory unless cases are full-length resized. Though it is sometimes possible to obtain satisfactory results with hand tools, the results are often disappointing in arms other than bolt-action or single-shot models. Cases to be reloaded using hand tools must generally be new, or must have been full-length resized before the first reloading in hand-held tools. Gun chambers differ slightly in dimensions, and cases fired in one gun often cannot be chambered in another of the same caliber without full-length resizing. It is possible to buy hand dies for full-length resizing, and use an arbor press, bench vise, or even a mallet to drive the cases into the die, but this increases the investment so that the purchase of an inexpensive bench-mounted press might be justified instead.

Reloading with hand-held tools is relatively slow. If the ammunition requirements are not great, and the user is not pressed for time, this is not a serious disadvantage. Hand tools are often purchased by a beginning reloader, and serve very well to introduce him to the enjoyable practice of handloading. In most instances, as the handloader becomes more experienced, he forms opinions on the more sophisticated equipment he would like to have, and chooses that equipment more intelligently. Hand-held reloading tools were used almost exclusively by handloaders from the 19th Century up to about 1940, and they served their purposes quite well. They are still good choices, provided their limitations are understood.

Most handloaders nowadays assemble their ammunition on bench-mounted reloading presses. These may be simple, or quite sophisticated. The practical difference between simple and sophisticated models is in the speed of operation. Nearly all models use dies of standardized design having a 7⁄8"–14 thread, so that dies made by one manufacturer can be used in presses made by other manufacturers as well. The quality of ammunition loaded depends far more on the quality of the dies than the sophistication of

the press, and the simplest presses can produce excellent reloads.

Another distinguishing difference among presses is the matter of strength. While the simplest presses designed for use with standard full-length resizing dies can perform all necessary reloading operations, they may not be strong enough for specialized uses such as reforming cartridge cases from one caliber to another, or swaging jacketed bullets. Special dies to perform such operations are available, and they should be used only in strongly made presses specifically recommended for such use. Many manufacturers produce both ordinary reloading presses, and, at higher cost, special heavy-duty presses for the advanced reloader who may wish to do case reforming or bullet swaging with his reloading press.

Bench mounted presses are usually permanently installed. The bench must be sturdy, because considerable force is required for full-length resizing of the larger cartridge cases. While a permanent reloading bench is the ideal arrangement, it is possible to utilize a bench press without one, where space limitations do not permit a permanent installation.

Before choosing his equipment, the beginning handloader should obtain descriptive literature from the major manufacturers who advertise in the *American Rifleman* and other journals devoted to the shooting sports. Having studied the brochures, he should visit a dealer who displays reloading equipment, and examine the items in which he is interested. Handloaders in the U.S. are the most fortunate in the world, having far fewer restrictions on handloading than their counterparts in most other major countries. Americans also have a far greater selection of handloading equipment from which to choose. The manufacturers of handloading equipment in the U.S. are, practically without exception, committed to high standards of quality and service for their products. Those who were not have not survived long in the marketplace, because experienced handloaders are very discriminating.

A beginning handloader should seek the advice of more experienced handloaders on his choice of equipment, but he should weigh carefully the advice from several sources where possible, because even veteran handloaders sometimes have ill-founded prejudices, just as have buyers of guns, fishing rods, sports cars, and other highly personal possessions. Items from well-established manufacturers can safely be chosen on the basis of intended applications and product features, because the buyer is virtually assured of good quality and value for his investment. ∎

SYMPATHETIC DETONATION OF PRIMERS

Q: *I have heard that primers can detonate "sympathetically", which I assume means that the explosion of one primer can cause others to explode. That seems to be a dangerous possibility. How can it be avoided?*

A: You are correct in your understanding of sympathetic detonation, and it is indeed a potential hazard if primers are not properly handled. I know of a recent incident in which a handloader was injured when he tapped vigorously with his finger on the side of a primer feed tube, to free a jam of primers in the tube. The primers detonated sympathetically, and chopped off half his finger. This accident was probably caused by an accumulation of primer "dust" in the tube or at the bottom of it. It could have been avoided by careful cleaning of the tube and associated parts after each occasion of use. Primer "dust" consists of fine particles that occasionally are dislodged from the pellet of explosive material in a primer, and it can accumulate in feed tubes or other parts of primer-handling machinery. It is removed by washing the parts in water with soap or detergent, rinsing and drying them after each use.

I know also of other instances in which primer feed tubes have exploded violently owing to some malfunction of the machine that caused the primer at the bottom of the stack to be detonated accidentally. Primers situated end-to-end, as they are in a primer feed tube, are especially susceptible to sympathetic detonation. Some handloaders place a short length of pipe or strong steel tubing over the feed tube when it is in use. The pipe is open at the top, so as to direct the blast upward and away from the operator in event of an accidental detonation inside the tube.

The packaging in which primers are packed for handloaders is very carefully designed to minimize the risk of accidental explosion, and more importantly to prevent sympathetic detonation in event of an accident in which one or more primers are individually detonated. Primers should be left in these original packages until they are required for use, and it is best not to handle more than 100 primers at a time outside the original packages.

Primers can be detonated by heat, shock or friction, and occasionally even by static charges of electricity. The prudent handloader will avoid any conditions which might expose his primers to these hazards.

WCD, Jr.

APARTMENT HOUSE HANDLOADING

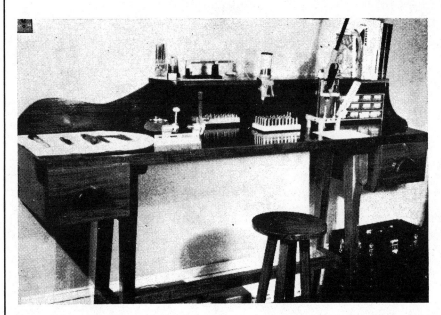

A small parts cabinet with plastic drawers is used to store small tools, dies, etc. This fits under the shelf, is out of the working surface, and is very accessible. Powder, primers, and bullets are kept in two 18"x12"x7" drawers on either end of the bench. A lock mounted on the side of the drawers is in order if you have small children in your home.

The height of the bench is entirely up to the individual. With a 25"-high stool and 36"-high bench, I can work comfortably sitting or standing. If you wish to do all your work sitting, you can make the bench standard table height and use an ordinary chair.

After the bench is completed, give practical thought to the matter of tool layout. Layout varies with right- and left-handed operators, and the method of handling the work sequence.—CHARLES R. SANDERS

THE sportsman who doesn't have 'spare' space in his home need not be deprived of the enjoyment of handloading. I converted my den into a very efficient handloading workshop and still retained the neatness of our small 4-room apartment.

If you can spare 18 sq. ft. of one of your rooms (approximately 6 ft.x3 ft.), you can convert it into a convenient handloading shop.

The work bench should be a presentable piece of furniture. I designed a saddle drawer bench and had a local cabinetmaker construct it. Made of black walnut wood for beauty (any type of wood that will finish satisfactorily would do), it was finished with 3 coats of Fabulon to toughen the surface and a few coats of furniture wax.

In designing a bench, consider the type of reloading you wish to do and the type of equipment you wish to use. I chose a leg-mounted down-leverage press because I wanted to full-length resize cartridge cases. Since this demands a great deal of leverage, I had to design the bench so the pull would not tip it over. This is not necessary if you can anchor the bench to the floor or wall.

I have found that powder scales mounted at eye level are much easier to read, so I designed a shelf extending ¾ the length of the bench to base them on. This also serves as a mounting base for the powder measure and a convenient spot for handloading books and literature.

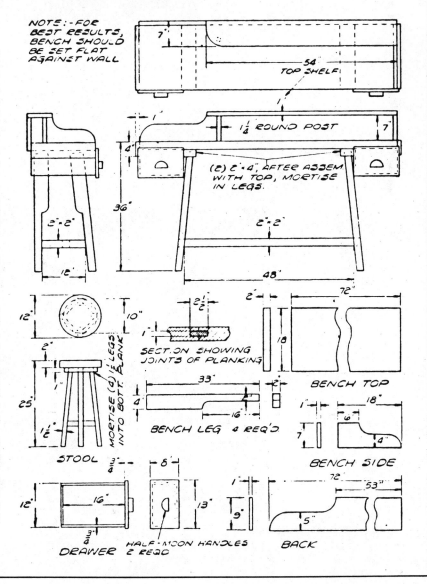

NOTE:- FOR BEST RESULTS, BENCH SHOULD BE SET FLAT AGAINST WALL

TOP SHELF

1¼ ROUND POST

(2) 2"x4" AFTER ASSEM WITH TOP, MORTISE IN LEGS.

SECTION SHOWING JOINTS OF PLANKING

BENCH LEG 4 REQ'D.

BENCH TOP

BENCH SIDE

STOOL

MORTISE (4) LEGS INTO BOTT. PLANK

DRAWER 2 REQD

HALF-MOON HANDLES

BACK

HAND-HELD LOADING TOOLS

For shooters with limited ammunition requirements

By JOE D. HUDDLESTON

LIGHTWEIGHT, hand-held reloading tools have several desirable characteristics not possessed by the heavier bench tools. The hand-held tools are sufficiently compact to be used anywhere, including field use by the hunter or target shooter. They require minimum storage space and are moderately priced.

Assuming care in assembly, there is no difference in practical accuracy of ammunition loaded with hand-held and bench tools. Hand-held tools are slower and less convenient in use than bench tools, but this is not important when ammunition requirements are limited.

Hand-held tools are not usually designed to full-length resize cartridge cases; a requirement for proper functioning of ammunition in some firearms. However, portable full-length case resizing dies are offered for this purpose.

Charging can be done with a dip measure, or by weighing the charges with a small hand-loader's scale. Dip measures, when properly calibrated, are sufficiently accurate for measuring moderate charges of smokeless powders.

Assembly of ammunition with a representative hand-held tool, the Lee Loader, is shown in the accompanying illustrations.

3 With decapping completed, drive case into neck sizing die with mallet until head is flush with end of die.

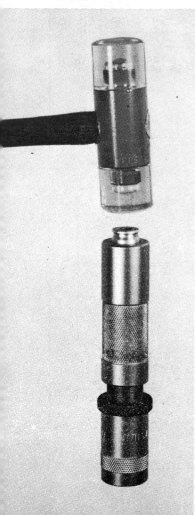

4 Priming is done after the case neck has been sized. With priming chamber on its base, place a primer, anvil up, in center of priming chamber (inset). Place sizing die with case into priming chamber, insert priming rod into case, and force case head down over primer with light blows from mallet. Primer can be felt bottoming in primer pocket of case head.

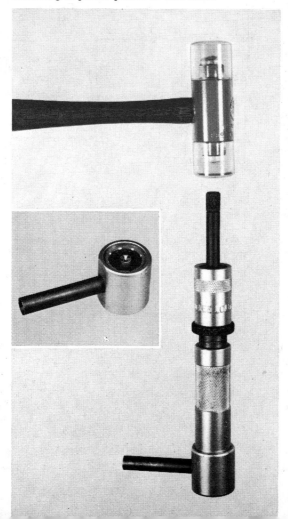

5 With priming completed, replace priming chamber with decapping chamber and knock case loose from die with light blow on head of priming rod. This step may not be necessary, as act of priming will usually loosen case so that it can be withdrawn from die with the fingers.

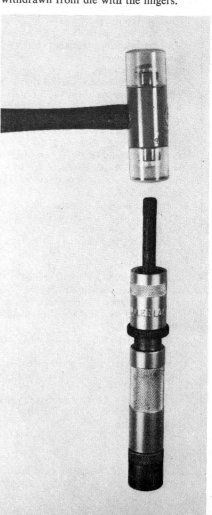

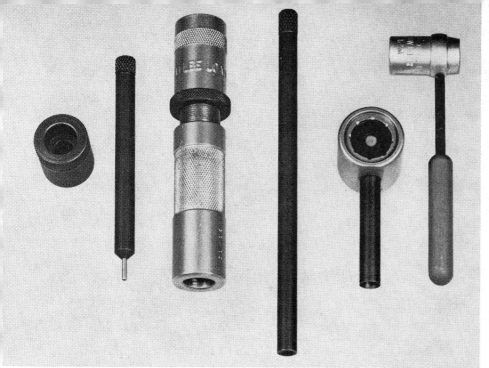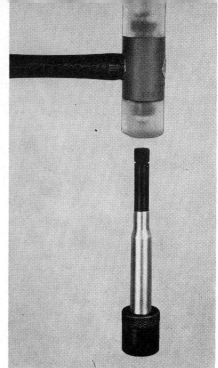

1 Designed for use with light mallet or block of wood, Lee Loader provides all implements needed to reload fired cartridge case. Cal. .30-'06 kit shown weighs 14½ ozs.

2 Decapping fired case is initial step in reloading sequence. Seat case in decapping chamber, and insert decapping punch in case mouth. Light mallet blow on head of punch expels fired primer.

6 With priming rod removed, pour level-full measure of recommended powder into case. (Charge table is furnished by the tool manufacturer.) Rap mouth of die assembly with powder measure to insure that all powder enters case and does not lodge in die opening.

7 Seat bullet in charged case using bullet seating punch in side of priming chamber. Drop bullet into die opening, insert punch, and drive home until it bottoms. Adjustments of stop collar (a) and lock nut (b) determine bullet seating depth. Depth adjustment is made by trial.

8 If required, crimping is done after seating bullet to full depth. Adjust die assembly by turning lock nut and stop collar down against die body. Place decapping chamber over end of case to shield primer and drive cartridge into die mouth until satisfactory crimp is obtained.

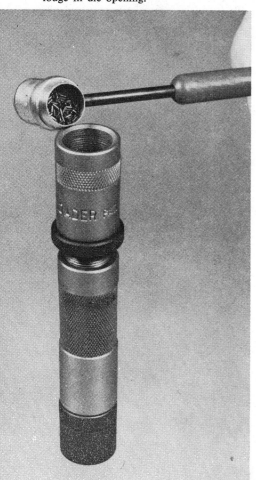
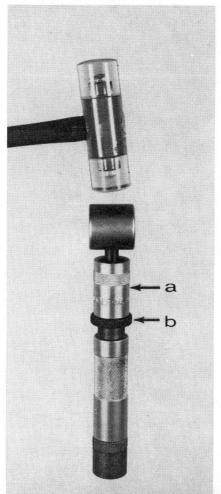
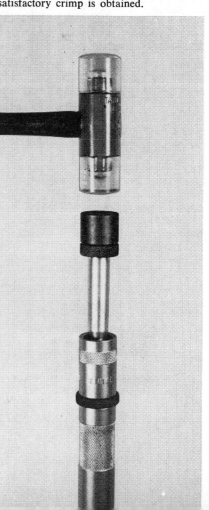

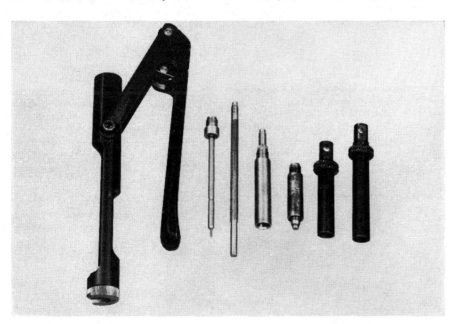

'Nutcracker' reloading tools have been in existence since the early 1870's. Lyman 310 tool shown weighs 1¼ lbs. in cal. .30-'06. It includes all implements necessary to assemble cartridge, but user must provide means of measuring powder. Accessory attachments are available in many calibers. Tool is designed for neck sizing cases only.

Hand-operated Pak-Tool weighs 1½ lbs. in cal. .30-'06. Accessory attachments for popular calibers are available. User must provide means of measuring powder and for resizing cases full-length.

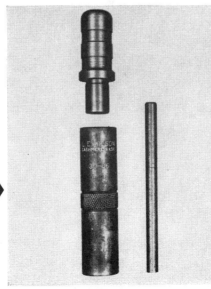

Auxiliary full-length case resizing dies are available for use with portable reloading tools. In Wilson non-adjustable die shown, fired case is pressed into die with drift. Sized case is then driven from die with punch. Die assembly weighs 11 ozs. in cal. .30-'06. Full-length resizing of cases may be necessary to prevent malfunctions in some guns. ■

High-Pressure .38 Loads

I read with interest the article (American Rifleman, Dec., 1978, p. 49) on the investigation of .38 Spl. revolvers blown up by supposedly light loads of Bullseye powder. Though it warns against pressures approaching 70,000 c.u.p. in good-quality, medium-frame revolvers, or 50,000 c.u.p. in light-frame guns, nothing is said about loads developing pressures lower than those, but above the 20,000 c.u.p. of .38 Spl. +P factory loads. Are loads in that category safe?

Answer: You should not load or fire .38 Spl. ammunition developing pressures that exceed those of the factory loads for which the guns are recommended. This point was spelled out in the original text of the article that you mention, but was omitted in the final printing, since the specific subject was the catastrophic failure of revolvers.

In the course of developing the improved military caliber .38 ammunition identified as the M41E2 and PGU-12/B (*American Rifleman*, Aug., 1976, pp. 62–63) for use in revolvers, considerable testing was done with ammunition that exceeded the 20,000-c.u.p. pressure limit of commercial +P loads. It was found that pressures only very moderately above that level, in the best medium-frame revolvers made for the .38 Spl., did seriously damage the guns, sometimes within as few as 100 to 200 rounds.

The manufacturers' warnings against the use of loads developing chamber pressures higher than those of factory ammunition for which the guns are recommended are soundly based, and should be scrupulously heeded. Inferences to the contrary are unwarranted.—W.C.D., Jr.

Kapok Fillers

I've read a lot about the use of fillers, such as kapok, in rifle reloads, but very little about fillers in pistol cartridges. It is my understanding that the less air space in a loaded round the better the accuracy. Is there any particular reason why fillers cannot be used in pistol loads as well as rifles?

Answer: Formerly, the use of fillers such as kapok was suggested for increasing uniformity of velocity in reduced rifle loads or improving cast bullet accuracy. It has never been recommended in near-maximum loads, because it increases chamber pressure. In recent years, however, a few rifles have been observed that developed ring-bulges in the chamber at the base of the bullet when reduced loads using fillers were employed. Therefore, we do not now recommend using any fillers in rifle or handgun loads. — W. C. D., Jr.

SPECIALIZED HAND-HELD RELOADING TOOLS

By WM. C. DAVIS, JR.

I N addition to the common and inexpensive hand-held tools, there is a specialized class of hand-held tools made primarily for benchrest shooters, and others seeking the highest degree of precision for competitive shooting. The only such tool currently made on a production basis is the Lee Target Model Loader illustrated here. The others are custom or semi-custom products, made by gunsmiths or craftsmen catering to the benchrest shooters' trade.

The Lee Target Model Loader includes a device for reaming the neck of the cartridge case, which assures a degree of concentricity and uniformity of wall thickness that cannot practically be attained in the drawing operations by which the cartridge cases are made. The same purpose is accomplished by hand-held neck-turning tools that operate on the principle of a lathe, cutting metal from the outside of the case neck while it is supported on a closely fitting mandrel.

The neck-resizing dies are often custom-made to conform to the dimensions of cases fired in one particular rifle, so that the minimum resizing and maximum concentricity are assured during the resizing operation. The custom tools are, of course, relatively expensive in comparison to mass-produced hand-held tools, but worth the price for their specialized applications. The shooter using any but a specialized benchrest or heavy match rifle is unlikely to find any noticeable advantage in the use of such tools, however.

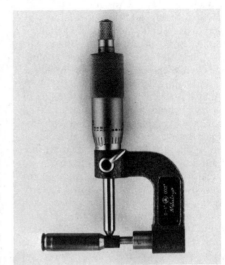

Neck thickness micrometer is specialized tool used by many benchrest shooters.

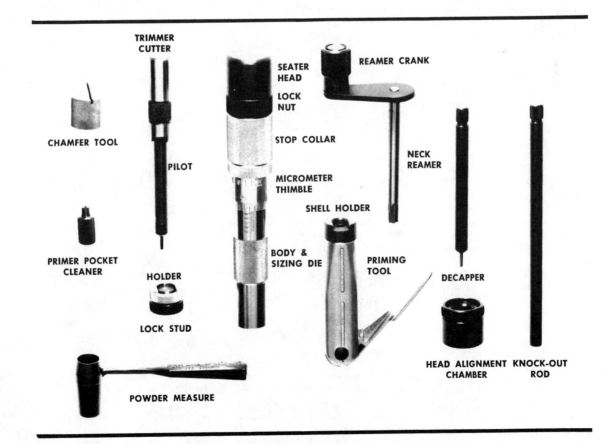

Components of the Lee Target Model Loader

(Labels: TRIMMER CUTTER, CHAMFER TOOL, PILOT, PRIMER POCKET CLEANER, HOLDER, LOCK STUD, POWDER MEASURE, SEATER HEAD, LOCK NUT, STOP COLLAR, MICROMETER THIMBLE, BODY & SIZING DIE, SHELL HOLDER, PRIMING TOOL, REAMER CRANK, NECK REAMER, DECAPPER, HEAD ALIGNMENT CHAMBER, KNOCK-OUT ROD)

Reloading ...Right Out Of

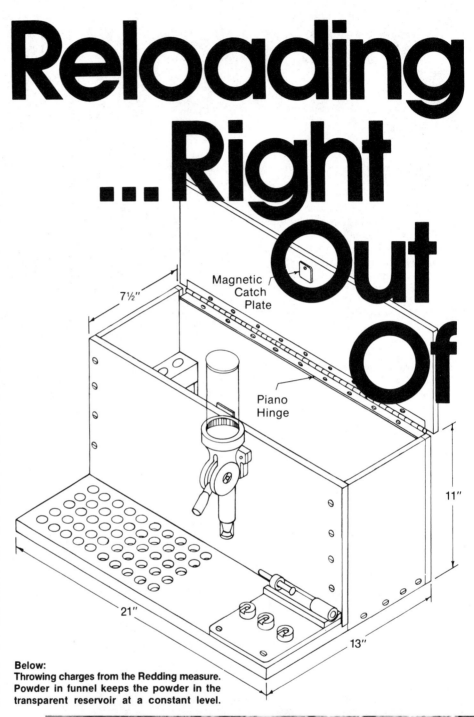

Magnetic Catch Plate

7½"

Piano Hinge

11"

21"

13"

HANDLOADERS often need something other than a fixed loading bench. Few apartment dwellers, for example, have the necessary space for one. Many shooters prefer to load their cartridges at the range.

The type of portable loading bench shown here suits both purposes. It is an excellent project for the home craftsman and a valuable addition to almost any handloader's equipment. It is basically a wooden box with an extended base. The box holds the loading tools and components while its extended base forms the actual loading bench.

Flat-bottomed holes in the left side of the bench hold 50 cartridge cases. Shell holders of three different sizes are attached to a 5/16"-thick steel plate at the right side of the bench. A powder measure is mounted on the front of the box.

The loading procedure depends on the tools used. A typical one begins with placing empty cases in the proper shell holder and tapping out the fired primers with a decapping rod. The spent primers drop through a hole in the bench. The cases are neck sized and primed in separate tools, and placed head-up in the holes in the bench. They are then charged from the powder measure and returned to the holes with their mouths up. Charging all the cases at once avoids the unwanted effects of jarring the measure by other operations.

Bullets are seated with straight-line dies such as the Wilson, or with ordinary seating dies threaded for a loading press. For threaded dies, a head which screws over the top of the seater stem is made. The charged case is placed in the shell holder and a bullet held over its mouth. The die is then dropped over both and the head pushed or tapped downward until the bottom of the die meets the top of the shell holder to seat the bullet. RCBS seating dies, or others which have a bullet-guiding diameter above the chamber portion, are best. When used as described, the case is well supported in the die as the bullet is seated and the results are practically the same as when a straight line seater is used.

Fastened to the steel plate behind the shell holders is a case trimmer. The cutter and shell holders as well as the neck reamers and deburring tool used with it are kept in specially made holes in the blocks built inside each end of the box. This protects the cutting edges. The blocks strengthen the box while keeping these and other often-used tools easily accessible.

The box cover swings on a piano-type hinge and is held closed by a magnetic catch at its front center. Lifting the cover by the ⅛" it overhangs the front of the box exposes about 1200 cu. ins. of storage space. It holds cleaning materials and

Below:
Throwing charges from the Redding measure. Powder in funnel keeps the powder in the transparent reservoir at a constant level.

Opening the cover exposes the loading tools and components carried inside the box. You can begin loading immediately. No loading press, which must be fastened down, is required. Other small tools and cleaning materials may also be kept in the box.

The Box

To fill his need for a compact reloading setup, the author built this self-contained unit. He's never been sorry.

BY ROBERT N. SEARS

Trimming cases with the Wilson tool. The cutter, case holders, neck reamers and burring tool are stored inside the box.

Special head at top of the die allows bullets to be seated by hand. The head also acts as a lock nut for the seater.

basic hand tools as well as cartridge cases, primers, powder and bullets. The powder measure is attached by two screws through the front of the box. It is taken off and placed inside when the portable loading bench is carried in an automobile.

The box walls and cover are 7/16" thick. The joints are glued and fastened with flat-head wood screws. The bottom which extends forward to form the loading bench is 1⅛" thick. It is grooved ¼" deep to hold the front of the box, and cut 7/16" deep for the sides. Rubber feet are screwed to the underside of the bench — one at each front corner and one at the center rear. This three-point support makes the bench stable even when it is placed on an uneven surface. It also prevents marring of any finely finished surface on which the bench might be placed.

Plans for this portable bench began nearly 30 years ago. Bench-rest competitors at that time would show up at matches with an amazing variety of loading equipment. Many brought presses which they bolted to the covered loading benches built at the range. Others loaded at the benches using hand tools brought in cigar boxes and components carried in paper bags. The variations were almost as numerous as the shooters. I well remember the late John Unertl loading on a bracket which he clamped to the bumper of his automobile.

From all this, I determined that I would build an easily portable loading bench which did not require fastening and would carry all the tools and components necessary for loading at the range. The material requirements were largely met when a friend gave me some of the sound lumber from a decaying maple tree which we cut from his lawn. The result is shown here. After more than a quarter century of use, I have found no reason to want to change either its form or dimensions.

Construction of the portable loading bench involved considerable time but little expense. The most costly single item was the length of continuous piano-type hinge. This kind of hinge is very strong and durable. It is also easily installed. A finish which enhances the grain of the wood improves the bench's appearance. Some of the newer polyurethanes do this and also seal the wood from the effects of oil and solvents. As a finishing touch, I added a nameplate to the box cover.

Operations such as case forming and full-length sizing require a fixed bench and press, but all ordinary reloading procedures may be accomplished easily and well with the kind of portable bench described here. It stores all tools and components in the same container in which they are carried. One of the most favorable results is that critical items are not likely to be left at home. ∎

BASIC HANDLOADING OPERATIONS

NRA Technical Staff

1 Inspect each cartridge case. Throw away any with cracked necks, any showing the least sign of separation ¼″ above the base, and any which are badly dented. Wipe carefully, since grit left on will scratch case and sizing die

2 Cases must be lubricated before being pressed into the sizing die. Loading tool makers supply grease or liquid lubricant, and also automobile chassis grease works well. Case necks require little lubrication, but case bodies must be well lubricated. Too much grease may leave 'oil dents' in case shoulders, which while somewhat unsightly are of little practical importance. Too little grease, however, may stick the case immovably in the die, which when the case rim has been pulled off by the loading tool, presents the handloader with a serious problem. A small amount of powdered graphite, molybdenum disulfide, or mica (at top of cut) supplies lubrication to inside of neck for pulling expanding plug through (see caption 3), since oil or grease should not be used inside the case. Dip case mouth into the dry lubricant, or preferably apply it to inside of case neck with brush

HANDLOADING is widely practiced by rifle shooters. The greatest motive is money-saving, not so much to make shooting cost less, as to get more shooting within financial means. The saving made is from half to three-fourths on the cost of ready-made ammunition. Of course the loading tools must be paid for before this saving begins.

Handloaders also discover much interest in the loading operation, and pleasure in using ammunition which they have prepared with their own hands. Special ammunition types, obtainable ready-made with difficulty or not at all—target ammunition for either medium or long range, varmint ammunition with light high-speed bullets, and reduced loads for small game or target shooting—are readily made up by the handloader. He can thus enjoy the use of his rifle the year round.

Considering the number of handloaders and the great quantity of ammunition loaded and fired, the safety record of handloading has been excellent. Ample loading information is available, and loading components for any requirement. THE AMERICAN RIFLEMAN publishes special loading articles for the more important rifle calibers, giving loads on which velocity and pressure have been measured. Information is also given by the suppliers of many components. It is foolish to disregard or exceed the loads given in instructions.

Loading tools have been developed to a remarkable degree. The basic tool is a bench press of considerable power, which by means of interchangeable dies performs all the reloading operations (except weighing and measuring powder charges) with maximum speed and minimum exertion by the user. However, there are also simple and inexpensive tools for the shooter who desires to load in limited quantities and keep his investment down.

Handloading begins with the empty brass case remaining from firing the factory cartridge (or purchased new if desired). It accounts for a large part of the original cost of the cartridge, and can be re-used many times. It was expanded slightly into the chamber of the rifle when it was fired, so the first step is to press it into a steel die which returns it to its original dimensions. Then the fired cap (primer) is knocked out and a new one pressed into place. The correct charge of the rifle powder being used is weighed or measured out and poured into the case. A bullet is pressed into the case mouth, which with final inspection completes the new cartridge.

These basic steps and some of the more important refinements on them are illustrated. The cartridge shown is the .30-'06, loaded by more American riflemen than any other, but the operations are applicable in general to any caliber.

◄3 The case (see arrow) is sized by the tool ram pushing it up into the die. Screw die down until lower face is just touched by ram at top of stroke, then secure die with lock ring. At this setting the case is fully resized. Some handloaders prefer to adjust the die to size the case a little less, finding that sufficient for their rifles; this should not be carried so far as to leave cartridge hard to chamber in rifle. At top of stroke, pin at bottom of die knocks out fired primer. Projection of this pin should be just enough to push primer clear of case, and is adjusted by screw and lock ring at top of die. As case is withdrawn it is pulled over a plug on the decapping pin stem, which slightly expands case neck to correct size to hold bullet tightly. If case develops unusual resistance in entering die, *stop instantly*. Cause probably is insufficient case body lubrication, and to continue may stick case in die

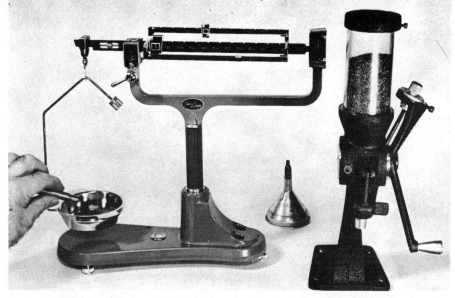

5 Most loading is done with an adjustable powder measure (on right) since weighing every charge is tedious. The measure graduations are useful in returning to a previous setting and in making small adjustments. Because of possibility of misreading or other error, the measure setting always should be checked by weighing sample charges thrown, as done here. Make sure you are using the powder specified

6 Settle powder in measure reservoir by throwing at least 10 preliminary charges of fine-grained powders or 20 of coarse-grained powders, otherwise first charges loaded may be light. Work the measure handle with unvarying speed and force, and use knocker uniformly if measure has one. Do not allow powder level in reservoir to become low

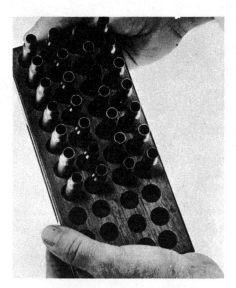

7 Systematic care must be taken to insure against excessive charges in some rounds and light or no charges in others. This requires alertness and the adoption of a standardized routine in loading. Inspection of the charged cases before seating bullets is indispensable. One of the best ways is to look into the cases while they are held in a charging block (see cut). With a good light from above, the powder level is plainly seen and any charges materially higher or lower than the others will be evident

4 While ram is still at top of stroke to size case, place new primer in cup of capping arm (see arrow) and swing arm into slot in ram. First motion of lowering arm seats primer. Raise ram slightly to release arm, then lower fully to withdraw case from die. Cup in capping arm is made with round or flat bottom to suit primers of those shapes, but round-bottomed cup may also seat flat-bottomed primers unmarked. Be sure primers are seated to bottom of primer pockets. Occasionally scrape hard deposit from primer pockets with small screwdriver

8 Last operation of loading is seating bullets. Screw seating die in top of tool, and adjust until at top of tool stroke the case just enters die without binding. Back out seating screw in top of die, and adjust by trial until full tool stroke seats bullet to correct depth. This is found by bullet cannelure, which should be flush with case mouth, or by comparison with over-all length of factory cartridge

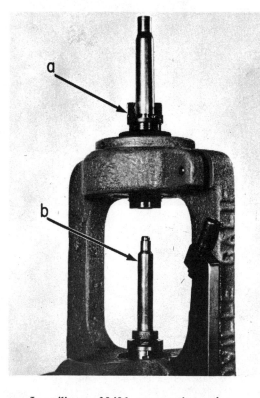

9 In military .30-'06 cases, edges of primer pockets are rolled inward to hold the primers positively in place. Special decappers are available for such cases, but most modern loading tools will knock out the fired primers. The rolled edge then must be removed before new primers can be put in. In a typical device, the fired case is fixed in a holder (a) at top of the loading tool. A hard steel plug (b) is raised by the tool ram until its rounded tip enters the pocket, pushing back the overhanging edge. The job can also be done with a small hand-operated reamer made for the purpose. By either method, this special operation need be done only once

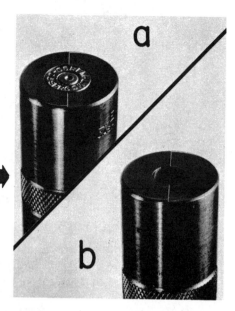

10 Another special operation is case-trimming. Under repeated reloading fired cases lengthen at the mouth, eventually becoming too long for the chamber, which can cause inaccurate shooting and excessive pressures. This is corrected with a shell trimmer, in which typically the case **(a)** is held by its base while its mouth is trimmed with a hand-turned cutter. The cutter depth stop can be set to a once-fired case. After trimming, lightly de-burr inside and outside of case mouth with the small hand tool **(b)**

11 Some handloaders like to gauge their cartridge cases as a check on sizing die setting, and to determine when cases need trimming. The illustrations show base and mouth ends of a combination gauge. When headspace (base-to-shoulder length) of the case is within allowable limits, its base will be between the maximum and minimum base steps of the gauge **(a)**. When over-all length of the case is correct, its mouth will be between maximum and minimum mouth steps of **(b)**

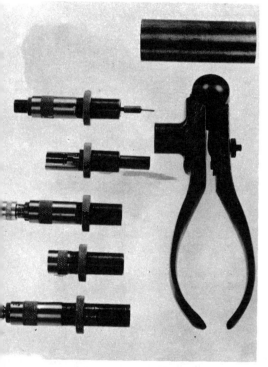

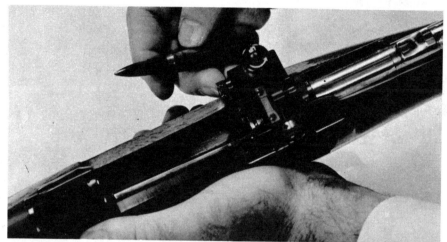

13 The work should be inspected at each step. For important match shooting or hunting, final inspection should include trial in rifle chamber to be sure action will close freely on cartridge. *Caution—remove striker mechanism from rifle bolt before this test.* If cases have not been completely resized, they may not be interchangeable between rifles even of same caliber, since rifle chambers differ slightly

14 Record details of the finished load. It is impossible to remember all these reliably, and then the ammunition is useless or worse. A clear record also shows on review which features of handloads tried have proved desirable and which not, and that information soon becomes highly interesting. Place clear identification on or in each box of handloaded ammunition——■

12 There are excellent loading tools available for the handloader who requires inexpensive equipment. These smaller, simpler tools produce at a lower rate which is ample for many requirements. Above is current model of the Ideal reloading tool which has been used successfully for decades. The inserts at left, which are screwed into the handles interchangeably, are (top to bottom) decapper, recapper, neck expander, neck sizer, and bullet seater. At top is an inexpensive full-length case-sizing die, which should also be bought since full-length sizing is required at least occasionally. Low-cost powder scales, powder measures, and case trimmers are available also

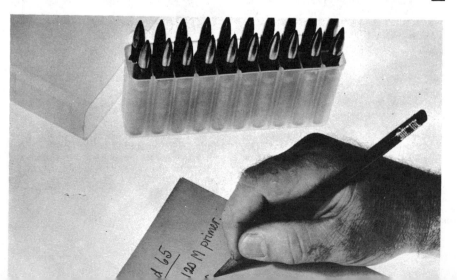

1 Reloader accustomed to using one scale should be alert to the fact that beam markings may differ according to make. Beam of upper scale is graduated in 5-gr. increments, of lower scale in 10-gr. increments. This may be overlooked when reloader owns more than one scale, or has occasion to use scale not his own

2 Inspect powder scale regularly to note condition of beam knife-edges and possible presence of oil or dirt in bearings. Scales must be kept clean and knife-edges sharp and free from burrs. A good mechanic can deburr knife-edges by stoning, but manufacturer is recommended for such repairs

SAFETY IN RELOADING

NRA Technical Staff

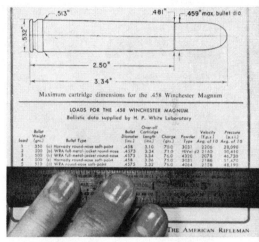

3 Use of straight-edge when extracting charge data from loading table will prevent misreading due to line jumping

THE reloading of small-arms ammunition is a safe and enjoyable hobby when practiced by those who are attentive to fundamentals and who exercise good judgment and due care.

The majority of accidents involving preparation and use of reloaded ammunition result from hazardous practices on the part of the reloader. The following are typical:

1) Smoking while reloading, or employment of any open flame too near to gunpowder or primers.

2) Use of intoxicants while loading.

3) Use of smokeless powder in firearms designed for blackpowder only.

4) Use of untested charge data.

5) Use of unidentified powders, the characteristics of which are unknown.

6) The attempt to develop full charges by 'cut-and-try' methods without measuring pressures.

7) Use of excessively charged ammunition in arms not designed for such ammunition.

8) The inerting of safety devices provided to prevent double charging on progressive-type reloading tools.

9) Reloading cartridge cases weakened by corrosion, or having obvious faults such as body splits, perforations, or incipient cracks in head area.

10) Continuing to shoot ammunition when signs of excessive pressure are evident from observation of the fired

case and primer, escape of gas from the gun breech, or abnormal functioning of the gun.

Mechanical errors

Some reloading errors may be classed as mechanical although often abetted by carelessness and faulty technique. Among these are:

1) Misreading of charge data.

2) Use of incorrect charge data due to confusion in cartridge identity.

3) Use of wrong weight or caliber of bullet.

4) Use of wrong powder.

5) Incorrect setting of scale weights.

6) Failure to balance scale.

7) Use of scale that is rendered insensitive or inaccurate by dirt or oil in fulcrum area, or burrs on beam knife-edges.

8) Failure to clear powder funnel when transferring it to next case in the loading block.

9) Failure to inspect level of powder in cases after charging.

10) Inadvertent mixing of powders by pouring unused powder into canister containing powder of different type.

The probability of mechanical error can be virtually eliminated if the reloader institutes a rigid system of checks and inspections covering every phase of the reloading operation and maintains an alert attitude at all times.

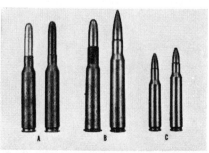

4 Confusion in cartridge identity is possible when nomenclature is similar. Relative powder capacities may differ greatly so that charge safe in one cartridge will give excessive pressure in another. Also, cartridges with similar nomenclature and powder capacity may have markedly different established maximum pressure levels based on relative strength of guns for which they were designed. Cartridge pairs illustrated are typical, and in each instance cartridge on right has greater powder capacity and/or is loaded to higher maximum pressure level. A) 6.5 mm. Mannlicher-Carcano (l.) and 6.5 mm. Mannlicher Schoenauer; B) .30 U.S. Army (.30-40 Krag) (l.) and .30 U. S. Government (.30-'06); C) .222 Remington (l.) and .222 Remington Magnum

5 An uncluttered reloading bench is a must. In this typical setup the reloader has before him only those components and equipment necessary. Note that only one canister of powder and box of bullets is in view. Other components are stored well away from bench so that mixup is virtually impossible. He has noted the desired charge on a scratch sheet and has verified correctness of powder number and bullet. Scale has been balanced and then set for desired charge weight. Unused powder will be returned to canister upon completion of charging

6 When charging cases with opaque metal or plastic funnel, check each time to insure that it is clear of powder before transferring it to next case

7 Final visual check of powder level in every case is mandatory before seating bullets. Good light source is required to illuminate case interiors. Some reloaders use a small flashlight ∎

Collapsed Case Shoulder

My .30-'06 rifle has been fired many thousands of rounds and has a severely eroded throat. The enclosed photograph is a case which I fired recently with 50.0 grs. of H-335 and a 150-gr. jacketed bullet. It has a dent in the shoulder and resulted in noticeable gas leakage. What is the cause of this?

Answer: A collapsed case shoulder is not common in the .30-'06, but happens occasionally in large capacity magnum cartridges, and sometimes in reduced loads. It is usually found in combination with one or more of the following conditions:

- A long throat, so that the bullet base can move forward to clear the case mouth before the bullet engages the origin of the rifling. This can be caused by "free boring," "long throating," or erosion from much firing.
- A case neck expanded to nearly the diameter of the bullet, so the grip of the case neck on the bullet is not very secure.
- A condition of rather slow ignition of the powder by the primer, due either to a powder that is inherently hard to ignite, or a low density of loading, which leaves much airspace in the case.

The probable cause of this denting is that the bullet is driven out of the case by the force of the primer explosion, at a pressure too low to cause radial expansion of the case neck and thus seal the chamber. Indented cases may show little or no expansion of the neck, and a bullet may not enter freely into the neck of the fired case, as it should in a case that is normally expanded. Powder ignition is slightly delayed, and gas flows into the space between the case neck and the chamber wall. As pressure rises, pressure of the gas between the case wall and shoulder momentarily exceeds the internal pressure in the case and the shoulder collapses. It is possible that a pressure wave is reflected from the base of the bullet during the delayed ignition of the charge, contributing to the high pressure between the case and chamber wall.

The phenomenon has not been systematically investigated, so far as I know, but the above explanation is consistent with the available evidence, although it must still be considered unproven.

Dent caused by neck failing to expand radially to seal chamber permitting gas to flow between case wall and chamber.

You can probably avoid the condition in full-power loads by using a more easily ignited powder such as W-W 760, IMR-4895 or IMR-4064 for your .30-'06, which will leave less airspace in the case. When indented shoulders occur with reduced loads, a solution is to use a more easily ignited powder such as Du Pont SR-4759 or Hercules Reloader 7.—W.C.D.,Jr.

Gas Check Seater

Only the Saeco lubricator-sizer seats gas checks as a separate operation before sizing and lubricating bullets. Can you suggest some simple way this can be done using the more common lubricator-sizer tools?

Answer: One way is to make the kind of small fixture illustrated here.

Easily made fixture (arrow—section view below) allows separate seating of gas checks with an ordinary lubricator-sizer.

It fits inside the sizing die nut of ordinary tools such as the Lyman and RCBS. Gas checks are set into the recess at the top of the fixture and are seated squarely onto the bullet bases by downward pressure of the top punch on the bullet noses. The fixture is then removed and the bullets sized and lubricated in the usual manner.

When gas checks are seated as part of the lubricating-sizing operation, inward pressure of the sizing die can crimp the gas check onto the bullet shank before the gas check is seated firmly and squarely against the bullet base. This is particularly true if the shank is tapered, and most are. Eliminating resulting irregularities is the principal advantage of seating gas checks as a separate operation.

The gas check seating fixture is easily turned on a lathe from 1" dia. bar stock. The recess at the top is made about .035" deep and about .005" larger in diameter than the gas check. The bottom is turned down to about ⅝" diameter to fit inside the nut which holds the sizing die. No change in the normal tool setup is required to use this fixture.—R.N.S.

THE USE AND HANDLING OF PRIMERS

By WM. C. DAVIS, JR.

Practically all reloading tools incorporate some more or less satisfactory means of priming the cartridge case. The strong bench-mounted reloading presses, unfortunately, are by design rather ill-adapted to primer seating, and the means provided are neither very convenient nor very satisfactory with most models. Some have an automatic primer feed available as an accessory, which somewhat increases the speed of operation, but many handloaders find they are susceptible to malfunctions and they do not overcome the inherent disadvantages of using the powerful bench-mounted press as a tool for seating primers.

The seating of primers requires very little force, in comparison to the force required to resize cartridge cases, and the powerful leverage of the bench-mounted press is a disadvantage for seating primers. It is most desirable that the operator be able to "feel" the difference between a primer being normally seated, and one that requires too little or too much force. Too little force during primer seating may be an indication of an expanded primer pocket in the case, and the operator should be aware of it. Too much force, or force beginning too early in the stroke of the tool, may be an indication that the primer is misaligned or cocked in the pocket, and should not be seated. Both of these conditions may escape attention, because of the powerful leverage of the bench-mounted press. Furthermore, many authorities believe that the most uniform results are achieved when primers are seated under a constant force, sufficient to bottom the primer in the pocket and produce a slight compression of the explosive pellet between the anvil and the cup, rather than to a predetermined depth below the face of the case head. A "feel" for this proper seating force is developed, with practice, if the leverage of the tool is not too great, but it is not possible with the heavy handle and powerful leverage of the bench-mounted reloading press.

For these reasons, experienced handloaders in recent years have turned more to the use of priming tools designed specially for that purpose. Manufacturers have provided a variety of good tools, ranging from simple and inexpensive ones, such as the Lee hand-held manual-feed model, to various bench-mounted models, with and without automatic primer feed, such as the RCBS. Such tools are reasonably priced, and practically all of them perform better than the priming arrangement typically provided on bench-mounted reloading presses.

Some words of caution are in order regarding the safe handling and use of primers. The primer is the only handloading component that contains high-explosive material, and the only one which will truly explode outside the gun. The quantity of explosive composition is small — typically about 0.3 to 0.4 grain for small primers and 0.4 to 0.6 grain for large primers — but nevertheless capable of inflicting serious injury if

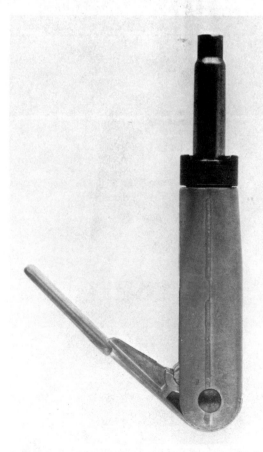 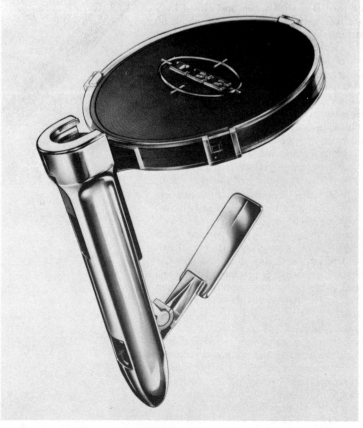

Lee Priming Tool (left) and Lee Auto-Prime, allow handloader to seat primers with just the right amount of force necessary. Handloaders develop a "feel" for seating primers with experience. These simple, inexpensive tools are often easier to use than priming arms on bench-mounted presses.

improperly handled. There are authenticated instances of loss of eyesight, caused by penetration of the eye by the cup of a primer accidentally exploded, so it is always prudent to wear impact-resistant glasses when handling primers. Painful injuries have been inflicted when the cup of an exploding primer imbedded itself in a hand or a finger.

Primers are somewhat unpredictable in their behavior if roughly handled, so it is not safe to assume that a questionable procedure is safe merely because it failed to explode one or two, or even a hundred primers, because the next one might explode under the same mishandling. One should never tamper with a live primer by trying to remove the anvil, or otherwise take it apart. Primers should be kept in their original packages, which are carefully designed for safe storage and handling, until they are used. Primers dumped into a glass jar or other such receptacle are especially dangerous, both because they are likely to explode from rough handling, and because more than one might explode sympathetically.

Live primers dropped on the floor should be promptly retrieved and disposed of, because they might explode when stepped on, and thereby cause injury. If the need arises to dispose of live primers that are damaged or otherwise cannot be used, the safest practice is probably to place them in a small bottle or jar filled with water and closed by a sealing cap, with not more than 50 primers in any container, and dispose of the waterfilled container along with other solid waste going to a land-fill, large incinerator or other such place.

When using a priming tool, one should see that it is always pointed in a direction that will carry the force of the explosion safely away from the operator and other persons, in event of the accidental explosion of the primer being seated, or other primers in the tray or tube if an automatic feed is being used.

It is also important that primer-seating tools be kept scrupulously clean, to prevent the accumulation of "dust" from the primer composition. This "dust" is exceedingly sensitive to shock or friction, and can cause the smypathetic detonation of primers in a primer-feed tube. Feed tubes should be washed frequently in water with soap or detergent.

In summary, primers are the most hazardous components used by the handloader, with the possible exception of blackpowder. They are quite safe to transport and store in the original packaging, and safe also if they are properly handled and used, but not at all tolerant of careless use and handling. Though small, they are surprisingly powerful, and quite capable of causing serious injury.

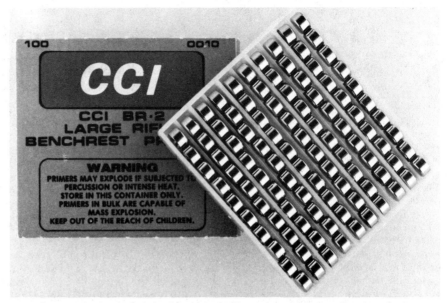

Store primers in original package. Never keep primers in glass jars.

Lachmiller Priming Tool

USING STANDARD RELOADING DIES

NRA Technical Staff

Most modern bench-mounted reloading tools are adapted for use with standard ⅞"x14-thread metallic cartridge reloading dies. These are commonly called Pacific-type, as they were introduced in 1930 by the Pacific Gun Sight Co. in conjunction with their first C-frame straight-line reloading tool. The Pacific reloading tool and die combination was an immediate success, as all reloading operations, including full-length resizing and priming, could be accomplished with speed, and only 2 dies were required. In comparison with other reloading equipment available at the time, the Pacific tool and its dies were revolutionary, and therefore did much to popularize the reloading hobby. Pacific dies were furnished in sets of 2, composed of a full-length case resizing die with centrally threaded spindle carrying a neck-expanding plug and decapping pin, and a bullet-seating die with internal crimping shoulder if required.

Many firms now make ⅞"x14-thread reloading dies that differ only slightly in minor details according to make. These do not affect adjustment procedures described in the accompanying illustrations.

Dies for loading pistol cartridges are usually furnished in sets of 2, but 3- and 4-die sets to separate operations normally carried out in single dies of the usual 2-die set are available for those who wish to take extra pains in loading their ammunition.

Headspace

It will be noted from Fig. 3 that normal practice when full-length resizing cartridge cases is to adjust the die until its base contacts the shell holder at top of the ram stroke. At this setting, the case is resized throughout its full length. If of rimless type, its end play in the gun chamber should be within the limits or tolerance specified for it. However, if the body cavity of the die is too short or the shell holder rim too shallow, the case body will be shortened and create excessive headspace. On firing, such cartridge cases tend to pull apart forward of the head. Conversely, if the body cavity of the die is too long or the shell holder rim too high, the opposite condition may be created, and difficulty encountered in fully closing the action on the loaded cartridge.

Normal practice is to full-length resize all cases, whether for rifle or handgun. Some reloaders prefer to neck resize their cases only, as they believe full-length resizing reduces case life and decreases accuracy of their ammunition. Most die manufacturers can furnish special resizing dies in this form which resize only the case neck.

The main requirements are that the reloaded cartridge fit the gun chamber, and that its neck grip the bullet securely in handling and gun functioning.

Crimping

With certain rifle cartridges and virtually all revolver cartridges, it is necessary to fold or crimp the case neck into the side of the bullet. This is true of cartridges to be functioned through tubular magazines, or carried in box magazines of rifles developing heavy recoil. Crimping prevents telescoping of bullet into case from impact with base of another cartridge or front face of the magazine box. Full-charge revolver ammunition must be crimped to prevent inertial dislodgment of the bullets.

Ammunition for semi-automatic pistols is rarely crimped as the bullets are not subject to inertial dislodgement as in the revolver. Most pistol cartridges are of rimless or semi-rimless construction with little or no body taper, and

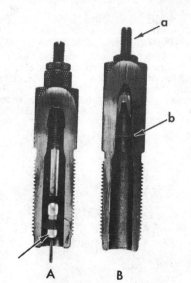

1 Sectioned 2-die rifle unit less exterior lock rings. Die A punches out fired primer, resizes case full length, and expands case neck. Bottom of expanding plug (arrow) should be positioned not less than 3/16" from bottom of die, or plug may strike interior of case and break or bend spindle. Die B contains adjustable bullet seating punch (a) and in some calibers has integral crimping shoulder (b)

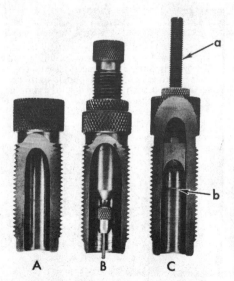

2 Sectioned 3-die pistol unit less exterior lock rings. Die A resizes case full length. Die B punches out fired primer and expands and flares case neck. Die C contains adjustable bullet-seating punch (a) and in most calibers has integral crimping shoulder (b). Nose cavity of bullet-seating punch should conform to nose profile of bullet. Otherwise, bullets may be deformed in seating

3 To full-length resize all types of cartridge cases, screw case-resizing die into tool frame until shell holder clicks against bottom of die at top of ram stroke, then tighten lock ring to secure die. With light C-frame tools, shell holder should bear hard against die to compensate for possible spring in tool frame and insure uniform head spacing

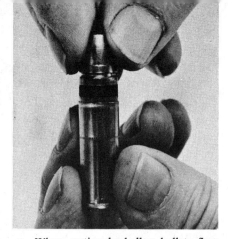

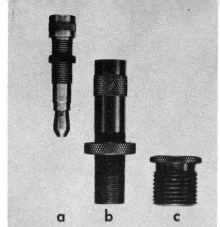

4 To adjust bullet-seating die when no crimp is desired, screw die into tool frame until shell holder contacts bottom of die at top of ram stroke. Then unscrew die ¾ of a turn as shown and tighten lock ring to secure die. Bullet-seating punch is then adjusted with fingers or screwdriver until bullet is seated to desired depth. Seating punch lock ring is then tightened. Adjust die as in Fig. 7 if case neck is to be crimped into cannelure on bullet. Do not attempt to crimp jacketed bullets lacking crimping cannelure

5 When seating lead-alloy bullets flare case mouth slightly to accept bullet base. This prevents crushing of case necks and shaving of bullet. Expanding plugs of most pistol dies have integral shoulders for this purpose. Only slight flare is required as excessive flare may split case neck, or prevent its entry into mouth of bullet-seating die. Neck flaring is usually not necessary with metal-jacketed bullets, but if interference is noted, slight inside chamfering of case neck with reamer will ease bullet entry

6 Lyman-Ideal 310 tool expanding plug (a), shell-expanding chamber (b), and ⅞"x14-thread adapter collar (c). This unit will flare case neck of rifle cartridge so that lead-alloy bullet will enter case mouth without damage to bullet or case. Flare is removed during final bullet-seating operation

7a With sized and flared, empty, unprimed case in shell holder, elevate ram to highest position and screw in die until its internal crimping shoulder bears firmly against case neck. Tighten lock ring to secure die

7b With bullet in case neck elevate ram fully and screw in bullet-seating punch until it contacts bullet. Then, by repeating trial, adjust punch until bullet is seated with lower edge of crimping groove, crimping shoulder, or cannelure opposite case neck. Tighten lock ring

7c Loosen die lock-ring and screw in die until desired crimp is obtained. Tighten die lock-ring and, if necessary, make final height adjustment of bullet-seating punch. Dummy cartridge should be kept with dies for use as gauge in subsequent resetting of die for same bullet

8 Standard 2-die rifle unit (l.) and pistol unit (r.). Major difference between pistol and rifle dies is that expanding plug of pistol die has integral neck-flaring shoulder not present on rifle die expanding plug

9 Three-die pistol unit consists of: (A) full-length resizing die; (B) decapping, neck-expanding, neck-flaring die; (C) bullet-seating and crimping die

10 Three-die pistol unit for 9 mm. Luger and similar straight or slightly tapered self-loading pistol cartridges consists of: (A) full-length resizing and decapping die; (B) neck-expanding and neck-flaring die (expanding plug assembly removed from sleeve unit shows construction): (C) bullet-seating die. Die C does not have integral crimping shoulder, but is constructed to remove case neck flare put in by die B

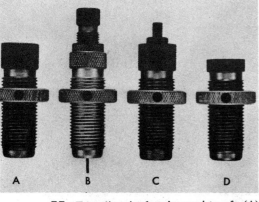

11 Four-die pistol unit consists of: (A) full-length resizing die; (B) neck-expanding, neck-flaring, decapping die; (C) bullet-seating die; (D) bullet-crimping die. Bullet seating and crimping are done in separate dies in this unit to eliminate possibility of bullet deformation sometimes experienced with single crimp-seat die

forward movement of the cartridge in the gun chamber is stopped by the case neck striking a shoulder in the front of the chamber. If the case neck is crimped, the cartridge may be driven too far forward in the chamber, resulting in ignition failures.

Trimming of cartridge cases to a standard length is necessary for uniform crimp from cartridge to cartridge.

Attempts to form a heavy roll crimp on revolver cartridges may result in outward bulging of the case neck and loss of neck tension between case wall and side of bullet. This becomes evident when the bullet can be readily

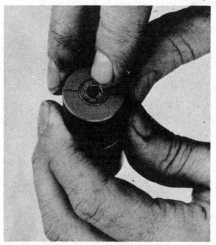

12 If head of full-length resized rimless case lies below lower step of cartridge case gauge, body cavity of die is too short or shell-holder rim too low. Both die and shell holder should be returned to manufacturer, or die can be unscrewed in tool frame to resize case within limits of case gauge. If head of full-length resized case extends above upper or maximum step of case gauge, body cavity of die may be too long or shell-holder rim too high. Removal of metal from bottom of die or reduction in height of shell-holder rim is required. However, before altering either die or shell holder, check unsized fired case from same rifle in case gauge to note if its head extends above upper step of case gauge. If it does not, resized cases are probably being stretched through failure to lubricate expanding plug, and die and/or shell holder are not at fault

turned with the fingers despite the roll crimp. Very slight backing off of the die will usually correct this condition.

A common oversight is failure to properly lubricate the expanding plug when resizing bottlenecked rifle and pistol cartridges. The result is that the cartridge case is actually elongated so that more than normal force is required to close the action on the loaded cartridge. Also, increased friction from the dry expanding plug shortens case life and accelerates wear of the plug. Case neck interiors are easily lubricated by dipping them in powdered graphite or mica and then knocking off the excess, or by lubricant applied with the fingers or small bristle brush. It is sufficient to lubricate every third or fourth case in this manner. Expanding plug friction is readily apparent from the screeching heard when the plug is pulled through the case neck.

A common failing of some rifle dies, and not restricted to those of moderate price, is that they size case necks excessively. This results in reduction of case life through excessive cold working of the brass, which induces neck splits. Such dies should be returned to the maker for replacement.

Rifles chambered for rimless or belted cartridges occasionally have excessive headspace due to manufacturing error, wear, or mis-matched bolts or breechblocks. This condition is usually revealed by gauge check of the rifle, or of the fired cases in a full-length case gauge. Fired cases from such rifles should not be full-length resized as this may result in incipient, partial, or complete separation on subsequent firing. Corrective action consists of backing out the case-sizing die in the tool frame so that the case shoulder is not re-formed by the die. This procedure is always justified when fired rimless or belted cases show evidence of strain or separation in the head area. Sizing die should be adjusted so that bolt or breechblock closes with slight resistance on the resized case. ∎

13 If over-all length of bottlenecked cartridge case is greater after full-length sizing than before, cases are being stretched by excess friction between expanding plug and interior of case neck. Lubrication of expanding plug is indicated. Cases are conveniently checked in commercially-available snap gauges, with a caliper, or in full-length case gauge

14 When headspace of rifle and of full-length resized cartridge cases is within tolerance, but cases will not readily enter rifle chamber, die is not reducing case body sufficiently. Micrometer check of chamber cast and resized case will indicate if necessary diameter clearance exists. If die is at fault, most die makers, given several fired cases from rifle, can make special die to reduce case body to chamber properly

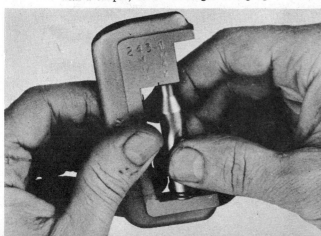

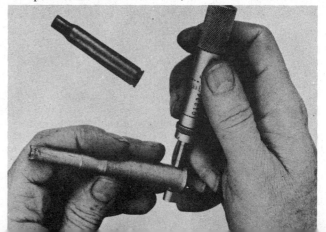

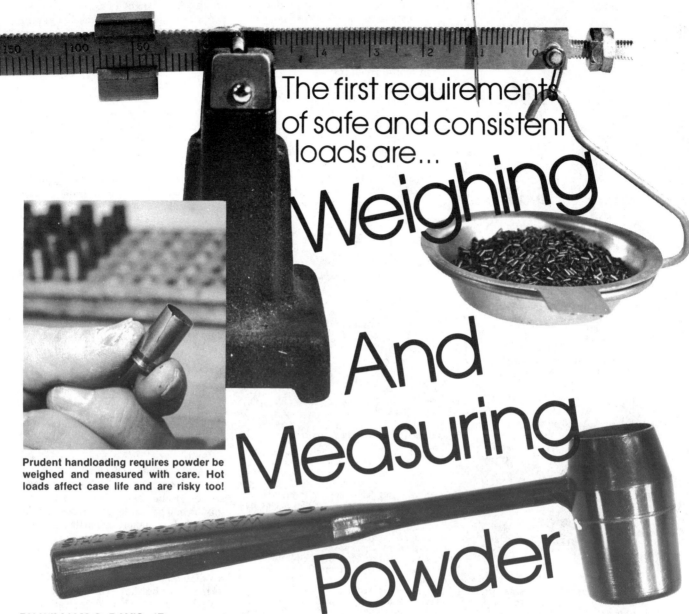

The first requirements of safe and consistent loads are...

Weighing And Measuring Powder

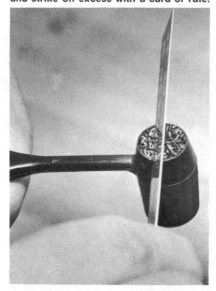

Prudent handloading requires powder be weighed and measured with care. Hot loads affect case life and are risky too!

BY WILLIAM C. DAVIS, JR.

THE powder scale, or "reloading balance" as it is more properly called, is the most important single piece of reloading equipment for metallic cartridges. In very few instances can the handloader safely and satisfactorily dispense with its use.

For shotshells, and for reloading handgun cartridges with well established mild charges in target loads, mechanical measures with non-adjustable powder-metering cavities are often used, and a powder scale is not then required. There are, furnished with the Lee hand-held loading tools and available separately, sets of charge cups suitable for measuring charges in mild loads, where a high degree of accuracy and uniformity are not required. Charge cups or dippers can actually measure powder with better uniformity than is commonly supposed, provided the operator is experienced and skilled in their use. (See *American Rifleman*,

When using a charge cup, let the powder flow into the cup of its own weight and strike off excess with a card or rule.

Sept., 1976, p. 74). Unfortunately, experienced reloaders are the group least likely to rely on powder dippers, which are most likely to be used by beginning reloaders because of their low cost. In the hands of inexperienced reloaders, dippers are safe only for loads that are sufficiently reduced to assure that possible variations in charge weight cannot cause hazardous increases in chamber pressure. Such loads are listed by the charge cup manufacturer, for selected cartridges, and the user of them should limit himself strictly to those recommended loads, unless he is thoroughly familiar with the precautions that must be observed in extending the use of dipped charges to other loads.

The only other applications in which dipped charges can be recommended are for loads of blackpowder, or Pyrodex, which is a special class of propellant described as "rep-

62

lica blackpowder." Those two propellants are designed and intended for loading by volumetric measure (though they can be loaded by weight if their characteristics are fully understood) and the accuracy achieved by use of powder dippers is satisfactory. A scale is highly desirable, however, even for blackpowder or Pyrodex loads, to assure that the dipper used is of the correct capacity.

The design of powder scales has been greatly improved during the last decade. Possibly the most notable improvement is magnetic damping, which greatly reduces the duration of the periodic oscillation of the beam before it comes to rest. It is accomplished by attaching a plate of highly conductive nonferrous metal, usually copper, to the beam, in such a way that it oscillates between opposite poles of a permanent magnet. The damping action depends upon the fact that the motion of the conductor in the magnetic field induces small electric currents within the plate, which are proportional to the speed of motion. These currents, which are called "eddy currents," produce their own magnetic field, which opposes the field of the fixed permanent magnet. The interaction of these magnetic fields exerts a damping force on the plate, and thus on the beam, to reduce its speed of oscillation. As the movement of the beam slows down, so does the magnitude of the induced eddy currents, and so does the damping force. As the beam approaches its position of rest, the damping force approaches zero, so it exerts no force on the beam

Magnetically dampened powder scales, like this one made for RCBS by Ohaus, are both accurate and convenient. Oscillations of beam should be observed on the same level with it to minimize errors. A powder trickler makes weighing many charges a lot easier.

to prevent its reaching the true point of equilibrium. The result is that oscillations are damped quickly, with no loss in sensitivity or accuracy of the scale.

Before the development of magnetically damped powder scales, damping was accomplished on some models by a paddle attached to the beam, arranged so that it moved in a reservoir of oil. The degree of damping depended upon the viscosity of the oil in the reservoir. Unfortunately, the damping force did not diminish as the beam approached the position of rest at equilibrium in the way that it does in magnetic damping. Furthermore, the oil was subject to thickening by oxidation, and contamination by solid particles of powder or dust that fell into it, so the paddle sometimes interfered with free movement of the beam and impaired the accuracy of the scale.

Handloaders who have scales designed for viscous damping are well advised to cut off the paddle and deactivate the system, because an undamped scale is much preferable to an inaccurate one.

For undamped scales, including models originally so designed and others on which the viscous-damping system has been deactivated, the technique of weighing should be somewhat different from that used for magnetically damped models. It is impracticable to wait until the beam comes to rest at equilibrium without interference, because the damping by frictional forces alone is very slow on a sensitive balance. Large oscillations can be reduced by gently touching the beam or the pan with the finger, but the oscillations should not be entirely stopped. When the oscillations are small, the midpoint of the oscillations can be accu-

Volumetric measures (left) must always be checked with a scale. Once verified, charges can be measured directly into the case, but rechecked periodically. Powder funnel in measure reservoir (center) helps maintain a uniform "head" to minimize variations in measured charges. This is very important with fast burning pistol powders. Belding & Mull measure (right) is a favorite of benchresters and high power shooters, as its sliding reservoir measures most rifle powders uniformly.

Measuring Powder

rately estimated by watching the movement of the pointer on the scale of index marks behind it. The midpoint of these small oscillations can be taken as the point of balance or equilibrium, without waiting for the pointer to come to rest.

Powder scales are essential for the accurate determination of charge weights. The sensitivity of good powder scales, which is the least change in weight that can be clearly detected, is about 0.1 gr. in most models. To preserve that sensitivity, the knife edges and their bearings must be kept clean, in accordance with the manufacturer's recommendations. The beam should not be allowed to rest on the bearings when the scale is not in use, and the scale should never be set on a bench where it is subjected to jarring by pounding, or by operation of a loading press, or other such violent disturbances. Sensitive scales are necessarily somewhat delicate, and they must always be treated with appropriate gentleness if they are to retain their sensitivity and accuracy. In storage, they should be boxed or covered so as to protect them from airborne dust. In short, the careful handloader must recognize conditions that might damage his powder scale, and avoid them. It is unfortunately not uncommon for a handloader to disregard the proper care of his powder scale, but nevertheless go to great lengths in the care with which he weighs his powder charges, and that is a futile gesture.

The accuracy of a powder scale, which is not the same as its sensitivity, is the proximity of the weight determined by it to the true weight of the specimen being weighed. Many years ago, the most common powder scales were of the substitution type. In use, a predetermined combination of weights was placed on the scale pan, the scale was balanced by adjusting the counterweights, and the weights were removed from the pan. The powder charge was then substituted for the weights in the pan, and powder was added or subtracted to balance the scale. For that type of scale, the accuracy was limited only by the accuracy of the weights with which it was adjusted, and the precision was determined by the sensitivity of the scale. It is a highly accurate system, but somewhat inconvenient to use.

Modern powder scales have movable weights, called "counterpoises," that are adjusted along a calibrated beam. There is typically a large counterpoise that is adjusted in 5-gr. or 10-gr. increments by positioning it in various notches cut into the top of the beam, and a much smaller counterpoise that is adjusted either into other notches, or by a micrometer arrangement, for fine adjustments. The accuracy of scales such as these depends not only on the accuracy of the counterpoise weights, but also on the accuracy of the mechanisms by which they are adjusted. Though such scales are sometimes advertised as having an accuracy of 0.1 gr., it may be found by comparing several different scales, weighing the same object, that differences as great as 0.3 gr. are not uncommon, and even larger differences are occasionally observed. It is a price we pay for the convenience of scales operating on this principle, and probably inevitable unless we are prepared to pay the much higher cost of laboratory-type balances. The sensitivity, which determines the uniformity of charges weighed at a given adjustment, is indeed 0.1 gr. or less in most models, and that is more than adequate for the purpose.

Some handloaders ascribe great importance to the accuracy of charge weight, and carefully weigh each and every powder charge. Others believe no significant advantage is gained by this laborious process, and use their scales only to adjust their mechanical powder measures, which are then used to meter the charges volumetrically, with only occasional weighing to assure that nothing has gone awry with the adjustment of the measure.

It is unquestionable that a scale should be used to adjust the powder measure, and also unquestionable that more uniform powder charges can be obtained by careful weighing than by measuring the charge volumetrically. The extreme variation in a sample of 10 weighed powder charges at the same scale adjustment should not exceed 0.2 gr., and many operators can do better than that. Making some reasonable statistical assumptions, we could expect the standard deviation of weighed charges, a more reliable measurement of uniformity, to be about 0.06 gr. It is informative to consider the effect of such variations on muzzle velocity, which is the principal characteristic we seek to control.

For the 7 mm Remington Magnum cartridge, a typical full-charge load with 150-gr. bullets produces a change in average muzzle velocity of about 50 f.p.s. corresponding to a one-grain change in charge weight. In the absence of all other factors that affect uniformity, a 0.1 gr. change in charge weight would result in a change of about 5 f.p.s. in muzzle velocity. The standard deviation in muzzle velocity ascribable to normal variation in charge weights of weighed charges, in the absence of all other factors, is therefore expected to be about 3 f.p.s. It is a matter of experience, however, that 7 mm magnum ammunition that produces velocity standard deviations as small as 20 f.p.s. is very good, and that producing standard deviations of 10 f.p.s. is superb. The statistics of the situation are such that the several causes of velocity variation are not arithmetically additive, but accumulate as the square root of the sum of the squares of the effects of separate causes. From that fact, it can be deduced that ammunition which produces a velocity standard deviation of 10 f.p.s., with charges weighed to the usual accuracy, would produce a standard deviation of about 9.5 f.p.s. if the variation in charge weight could be entirely eliminated. Even more interesting is the fact that, if the extreme variations in charge weight of such ammunition were increased to 1.0 gr., which might occur with volumetric measurement of very coarse-grained powders, the standard deviation of velocity would be increased only to about 19 f.p.s., which is still quite acceptable for most purposes.

Weighing powder charges is laborious, in comparison to throwing charges from a mechanical powder measure. Nevertheless, many handloaders attempt to weigh charges for every round, with great exactitude. They may even be perfunctory about their choices of components, and about the performance of the other loading operations, as if weighing the charges with great care could somehow assure uniformity of ballistic performance. In fact, for all but the most critical requirements, in loads that are established as capable by design of giving a high degree of uniformity, weighing powder charges is labor not rewarded by any material improvement in ballistic uniformity.

When the circumstances warrant weighing each powder charge, as they do for ammunition to be used in 1000-yd. match shooting, for example, the process can be done more quickly by using a powder trickler. This is a device designed to drop powder granules on the scale pan very slowly, as the operator rotates the feed tube slowly between thumb and finger. The technique is to set the powder trickler in position beside the scale, so that the mouth of the drop tube projects over the edge of the pan. The powder measure is then adjusted to throw charges slightly less than the desired charge weight. The charge from the measure is dropped into the scale pan, the pan is placed on the scale, and the trickler is used to add the small amount of powder required to balance the scale.

Mechanical powder measures have not changed significantly in design for many years. The most popular type consists of a metering chamber that is attached to, or integral with, a rotating drum that connects alternately with a powder reservoir or hopper at the top, and a drop tube at the bottom. It is rotated by a handle or crank, first to fill the metering chamber from the reservoir, then to empty it through the drop tube into the cartridge case. The metering chamber is adjustable, usually by a micrometer arrangement, for various weights of charge.

The head of powder (the depth in the reservoir) does affect the weight of charge thrown, to some degree. Some measures have a baffle located near the bottom of the reservoir which bears most of the weight of powder above it, minimizing the effect of the head on the weight of charge. Much the same effect can be achieved by placing a funnel in the top of the reservoir, and keeping some powder always in the funnel. The level of powder in the reservoir is then maintained at the bottom of the funnel opening, so its height is constant.

For target loads in pistol cartridges, particularly the .38 Special, small mechanical measures are made having fixed (non-adjustable) cavities in the metering chamber. These are drilled for various popular charges, usually from about 2.2 to 3.5 grs. of Bullseye powder, or comparable loads of other powders such as Winchester-Western 231 or Du Pont Hi-Skor 700-X. This is the only type of mechanical measure for metallic cartridges that need not be adjusted by use of a powder scale.

The technique of operation is at least as important as the design of the measure itself to the uniformity of charges thrown. After the reservoir has been filled, several charges should be thrown and turned back into the reservoir to achieve a constant degree of settling of the powder in the reservoir. Trial charges should then be weighed on the scale, and the metering chamber adjusted to obtain the desired charge. For light charges, it is useful to weigh five or 10 charges simultaneously in the scale pan, as that automatically "averages" the charge weight from the measure. Thus, if the desired charge is 2.7 grs., the scale should be adjusted to 27.0 grs., and the metering chamber adjusted until 10 charges balance the scale.

It is very important that the measure be operated in a uniform cadence, and with uniform force. The metering chamber must be connected with the reservoir long enough to assure that it is filled. Rotation of the drum should be done in a smooth motion, firmly but without excessive force at the stops. When beginning the use of a new measure, the operator should practice the technique, weighing each charge, and refine his technique to achieve the best uniformity of charge weights.

It is good practice, when loading with a powder measure, to weigh a charge occasionally to assure that the correct charge is being thrown. At least every 50th charge should be weighed, and at least one should be weighed at the end of the series being loaded. If agreement is not satisfactory, the operator should empty all of the charged cases, re-adjust the measure, and begin again.

Whether weighing or measuring powder, it is essential for safety that *every charged case be visually inspected* before the bullet is seated. This can be accomplished as the cases are charged, if the operator prefers to seat bullets at once. Otherwise, it is best accomplished by setting all of the charged cases in a loading block, holding the block under a light so that the surface of the charge is clearly visible, and examining each case in turn. It is not sufficient to glance at the whole block of cases. The best technique is to begin with the left-hand case in the top row, looking at each in turn from left to right, then dropping to the next row, and repeating the procedure, as if reading a printed page. An operator having normal depth perception can easily detect a double charge, even with target loads of pistol powder, by this technique. It also serves to identify any case that has received no charge, as may happen occasionally if the operator is not constantly alert.

Special care is required when cartridges are loaded in a progressive loading machine. These machines are normally used for target loads in cartridges such as the .38 Special. The cartridge case will accommodate multiple charges for most such loads, and multiple charges can easily blow up guns. As a matter of experience, veteran handloaders have made errors in the operation of progressive loaders that resulted in enormously excessive chamber pressures, and so have blown up revolvers. Of all types of reloading, the one potentially most hazardous is probably assembling target handgun loads on a progressive loading machine. Such machines do not ordinarily afford the opportunity for visual examination of charged cases, so it is especially necessary that the operator have a thorough understanding of the machine and its operation, that he establish a safe routine, and that he adhere invariably to the safe routine. The utmost vigilance is required to avoid accidents that can destroy guns and possibly cause personal injury. ■

"BRISANCE" IN PRIMERS

Q: *I have read that a primer of "high brisance" is required to ignite the heavy charges of slow-burning powders used in magnum rifle cartridges. Which primers have "high brisance", and what does that term actually mean?*

A: The term "brisance" refers specifically to the shattering effect of an explosive. It is measured in the laboratory by detonating a specified quantity (about 6.16 grains) in a bed of special sand, and determining the degree to which the grains of sand have been shattered into finer particles by the effect of the explosion. It is not necessarily indicative of the energy or heat liberated by the explosion, but depends largely upon the suddenness with which the gaseous products are released.

The term "brisance" is misunderstood, and misused when applied to primers in the sense you describe. The primer is intended to ignite the powder charge, and certainly not to shatter it. High brisance is a property always avoided, insofar as possible, in the design of a primer.

Ignition of the powder charge in a cartridge is accomplished basically by two different mechanisms. One is the evolution of hot gases, which raise the surface temperature of the powder granules to the ignition point, and thus set them afire. The other mechanism is by a shower of white-hot particles that may be ejected from the explosion of the primer composition and cast among the powder granules. Most primers function by a combination of these two different mechanisms.

Designers of primers can regulate the performance, both by a choice of the ingredients in the primer composition, and by the quantity of composition used in each primer. For primers intended to ignite heavy charges of heavily deterrent-coated powders, the ingredients are chosen to provide the most favorable conditions for ignition under those conditions, and the maximum practicable quantity of compositon may be used. Such primers are called "magnum" primers by most manufacturers, because their principal use is in magnum cartridges. In exception to this usual practice, Winchester-Western does not produce a special magnum primer for use in rifle cartridges. Their No. 6½-116 small rifle primer and No. 8½-120 large rifle primer are formulated to produce satisfactory ignition in all rifle loads, both regular and magnum. The best policy in choosing primers is to follow the recommendations of the laboratory in which the load was developed. Most manuals nowadays include information on the type of primer used in development of the loads listed.

WCD, Jr.

.45 ACP Headspace

Accurizing procedures for the Colt Government Model .45 ACP often include installation of a long-hooded barrel to reduce play of the barrel and slide. Does this increase effective chamber length, and therefore affect headspace? Chamber length of my pistol from the rear of the hood to the chamber seat is .9176". Maximum case length of the .45 ACP is .898", but most cases are shorter than that, so there is usually more than .020" end play of rounds in the chamber. What is the maximum headspace consistent with match accuracy?

.45 ACP round *should drop into chamber without case head being below the rear face of the hood, and should not protrude enough to prevent the slide from closing during the firing cycle.*

Answer: Your .45 ACP pistol has an excessively deep chamber and should be rebarreled by a competent gunsmith familiar with the requirements of target pistols. Long hoods on .45 ACP match barrels are measured from the locking surfaces, not the chamber. Correctly manufactured barrels are chambered to provide correct headspace, though chamber depth may be close to maximum to permit shortening the hood somewhat during fitting. Match barrels made for gunsmith installation are occasionally "short-chambered," so that headspace can be corrected by deepening the chamber after the barrel hood has been fitted to the slide. When the hood of a standard barrel is built up by welding, it may create excessive headspace. The breeching space of the M1911A1 National Match pistol, measured from the breech face of the slide to the chamber seat is .879" minimum, up to .901" maximum. This should be used as a guide in accurizing .45 ACP pistols.

Excessive end play of the cartridge in the chamber is not conducive to best accuracy. Some of the firing pin energy is used to drive the cartridge forward in the chamber until it stops against the chamber shoulder. This causes erratic ignition and greater velocity spread. Handloaders some-times aggravate this condition by crimping cases excessively, since this tends to increase and play. Risk of this happening is reduced, but not eliminated, by using a taper crimp instead of a roll crimp. Lead bullets should have .015" to .025" of the shoulder exposed forward of the case mouth, but the amount must not be enough to prevent the slide from closing fully, and seating depth should be determined by trial according to the individual gun and bullet design.

I have never found a lot of .45 ACP cases approaching the .898" maximum length. Most cases will be .885"-.890".

Because of the aforementioned conditions, trimming .45 ACP cases is not necessary or recommended. Handloaded cartridges with lead semi-wadcutter bullets should be tried in the barrel, adjusting seating depth until the case head protrudes very slightly, or is flush with the rear of the hood when the loaded round is dropped into the chamber. Ammunition should then be test fired to insure that the slide closes positively during the firing cycle.—E.L.

Case Head Separation

I have an M1A match rifle for the 7.62 mm NATO cartridge which has been fired about 1000 rounds. I reload military cases using 168-gr. match bullets and IMR-4895 powder to approximate the performance of National Match ammunition. Cases are full-length sized, using RCBS dies. After two or three reloads, I get partial head separations. My loads give no signs of high pressure and the rifle functions well. What is the problem?

Answer: Fired cases which show partial or complete circumferential ruptures, such as you describe, are not usually a sign of excessive pressure in guns with a front locking bolt, such as the M14 or M1A, but of excessive headspace. This condition can be caused either by a combination of resizing die and shell holder which pushes the shoulder of the case back too far during resizing, or by a rifle having excessive headspace.

I suggest you get a cartridge case gauge, which checks the head-to-shoulder dimension of your cases, such as those made by Forster, 82 E. Lanark Ave., Lanark, Ill. 61046, or by L. E. Wilson, Box 324, Cashmere, Wash. 98815. Either gauge will tell you if your reloads have correct head-to-shoulder length. If they are too short from excessive sizing, you can adjust your sizing die, backing it off by trial until the correct dimension is obtained. You should also have a qualified gunsmith check the headspace of your rifle. If the bolt closes fully on an accurate "No-Go" gauge, the rifle should be returned to the manufacturer for correction.—W.C.D., JR.

Testing Handguns

I read with considerable interest the Q&A in the July American Rifleman, *p. 68, entitled "Machine Rest vs. Hand Hold." I test my handguns from sandbags, and have confidence in the results, but I am curious as to how the Technical Staff does it. Could you elaborate briefly?*

Answer: The test methods used by the Technical Staff were standardized by the late M. D. Waite, who was then Technical Editor of the *American Rifleman.*

Accuracy testing is usually done with a two-handed hold. In addition to the front sandbag rest, or pedestal, one, or sometimes a pair of rear bags (usually 25-lb. shot bags) are used as support for the forearms and elbows. The height of the rest, bench and chair is adjusted so that shooting can be done sitting upright in a natural position, with the head erect. This reduces fatigue on the muscles of the arms, neck and shoulders. The eyes then gaze straight through the lens of the shooting glasses, thus reducing eyestrain and permitting a clearer sight picture. When shooting iron sights, a small aperture is usually placed over the lens of the shooting glasses to sharpen the sight picture. When firing scoped handguns at short range, where parallax is noticeable, an aperture is similarly placed over the eye lens of the scope. Lighting on the indoor range is controlled so as to reduce glare off the target, while having it well lighted, and reducing stray backlight and sidelight from behind the shooter.

Aside from getting a comfortable shooting position and good lighting, the method of supporting the handgun is also important. Most revolvers and semi-automatic pistols shoot best if the barrel or slide is free of any contact with the rest. The front of the gun frame or trigger guard is the usual point of contact with the rest. A sandbag is placed under the heel and wrist of the shooting hand, to support the butt comfortably without having any direct contact of the gun butt with the rest. An alternative for small frame handguns is to use the rest only to support the hands in the two-handed grip, avoiding direct contact of the gun frame or butt with the rest.

Some handguns, such as the Thompson/Center Contender, require different techniques. With the Contender pistols, Steve Herrett's suggestion of resting the fore-end on the sandbag, with the non-shooting hand resting on the scope for support, seems best. The butt does not contact the bench or bags, but the grip is held firmly in the hand. A bag can be used under the forearm of the shooting hand for additional support, if desired.

Handguns zeroed from sandbags will usually shoot to the sights when fired offhand also, provided you use a relaxed position which lets the gun recoil normally, and you take care to maintain the same erect head position you use in offhand shooting. — C. E. H.

HEADSPACE... AND HOW IT IS MEASURED

By MAJ GEN. J. S. HATCHER

(Gen. Hatcher was Technical Editor of THE AMERICAN RIFLEMAN until his death on Dec. 4, 1963.)

ACCORDING to the dictionary, head-space is "in the bolt type rifle, the space between the rear end of the barrel and the front end of the bolt when the bolt is closed". While this is a good definition for headspace in guns using rimmed cartridges, it leaves questions unanswered. For example, the cal. .30-40 Krag cartridge and the cal. .30-'06 cartridge look much alike and are much the same size, yet the minimum headspace for the Krag is given as .064" and for the cal. .30-'06 as 1.940". In the Krag rifle, the distance from the rear face of the barrel to the front face of the bolt will be found to be close to .064", but in the cal. .30-'06 rifle the space occupied by the cartridge head is nothing like the figure of nearly 2" stated for the headspace. What is behind this apparent discrepancy?

Headspace measurement

The answer is that the headspace is measured from the face of the bolt to the point where the cartridge is stopped from going any farther into the chamber when the bolt is closed. The Krag cartridge is stopped on the front edge of the rim, which is .064" thick, while the cal. .30-'06 cartridge, which is rimless, cannot be stopped on the rim, so it is stopped on the shoulder of the chamber, which is nearly 2" forward of the cartridge head (see Fig. 1), and this distance to the stopping point is still called *headspace* though it is in reality *cartridge space*.

The purpose of this article is to explain how headspace is defined and measured for all the different types of cartridges the shooter is likely to encounter, and to give the shooter an understanding of the practical importance of headspace.

Rimmed cartridges, either rimfire or center-fire, have a head which is larger in diameter than the body of the case, and this forms a rim which makes an ideal point for positioning the cartridge in chambering (see Figs. 2a & 2b). The rim is easily held to close tolerances in manufacture, and the headspace in the gun is also easy to hold to close tolerances. There is no danger of changing the headspace by too much resizing of the cartridge as is the case with rimless cartridges which make contact on the shoulder in chambering. In rimmed cases which have a shoulder, such as the cal. .30-40 Krag, a good clearance is left at the shoulder to insure that the contact is only at the rim. All rimfire rifles and pistols, most early center-fire rifles, all shotguns, and nearly all revolvers use rimmed cartridges.

Because rimmed cartridges present difficulties in feeding from box magazines, most center-fire automatic pistols and many late-model center-fire rifles use rimless cartridges. The head of a rimless cartridge is no larger than the body of the case, but it does have a groove, or *cannelure,* for the extractor cut into the body of the case just forward of the rear end. As the rim thus formed is no larger than the body of the case forward of the head, there is no convenient way of using the rim for stopping the cartridge in chambering, and the cartridge stops by having its conical shoulder come in contact with the corresponding shoulder in the chamber.

For such cartridges, headspace is measured from the face of the closed bolt to a point where a circle of a certain size, called the *datum circle,* would intersect the cone of the shoulder on the chamber (see Fig. 3). The table gives the shoulder angle, diameter of the datum circle, and the headspace measurement for most modern rimless center-fire cartridges now being made in the U. S. An exception is the cal. .30-'06 cartridge as made for the U. S. Government. While commercial specifications for the cal. .30-'06 use the datum circle system, the Government drawings call for a measurement of headspace to a different point, the point at which the cone of the shoulder would intersect the cone of the body (see Fig. 4). A cartridge having the standard Government minimum headspace of 1.940" according to this drawing would have a minimum headspace of 2.0479" when measured to the datum circle of .375" diameter used as a measuring point on commercial drawings. The figures stated are different only because the commercially made cartridge of identical dimensions is measured to a different point on the shoulder.

Why 2 methods?

A fair question would be, "Why the 2 different methods of measuring?" The answer is that the cal. .30-'06 is the earliest of all the American rimless cartridges now made. After a method of headspacing was developed and incorporated in Government drawings, other rimless cartridges appeared on the market. Then companies making them developed a simpler method of measuring and stating headspace.

Headspacing on the shoulder of the case and the chamber, as described for rimless rifle cartridges, is not a very satisfactory way of doing the job because the stopping surface of the cartridge is the conical shoulder made of the relatively soft and yielding brass of the

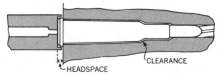
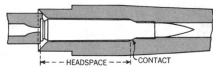
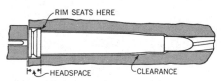

1 (Left) Headspace in a rifle using rimmed center-fire cartridge. Note that before firing, the cartridge is provided with clearance on the body, neck, and shoulder to insure it will stop on the rim when chambered and not at some other point. (Right) Headspace in a rifle using a modern rimless cartridge. The body and neck of the cartridge have a slight clearance, but there is no clearance at the shoulder, for the cartridge seats here when it is chambered. Headspace is measured to datum diameter (see Fig. 3).

7 Belted cartridge showing headspace which, except for greater depth, corresponds with that of rimmed cartridge.

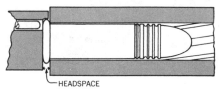

2a Headspace in a rifle using a cal. .22 rimfire cartridge.

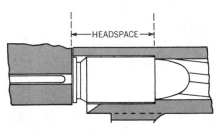

5 Headspace in a pistol using a true rimless cartridge, such as the cal. .380 ACP or the cal. .45 ACP (shown here). As the rim is no larger in diameter than the body of the case, it cannot be used as a seating point. Case mouth is left square, and seats against square shoulder at front end of chamber.

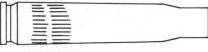

STRETCHED CASE

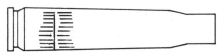

INCIPIENT SEPARATION

2b Headspace in a revolver using a rimmed cartridge.

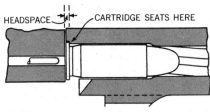

6 Headspace in an automatic pistol using a semi-rimmed cartridge such as the cal. .38 ACP. Rim is larger than the body of the case, and there is a clearance between the mouth of the cartridge and the front end of the chamber. In chambering, cartridge stops on the rim.

COMPLETE SEPARATION

8 Typical results of excess headspace. When any of these 3 effects is observed on a fired case, it is certain that headspace is excessive, though the gun may not be at fault. A cartridge that has been made too short by too much full-length resizing will give too much headspace, even if the gun is correct in dimensions. *Stretched case* is due to moderately excessive headspace. *Incipient separation* is due to somewhat greater excess headspace. *Complete separation* is due to excessive headspace. It may permit an unpleasant and perhaps dangerous escape of gas as much of the obturating property of the case has been lost.

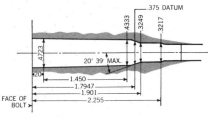

3 7 mm. Mauser minimum chamber showing headspace datum diameter.

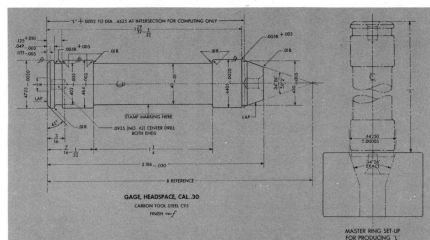

GAGE, HEADSPACE, CAL. .30
CARBON TOOL STEEL C95
FINISH

4 Headspace gauge for U. S. Service rifles cal. .30. "L" is the headspace, and "B" is the breeching space, used for purposes of computation only; it is equal to "L" plus .714″. Values of "L" are as follows: For manufacture of the U. S. Rifle, Caliber .30 M1: minimum, 1.942; maximum, 1.944. For the manufacture of other rifles: minimum, 1.940; maximum, 1.944. As a maximum gauge for inspection of overhauled rifles: 1.946. For inspection as a field headspace limit for serviceable rifles: 1.950. A semi-circular groove may be cut in the head to clear the ejector in the M1 Rifle.

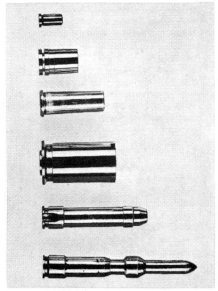

9 Headspace gauges: (top to bottom) .22 rimfire, belted cartridge, .303 British, shotgun, .30-'06, adjustable .30-'06.

cartridge case. This is hard to hold to close dimensions. Also, the headspace is too easy to change if the cartridge is full-length resized. If the cartridge is pushed too far into the resizing die, the shoulder will be pushed back and excess headspace will result. Moreover, the fact that the headspace is measured to some hypothetical point on a cone makes it less definite and less easy to produce correctly in the first place, and decidedly more difficult to measure, than when headspace is measured to definite surfaces as it is in a gun made for a rimmed cartridge.

Some rimless cartridges, notably those for the cal. .45 ACP, the 9 mm. Luger, and the cal. .380 ACP, do not have a conical shoulder but stop on the square edge of the case mouth which in turn butts against a square edge at the rear end of the bore or the front end of the chamber (see Fig. 5). These avoid the disadvantages mentioned above.

Avoiding feeding troubles

In an effort to get away from the feeding troubles in box magazines caused by the cartridge rim, and still retain the headspacing advantages of using the rim as a contact point for chambering, the semi-rimmed (or semi-rim) cartridges were developed. These look like rimless cartridges, but on closer examination it will be found that the part of the rim behind the extractor groove is actually just a small amount larger in diameter than the body of the case forward of the groove. This small semi-rim does not project enough to cause feeding difficulties from the magazine, and yet it is too big to go into the chamber, so that it makes a stopping point for chambering (see Fig. 6). The cal. .25 ACP, the cal. .32 ACP, and the cal. .38 Super Automatic are examples of semi-rimmed cartridges.

There no longer are many semi-rimmed cartridges used in rifles; the cal. .351 Winchester Self Loading is an example. The cal. .220 Swift is technically a semi-rimmed cartridge, having been developed from the old and long-obsolete 6 mm. U.S.N., but actually the Swift does not use the semi-rim at all. The rear end of the barrel is cut away so far that the cartridge case rim never comes in contact with it, and the shoulder is used for headspacing just as if the semi-rim did not exist.

The belted cartridge is another type that at first glance looks like a rimless, but isn't. It is made with the walls of the cartridge case quite thick at the rear, and it has a typical rimless rear end formed on this thick rear portion. But then comes the difference—for a little less than ¼" forward of the breech end of the cartridge there is a step, .01" deep, cut into the body of the cartridge case which is used as

a stop in chambering (see Fig. 7).

This system, which has the advantages of a rimless case so far as ease of magazine feeding is concerned and also results in greater strength in the rear end of the cartridge case, is popular for the extra-high-power cartridges called Magnums.

Wrong headspace

Headspace can be either too small or too great. If it is not large enough, then the bolt will not close completely on a rifle, automatic pistol, or shotgun cartridge. With a revolver, the cylinder cannot be swung fully into place because there is not room for the cartridge to go all the way in.

With shouldered rimless cartridges, the headspace may be found too small because the cartridge has been stretched (in the case of reloads) by firing it in a gun that has excess headspace. If it is then reloaded without full-length resizing and an attempt made to use it in a gun with tight headspace, it may be found impossible to close the bolt.

Much more common is trouble with headspace that is too large—excess headspace. This may occur from natural wear even if the headspace is correct when the gun is new. If a gun has excess headspace, ignition trouble (misfires or hangfires) may occur because the firing pin may not be able to give the primer a proper blow. This is especially likely in weapons such as handguns, which do not have an extractor to hold the cartridge back close to the bolt face; it can also happen in other weapons if the cartridge is shoved into the chamber ahead of the extractor and not hooked into it.

If the headspace happens to be much too great, but the firing pin can still reach the primer sufficiently to explode it, a curious effect may occur. The primer may blow all the way out and spread into a disk before the main charge explodes fully enough to drive the cartridge back. Then the cartridge is blown powerfully back against the breech, flattening the disk of the primer against the head of the cartridge. Sometimes a ring of metal from the primer is forced so tightly around the point of the firing pin that the pin is held forward and difficulty may be experienced in opening the gun.

Ruptured case

When a gun such as a high power rifle with excess headspace does fire, a stretched or ruptured cartridge is likely to result, with possible dangerous escape of gas to the rear around the bolt head. This rupturing of the cartridge occurs because the firing pin blow drives the cartridge forward and then the internal pressure of the explosion expands the neck and sidewalls of the case out-

ward and causes them to grip the walls of the chamber. The friction of the case walls against the chamber, together with the forward pressure of the gas on the inside of the case shoulder, combine to hold the front portion of the case forward, while the pressure of the powder gas acting on the inside rear of the case blows it back, causing a stretching, or even a separation, between the front and rear portions of the cartridge case (see Fig. 8).

Just how much excess headspace it takes to make a gun dangerous depends on several things, including the pressure level to which the cartridge is loaded, and especially the temper of the brass. From .004" to .006" tolerance on headspace is allowed in new manufacture, so that guns with headspace anywhere from the minimum headspacing to .006" above it may be accepted, while on an inspection in the field a gun with more than .010" above the minimum figure is returned to the shop for overhaul, according to military practice. A practical attitude would be to follow the military rule and refuse to shoot any gun that has a headspace over .010" above minimum. While such excess headspace can sometimes be cured by fitting a new and oversized bolt, the most practical cure usually is rebarreling.

Headspace gauges

To tell whether or not the headspace of a gun is satisfactory, it is necessary to make use of a headspace gauge, which is a piece of steel made to the same shape as the cartridge to which it pertains, and to the dimensions of the standard minimum chamber drawing. To avoid interference and insure that the gauge does not make contact with the chamber anywhere except on the chambering point (shoulder or rim or mouth of case, according to circumstances), it is usual to omit the neck and to allow a slight relief at other points where unwanted contact might occur. In using headspace gauges in bolt-action rifles, the extractor and firing mechanism of the gun should be removed so they will not interfere with the delicate feel of contact when the surfaces of the gauge come in contact with those of the gun.

The minimum, or 'go', gauge is inserted and the gun should close with ease, no contact being detectable. Then the maximum or 'no go' gauge should be tried, and it should prevent the bolt being closed completely.

With a skilled and experienced operator, it should be possible to estimate rather closely just what the headspace figure is by noting the amount by which the bolt fails to go completely down before the gauge is felt. Of course a delicate touch should be used and force should never be employed. ∎

RESIZING CHANGES THE CASE

Tests show how reduction of case diameter affects other cartridges case dimensions.

By L. E. WILSON

WOULD you believe that the cone-to-head length of a cartridge case is increased during full-length resizing? In other words, that the cone-to-head length gets longer before it gets shorter?

That is actually what happens. As diameter of the case is reduced almost from one end to the other, the cone-to-head and over-all length must both increase. This continues until the shoulder cone contacts the mating portion of the die; then, if the die is correctly made and properly adjusted, the cone is pushed back the amount necessary for proper chambering. The increased over-all length remains.

The following will point out the troubles one may have from incorrectly adjusted dies, or from the use of full-length dies for a purpose not intended by the maker.

To determine the extent of this length increase, a number of fired cases were tested in lots of 5, in 3 common calibers: .250 Savage, .308 Winchester and .30-'06. The body tapers of these are .041", .012", and .016" per inch, respectively. A die of the type shown in the illustration was used in each caliber, and was closed in an arbor press. Before resizing, the cases in each caliber were trimmed to uniform length and the cone-to-head length checked relative to minimum chamber dimensions. The cases were numbered so each could be followed through.

If the die were completely closed on each case it would not be known how much, if any, the cone advanced before it reached the die shoulder and was pushed back. So spacers were made to prevent complete closing. The spacer was .020" thick for the .308 and .30-'06 cases, but was made .030" thick for the .250 cases because they were .010" to .014" over minimum to start with. Probably they had been fired in a lever-action rifle—a bolt action would have held them closer to minimum.

The table contains the case lengths resulting (all figures in inches).

Results should be the same with the usual 7/8" x 14 threaded die, and the reloader can make the test himself by placing a spacer between the die and the shell holder of his press. Before any resizing, he should trim the case to correct minimum over-all length, and check the cone-to-head length in a cartridge case gage. After resizing with the spacer, the case will stand higher in the gage than before. Then resize fully, and if the die is correctly made and adjusted, the case head will drop down to the desired level in the gage. The extra over-all length will still show on the gage.

The growth in case over-all length indicates the need to watch this dimension if you full-length resize each time you reload. Without trimming, the cases would soon be bottoming in the chamber.

The non-threaded dies used in these experiments are reamed to a uniform depth, using a stop, but slight dimensional changes in hardening make it necessary to number the dies and drifts and individually fit them, which is done after polishing the interior. We find that during hardening there is often an unpredictable slight change.

Problems with dies

If the popular 7/8" x 14 threaded dies are not corrected after hardening, I would expect difficulty in obtaining the correct shell holder-to-die end fit. When such a die is reamed too deep, or becomes so in hardening, the cone-to-head length of the case will be increased in resizing and the loaded ammunition will not chamber readily in the rifle. This will be especially bothersome in rapid fire. If cases are resized with the shell holder brought up firmly against the die, and the cases then stand up higher in the case gage than before sizing, the die is too deep and some of the the end should be ground off. If, on the other hand, full-length resized cases drop into the gage below the lower step, the die must be unscrewed enough to give the correct reading. Better yet would be to insert a spacer of the right thickness between die end and shell holder.

These experiments point out a rather serious disadvantage in trying to neck size with a full length die. If the die is backed away a half-turn or a turn for this purpose, with most body tapers the case body will be reduced enough to increase the cone-to-head length noticeably, with the result that the cases can become difficult to chamber. ∎

RESULTS OF TESTS

	OVER-ALL LENGTH			CONE-TO-HEAD LENGTH*		
Fired and Trimmed	Resized With Spacer	Fully Resized		Fired and Trimmed	Resized With Spacer	Fully Resized
Frankford Arsenal .30-'06						
2.480	2.491	2.491		+.005	+.011	+.003
2.480	2.490	2.490		−.002	+.002	+.002
2.480	2.490	2.490		+.002	+.007	+.002
2.480	2.492	2.492		.000	+.008	+.001
2.480	2.490	2.490		+.003	+.007	+.003
Remington .30-'06						
2.484	2.492	2.492		+.001	+.004	+.002
2.484	2.494	2.494		−.002	+.001	+.001
2.484	2.493	2.493		+.006	+.008	+.003
2.484	2.494	2.494		+.003	+.007	+.003
2.484	2.494	2.493		+.002	+.006	+.003
Winchester .308						
2.005	2.008	2.010		+.007	+.009	+.002
2.005	2.010	2.011		+.007	+.007	+.001
2.005	2.008	2.010		+.008	+.009	+.002
2.005	2.010	2.010		+.007	+.008	+.002
2.005	2.010	2.011		+.007	+.009	+.003
Savage .250						
1.902	1.909	1.910		+.013	+.018	+.002
1.902	1.910	1.912		+.013	+.019	+.002
1.902	1.909	1.910		+.011	+.016	+.003
1.902	1.912	1.914		+.014	+.021	+.004
1.902	1.911	1.914		+.010	+.017	+.003

*With respect to the minimum allowable headspace length.

CASE TRIMMERS AND GAUGES

NRA Technical Staff

IT is sometimes necessary to cut back the case mouth slightly when preparing metallic cartridge cases for reloading. This operation, known as trimming, is done for several reasons.

Cartridge cases may be trimmed to bring all cases within a particular lot to the same over-all length. This insures uniformity of bullet crimp within that lot, which is not possible when the cases vary in length. Unevenness of the case mouth is also correctable by trimming.

Cracks weaken crimp

Longitudinal cracks usually develop around the mouths of revolver cartridge cases after repeated reloading. These cracks weaken the bullet crimp and have an adverse effect on performance of the ammunition. The bullets may dislodge forward from failure of the crimp to hold them in place, and can prevent rotation of the revolver cylinder if they engage the frame of the gun.

It is the usual practice to discard revolver cartridge cases which develop neck cracks, but many can be salvaged for additional use by trimming away the cracked portion if it is not too deep. The powder capacity of these shortened cases is reduced somewhat and this must be allowed for in establishing the charge. All cracked cases within a lot must be trimmed to the same over-all length and a special short die may be required to crimp the case neck around the bullet. The regular die,

if shortened slightly, can be used to seat and crimp bullets in both shortened and standard-length cases.

Trimming may be done to convert a case to a shorter type. Typical would be trimming of .357 S&W Magnum to .38 S&W Special, or .44 Remington Magnum to .44 S&W Special.

Some accurized M1911-type pistols are headspaced so tightly that a slight trimming of the cartridge case is required to insure proper functioning. Otherwise, the breech end of the barrel will not rise and lock fully into position as the cartridge is chambered.

Rifle cartridge cases must be trimmed when their over-all lengths exceed stated maximums. If the neck portion of the case is too long, the case mouth may lodge against the shoulder at the front end of the chamber and prevent complete closing of the action. Self-loading and slide-action rifles will usually malfunction when this occurs. In bolt-action and lever-action rifles, more than ordinary force is required to close the breech on the loaded cartridge and there is the possibility that chamber pressures may be increased if the case mouth is compressed around the bullet so that it cannot expand normally when fired.

Maximum case-length dimensions of standard rifle and handgun cartridges can be obtained from cartridge drawings and data tables incorporated in reloading articles or handbooks. The

nominal case length can also be determined by measuring a new unfired case of the same type. In rare instances it may be necessary to make a cast of the rifle chamber to obtain this and other pertinent dimensions.

There are many case trimming devices available to the handloading hobbyist and basic types are illustrated. It will be noted that some of these devices are universal, whereas others are made to trim a specific case.

Case measuring devices

A variety of case-measuring devices is offered for determining whether trimming is required. Some are adjustable; others are of fixed-type with paralleled gauging surfaces spaced for a particular cartridge, or with several gauging surfaces for cartridges of different lengths. In use, attempt is made to insert the cartridge case between the gauge jaws. If it does not enter, it must be trimmed until it will.

A vernier caliper accurate to .001″ is very useful to the handloader in measuring case and cartridge lengths and other dimensions. When set to a desired reading, it can be used as a snap gauge.

Cartridge cases should always be decapped before attempting to gauge or measure their over-all length. This precaution eliminates any possibility of error from contact of a gauging or measuring surface with the primer rather than the case head.

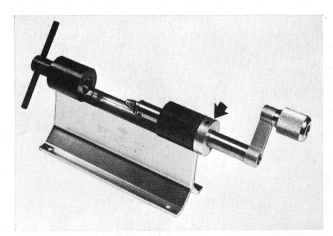

1 Typical hand-operated bench trimmer. Head of case is gripped by draw-in collet on left. Trimming is done by cutter on end of crankshaft. Cutter is aligned with case neck by detachable pilot of such diameter that it will just enter case mouth without binding. Depth of cut is determined by adjustment of stop collar (arrow) on shaft

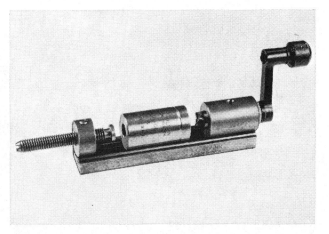

2 Hand-operated trimmer in which case is held friction tight in sleeve bored to approximate body taper of cartridge. Sleeve rests in trough to insure precise alignment of case with crank-operated cutter. Depth of cut is determined by adjustment of large screw in tailstock

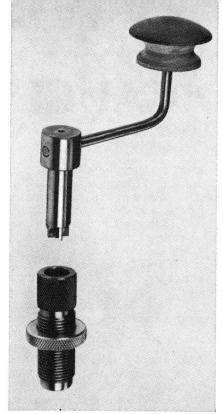

5 File trim die, for use in standard 7/8" x14 thread reloading tools, is designed primarily for forming cases from a larger and longer case type of same nominal head diameter. Die shown will form 7.65 mm. Mauser cases from other cases such as 8 mm. Mauser, .270 Winchester, or .30-'06. In use, case is lubricated sparingly and then forced into die until shell holder contacts base of die. Excess case metal extending above mouth of die is cut off with hacksaw with final finishing done with fine-cut file. Case neck is filed flush with upper surface of hardened die

3 Mill-type hand-operated trimmer for use in standard 7/8"x14 thread reloading tools. In use, cartridge case is run all the way into die body, after which cutter is rotated by hand to trim case.

This trimmer is not adjustable, but is so made that cases are trimmed to correct length when shell holder contacts base of die. Cutter is universal but each cartridge type requires separate body

8 Combination micrometer and case trimmer. Micrometer on left side is used to measure over-all length of cases to .001", or can be locked at desired setting and used as a snap gauge to segregate cases which require trimming. Micrometer also aids in precise adjustment of case trimmer at right.

Case is trimmed to desired length as verified by trial measurement with micrometer. Case is then returned to trimmer and stop collar (arrow) on trimmer shaft adjusted so that all succeeding cases will be trimmed to same length. Base of cartridge case is gripped by draw-in collet and centered at neck end by detachable pilot secured in cutter head

6 Manual trim die for use with fine-cut file. Case is dropped into the die and held in place with the fingers while mouth is filed flush with end of hardened die

4 Drill press trimmers are convenient and fast for processing large numbers of cases. Base of trimmer shown is clamped in drill press vise. Cutter head with detachable neck pilot is held in chuck. Depth of cut is adjusted with stop on drill spindle. Case head is clamped by draw-in collet

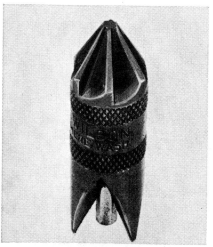

7 Trimming leaves sharp wire edges on exterior and interior of case mouth. These are readily removed with simple deburring tool shown

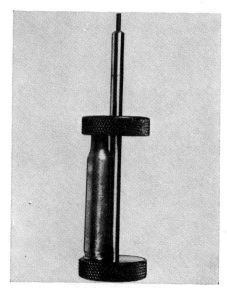

9 Adjustable snap gauge can be pre-set to any desired spacing between gauging surfaces. Vernier caliper, or new unfired case, can be used to set gauge spacing

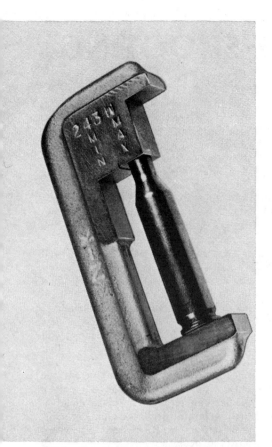

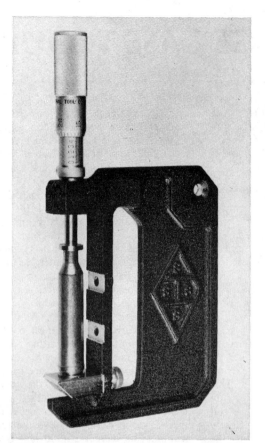

13 Full-length case gauge made for specific cartridge is designed to measure base to shoulder length (headspace) as well as over-all case length. There are minimum and maximum gauging steps on base and mouth ends of gauge.

When over-all length of case is correct its mouth will lie between the steps on mouth end of gauge. If case mouth extends beyond upper (maximum) step, it should be trimmed until it does not.

When headspace of case is correct, its head will lie between minimum and maximum steps on base of gauge

10 One-piece non-adjustable snap gauge for specific cartridge has both minimum and maximum case-length gauging surfaces plus additional surface for determining if over-all cartridge length is within established maximum

12 Micrometer case gauge, accurate to .001", with adjustable anvil. Anvil can be moved to any one of 3 positions on the beam, depending on over-all case length.

This gauge can be used to measure case lengths and in adjusting case trimmers. Micrometer spindle can be locked at desired setting and the gauge then used as a snap gauge

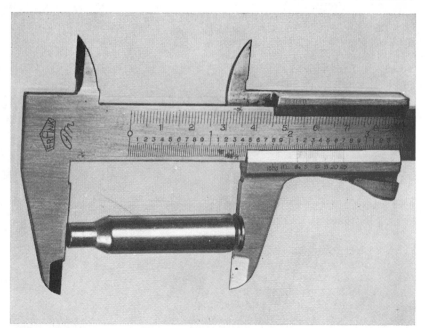

11 One-piece multi-caliber snap gauge has maximum case-length measuring surfaces for variety of popular pistol and rifle cartridges

14 Vernier caliper, accurate to .001", is most versatile instrument available to the handloader for determining cartridge dimensions and adjusting case trimmers precisely. When set to desired reading, it can be used as snap gauge to segregate quickly those cases which require trimming ∎

CARTRIDGE CASE TROUBLE-SHOOTING

By L. E. WILSON

RELOADED ammunition which does not chamber properly is a nuisance. At worst, it can become impossible to chamber and fire, spoiling a day at the range or a hunting trip.

Most such trouble originates in the resized cartridge case. Its exact location can be pinpointed by checking only 4 dimensions of the case.

In the .30-'06, for example, maximum allowable over-all case length is 2.494". If that length is not exceeded, it will cause no interference. Check length with a case gage, a 2" to 3" micrometer, an indicating caliper, or a plain outside caliper together with a scale graduated in hundredths.

For the other 3 decisive dimensions —body diameter, cone-to-head length, and neck diameter—a fired case from the handloader's rifle is the master. This should be a case that chambered readily in the rifle and was fired with a full load. This case will then very closely represent these 3 dimensions of the rifle's chamber.

The body diameter of cases to be reloaded need not be actually measured, but should be compared with the master fired case after resizing. In this shop we would do it by "bumping" the master case into a trimmer shell holder, which contacts only the tapered case body, and measuring the amount the head projects. This is compared with the projection of the resized case. The '06 case, which has a body taper of .016" per inch, enters the holder 1/16" farther for each .001" of body reduction. If the resized case enters ⅛" to 3/16" more than the master, you know you have .002" to .003" of body clearance in the chamber and no interference there.

Next check the cone-to-head length. For the reloader this is best done in a cartridge case gage. If the resized case stands the same height in the gage as the fired one, the case should chamber in the rifle without interference in this dimension. For rapid-fire work I would prefer a cone-to-head length about .001" to .003" shorter than in the master fired case, for smooth working of the bolt. If the resized case stands any higher in the gage than the as-fired one, some correction is required for easy chambering. If it drops as much as .005" lower than the as-fired case, a correction in the opposite direction is needed for the sake of longer case life.

Last, check neck diameter of the loaded cartridge. This can best be done with a micrometer or indicating caliper. A fair job can be done with only a plain outside caliper, if you are careful. Set the caliper to just "feel" the as-fired case neck and try it on the loaded round in the same location. Case necks are tapered, so be careful to use the same location. The caliper should slip freely over the loaded round and, better yet, with some daylight showing. If the neck of the loaded round is as large or larger than the as-fired case you may have neck interference which, if the wedging effect is great enough, will cause not only difficulty in chambering but possibly dangerous pressures. A minimum clearance of .0025" to .003" on the diameter is desirable.

The remedy for excessive neck wall thickness is neck reaming. Neck reamers are .0025" to .003" larger than the bullet in each caliber, and if case necks have thickened until the chamber clearance with a bullet seated is less than the above amount the reamer will cut. Otherwise it will not, and in that respect acts as a gage. Extra wall thickness could be removed from the outside up to the shoulder, but only a reamer can remove the extra metal at the junction of neck and shoulder. This is important when bullets are seated past the neck. ∎

Instruments illustrated (R.) are:

1. Common 2½" outside caliper, and steel scale graduated in hundredths on upper edge.
2. Indicating caliper of 4" capacity, useful for measuring over-all length and outside and inside neck diameters.
3. Trimmer shell holders, showing difference in case head projection before and after resizing.
4. Typical case gage with .30-'06 case.
5. Micrometer checking neck diameter.

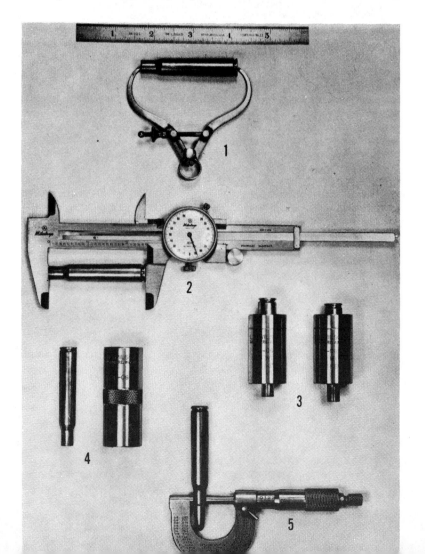

CLEANING CARTRIDGE CASES

NRA Technical Staff

CLEANING rifle and handgun cartridge cases before reloading has always been of interest to handloaders. It seems appropriate that the case be put into the best possible condition, to make it worthy of the labor to be spent on it and also to make the finished ammunition as attractive as practicable.

Handloaders generally appreciate that cartridge cases must be carefully cleaned of dirt and grit before resizing, or they will damage resizing dies (straight handgun cases may be resized in carbide dies after only light wiping). The problems usually arise from more extensive cleaning that is done with the idea of case preservation or of beautifying the product.

These processes also leave the cases ready for sizing and loading without wiping. Some of these processes thus constitute the most practical method of preparing large quantities of cases for reloading, and they may be well justified for this purpose even when appearance is not a consideration.

The situation is quite different between cartridge cases that have been fired with blackpowder and those fired with smokeless powder.

Must be washed soon

Brass cartridge cases fired with straight blackpowder must be washed soon after firing, or the fouling will corrode and ruin them. Decap, wash with warm water and soap using a bristle brush to dislodge solid fouling inside the cases, rinse in hot water, and allow to drain and dry. The cases eventually turn black but remain serviceable.

Cartridge cases fired with smokeless powder do not require cleaning for preservation. Their strength and serviceability are often impaired by cleaning.

This was explained by the late Gen. J. S. Hatcher, from his own experience. In the middle 1920's, Frankford Arsenal gave consideration to the cleaning of small-arms cartridge cases to remove the slight smoky residue and oxide colors left by the final neck anneal. Experimental lots of cases were polished by tumbling, and exposed on a roof of the Arsenal in the corrosive atmosphere of that area which contains a number of chemical manufacturing plants. Untreated cases just as they came from the manufacturing operation were exposed in the same place. Within a year the cleaned cartridge cases had cracked to a serious degree. The uncleaned cases were not affected. As a result of this and other tests, military procurement regulations require that the surface oxides that are remaining after manufacture be left on the cartridge case.

Handloaders, however, may wish to clean up salvaged, weathered, or otherwise discolored cases, and occasionally to polish them for some special effect. Or they may wish to clean them in quantity as preparation for reloading, as already mentioned.

Brass cartridge cases can be cleaned by: (a) buffing, (b) tumbling, (c) chemical washing.

Whatever the method used, the cases should first be decapped to let the cleaning material pass through them as freely as possible. This will also have a marked cleaning effect on the primer pockets of the cases.

For buffing, more or less ingenious arrangements can be devised. A simple and effective one is a small electric motor with an inexpensive chuck to carry a brass bore-brush. Each case is pushed onto the rotating brush and allowed to spin while the outside is buffed with a cloth and mild polishing compound, then polished with a clean cloth, and pulled off. Inside of the case can be cleaned by holding the case tightly a moment while the brush turns inside it. The next case is put on without stopping the motor. Though cases must be handled singly, the process is fast enough for a limited number. Of course, other buffing arrangements are possible, including automatic ones.

Ammonia can weaken brass

Most liquid brass polishes contain ammonia. Such polishes must not be used on cartridge cases which are to be fired, since ammonia can weaken brass seriously. A cloth with a little rouge has ample polishing action.

Buffing leaves a very bright, smooth finish, so smooth as to make later small dents and scratches quite conspicuous. The finish is not like that of a new case. A considerable amount of brass is removed by heavy buffing, and some by even light buffing.

Tumbling, also often called rumbling, is done by rolling the cases in a rotating barrel with a dry, cleaning material. This is done as a final operation on commercial cartridge cases. The usual material is ground corncobs, such as the product available under the trade name Maizorb. The tumbling barrels are large or very large, and the method is effective. The cases acquire a great number of tiny nicks and dents, which while not conspicuous determine the character of the finish to a great degree.

Small, motor-driven tumbling drums have been offered to handloaders for case cleaning. Most are simply the devices of this kind which have long been used by amateurs for tumbling mineral specimens. Such specimens are put into the drum with a quantity of abrasive material and run as long as necessary, sometimes several days. For cleaning cartridge cases in these devices the directions have usually prescribed the use of sawdust.

These small machines have been ineffective in cleaning and brightening cartridge cases. Some improvement can be obtained by adding scouring powder to the sawdust, but the improvement is limited and this addition introduces a new problem of cleaning the scouring powder off and out of the cartridge cases one by one. The trouble is evidently that the very small drums do not provide sufficient fall of the contents.

A successful construction

The sketch details a successful tumbling keg construction. The keg is of 2-gallon size and in operation turns end over end. Ends of the staves are chipped out so the head can be lifted off for charging and emptying. It is held in place by a screen-door spring, doubled to give a strong clamping action and passed over a cleat on the head as shown.

Frame uprights are oak, drilled for the shafts and small oil holes then drilled in from the top for lubrication. Shafting, pulleys, setscrew collars, and belts are readily available hardware items. Any small electric motor of 1/30-horsepower or larger is sufficient. For a 1750-rpm motor, suitable pulley sizes are 1″ on the motor driving 6″ on the jackshaft, and 1½″ on the jackshaft driving 6″ on the keg. This turns the keg at 60-65 rpm, which should not be exceeded since higher speed might throw off the keg head.

Fill the keg about ⅓-full of cartridge cases, put in an equal volume of ground corncobs, close securely, and run for 30 minutes for pistol cases, longer for rifle cases as required. The time creates no problem since if construction is correct the machine does not have to be watched closely. After cleaning, separate cases and polishing material by sifting on a screen made of ¼″ hardware cloth, a wire mesh which is available under that name at hardware stores.

Chemical cleaning can be done by washing in several available materials. Commercial brass-cleaning chemicals are offered from time to time for cleaning cartridge cases. These vary in content, but they all operate by dissolving copper oxides from the surface. This is often accompanied by the removal of more or less brass, or of copper or zinc taken out of the brass. There is also the distinct possibility of an intergranular effect, seriously weakening the case. Some of these chemicals literally eat the brass up. Others leave the case a glaring yellow, which may be considered unattractive and certainly is unlike a new cartridge case of sound metal. The inconvenience and cost of purchasing these proprietary materials are also unfavorable factors in their use.

There are means of chemical cleaning which remove very little of the surface and which do not weaken the remaining brass.

The military arsenal method of cleaning cases is by 4% sulfuric acid dip. Commercial- or technical-grade sulfuric acid is satisfactory. Battery acid can be used if an acid hydrometer is available to adjust the solution to 4% strength. Mix and keep in a large crock. In mixing, *always pour the acid into the water,* never the water into the acid as then the heat developed on mixing might throw acid out of the vessel. A couple of pieces of potassium dichromate added to the solution give a brighter finish to the cartridge cases. The solution can be used a long time.

Make a small dipping basket of copper screen, *not iron.* Heat the solution until bubbles rise slowly but do not boil it. Dip the cases 4 to 5 minutes. Lift out, rinse in hot water, and if desired rub any stubborn spots with fine steel wool. Rinse again in slightly soapy water made with Ivory or other pure soap, and dry in a warm place to drive off trapped water. Do not worry about leaving a soapy film on the brass; it helps in resizing later.

This method is effective and safe for the cartridge case, as shown by its large-scale arsenal use. The acid costs very little. However, in small-scale use there are the practical inconveniences of heating the acid solution during employment, of keeping it off clothes in which it will eat holes, and in storing it between uses.

Vinegar and salt solution

Vinegar and table salt, long known as an improvised brass polish, have been used to clean cases. The cases are soaked for 15 to 20 minutes in a solution of 2 tablespoons salt to the quart of vinegar, shaking or stirring occasionally. They are then drained, and washed in running water at least 5 minutes. After washing, the necks of especially dirty cases may be wiped with a cloth. At the same time a cotton or cloth swab easily clears the primer pockets of residue, which is much softened by the treatment.

This solution cleans serviceably, but the cleaned cases soon tarnish. A rinse in straight vinegar before the water rinse has been recommended. In RIFLEMAN trial this did not prevent tarnishing.

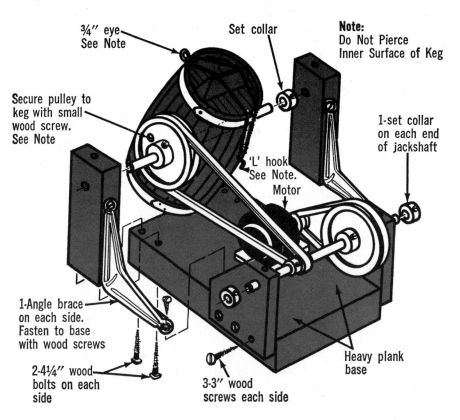

¾″ eye
See Note

Set collar

Note:
Do Not Pierce
Inner Surface of Keg

Secure pulley to keg with small wood screw.
See Note

'L' hook
See Note.
Motor

1-set collar on each end of jackshaft

1-Angle brace on each side. Fasten to base with wood screws

2-4¼″ wood bolts on each side

3-3″ wood screws each side

Heavy plank base

Inquiry of Frankford Arsenal established that this cleaning method does not harm cartridge brass.

The Arsenal remarked that another method which cleans quite satisfactorily is to soak the cartridge cases 5 to 10 minutes in 5% citric acid solution (a higher percentage in hard water), then thoroughly rinse in water. A final rinse in slightly soapy water can well be used as after the sulfuric acid dip. Citric acid is inexpensive and easily procured from drug suppliers, and it is not corrosive. A RIFLEMAN trial of this method gave very good results, and the cleaned cases did not tarnish unduly. This method leaves the cases not conspicuously bright, but obviously clean and in good condition.

Observation soon shows the extent of cleaning and brightening which can be obtained, and there is no need to soak beyond that.

A review of the above methods shows where each is most useful, either for giving a bright appearance to the cases or for cleaning large quantities of cases for sizing.

Care required in buffing

Buffing usually requires handling the cases one at a time, so is usually applicable to only limited quantities. Great care must be taken not to buff off any more metal than necessary. The finish produced is desirable only when cases as bright and smooth as possible are wanted, even though their appearance is somewhat artificial.

Tumbling in a barrel of adequate size works well. It is suitable for large quantities of cases, either to polish for appearance or to clean as preparation for reloading. It requires a barrel big enough for satisfactory action. The style and dimensions given in the illustration appear minimum. Industrial tumbling barrels are available, and represent one of the very best solutions to the problem of processing large quantities of cases.

The sulfuric acid dip gives excellent results for either purpose. It is suitable for large-scale or continuous employment. An individual handloader will have to consider whether his situation permits handling and storing this material in intermittent small-scale use.

Washing in citric acid solution involves low cost for materials, no equipment other than containers ordinarily available, safety, and effective cleaning. It is suitable for either large or small quantities of cases. It appears to be in many ways the best method for the handloader desiring the above characteristics and a finished case which is clean, of unimpaired strength, but only moderately bright. ∎

From The Loading Bench

An Effective Way To Anneal Cases

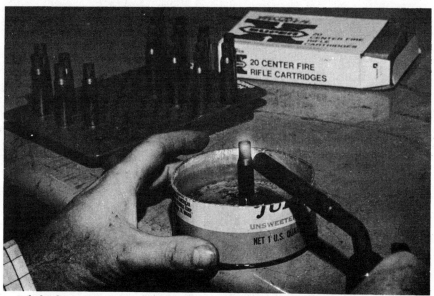

While the method of annealing case necks using a 700°F temperature-indicating crayon is excellent and preferred, an adequate job can be done without the crayon. A propane torch and an empty beverage can provide all the equipment required.

The can should be cut off at a height equal to about two-thirds the body length of the cases to be annealed, or 1¼" for cases such as the .30-'06. Aluminum beverage cans are most easily cut. The can should be filled with water to a depth equal to about one-half the body length of the case, or 1" for cases such as the .30-'06, or .270.

Cases should have empty primer pockets during annealing. If die-forming is required, as in converting cases from one caliber to another, that should be accomplished before annealing. If fire-forming of the neck and/or shoulder is required, that should be done after annealing.

The work area for annealing cases by this method should be as dark as practicable, with only enough light to carry on the operation. The shortened can should be set a few inches from the edge of the workbench, where it can easily be grasped and rotated between the thumb and finger of one hand.

The torch should be adjusted so that the blue inner cone of the flame is about ¾" long. It will burn steadily at that length, after proper throttle adjustment is made, so long as the tank is inclined downward, with the burner head approximately horizontal. The reason for working near the edge of the bench is that the tank must project beyond the edge of the bench to maintain the proper position of the torch.

The flame should be applied to the case neck, with the tip of the blue central cone about ¼" from the surface. The can should be rotated steadily, so that the case neck is heated evenly around its circumference. As soon as the neck is seen to reach a dull red glow, the flame should be removed. The case can then be tipped over into the water. Long cases will rest against the side of the can before they are completely submerged, but they can be handled by reaching beneath the water surface to grasp them near the bottom, between the thumb and finger. A can of larger diameter may be used for longer cases, of course, so that they are completely submerged after tipping over, but if the can is too large, it is inconvenient to grasp and rotate during heating of the neck.

The key to success by this method is to work in a darkened area, and learn to recognize the first appearance of dull-red heat in the case neck. Overheating the case does not create a dangerous condition, so long as the lower body is immersed in water, but it softens the neck excessively. With short-necked cartridges having fairly long bullet protrusion, a dead-soft case neck may not be strong enough to hold the bullet securely, and may bend if the cartridge is roughly handled.—W.C.D., JR.

CASE NECK ANNEALING

By WILLIAM DRESSER

Annealing necks of commercial cartridge cases to be reloaded is seldom necessary, provided reloading dies do not excessively resize the necks. Annealing may be necessary for cases to be used in a rifle whose oversize chamber permits too much neck expansion.

Frequently, however, cases are reformed from one caliber to another, often by drastically shortening the original case, necking down part of the body, and blowing out the forward portion of the remaining body to decrease its taper. The widespread availability of military cases makes such reforming appealing to economy-minded reloaders. Unless given some anneal, such cold-worked brass is certain to have a short useful life, and annealing becomes necessary. Often it is done in a rough-and-ready manner, but actually the operation calls for considerable care and uniformity for best results.

Case necks are finally annealed in manufacture to reduce their hardness to the point that season-cracking, the once common tendency of the necks of cases loaded and stored for a long time to split, has almost disappeared. Incidentally the splitting of case necks from repeated reloading is greatly reduced. At the same time, sufficient hardness and resilience must be retained to hold the bullet securely. Such annealing of necks in manufacture is closely controlled.

The marked cold working of cartridge brass in forming cases to other calibers work-hardens the brass to an excessive degree. It is unable to withstand repeated reloading and may fail on the first firing. Only careful heating of the work-hardened brass will permit a reasonable length of life for such cases.

Avoid excessive heat

Most reloaders excessively heat the necks, causing formation of a large-grain brass structure, extreme softness, and lack of 'spring', or ability to hold the bullets in the necks. This results from the usual advice, "Heat the case necks until red hot and then knock the cases over into water". While the necks so treated are indeed unlikely to crack, they may be so soft that they can be squeezed together between the fingers, which is a good way to judge their relative softness.

Metallographers tell us that temperatures up to approximately 500° F. do very little to break down a hard, cold-worked brass structure. By the time the temperature reaches approximately 700° F., the cold-worked structure is gone entirely. A new, fine-grained structure exists with almost all internal stresses removed, making an ideal form of brass for case necks and shoulders with adequate hardness and springiness but without any tendency to split. Such a process is termed 'grain refining'. This is the proper annealing process for most reloaders and for most case reforming, rather than the complete annealing so often practiced.

Further raising the temperature would only coarsen the grain structure, increasing the softness of the brass, lowering its resilience, and in no way improving its qualities. By the time a temperature of 1400° F. is reached, the brass is completely annealed and dead soft. Still higher temperatures 'burn' the brass and make it useless.

Actual 'red hot' temperature varies depending on the observation conditions, particularly the lighting. But even when only barely visible in pitch darkness, brass has already been heated far beyond the grain refining stage and made unnecessarily soft.

While an expert can more or less judge when this grain-refining temperature is reached by the bluish heat colors of the surfaces of highly polished case necks and shoulders, it is by no means easy to do with uniformity. The only consistent method for most persons is the use of a temperature crayon.

Such crayons are available from welding suppliers, etc. The ones I use are "Tempilstiks" and sell at $2 apiece. One crayon lasts for probably more cases than

Case necks annealed too soft can be detected by pressing them under the thumb (vary the hand grip by trial until greatest force is available)

Annealing case necks by heating with propane torch and dropping them into water

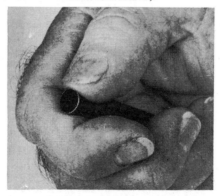

the average user will ever anneal. As the metal is heated, one runs the crayon across the surface (not in the flame) and when the metal reaches the temperature for which that crayon is made, the mark melts. Crayons are made for temperatures only 12° or 13° F. apart but most suppliers stock only those in 50° and 100° F. steps. I find that such crayons work better on cases as they are than on polished ones, eliminating an unnecessary operation. ("Tempilac" is a liquid material for the same purpose, and is applied with a brush. It is available from Brownells, Inc., Montezuma, Iowa.)

Method of work

A small but hot flame is essential. A propane torch is fine. I use the Bernz-O-Matic "Master" torch with utility burner unit, and work sitting down with knees spread wide apart. The gas cylinder is held under the left thigh with the burner sticking well out and up so that the flame comes about midway between the knees and shoots outward and upward. A pail of water is placed below to catch cases heated to the right temperature and dropped. Each case is held in the fingers of the right hand so the flame bathes the neck and part of the shoulder, and is rotated to spread the heat evenly.

Quick strokes of the temperature crayon are repeatedly made down the neck and shoulder, keeping the crayon out of the flame, until the marks liquify on the neck and also on the shoulder. The case is then dropped into the water. Except with very short cases, the heat should not come back to the head of the case enough to uncomfortably heat the fingers or in any undesirable way affect the case.

I use a 700° F. crayon for such annealing but the best one for you may depend somewhat on your technique, heat source used, recognition of liquification of crayon marks and, of course, on the cartridge cases that are being treated.

The real test is of the springiness of the annealed necks as compared to those of once-fired military or commercial cases of the same caliber. Give them the 'squeeze test' described, and be sure to intentionally overheat a few cases at first, some to the red stage, for comparison. A few trials with the crayon will enable you to establish a technique that results in quite uniformly annealed necks of the desired characteristics.

Such grain refining ordinarily works best as a final operation in reforming cases. It is quite unnecessary or of questionable desirability with many minor case reformings, and may do more harm than good if unnecessarily or incorrectly applied. In the more drastic reforming operations, with cases exceptionally hard originally in neck and shoulder areas or to be blown out to a caliber larger than the original, it may become desirable to do such work as an intermediate step, and again as a final operation. If it is done as an intermediate step, water cleaning and polishing before further forming operations are as necessary for you as for the cartridge case manufacturer. ∎

OLD CARTRIDGES FROM NEW

By KENNETH L. WATERS

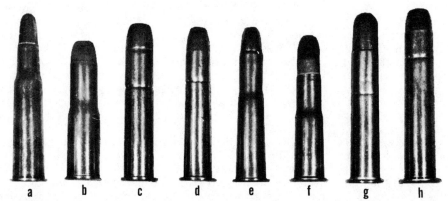

Old cartridges from new (l.-r.): (a) .348 WCF; (b) .45-75 WCF, which may be formed from .348; (c) .45-70-405, followed by three cartridges using the same case—(d) .40-65 WCF, (e) .38-56 WCF, and (f) .40-50 Sharps B.N.; Last pair, (g-h) .45-70-500 and .45-90-300, illustrate how shorter case of same diameter may be adapted for use in a rifle chambering a longer case by seating bullet out farther than normal

THIS article presents specific suggestions as to how cartridge cases for old rifles and one caliber of revolver can be formed from what is *actually available* today. It was thought that by this means many a fine old gun can again be used and enjoyed.

The actual dimensions of the various cartridges — unfired factory specimens, measured with a micrometer caliper— are listed on page 38 in tabular form in order of calibers, arranged for comparison. This table is a *guide only*. Dimensions vary, even between cases of the same caliber designation, and the nearest average figures have been given. Let the 'handloader' take care!

With only a few exceptions, the old cartridges were rimmed. However, a look at the table shows considerable variation in both the diameters and the lengths of the various cases, so a separation by head size (small, medium, and large) and by case length (short, medium, and long) is indicated. Too, some cases are straight, some tapered, and others bottle-necked in shape. These factors have a direct bearing, not only on the case to be selected for reforming, but also on the amount of difficulty which will be encountered, and the number (and therefore expense) of forming dies needed.

As an illustration of this, we will point out three examples, ranging from the simple to the more difficult.

All that is necessary to produce the old .38-50 Ballard Everlasting case is to shorten a .38-55 case by 3/16". The very slight difference in body diameter is negligible as being within normal chamber tolerances. Chambers of the older lever-action repeaters, especially, are usually found to be somewhat oversize, and will therefore generally accept a cartridge which is a few thousandths oversize. Rim diameter can vary even more and still work safely, but should always be large enough to assure the extractor catching on it. Case rim thickness also varies, particularly between foreign-made brass and American, and occasionally between certain of the early American cases. It may therefore be necessary to reduce the thickness of a case rim, either by hand filing, or by turning on a lathe. In either method, the metal must *always* be removed from the *front* of the rim, never from the base, as this would cause the primer to protrude.

The .40-65 WCF for the Model 1886 Winchester is a tapered case made from the well-known .45-70, which must be forced into a die to reduce the neck diameter from .45 caliber to .40 caliber. The length remains the same, that is 2-1/10", so no shortening is required. Dies for forming are available.

More work still is involved with the .40-50 Sharps bottle-neck case. The .45-70 case must be forced into one or more full-length sizing dies to reduce the neck diameter and, further, to form the bottle-neck shape. While the case is still in the die, it must be shortened to 1-11/16" by cutting the projecting neck off flush with the end of the die, using a three-cornered file ground smooth on the bottom flat, or by trimming to the proper length with a case trimmer.

Obtain sizing dies

The first problem is to find someone with the skill, tools, and willingness to make up the necessary sizing dies. I have been fortunate in this respect.

Forming the case is the biggest single step in our progress toward getting an "Old Veteran" firing again, but it is by no means the end. Those empty cases must be loaded, and this means more tools. For the single-shot rifle not requiring full-length resizing of the case or crimping of the bullet in the case neck, it is a relatively simple task, principally involving neck-sizing and bullet seating. For the lever-action or early slide-action rifles however, with their tubular magazines and more tolerant chamber dimensions, full-length resizing is a *must*. This can be accomplished in the die acquired for case forming, but the process is slower and involves considerably more time and work. Then, too, you'll need either a loading tool with crimping die, or one

KENNETH L. WATERS, *New Canaan, Conn., a firearms collector, bench-rest shooter, and handloader, had to make his own cases in order to shoot some of his single-shot rifles.*

of the old shell indentors, to hold the bullet firmly in the neck of the case against the pressure of the tubular magazine follower-spring. To a certain extent, homemade tools and kitchen-table methods can be improvised by the shooter who is not too particular about fine accuracy, but that sort of loading had best be left to the fellow who is satisfied with a loud bang.

Most manufacturers of reloading equipment can supply reloading dies for certain obsolete cartridges. Thus it would be advisable to obtain their die listings or query them concerning desired calibers.

Some reloading tools will neck-size only. If the rifle is a repeater it is advisable to select a tool that has the power to full-length resize, unless, that is, you are willing to follow the more arduous task of full-length resizing in a plain straight-line die used in a vise or arbor press.

An important word of caution. Many of the older rifles should definitely *not* be loaded with smokeless powders. These include the Maynard, Winchester Models 1873 and 1876, Marlin Model 1881, and cast-iron-frame Ballards. For cleaner shooting they may

actions of more modern steels, such as the Winchester High Walls, Winchester repeaters Models 1886, 1892, 1894, and 1895; the Sharps-Borchardt, Remington-Hepburn, Stevens #44½, and Marlin repeaters 1892, 1893, and 1895, all in calibers for which tested smokeless loading data are available.

If you're not sure of caliber . . .

If one is not *absolutely sure* of the cartridge his old rifle uses, he should by all means have a gunsmith make a metal or sulphur cast of the chamber and measure the cast with a micrometer caliper to determine what cartridge the rifle uses. At the same time, the bore should be 'slugged' by forcing a soft lead slug through the barrel with a brass rod, and measuring the slug to get the groove diameter. This is both a safety and an accuracy measure and will enable the shooter to order a bullet mold casting bullets of the proper size. Oversize bullets will cause a rapid rise in chamber pressures, and be deformed in a way to reduce accuracy. Undersize bullets will fail to grip the rifling properly and will be inaccurate.

While measuring the bore of a rifle, the rate of rifling twist should also be

grooves in the rifling. The steeper the rate of twist, the longer a bullet which may be fired accurately. A long, heavy bullet in a barrel of slow twist will almost certainly 'key-hole' (turn sidewise and tumble), ruining accuracy.

The Lyman Ideal Handbook lists the various rates of rifling twist for the common American makes of rifles, and the standard weight and style of bullets intended for them. This is good information except for special barrels and unlisted makes, which data can only be obtained by inspection and measurement as outlined above. Fortunately, Lyman still makes bullet molds for practically all of the old cartridges, including the big .50 calibers, which is a real 'break' for those who enjoy shooting the big old guns.

Chambers of individual rifles may vary somewhat, even more than do the cartridge cases. If a case proves too large for a push-fit in the chamber of your rifle, either the case must be sized down or the chamber of the rifle relieved slightly (if repeatedly found to be too tight). This latter procedure is quite acceptable within reasonable limits, such as the .45-2-4/10-inch Sharps being relieved to accept the .45-

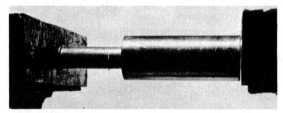

Using heavy-duty bench vise or arbor press, force case into full-length sizing die. Case should be lightly lubricated; too much oil will cause indenting of the case

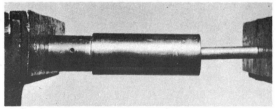

Formed case is ejected from die with knockout rod inserted in mouth of case. Hollow collar placed against base of die facilitates operation. Case is now trimmed to length and neck opening adjusted to fit bullet used. Inside edge is beveled to avoid shaving bullet

(l.-r.) .45-70 case; .40-50 Sharps bottle-neck full-length sizing die; reformed .45-70 case after ejection from die; reformed case trimmed to correct length; fire-formed .40-50 Sharps bottle-neck case

be loaded with about five grains of #4759 or DuPont Shotgun Smokeless in the base of the case as a priming charge, with the rest of the space loaded with blackpowder. This was an old Schuetzen method that produced good results and still will.

Heavier loads of smokeless powder are best restricted to the later, stronger

determined as it too will seriously affect accuracy unless a bullet of the proper weight in relation to caliber is used. This measurement is easily taken by pushing a cleaning rod with swivel handle through the bore and noting the distance the rod moves through the bore while making one complete revolution, its patch-fitted tip following the

90 Winchester case, which is exactly the same as the Sharps case except for thicker brass at the case mouth. In any event, do *not* spoil original, fine rifles by cutting barrels off at the breech and rechambering. The rifle's value will depart with that cut-off section.

Where modern cases are too short to duplicate the original, loading the bullets farther out in the case to give the same overall length will generally prove quite satisfactory and should not materially affect accuracy.

It is not claimed that all the conversions listed will make perfect replicas of the old cases. In some instances they will; in others, they will not. Every conversion listed in the table is considered both safe and reasonable in practice, subject, of course, to proper workmanship.━━━ ■

COMPARATIVE CARTRIDGE DIMENSIONS

Old Case	Length	Body Diameter	Rim Diameter	New Case	Length	Body Diameter	Rim Diameter	Comments
.22 Savage H.P.	2.05"	.418"	.498"	.25-35 WCF	2.04"	.413-4"	.501"	Full-length size
6 mm. Lee Navy	2.34"	.442"	.444"	.220 Swift	2.20"	.442"	.468"	Ream chamber for Swift rim. Seat bullet out
.25-20 Single Shot	1.62"	.314"	.375"	.22 Lovell	1.62"	.314"	.376-8"	Open up neck to .25 cal.
.25 Remington	2.05"	.417"	Rimless	.30 & .32 Remington	2.05"	.418-9"	Rimless	Full-length size
.25-36 Marlin	2.12"	.417"	.500"	.30-30 WCF	2.03"	.416"	.503"	Full-length size & seat bullet out
.256 Newton	2.44"	.468"	Rimless	.270 or 30-'06 .270	2.49" 2.54"	.466-70"	Rimless	Trim to 2.44" and full-length size
.30-30 Wesson	1.65"	.377"	.436"	.357 S&W Magnum	1.28"	.375-8"	.429-36"	Full-length size & seat bullet out
7.65 mm. Mauser	2.12"	.469"	Rimless	8 mm. Mauser	2.24"	.468"	Rimless	Trim to 2.12" and full-length size
.32 Extra Long Ballard	1.21"	.317"		.22 Lovell	1.62"	.314"	.376-8"	Trim to 1.21" and fire-form
.32 Ideal	1.75"	.350"	.404"	.32-20 WCF	1.31"	.348"	.403"	Seat bullet out & fire-form
.32-30 Remington	1.62"	.377"	.432"	.357 S&W Magnum	1.28"	.375-8"	.429-36"	Full-length size, seat bullet out, & fire-form
.32-40 Remington	2.12"	.455"	.534"	.303 British	2.21"	.452-5"	.525"	Trim to 2.12", full-length size, & fire-form
.32-35 Stevens & Maynard	1.87"	.400"	.498"	.32-40	2.12"	.417"	.498"	Trim case to 1.87" & relieve chamber
.32-40 Bullard	1.84"	.450"	.508"	.303 British	2.21"	.452-5"	.525"	Turn rim down, trim to 1.84", full-length size, & fire-form
8 x 50 Mannlicher (Model 1895)	1.97"	.488"	.560"	7.62 mm. Russian	2.11"	.484"	.564"	Trim to 1.96", open neck to 8 mm. (.321") and fire-form
8.15 x 46 R.	1.81"	.421"	.506"	.32 Win. Special	2.06"	.419"	.503"	Trim to 1.81", full-length size and fire-form
.33 Winchester	2.10"	.500"	.598-607"	.45-70	2.10"	.502"	.598-605"	Full-length size, trim & fire-form
.35 Winchester	2.41"	.457-9"	.539"	.405 Winchester	2.58"	.459"	.540"	Trim to 2.41" and full-length size
.35-30 Maynard 1882	1.56"	.400"		.38-55	2.13"	.418"	.499"	Trim to 1.56" and full-length size or relieve chamber
.35-40 Maynard 1882	2.06"	.400"		.38-55	2.13"	.418"	.499"	Trim to 2.06" and full-length size or relieve chamber
9 x 57 Mauser	2.24"	.468"	Rimless	8 mm. Mauser	2.24"	.468"	Rimless	Open neck to accept .357" bullets
9 x 56 Mannlicher	2.21"	.469"	Rimless	8 mm. Mauser	2.24"	.468"	Rimless	Full-length size & open neck for .357", trim to 2.21"
.375 Nitro Express British Flanged	2.50"	.457"	.510"	.405 WCF	2.58"	.459"	.540"	Trim to 2.50", turn down rim to .510" diameter and full-length size
.38-40 Remington Straight	1.75"	.454"	.534-5"	.30-40 Krag	2.30"	.457"	.541"	Trim to 1.75", size down, and fire-form
.38-45 Bullard	1.75"	(This is same case as .38-40 Remington—Use Krag case)						As above
.38-50 Remington Straight	2.25"	.454"	.535"	.30-40 Krag	2.30"	.457"	.541"	Trim to 2.25", size down to .454" and fire-form
.38-50 Maynard 1882	2.09"	.417"		.38-55	2.13"	.418"	.499"	Trim to 2.09"
.38 Extra Long	1.62"	.377"	.439"	.357 S&W Magnum	1.28"	.375-8"	.429-36"	Seat bullet out
.38-50 Ballard Everlasting	1.93"	.417"		.38-55	2.13"	.418"	.499"	Trim case 3/16"
.38-56 WCF	2.10"	.503"	.604-5"	.45-70	2.10"	.502"	.598-605"	Full-length size, trim & fire-form
.38-70 WCF	2.40"	.503"	.603"	.45-70	2.10"	.502"	.598-605"	Full-length size, fire-form, & seat bullet out
.38-72 WCF	2.58"	.458"	.521"	.405 WCF	2.58"	.459"	.540"	Full-length size & fire-form. May require turning down rim slightly
.400/.350 British Express	2.75"			9.3 x 74 mm.	2.91"	.465-6"	.523-5"	Trim to 2.75", size and fire-form
.400/.360 British Express	2.75"			9.3 x 74 mm.	2.91"	.465-6"	.523-5"	Trim to 2.75", full-length size, & fire-form. Neck-sizing to shoulder sometimes sufficient
.450/.400- 2⅜" British	2.37"	.550"		.348 WCF	2.25"	.546-53"	.604-10"	Thin rim from front end & fire-form
.40-40 Maynard 1882	1.75"	.454"		.303 British	2.21"	.452-5"	.525"	Trim to 1.75" and fire-form
.40-60 Maynard 1882	2.21"	.454"		.30-40 Krag	2.30"	.457"	.541"	Trim to 1.75", size down and fire-form
				.303 British	2.21"	.452-5"	.525"	Fire-form only
.40-70 Maynard 1882	2.37"	.454"		.30-40 Krag	2.30"	.457"	.541"	Trim to 2.21" and size down
.40-45 Remington Straight	1.87"	.454"	.549"	.30-40 Krag	2.30"	.457"	.541"	Fire-form only
.40-50 Sharps Straight	1.87"	.454"	.549"	.30-40 Krag	2.30"	.457"	.541"	Trim to 1.87", size down and fire-form
.40-50 Sharps Bottle-neck	1.68"	.503"	.599"	.45-70	2.10"	.502"	.598-605"	Trim to 1.87", size down and fire-form
.40-70 Sharps Bottle-neck	2.25"	.504"	.606"	.45-70	2.10"	.502"	.598-605"	Full-length size & trim to 1.68"
.40-70 Sharps Straight	2.50"	.453"	.537"	.30-40 Krag	2.30"	.457"	.541"	Fire-form and seat bullet out. May need sizing
.40-60 WCF	1.87"	.505"	.620"	.45-70	2.10"	.502"	.598-605"	Full-length size & trim to 1.87"
.40-65 WCF	2.10"	.503"	.603"	.45-70	2.10"	.502"	.598-605"	Full-length size
.40-70 WCF	2.40"	.504"	.604"	.45-70	2.10"	.502"	.598-605"	Full-length size & seat bullet out
.40-82 WCF	2.40"	.504"	.604"	.45-70	2.10"	.502"	.598-605"	Full-length size & seat bullet out
.40-72 WCF	2.58"	.459"	.519"	.405 WCF	2.58"	.459"	.540"	Same case as .405. Turn down rim
.40-110 Winchester Express	3.25"	.543-9"	.651"	.450/.400-3¼"*	3.25"	.542"	.618"	Full-length size & fire-form
.40-63 & .40-70 Ballard	2.37"	.475-7"	.555-61"	9.3 x 74 mm.	2.91"	.465-6"	.523-5"	Trim to 2.37" and fire-form
.40-85 Ballard	2.93"	.478"	.556"	9.3 x 74 mm.	2.91"	.465-6"	.523-5"	Fire-form. Rim may be too small
.43 Egyptian	1.91"	.574"	.652"	.500-3" Express (British)	3.00"	.573"	.641"	Trim to 1.91", full-length size, & fire-form
.44 Evans (New)	1.56"	.450"	.511"	.303 British	2.21"	.452-5"	.525"	Trim to 1.56" and fire-form
.44-60 Maynard 1882	1.75"	.499"		.45-70	2.10"	.502"	.598-605"	Trim to 1.75" and full-length size
.44-70 Maynard 1882	2.21"	.499"		.45-70	2.10"	.502"	.598-605"	Full-length size & seat bullet out
.44-77 Sharps & Remington Bottle-neck	2.25"	.512"	.625"	.43 Mauser (11 mm.)	2.34"	.510"	.584"	Trim to 2.25", full-length size. Rim may be too small
.44-100 Remington Straight	2.59"	.503"		.45-70	2.10"	.502"	.598-605"	Seat bullet out
.45 S&W American Revolver	1.09"	.478"	.520"	.45 Auto Rim	0.88"	.473"	.510-11"	Seat bullet out
.45-60 WCF	1.87"	.504"	.627"	.45-70	2.10"	.502"	.598-605"	Trim to 1.87"
.45-75 WCF	1.87"	.559"	.623"	.348 WCF	2.25"	.546-53"	.604-10"	Full-length size, trim to 1.87", & fire-form
.45-90 WCF & .45-85	2.40"	.500"	.602"	.45-70	2.10"	.502"	.598-605"	Seat bullet out
.45-85 Marlin	2.10"	.502"	.602"	.45-70	2.10"	.502"	.598-605"	Same case as .45-70
.45-55 Carbine	2.10"	.502"	.602"	.45-70	2.10"	.502"	.598-605"	Same case as .45-70
.45-75 Sharps (2-1/10")	2.10"	.500"	.597"	.45-70	2.10"	.502"	.598-605"	Use .45-70 as is
.45-2-4/10" Sharps Straight	2.40"	.500"	.597"	.45-70	2.10"	.502"	.598-605"	Seat bullets out. Neck may need thinning
.45-125 Winchester Express	3.25"	.553"	.601"	.450 Express* (British)	3.25"	.544"	.614"	Full-length size
.50-70 Government	1.75"	.563"	.660"	.500 Express	3.00"	.573"	.641"	Trim to 1.75" and turn down case
.50-95 Winchester Express	1.93"	.560-3"	.625-7"	.450 Express	3.25"	.544"	.614-6"	Full-length size, trim to 1.93", & fire-form
.50-110 Winchester Express	2.38"	.551"	.605"	.450 Express	3.25"	.544"	.614"	Trim to 2.38" and fire-form
.50-100 Winchester	Same case as .50-110							As above
.50-140 Winchester Express	3.25"	.551"		.450 Express*	3.25"	.544"	.614"	Fire-form only
.50-90 Sharps	2.50"	.563"	.663"	.500 Express	3.00"	.573"	.641"	Trim to 2.50" and turn down case
.50-3¼" Sharps	3.25"	.565"		.500-3¼" Express	3.25"	.573"	.641"	Turn down case to .565" body diameter
.50-50 Maynard 1882	1.37"	.553"		.348 WCF	2.25"	.546-53"	.604-10"	Trim & fire-form
.50-70 Maynard 1882	1.75"	.553"		.348 WCF	2.25"	.546-53"	.604-10"	Trim & fire-form
.50-100 Maynard 1882	2.31"	.553"		.348 WCF	2.25"	.546-53"	.604-10"	Fire-form only. Case necks may split here

*(British rim thinner)

81

MAKING CARTRIDGE

is the way to go when you've got the gun but the ammunition is obsolete or unobtainable.

To prepare a basic case for fireforming, load 10-15 grs. of fast burning powder and fill the case with dacron or cotton.

THE handloader may have various reasons for wanting to convert cartridge cases from one caliber to another. A common one, though not a very good one, is economy.

It is possible to produce cartridge cases for the 6 mm Remington, for example, by converting .30-'06 brass which is sometimes more plentiful and therefore cheaper. To do a satisfactory job, however, requires special case forming dies, and a reamer or neck-turning tool to thin the case necks. Annealing is usually required to obtain reasonable case life after such drastic reforming. The special equipment required will cost from $35 to $50, there is considerable tedious labor involved, and the cases will generally be inferior to new or once-fired 6 mm factory cases. About 200 new factory 6 mm cases can be purchased for the $35 cost of the dies and reamer, at current prices, and these cases will survive many reload-

ings if they are properly cared for. In this and most other instances, it is poor economy to convert cases from one caliber to another merely to avoid paying the price of new cases or factory loads that are readily available.

It often happens, however, that the handloader wants to prepare ammunition for use in a gun chambered for a foreign or obsolete type of ammunition that is not obtainable in the U.S. market. In that event, it is usually practicable to form the cases from another type of case that is obtainable.

There are literally hundreds of different calibers of unobtainable foreign and obsolete American ammunition for which serviceable guns exist, and detailed instructions for forming all of them are beyond the scope of this article. Only the general principles can be covered here. For more detailed information on the subject, there are two excellent books available. One is *The Home Guide to Cartridge Conversions*, by the late George Nonte, published by the Gun Room Press, 127 Raritan Ave., Highland Park, N.J. 08904. The other is *Cartridges of the World*, by Frank C. Barnes, published by DBI Incorporated, 540 Frontage Rd., Northfield, Ill. 60093. Both books give detailed dimensions of many different cartridges. Nonte's book also includes detailed text on the procedures for cartridge conversions, and suggests the cases of available types from which the cases of unavailable types

The versatility of one cartridge case is amply demonstrated below. To the left, a .30-'06 case has been sized, and trimmed and formed to yield a .22-250 cartridge half its size. At right is another .30-'06 and cases that can be made from it: .22-250, 6mm Rem., .25-'06 Rem., and .35 Whelen.

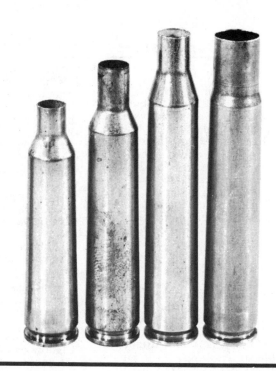

CONVERSIONS...
BY WILLIAM C. DAVIS, JR.

To see if neck reaming is required, try to slide a bullet into the neck of a fired case. If it goes in, reaming is unnecessary.

can be successfully formed. Both books also include information on recommended loads. The handloader who has a requirement that cannot be met by following the general procedures described here should refer to these more detailed references.

The first requirement for finding a case that is suitable for conversion is to know the chamber dimensions of the gun for which the ammunition must be prepared, or the dimensions of a cartridge that properly fits that gun. If the caliber can be identified,

at least one or two specimens of the proper cartridge can usually be obtained from cartridge collectors for measurement, or the dimensions can be found in one of the references mentioned above. If the caliber of the gun cannot be positively identified, then a chamber cast should be made. Most gunsmiths are prepared to perform this service, if the handloader is not able to do it for himself.

The principal requirements for a cartridge case to be converted are that it must have the same head configuration (rimmed, semi-rimmed or rimless) as the proper cartridge for the rifle; it must have very nearly the same diameter in the solid head just forward of the rim or extractor groove; and it must be practically as long, or longer, than the case to which it is to be converted. There are some exceptions to these requirements that are of interest to advanced and well-equipped handloaders, who may have a lathe to turn off the rim and cut an extractor groove in rimmed cases for conversion to rimless, or a heavy arbor press and special dies in which to swage the solid case head to smaller diameter, but these are beyond the capabilities of most handloaders.

The operations by which cases are converted from one caliber to another are die-forming, expanding, shortening, and neck-reaming or turning. One or more of these operations may be required for any particular conversion.

Die-forming can sometimes be performed in a single operation, using a full-length resizing die of the proper caliber for the gun, but only where the dimensional changes required are fairly minor. In most instances, special forming dies are required for best results. Depending on the extent of the dimensional changes required, one, two or three dies may be required. Forming dies for many common conversions are available from the RCBS Company, P.O. Box 1919, Oroville, Calif. 95965. The die-forming operation serves to reduce diameters on the case, and to reform the case shoulder where that is required. Die-forming should generally be done before the case neck and shoulder are annealed.

Thinning of the case neck is often required if the neck has been reduced in diameter during forming. To determine whether thinning is required, one test is to try a bullet of correct diameter in the neck of a case that has been expanded to fit the chamber. If the bullet does not enter freely, the case neck must be thinned, either by reaming, or by neck-turning on a tool made for that purpose. Another test is to seat a bullet in the resized case neck, and measure the diameter of the neck with a micrometer caliper. If the neck is not at least .002″ smaller than the neck of the chamber, as determined from a chamber cast, the neck should be thinned. Reaming or neck-turning is

Cartridge Conversions

seldom required if the neck has been expanded in the conversion, but it is occasionally required if the case that has been reformed had much thicker walls than the original cases of the caliber to which it was converted. The test should always be made, even when case necks have been expanded, because a case neck that is too thick can cause hazardous increases in chamber pressure. If bulleted loads are to be used for fire-forming, then of course the case neck must be of the proper thickness before assembling the fire-forming loads.

Expanding the case necks alone can sometimes be accomplished by use of a special tapered plug, comparable in function and use to the expander plug that is normally installed in a full-length resizing die. If expansion of the case body is required, it is most conveniently done by fire-forming. If the neck has been die-formed to the proper diameter, and the case trimmed to proper length, fire-forming can be accomplished by loading the case with a moderate powder charge and bullet, and firing it in the gun for which it is intended. It is also necessary that bulleted fire-forming loads have means of controlling headspace within acceptable limits. For rimless cases, this requires that an adequate shoulder be formed, in the correct position, before the case is fire-formed. The rim performs this function in rimmed cases.

Another method of fire-forming that works very well when both the case neck and the body require considerable expansion, as in forming .38-55 cases for a .30-30 brass, does not require use of a bullet. The case to be expanded is primed, loaded with a moderate charge of relatively fast-burning powder such as Hercules Red Dot, filled nearly to the mouth with Cream-O-Wheat cereal, and the mouth is plugged by a wad of cotton. The unbulleted cartridge is then fired in the chamber of the gun. The powder charge used should be no more than sufficient to form the case, and must be found by trial. A charge of 10 to 15 grs. is required to form .38-55 cases from .30-30 brass. More or less powder is required for larger or smaller cases. Initial trials should be with a charge small enough to be surely safe, and the charge should be increased in small increments until the case is formed satisfactorily. The .38-55 cases formed from .30-30 brass are somewhat shorter than original cases, incidentally, but are serviceable, though the seating die must be correspondingly shortened so the shorter case reaches the crimping shoulder if crimped

ammunition is required.

It is generally advisable to anneal the neck and shoulder of the case before fire-forming, to reduce the incidence of splitting in the forward body that sometimes occurs during the fire-forming operation. Trimming to a length slightly longer than that of the finished case required is good practice before fire-forming with unbulleted loads, because the expansion sometimes leaves the case mouth not quite square with the axis of the case. Trimming again after fire-forming will correct this condition, and bring the case to proper length. For fire-forming with bulleted loads, it is necessary to trim the case to proper final length before forming.

Shortening of cases converted from another caliber can be accomplished in the same way as trimming during ordinary reloading operations, but if much metal is to be removed, that is a laborious process. Time and labor are saved by cutting off the necks with a fine-toothed hacksaw blade, or with a jeweler's saw, to a length a little greater than the final length, and finishing the job accurately with a case trimmer.

For many of the large, obsolete blackpowder cartridges, none of the cases currently made by major manufacturers can be used for conversion. That also applies to some of the large English rifles made for African hunting. Fortunately, a few smaller manufacturers cater to the special requirements of such guns. These manufacturers usually advertise in the *American Rifleman* and other journals of the shooting sports. Some large cases of this type are currently available from Brass Extrusion Laboratories Ltd., 800 W. Maple Lane, Bensenville, Ill. 60106; RCBS Inc., P.O. Box 1919, Oroville, Calif.; and Dixie Gun Works, Highway 51 South, Union City, Tenn. 38261.

Cartridge conversion is a fairly complicated process, and the exact procedures vary considerably from one case to another. It is potentially hazardous, if incorrectly done. The handloader who undertakes it should have a thorough knowledge and understanding of the dimensional relationships that must exist between cartridge cases and chambers, and of the practical aspects of interior ballistics. This knowledge and understanding must generally be acquired by extensive experience in conventional reloading practices. Cartridge conversion is best left to the advanced handloader, who is familiar with all the appropriate safety precautions to be taken in such experimental work. It is not recommended for beginning handloaders, or those having only a casual interest and limited familiarity with the theory and practice of handloading. ∎

Load Switching

I have a strong bolt-action rifle chambered for the .35 Rem. cartridge. Since my rifle could safely withstand the pressures developed by the more powerful .358 Win. cartridge, it seems to me I could safely use .358 Win. loads in my .35 Rem. cases, and enjoy more powerful performance from my handloads. Do you agree?

Answer: What you propose could be extremely hazardous. The .35 Rem. cartridge has about 15 percent less case capacity than the .358 Win. Therefore, if you could manage to get a full .358 Win. powder charge into a .35 Rem. case, the density of loading would be about 15 percent greater than that of the same charge loaded in the .358 Win. For normal full-charge loads, the relationship between loading density and peak chamber pressure is such that the 15 percent increase in loading density would increase chamber pressure by about 25 percent. Thus, if the load developed 52,000 c.u.p. in the .358 Win. cartridge, it would develop about 65,000 c.u.p. in the .35 Rem. cartridge. That is definitely too much.

You should never try to adopt loading data from one cartridge to be utilized in another. Even professional ballisticians do not trust calculation as a basis for establishing safe maximum powder charges, without confirmatory pressure testing. There are no simple rules by which you can safely translate loading data from one cartridge to another, but the calculations are sufficient to show that what you suggest would be dangerous practice. — W. C. D.

Ball Definition

Why is the term "ball ammunition" used for service rounds when the bullets are not spherical but elongated?

Answer: "Ball," as applied to U.S. military small arms ammunition, usually designates a jacketed conical lead projectile used for training and competition or against enemy personnel and light materiel targets. The word itself is an anachronism dating back to the days when military projectiles were spherical rather than conical. By 1865, when both types of projectiles were in use, the Army Ordnance Bureau used the terms "Musket, elongated ball" and "Musket, round ball" to differentiate between the two types.

Today the word serves as a term for the most common service rounds as opposed to more specialized loadings such as armor-piercing, incendiary, tracer and blank.—P. D.

HOW TO MAKE CHAMBER CASTS

By WILLIAM E. POOLE

I⊤ is often necessary to determine the dimensions or configuration of a gun bore or chamber. The most convenient way to do this is by making a cast. The most suitable casting material is Cerrosafe, a low melting-temperature (158°-194°F.) bismuth alloy sold by gunsmith supply houses as chamber-cast metal. The technique for making bore and chamber casts is shown in the accompanying illustrations.

The gun bore and chamber should be cleaned before casting and then either oiled lightly or left dry. Quality of the casts will be improved if the barrel is preheated with hot water. This delays solidification of the metal, which helps prevent voids or seams in the cast.

Sulfur, paraffin, and lead are sometimes used for making chamber casts, but they are inferior to Cerrosafe for this purpose.

3 A small funnel with attached tube facilitates pouring the molten alloy into gun chamber. Tube was made by rolling aluminum foil around a rod. A cardboard or sheet-metal trough can also be used.

Tilting the barrel slightly, improves the quality of the casts by helping to release trapped air. The chamber should be filled to the mouth, but avoid overfilling since excess metal may enter action recesses and lock the cast in place.

The bore must be plugged to contain the molten alloy. This is done by inserting a tightly patched cleaning rod into the bore and leaving it in place until the cast has solidified. Light taps on the end of the rod will then loosen and eject the cast. Casts must be removed promptly. The alloy expands after cooling and the cast will seize if left in the barrel too long.

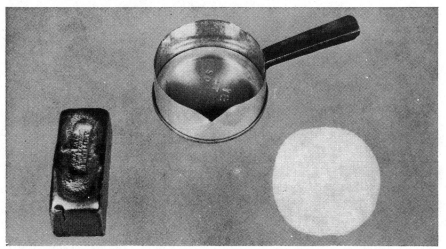

1 Materials required for casting include an ingot of Cerrosafe chamber-cast metal, pouring ladle, and cleaning patches to plug gun bore. Ladle shown was made by cutting down a small tin can. A well-cleaned bullet-casting ladle can also be used.

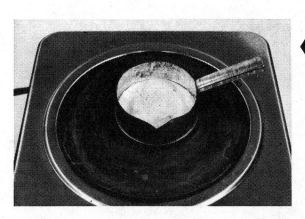

◄ 2 Cerrosafe alloy can be melted over any low-intensity heat source, including an electric hot plate, alcohol lamp, gas flame, or boiling water. For added convenience, melt the alloy in the ladle.

4 Making a cast at the rifle muzzle. A cast approximately 1½″ long will generally suffice. Spillage may be avoided by encircling the muzzle end of the barrel with a dam of masking tape.

5 Chamber and bore casts. Usual practice is to include a section of the rifled bore when making chamber casts. Cerrosafe shrinks slightly in initial cooling, but then expands. Expansion equals shrinkage approximately one hour after casting. Accurate measurements may then be taken. ■

Small-Base Sizing Dies

I handload for two .30-'06 rifles, a bolt-action Springfield and an autoloading Remington Model 742. I use a small-base sizing die for the Model 742 and have had no problems, but I don't fully understand the differences in rifles which make this necessary. Could you explain?

Answer: Proper functioning of semi-automatic rifles requires that the force required to extract the fired cartridge case be minimized. One of the factors affecting extractive effort is the initial clearance between the cartridge case and the chamber walls. If there is too little clearance, extraction effort is increased, and functioning may be less reliable. This is the reason that RCBS makes special small-base and ultra small-base sizing dies which reduce the case to smaller dimensions than standard dies for autoloading, pump and some lever-action rifles.

Another consideration is that the camming force for chambering the cartridge is limited and if too much effort is required for final closing and locking of the bolt, the bolt may not lock fully and the rifle will not fire. In bolt-action rifles such as the Springfield or Mauser, turning down the bolt handle exerts a powerful force through the mechanical advantage of bolt handle leverage and camming surfaces which move the bolt forward. Cases that are neck sized only will generally have some interference in the fit between the bolt face and the shoulder of the chamber, but in most bolt-actions this is easily overcome and goes unnoticed in most instances. In an autoloader, however, failures to fire may result if the case shoulder is not set back during resizing to provide headspace about equal to that of factory loads or new unfired cases.—W.C.D.,Jr.

Sabot Separation

Does the 55-gr. bullet used in the Remington Accelerator .30-'06 cartridge gain any velocity as the sabot is separated from it?

Answer: The bullet in the Remington .30-'06 Accelerator cartridge could not gain velocity when the sabot is separated from it. No moving body can increase its speed unless acted upon by a force exerted in the direction of its motion.

As soon as the bullet and sabot are far enough from the muzzle that the expanding powder gas is no longer pushing against them, within a few inches at most, both of them start to decelerate. The sabot cannot continue to push or even keep up with the bullet, so it falls away.—W.C.D., Jr,

BULLET TILT GAUGE

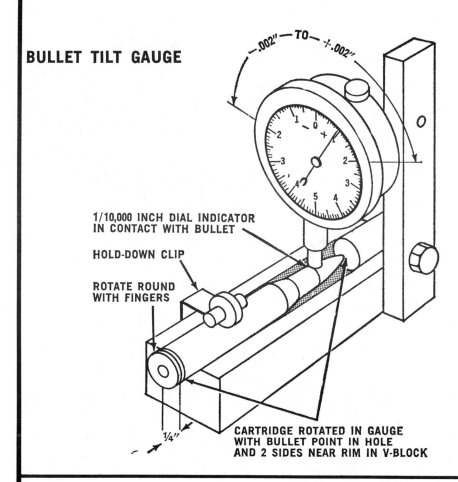

.002" — TO — +.002"

1/10,000 INCH DIAL INDICATOR IN CONTACT WITH BULLET

HOLD-DOWN CLIP

ROTATE ROUND WITH FINGERS

1/4"

CARTRIDGE ROTATED IN GAUGE WITH BULLET POINT IN HOLE AND 2 SIDES NEAR RIM IN V-BLOCK

DISTRIBUTION OF BULLET TILT

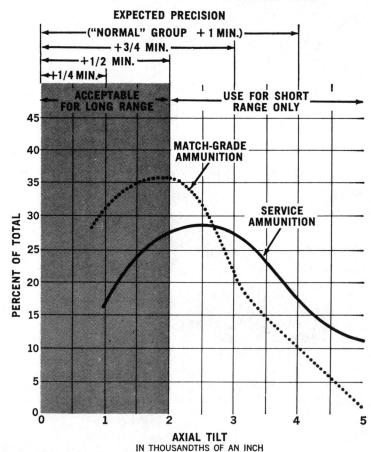

EXPECTED PRECISION

("NORMAL" GROUP + 1 MIN.)

+3/4 MIN.

+1/2 MIN.

+1/4 MIN.

ACCEPTABLE FOR LONG RANGE

USE FOR SHORT RANGE ONLY

MATCH-GRADE AMMUNITION

SERVICE AMMUNITION

PERCENT OF TOTAL

AXIAL TILT IN THOUSANDTHS OF AN INCH

GAUGING BULLET TILT

The most precise ammunition can be selected with a bullet alignment gauge

By A. A. ABBATIELLO

OTHER factors being normal, bullet tilt with respect to the case center-line affects group size. If the barrel length and twist are known, it has been found possible to predict the direction from the group center in which the tilted bullet will strike. If the amount of tilt is known, the distance from the group center can be predicted.

Significant score improvement has been noted by those who have tried such gauged ammunition.

In cal. .30 long-range shooting, the best match-grade ammunition will group in one to 2 minutes of angle under test conditions. Part of this spread is due to the bullet tilt with respect to the case centerline, imposed by the bullet-seating tool. This tilt displaces the bullet's center of gravity slightly to one side; in bullets such as the cal. .30 M1, the amount is about ⅛ the displacement of the bullet point. It enlarges groups by amounts up to one minute. These deviations become proportionately less as the tilt is reduced. Tilts over .004″ do not seem to increase the dispersion of the group beyond the expected one minute. Perhaps this is because a well-fitting chamber has a tendency to straighten any rounds which are excessively tilted. Other explanations are possible.

The gauge consists of a V-block which permits rotating the round about the bullet point and 2 tangent spots near the case head. A dial indicator which reads in tenths of thousandths of an inch (.0001″) bears on the bullet near the case neck. Half the total indicator reading is used as the displacement for determining the classes into which the rounds are separated. The high point is also marked at this time for orientation of the round in the rifle chamber.

Rounds with .002″ tilt or less can be considered good enough for long-range use, while those with .003″ and .004″ tilt are best used only at short ranges. In general, it was concluded from target results that each .001″ of tilt will increase the group spread about ¼ minute of angle, up to a maximum of .004″ as mentioned above.

Under test conditions, it was found that when the rounds were chambered with the high point always in the same orientation, the groups were smaller than when it was randomly oriented. Gauging and orienting the rounds can produce the smallest groups of which that ammunition is capable.

These ammunition refinements are becoming important, particularly in long-range matches.

The essentials of the tilted bullet were discussed in detail no less than 50 years ago by Dr. F. W. Mann in his book *The Bullet's Flight*. He pointed out that the balance of the bullet and the spiral path of the center of gravity are of high importance in accuracy.

Following a discussion between George L. Jacobsen of Frankford Arsenal and the writer at the 1959 National Matches, a trial of the effect of neck eccentricity was carried out by Jacobsen. He described his results in ".30-'06 Cartridge Cases And Accuracy", which appeared in THE AMERICAN RIFLEMAN, January 1960, page 20.

Seating tool a factor

The effects which Jacobsen found, though small, are essentially in agreement with the work reported here. However, he did not separate the effects of neck eccentricity and the bullet center-of-gravity location with respect to the bore. The angular direction of the bullet seating tool is a controlling factor in the initial position given to the bullet, rather than merely case neck eccentricity. Case necks can be centered or eccentric, and the bullet can be inclined in completely random directions. The tilted bullet is believed to be the main cause for center-of-gravity side shift.

The cal. .30 boattail bullet of 173 grs. weight was selected for these tests because it is in common use and is of sufficiently high quality for use in the National Matches.

Using the gauge shown, 42 ammunition lots were sampled and the high point was marked on each round gauged. These rounds were grouped in steps of .001″ bullet tilt, and the data tabulated. The results gave a bell-shaped curve for 829 rounds of match ammunition, peaking at about .002″ (see illustration). Measurements on Service ball ammunition produced a curve of similar shape, but peaking at about .0025″ tilt.

This graphically illustrates that even match-grade ammunition has appreciable variations. There is a large spread among particular lots and boxes. In general, 10% to 20% of each lot, depending on ammunition quality, falls into .003″, .004″ or even up to .010″ tilt. Run-of-the-mill ammunition can thereby enlarge groups to about twice the size which the same ammunition can show when it is gauged before firing.

Since the tilt angle of the bullet is so small (about ¼°) it is difficult to perceive visually. The gauge, however, makes the sorting a fast, routine step.

A mathematical solution of this problem was also tried (see box) and is in good agreement with the results obtained. It is gratifying to find the mathematical solution and the experimental results in agreement. ∎

Mathematical Solution

A laterally displaced center of gravity moves through the rifle bore in a helical (screw) path. The pitch of this helix is the pitch of rifling, and its radius is the lateral displacement of the center of gravity. On leaving the muzzle, the center of gravity continues in the direction it had at that point. For example, if it leaves at top of the bore and rifling is to the right, the departure will be to the right. The bullet travels approximately 21.5″ in a 24″ barrel, making 2.15 turns in the 10″ twist of rifling. The number of turns shows the orientation on emergence compared with that in the chamber before firing. The angle of emergence is that angle whose tangent is 2π times the lateral displacement divided by the rifling pitch. For .004″ point displacement and 10″ rifling pitch, the tangent is ⅛(2π) (.004)/10 and the corresponding angle is 1.1 minutes.

The displacement on target from this cause is proportional to the range and can be obtained without noting the angle. For example, .004″ point displacement gives in 10″ rifling pitch, so far as this mechanism goes, a target displacement at 100 yds. (3600″) indicated by the proportion .001π/10 = x/3600, from which x = 1.1″.

DETERMINING RIFLE ACCURACY

*How to deduce from a few test groups
the typical accuracy to be expected
from a rifle-ammunition combination.*

By WM. C. DAVIS, JR.

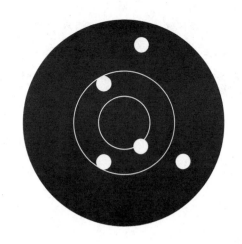

IN BRIEF

Riflemen all appreciate that successive target groups differ in size even when fired with the same rifle and ammunition. The aim of most accuracy testing is to learn what can be expected of a rifle-ammunition combination. This article provides the means of deducing, from only a few test groups, the typical accuracy which probably will be obtained in the long run. The amount of variability also can be forecast, so the rifleman can know the proportion of very large and very small groups to expect and not be misled by them.

THE riflemen-experimenter making accuracy tests of equipment is meticulous about certain details. He often weighs powder charges, and perhaps also his bullets, to .1 gr. He fires from bench rest, using a high-power telescope to minimize his aiming error. He measures the spread of each group carefully, sometimes to .01″ or .001″.

The worth of conclusions which he draws from all of this is still dependent on the care with which he analyzes his data. At this point the exactitude of his methods often breaks down.

There is in each of us a certain intuitive conception of statistics, chance, and probability, though this intuition is not refined enough for evaluating technical experiments. Laplace, a famous mathematician, once wrote that ". . . the theory of probabilities is at bottom only commonsense reduced to calculation: it makes us appreciate with exactitude what reasonable minds feel by a sort of instinct."

It is not tiresome, and one need not be a mathematician, to make use of certain statistical principles in analysis of

accuracy-test data. Most who conduct careful experiments in accuracy will indeed find satisfaction in analyzing their data according to sound principles.

Basically, the rifleman is interested in 2 accuracy characteristics of his rifle-ammunition system. First, what is the typical group size which it produces? Second, how dependably does it produce groups which are close to this size?

Often it is said that a particular rifle-ammunition system is "capable of minute-of-angle groups", or some similar performance. Not infrequently, such a statement is based on the fact that one or 2 such groups have been made. It is argued that if even one such group has been produced, then the capability has been demonstrated, and all larger groups must be ascribed to some error of the rifleman or the external conditions. Larger groups are often charged rather vaguely to poor holding or a changing breeze, and arbitrarily disregarded in evaluating performance. The fallacy here is that the manifestation of chance is being ignored.

Fortunately, there are means of deducing from limited data the **typical** accuracy which can be expected from a rifle-ammunition combination. It is possible even to estimate the probability of producing groups which are more than or less than a specified size.

In recent years, Frankford Arsenal and some other technical and scientific establishments have carried out certain investigations into both the experimental and theoretical aspects of rifle-ammunition accuracy. Details of these studies are voluminous and complicated, but the results have given certain simple and useful relationships. These can be easily applied by experimenters who have no special familiarity with statistics or mathematics beyond the solving of simple formulae.

Perhaps the most significant observa-

tion is that rifle accuracy performance is statistically 'well behaved'. The long-run results follow well-established and predictable patterns. In various experiments, gun-ammunition combinations were used which produced small extreme spreads, and others which produced large extreme spreads. For any given gun-ammunition combination, whether its long-run average was large or small, the same statistical patterns were found so long as the conditions remained unchanged.

It is further of interest that the relationships observed in actual tests were in good agreement with those which a statistician would predict, making only certain basic assumptions about the distribution of the pattern of shots and without necessarily examining any data from actual targets. The results of various experiments have been thus consistent not only with each other but with statistical theory as well. This leads to confidence in the general applicability of the conclusions.

Only 5-shot groups

Although accuracy investigations included both 10-shot and 5-shot groups, only 5-shot groups will be discussed here. In terms of statistical reliability, it makes little difference whether one fires his ammunition in 5-shot groups or 10-shot groups. Ten rounds of ammunition yield information of about the same reliability whether fired in one group of 10 shots or 2 groups of 5 shots each. However, careful attention to sight picture, firing position, trigger control, and wind conditions is more easily maintained for 5 shots than for 10. This is especially true if the rifle has appreciable recoil or muzzle blast, and if the rifleman is not highly trained and in top shooting condition. Consideration of the human element, therefore, indicates that dividing the ammunition to be fired into 5-shot groups, with rest periods between, probably is better for most nonprofessional experimenters who are testing for equipment accuracy.

The long-run average for extreme spread of 10-shot groups is about 1.3 times the average for 5-shot groups. Thus, if the average for 5-shot groups is 2.0″, the average for 10-shot groups would be about 2.6″ under the same conditions. If the average for either is known, the average for the other can easily be estimated. However, the group-to-group variation for 10-shot groups is generally a bit less than that for 5-shot groups. There is no very simple and accurate way to estimate the variation of the one from the known variation of the other.

The formal technical investigations of accuracy usually include mean radius and other measurements of dispersion besides the extreme spread. Only the extreme spread will be considered here. Some of the other dispersion measures are slightly more reliable than extreme spread on statistical grounds, but for 5-shot groups the improvement is not very great. Furthermore, the extreme spread is so universally used in America that few have any intuitive appreciation for other dimensions.

Typical accuracy

Generally, the rifleman wishes first to establish the **typical** accuracy which his rifle-ammunition system will produce. It is basic to our intuitive concepts, and generally acceptable to statisticians as well, that an **average** gives a satisfactory representation of a typical value. It is also obvious to us intuitively that the average of 10 groups is more meaningful than the average of 2, and the average of 20 groups would be better than 2 or 10. In fact, we should like to know the average of an unlimited number of groups, all fired under the same given conditions. This concept of the average of an unlimited number of observations is often called by statisticians the population mean; we shall call it the **long-run average.**

The actual long-run average cannot, of course, be precisely known, as we cannot fire an unlimited number of groups to ascertain it. We can estimate it within certain limits by firing only one group, although an estimate based on one group would be quite crude, and the error might be quite large. We can estimate it more closely by firing 2, or 10, or 20 groups. The averages of 2 or 10 or 20 groups are called by statisticians sample means; we shall call them **test averages.**

In general we must always be satis-

fied with a test average which is only an approximation of the actual long-run average. However, we can refine our estimate of the long-run average to any desired degree by increasing the number of groups we are willing to fire.

Let us, for convenience, designate the **long-run average** by the letter **L,** and the **test average** by the letter **T.** Use the letter **N** to indicate the **number** of 5-shot groups included in our tests to find **T.** Fig. 1 enables us to see how reliably we can estimate the long-run average **L** from the firing of **N** test groups which give a test average of **T.**

The shaded bars in Fig. 1 indicate the limits of the range within which we can say that the long-run average probably will lie. We must here define our use of the word 'probably'. For our purposes in Fig. 1, we may consider that 'probably' implies 9 chances in 10 of our being correct. If we used Fig. 1 in a great many cases to estimate the

range within which **L** will lie, we should expect to be correct in about 90% of those cases. In about 5% of them we would expect **L** to fall below the estimated range, and in about 5% we would expect it to fall above the estimated range. We could, of course, use another definition of 'probably', and adjust Fig. 1 accordingly. The definition of 'probably' is arbitrary, but consistent with our usual concept of the term.

The shaded bars in Fig. 1 illustrate graphically how our estimate of the long-run average improves as we fire a larger number of test groups.

To use Fig. 1, we first determine the average extreme spread of all of our 5-shot test groups, and designate this **T.** The number of groups which make up this average we designate **N.** Looking now in the **N** column for the appropriate number of groups, we observe in the **L** column the corresponding limits. These are given in terms of **T.** Between

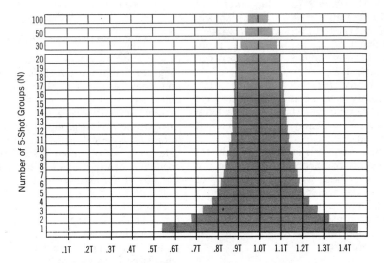

Fig. 1 Probable Limits of Long-Run Average (L) in Terms of Test Average (T)
(Extreme Spread of 5-Shot Groups)

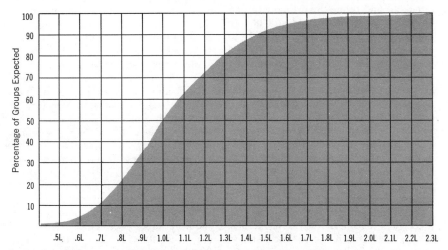

Fig. 2 Group Sizes in Terms of Long-Run Average, L (Extreme Spread of 5-Shot Groups)

these limits, our long-run average probably will lie.

To illustrate, let us consider some data from a shooter's notebook. A test was being conducted to develop a low-power practice load for a .30-'06 Model 70 Winchester rifle. The bullet was Ideal No. 311334, with a charge of 14.5 grs. IMR 4227 powder. Twenty bullets were sized to .308″ diameter and an equal number to .310″. Four 5-shot groups were fired from bench rest with each size of bullet at 100 yds. Following were the extreme spreads:

	(.308″ Bullet)	(.310″ Bullet)
Group 1	1.46″	1.97″
Group 2	1.33″	1.97″
Group 3	1.18″	3.07″
Group 4	1.61″	1.73″
Test Average (T)	1.40″	2.18″
Number of Groups (N)	4	4

Considering the load with .308″ bullets, we find in Fig. 1 that for $N = 4$, the corresponding limits are from .77T to 1.23T. Our upper limit is therefore 1.23 x 1.40″ = 1.72″. Our lower limit is .77 x 1.40″ = 1.08″. We can say then that the test average (T) was 1.40″, and that the long-run average (L) probably lies—in round figures—between 1.1″ and 1.7″.

Similarly, for the load using .310″ bullets we have obtained a test average of 2.18″, and can show that the long-run average probably lies between about 1.7″ and 2.7″.

These are reasonably meaningful statements of accuracy. They give not only the best available estimate of average performance, but also some idea of the precision with which this estimate was made. It is clear in this instance that the .308″ bullet diameter is to be preferred.

Variations from typical

We now know how to estimate our long-run average group size from our test data, and refine the estimate to any desired degree. We should still like to know how our group sizes are likely to vary around this typical value. This can be determined directly, of course, by firing a sufficiently large number of groups and observing the actual variation among them. The statistical procedure for this was described in a very informative article by Kermit LaFleur (THE RIFLEMAN, May 1958). A difficulty with this procedure is that a rather large number of groups—usually at least 20—must be fired to obtain any reasonable accuracy.

Fortunately, extensive tests (and also theoretical considerations) have recently shown that the **long-run variation** in group sizes is reliably related to the

NOTE ON THE STATISTICAL METHODS

The basic 'model' used by statisticians for the theoretical study of accuracy is the circular normal distribution. The hypothesis is that a large number of shots fired at a vertical target form a pattern of impacts in which the vertical coordinates are normally distributed, the horizontal coordinates are normally distributed, the variances of the 2 distributions are about equal, and the vertical and horizontal coordinates are uncorrelated. The properties which statisticians have predicted from this model agree very well with the properties actually observed in extensive testing.

Figs. 1 and 2 are based on a somewhat simplified analysis of empirical data from several thousand rounds of firing. However, they are substantially consistent with the properties of the theoretical model of dispersion.

Fig. 1 is based specifically on the following premises:

1. The coefficient of variation of a 'population' of 5-shot extreme spreads is 28%.

2. If the population is divided arbitrarily into subgroups of **N** targets each, the means of these subgroups are nearly normally distributed, with a variance inversely proportional to **N**. (Actually, the distribution of individual extreme-spread values is characteristically skewed, but no great error in probabilities is introduced by treating the distribution of means of such values as a normal distribution.)

3. The fiducial probability that the population mean lies between the limits shown in Fig. 1 is .90.

Fig. 2 is based on a log-normal curve fitted to the distribution of extreme spreads obtained from about 300 actual targets. If a fitted log-normal curve and the actual data are made to agree as to the number of targets, the mean, and the standard deviation, the observed and predicted frequencies in class intervals thus obtained are in good agreement, although a more sophisticated analysis might yield a still better representation than the log-normal curve for this type of distribution.—W.C.D.

long-run average itself. This is an uncommonly useful fact, because it enables us to obtain from the average extreme spread alone a very good estimate of the typical group-to-group variation. (Theoretical considerations indicate a value of about 28% for the coefficient of variation of 5-shot extreme spreads. Test experience agrees very well with this figure.)

Fig. 2 enables us to deduce some facts about group-to-group variation from our estimates of long-run average group size. Suppose we wish to know what size group we can expect to equal or better in 90% of our firings. Consulting Fig. 2, on the vertical scale at the left we find that the 90% line intersects the curve at about 1.46L. This means that about 90% of our groups should have extreme spreads not exceeding 1.46 times our long-run average.

For example, suppose we have fired a fairly large number of 5-shot groups and arrived at a satisfactory estimate of our long-run average (L), and this estimate is 1.50″. We can therefore expect about nine-tenths of our groups to be 1.46 x 1.50″ = 2.19″ or less. If we look at the 10% line on Fig. 2, we see that it intersects the curve at about .68L. The best 10% of our groups should therefore be .68 x 1.50″ = 1.02″ or less. We should not be surprised, then, if this rifle which averages 1½″ should produce occasional groups which are larger than 2″ or smaller than 1″. Such occasional groups reflect merely

the inevitable variations of chance.

However, should our group sizes vary much more widely than this on frequent occasions, then there is reason to suspect that our test conditions are not unchanging, and we should seek out the cause. Groups varying much more widely than we can expect from chance may indicate imperfect wood-to-metal contact in the bedding, loose or binding elements in the sighting system, or some other mechanical defect, or errors in loading the ammunition. Such defects can actually change the test conditions during the course of our firing, and give erratic and unpredictable results from group to group. On the other hand, it is futile to be trying continually to correct fancied errors in our equipment because of variations which are merely manifestations of chance.

Another example of data from a shooter's notebook illustrates the practical usefulness of Figs. 1 and 2. A new barrel had recently been fitted to a single-shot .219 Donaldson rifle. The Winchester high-wall action had previously been barreled in the same caliber, but chambered for an earlier version of the .219 Donaldson case which had a slightly shorter neck. A supply of cases remained which had been trimmed for the earlier chamber. The question to be settled was whether these cases, with their rather short necks, could be used with satisfactory accuracy in the chamber of the new barrel.

Twenty new cases were formed, and

trimmed to the maximum permissible length for the new chamber, which was 1.785". Twenty of the older cases, trimmed to 1.750", were taken for comparison. Both groups of cases were assembled with the same components and loaded to the same over-all length of cartridge. The load, which had previously been used with good success, was 30.0 grs. IMR 4064 powder and a 55-gr. Sierra spitzer bullet.

Four 5-shot groups were fired from bench rest at 100 yds. with each ammunition sample, giving extreme spreads as follows:

	Sample A (1.750" Cases)	Sample B (1.785" Cases)
Group 1	.73"	.91"
Group 2	.66"	1.10"
Group 3	1.00"	1.38"
Group 4	.93"	1.10"
Test Average (T)	.83"	1.12"
Number of Groups (N)	4	4

For Sample A, the test average was .83". Since 4 groups were fired with Sample A, **N = 4**. The limits for the probable long-run average shown in Fig. 1 at **N = 4** are .77**T** to 1.23**T**. The lower limit in this case is therefore .77 x .83" = .69". The upper limit is 1.23 x .83" = 1.02". The long-run average of 5-shot groups probably would lie between about .69" and 1.02" for cartridges like those of Sample A. Similarly, for Sample B, the lower limit is .77 x 1.12" = .86", and the upper limit is 1.23 x 1.12" = 1.38". Thus the long-run average for cartridges like those of Sample B would probably lie between about .86" and 1.38".

We see that the Sample A, with the shorter cases, actually gave a somewhat smaller test average than did Sample B. From this we might be tempted to conclude that the accuracy was improved by trimming the cartridge cases some .035" shorter than necessary. (This might, in fact, be true, or perhaps there were other differences between the old and new cases.) However, we also see that our long-run average with Sample A might well be as large as 1.02", whereas the long-run average for Sample B might well be as small as .86". We have not proved which was better. If there is a real difference in accuracy associated with the difference in case length, it is too small to be detected reliably by firing eight 5-shot groups. In any event, it seems unlikely that the short cases had any seriously bad effect on accuracy, and from this viewpoint at least they are suitable for use. This was the point to be determined.

To carry this experiment further, records were maintained for a time on the 5-shot groups later fired with this same rifle and load during sighting-in on various occasions. These groups were

as follows, including the first 4 groups which were shown above for Sample A:

Group Number	Extreme Spread	Group Number	Extreme Spread
1	.73"	12	.75"
2	.66"	13	1.04"
3	1.00"	14	.65"
4	.93"	15	.71"
5	.84"	16	.82"
6	.85"	17	.67"
7	.79"	Test Average (T)	.87"
8	1.34"		
9	.92"		
10	.97"	Number of Groups (N)	17
11	.86"		

Having data now on 17 groups, we have a rather good estimate of the long-run average. In Fig. 1 we see that the limits for **N = 17** are from .89**T** to 1.11**T**. Since our test average is now .87", we estimate that our long-run average **L** should lie between about .77" and .97".

If we accept .87" as a satisfactory estimate of our long-run average **L**, then we can obtain some interesting data from Fig. 2. Since that figure shows that about 90% of our groups should be 1.46**L** or less, we can expect about nine-tenths of our groups to be 1.46 x .87" = 1.27" or less, if our estimate of the long-run average is a good one.

Suppose we wish to know how often our groups are likely to be smaller than 1" with this rifle and load. Assuming that our long-run average **L** is .87", we divide 1.00 by .87 and get 1.15. This means that a 1" group is 1.15 times our long-run average, or 1.15**L**. This value on the horizontal scale of Fig. 2 corresponds to about 67% on the vertical scale. We can therefore expect to obtain groups of 1" or better about 67% of the time, or about 2 times out of 3, in the long run. Of the 17 groups fired, 14 of these, or about 82% were less than 1". This percentage is slightly better than we can expect in the long run.

Procedures easily learned

These procedures are very easily learned by practice, and are not laborious. This is not a sophisticated treatise in statistics. Statisticians, with their special skills, can make a much more precise and thorough analysis of data than we have done here. These methods are simple and reasonably accurate ones for those of us who are not statisticians; they are very much more reliable than the unguided intuition which is often our only alternative. Application of these principles to our accuracy testing will enable us to speak to each other with some common understanding of our results. It can help us to interpret meaningfully the data which we have acquired, and guide us in the design of new and more interesting experiments in rifle accuracy. ∎

Washing Cartridge Cases

I'd like to use a dishwasher for cleaning powder residue and sizing lubricant from decapped rifle and pistol cases. They will be held in racks, neck down in wire baskets to drain, and when the wash cycle is complete, a heater coil will evaporate any remaining water. What detergent can I use which won't harm the brass?

Answer: Your idea for cleaning cases in a dishwasher sounds like a good one. I believe it would be hard to improve upon detergents made for automatic dishwashers, such as Cascade, for washing cases. I have used this product for cleaning very dirty cartridge cases, though not in a dishwasher, and it seems to do a very good job.

It is a powerful degreaser, and does not attack the brass. I left a case immersed in a solution of Cascade for seven days and there was no evidence of action on the brass itself, only on the dirt. The active ingredients are various phosphates of sodium, and are not harmful to brass as far as I know, or as far as my experience indicates.—W.C.D., Jr.

Case Tumbler Caution

I have some ammunition which has become dirty and discolored, though it doesn't show deep corrosion. Can a case tumbler be used on loaded ammunition?

Answer: I haven't heard of accidental firing of a cartridge cleaned in a tumbler, but I cannot assure you that it positively will not occur. I would not advise tumbling loaded ammunition.

Dirt can be cleaned from ammunition by wiping cartridges with a soft cloth, moistened slightly with mineral spirits (paint thinner), if necessary, but be careful to use only a small amount of thinner, as too much will seep into the cartridge, spoiling the powder or primer.

Discoloration due to corrosion will do no harm when you fire the ammunition. If cases are deeply pitted from corrosion they may rupture if fired, so it is best not to fire heavily corroded ammunition. After firing, the cases can be cleaned in your tumbler before reloading them; that is the safest practice.—W.C.D., Jr.

BY WILLIAM C. DAVIS, JR.

Handgun Cartridges In Rifles (And Vice Versa)

Cartridge characteristics, not barrel length, determine the most efficient powders for rifle-revolver loads.

THE idea of a handgun and rifle using the same ammunition was popular more than a century ago. Shortly after the .44-40 cartridge was introduced with the Winchester Model 1873 rifle, Colt offered their famous Single Action Army revolver chambered for the same cartridge. Later cartridges offered for these guns included the .38-40 and .32-20, both popular calibers in blackpowder days.

Men on the Western frontier in the 1800s saw an advantage in owning a rifle and handgun that fired the same ammunition. A frontiersman carrying such a rifle and revolver, and transporting all of his own provisions for months, far from a source of resupply, was relieved of carrying two different types of ammunition. The logistic necessity no longer exists, but for different reasons there has been a revival of interest in rifles that can fire handgun ammunition, and vice versa.

Cartridges chosen for testing here were the .222 Rem. and .30-30 Win., both popular rifle cartridges offered in the Contender pistol; and the .357 and .44 Mag. handgun cartridges that are often used in rifles. Guns used for the .222 were a Sako custom rifle with 20″ barrel and a Contender pistol with 10″ barrel. For the .30-30, a Winchester Model 94 carbine with 20″ barrel and a Contender pistol with 10″ barrel were used. Guns for testing .357 Mag. loads were a Ruger Security Six revolver with 6″ barrel, and a custom Martini Cadet rifle with 25″ barrel. The .44 Mag. ammunition was fired in a Herter's Powermag single-action revolver with 6½″ barrel and a Remington Model 788 rifle with 22″ barrel.

Table 1 gives results obtained in the .222 Rem. rifle and in the handgun of the same caliber. These indicate that highest velocity obtainable at acceptable chamber pressure is obtained with IMR-4198 powder, among the three types tested in this

TABLE 1 — .222 REM. CARTRIDGE WITH 50-GR. SOFT-POINT BULLET

DU PONT POWDER	CHARGE WEIGHT (grs.)	VELOCITY IN 20″ RIFLE BARREL (f.p.s.)	VELOCITY IN 10″ PISTOL BARREL (f.p.s.)	VELOCITY DIFFERENCE (f.p.s.)
IMR 4198	20.5	3153	2631	522
IMR 4227	17.5	2990	2570	420
SR 4759	16.5	2698	2278	420

TABLE 2 — .30-30 CARTRIDGE WITH 150-GR. SOFT-POINT BULLET

POWDER TYPE	CHARGE WEIGHT (grs.)	VELOCITY IN 20″ RIFLE BARREL (f.p.s.)	VELOCITY IN 10″ PISTOL BARREL (f.p.s.)	VELOCITY DIFFERENCE (f.p.s.)
IMR 4227	20.0	1758	1518	240
IMR 4198	28.0	2220	1932	288
IMR 3031	35.5	2285	1969	316
WW 748	34.5	2181	1829	352
RELOADER 7	25.5	2040	1788	252

TABLE 3 — .357 MAG. CARTRIDGE WITH 125-GR. JACKETED SOFT-POINT BULLET

POWDER TYPE	CHARGE WEIGHT (grs.)	VELOCITY IN 25″ RIFLE BARREL (f.p.s.)	VELOCITY IN 6″ REVOLVER BARREL (f.p.s.)	VELOCITY DIFFERENCE (f.p.s.)
UNIQUE	9.0	1709	1383	326
BLUE DOT	15.5	2204	1593	611
2400	17.8	2037	1360	677
WW 231	8.1	1668	1302	366
WW 630	15.4	1949	1400	549
WW 296	18.5	2038	1343	695
IMR 4227	19.0	1977	1387	590
FEDERAL 357B	—	2286	1623	663

TABLE 4 — .44 MAG. CARTRIDGE WITH 240-GR. JACKETED SOFT-POINT BULLET

POWDER TYPE	CHARGE WEIGHT (grs.)	VELOCITY IN 22″ RIFLE BARREL (f.p.s.)	VELOCITY IN 6½″ REVOLVER BARREL (f.p.s.)	VELOCITY DIFFERENCE (f.p.s.)
UNIQUE	10.6	1414	1146	268
BLUE DOT	18.5	1788	1369	419
2400	22.0	1677	1271	406
WW 231	11.2	1442	1203	239
WW 630	19.6	1705	1328	377
WW 296	24.0	1768	1344	424
IMR 4227	24.0	1714	1306	408
REM. FACTORY LOAD	—	1737	1288	449

cartridge. Although the velocity difference between the rifle and the pistol was greatest with this powder, as was expected because it has the slowest burning rate, IMR-4198 still produced higher velocity than did either of the faster-burning powders, even in the 10″ pistol barrel. IMR-4227 is a relatively slow-burning powder for handgun loads, yet it is clearly too fast burning for best velocities at acceptable pressure in the 10″ Contender barrel. It is clear that the faster-burning handgun powders would compare even less favorably with IMR-4198 in loads for a .222 handgun. Powders slower burning than IMR-4198 would also be less advantageous in the handgun. The charge weight of such powders is limited by the capacity of the cartridge case, and they cannot match the velocity performance of IMR-4198, even in rifle barrels, much less so in the 10″ barrel of a handgun.

Table 2 gives the results for the .30-30 Win. cartridge fired in the Model 94 Winchester carbine and the Contender pistol. Results are similar to those obtained with the .222 Rem. The powder producing highest velocity in the 20″ .30-30 barrel, IMR-3031, also produced the highest velocity in the handgun. The difference between IMR-3031 and IMR-4198 in velocity performance in the handgun is small, with the 150-gr. bullet used for these

tests. Possibly IMR-4198 would produce higher velocity than IMR-3031 with the lighter bullets often used in the Contender, but the difference would not be great for moderately lighter bullets such as the 125-gr. For bullets heavier than 150 grs., the superiority of IMR-3031 over IMR-4198 would be even greater in both handgun and rifle. Probably powders even slower burning than IMR-3031 would produce higher velocity, at acceptable pressure, with bullets heavier than 150 grs. in the .30-30 rifle, but they might not do so in the handgun. Du Pont data list a compressed charge of slower-burning IMR-4064 at a velocity only 10 f.p.s. above that produced by IMR-3031, with a 170-gr. bullet in a 20″ test barrel. This very small advantage of IMR-4064 over IMR-3031 for the heavier bullets in rifle barrels might be offset by the greater velocity loss with the slower-burning IMR-4064 in the 10″ pistol barrel.

It should be mentioned here that differences obtained between the rifle and handgun velocities in these tests are not attributed solely to barrel length. The throating of the .30-30 Model 94 Winchester allowed free run of about .120″ before the bullet engaged the origin of rifling, whereas the .30-30 Contender barrel allowed only .030″ of free run, when the bullets were seated to the same stand-

ard overall length. The shorter throat of the Contender barrel certainly contributed to both higher velocity and higher chamber pressure, in comparison to the long throat of the Winchester carbine. Had it not been for this difference in dimensions of the throat, the difference in velocity between the carbine and the pistol would undoubtedly have been greater, but the relative performances of the powders would have been the same.

In .357 and .44 Mag. revolver cartridges, results were much the same as those obtained with the .222 Rem. and .30-30 Win. Results are in Table 3 and Table 4. The same powder that produced highest velocities in the rifles also produced highest velocities in the revolvers. Hercules Blue Dot and Winchester-Western 296 were the outstanding performers in both of these magnum handgun cartridges. As with the rifle cartridges, the velocity differences between the rifles and handguns were greatest with these relatively slow-burning powders, but these powders nevertheless produced the highest velocities in short barrels as well as in long ones.

Single-shot pistols such as the Thompson/Center Contender and assorted custom conversions of the Remington XP-100 have become popular and are chambered for a variety of cartridges that were traditionally

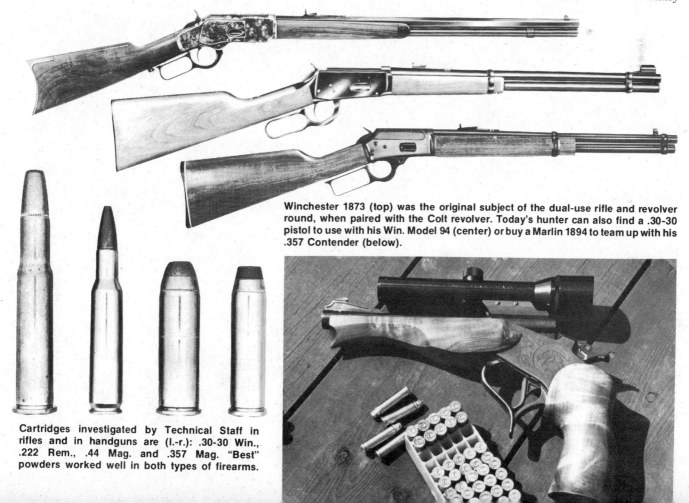

Winchester 1873 (top) was the original subject of the dual-use rifle and revolver round, when paired with the Colt revolver. Today's hunter can also find a .30-30 pistol to use with his Win. Model 94 (center) or buy a Marlin 1894 to team up with his .357 Contender (below).

Cartridges investigated by Technical Staff in rifles and in handguns are (l.-r.): .30-30 Win., .222 Rem., .44 Mag. and .357 Mag. "Best" powders worked well in both types of firearms.

used only in rifles before these guns were introduced. Some of these rounds include the .22 Hornet, .222 Rem., .25-35 Win., .30 Carbine, .30-30 Win., and .35 Rem. Rifles such as the Ruger autoloading carbine, Marlin Model 1894, and the Browning and Rossi copies of the Winchester Model 1892 are being chambered for the .44 Mag. or .357 Mag. rounds, both originally conceived as handgun cartridges. Navy Arms imports reproductions of Winchester lever-action rifles for the .38 Spl. cartridge. Various single-shot actions and Winchester Model 1892 rifles have frequently been converted to these rounds on a custom basis.

Many owners of pistols chambered for rifle cartridges, or rifles chambered for handgun cartridges, are handloaders. Observing that handguns and rifles usually use different types of powder, they often seek to improve the performance of their arms by more advantageous choices of powders for their handloads.

The technical problems of interchangeable ammunition for rifles and handguns did not arise when blackpowder was the only propellant used, because all blackpowder was of practically the same composition and grain form, and its burning rate was controllable only to a limited degree by different granulations, such as FFg, FFFg, etc. The situation is quite different with smokeless powders, which differ in both composition and grain form, and are designed for a specific range of ballistic performance. Handgun powders are traditionally characterized as "fast-burning," whereas rifle powders are regarded as relatively "slow-burning," although a considerable range of burning characteristics is exhibited within the different types of powders available for each type of gun. A logical question is whether a "handgun" cartridge to be fired in a rifle ought to be loaded with a "rifle" powder or a "handgun" powder, and vice versa. Some tests were therefore undertaken to examine the performance of potentially useful powders in these two different classes of arms.

Powders chosen for testing represented a range from the fastest to the slowest-burning types showing promise of being useful for full-charge loads in either type of gun. Loads are representative, taken from various sources of reloading data, and are maximum or near-maximum loads on the basis of acceptable chamber pressures. *The loads used are not necessarily recommended loads.* For detailed loading data, including specific brands and types of components to be used, the various reloading handbooks and publications of component manufacturers should be consulted. The loads used in these tests are intended only to demonstrate the performance that can be expected of full-charge loads using the various types of available powders, in these respective rifle and handgun cartridges.

Another interesting point was the excellent performance of the .357 and .44 Mag. factory loads, in rifles as well as in revolvers. Federal 125-gr. factory loads in the .357 Mag. produced higher velocities than any of the handloads, in both the rifle and the revolver. Remington factory 240-gr. loads in the .44 Mag. guns produced velocities comparable to the best of the handloads in the rifle, but did not equal the performance of most of the handloads in the revolver. Uniformity of velocity with the factory loads was also very good. Velocity standard deviation, which is the most efficient statistical measure of uniformity, was only 10.6 f.p.s. for the Federal .357 Mag. factory loads, and 9.1 f.p.s. for the Remington .44 Mag. factory loads in the rifles. In the revolvers, standard deviations for the .357 and .44 Mag. factory loads were 17.7 and 17.2 f.p.s. respectively. None of the handloads in the .357, and only two of the handloads in the .44 Mag., showed better uniformity than the factory loads, although all of the powder charges in the handloads were carefully weighed.

The conclusion drawn from these tests is that choice of the most suitable powder depends much more on the characteristics of the cartridge than on the length of the barrel from which it will be fired. For a given level of acceptable chamber pressure, the most important factors in powder selection are the capacity of the cartridge case and the sectional density of the bullet, both of which are characteristics of the cartridge rather than of the gun. The plausible idea that faster-burning powders produce higher velocities than do slower-burning powders in short barrels is not borne out in practice. Although the slower-burning powders show greater velocity loss as the barrel length is decreased (or less velocity gain as barrel length is increased) this effect does not offset the inherent advantage of the slower-burning powders in their ratio of velocity to chamber pressure, at least for barrels of moderate length. For very short handgun barrels, of course, this might not be the case, but it clearly applies to the magnum handgun cartridges fired in barrels longer than 6", and to rifle cartridges such as the .222 and .30-30 fired in 10" or longer barrels. ■

Above, the author is chronographing some loads from the Thompson/Center Contender pistol in .30-30 Win. caliber. It is available in a variety of popular rifle and handgun calibers. Below, some .357 Mag. loads are being chronographed from a custom Martini Cadet rifle with 25" barrel, the chronograph screens are in front of the bench, mounted on the wooden supports.

Cast Bullets Must Fit The Bore

By Robert N. Sears

Size is More Important than Shape

Cast bullet shooters often buy a succession of molds. The hope is always that the bullet of the next design will give fine accuracy in their particular rifle. Repeated disappointments can be avoided and the chances of success greatly improved when it is recognized that a cast bullet's dimensions are more important than its form. The bullet must fit the bore.

Proper fit is necessary to maintain the bullet's alignment in its travel down the barrel. Any tilt of a bullet's axis relative to that of the bore is accentuated during its flight through the air. Reliable grouping is then impossible.

Cast bullets, probably because they are relatively soft, require a longer bearing length than jacketed bullets to provide proper alignment. The most successful cast bullets for use in rifles firing fixed cartridges have a bearing length of at least twice their diameter. The driving bands at the rear of the bullet are always larger than the bore diameter so they always form part of the bearing length. But the driving band portion of most bullets is less than two diameters long, leaving the cylindrical bore-riding portion to make up the difference.

To contribute effectively, this cylindrical portion between the foremost driving band and the nose ogive must ride on and be guided by the tops of the rifling lands. In other words, its diameter must be at least as large as the bore. Too often it is not. In many .30 cal. bullets it measures .299″ or less while the rifle bore measures at least .301″.

Unfortunately, more attention is usually given to the diameter of the driving bands which are sometimes sized and measured to within .0005″. This can be futile when the diameter of the bore-riding portion is ignored. The driving bands contribute to the bearing length in any event, but the forward cylindrical portion contributes only when it fills the bore.

A most revealing check of a bullet's fit can be made by simply placing it nose first into the rifle muzzle. If it drops in of its own weight up to the driving bands no more than mediocre accuracy can be expected. The lands should, at least, provide felt resistance to thumb pressure. This very effective check requires no measuring devices and provides instant preliminary information on a bullet's suitability for that rifle.

If it passes the muzzle check, test the bullet's fit at the breech. This is the critical point. Many barrels have bore diameters larger at the breech end than at the muzzle. Some leave the factory so tapered. Erosion tends to wear them all that way.

Cylindrical part of a cast bullet must not enter the rifle muzzle. This simple check for bore fit requires no measuring devices.

Seat the bullet in a sized empty case and chamber it in the rifle. A slight resistance felt as the breech is closed gives an indication of proper fit even before the extracted bullet is examined.

The lands should mark the bore-riding cylinder evenly to the point where it joins the nose portion. The farther rearward the marks extend the better. Any amount of interference which does not result in leaving the bullet in the bore when a loaded cartridge is extracted does no harm. Cartridges which debullet when extracted are unacceptable in the hunting field, but often give splendid accuracy for target shooting where it is unnecessary for loaded rounds to be extracted from the chamber.

Molds which cast the cylindrical portion of the bullet smaller than the bore by only .001″-.002″ can often be improved by lapping. This can also help to correct out-of-roundness present in many molds.

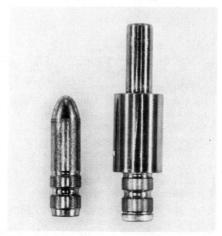

Specially bored top punch controls expansion of cylindrical bore-riding portion of the bullet when it is sized and lubricated.

An alternative which does not require modification of the mold is to expand the cylindrical portion of bullets after they are cast. This has been successfully done with ordinary lubricator-sizer tools adjusted so that pressure is exerted on the bullet nose at the end of the sizing stroke. The driving bands are then fully supported in the sizing die so the resulting compression expands only the unsupported cylindrical portion. No addition to the tool or change in the usual lubricating-sizing operation is required.

Use only enough force to barely expand the bullet. Excessive force not only causes the bullet to stick in the special top punch described here, but can also break the toggle linkage of the lubricator-sizer.

The requirement for an effective bearing length of at least two diameters applies mainly to cast bullets loaded in fixed cartridges. Bullets loaded from the muzzle with a guide starter are aligned with the bore by the loading procedure. Even conical shaped "picket" bullets having a bearing length of less than one-half their diameter give outstanding accuracy when their alignment is properly established in a false muzzle and maintained while being pushed down the bore with the ramrod.

Breech seating the bullet into the rifling with a guide starter as a separate operation before chambering the powder-charged cartridge case as allowed by American Single Shot Rifle Association rules can provide the same kind of initial guidance.

With fixed ammunition, as required by Cast Bullet Association rules, the bullet's alignment is always subject to influence of the cartridge case. Even when the inside of case necks are uniformly concentric with the outsides, misalignment of the chamber with the bore or case body within the chamber will tilt the bullet at the critical moment it starts down the bore. An effective bearing length of at least two diameters (three is much better) serves to overcome unwanted influence of the case.

The Lyman #311335 shown here is typical of the two-diameter bullets used successfully in .30 cal. fixed cartridges. Its total bearing length (including the gas check) is 3.2 diameters. More than half of this length is in its cylindrical bore-riding portion.

This and other bullets designed 75 years ago perform splendidly if their dimensions are correct. Success with cast bullets does not depend upon minor variations in shape, but rather upon how well their diameter and bearing length align them in the bore.

WHAT MAKES A

Hitting the target is only half the answer – here's the other half.

BY WILLIAM C. DAVIS, JR.

IT is widely believed among silhouette shooters that the construction of a bullet is a very important factor in its ability to topple the steel targets. Two terms often heard are "knockdown effect" and "energy transfer." They are supposed to be less favorable with conventional soft-point or hollow-point bullets than with full-jacketed bullets. The gist of the argument is that bullets which strongly resist deformation must transmit more energy to the steel target before they disintegrate than do those bullets which disintegrate more quickly and easily on impact. This intuitively plausible idea has been widely accepted without verification because it sounds as if it ought to be true.

To examine the argument critically, it is necessary to consider the natural laws which invariably govern the behavior of two colliding bodies. At the risk of seeming pedantic, we must review some of Newton's basic Laws of Motion.

Law of conservation of momentum

Of first importance is the Law of Conservation of Momentum, which invariably applies when one body collides with another. It states that the total momentum of the colliding bodies is unaltered by the collision. The ballistic pendulum, invented by Benjamin Robins about 1740 and used for more than 100 years thereafter for determining the velocities of all gun-fired projectiles, is based on this principle. A bullet strikes the stationary bob of the ballistic pendulum, and is imbedded in it. The momentum of the bullet is thus transferred to the pendulum and imparts some velocity to the pendulum bob. The height to which the pendulum swings is determined by suitable measurements, and from that its initial velocity, and its momentum, can be calculated. Since the pendulum bob had no momentum prior to bullet impact, its momentum after impact must be exactly equal to the momentum of the bullet just before impact. The momentum of the bullet is thus determined.

Since the momentum of a body is the product of its mass multiplied by its velocity, its momentum divided by its mass equals its velocity. The mass of the bullet is known from its weight, and its velocity upon striking can thus be determined from the observed momentum imparted to the pendulum bob.

Momentum is a directional (vector) quantity, as is velocity. If a body is moving

Bullet Type	No. of Shots	Momentum Ratio		Difference Significant? (I)
		Average	Std. Dev.	
.224 Spire Point 55-gr.	6	1.163	.017	Yes
.308 BTHP 168-gr.	6	1.137	.029	No
.430 FMJ-FP 240-gr.	8	1.136	.039	No
.430 JHP 240-gr.	8	1.135	.046	No
.308 SJSP 100-gr.	4	1.129	.011	No
.358 RNSP 200-gr.	4	1.108	.028	No
.358 Lead RN 158-gr.	4	1.101	.011	No
.357 JHP 158-gr.	6	1.093	.023	No
.430 Lead SWC 240-gr.	7	1.080	.062	No
.243 Spire Point 100-gr.	11	1.073	.019	Yes
.355 FMJ-RN 100-gr.	10	1.073	.030	Yes

TABLE 1

Grand Average Momentum Ratio For All Bullets: 1.112

(I) Indicates whether average momentum ratio is significantly different from grand average at .95 confidence level.

SILHOUETTE FALL?

eastward and its momentum is considered arbitrarily to be positive (having a plus sign), then any westward movement of a body in the same system is opposite in direction, and its momentum must be considered negative (having a minus sign). Thus, if a moving body strikes a stationary one in such a way that the moving body rebounds backward in the direction from which it came, and if the velocity (and momentum) of the moving body was positive before the collision, then it must be negative after the collision. The momentum gained by the stationary body from the collision must therefore be equal to the momentum of the moving body at the instant before collision, plus the momentum required to reverse the direction of the moving body and cause it to rebound. A collision of this type is called an elastic collision, whereas a collision in which the moving body sticks to (or is imbedded in) the stationary body is called an inelastic collision.

Energy is a non-directional (scalar)

This shooter uses 200-gr. bullets on the 500 m sheep; 165-gr. on chicken, pig, and turkey targets used at shorter distances.

The fourth of a bank of five silhouette chickens falls. Momentum is the best measure of a bullet's efficiency in toppling targets made of tough steels used in mining and construction equipment.

quantity, unlike velocity or momentum. In an elastic collision, some of the energy is returned to a light moving body which has collided with a heavy stationary body, by virtue of the velocity with which the light body rebounds after impact. Some kinetic energy is transferred to the body which was struck, by virtue of the velocity which it acquired from the impact.

In the practical case, some energy is always lost in a collision, from work done in deforming the bodies permanently, and/or in heating the region where impact occurred. In the theoretical case of a perfectly elastic impact, to be described later, no energy is lost, and the total kinetic energy in the system after impact is the same as before. Most of that kinetic energy is returned to the light body as it rebounds, and only a little energy is transferred to the heavy body in the collision.

In the case of the classic ballistic pendulum, the bullet is imbedded in the pendulum bob, so there is no rebound whatsoever, and the collision is said to be perfectly inelastic. The other extreme would be a perfectly elastic collision, in which the one body rebounds from the other with exactly the same relative speed that it had before striking, losing no energy whatsoever in the impact. In nature, a perfectly elastic collision never occurs between two bodies of appreciable size. Every collision between a bullet and a target must therefore be either inelastic, or somewhat elastic. It is never perfectly elastic. This fact allows us to determine the upper and lower limits, between which the transfer of momentum must always lie when a bullet collides with a target and does not pass through it.

In a perfectly inelastic impact, such as that which occurs when the bullet is imbedded in the bob of a ballistic pendulum, the momentum gained by the stationary body is exactly equal to that possessed by the moving body at the instant before collision. In a perfectly elastic impact (if that were possible) the bullet (or the pieces of it) would rebound

Hitting the silhouette target is the first requisite. The standard high power rifle course includes chickens at 200 m, pigs at 300 m, turkeys at 385 m and sheep at 500 m. All shooting is done standing.

toward the gun with exactly the same relative speed that it had upon striking, and the momentum gained by the pendulum bob would be twice that which the bullet had before striking. This may be intuitively apparent to some people. It is also easily proved by those inclined to solve the problem mathematically. These limits apply to every collision, whether or not the bodies are permanently deformed, and even if one or both disintegrate into smaller pieces in consequence of the impact. There is no other mechanism by which a moving bullet can transfer its momentum to a body with which it collides, irrespective of the way in which it does or does not disintegrate.

Whenever a bullet strikes a hard target to which it does not completely adhere,

therefore, the momentum which is transferred from the bullet to the target must be between one and two times the momentum of the bullet upon striking. If we express this as a ratio of the target momentum after impact to the bullet momentum just before impact, the ratio must always be between 1.0 and 2.0. To the extent that one bullet transfers its momentum more efficiently than another, it must be reflected quantitatively in that ratio, which we call the momentum ratio. The momentum ratio, a number always between 1.0 and 2.0, is a meaningful quantitative way to compare bullets of different construction. Since we know that bullets do not rebound from a steel target with a velocity nearly equal to their striking velocity, we should expect the

momentum ratio to be much closer to 1.0 than 2.0, and so it proves to be.

The experimental data were acquired by use of a special ballistic pendulum having a hard steel plate on the face of the bob. The bullets are not imbedded in the bob but are deflected as they are when they strike a steel silhouette target. We are greatly indebted to Ed Heers and the Hornady Manufacturing Company, who conducted the necessary experiments and made their data available to us. Heers, Project Engineer for Hornady, constructed the ballistic pendulum weighing 77 lbs., suspended at an effective length of 56.3". The bob was faced with 1/2" thick tempered T-1 steel plate. The instrumental velocity of each shot fired at the pendulum was measured by means of a chronograph system, and the striking velocity at the pendulum face was calculated from the established ballistic coefficients of the bullets. The horizontal swing of the pendulum was carefully measured for each shot. From that dimension the height of swing, pendulum energy and momentum were calculated.

The momentum of the bullet was calculated from its weight and striking velocity. The ratio of the pendulum momentum to the bullet momentum was calculated, as described before. The results for each shot are shown in **Table 2**. The striking energy of the bullet and the kinetic energy imparted to the pendulum are also shown for comparison. Momentum transfer is independent of target weight, so it would be the same for a steel silhouette as for the 77-lb. pendulum bob. The transfer of kinetic energy would be somewhat greater for lighter targets, but that is of little use in evaluating bullet construction, as we shall later see.

As must be expected in any mechanical experiment, the results from shot to shot are not perfectly consistent, though the overall consistency of the results is generally very good. The experiment was evidently carefully done. It is interesting to note that the momentum ratio does indeed appear to be characteristic of the bullet and substantially independent of the striking velocity, at least for the range of velocities investigated.

In a few instances, Heers reported, the bullet struck a region of the plate that had been damaged or "cratered" by a previous impact, and this increased the pendulum deflection for those particular shots, which were not included in the record. That result is to be expected, since the effect of a bullet striking in a previous crater (or producing a crater itself) would be to increase the "back-splatter" of bullet fragments toward the gun. That is, of course, equivalent to increasing the effective "rebound" velocity of the bullet, producing the same result as a more highly elastic impact. The momentum transfer, in

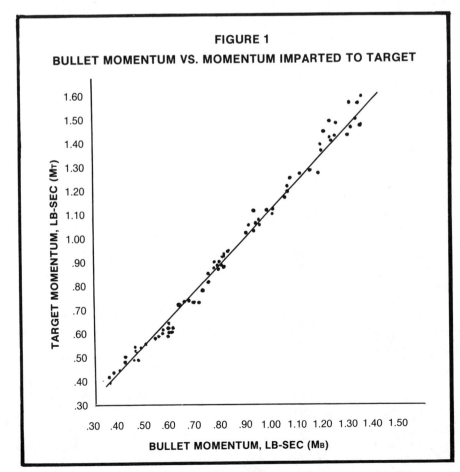

FIGURE 1
BULLET MOMENTUM VS. MOMENTUM IMPARTED TO TARGET

TARGET MOMENTUM, LB-SEC (M_T)

BULLET MOMENTUM, LB-SEC (M_B)

that case, would certainly be greater than that effected by a bullet which produced less "back-splatter." The "splatter" effect can be illustrated by directing a stream of water out of the faucet into the bowl of a spoon, as compared to directing the stream against a flat surface.

It is only by virtue of the weight and effective velocity of the bullet fragments which "back-splatter" that a bullet is able to impart to the target any greater momentum than the momentum of the bullet itself prior to impact. The idea that a strongly constructed bullet is advantageous because it "pushes harder and longer"

before it disintegrates might seem plausible, but it does not bear scrutiny in accordance with the laws of physics which unavoidably apply to all such collisions. Indeed, if a bullet were so strong and hard as to penetrate the steel plate undeformed, and lodge in it, the momentum ratio would be exactly 1.00, as it was in the classic ballistic pendulums formerly used to determine the velocities of bullets. All of the bullets in the Hornady tests did produce some "back-splatter," of course, and for that reason produced a momentum ratio greater than 1.00.

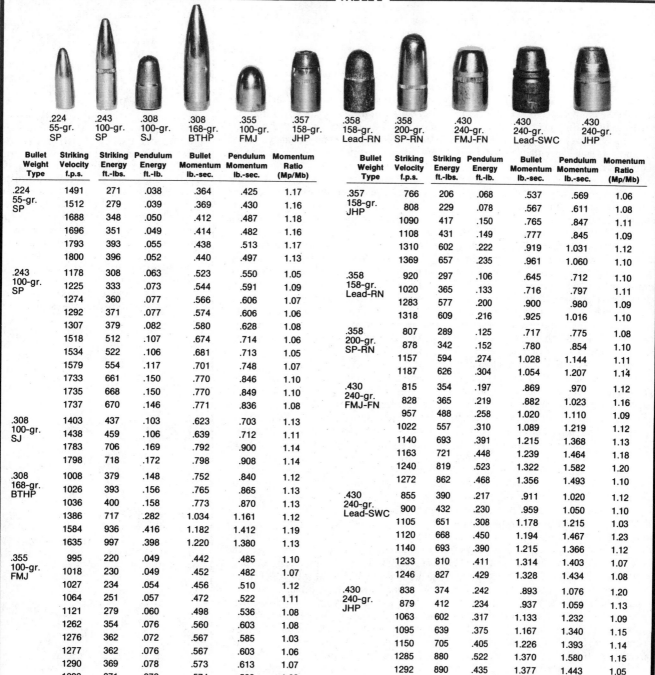

TABLE 2

Bullet Weight Type	Striking Velocity f.p.s.	Striking Energy ft.-lbs.	Pendulum Energy ft.-lb.	Bullet Momentum lb.-sec.	Pendulum Momentum lb.-sec.	Momentum Ratio (Mp/Mb)
.224 55-gr. SP	1491	271	.038	.364	.425	1.17
	1512	279	.039	.369	.430	1.16
	1688	348	.050	.412	.487	1.18
	1696	351	.049	.414	.482	1.16
	1793	393	.055	.438	.513	1.17
	1800	396	.052	.440	.497	1.13
.243 100-gr. SP	1178	308	.063	.523	.550	1.05
	1225	333	.073	.544	.591	1.09
	1274	360	.077	.566	.606	1.07
	1292	371	.077	.574	.606	1.06
	1307	379	.082	.580	.628	1.08
	1518	512	.107	.674	.714	1.06
	1534	522	.106	.681	.713	1.05
	1579	554	.117	.701	.748	1.07
	1733	661	.150	.770	.846	1.10
	1735	668	.150	.770	.849	1.10
	1737	670	.146	.771	.836	1.08
.308 100-gr. SJ	1403	437	.103	.623	.703	1.13
	1438	459	.106	.639	.712	1.11
	1783	706	.169	.792	.900	1.14
	1798	718	.172	.798	.908	1.14
.308 168-gr. BTHP	1008	379	.148	.752	.840	1.12
	1026	393	.156	.765	.865	1.13
	1036	400	.158	.773	.870	1.13
	1386	717	.282	1.034	1.161	1.12
	1584	936	.416	1.182	1.412	1.19
	1635	997	.398	1.220	1.380	1.13
.355 100-gr. FMJ	995	220	.049	.442	.485	1.10
	1018	230	.049	.452	.482	1.07
	1027	234	.054	.456	.510	1.12
	1064	251	.057	.472	.522	1.11
	1121	279	.060	.498	.536	1.08
	1262	354	.076	.560	.603	1.08
	1276	362	.072	.567	.585	1.03
	1277	362	.076	.567	.603	1.06
	1290	369	.078	.573	.613	1.07
	1293	371	.072	.574	.589	1.03

Bullet Weight Type	Striking Velocity f.p.s.	Striking Energy ft.-lbs.	Pendulum Energy ft.-lb.	Bullet Momentum lb.-sec.	Pendulum Momentum lb.-sec.	Momentum Ratio (Mp/Mb)
.357 158-gr. JHP	766	206	.068	.537	.569	1.06
	808	229	.078	.567	.611	1.08
	1090	417	.150	.765	.847	1.11
	1108	431	.149	.777	.845	1.09
	1310	602	.222	.919	1.031	1.12
	1369	657	.235	.961	1.060	1.10
.358 158-gr. Lead-RN	920	297	.106	.645	.712	1.10
	1020	365	.133	.716	.797	1.11
	1283	577	.200	.900	.980	1.09
	1318	609	.216	.925	1.016	1.10
.358 200-gr. SP-RN	807	289	.125	.717	.775	1.08
	878	342	.152	.780	.854	1.10
	1157	594	.274	1.028	1.144	1.11
	1187	626	.304	1.054	1.207	1.14
.430 240-gr. FMJ-FN	815	354	.197	.869	.970	1.12
	828	365	.219	.882	1.023	1.16
	957	488	.258	1.020	1.110	1.09
	1022	557	.310	1.089	1.219	1.12
	1140	693	.391	1.215	1.368	1.13
	1163	721	.448	1.239	1.464	1.18
	1240	819	.523	1.322	1.582	1.20
	1272	862	.468	1.356	1.493	1.10
.430 240-gr. Lead-SWC	855	390	.217	.911	1.020	1.12
	900	432	.230	.959	1.050	1.10
	1105	651	.308	1.178	1.215	1.03
	1120	668	.450	1.194	1.467	1.23
	1140	693	.390	1.215	1.366	1.12
	1233	810	.411	1.314	1.403	1.07
	1246	827	.429	1.328	1.434	1.08
.430 240-gr. JHP	838	374	.242	.893	1.076	1.20
	879	412	.234	.937	1.059	1.13
	1063	602	.317	1.133	1.232	1.09
	1095	639	.375	1.167	1.340	1.15
	1150	705	.405	1.226	1.393	1.14
	1285	880	.522	1.370	1.580	1.15
	1292	890	.435	1.377	1.443	1.05
	1303	905	.549	1.389	1.621	1.17

Bullet types illustrated (left to right): .224 55-gr. SP · .243 100-gr. SP · .308 100-gr. SJ · .308 168-gr. BTHP · .355 100-gr. FMJ · .357 158-gr. JHP · .358 158-gr. Lead-RN · .358 200-gr. SP-RN · .430 240-gr. FMJ-FN · .430 240-gr. Lead-SWC · .430 240-gr. JHP

Silhouette Knockdown

The fact that the "hardest" bullets do not necessarily transfer momentum most efficiently is established by the Hornady tests. The bullet which showed the highest momentum ratio was the 55-gr. .22 cal. soft-point, certainly among the most frangible of the bullets tested. Heers reported that the .22 cal. bullet was fired after the surface of the target plate had been somewhat roughened by the impacts of previous shots, and that condition might have increased its apparent effectiveness by increasing the "back-splatter." Nevertheless, the bullet ranking next among those tested was the .30 cal. 168-gr. hollow-point, which is also relatively "soft" and easily deformed on impact.

Since the results indicate that the momentum ratio is substantially independent of the velocity at impact, all of the shots made with each specific bullet are grouped together in **Table 1**. The bullets are ranked from highest to lowest in order of their indicated momentum ratios.

Among the hollow-point, soft-point, lead and full-jacketed bullets tested, there is no clear indication that one bullet construction is superior to another. Other factors, not yet clearly identified, seem to be more important than these particular details of construction.

A word should be said here about the concept of "energy transfer," a term that is much used but apparently little understood. Except for bullets of the same weight, there is no reason to be found in theory for supposing that a correlation exists between bullet-impact energy and the kinetic energy imparted to the target. Practice confirms the theory, as is apparent from a study of **Table 2**.

A heavy target struck by a much lighter bullet receives only a very small percentage of the bullet's kinetic energy in any case. With the 240-gr. bullets and heaviest loads tested, the greatest kinetic energy imparted to the pendulum was about .5 ft.-lb., though the striking energy of the bullet was more than 800 ft.-lbs. That energy ratio is about .0006. With the 100-gr. bullets and heaviest loads, the pendulum energy was about .15 ft.-lb., whereas the striking energy of the bullet was about 700 ft.-lbs., and that energy ratio is only about .0002. It is meaningless to speak about "energy transfer" as if it depended solely on bullet construction. Bullet weight is by far the more important factor.

Bullet momentum at impact should correlate well with the momentum imparted to the target. The Hornady tests confirm that it does. The results are illustrated in **Fig. 1**, which is a plot of every shot recorded in the Hornady tests, irrespective of caliber, bullet weight, or bullet construction. Some of the 74 plotted points fall so closely together that

they cannot be separately distinguished. The relationship between bullet momentum and the momentum imparted to the target is practically linear, and is adequately represented by the equation:

$$M_t = 1.112 \times M_b$$

where M_b = striking momentum of the bullet and M_t = momentum imparted to the target.

A statistical analysis of the results obtained for each bullet in the Hornady tests indicates that only the 55-gr. .22 cal. bullet produced a momentum ratio significantly higher than the average of 1.112 for all bullets, whereas only the 100-gr. .243" soft-point and the 100-gr. .355" full-metal jacket produced momentum ratios significantly lower than the average. A .95 level of confidence applies to both results.

The relative "knockdown" effectiveness of loads can easily be estimated, provided that the weights and striking velocities of the bullets are known. The striking velocities corresponding to various levels of muzzle velocity are given for each bullet in some reloading manuals, such as the *Hornady Handbook of Cartridge Reloading* and the *Sierra Bullets Reloading Manual*. For ranges and muzzle velocities not listed, the striking velocities can be estimated by interpolation in the tables, remembering that one meter equals about 1.1 yds. The Speer Ballistics Calculator can also be used to determine striking velocities at any range, provided only that the muzzle velocity and ballistic coefficient (C_1 or Ingalls) are known. The ballistic coefficients are listed in most reloading manuals, including those of Speer, Hornady and Sierra.

When the striking velocity and bullet weight are known, the striking momentum can be calculated (in the usual engineering units of lb.-sec.) from the following equation:

$$M_b = W \times V / 225200$$

where W = bullet weight (grs.)
and V = striking velocity (f.p.s.)

The Hornady tests show that striking momentum is overwhelmingly more important than bullet construction. Furthermore, the test results contradict the widespread notion that full-jacketed bullets are categorically superior to other types for shooting silhouettes. The results do not yield any clue as to which type of construction is characteristically "best" in that respect. In the ranking from "best" to "worst" on the basis of efficiency in transmitting momentum to the target, the soft-point, hollow-point, lead or full-jacket types do not appear together in any particular region of the table.

The silhouette shooter would be well advised to choose his loads on the basis of striking momentum. He can wisely choose his bullets on the basis of their weight, ballistic coefficient and accuracy. Then let others argue about what particular bullet construction gives the best "energy transfer" on the steel targets. ∎

Reloading Blank Cases

I have a quantity of 7.62 mm blank cases which I would like to reform and use. Would it be safe to do so? I have heard that .30-'06 blanks were made from reject cases, but I don't know if the same is true for 7.62 mm blanks.

Answer: It is true that some cal. .30 M1909 (.30-'06) blank cartridges have been assembled using cartridge cases that did not meet all requirements for bulleted ammunition. Some were also loaded in previously fired cases that had been returned from the field. Because of the uncertain quality of such brass, I would not recommend reloading any cases salvaged from .30-'06 blanks.

The situation is not the same with 7.62 mm NATO M82 (.308) blanks. These cases are much longer than cases used for bulleted ammunition, so it is impossible to utilize standard 7.62 mm cases of substandard quality for reloading blank ammunition. However, the metallurgical properties of cases for loading blanks are not as strictly controlled as they are for bulleted ammunition, because such great strength is not required.

The cases are produced by similar processes, and most cases from blanks could probably withstand the chamber pressures of bulleted loads. Some blank cases, however, with undetected flaws, not significant as long as the cases were used for blank ammunition, might cause the case to fail disastrously with a full load.

For this reason I would not recommend reloading cases salvaged from 7.62 mm M82 blanks for full-charge bulleted loads. The same caution would hold true, of course, for cases of other calibers made by reforming brass salvaged from blanks.—W.C.D., Jr.

Energy Calculation

What is the formula for calculating muzzle energy in ft.-lbs. when the weight of the bullet is given in grains, and its velocity in feet per second?

Answer: To calculate muzzle energy in ft.-lbs., given the bullet weight (W) in grains, and the muzzle velocity (V) in feet per second, you can use the formula:

$$E = \frac{W \times V^2}{450,400}$$

For example, a 100-gr. bullet having a muzzle velocity of 3000 f.p.s. would have a muzzle energy of

$$E = \frac{100 \times 3000 \times 3000}{450,400}$$

$$E = 1998 \text{ ft.-lbs.}$$

—W.C.D., Jr.

1 Hensley & Gibbs gang mold teamed with Saeco 20-lb.-capacity electric melting furnace is efficient combination where large quantities of bullets are required. Single- and double-cavity molds are less costly and are quite adequate when ammunition consumption is nominal

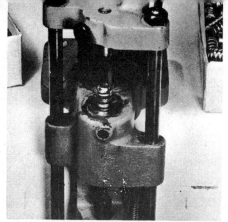

2 Typical sizer and lubricator, the Lyman No. 45, consists of a lever-operated punch-and-die arrangement to simultaneously size and lubricate bullet. Material sizing-down damages bullets. Cast bullets should always be handled carefully and stored in clean containers with protective dust covers

3 Full-length case sizing in sleeve die removes bulges and reduces case body diameter to insure proper chambering of finished round in revolver cylinder. Cases should be wiped clean and lubricated lightly prior to insertion in die. Sizing of dry or dirty cases in ordinary steel die usually results in stuck case or scoring of die walls

HANDLOADING FOR HANDGUNS

By M. D. WAITE

THE quantity handloading of accurate revolver ammunition is simple and interesting once the technique is understood and mastered. Basic equipment required includes a sturdy straight-line reloading press, dies of the desired caliber, and a powder measure to meter the charges. An accurate scale to verify settings of the powder measure is also a must. A block to hold the cartridges can be made or purchased at small cost.

Prelubricated cast or swaged bullets are obtainable from several sources, or, if desired, one can purchase equipment

to make bullets by casting or swaging methods. The more common method involves use of a mold to cast the bullets from lead alloy.

The alloy can be melted on the kitchen stove in a simple cast-iron vessel, or in a gasoline- or electrically-heated melting furnace designed for the purpose. A pot holding about 12 lbs. of metal is adequate for single- or double-cavity molds, but gang molds demand use of a furnace of greater capacity to insure a continuous supply of alloy at proper pouring temperature.

Most cast bullet designs incorporate annular grooves to hold bullet lubricant, with an additional groove for crimping. The usual practice is to force the cast bullet through a sizing die to make it round and of desired diameter; ordinarily, means are provided by conventional sizer-lubricators to simultaneously fill the grease grooves with lubricant. This is the most convenient procedure, although the bullets can be sized and lubricated in separate operations. The disadvantage of the latter system is the much greater time re-

4 After initial full-length sizing, case is inserted in second die which expels fired primer, expands neck, and bells case mouth slightly. If case necks are not belled, metal is likely to be shaved from side of bullet during subsequent seating operation. Cases may be primed during this operation

5 Cases need not be cleaned or lubricated prior to sizing if carbide-faced sizing die is used in lieu of ordinary steel die. 'Perfection' carbide die shown here imparts high scratch-free polish to case walls and is especially good for sizing nickel-plated cases. It simultaneously expels fired primer, expands neck, and bells case mouth

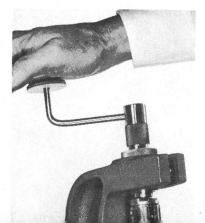

6 Uniform bullet crimp is assured if cases are trimmed to identical length. R.C.B.S. mill-type trimmer shown here allows rapid full-length sizing and trimming of cases. Trimming can also be accomplished in bench and hand type tools of which a variety are available

7 Virtually all reloading tools incorporate a priming punch to insert fresh primers. Priming or capping may be performed during initial case-sizing operation or as separate operation as shown here. Automatic-feed priming devices are available as an accessory for most tools to eliminate handling of each primer

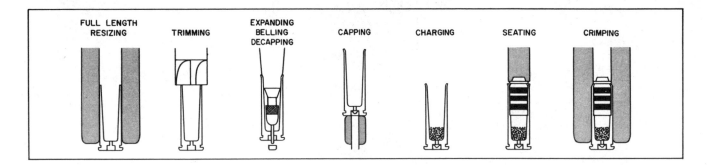

FULL LENGTH RESIZING | TRIMMING | EXPANDING BELLING DECAPPING | CAPPING | CHARGING | SEATING | CRIMPING

quired to process the bullet.

Molds are available in single- or multiple-cavity type. A mold casting 4, 6, or 10 bullets simultaneously is known as a gang mold and is particularly recommended when large quantities of ammunition are to be prepared.

When ordering the mold, particular care must be taken to specify the 'as-cast' bullet diameter desired. It will be of some assistance to the mold maker if the purchaser will indicate the alloy or alloys to be used. The bullets as they come from the mold should require little if any reduction in diameter during subsequent sizing and lubricating operations as it is impossible to obtain uniform accuracy from oversized bullets subsequently distorted by excessive sizing. The 'as-cast' diameter of the bullet should not exceed the groove diameter of the gun barrel by more than .002". Less is better.

The assembling of the finished round, starting with the fired case, can be accomplished using 2, 3, or 4 dies, depending on how much care and attention one wishes to devote to the job. With the 2-die system, the initial die full-length resizes the case, ejects the fired primer, and at the same time expands and bells the case mouth to accept the bullet. As the case is extracted

from the die, a fresh primer can be inserted in the primer pocket to complete the case-preparation cycle. After charging and insertion of a bullet in the case mouth, the second die is used to simultaneously seat and crimp the bullet to complete the loading of the round.

With the 3-die system, the first die full-length resizes the case but does nothing else. The second die ejects the fired primer and expands and bells the case mouth. As the case is extracted from the die, a fresh primer can be inserted in the primer pocket to complete the case-preparation cycle. After charging and insertion of a bullet in the case mouth, the third die is used to simultaneously seat and crimp the bullet to complete the loading of the round.

Reloading with the 4-die system is similar to the above except that the bullet-seating and crimping operations are accomplished in separate dies. Separate bullet seating and crimping can also be accomplished with the regular crimping-seating die by altering body and seating punch adjustments, but users of turret tools in particular can save time by purchasing separate-function dies requiring initial adjustment only.

Each of the die systems noted has its advantages and disadvantages. The 2-die set will prove least costly, but many handloaders do not like to bell and expand the case mouth, then remove most of the flare or bell from the case as it is withdrawn from the die. If the case mouth is not sufficiently belled, metal is likely to be shaved from the side of the bullet during the seating and crimping operation. If the die is adjusted to provide a prominent bell sufficient to withstand removal from the die body, there is every likelihood that the cases will eventually split at the mouth from excessive cold working of the metal.

This objection is eliminated with the 3-die system, as the initial die full-length resizes only and the belling-expanding-decapping operation is completed in the second die. Cases will last longer when the operations are thus separated, but the extra case handling and cost of the additional die must be considered.

The 4-die set is similar in operation but seating and crimping are carried out in separate dies. Advocates of this practice claim that the bullet is less likely to be deformed when a heavy crimp is required. Again, the cost of the extra die must be considered. ■

8 When loading press is of heavy-duty type, priming may be more conveniently done with auxiliary device such as the Lachmiller priming tool shown here

9 Powder charges can be weighed individually on a scale, but much time is saved by using measure to meter powder directly into cartridge cases held in loading block. Charged cases should be carefully inspected for double charge prior to insertion of bullets

10 Bullets may be simultaneously seated and crimped, or seated with one die and crimped with another. Die shown is R.C.B.S. seating die minus usual internal crimping shoulder. Time is saved if bullets are lightly pressed into case neck prior to insertion of cartridge into die

11 Final operation with 4-die system is crimping of case neck into crimping groove in side of bullet. An adequate crimp protects powder charge against oil and moisture and also prevents dislodgment of bullet under shock of recoil. After inspection the reloaded cartridge is ready to be shot

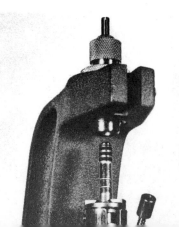

MAKING ACCURATE .38 HANDLOADS

How to reload .38 Special ammo that's reliably accurate

By E. H. HARRISON

THE .38 Special is reloaded by more shooters than any other cartridge except the .30-'06 and the 12-ga. shotshell, according to information gathered by THE AMERICAN RIFLEMAN.

Police departments reload the .38 Special to extend their training. Clubs and individuals reload it to obtain target ammunition for practice and competition. Not many shooters consider they could otherwise afford the quantity of ammunition which must be fired to reach and retain match proficiency.

The .38 Special ammunition loaded for this purpose is standardized with a light powder charge and a "wadcutter" (flat-ended) bullet. The purpose is target accuracy.

Indications of failures

There have been increasing indications of failure in this purpose. Few leading handgun competitors fire reloads in important competitions. Reports reach THE RIFLEMAN of reloaded .38 Specials giving yawed impacts, almost keyholes, in the target, or producing much poorer scores than obtained on changing to better ammunition. Poor ammunition is self-defeating where shooting accuracy is required. Its value may be questioned even for practice.

This does not, of course, mean that all handloaders obtain such results. There are individuals and organizations who produce excellent .38 Special target ammunition, and others whose product sufficiently meets the demands made on it. But as to reality of the general problem, when target scores are counted, there appears to be no doubt.

Few handgun target shooters have a reliable idea of their ammunition's performance. They might get it by firing several hundred rounds of factory wadcutter ammunition and their reloads at targets under the same conditions, and comparing results. This would require keeping an accurate record of all scores. The comparison would have to be made in presence of the shooter's own target dispersion, which may be greater than that of the ammunition. Appreciating this, not many shooters go through with the comparison.

Rifle handloaders can test their ammunition with relative strictness by firing from a rest. Pistol handloaders, however, in general are at a serious disadvantage in having no equivalent way

in which they can check their product. Some shooters have improved their scores by buying custom bullets for loading instead of casting the bullets themselves. There has been little further definite information on the effect of components and loading procedures.

THE RIFLEMAN therefore carried out a thorough investigation to determine the factors in .38 Special target ammunition accuracy, and to establish the accuracy level obtainable with handloads. The findings proved definite enough to guide the loading of reliably accurate ammunition.

The principal firing was done from 2 Smith & Wesson K-38 revolvers and a Colt Officers Model revolver. The Colt had the small .354" barrel groove diameter which formerly was standard in that make. It was used because of the great number of guns with that groove diameter in service, and also to obtain an idea of the effect of a barrel bore considerably smaller than the cylinder throat diameter. Extensive check firing was done in a Winchester single-shot rifle with heavy barrel of target quality, 16¼" long. Barrel groove diameters in the S&W revolvers and the rifle were .357".

The semi-automatic pistol has as-

sumed the leading position over the revolver in .38 Special competition. Nevertheless, this investigation was done mainly with the revolver because its fixed barrel can be held reliably in a machine rest. Also, the revolver presents certain special obstacles to ammunition success in its chamber throats larger than barrel groove diameter, its gap between cylinder and barrel, and its large, roughly reamed cone in rear end of the barrel. Ammunition successfully surmounting these difficulties should do well in the easier conditions of the semi-automatic chamber and barrel. (It is not meant that the semi-automatic is more accurate than the revolver; the revolver may be the more accurate.) Check firing was also done with 2 semi-automatic target pistols, one in .38 Special and the other in .38 AMU.

The revolvers were fired from Phelps machine rests, in which the barrel is held solidly in a block which slides to the rear in recoil. This type of machine rest was chosen because it is insensitive to small variations in handling, and is capable of giving very small target grouping. The rifle was fired without stock from a 6-point rest, and the pistols from a Broadway rest. The results

Author E. H. Harrison, using the Phelps machine rest in testing the accuracy of .38 Special loads.

are therefore representative to the maximum possible extent of the ammunition's capability.

The firing was done in indoor test ranges at 50 ft., 75 ft., and 50 yds. It was found that group sizes at 50 ft. and 50 yds. were substantially in proportion to the range, and the final firing was carried out at 75 ft. (25 yds.). Groups were recorded in minutes of angle to make them comparable regardless of range—the reason rifle groups are often reported in that manner. A minute of angle is very nearly ½″ at 50 yds.

In tests of handgun ammunition the groups obtained have often been compared with the regulation target 10-ring, and if as small as the 10-ring they have been called good. Diameter of the 50-yd. target 10-ring is 3.39″ or about 6¾ minutes of angle. In reality, the firer's dispersion in holding and let-off are added to the gun and ammunition dispersion as given by machine-rest firing (just how they are added need not be gone into here), and if the firer's group is not perfectly centered on the 10-ring there is a further loss of score. Consequently, ammunition which groups as large as the 10-ring cannot score possibles except by accident. As will be seen, group sizes of 6 minutes of angle (3″ at 50 yds.) are poor. They must be very small to be good.

The test firing comprised approximately 360 groups of 10 shots each. Some of these were fired incident to an investigation of half-jacketed bullets, but most were fired for this investigation. Approximately 295 of the groups were with handloads, the rest with factory wadcutter target ammunition fired at intervals as control. Gun bores were cleaned only after each 50 rounds, since it was considered that handgun target ammunition used in competition should perform that long. The number of load variations and the great number of machine-rest groups, all of which were accurately recorded, made definite conclusions possible.

Following are the results. They are described first by the components tried.

Primer choice significant

The Remington No. 1½ small pistol primer was used in most loads. A magnum small pistol primer was also tried, but the result was nearly a doubling in group size.

Most loads were fired with the widely used charge of 2.7 grs. Hercules Bullseye powder. Extensive check firing was done with Du Pont PB powder, in the charge of 3.4 grs. recommended by Du Pont for .38 Special target loads. Other powders could have been chosen; however, among powders in this range PB

Target revolver in Phelps machine rest for test of .38 Special handloads.

is about as unlike Bullseye as can be obtained. PB measures with outstanding smoothness and regularity in this small charge. In the outcome, average group size with PB was substantially the same as with Bullseye. The amount of barrel leading with the 2 powders was also about the same.

The revolver load of 2.7 grs. Bullseye failed to function the auto pistols when held in the rest, making it necessary to fire them single shot. The load was therefore increased to 2.9 and then 3.0 grs. in these guns to get functioning. The 3.0 gr. load was then check fired in a revolver, and gave groups averaging ½ minute of angle larger than the 2.7 gr. load. It also showed greater leading tendency.

Examination of factory .38 Special target ammunition showed powder of different types in different ammunition lots. Samples from a single lot were less uniform in charge weight from round to round than is usual in handloading.

Effect of crimp

Case mouth crimp was long thought necessary to regular ignition and good groups. That did not prove true in these tests. Changing from heavy crimp to light, and to no crimp at all, had no detectable effect on grouping. (This does not refer to need for crimp in heavy revolver loads to hold bullets in place during recoil.) It did not even matter whether the case was sized or not. There was usually enough grease friction to hold the bullet in the unsized case until some crimp could be applied, and the loads still grouped the same.

This does not state that crimping has no effect. Different crimps may (not necessarily will) give different centers of impact, and if mixed might enlarge groups. There is no need for mixing.

Taken singly, the different degrees of crimp, and no crimp, gave about the same target dispersion.

There was one exception. By selection among crimping dies it was possible to form the case mouth fully into the rounded crimping groove in the bullet (illustration below). This form of crimp, with mouth edge turned outward, was intended to allow smooth passage of the bullet, while the unusual length and depth of crimp behind the mouth provided strong resistance. Ammunition so crimped showed a marked tightening of the central 5 to 8 shots in each group. The remaining shots, however, always enlarged the over-all group diameters beyond those given by normal crimping.

Factory .38 Special target ammunition shows one or 2 case cannelures rolled into the bullet (not counting the one below the bullet to insure against receding). Position of these cannelures varies among ammunition lots of different date, even in the same make. Few handloaders have any way to indent such case cannelures into the bullet after loading. If they had, they would still be unable to test the effect on target grouping and make adjustments before loading the ammunition lot, as the factories can do.

After taking all these points into con-

Specially formed heavy crimp (arrow, r.) was unsuccessful in improving grouping. Standard crimp shown for comparison.

sideration, the tests were completed with moderately resized cases, moderately crimped. This procedure is applicable on normal loading equipment, is suitable for reloads in both pistols and revolvers, and appears to give grouping as good as any.

Much .38 Special loading is done with sets of 3 or even 4 dies, instead of the 2 dies which are conventional in loading bottle-neck rifle cartridges. Purpose of the additional die in 3-die sets is to bell the case mouth as a separate operation after sizing; this works the mouth less than in belling during sizing, and the cases last longer. A 4th die separately crimps after seating the bullet, to avoid possibly shaving the bullet at that stage. Most loading for the present tests was done in 3-die and 4-die sets. These are successful in the respective purposes. There was nothing, however, to indicate that they load better ammunition than a 2-die set correctly adjusted. The loads making the smallest groups among handloads in these tests were assembled on a 2-die set.

It has often been pointed out that cases of variable length result in variable crimping. The condition is most likely in cases picked up at random on the range, or otherwise mixed. The present tests were done with cases bought new or left from control firing of factory ammunition, and kept together throughout use. They were found to crimp uniformly.

While most factors in connection with the cartridge case thus proved to be of

Case mouth cracks (arrows) in crimped ammunition have very bad effect on grouping, and must be inspected for.

no special importance, this was not true for case mouth condition. A small crack in the case mouth (illustration below) was found to throw the shot out of the group. A deviation of 3 to 4 minutes of angle appeared to be typical. Such cracks probably would have little effect if the case mouth were not crimped onto the bullet. Since crimping is usual, the cracks are serious.

Bullet is most important

We come now to the bullet, the only remaining component. These tests showed the bullet to be by far the most important factor in .38 Special target ammunition accuracy.

The following bullets were tried (see illustration on page 37).

a. *Hensley & Gibbs No. 50 BB.* A wadcutter bullet of form which has become usual in revolver target bullets. The 50 BB has, however, a markedly beveled base edge, intended to simplify starting the bullet into the case mouth during loading. This and the 2 other cast bullet types tried (listed below) were cast in Hensley & Gibbs (H&G) gang molds bought new for these tests, in separate sizes for .357" and .354" barrel groove diameters. These high quality, beautifully working molds were valuable both in quantity production of bullets and in obtaining consistent test results.

b. *Hensley & Gibbs No. 50.* The same design without base bevel, the base edge coming to substantially a sharp edge in the conventional way.

c. *Hensley & Gibbs No. 73.* Body with sharp leading edge for wadcutter effect, and long conical nose with flat end. Essentially same form as the similar revolver bullet used by handloaders for field shooting.

d. *Custom target wadcutter.* Machine-swaged (not cast) bullet of substantially same form as H&G 50 BB, of a leading make. Sold lubricated ready for loading.

e. *Custom hollow-base target wadcutter.* Machine-swaged (not cast) bullet of the same make, of somewhat similar form, but with large base cavity like that of bullet in factory target cartridge. Sold lubricated ready for loading.

f. *Remington No. 22850 factory hollow-base target wadcutter.* Machine-swaged bullet used in Remington .38 Special target ammunition. Sold lubricated ready for loading.

All these bullets are of nominal 145 to 148 grs. weight.

The H&G No. 73 long-pointed bullet can be disposed of first, as being not normally considered suitable for competition with the target wadcutters. Results of the present tests confirmed that view. Groups were about one min-

ute of angle larger than those obtained with H&G No. 50 BB. Note that this comparison relates to ammunition for competitive target shooting. The No. 73 would be preferable for field shooting at higher velocity.

The H&G No. 50 BB gave best results among the cast bullets tried. Correctly made and loaded, it averaged not over 3.5 minutes of angle in the 10-shot groups fired in all this testing.

The H&G No. 50 grouped about as well. It was, however, less convenient to load, and also leaded the barrel cone more than No. 50 BB.

The custom wadcutter bullet of solid form gave 2.5 to 7.9 minutes of angle in individual 10-shot groups, averaging 5.1 minutes. This bullet was loaded with the same equipment and care as the other bullets and machine-rest fired in the same way. Its comparatively wide and variable grouping thus had to be considered the measure of its target quality. (These and all other group diameters given in this article refer to groups made by the target revolvers.)

The custom hollow-base target wadcutter also gave variable results. While a few of its groups were under 4 minutes of angle, others were over 6 minutes, and the average was 4.8 minutes.

The Remington No. 22850 factory hollow-base wadcutter bullet, in startling contrast, averaged between 2.5 and 3.0 minutes of angle. Some details of this performance are examined later in this article.

Remington and Winchester-Western factory .38 Special target ammunitions were fired at intervals, as control. Their groups averaged within 2.5 minutes of angle. Also, while an occasional series with the H&G No. 50 BB was more uniform from group to group, the factory ammunition performed most uniformly in the long run. *The factory .38 Special target ammunition is the standard against which handloads must be judged.*

Within the ranking of bullet types resulting from these tests, it is useful to consider the procedures found necessary for best grouping.

Best loading procedures

The bad effect of case mouth cracks shows clearly that cases should be individually inspected at every loading. Mouth cracks can appear during the final crimping; hence if the inspection is made on the empty cases before loading, the finished ammunition still may contain cracks. It is therefore best to inspect for this defect after loading. Only a few rounds are lost in this way—any more would call for scrapping the entire lot of cases.

Only linotype alloy is adequate for

Bullets used in handloads in these tests. (l. to r.) H&G No. 50 BB, H&G No. 50, H&G No. 73, custom target wadcutter, custom hollow-base target wadcutter, Remington No. 22850 hollow-base target wadcutter.

best grouping. Since some handloaders still use traditional compositions of bullet alloys, and very many use salvaged metal, the tests included an alloy softer than linotype for comparison. A Brinell of 10 (about half as hard as linotype) was chosen, since this is the hardness of the 1-to-20 tin-lead mixture long recommended for bullets of this kind, and also might roughly represent recovered bullets and other salvage. Groups averaged about one minute of angle larger than with linotype metal, and their uniformity was poorer.

Effect of bullet lubricant

THE RIFLEMAN has pointed out ("Bullet Lubricants", page 124, and other articles) that the bullet lubricant used has a strong effect on shooting accuracy. The effect, as expected, proved to be less marked in the short, wide bores of handguns, which give less opportunity than in rifles for bore conditioning to influence the bullet. Nevertheless, the effect still exists. Some lubricants tried, though satisfactorily preventing leading, increased group diameters by more than 50%. Attention was therefore concentrated on a few lubricants which were found to deliver good groups.

Bullet lubricant in the final tests was applied with either a Schuetzen lubricating pump, leaving the bullet unsized; or with a SAECO Lubrisizer, reducing the diameter by .0005" to .001". There was no distinguishable difference in the grouping. The finely made, accurately aligned SAECO Lubrisizer, with its smooth dies incorporating the correct tapered mouth to center the bullet base entering the die, was largely responsible for the success of bullets lubricated in this manner.

While the lubricant chosen has a very marked effect, bullet lubrication itself is a necessary evil. These tests showed conclusively that the less lubricant used, the better the grouping. The limitation on this is, of course, the disastrous lead fouling which appears when lubrication is reduced too far. Lubricants, otherwise good, differ in the quantity that must be used.

Lyman and SAECO bullet lubricants, applied in all 3 grease grooves of the cast bullet, produced the full accuracy of which the load appeared capable. Leaving them out of one or 2 grooves resulted in excessive barrel and cylinder leading after 2 or 3 groups. The Alox-beeswax lubricant described in THE RIFLEMAN article gave equally good accuracy, and no undue leading, when used in only one bullet groove and the other grooves left dry. It can be used in all 3 grooves if extra lubrication is desired, though target groups are somewhat enlarged. In that case it provides so much lubrication that after 50 rounds the revolver muzzle is covered with grease. Advantages of the Alox lubricant in .38 Special loads are thus limited to use of less lubricant, giving convenient handling of the greased bullet and less smoke in indoor ranges; or much greater lubrication if desired, with enlargement of groups. These advantages, while real, are less decisive than this lubricant possesses in cast-bullet rifle loads, in which it is superior in all circumstances.

A final point in connection with lubrication is its effect on the factory bullet.

Lubricant applied

The Remington hollow-base wadcutter target bullet, as supplied, has so little lubricant on it that at first sight there appears to be none. The bullets seem merely to have been tumbled in some solid lubricant leaving a trace on or in the surface. To prevent possible lead fouling of the test gun the first loadings of the factory bullet were done with Alox bullet lubricant applied in 2 of the bullet grooves, all of which appeared empty. Groups averaged about 3.5 minutes diameter. Grease on the revolver muzzle indicated much more lubrication than necessary. The bullet was then loaded with Alox lubricant in only one groove; the result was 3-minute groups and still a quantity of grease on the muzzle. Eventually the bullet was loaded simply as received. In that condition it grouped only a little larger than the 2.5 minutes of the factory ammunition, and with no more bore

leading than from best loads of cast and custom bullets.

During the experimentation it was observed that this bullet with Alox lubricant added, even in only one groove, left no leading at all in the revolver barrel cone. This was the only bullet and manner of loading which left no leading at all (even the excessive lubrication provided by Alox lubricant in all grooves of the No. 50 BB cast bullet did not completely prevent it).

At this point we leave the tests, and turn to use of the information as directly as possible for the handloader.

It is absolutely necessary not to assume that such excellent results will automatically follow from handloading. All available indications are that .38 Special target handloads vary in practice from very good to highly unsatisfactory. Only reasonable care was taken with the handloads in these tests. Why then do not all handloads perform well?

The primer is not to blame. The standard small pistol primer appeared consistent throughout these tests, and evidently compatible with the target powder charge.

The powder is not to blame. Two quite different powders performed well in these tests. Powders of various types have been used by the factories in .38 Special target ammunition, and round-to-round uniformity of the powder charges is only fair at best; yet the factory ammunition shoots with superior accuracy.

The cartridge case does not appear basically to blame. Irregular crimping admittedly is undesirable in principle, though crimped and uncrimped rounds shot into the same group in one of the tests. Case mouth cracks do have a very bad effect, as already explained. It seems unlikely, however, that reasonably careful handloaders would load cases showing widespread cracking, which would be necessary to produce a generalized condition of poor grouping.

The home-cast bullet is without any doubt the main cause of poor performance. Some handloaders have found this out for themselves, when a change to purchased bullets brought immediate improvement in scores.

That points to a simple solution—buy the bullets for loading. A still simpler one is to buy the factory ammunition, thus obtaining best possible results and skipping all the trouble of handloading. However, comparatively few users, either individuals or organizations, consider they can afford the cost of this solution for the quantity of ammunition they wish to fire, or need to fire for proficiency.

Cost comparison

Since cost is an unavoidable consideration, a rational choice among methods includes comparison of their costs. These are for 1000 rounds.

	Factory Ammunition	Handloads, Bullets Bought	Handloads, Bullets Cast
Cases	—	$ 7.00	$ 7.00
Primers	—	9.00	9.00
Powder	—	3.00	3.00
Bullets	—	40.00	15.00
	$180.00	$59.00	$34.00

Components costs are approximate; for cases and bullet metal they are frequently less than those shown. Loading tools are assumed to have been paid off.

These figures provide a clear-cut comparison. Many shooters are also interested in handloading for its own sake, including making their bullets.

The problem, then, is to find and eliminate the causes of poor bullets.

Unlike the investigation up to this point, which produced firm information from specific tests, there are obvious difficulties in reaching conclusions about the product of many individual handloaders. Still, the available information points to the following 3 factors as controlling:

1. Bullet casting.
2. Bullet sizing, including the dies used.
3. Bullet lubricants.

The short, fat handgun bullets cast easily. A glance at the bullets produced shows whether they are filling out cleanly in the mold. Any trouble in this respect is normally soon corrected as the mold gets up to temperature, aided if necessary by cleaning the mold.

But even when it appears acceptably filled out, a bullet may be partly hollow. The illustration shows cavities produced by not allowing time for the mold to fill completely and the sprue to solidify, before knocking the sprue plate around.

Undesirable as such cavities are, much worse ones can occur. These may be very large (described as sometimes large enough to contain a small pistol primer) and may be in any part of the bullet base, even near the edge. The unbalancing effect obviously is severe. The cavity may be covered by a thin layer of metal, so that the bullet looks solid; or instead of one large hole there may be a honeycombed condition.

Defects of this type were described, with illustrations, in the article "Cast Bullets And Fliers" (THE RIFLEMAN, February 1957). They were attributed to bullet metal not hot enough, to an unvented spout on the bottom-feed electric pot used with a single-cavity bullet mold (not a gang mold with its

Poorly cast bullets with base defects. Bullets with defects such as these appear to be often cast and loaded.

open-trough sprue plate), and to excessive speed in casting without inspecting the product.

Cast bullets cannot be perfectly uniform. The following summarizes the weights of 30 linotype bullets cast in a 4-cavity Hensley & Gibbs No. 50 BB gang mold, compared with the same number of Remington No. 22850 hollow-base wadcutter bullets. The cast bullets were well cast and then given only a rapid visual inspection. The Remington bullets, taken from a single box, were boiled in detergent solution before weighing to remove the lubricant which might be a cause of variation (boiling did not seem to affect the lubricant much). Weights were obtained on a laboratory balance and recorded to the nearest .01 gr.

	Average	Lightest	Heaviest	Spread	Standard Deviation*
Cast	136.13	135.24	136.77	1.53	.432
Factory	147.82	147.47	148.07	.60	.156

* A measure of dispersion which takes each individual value into account, and thus gives more information than merely the spread between highest and lowest values. It is included here for use by statisticians who may desire it.

The factory wadcutter, with a maximum spread of only .6 gr. in 30 sample bullets, proved to be highly uniform. It is comparable in this respect with cal. .30 Match bullets of the large custom bullet manufacturers, and bullets of the .30-'06 and 7.62 mm. National Match ammunition. Such uniformity in quantity production is possible only with heavy bullet-making machinery, expert-

Accurized M1911 pistol of cal. .38 AMU in Broadway machine rest. Light and heavy return springs at front provide choice depending on recoil.

ly operated, and Remington is to be complimented on such a product.

Even though extremely uniform, this factory wadcutter bullet groups in about 2½ minutes of angle instead of the 1 minute or less of cal. .30 Match bullets. Evidently, other factors are decisive in determining the size of target groups. Reasons for grouping superiority of the factory bullet will be investigated later.

The cast wadcutter showed a weight spread of 1.5 grs. in 30 bullets, or about 2½ times the factory spread. It appears the difference is due mainly to a small variation among the cavities of the gang mold, since staff experience with single-cavity molds indicates a weight spread of about ½ gr. in well-cast bullets of both rifle and pistol types. This is about the same uniformity as in factory wadcutters and cal. .30 jacketed Match bullets.

Cast vs. swaged bullets

It has at times been stated that swaged bullets, being free of internal voids, must shoot better than cast bullets. The statement, made without proof, appears to be based on a belief that it should be true. Here it is sufficient to note that the cast bullets in these tests performed excellently, grouping only slightly larger than the factory bullet, while the custom swaged bullets did comparatively poorly.

The answer, as to cast bullets, is found in the words "well-cast bullets" used above. It is absolutely necessary to give the mold time to fill. Then weighing a few bullets verifies that there is no other condition causing non-uniformity. Such check weighing need be done only until the casting procedure is established. Production is obtained not by hurriedly casting poor bullets in a one- or 2-cavity mold, which cannot give quantity in any case, but by using a gang mold. Ten-cavity molds are available, giving real quantity. Even a 4-cavity gang mold turns out with ease all the bullets an individual will wish to shoot.

The bench sizer-lubricator is a decided convenience in preparing even a few bullets. In production it is an unquestioned necessity.

Two past practices were damaging— casting bullets too large and then heavily sizing them, in the hope of improving poor bullets, and doing the sizing in dies which deform the bullets eccentrically (see illustration above). The present, correct practice is to cast bullets only very slightly above finished diameter, and to use lubricator dies with a conical mouth which centers the bullet for the small amount of sizing done.

Many poorly dimensioned molds and sizers are still in existence. The owner can readily replace the dies, which are comparatively inexpensive, with dies of the centering type which at least minimize the disadvantage of starting with excessively large bullets.

The final factor in performance is the bullet lubricant. The lubricant must work satisfactorily through the sizer-lubricator and then remain in place until the bullet is put into the cartridge case. It is easy to produce a lubricant which does that. It is much harder to provide the bore-conditioning action which makes bullets group well. This is true even though handgun requirements are not so difficult to meet as those of rifles. Lyman, SAECO, and Alox-beeswax bullet lubricants gave about equal grouping in these .38 Special target loads.

Some others were much less successful. The Alox lubricant has the advantages of use in only one groove on the bullet instead of all 3 grooves, and of preventing all revolver bore leading when added to one groove of the factory wadcutter.

Comparatively little has been said in all the foregoing about swaged target wadcutters from the custom bullet manufacturers. The solid and hollow-base custom wadcutters, of a single make, tried in these tests, did not perform nearly so well as factory and cast target bullets. The custom manufacturer has changed the design of both bullets since the time of the tests. The products of other makers are, of course, different also. It would, therefore, be wrong to take the present results as unfavorable to custom .38 Special target bullets in general. Leading bullet makers provide superior jacketed target bullets for rifles, and certainly can be expected to develop correspondingly good .38 Special bullets. But since the bullets differ from maker to maker, their performance can be known only by adequate test of each make and production style. Test of rifle bullets is readily within the ability of a good rifle shot. It is not within the capability of most pistol shooters, and this greatly limits their ability to select accurate target ammunition.

Prices of the factory wadcutter bullets and most of the custom bullets are the same.

Findings summarized

This completes the account. Because of its length, necessary for reasonable completeness, the most important points are summarized:

1. The ammunition's target spread is added to that of the shooter. Thus there is no given ammunition dispersion (10-

Bullet (r.) damaged by sizing down .004" in a die of non-centering shoulder type. Shown with bullet correctly sized down ½ of .001" incident to lubricating, in die of centering type.

ring diameter, X-ring diameter, or any other) which is as small as desirable; it can only be desired that the ammunition have no dispersion.

2. The factory target wadcutter ammunition proved best, showing itself capable in high-grade target revolvers of averaging 2½ minutes of angle in 10-shot groups, or 1¼" at 50 yds.

3. Handloads made up with the factory wadcutter bullet were very nearly as good. Factory bullets are sold for handloading at the same price as most custom bullets.

4. Handloads made up with *correctly prepared* wadcutter cast bullets averaged within 3½ minutes of angle in 10-shot groups, or 1¾" at 50 yds.

5. Handloads made up with solid and hollow-base wadcutter custom bullets, of designs being produced at that time by a large manufacturer, averaged considerably larger groups.

6. Cartridge case, primer, powder charge, and crimp, so long as suitable for the load and assembled with reasonable care, have little effect on the grouping of .38 Special target handloads. The bullet is the decisive component.

7. Successful cast bullets must be:

    a. Well cast, allowing the mold to fill completely; and made of metal which is sufficiently hard and strong.

    b. Sized only lightly, in a die that centers the bullet; or not sized. A correctly made die makes best use of an oversize bullet.

    c. Lubricated with a bullet lubricant which conditions the bore for close grouping.

This investigation was directed entirely to fundamentals. It may still be possible, by refinements, to equal or perhaps even surpass the factory ammunition and bullet. ∎

HANDLOADING THE .45 ACP

By M. D. WAITE

THE handloading of good-quality ammunition for the Colt cal. .45 automatic Service pistol is not likely to be difficult so long as certain precautions are observed.

Reliable functioning of this pistol requires ammunition which works the mechanism with some reserve of power. The Service cartridge with 230-gr. metal-jacketed bullet at 830 feet per second (f.p.s.) is somewhat more than adequate for this purpose, and is unnecessarily powerful for target shooting at the maximum competitive range of 50 yds.

One can purchase commercial match ammunition loaded with a wadcutter bullet of lighter weight and lower velocity. This is more pleasant to shoot than the 230-gr. Service load and will function through the as-issued Service pistol with reliability. However, many shooters either cannot afford to use match ammunition or must restrict its use to important matches. The only alternatives are to handload one's ammunition or to purchase it from a custom loader.

The cost of a good handloading outfit, including press, dies, powder measure, powder scale, bullet mold, sizer-lubricator, and lead melting pot, will exceed $100 and can be as much as $200 depending on choice of equipment. Even the latter estimate will be more than doubled if a semi-automatic turret tool is purchased.

Factors affecting decision

The decision to handload one's ammunition depends on several factors, including time available for handloading, expected ammunition consumption, and the size of one's pocketbook. Economies amounting to several cents per round can be effected by handloading or by using lower priced custom-loaded ammunition. Obviously the greater saving will accrue to the handloader and in time will more than pay for equipment used. Also, handloading is a challenging hobby. The mechanical processes involved are simple and attention to details can result in ammunition of good quality.

The components of the cartridge are case, primer, powder charge, and bullet. The only item likely to be made by the handloader is the bullet, which can be formed in a die or cast in a mold. Bullets can also be purchased. The cartridge case, the costliest component, can be reused several times and it is this fact which explains much of the saving possible through handloading.

The fired case ejected from the gun has been expanded by gas pressure to fill the gun chamber. Although relatively elastic, it does not return all the way to its original size. The case must there-fore be full-length resized in a die. This insures that the case will re-enter the gun chamber easily and also be small enough to grip the bullet. In automatic pistol ammunition loaded with lead-alloy bullets, it is usually necessary to crimp or bend the edge of the case mouth into the side of the bullet to secure it. Otherwise the bullet may be pushed back into the case on striking the feed ramp or breech, with a malfunction resulting.

Crimping of the relatively straight case of the .45 ACP cartridge is complicated by the fact that it headspaces on the mouth of the case. That is, forward movement of the cartridge is stopped by the mouth of the case reaching a shoulder at forward end of the chamber.

End play minimized

The end play of the cartridge within the chamber is normally very small and especially so in pistols made, or 'accurized', for target shooting. Minimum end play is desired for uniform primer ignition from shot to shot. If excessive end play or headspace exists, a portion of the firing pin blow is wasted in driving the whole cartridge forward to its stopping point. The amount of drive-in is not uniform from shot to shot and the same holds true for ignition of the primer and powder charge. This causes a greater than normal velocity spread, with loss of accuracy. The identical condition can be created by improper crimping or bullet-seating practices which increase cartridge end play.

Crimping is done in special taper-crimp dies by inserting the cartridge into the full-length sizing die, or in the crimping die regularly furnished in the

1 Full-length case resizing in sleeve die removes bulges and reduces case-body diameter to insure proper chambering in gun. Light application of lanolin lubricant is applied to case with fingertips before inserting it in die. This reduces friction and prevents cases from seizing or galling in die

2 After initial full-length resizing, case is inserted in second die which expels fired primer, expands neck, and bells case mouth slightly to prevent shaving of bullet on seating. Cases may be primed concurrent with this operation

die sets made for reloading the .45 ACP cartridge. Regardless of the crimping device, the bullet should be well secured in the case. A simple test is to hold the cartridge in the fingers, press the bullet nose straight in against a solid surface, and note if the bullet remains in place under firm pressure. If not, amount of crimp must be increased.

Most lead-alloy wadcutter bullets designed for the .45 ACP cartridge lack the crimping groove customarily found on revolver bullets. Therefore, the case mouth must be crimped into the smooth side of the bullet near the top edge of the body. A little lead should extend above the case mouth. The exposed lead acts as a lubricant against the barrel feed ramp and also engages the rifling when the round is fully chambered. This tends to reduce cartridge end play within the chamber, and also explains why a relatively heavy crimp is possible when handloading lead-alloy wadcutter bullets in this cartridge (see Fig. 11). The amount of bullet shoulder exposed will largely depend upon hardness of alloy used but should not be so great that the slide fails to close completely. Bullet seating depth should be determined experimentally according to the individual gun and bullet design.

Barrel condition affects accuracy

Light barrel pitting will have little effect on accuracy, but worn rifling will. To check a barrel, remove it from the gun and with firm thumb pressure force a 230-gr. Service round into the chamber. Then slowly tilt the chamber end down. If the round does not drop freely from the chamber one can assume that the throat and possibly the rifling are badly worn. Replace such a barrel.

Insufficient seating of primers is a prime cause of misfires with handloads in the Service pistol. It is extremely important that primers be seated to full depth and that all cases be inspected after priming to assure that such is the case. Top of the primer should lie slightly below base of the case. A check of the primer with the fingertip upon removal of the primed case from the shellholder should become habitual.

It is wise to segregate cases according to manufacturer and to clean them before resizing. Grit on the cases will score even the hard carbide-faced dies, and is destructive to ordinary steel dies.

Cases are readily cleaned of grit and fouling with a suitable solution. Quart screw-top mayonnaise or fruit jars with top seal are convenient; at least 2 are required. The proportions of the cleaning solution are: 1 pt. water, 1 cup white vinegar, 1 tablespoon salt, and 1 teaspoon detergent.

Mix the solution in one of the jars. When all solids are dissolved, fill jar half full with decapped cases, screw on cap, and shake about 10 minutes, or until cases are visibly cleaned of fouling. Brass cases will brighten appreciably in cleaning, as the solution is mildly acidic. After cleaning pour off solution into another jar also half filled with cases and place jar of cleaned cases under water tap to wash with occasional agitation for at least 10 minutes. While this jar is washing, the cleaning process is repeated with the second jar, etc. After rinsing and draining, cleaned cases can be sun dried or placed on pie tins and dried in a mild oven for a few minutes.

Note that cases are best decapped before cleaning. This is conveniently done with a hand punch and base unit.

If cases are washed before decapping, the primer pockets are likely to corrode from trapped cleaning solution reacting with primer residue. Also, water may remain in the pockets even after prolonged drying.

During decapping and cleaning, inspect constantly for split cases or other serious defects. Doubtful cases should be rejected as early as possible to avoid waste of primers, powder, and bullets.

Trimming not recommended

Trimming .45 ACP cases is not recommended because shortening them increases end play in the chamber. Chamfering of case mouths is also inadvisable as it tends to weaken the crimp.

Relatively hard bullets are best in this cartridge as they feed more reliably than soft bullets and are less susceptible to deformation in the bore. Suitable alloys are commercially available. As most shooters use reclaimed lead, it is often necessary to adjust hardness by addition of lead when the alloy is too hard, or to add tin or antimony as hardening agents when the alloy is too soft. A bullet which will just take impression of the fingernail is about right for hardness. Some shooters use straight type-metal alloys, but these are unnecessarily hard and can be difficult to size.

Batches of alloy should be thoroughly blended and bullets cast from each batch kept separate.

Gang molds casting 4 or more bullets are advisable when much shooting is to be done. At best, bullet casting is tedious and the increased production possible from gang molds more than offsets their higher cost. Efficient use of gang molds demands a melting pot holding at least 10 lbs. of alloy, and double that capacity is better to mini-

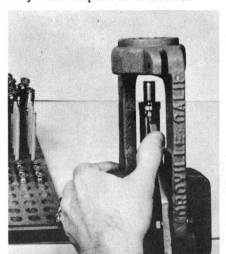

3 Priming may be performed in separate operation. Automatic-feed priming devices, available as accessory for many tools, eliminate handling each primer

4 Charge of powder is metered directly into cartridge case. Accurate scale is used to adjust measure setting and occasionally to verify weight of charge thrown. Cases should be inspected for possible double charge

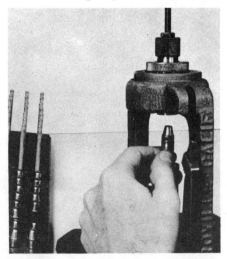

5 Time is saved if bullets are lightly pressed into case necks by hand after charging with powder. Bullets are then seated to desired depth in seating die

6 Final operation with 4-die system shown is crimping of case neck into side of bullet, or crimping groove if present. An adequate crimp prevents telescoping of bullet into case on feeding and also protects powder charge against oil or moisture. After final inspection and wiping, the cartridge is ready to be shot

7 Typical bullet casting setup. Lead alloy has been melted in electric pot. Operator is transferring molten alloy from pot to mold using a dipper with integral pouring snout. Upon cooling, excess metal (sprue) is sheared from bullet base into can behind melting pot by tapping mold cut-off plate with wooden mallet or heel of gloved hand, after which mold blocks are opened to release bullet onto soft surface such as folded towel. This prevents deformation likely to occur if bullets are dropped on hard surface. Bullets are inspected upon cooling

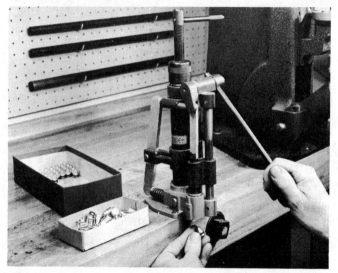

8 Typical sizer-lubricator which simultaneously trues up bullet and fills grease grooves with lubricant. Finished bullets should be stored in clean, covered boxes until ready for use

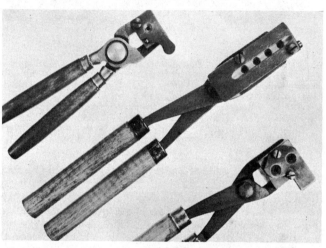

9 Typical bullet molds for casting lead alloy bullets. Gang mold (center), casting 4 bullets simultaneously, is recommended when much shooting is to be done, or when time available for handloading is limited. Gang molds casting up to 10 bullets are available. Single- and double-cavity molds shown are cheaper, and are adequate for average shooter with limited ammunition requirement

mize time lost between melts.

All bullets should be inspected after cooling and defective ones returned to the pot.

The sizing and lubricating operations are critical. An imperfectly sized bullet will not shoot accurately. The sizing die *should not* have a pronounced interior shoulder as this feature will almost always result in bullets sized more on one side than the other. The throat of the best die is cut on a gentle taper which centers the bullet as it enters the constriction. By design such dies cannot size a bullet off-center where the as-cast diameter of the bullet is the same or greater than the diameter of the main die bore.

The mold maker should be advised of the approximate alloy to be used in the mold. He can then estimate the shrinkage and furnish a mold casting bullets of proper diameter. Ideally, the bullet should require only minor truing up in the sizing operation as any significant reduction in diameter will usually result in distortion and subsequent inaccuracy.

Usual sizing diameter for .45 ACP bullets is .452″, although bullets for use in thinner walled, nickel-plated cases are less likely to jump their crimp if sized to .453″.

A variety of excellent commercial bullet lubricants is available in stick form for use with available sizer-lubricators, and it is doubtful if significant saving is effected by preparation of homemade lubricants.

Bullets as they come from the sizer-lubricator may have grease on their bases. This should be carefully removed as powder can adhere to the grease and remain unburned on firing. To do this efficiently, tack several layers of sturdy cloth to a board and saturate the cloth with a solvent such as Varsol. As the bullets come from the sizer-lubricator, slide their bases across the cloth before placing them in boxes.

Measuring powder

Use of a mechanical powder measure is the only practical method for rapidly metering the small charges of powder required for .45 ACP target loads. Relative precision of most measures is good, but they cannot be expected to deliver exact charges. Some deviation in weight may therefore be expected from charge to charge. Experience with good quality measures indicates a probable plus or minus deviation of .2 (two tenths) gr. when metering Bullseye or similar flocculent powders. Most manufacturers of drum-type powder meas-

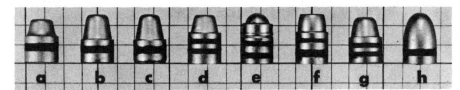

10 Some popular cast bullet designs for use in .45 ACP cartridge: **(a)** Hensley & Gibbs #130; **(b)** Hensley & Gibbs #68; **(c)** Hensley & Gibbs #68 bevel-base; **(d)** Hensley & Gibbs #78; **(e)** Lyman #454309; **(f)** Lyman #452423; **(g)** Lyman #452460; **(h)** Lyman #452374. (On ¼" grid)

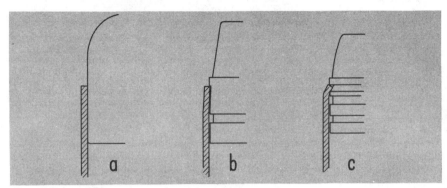

11 Bullets are secured in case necks by (a) friction, (b) taper crimp into sidewall, or (c) by roll crimp into sidewall, or crimping groove. Metal-jacketed cal. .45 bullets do not ordinarily require crimping as friction alone is sufficient to secure them in properly sized case necks. Lead bullets, by their nature, have a low coefficient of friction, which may be further decreased by presence of lubricant film. They must be secured by crimping as friction alone will not hold them in place. Either taper or roll crimp can be used in .45 ACP handloads. Roll crimp is necessary when loads are to be used in revolver where bullets are subject to inertial dislodgement

ures can furnish drums designed for accurate metering of relatively small charges of pistol powder. Also available are electrically operated powder scales which are more accurate than mechanical measures, but are necessarily costly.

Reloading of the .45 ACP cartridge can be accomplished with 2, 3, or 4 dies, depending on how much care and attention one wishes to devote to the job. With the 2-die system the initial die full-length resizes the case, ejects the fired primer, and at the same time expands and bells the case mouth to accept the bullet. Priming can also be accomplished at this stage. After charging with powder and inserting a bullet into the case mouth, the second die is used to simultaneously seat and crimp the bullet to complete the loading of the round.

With the 3-die system, the first die full-length resizes the case but does nothing else. The second die ejects the fired primer and expands and bells the case mouth. As the case is extracted from the die, a fresh primer can be inserted in the primer pocket to complete the case preparation cycle. After charging and inserting a bullet into the case mouth, the third die is used to simultaneously seat and crimp the bullet.

Sequence of operations with the 4-die system is shown in Figs. 1 through 6. This system is preferred by many careful handloaders as bullet seating

and crimping operations are separate, which eliminates any possibility of lead being shaved from the bullet during crimping. Also, resizing and neck expanding-belling operations are separate, which reduces cold-working of case necks and incidence of splits.

Special carbide-faced dies are commercially available which have several advantages over ordinary steel dies. Cases require no lubrication for resizing and are burnished to a high scratch-free polish. These dies are recommended for steel and nickel-plated cases. They will also last much longer than ordinary steel dies.

Mid-range loads

Rearward movement of the Service pistol slide on firing compresses the large recoil-spring within the slide and the smaller mainspring within the mainspring housing. Considerable energy is required to compress these springs. Excessively reduced charges in the .45 ACP cartridge often result in malfunctions as the slide does not move back far enough to cock the hammer and pick up a fresh round from the magazine. Removal of a coil or 2 from the recoil spring will often correct this condition, but once a gun has been 'balanced' for reduced-charge loads it should not be fired with full-charge loads unless re-equipped with an unaltered recoil spring. ∎

REDUCED LOADS

By WM. C. DAVIS, JR.

ONE of the great advantages and most enjoyable aspects of handloading is developing and shooting reduced loads. It is unfortunate that this is not recognized by many modern-day handloaders as it was years ago. Possibly that is due to the preoccupation with high-velocity loads that developed among handloaders in the years following World War II. High-velocity cartridges proliferated in that period and handloaders were eager to explore their new capabilities. In the publicity attending the introduction of new high-velocity cartridges, the great virtues of versatility and economy afforded by handloading were neglected and a generation of handloaders evolved whose principal object was the achievement of the highest possible velocity. This excessive preoccupation with high velocities has moderated in recent years as is evident from the resurgence of interest in such cartridges as the .45-70 and in rifles chambered for handgun cartridges and interest in blackpowder shooting. Meanwhile, however, the advantages of using reduced loads and their true capabilities had been so long neglected that most handloaders were quite unfamiliar with them. That is regrettable.

Two big advantages of reduced loads are the versatility they afford the handloader and the economy of using reduced loads with cast bullets. Other benefits are the mild recoil and report which make reduced loads a pleasure to shoot, particularly in guns which otherwise kick hard and produce unpleasant muzzle blast. The reduced-load shooter can fire his centerfire rifle or handgun in practically any location where the use of .22 rimfire arms is appropriate, with equal safety and no greater disturbance to the surroundings. A handloader who has a .222 Remington or .22-250, for example, can approximate the performance of the rimfire .22 short, long or long rifle cartridges at costs actually lower than those of the inexpensive rimfire ammunition. He can duplicate the performance of the .22 Winchester Magnum Rimfire and .22 Hornet with even greater savings. The .30-06 and .308 can be loaded to produce the performance of a .32 revolver cartridge or the .32-20, .30 Carbine or .30-30.

In addition, cast-bullet reduced loads can be developed by the serious target shooter to produce accuracy fully equal to that of factory loads in most calibers, and to compare favorably with that obtained from the best full-charge jacketed-bullet handloads at ranges up to 200 yards. Though cost may not be an important incentive for many serious target shooters, the savings realized by cast bullet shooting is generally welcome and there is a certain fascination in developing highly accurate cast bullet loads.

Loads are versatile

Quite apart from the cost saving of cast bullet loads, reduced loads using jacketed bullets are attractive because of the versatility they offer. The shooter who wants to hunt wild turkey, fur-bearing animals, or even rabbits, with a centerfire rifle can develop reduced loads that are not excessively destructive to meat or pelts, using jacketed bullets. The handloader who has a .300 Winchester Magnum for long-range big-gun hunting but wants to use it for woods hunting of whitetail deer without excessive destruction of meat, can load it down to the ballistics of the .30-30 or .308 for that purpose.

For the shooter who enjoys competition, there are organized matches held by the Cast Bullet Association constantly. Some are postal matches, where the shooter fires targets on his own range under prescribed rules and submits them by mail for scoring. Others are shoulder-to-shoulder matches fired at local clubs or at the annual national match sponsored by the Cast Bullet Association. Cast bullet shooting is a good group activity for small clubs whose members do not wish to invest in highly specialized equipment or elaborate range facilities. It can be practiced with ordinary hunting and varmint rifles.

For the handloader who is equipped to assemble full-charge loads, no additional equipment is required to assemble reduced loads with jacketed bullets; he need only buy appropriate powders. As the term is applied generally (and in this article) reduced loads are those producing less than about 90 per cent of the velocity of maximum loads in the same cartridge. In a few instances, powders suitable for full-charge loads are also suitable for moderately reduced loads, but in many instances they are not.

Because smokeless powder burns at a rate strongly dependent on pressure, powders suitable for full-charge loads often do not burn completely in low-pressure reduced loads and many produce poor results. Powders of finer granulation, designed for more rapid burning, are then required. Another consideration dictating the choice of faster-burning powders for reduced loads is the reliable and uniform ignition of the charge by the primer. Reduced loads usually occupy less than the full powder space in the case. This condition is not favorable to quick and uniform ignition. Powders intended for full-charge loads in high-velocity cartridges are usually of large granulation and have deterrent coating in the outer surface of the grains to achieve favorable velocity-pressure relationships in maximum loads. These characteristics are unfavorable for ignition, particularly when there is much free air-space in the case. Powders of finer granulation and those not heavily deterrent-coated ignite more easily and burn more completely and uniformly in reduced loads.

Cartridges with large powder capacity and using small-diameter bullets require special caution when reduced loads are being prepared. These cartridges include the magnum rifle ones less than .35 caliber, and even such cartridges as the .270, .25-06, .243 and 6mm Remington. For reasons not completely understood, reduced loads of slow-burning deterrent-coated powders in such cartridges will, on rare occasions, develop destructively excessive chamber pressures when fired. In general, the powders suitable for full-charge loads in such cartridges — for example IMR-4831, IMR-4350, H-205 and H-450 — should never be used in those cartridges at charge weights less than 90 percent of maximum charges. Another powder often used in those cartridges, Winchester-Western 785, should never be loaded in any charges except those specifically recommended by the manufacturer or some other source of thoroughly tested data. Winchester-Western 296 is a handgun powder that also should be used only in the charges specifically recommended, and never in reduced loads. Though some of the slow-burning powders can be used satisfactorily in full-case loads for smaller cases, in which they give reduced-load performance, it is best to avoid their use in any reduced loads where other powders will give comparable performance.

The phenomenon of excessive chamber pressures developing from reduced loads of slow-burning powders has been widely publicized. Shooters not entirely familiar with the problem may wrongly think that all reduced loads are hazardous. When suitable powders are used, this is not the case, according to information available to the NRA.

It is widely known that some .38 Special and .357 Magnum revolvers have been destroyed by supposedly small charges of Bullseye powder — traditional target loads in the .38 Special for many years. These are, in effect, reduced loads. An extensive investigation by Hercules, the powder manufacturer, failed to confirm any phenomenon comparable to that which occurred with slow-burning powders in rifles, despite the most severe tests that could be contrived. Convincing evidence was developed that the guns were blown up probably because two or more charges were inadvertently put into the case by the handloader.

Some important precautions

Multiple charges are indeed a potential hazard, whether in rifles or handguns, and extra precautions are warranted. With most reduced loads, the cartridge case will accommodate two or more charges without overflowing. Most handloaders of long experience have tried, at some time or other, to put two full-charge loads in the same case only to be reminded of their carelessness when the case overflowed. Because reduced loads may not give that warning, it is of vital importance to check loading precedures to guarantee against any such mistake.

Reduced loads for handguns are more common than for rifles, and practically all reloading manuals list such loads, though they are not usually so identified. In the .357, .41 or .44 Magnum cartridges, for example, full-charge factory loads are approximated with handloads using powders such as Blue Dot, 2400, SR-4756, IMR-4227, WW 296 or H110. When somewhat less powerful loads are desired, suitable powders are Unique, PB, WW 630 and HS 6. For light target loads using lead bullets, Bullseye, 700X, WW 231, and HP-38 are available.

The only special precaution required in assembling reduced loads for handguns, except extra vigilance to guard against double or multiple charges, is to avoid the use of jacketed bullets with very light powder charges. Especially in revolvers, there is a real possibility that a jacketed bullet might lodge in the barrel when fired with a very light powder charge. With body-jacketed or "half-jacketed" bullets, the jacket may lodge in the barrel, even though the core may be expelled and strike the target, so detecting the malfunction is unlikely unless the bore is examined after each shot. If a succeeding round is fired into a lodged bullet or jacket lodged in the barrel, the barrel may be bulged and ruined. For these reasons, jacketed bullets should not be loaded in handgun cartridges using powder charges less than those listed in a reliable data source, with any type of powder.

In rifles, there are only a few extra precautions necessary from the safety standpoint. One is to guard against double or multiple charges, as mentioned before. Another is to avoid use of slow-burning powders in reduced loads, as also mentioned before. A third is to segregate the cases used for reduced loads in bottle-necked rimless cartridges, and not reload these with full-charge loads unless the cases have been checked in an accurate gage for head-to-shoulder-cone length. This is necessitated by the fact that the head-to-shoulder-cone length of the case, which controls headspace in bottle-necked rimless cartridges, may be shortened slightly by firing reduced loads. It is not essential for safety to understand the mechanism by which this occurs, but possibly it is interesting enough to warrant description.

When the primer is fired, whether or not with a reduced powder charge, the force of the explosion drives the case forward in the chamber causing the head of the case to separate momentarily from contact with the bolt face. The force of the primer explosion is sufficient, in some instances, not only to take up any free movement of the cartridge in the chamber, but actually to force the case shoulder slightly backward, increasing the space between the case head and the bolt face. Very soon, the rising pressure from the burning powder charge exerts a force inside the case tending to push it back into contact with the bolt face. With full-charge loads, the case is almost invariably forced back to the bolt face, the case shoulder is blown forward against the shoulder in the chamber, and the head-to-shoulder length of the case then corresponds to the headspace dimension of the rifle. With reduced loads, however, the combined forces of friction between the case walls and the chamber walls and the gas pressure acting against the inside of the shoulder in the case which tend to push it forward, are not overcome by the force tending to thrust the case backward against the bolt face. The case remains in the forward position with its head-to-shoulder dimension permanently shortened. A clue to the occurrence of this is that the primer of the fired case will be protruding slightly by the amount that the head-to-shoulder dimension of the case has been shortened. The condition is occasionally noticed even in factory loads for low-pressure cartridges. Some old .30-30 rifles that have seen much use develop excessive headspace. The rim does not prevent forward movement of the case as it is intended to do and the cases from factory loads fired in such rifles sometimes show slightly protruding primers. With rimless cases, of course, the shortened head-to-shoulder length of the case presents exactly the same situation as a rifle with excessive headspace and that is the reason such cases should not subsequently be fired with full-charge loads. For reduced loads, the condition does no serious harm and the cases can be reloaded again with comparable low-pressure loads.

For convenience, reduced loads can be categorized as midrange, short-range and minimum loads. Midrange loads are those that develop from about half to three-fourths the velocity of full-charge loads in the same caliber, usually with bullets of normal weight. Short-range loads are those developing less than half the velocity of full-charge loads, either with bullets of normal weight or lighter bullets. Minimum loads are those that contain only enough powder to expel the bullet reliably from the bore and give acceptable accuracy for the intended purpose.

Midrange loads are often successful using the same powders suitable for full-charge loads, except in cartridges for which full-charge loads normally employ very slow-burning powders. Powders such as IMR-4895, IMR-3031 and IMR-4198 can be used successfully for the more powerful midrange loads in cartridges such as the .30-06 and .308. IMR-4198 and Reloder 7, often used for full-charge loads in the .222 and .223 Remington, can also be used in midrange loads. At lower midrange velocities with lighter bullets, faster burning powders are required.

Short-range loads almost always require faster burning powders for best results. In a wide variety of centerfire rifle cartridges, the most suitable powders are those such as SR-4759, SR-4756, Unique, 2400 and WW 630. In cartridges for which the velocity of full-charge loads exceeds about 2,000 fps, jacketed bullets should not be used in low-power loads developing less than about 1,200 fps. The friction of jacketed bullets passing through the bore is much greater than that of lubricated cast bullets, and it is also more variable. With very light powder charges, the energy of the charge might not be enough to overcome the bore friction, and the bullet might lodge in the bore. Even if bullets do not lodge, jacketed bullets may shoot poorly in very low-velocity loads, giving large vertical dispersion. This is because variation in bore friction from shot to shot causes comparatively large variations in velocity. The effect is especially noticeable when firing from a cold uncleaned barrel, where the first shot may characteristically strike quite low on the target. For cartridges having a relatively large diameter bullet in comparison to case capacity, such as the .32-20, .44-40, .45-70 or rifles chambered for handgun cartridges, jacketed bullets are usually satisfactory down to about 1,000 fps. At velocities less than about 1200 fps in high-velocity rifles, or about 1,000 fps in low-velocity rifles, lubricated lead bullets should be used. They often can be made to perform satisfactorily down to 800 fps or lower.

Choose the right powder

Powders for reduced loads should be easily ignited by the primer, burn completely enough to avoid a troublesome residue of partially burned granules, and be of low bulk density so they occupy as much space as possible in the cartridge case. Double-base powders such as Unique, 2400 and WW 630 meet the requirement of easy ignition, and usually give good results. Both 2400 and WW 630 are quite dense and occupy relatively little space in the case. Both leave considerable amounts of unburned powder if they are used in light loads. Nevertheless, they perform very well in many reduced loads and are well worth trying. IMR-4227 and IMR-4198 perform well in many midrange and some short-range loads, as do H-4227 and H-4198. Hercules Reloder 7 gives outstanding results in some midrange and short-range loads, specially with cast bullets in cartridges such as the .30-30, .308 and .30-06.

Du Pont SR-4759 is possibly the most useful reduced-load powder for rifles. It combines all the desirable characteristics of easy ignition, relatively clean burning and low bulk density. It is a single-base powder, of the porous-base type (as are PB, SR-7625 and SR-4756) which facilitates quick, uniform ignition in reduced loads. Low bulk density is achieved both by the porous-base grains, and the fact that its grain form is tubular with an unusually large perforation through the center. The tubular grain form imparts, by its geometry, a relatively large initial surface area for prompt ignition, but a measure of progressivity in burning. This gives a favorable velocity-pressure ratio in a wide range of applications. The progressivity imparted by the geometry of the grain is achieved without the use of a deterrent coating, which would otherwise inhibit ignition undesirably. SR-4759 was the powder chosen for most of the reduced loads in the excellent Speer Reloading Manuals Numbers 9 and 10, two of the few manuals in which reduced-load data are now published. The only obstacle to this powder's wider use is its relatively limited availability on the shelves of retail dealers.

This limited availability is due to an unfortunate combination of circumstances. SR-4759 is Du Pont's replacement for No. 80 powder, which was extremely popular in the heyday of reduced loads before World War II. SR-4759 is fully as good as No. 80 was, better in some respects, but it was introduced in 1941, just as handloading components disappeared from the market for the duration of the war. It was originally available in 8-ounce canisters, as SR-4756 and SR-7625 are now. Unfortunately, owing to the decline in popularity of reduced loads after World War II, SR-4759 did not sell well, and it was discontinued in 1965. As a result of many requests, most of them from readers of *The American Rifleman*, Du Pont resumed manufacture and distribution of SR-4759 in 1973, but only in 4-pound caddies and 12-pound kegs. It is the only Du Pont canister powder not available in half-pound or 1-pound canisters. Being designed specifically for reduced loads in rifles, SR-4759 is not very suitable for other uses, and Du Pont felt that the limited market for such a single-purpose powder would not justify the additional expense of marketing it in smaller canisters. Retail dealers, on the other hand, refused to stock the 4-pound caddies because they felt the powder would be hard to sell in such large packages. Being practically unavailable at retail stores, SR-4759 is completely unknown to many of today's handloaders, and indeed it has not sold well under those circumstances. The poor sales record apparently reinforces the manufacturer's opinion of a low potential market for the powder, and the unfortunate circle of circumstances is complete.

SR-4759 is available for handloaders who have knowledge of its excellent qualities and perseverance to seek it out. The manufacturer has advised that there is ample stock on hand. Any dealer in Du Pont powders can order SR-4759 from a Du Pont distributor. For handloaders who want to try SR-4759 but hesitate to invest in 4 pounds of it, one solution is to pool requirements with other shooters in the same area, and place the order through a Du Pont dealer. For some reduced-load requirements, especially large magnum rifle cartridges, no other powder serves as well as SR-4759. It is *the* powder designed exclusively for reduced loads in rifles, and its performance is excellent in the whole range of applications from low-velocity to moderately powerful midrange loads.

Minimum loads in rifles and handguns require the use of lubricated lead bullets and fast-burning pistol or shotgun powders. They are special loads for target practice in a basement range or shooting small pests in the barnyard or garden. They can produce dangerous ricochets, just as .22 rimfire cartridges can, and must be used with the same precautions required of .22 rimfire rifles.

Minimum loads in rifles perform best with light bullets because the shorter bearing surface of the bullet in the barrel causes less bore friction. Cast bullets weighing 80 to 120 grains in .30 caliber, 60 to 70 grains in .25 caliber, and 35 to 45 grains in .22 caliber are suitable. There are, unfortunately, no comparably light cast bullets available in other popular calibers such as the .243, .270 and 7mm, but dies for swaging such bullets from lead wire or cast slugs are available on order from firms such as Corbin (P.O. Box 758, Phoenix, Ore. 97535). One type of die is available for use in most ⅞-inch x 14 threaded bench-mounted reloading presses. Die-forming has the advantage of allowing bullets of different weights to be made using the same equipment.

For handguns, especially those with non-adjustable sights, bullets of normal weight are best even in minimum loads because very light bullets do not produce a normal point of impact on the target. Regular 148-grain wadcutter bullets are best suited to .38 Special and .357 Magnum handguns.

Reduced loads using jacketed bullets introduce no special problems for the handloader who can prepare good full-charge loads. Success is usually achieved with any of several powders that are suitable to the desired velocity. Cast-bullet loads, on the other hand, are more critical in their requirements.

As mentioned before, a large amount of air space in reduced loads is a detriment to their performance. Much can be done to overcome this problem with the proper choice of powders. It is impossible, however, to avoid the existence of airspace in most reduced loads. One consequence of this is that the powder charge is not uniformly positioned in the case before each shot and variations in the powder position cause variation in muzzle velocity. One way this problem can be solved is to use a light tuft of fibrous filler, such as the Dacron intended for stuffing pillows, pressed lightly down on the powder charge. That procedure is effective and often significantly improves the accuracy of certain cast bullet loads. Many handloaders have practiced this method for years with no untoward results. There are, however, a few instances in which loads employing such filler material have produced ring-bulges in the gun chamber at the position corresponding to the base of the bullet in the assembled cartridge. For this reason, the general use of such fillers cannot be recommended, though in some loads it has worked very well. An alternative procedure, which produces similarly beneficial results, is to elevate the muzzle of the gun at a high angle just before aiming at the target and firing the shot. This assures that the powder is uniformly positioned at the head of the cartridge case from shot to shot.

If the handloader is not already acquainted with the many advantages of reduced loads, he is well advised to try them. Handloaders of an earlier generation used them widely with great success. This made one center-fire rifle suitable for such diverse purposes as shooting grackles in the garden, squirrels in the woodlot, and deer on the mountain. It is a fascinating aspect of handloading, too long neglected.

MINIMUM LOADS IN HANDGUNS

By WILLIAM DRESSER

Development and use of low-power .38 Spl. loads

DESPITE the popularity of midrange and high-velocity handgun ammunition, there are many uses for loads of absolutely minimum practicable power. Among such uses is shooting on a basement range where noise must be held at minimum. Equally important may be the use of such loads to instruct noise- and recoil-shy beginners.

Although the desirability of using the .22 rimfire counterpart of a center-fire gun for training is evident, no rimfire guns similar to certain center-fire guns exist. The cost of a similar rimfire gun is considerable if it is to be used only for instruction. The saving in ammunition cost resulting from use of rimfire ammunition is slight if one already has reloading equipment or plans to acquire such equipment anyway.

Properly employed, minimum-power center-fire loads permit immediate use of a much more powerful caliber than might be thought possible. There is a definite psychological advantage to the use of one gun throughout training with loads of gradually increasing power. Lightweight, powerful weapons of heavy recoil, such as snub-nosed revolvers, particularly call for minimum first loads. Many men might shoot such guns more competently if they had worked the charges up from a very low-powered first load.

Wadcutters are best

Full wadcutter bullets seated deeply in the case are best for all light revolver loads regardless of caliber. The reduced powder space permits best ignition of light loads and burns them at a favorable pressure level. Very light bullets, usually round-nosed or semi-wadcutter, which are sometimes suggested for light loads, are of dubious usefulness. They fail to reduce powder space and lack the weight to give good burning of light charges. Their centers of

impact with any powder charge will be found far different from those of more usual bullet weights. This is even more true of lead balls or buckshot, which are especially unsatisfactory with light charges in fixed-sight revolvers.

Development of minimum loads is a safe and highly desirable experience for even the beginning reloader. One starts out by finding the minimum load listed for the given caliber, bullet, and powder. Bullseye pistol powder is desirable due to its ease of ignition. The minimum powder charge listed is cut in half, and one cartridge is loaded and fired. If the bullet of this first cartridge leaves the barrel, the powder charge is cut in half again, a cartridge is loaded and fired, and this process continued until a bullet fails to leave the barrel.

No one can work out a near-minimum load without loading a number of cartridges whose bullets do not leave the barrel. So long as every bullet is removed before another shot can be fired, no harm at all is done and lead alloy bullets can be knocked out easily.

Jacketed bullets are much harder to remove. If another cartridge is fired before a stuck bullet is removed, there is considerable chance even with very light loads that the barrel will be bulged and perhaps ruined.

The only tools needed to remove a bullet from the bore are a hammer with head of lead, plastic, or rawhide, and a 1/4" or 5/16" aluminum, brass, or copper rod slightly longer than the barrel. Free from grit, such a rod cannot damage the rifling. The cartridges and fired cases are ejected, careful check made that the gun is empty, and the cylinder is closed. The gun is then held upside down with the gloved left hand around the cylinder area and the gun butt resting in the pit of the stomach, not on a hard surface. The rod is placed against the bullet and tapped to drive the bullet back into the cylinder. No great force is necessary. The bullet can then be shoved out of the cylinder with the rod and hand pressure alone.

Bullet sticks in barrel

Once the first bullet sticks in the barrel, real progress has been made toward a minimum load. The next load tried should be halfway between the load that stuck a bullet and the lightest load that did not. When such loads are only a few tenths of a grain apart, the use of single cartridges and weighed powder charges should be discontinued. From this point on, every load should be tried in 10 cartridges using measured powder charges. Rather than set the measure by weighing single thrown charges, measure out 10 or more such charges, check the total weight against that proper for such a number, and continue adjusting the measure this way. This procedure gives no information on variation among the charges thrown, but it is an excellent way to set the measure, even with heavy rifle charges.

During test firing the powder charge

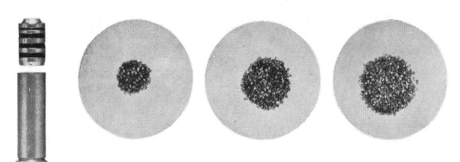

Hensley & Gibbs No. 50BB .357″, 146-gr. full wadcutter bullet can be used in .38 Special with Bullseye charge as little as .75 gr., with midrange target load of 2.7 grs., and with full-charge load of 3.5 grs.

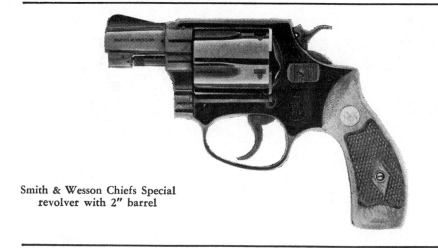

Smith & Wesson Chiefs Special
revolver with 2" barrel

should be shifted before each shot by tilting the muzzle up or down or by holding the gun level and shaking it gently. This is necessary to make sure that the load will invariably expel bullets from the muzzle regardless of the position of the powder. It is also important that bullet bases be kept free from grease, both when preparing minimum loads experimentally and in later regular loading, as a small amount of grease can 'kill' a light powder charge.

When the very minimum load that will expel bullets every time has been found, it is increased slightly to give a safety margin in regular use.

Little information available

Little information on minimum loads will be found in reloading manuals and books. The current Lyman Handbook goes down only to 2.5 grs. Bullseye pistol powder with a 148-gr. wadcutter bullet in the .38 Special. Even Sharpe's *Complete Guide to Handloading* goes no lower than 2.0 grs. Bullseye for wadcutter bullets, although loads are given as light as 1.5 grs. Bullseye for lighter and heavier bullets of other types.

Loads less than half the minimums listed by most sources can be successfully used for specialized purposes.

As an example, the Hensley & Gibbs No. 50BB full wadcutter bullet of .357" diameter and 146 grs. weight can be used in .38 Special with as little as .75 gr. Bullseye. Experimental loads of .55 gr. expelled all bullets from the barrel, so the charge was increased .2 gr. for an adequate safety margin.

This above load was used in my 2" barreled S&W Chiefs Special revolver. As in other Chiefs Specials, the actual barrel length is only 1-27/32" instead of the listed 2" but it still permits fine accuracy.

A comparison of this light charge with a midrange target load and the listed maximum of Bullseye shows this:

Charge Bullseye (grs.)	Muzzle Velocity (f.p.s.)	Muzzle Energy (ft.-lbs.)
.75	195	12.3
2.7	635	131.5
3.5	771	193.5

The muzzle energy for this minimum load in .38 Special is only about a quarter as much as that for the standard velocity .22 short cartridge in a 6"-barreled revolver. Even in this small, light .38 Special gun, the perceptible recoil is less than that of the .22 short in the usual .22 rimfire revolver.

Although not notably accurate, this minimum load permits placing ten consecutive shots in the black of a 50-ft. pistol target at a basement range of 35 ft., from a normal standing position. This is adequate for preliminary instruction. Increasing the load somewhat will improve accuracy materially.

This minimum load is not enough for longer barreled guns. In a 6" barreled S&W K-38, bullets invariably stopped 1¼" or more from the muzzle. The minimum that would invariably expel bullets from that gun proved to be 1.05 grs. Bullseye, so 1.25 grs. Bullseye became the minimum working load. This gave a muzzle velocity of 272 f.p.s. Even this load has only half the muzzle energy of the regular velocity .22 short cartridge, but is noisier, noticeably more so than the .75 gr. Bullseye load used in the 2" Chiefs Special.

Instrumental velocities were measured at 10 ft. from the muzzle with the Avtron Counter Chronograph and muzzle velocities were calculated from these figures. Hensley & Gibbs No. 50BB bullets cast in a 1-16 tin-lead alloy, of .357" diameter and weighing 146 grs., were used throughout.

These loads may or may not be suitable minimums for your .38 Special revolver, but the methods and principles outlined are universally applicable, regardless of caliber. ∎

CHRONOGRAPHING FOR THE HANDLOADER

By WM. C. DAVIS, JR.

Early Velocity Measurements

Though guns were in use before 1320 A.D., the velocities of gun-launched projectiles could not be measured with reasonable accuracy until the invention of the ballistic pendulum, about 1740, by Benjamin Robins, a British engineer and ballistician. Robins' understanding of both interior and exterior ballitics was truly remarkable for his time, and his measurements of projectile velocities provided the first sound basis for the science of gunnery. His ballistic pendulum was the only instrument for measuring bullet velocities for more than 100 years after its invention, and it still serves a useful purpose for recoil measurements in modern laboratories.

The ballistic pendulum is not truly a chronograph since it does not measure time. Its operation depends on principles of the conservation of momentum, which applies when the bullet strikes and is imbedded in the pendulum bob, and the conservation of energy, which applies when the kinetic energy of the moving pendulum (imparted by the bullet at the lowest point of pendulum swing) is converted to potential energy, as the pendulum bob is lifted to the highest point of its swing.

The first practical chronograph for measuring bullet velocities was invented by a Belgian officer about 1850, and was called the Boulenge' (pronounced Boo-lon-jay). Its essential principle is based on the fact that the acceleration of gravity is practically constant, and, therefore, that a freely falling body always falls practically the same distance in a given interval of time after it has been released. The relationship is expressed in the equation $s = \frac{1}{2}gt^2$, where s is the distance fallen (in feet), t is the time falling (in seconds) and g is the acceleration of gravity, commonly standardized at 32.17 fps. In the Boulenge' chronograph, a long metal rod is suspended vertically from an electromagnet, and a wire near the muzzle of the gun is arranged so that the current to the magnet coil must pass through it. When the wire is broken by the bullet, the rod begins to fall. A second wire (or some other circuit-breaking device) is placed downrange at a measured distance, usually 100 or 150 feet, so it will be broken as the bullet strikes it. The second wire actuates an electromechanical trigger which marks the falling rod as it passes. the distance that the rod has fallen is determined by the marks made on it, and that distance is the value of s in the equation above, from which the time t can then be calculated. The distance between the wires broken by the bullet (in feet) is then divided by the time t (in seconds), and the result is the "instrumental" velocity of the bullet, in feet per second. The Boulenge' chronograph was in use for nearly 100 years, during which many refinements were made to improve its accuracy and convenience of operation.

Other more or less successful electromechanical chronographs were also invented between about 1865 and 1940. Most of them depended on marking the periphery of a rapidly revolving drum or cylinder, the rotational speed of the drum being accurately known. One mark was made when the bullet broke the first circuit, another when it broke the second circuit. The distance between the marks could then be converted to a measurement of time.

The first such chronograph was probably that of Bashforth, in England, about 1865. A very sophisticated development, employing the same basic principle, was the drum chronograph developed at the U.S. Army Aberdeen Proving Ground, used as recently as the 1950's.

Choosing a Chronograph

Great strides have been made in the development of ballistic chronographs during recent years. An important turning point in design of chronographs for professional use occurred during the 1940's. At this time practical chronographs were designed to utilize a crystal-controlled electronic counter as the basis for measuring extremely short intervals of time. This gave accuracy previously unattainable. These instruments depended for many years on the use of vacuum tubes for the electronic circuitry, which had many disadvantages. The instruments were relatively large, demanded power not conveniently supplied by portable batteries, required frequent maintenance by skilled electronic technicians, were subject to malfunctions due to microphonic effects of muzzle blast, and were expensive. Though these obstacles did not prevent their practically universal use in professional laboratories, they were nearly insurmountable obstacles to their use by individual handloaders. The great technological breakthrough in the use of solid-state electronic components, which paved the way for development of reliable and inexpensive portable radios, pocket calculators, electronic timepieces and other such items, also made handloaders' chronographs eminently practicable for the first time. The development of electronic counter-type chronographs, like that of many other electronic devices, has resulted in great improvements in performance and convenience of use, and substantial reductions in cost. Handloaders now have a wide variety of excellent instruments from which to choose, at prices comparable to those of one new gun.

The great proliferation of available models has, however, resulted in some confusion on the part of a prospective purchaser as to which type of chronograph best suits his needs. The answer to that question depends on the anticipated frequency of use and the price the handloader is prepared to pay for convenience.

The simplest and least expensive models are those that employ printed screens through which the bullet must pass to produce signals for the counter. These do not provide a direct digital readout of velocity or time. Such instruments may have inherent accuracy fully equal to that of more sophisticated types, and they are attractive because of their low initial cost. If your budget is limited, and you do not expect to chronograph a great many shots, the simplest types offer the best value at prices often below $100.

The slow and less convenient operation, and the cost of the expendable screens that they require are disadvantages.

The printed screens usually cost about $8 to $12 per hundred, and two screens are required for each shot. The cost of operation is therefore about 20¢ per shot, or $20 per hundred shots. If you chronograph 100 or 200 shots per year, this is no great burden, and the cost of a more expensive instrument that uses non-expendable screens may not be justified. The readout on simple models usually involves the manipulation of one or more multi-position switches from which numbers are read and recorded. These numbers are then used to refer to a table provided by the manufacturer of the instrument which gives corresponding velocities. With most such instruments, recording the readout and determining the velocity requires less than one minute per shot, after a little familiarization and practice.

Somewhat more sophisticated models use photoelectric detectors or "sky-screens" that produce signals to the chronograph when the bullet passes a few inches above them. The first cost of these models is higher, as might be expected, but the cost of expendable screens is eliminated. Only a little arithmetic is required to determine how many rounds must be chronographed to recover the difference in initial cost of the system by savings on the cost of screens. The anticipated frequency of use is, of course, the determining factor.

The next step up in sophistication is the direct digital readout instrument where numbers are actually displayed after each shot and you need only to copy them down. In some models, the number displayed is an interval of time, and you must refer to tables or divide the interscreen distance by the time interval to obtain velocity. In other models, the predetermined interscreen distance is set into the instrument (usually 5 or 10 feet, but sometimes shorter distances) and the instrument performs the necessary computation and displays the velocity directly. These refinements add to the complexity of the instrument and are reflected in higher prices.

In the most sophisticated handloaders' chronographs, additional circuitry may provide a memory function, and even automatic computation of the important statistics for analyzing a series of shots. In the Oehler Model 33 system, for example, you fire a series of shots (up to 255) giving no attention to the instrument. After each shot is fired, the velocity is automatically displayed in the LED readout, along with the number of the shot in the series, the information is stored in memory, and the instrument is automatically reset for the next shot. At any time during the series, you can push a button labeled *Summary*, whereupon

the LED displays the lowest velocity recorded, followed successively by the highest velocity, the extreme variation, the average, and the standard deviation (which is a statistical measure of uniformity more efficient than the extreme variation). A final push of the *Summary* button makes the instrument ready for the next shot, and the memory retains the previous information for further computations. At the end of the series, the final statistics are recalled and recorded, and the instrument is then made ready for the next series simply by switching it off momentarily, then back on again. Although this degree of sophistication has been incorporated in professional laboratory instruments for many years (at prices of several thousand dollars each) it has only recently been introduced in a handloaders' system, at a price of a few hundred dollars. If you do a great deal of chronographing and wish to analyze results in considerable detail, this type of system is a great convenience and time saver. Even handloaders without such sophisticated requirements are attracted to the instrument by its entertaining display of versatility, and that is sufficient reason to justify the purchase, if price is not a consideration.

You should request literature and prices from several of the well established manufacturers who advertise in *The American Rifleman* and other journals of the shooting sports, and study this literature carefully. Weigh the advantages of each model in light of your particular circumstances.

In the highly competitive market during the last decade, some manufacturers of chronographs appeared briefly on the scene and then ceased operations. It is extremely difficult to obtain service on an instrument whose manufacturer is no longer in business. This is one factor favoring the products of well established manufacturers.

Use of Chronographs

Whatever chronograph is chosen, you will get the best value from your investment if you learn how to use the instrument correctly. Most manufacturers provide adequate instructions for their particular instruments, and these should be studied carefully before the chronograph is set up on the range and operated. There are some general instructions, however, that apply to practically all chronograph systems.

Possibly the greatest source of error in chronograph results is inaccurate placement of the screens. Velocity is determined by dividing the measured time between signals from the first and second screens into the measured interscreen distance. It is obvious that an error in the interscreen distance causes a corresponding error in velocity. If the correct interscreen distance is 5 feet, for exam-

ple, and the error in measurement is ½ inch, the interscreen distance is in error by about 0.83 per cent. At a velocity of 3,000 fps, the error introduced is about 25 fps.

The effect of a given error in screen placement is obviously reduced by increasing the interscreen distance, since it is the *percentage* error that is reflected in the velocity. An error of ½ inch in an interscreen distance of 10 feet is only about 0.42 per cent (or about 12 fps at a velocity level of 3,000 fps). It is also obvious that the error, in terms of feet per second, is greatest at high velocities, and least at low velocities. Thus, a ½-inch error in an interscreen distance of 5 feet introduces an error of about 7 fps into the velocity measurement of a pistol bullet at 800 fps, but 25 fps into the velocity measurement of a rifle bullet at 3,000 fps.

Interscreen distances should be carefully measured, and they should be as long as practicable. As a general rule, a 5-foot interscreen distance is satisfactory for velocities up to about 1,500 fps, but a 10-foot interscreen distance is best for higher velocities. Different chronographs use counters with different frequencies. The use of higher frequencies theoretically permits the use of shorter interscreen distances on grounds that the time is measured more precisely. But this has no effect on errors of interscreen distance, so longer interscreen distances are, nevertheless, preferable.

The distance from the muzzle to the midpoint between screens is much less important. It is common practice in the ammunition industry to place the screens so the midway point is 15 feet from the muzzle. Many handloaders find a 10-foot midpoint distance more convenient. In any case, an error in this measurement is less important than an error in interscreen distance. This subject will be discussed later, in connection with the relationship between muzzle velocity and instrumental velocity.

The most convenient way to mount chronograph screens is on the same bar of wood or metal. It is possible to make a satisfactory bar of 1x3-inch lumber, arranged so the 3-inch dimension is vertical to provide the required stiffness. A bar providing a 10-foot interscreen distance can be assembled from two pieces about 6 feet long, or three pieces about 4½ feet long. They can be held together by lapping the ends 1 foot, and drilling two holes through both, about 8 inches apart, through which ¼-inch bolts will pass. The bolts should be provided with washers and wingnuts for convenient disassembly.

A sturdier and more convenient arrangement is to make the bar of 1x⅛-inch aluminum or steel angle stock. The ends of pieces should be prepared for joining by lapping at least 6 inches, with the outer angle of one piece fitted into the inner angle of the next. Clamp both in position and drill through one side of both pieces with a number 7 drill at two points 4 inches apart. The pieces are then separated, after marking the inner and outer pieces at the lap joint. The holes in the outer piece should be enlarged to provide clearance for a ¼-inch bolt, and the holes in the inner piece should be threaded with a ¼″-20 tap. Two round-head stove bolts ¼″-20 by ¾ inch long should be screwed tightly into the tapped holes of the inner piece of angle, heads inside, where they will remain. To assemble the pieces, the projecting bolts on the inner bar are passed through the corresponding holes in the outer bar, and secured by wingnuts. In use, the assembled bar should be mounted so the wingnuts are at the side, and the top is unobstructed. It is wise to number the pieces and mark the direction of fire on top of each piece with a permanent-ink marker. This facilitates correct assembly. Unless the holes are spaced the same on each piece, they will not be interchangeable, but must be reassembled in the same order each time. The method of mounting the screens on the bar will depend on the configuration of the screens and must be designed accordingly.

The screen bar should be adjustable for height to conform to different heights of shooting benches, if the equipment is portable. Camera tripods are excellent for supporting the screen bar, but are more elaborate and expensive than necessary. Light stands used by photographers are less expensive and serve equally well. The least expensive models adjustable for height are suitable, and cost about $10 each from photographic mail-order houses such as Spiratone (135-06 Northern Blvd., Flushing, N.Y. 11354). The light stands have a threaded ¼″-20 stud projecting from the top for mounting purposes. The bar can be conveniently mounted on the stands by means of L-shaped brackets bent from ⅛x¾-inch flat steel or aluminum stock. The horizontal leg of the L should be about 1½ inches long, and the vertical leg of a length that suits the design of the bar. Holes of ¼-inch diameter through both legs of the L permit the horizontal leg to attach to the stud on the light stand and the vertical leg to a ¼ inch bolt passing horizontally through the screen bar. If the screen bar is of metal, the horizontal mounting bolts can be permanently threaded into the bar. Wingnuts are used to secure the mounting brackets to the light stands and the screen bar. The mounting brackets should be located about 2½ feet from each end of a 10-foot bar, or 1 foot from each end of a 5-foot bar.

Another excellent material for making a screen bar is thin-walled steel electrical conduit of ¾-inch diameter. It can be jointed for easy portability. Couplings fastened by setscrews are available for joining pieces of conduit together. To achieve the necessary stiffness in the joint, however, a wooden dowel should be fastened in the end of each joint, with the end protruding about 3 inches so that it can slip inside the other piece at assembly. The setscrew coupler is used to secure the joint. The light stands usually have a ¼-inch threaded stud protruding from a slightly larger stem at the top — perhaps ⅜-inch in diameter. The conduit can be drilled through both walls with a ¼-inch drill, then the hole in one wall can be enlarged to ⅜-inch, or whatever diameter provides for passage of the stem from which the ¼-inch stud on the light stand protrudes. The larger hole is placed at the bottom of the bar, and the stem of the light stand is passed through it, with the ¼-inch stud protruding through the smaller hole in the top wall, where it is secured by a wing nut. The joints should be made, and the bar assembled, before locating and drilling the holes for attachment of the screens. This will assure that the interscreen distance will be as accurate as possible.

The problem of aligning the gun and screens so the bullet passes accurately over the screens (or through them in the case of printed screens) is a critical, difficult task. Efforts to aim the gun by "eyeballing" the position of the barrel with respect to the screens will, sooner or later, result in a bullet hole through an expensive photoelectric screen, or a clip shot off the printed-screen holder. The correct alignment is most easily accomplished by the following procedure:

1. Put a target on the target frame down range.
2. Set a rifle in firing position on the shooting bench, supported by sandbags or a benchrest pedestal. The pedestal and "rabbit-ears" type of rear bag are most convenient. It is important that the front bag or pedestal isn't moved after the rifle is in final firing position.
3. Remove the bolt or open the action of the rifle and place a small piece of white paper in the breech opening so it will reflect light through the bore.
4. Aim at the target, and support the rifle by manipulating the sandbags. If the bolt has been removed, place a white sheet of paper on a box, or some such support, behind and above the butt of the rifle, where it will reflect light through the bore. Recheck the alignment of the sights on the target.
5. Set up the screen bar and screens and adjust their position so the bar is directly beneath the centerline of the bore. Looking from the screen position, the centerline of the bore can be seen by sighting back through the bore toward the white paper behind it.
6. Adjust the stands vertically so the

centerline of the bore passes about 4 inches above the centers of the photo-electric screens, or between the clips of the printed-screen holder.

For iron-sighted rifles and printed screens, it may be necessary to adjust the centers of the screens slightly below the centerline of the bore. The line of sight will barely clear the tops of the printed screens and the target will be visible when aiming. For scope sights, the line of sight will be sufficiently high so this is not necessary.

For photoelectric screens, the alignment is made more accurately and conveniently if you improvise some means of attaching a card or wooden peg that will project 4 inches above the centers of the screens, and align these with the centerline of the bore. For screens in flat-top boxes, a ¼-inch dowel 4 inches long, set perpendicularly into the center of a flat piece of wood about 3 inches square, can be put on the screen boxes and secured temporarily with masking tape. For small screens, such as the Oehler Skyscreen II, a piece of cardboard can be cut to slide into the screen slot and project 4 inches above the screens, with the top trimmed to form a point for easy alignment.

7. Remove the alignment devices from the screens. Make the necessary chronograph connections, and begin firing. If the gun is aimed carefully, and the front sandbag or pedestal has not been moved, the bullet will pass accurately over or through the screens.

It is best to use a rifle for the initial alignment procedure, even if a handgun is to be tested. The longer barrel of the rifle permits accurate and convenient determination of the bore's centerline.

If a handgun is to be fired, the barrel should rest on the front sandbag or support in the same position as the rifle barrel. Because handgun sights may be located closer to the bore than those of a rifle, it may not be possible to see the target when the gun is aligned. In that event, aim directly at the first screen, somewhat above its center. In this case, it is best to attach a piece of cardboard to the back of the second screen holder, with a slot about 2 inches wide cut in the top. The two "ears" of the cardboard should project about 2 inches above the top of the screen. When aiming at the first screen, be sure the line of sight passes midway between the "ears" projecting above the second screen.

For instruments that do not provide automatic resetting between shots, this must be accomplished manually as described in the manufacturer's instructions. A common error is forgetting to reset the counter before firing the next shot. In this event, the reading from the previous shot remains in the instrument and it fails to record the next shot fired. The new reading is, therefore, the same as the previous one, and probably incorrect.

Whenever two consecutive readings are identical, the second reading should be regarded as suspect unless you are sure you remembered to reset the instrument. The best way to avoid this error is to establish a routine procedure, where resetting is always done at the same point in the sequence of operations. Some operators reset the chronograph twice, once immediately after copying the readout, and again after loading the gun for the next shot. This reduces the likelihood of a mistake.

Analysis of Chronograph Data

Any velocity data on a load is certainly better than none, and measuring the velocity of even one shot tells you more than you knew before. It is obvious, however, that more shots give more reliable information.

If you fire one shot each of two different loads, you can make some kind of comparison as to which load produces higher velocity. If the difference is great — say 2,500 fps and 3,000 fps — your probability of making the correct judgement is fairly high. If the difference is small — say 2,500 fps and 2,530 fps — your probability of making the correct judgement is little better than 50 per cent.

The odds of making the correct judgement depend not only on the number of shots fired and the difference between average velocities, but also on the shot-to-shot uniformity of both loads. By looking at the difference in average velocities, the shot-to-shot variations, and the number of shots fired, you can get some idea of how reliably you can make the judgement, but intuition can be deceiving in such cases, and a little arithmetic can provide a much better answer.

With the aid of the ubiquitous and inexpensive pocket calculator, it is easy to make an analysis that provides more useful information. The most sophisticated chronographs, such as the Oehler Model 33, automatically compute the essential statistics, and that is certainly most convenient. However, pocket calculators are now commonly available, at prices as low as about $30, that can compute the necessary statistics by a procedure no more complicated than entering the individual velocities, and pressing the appropriate keys to call forth the mean and the standard deviation of the series. Even the least expensive calculators that have a square-root key can be used with only a little more trouble.

The most important statistics are the mean (average) and the standard deviation. The method of computing the mean is so widely known as to require no explanation. While the formula for computing the standard deviation might look formidable to those not accustomed to mathematical exercises, it can be computed easily by a series of simple arithmetic operations, using any pocket calculator having the square-root capability. The procedure should be clear from the following description and example, based on a five-shot series of velocity data.

EXAMPLE
Step I

Round Number	Velocity (V)	Differences (V-V̄)	Differences Squared (V-V̄)²
1	2931	−17	289
2	2961	13	169
3	2936	−12	144
4	2950	2	4
5	2962	14	196
Sum	14740		802
Average (V̄)	2948		

Step II
Number of shots in series (N) = 5
(N−1) = (5−1) = 4

Step III
Sum of squared differences, divided by (N−1), equals 802 ÷ 4 = 200

Step IV
Square root of the answer obtained in Step 3 equals $\sqrt{200} = 14$ (This is the standard deviation.)

PROCEDURE:
Step I
a. Set up a table with headings as indicated in the example, and enter the velocity of each shot, identified as "V" in the table.
b. Determine the average velocity, identified as "V̄" in the table (pronounced "V-bar").
c. Subtract the average velocity (V̄) from the velocity of each shot, and enter the difference (V-V̄) in the third column of the table. While the difference is still displayed on the calculator, square it (multiply by itself) and enter the squared difference in the fourth column of the table under (V-V̄)².
d. Add all the numbers in the fourth column, and enter their sum at the bottom.

Step II
Subtract 1 from the number of shots in the series, and identify it as (N-1).

Step III
Divide the sum under the fourth column by (N-1).

Step IV
Calculate the square root of the answer obtained in Step III, and identify that as the "Standard Deviation."

Having obtained the mean (average) and the standard deviation of the series, you can learn much more from the velocity data by referring to Table 1, which is reproduced here in slightly

TABLE 1

Standard Deviation	Number of Rounds					
	3	5	10	20	50	100
2	3	2	1	.8	.5	.3
3	5	3	2	1	.7	.5
4	7	4	2	2	.9	.7
5	8	5	3	2	1	.8
6	10	6	4	2	1	1
7	12	7	4	3	2	1
8	13	8	5	3	2	2
9	15	9	5	4	2	2
10	17	10	6	4	2	2
12	20	11	7	5	3	2
14	24	13	8	5	3	3
16	27	15	9	6	4	3
18	30	17	10	7	4	3
20	34	19	12	8	5	3
25	42	24	14	10	6	4
30	51	29	17	12	7	5
35	59	33	20	14	8	6
40	67	38	23	15	10	7
45	76	43	26	17	11	8
50	84	48	29	19	12	8
60	101	57	35	23	14	10
70	118	67	41	27	17	12
80	135	76	46	31	19	13
90	152	86	52	35	21	15
100	169	95	58	39	24	17

Table 1. Plus-or-minus limits within which the long-run average will lie (with 90% confidence) based on the number of rounds fired and the observed standard deviation.

modified form, by permission of Dr. Ken Oehler (manufacturer of Oehler chronograph systems), from an excellent paper published by Oehler titled "Velocity Decisions." The numbers in the body of Table 1 are the limits, above or below the average velocity based on the series fired, within which the true velocity (or long-run average) will probably lie. "Probably" is here taken to mean that the statement can be made with 90 per cent confidence. For the example used above to illustrate the computation of standard deviation, it is recalled that the number of rounds in the series was five, and the standard deviation was 14 fps. Entering Table 1 with this information, it is seen that the number in the table (beneath five in the column for number of rounds, opposite 14 in the line for standard deviation) is 13. This means that the mean or average velocity obtained in the series (which was 2,948 fps), is probably within 13 fps of the long-run average that would be obtained if a great many rounds of the same load were fired under the same conditions. Stated differently, it can be said with 90 per cent confidence that the true long-run average for the load lies within the bracket 2,948 ± 13 fps, or between 2,935 fps and 2,961 fps. For values not specifically listed in the table, the limits can be estimated by interpolation between values on either side. Thus, if the standard deviation were 15 fps in the example above, the limits would be between that listed for 14 fps (which is 13) and that listed for 16 fps (which is 15), indicating limits of 14 fps.

It can be seen from Table 1 that the accuracy with which the average is determined by the test depends on the standard deviation obtained, and on the number of rounds fired. It is, of course, intuitively obvious that the average should be less reliable if the uniformity of velocity is poor, and more reliable if it is based on a larger number of rounds, and this is exactly what the table indicates in quantitative terms.

The other point of interest is how one load compares with another in terms of uniform velocity. It is far from certain that the load showing the smaller extreme variation is truly the more uniform load. The difference might be due to random variations in the experiment, and if the test were repeated, the results might be different as a matter of chance.

The standard deviation is a more efficient measure of uniformity than is extreme variation, but even so, the difference between observed standard deviations must be surprisingly great to justify the conclusion that one load is more uniform than another. Table 2, which is also reproduced here by permission of Dr. Oehler from his "Velocity Decisions," enables you to make a more reliable comparison between two loads on the basis of uniformity. It is used in much the same way as Table 1, by entering the table at the column headed by the number of rounds fired, and following that column to the line of observed standard deviation. The key number found in that column and that line is the standard deviation in Load B, for example, that must be exceeded to establish with 90 per cent confidence that Load A (with which you entered the table) is more uniform than Load B.

Suppose that you loaded two samples of ammunition, each with a different powder, and that the charges were adjusted to produce about the same velocity. You now wish to determine whether the powder in Load A produces better uniformity than that in Load B.

Suppose that Load A is the one used in the previous example, for which the mean and standard deviation have been calculated, and that you have calculated the mean and standard deviation for a 5-round series of Load B in the same manner, with the following results, including the extreme variations for the sake of further comparison:

	Load A	Load B
Round 1	2931	2980
2	2961	2918
3	2936	2945
4	2950	2958
5	2962	2921
Mean	2948	2944
Extreme Variation	31	62
Standard Deviation	14	26

Since the extreme variation with Load B was twice that obtained with Load A, and the standard deviation with Load B was nearly twice that with Load A, you are tempted to conclude that Load A is the more uniform. Refer to Table 2, however, to see whether that statement can be made with 90 per cent confidence of being correct. Entering the approp-

riate column for 5-round samples, and following it down to the line for 14 fps which was the standard deviation obtained with Load A, you find the key number is 35. Since the standard deviation obtained with Load B was 26 fps, it does not exceed the key number, and therefore you cannot conclude with 90 per cent confidence that Load A is more uniform than Load B. It might indeed be more uniform, and you have not proved to the contrary, but more testing would be required to prove the point with 90 per cent confidence. (It should be mentioned that there is an esoteric point of statistics involved in the confidence level associated with Table 2, and some statisticians might argue that it is 95 per cent rather than 90 per cent under the conditions stated. Possibly that is correct, but the matter is of small practical consequence, since you are concerned only with making a judgement with a reasonably high probability of being right.)

TABLE 2

Standard Deviation Load A	Number of Rounds Each Load					
	3	5	10	20	50	100
2	9	5	4	3	2	2
3	13	8	5	4	4	4
4	17	10	7	6	5	5
5	22	13	9	7	6	6
6	26	15	11	9	8	7
7	31	18	12	10	9	8
8	35	20	14	12	10	10
9	39	23	16	13	11	11
10	44	25	18	15	13	12
12	52	30	21	18	15	14
14	61	35	25	21	18	17
16	70	40	28	24	20	19
18	78	46	32	26	23	22
20	87	51	36	29	25	24
25	109	63	44	37	32	30
30	131	76	53	44	38	36
35	153	89	62	51	44	42
40	174	101	71	59	51	48
45	196	114	80	66	57	54
50	218	126	89	74	64	60
60	262	152	107	88	76	72
70	305	177	125	103	89	84
80	349	202	142	118	102	96
90	392	228	160	132	114	108
100	436	253	178	147	127	120

Table 2. The standard deviation of Load B must exceed the value shown in the table for 90% confidence that Load A is the more uniform.

It is informative to note that larger samples produce more discriminating data in Table 2, just as they did in Table 1. If 10-round series had been fired with Loads A and B instead of 5-round series, and if the standard deviations had been found to be 14 and 26 fps respectively, then the key number from Table 2 would have been 25 fps, the standard deviation of Load B would have exceeded the key number, and you could say with 90 per cent confidence that Load A was indeed the more uniform.

As can be seen from the foregoing tables and their use, the standard deviation is an uncommonly useful statistic. It has been little used in analyzing ballistic data, outside of professional laboratories, probably because it has been considered too difficult to compute, and possibly also because non-statisticians

do not generally have a very satisfying intuitive concept of what it is or what it means. The extreme variation (called "range" by statisticians) is easier to compute, and easier to appreciate intuitively, and these are probably the reasons it has been used much more often in non-professional ballistics.

You have seen, however, that standard deviation is really not difficult to compute, with the aid of a pocket calculator, and it can be very useful. It is worthwhile to look briefly at the other objection to its use, and to another use for it.

There are two statistics relating to uniformity of variables, such as velocity variations, that are easily appreciated intuitively. One is the extreme variation to be expected in a series of a given number of shots. It is intuitively obvious that the extreme variation expected from a series of five shots is less than that expected from 10 shots or 100 shots, but 5-shot and 10-shot series are probably the ones for which the extreme variation is most often quoted. If only one or a few series have been fired, it so happens that the extreme variation to be expected in future series can be predicted more accurately from the observed standard deviation than from the extreme variation actually observed in the limited data. If the standard deviation has been computed as described earlier in this article, the expected value of extreme variation in future series is about 2.3 times the standard deviation for 5-shot series, and about 3.1 times the standard deviation for 10-shot series. Finding exactly that relationship in any particular series is unlikely, of course, because of chance variation in small samples, but if a large number of series are fired, that relationship between standard deviation and extreme variation will be found to exist.

The other measure of uniformity that is intuitively satisfying to many people is the "probable deviaton" from the average or mean value. It is more commonly called the "probable error," though that is a less descriptive term for many applications of it. It can be defined as the deviation from the mean that is as likely as not to be exceeded by any particular shot, or in the long run will be exceeded by 50 per cent of the shots in the series. It is equal to about 0.67 times the standard deviation (computed as described before), and unlike the extreme variation, it does not then depend on the number of shots in the series. If the standard deviation is 14 fps, as it was in one of the previous examples, the estimated "probable deviation" or "probable error" for the load is about .67x14 = 9 fps. In future series under the same conditions, it is expected that about half the shots fired would be within 9 fps above or below the mean.

Another useful application of the standard deviation is to identify "flyers," or shots that are outside the range expected on the basis of the normal shot-to-shot variation for the load. It is not sufficient to decide intuitively or arbitrarily that the record would be improved by omitting one shot from consideration, and thereupon declare it a "flyer." The decision must be somewhat arbitrary at best, but there are guidelines for making it that are much more reliable than intuition.

In a normal distribution of velocities in a series, only about 1 shot in 100 is expected to deviate from the mean by more than 2.5 times the standard deviation. If one shot is suspected of being a "flyer," it is useful to apply this rule before deciding to disregard it. In one of the previous examples, the mean velocity was found to be 2,948 fps and the standard deviation 14 fps. Applying the rule, 2.5x14 = 35 fps. Therefore, any shot differing by more than 35 fps from the mean (that is, greater than 2,983 fps or less than 2,913 fps) might be reasonably considered a "flyer," and disregarded in recomputing the average. Statisticians use much more sophisticated procedures and would not consider this one rigorously correct, but it is simple, and much more reliable than unguided intuition for deciding which shots are "flyers" and ought to be thrown out. The reason for a "flyer" in a velocity series cannot be found in statistics, of course, but the fact is, accuracy of the mean will probably be improved by disregarding it in the computation, and recomputing the mean and standard deviation on the remaining shots.

It is clear that intuition is not to be trusted very far in comparing different loads, and that the averages we obtain by firing a few rounds are only estimates.

The handloader who invests his money in chronograph equipment, and his time in loading ammunition and firing tests, is well repaid for the small additional effort expended to analyze his data systematically before passing judgement on the qualities of his loads.

Muzzle velocities and instrumental velocities

The handloader who determines velocities by use of his chronograph is obtaining instrumental velocities or "IV's." They are, for practical purposes, the actual velocities of the bullets at a point midway between the first and second velocity screens. Thus, if the first screen is five feet from the muzzle, and the screens are 10 feet apart, the midpoint between the screens is 10 feet from the muzzle, and the velocities are said to be "instrumental at 10 feet." It often happens that you wish to convert this instrumental velocity to a muzzle veloc-

ity, for comparison with factory ballistic tables or the data from reloading manuals which usually quote muzzle velocities.

Because you will seldom measure instrumental velocities at distances more than about 20 feet from the muzzle, the corrections to be applied are relatively small, and simplifying approximations can be made without introducing any serious error. The same methods cannot be used to determine the velocity with acceptable accuracy at 200 yards, for example, because the simplifying approximations introduce too much error at that range, but at 20 feet or less, the error is of no practical consequence.

Table 3 gives the corrections that may be added to the instrumental velocity at 10 feet to obtain muzzle velocity, provided only that the ballistic coefficient of the bullet is known. It is based on the Ingalls or C_1 ballistic coefficient, which is the one given by practically all bullet manufacturers for all sporting bullets. Most bullet manufacturers supply information on the ballistic coefficients of their bullets in the reloading manuals that they publish, or will furnish the information on request.

For the purpose of Table 3, it is not necessary that the ballistic coefficient be known very accurately, because a small error in the ballistic coefficient introduces only a very small error in the retardation (velocity loss) of the bullet over short distances. For most home-made bullets, or others for which the ballistic coefficient is not known, it can be approximated with satisfactory accuracy for use in Table 3. Round-nose, flat-point or other bullets having short ogives can be categorized as "blunt." Spitzer bullets and others having a relatively long ogive and either a pointed nose or only a small hollow-point can be categorized as "sharp." For purposes of using Table 3, the ballistic coefficient can be calculated approximately from the following formulas:

For "blunt" bullets: $C = \dfrac{G}{d^2} \div 7000$

For "sharp" bullets: $C = \dfrac{G}{d^2} \div 5000$

where **G** = **bullet weight in grains** and **d** = **bullet diameter in inches.**

Table 3 can also be used to calculate the retardation over instrumental distances other than 10 feet, because for short distances it is acceptable to assume that the retardation, or loss of velocity, is exactly proportional to the distance. Thus, for any instrumental distance of D feet, the numbers in Table 3 may be multiplied by the ratio $D/10$, and the result added to the instrumental velocity to obtain muzzle velocity. At seven feet, for example, the numbers in the table must be multiplied by 7/10 or 0.7 to obtain the proper correction. At 15 feet, the numbers must be multiplied by 15/10 or 1.5 for the proper correction.

In general, for velocities and ballistic coefficients between those listed in Table 3, satisfactory values can be obtained directly by using the tabulated numbers closest to the actual ones, since the differences are in most instances less than 2 fps. Where the differences are greater, as in the case of light bullets at high velocities, the values can be obtained by interpolation in the table.

Trouble-shooting

Most modern chronograph systems are remarkably reliable, but sooner or later, some problem will arise. You should, of course, avoid placing the counter (or the screens) too close to the muzzle, or to the barrel-cylinder gap when firing a revolver. Shock waves are very strong in those positions, and might damage the instrument, or at least cause it to malfunction.

The shock wave produced by muzzle blast can cause another problem when photoelectric screens are used with loads that produce velocities below the velocity of sound, which is about 1,120 fps. It sometimes happens that the shock wave from the muzzle (which travels at the velocity of sound) arrives at the screen ahead of the bullet and produces false triggering. The velocity is then in error, of course. Shock-wave triggering may occur on some shots, but not on others,

TABLE 3

Ballistic Coefficient, Ingalls (C.)	Instrumental Velocity, FPS													
	800	1000	1100	1200	1400	1600	1800	2000	2400	2800	3200	3600	4000	4400
.14	3	5	7	10	13	15	17	18	20	22	24	26	29	32
.16	2	4	6	9	12	14	15	16	17	19	21	24	25	28
.18	2	4	6	8	10	12	13	14	16	17	19	21	23	25
.20	2	3	5	7	9	11	12	13	14	15	17	19	21	22
.22	2	3	5	6	8	10	11	12	13	14	15	17	19	20
.24	2	3	4	6	8	9	10	11	12	13	14	16	17	19
.26	1	3	4	5	7	8	9	10	11	12	13	14	16	17
.28	1	2	4	5	7	8	9	9	10	11	12	13	15	16
.30	1	2	3	5	6	7	8	9	9	10	11	12	14	15
.32	1	2	3	4	6	7	8	8	9	10	10	11	13	14
.35	1	2	3	4	5	6	7	7	8	9	9	10	12	13
.40	1	2	3	3	5	6	6	6	7	8	8	9	10	11
.45	1	2	2	3	4	5	5	6	6	7	7	8	9	10
.50	1	1	2	3	4	5	5	5	6	6	7	7	8	9
.60	1	1	2	2	3	4	4	4	5	5	6	6	7	8

Table 3. The numbers in the table may be added to the instrumental velocity at 10 feet to obtain muzzle velocity. For any other instrumental distance, D, multiply the numbers in the table by D/10 before adding to the instrument velocity.

so large shot-to-shot velocity variation on a load producing less than about 1,150 fps is a clue to possible shock-wave problems. The problem can sometimes be solved by placing the screens farther from the muzzle, because the intensity of the shock wave diminishes at longer distances from the gun. Another remedy is to emplace a blast screen about three feet square between the gun and first screen, with a hole through the center as small as possible. Celotex building board makes a good blast screen. The blast screen should be placed about midway between the muzzle and first velocity screen for best results.

When a new load produces much higher or lower velocity than you expect, the common reaction is to doubt the accuracy of the chronograph. In professional laboratories, the chronograph system is checked periodically by firing specially loaded reference ammunition, in a test barrel with which the velocity is well established. Reference ammunition and test barrels are not available to handloaders, but a good substitute is .22 long-rifle rimfire match ammunition. Ammunition such as Eley Tenex is remarkably uniform in velocity, usually at about 1,080 fps. The velocity of .22 rimfire ammunition is little affected by differences in barrel length, or other gun-to-gun differences that produce large velocity differences in centerfire rifles. Practically any .22 rimfire rifle having a barrel from 22 to 28 inches long should produce quite uniform velocities with match ammunition, generally averaging quite close to 1,080 fps at normal ambient temperatures. You are well advised to buy a few boxes of .22 match ammunition, establish the velocity level you can expect from it in your .22 rifle, and fire a few rounds occasionally to check the chronograph set-up.

In case of real trouble with a counter or photoelectric screen, return it to the manufacturer for repair. Tinkering with the chronography circuits is not recommended for do-it-yourself enthusiasts.

Handloaders' chronographs are very useful and interesting instruments, a fact to which their ever-increasing popularity attests. They are capable of excellent accuracy, and more or less convenience in use, according to the degree of sophistication, which is reflected in their prices. Serviceable models are available at less than $100, and very sophisticated ones at about $300. A handloader can learn much more about ballistics with a chronograph than without one, and derive considerable enjoyment from the process. The benefits to be obtained, the lessons to be learned, and the enjoyment derived are all increased by exerting the small effort required to use the equipment properly, and analyze the results with the care and thoroughness that they deserve. ∎

Case Splits

While reloading some military 7.62 mm cases, I came across one which had a large crack. What is the cause of this type of case failure?

Answer: The type of case casualty found in the fired 7.62 mm NATO case that you sent for examination is called a "j-split" in the classification of firing defects for military ammunition. It can be caused by a lamination or a non-metallic inclusion in the brass cup from which the case was drawn, or by inadequate heat-treatment of the case at some stage of its manufacture. It can also be caused by a defective punch or die which produces a "draw-scratch" either inside or outside of the case during manufacture. A deep scratch produced by some accident after the cartridge is loaded can also cause the case to split upon firing.

Occasionally a magazine for the M14 rifle or clip for the M1 rifle is found to have a sharp edge inside the lip, rather than a slightly rounded edge as it should have. This can

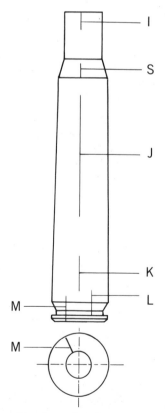

Classification of *defective cartridge cases depending on location of split as shown in Military Standard 636, Visual Inspection Standards for Small Arms Ammunition Through Cal. .50, dated June 5, 1958. Splits in the "k", "l" or "m" regions are considered "critical" or hazardous defects.*

cause a deep scratch down the side of the case during stripping from the magazine into the chamber. This can cause a j-split, especially if it occurs on the right-hand side, because the body of the chambered case in the M1 or M14 is usually pressed against the left-hand side of the chamber by the force of the extractor spring, and the case expands more on the right than on the left when it is fired.

Although a positive determination of the cause cannot be made without a metallurgical examination, I believe that the failure of the case that you sent was due to inadequate inter-draw annealing during manufacture. It is not due to any fault of your rifle.

J-splits do not allow any appreciable gas leakage, and so are not classified as hazardous or "critical" defects in military ammunition. Splits that extend farther toward the case head are called "k-splits" or "l-splits," and they may allow enough gas leakage to cause injury if the shooter is not wearing glasses. A split that extends through the head of the case and into the primer pocket is called an "m-split," and is always dangerous. One m-split in a lot of ammunition will cause removal of the whole lot from service. Fortunately, they are now very rare.

Cases that show occasional j-splits are not necessarily susceptible to the

An "m" split (left) is always dangerous. A "j" split ruins the case, but seldom presents any danger to the shooter.

dangerous m-splits, and so the occurrence of a j-split is not usually sufficient cause to remove the lot from service. You should always be sure to wear shooting glasses, especially when firing ammunition in which any body split has occurred. You should not reload those cases.—W.C.D., Jr.

CHAMBER PRESSURES IN HANDLOADING

BY WM. C. DAVIS, JR.

What is chamber pressure?

Chamber pressure is the result of the evolution of hot gases produced by the burning of a charge of propellant in a gun. It is the expected and necessary consequence of igniting a charge of powder in the gun chamber. It is the agent that propels the bullet or shot charge through the barrel. It begins to rise very soon after the primer is fired, reaches a peak value (in rifles, shotguns and handguns) within about ½ to 1 one-thousandth of a second, and thereafter falls rapidly, in a smooth curve, until after the projectile has left the muzzle. In high-velocity centerfire rifles, the bullet typically has moved several inches when the peak pressure is reached, more or less depending on the characteristics of the load. In a .30 Carbine, for example, the bullet has traveled less than one inch, and in most shotshell loads the shot have traveled about ½ to 1½ inches, for light and heavy loads respectively. In handguns, using quick-burning powders, peak pressure is sometimes reached before the bullet base has cleared the case mouth. It is because of this very rapid rise and fall of the chamber pressure that it is so difficult to measure accurately.

It is the peak chamber pressure that is of particular interest to handloaders, because that must be limited to the level which the gun and/or cartridge case can safely withstand. The upper limit of peak pressure differs for various guns, and for different cartridges, as handloaders generally know. In most bolt-action rifles, and other rifles having strong locking mechanisms, the upper limit is usually imposed because of the cartridge case. Most brass cartridge cases of modern construction, intended for use in strong rifles, can withstand pressures up to at least 55,000 pounds per square inch (psi), as measured in a crusher-type pressure barrel or gage, provided they are adequately supported by the chamber and the bolt or breech-block. Some brass cases can withstand much higher pressures — up to about 75,000 psi — though no brass cartridge case should be depended upon to withstand consistently

pressures above about 55,000 psi. In weaker rifles, and in practically all handguns, the upper limit of chamber pressure depends on the gun rather than on the strength of the cartridge case. Cases intended for use in those weaker guns might not be able to withstand pressures much higher than those for which the guns are designed, even though they are fired in stronger guns.

Pressures in U.S. commercial practice are now generally expressed in "c.u.p." or "l.u.p.". These are abbreviations for "copper units of pressure" and "lead units of pressure". They indicate that the pressures were measured in a radial crusher-type pressure gage (pressure barrel), using copper or lead crusher cylinders. Such measurements were formerly expressed in psi (pounds per square inch), but that term, in commercial practice in the U.S., is now reserved for measurements made by an electronic-transducer gage. Pressures recorded in a crusher-type gage are typically lower than those measured in an electronic-transducer gage with the same ammunition. Further details on this subject are given in the article "Measurements of Chamber Pressure", found elsewhere in this book.

Pressures of maximum loads

The maximum acceptable chamber pressures for various cartridges manufactured in the U.S. are established by the Sporting Arms and Ammunition Manufacturers' Institute (SAAMI), or by military specifications in the case of military ammunition. The pressures established by SAAMI are carefully considered, in the light of the types of guns for which the ammunition is intended, and the SAAMI limits should be carefully respected. In a few instances, as in the .45-70 for example, SAAMI limits are established in consideration of the strength of some relatively weak guns in which the ammunition is likely to be fired. If such ammunition is to be fired *exclusively* in much stronger guns, then the SAAMI limits can safely be exceeded

in handloading. Some handloading books (including this one) take account of this situation, and different loads will be found in them, clearly identified as to the type of gun for which the loads are intended. In some cartridges, SAAMI recognizes different pressure levels for use in different guns, as in the case of .38 Special ammunition for which ammunition developing higher than normal chamber pressure is identified as "+P" ammunition, and its use is recommended only in specific models as approved by the gun manufacturers.

Some sources of handloading data list the pressure of the loads suggested, and others do not. Where the pressure level is not stated, it is generally assumed to be within acceptable SAAMI levels, although that is not always the case when the loads have been developed on the basis of subjective pressure signs instead of in pressure barrels. The maximum loads listed in reloading manuals should be assumed to develop the highest acceptable chamber pressure, and should not be exceeded. Most sources of handloading data recommend reducing the maximum charge by 10 percent, or using a more moderate charge specifically listed, for initial trials. The trial charge should be increased only in small increments, until either the listed maximum charge is reached, or until some sign of excessive pressure appears. In custom-chambered guns, which sometimes have chambers not complying with SAAMI dimensional requirements, it is especially necessary to begin with reduced charges, and proceed with caution. It is also prudent to reduce the charge for initial trials when any change has been made in the brand, type or lot of cases, primers or bullets. There are a few exceptions to the use of reduced initial charges, as in the case of certain Ball powders (specifically 785 and 296), and a few cartridges when loaded with Ball powders of any type (specifically the 8x57mm Mauser and .338 Winchester Magnum). In those particular instances, the loads should be assembled exactly as specified by Winchester-Western, the powder manufacturer.

Gun characteristics affect chamber pressure

The handloader should be aware that variations in interior dimensions of the barrel can affect chamber pressures very appreciably. The minimum chamber dimensions and maximum cartridge dimensions agreed by the principal manufacturers of arms and ammunition will assure that there is adequate clearance, both diametrically and longitudinally, between the cartridge and the chamber. For custom chambers, which might not meet the industry-agreed requirements, a chamber cast should be made and compared with the dimensioned drawings of cartridges and chambers given elsewhere in this book. Comparision of the cartridge and chamber drawings for a particular caliber will show the clearances that are necessary to comply with safe practice, as agreed by the firearms industry. Provided these clearance conditions are met, the characteristic having the greatest effect on chamber pressure is the configuration of the throat, that region of the barrel between the mouth of the chambered case and the point where the lands reach their full height, ahead of the origin of rifling. The throat configuration determines the amount of "free run" that the bullet is allowed, from the instant it starts to move forward, until it encounters the lands (rifling) and begins to be engraved. It is easily determined for rifles by the following procedure.

1. Put the barrel in a vise, barrel horizontal, breech closed and locked, and insert a flat-tipped cleaning rod from the muzzle until it touches the bolt face. Mark the rod by wrapping a piece of adhesive tape around it, with the edge of the tape exactly even with the muzzle.

2. Remove the rod from the barrel, and the gun from the vise. Open the breech, point the barrel downward, and drop a bullet into the chamber, point forward, being sure that it falls into the throat in that position.

3. Put the rifle back into the vise, barrel horizontal, and with a short rod or pencil inserted through the chamber, press the bullet into firm contact with the origin of rifling. Insert the flat-tipped cleaning rod part-way again from the muzzle, hold the bullet in position against the lands, and gently advance the cleaning rod until it touches the tip of the bullet. Mark the rod at the muzzle with tape, as before, and remove it.

4. Measure carefully, preferably with a vernier or dial caliper, the distance between the forward edges of the two wrappings of tape. This is the overall length of a cartridge, with the bullet seated in it, that would provide land contact (zero free run) with that particular shape of bullet. The difference between that dimension, and the actual loaded length of the cartridge, is the free

run for that particular bullet and seating depth, in that particular rifle. The length of free run depends not only on the location of the origin of rifling, but also on the included angle of the throat cone, so it cannot be determined accurately with a bullet-diameter plug gage, or a flat-base bullet reversed in the case, as is sometimes advocated.

Other conditions being the same, it will be found that a rifle allowing more free run with a particular bullet-seating depth produces lower pressure (and lower velocity) than a rifle allowing less free run. In other words, shorter throats produce higher pressures and velocities. The difference can be quite considerable. That was illustrated by the results of a test done some years ago in a 5.56mm pressure barrel, on which the throat was advanced by careful reaming in increments of .020 inch, from zero to .060 inch of bullet free run. Reference rounds were fired at each stage of the throat advancement. The pressure decreased, almost linearly, by a total of about 4000 psi as the throat was reamed progressively deeper. The results probably would have been quantitatively different with another caliber or another load, but qualitatively the same. It should be mentioned, however, that the velocity also decreased as the throat was advanced. In fact, when the powder charge was increased to produce the same velocity in the long throat that had been achieved in the short throat before, the pressure was nearly the same as before. Lengthening the throat provides only limited benefit toward increasing the velocity at acceptable pressure. It does provide a small improvement in the pressure/velocity relationship, however, and that is the purpose of "free-boring" which is sometimes found in high-velocity rifles. Free-boring is simply providing a very long throat ahead of the chamber. Whether its advantages outweigh its disadvantages, however, is very questionable.

Loading practices and components affect pressure

It is obviously possible also to increase the free run simply by seating the bullet more deeply in the case. That has two effects on chamber pressure, which are in opposite directions. The increased free run tends to decrease pressure, but the decrease in powder space increases the loading density, which tends to increase pressure. Which effect will predominate depends on the characteristics of the particular load and gun. In most full-charge loads, it is found that the pressure decreases at first as the bullet is seated farther away from the lands, but beyond some particular seating depth, the pressure begins to rise again as the powder space is further reduced. In revolvers, the free run through the

cylinder is always relatively great, and increased seating depth always increases the chamber pressures.

Some dimensional relationships between the cartridge case and the chamber also affect the pressure strongly, and must be carefully monitored from the ammunition standpoint. If the diameter of the neck of the cartridge is too large for the chamber, pressures are increased, because the bullet is held tightly in the case neck and cannot move forward freely as the pressure begins to rise within the case. This condition can be caused by excessively thick case necks, bullets too large in diameter, or excessively small chambers. A reliable check, provided the chamber meets industry-agreed requirements, is to measure the diameter of the case neck, with a bullet seated in it, and compare this diameter with that given on the cartridge drawing which can be found elsewhere in this book. If the neck of the cartridge is too large in diameter, then it must be thinned by reaming or turning to the correct thickness. Another simple test is to try to insert a bullet into the neck of a case that has been fired in the gun, and not resized. The bullet should enter freely. If it does not, then the case neck must be thinned before the case is reloaded.

Another condition that increases chamber pressure is cases that are too long. They may jam into the front shoulder in the chamber mouth, and be crimped tightly against the bullet as the bolt is closed. This has the same effect as a tight chamber neck, and is especially hazardous with ammunition in which the case mouth is crimped into a cannelure on the bullet.

Summary — Be safe!

It is impossible to overemphasize the importance of chamber pressure to the handloader. Handloading is a relatively safe pursuit for those who know the rules of safety, and respect them. Foremost among those rules is to avoid any practice that might produce excessive chamber pressure in the ammunition being loaded. Some handloaders, even some of long experience, seem to feel that chamber pressure is only of academic importance, and that "practical" experience is a sufficient basis for disregarding chamber-pressure data. That is a naive and dangerous attitude, not at all a mark of experience as it is sometimes purported to be. It is unfortunate that the technology of instrumentation has not yet provided the handloader with practicable means of measuring chamber pressures for himself, as he now can measure his velocities. Until those means are available, however, the prudent handloader will study carefully the pressure data developed in professional laboratories, and heed their advice.

MEASUREMENTS OF CHAMBER PRESSURE

By WM. C. DAVIS, JR.

In historical perspective, the measurement of chamber pressure is a rather recent innovation in ballistics. Guns have been in use since the first years of the 14th century. The first practical pressure gage for guns was invented by Sir Alfred Noble about 1860. Therefore, for about 550 years after guns were first invented, the only clear evidence a shooter might have that he had exceeded the safe limit in weight of powder or shot was that something blew up. Some shooters still develop their loads that way, but better methods have now been available for more than 100 years.

Crusher-type gages

Noble's invention was a pressure gage of the type now called a "crusher gage." In that type of gage, the powder gases are allowed to act on a piston of accurately known area, and the piston, at the other end, bears against one end of a cylinder of soft metal (copper or lead), which in turn is solidly supported by an "anvil" at its opposite end. The soft metal cylinder is called a "crusher." Lead crushers are used for shotshells and some other types of low-pressure ammunition, and copper crushers are used for higher-pressure centerfire metallic cartridges. Since the force exerted on the piston by the powder gas exceeds the compressive strength of the crusher, the crusher is compressed ("crushed"), more or less, depending on the amount by which its compressive strength has been exceeded. Since pressure is, by definition in physics, the force exerted per unit area on which the force acts, the pressure of the powder gas is obtained by dividing the force exerted on the piston, by the cross-sectional area of the piston. In the British and American dimensional systems, the units of force are pounds, and the units of small area are square inches. If the force on the crusher in pounds (deduced from its compression or shortening) is divided by the area of the piston in square inches, the result is a pressure, in pounds per square inch. This is commonly abbreviated as *psi*.

The crusher gage has some imperfections, and so indeed have all other pressure gages so far invented. In the crusher gage, the fundamental flaw is that the deformation of the crusher is not quite instantaneous, since the piston must actually move some finite distance in order to shorten the crusher. If, while the piston is moving, the rapidly changing pressure reaches its peak and begins to diminish, the shortening of the crusher is halted before it reflects the true peak pressure acting on the piston. For this reason, the pressures indicated by a crusher gage are almost always a little less than the true peak pressures. It is impossible to say exactly how much less, since that depends on the "sharpness" of the pressure-time curve near the peak pressure. In a few instances, in which the pressure is applied very suddenly to the piston, crusher-gage pressures may be equal to, or even slightly higher than, true peak pressures. This occurs only in gages in which the piston hole is located ahead of the chamber, as in measurement of gas-port pressures along the barrel, or some chamber-pressure gages of unusual design.

Pressure terminology

In small arms, pressures measured by crusher gages are usually about five per cent to 20 per cent below true peak pressures, more or less depending on the characteristics of the load and of the particular type of crusher gage em-

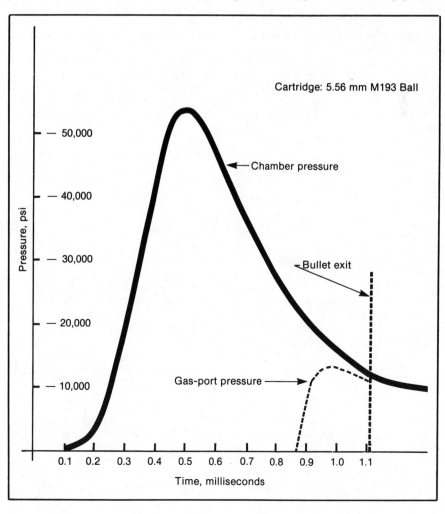

Cartridge: 5.56 mm M193 Ball

Chamber pressure

Bullet exit

Gas-port pressure

Pressure, psi

— 50,000

— 40,000

— 30,000

— 20,000

— 10,000

0.1 0.2 0.3 0.4 0.5 0.6 0.7 0.8 0.9 1.0 1.1

Time, milliseconds

ployed. That type of error is called a "systematic error," because it is quite consistent, and in the same direction from shot to shot. Because of this systematic error, some ballisticians have felt that it is academically inaccurate to refer to crusher-gage measurements as pressures in pounds per square inch (psi). Apparently because of these objections, it has become the practice in U.S. commercial parlance to speak of crusher-gage measurements in terms of "copper units of pressure (c.u.p.)" and "lead units of pressure (l.u.p.)." These new terms are used to distinguish crusher-gage measurements from those made by electronic-transducer gages (to be explained later) which are now expressed in psi or "psia" for "pounds per square inch, absolute." The choice of these new terms is unfortunate.

If the terminology "pressure in pounds per square inch" is academically objectionable when applied to crusher-gage measurements, it is the word "pressure" rather than "pounds per square inch" that ought reasonably to be questioned. The crushers are actually calibrated by subjecting a sample of each lot, in a specially designed press, to various levels of force, measured in pounds, and determining the shortening that results from each level of applied force. In military practice, the usual procedure is to compress 20 crushers at each of 20 levels of applied force, for a total sample of 400 crushers from each lot. Each crusher is measured both before and after compression, to determine the degree of shortening. The degree of shortening is then plotted against the applied force, to yield a curve fitting the 20 data points, each point representing a sample of 20 crushers. From this curve, a "tarage table" is then constructed, for the type of pressure gage (pressure barrel) with which the crushers will be used. If the gage has a piston of 1/30 square inch cross-sectional area, for example, the pressures in the tarage table are derived by dividing the applied force in pounds by 1/30 square inch. Thus, a force of 1,000 pounds, divided by 1/30 square inch, corresponds to a pressure in the table of 30,000 pounds per square inch, as of course it must, by the rules of dimensional analysis.

The terms c.u.p. and l.u.p. are, unfortunately, not specific, but ambiguous. In other countries, for example, crusher-type gages are also used, and the procedures are substantially the same. However, different units of force, and sometimes of area, are customarily employed. In England it is customary to express the force in long tons (2240 pounds) and the pressure in square inches, so the units of pressure are tons per square inch, abbreviated t.s.i. In countries using the metric system, the force was for many years customarily

expressed in kilograms-force, and the area in square centimeters, so the units of pressure were in kilograms per square centimeter, abbreviated kg/cm^2. If the ambiguous terminology of U.S. commercial practice were extended to measurements made in other countries, ammunition that produced 50,000 c.u.p. in the United States would produce about 22.3 c.u.p. in England, and about 3,515 c.u.p. in France or Germany, for example.

These ambiguities have, unfortunately, been introduced with no redeeming advantages in the academic purity of the terminology. Since it is the term "pressure" rather than the units themselves that might be in question, and that term is still used in connection with c.u.p. and l.u.p., the specificity of the former terminology has been lost, the academic purity of expression has not been improved, and the confusion has been more compounded than dispelled. The new terms do serve to distinguish between crusher and electronic-transducer measurements, for those among us by whom the convention is understood. But that was also done, more accurately and meaningfully, in terms "psi (copper)" and "psi (lead)" which were formerly used, when distinction was necessary, but have now been abandoned in U.S. commercial practice.

To summarize on the confusing matter of current terminology in pressure measurements in the United States, the terms c.u.p. and l.u.p. mean that the pressure measurements are in fact in pounds per square inch, and they have been made in crusher-type gages, employing copper or lead crushers, respectively. Exactly the same kind of measurements were formerly expressed in psi, with the type of gage identified elsewhere in the context, or as "psi (copper)" or "psi (lead)." In military practice, and in data of foreign origin that have been converted for the convenience of American readers, the terms c.u.p. and l.u.p. will seldom be found, and crusher-gage measurements are still expressed in psi. The terms psi and psia, in current U.S. commercial practice, now indicate that the measurements have been made with some type of electronic-transducer gage, and they are in pounds per square inch.

The movement to standardize dimensional systems on an international basis has led to the appearance of several other units not formerly seen in interior-ballistic literature, each apparently having its own advocates. For many years, countries using metric dimensional systems commonly expressed chamber pressures in kilograms-force per square centimeter (kg-cm²). One kg/cm² equals about 14.2 pounds per square inch. More recent usage has included the "atmosphere" (abbreviated atm), and the bar, and most recently the

megapascal (abbreviated MPa). One atm is equal to the standard atmospheric pressure at mean sea level, which is about 14.7 pounds per square inch. The bar is based on units of the metric centimeter-gram-second (cgs) system, and is equal to one million dynes per square centimeter, or about 14.5 pounds per square inch. The MPa is based on units of the metric meter-kilogram-second (mks) system, and is equal to one million newtons per square meter, or 10 "bar", or about 145 pounds per square inch. One must try to take comfort in the assurances of academic scientists that this proliferation of unfamiliar units is leading toward simplification, since that is hardly apparent on the face of the matter.

Crusher-type gages still useful

The crusher-type pressure gage has been much maligned in recent years, sometimes by research-oriented scientists whose purposes it does not serve as well as do electronic-transducer gages, and sometimes by other men who hear and repeat the criticism, having only limited experience and superficial knowledge of any pressure-measuring system themselves. In fact, crusher gages have served very well for the great preponderance of pressure measurements for many years, as they still do. Though it is unquestionably true that they indicate pressures somewhat lower than true peak pressures in most applications, it has not been convincingly demonstrated that crusher-gage pressures are less useful than electronic-transducer measurements in predicting the likelihood of excessive-pressure malfunctions in either guns or ammunition. The most common consequences of excessive pressure in small arms are the deformation of case heads, swelling of chambers, or permanent deformation of locking members that "stretch" the headspace of the gun. These are all consequences of failure of ductile and malleable metals that are stressed beyond their elastic limits, and it is not unreasonable to argue that their occurence is as closely related to the phenomenon of crushing a metal cylinder as to the instantaneous peak pressure indicated by an electronic-transducer gage. It is significant that the arms and ammunition manufacturers, and government ballistics laboratories as well, have continued to use crusher-type gages for about 40 years after practical electronic-transducer gages were developed. It is preposterous to suppose that they did so because they were unaware of technological developments, or too obtuse to appreciate the advantages of more sophisticated equipment, though those explanations have sometimes been put forth. The fact is that both crusher-type gages and electronic-transducer gages have been very useful in professional laboratories for about 30 years, each for the purposes to which it was best suited. For routine testing of ammunition manufactured to an established design, crusher-type gages were generally preferred. The technique of manufacturing crusher cylinders of excellent uniformity, and of calibrating them accurately for construction of tarage tables, has been highly perfected. A lot of crushers, once calibrated, does not change thereafter, whereas an electronic transducer may in fact change in calibration during use, and therefore requires periodic recalibration for reliable results. The equipment required for both calibration and use of crusher gages is simple, purely mechanical, and easily maintained. That required for calibration and use of electronic-transducer systems is relatively complicated, and requires the frequent attention of highly skilled technicians, if reliable results are to be maintained. Some experimenters who undertook the use of electronic-transducer systems, without having adequate facilities or understanding for their proper calibration and maintenance, soon found that their results were unreliable. The common notion that differences in pressure-test results among different laboratories testing the same ammunition (or ostensibly the same) are due primarily to the unreliability of crusher-type gages, is mistaken.

This writer was, for about ten years, a member of an international working group, whose goal was to establish electronic-transducer systems of pressure measurement as the standard for NATO-standardized ammunition. After each of several countries had developed a candidate electronic-transducer system, a comparison was conducted between the standardized crusher-gage system and the respective transducer systems, in each of the national laboratories, all using the same lot of reference ammunition. The result was that the agreement among laboratories was appreciably better with the crusher system than with the transducer systems. That was about ten years ago, when electronic-transducer systems had been in common use for more than twenty years. It is clear, therefore, that the transition from crusher systems to electronic-transducer systems, for many purposes in the ammunition industry, has been deferred for very good and practical reasons.

Within the past decade, the situation has changed somewhat, for two reasons. The first reason is that rapid advances in the general technology of electronics have eliminated many of the former technical problems. The other is that ammunition testing for routine production has become increasingly automated, as has the production process itself. The mechanical operations of pressure testing with a crusher-type system are practically impossible to automate, whereas the electrical signals of an electronic transducer are readily accepted by electronic data-processing systems. For these reasons, the transition to electronic-transducer systems for routine testing has been accelerated. Meanwhile, however, the crusher-gage data that are still furnished by practically all of the major manufacturers, and the laboratories in which loading data are compiled, should not be disparaged. It is fully as reliable as data obtained from the sophisticated transducer systems, and far more reliable than data taken by a sophisticated electronic system that is operated and maintained by personnel not fully aware of its sophisticated requirements and idiosyncrasies for operation and maintenance.

Though the invention of the crusher-type pressure gage in the 1860's was a great step forward in the science of ballistics, its serious limitation is that it can measure only the peak pressure. Understanding of the more complex problems of interior ballistics requires a continuous record of pressure, from the time the primer is fired until the projectile has cleared the muzzle. Various mechanical contrivances have been developed to obtain pressure-time records since about 1880, but these were only marginally successful. It was not until the development of the cathode-ray tube (of which the modern television tube is a well known example) that reasonably accurate pressure-time gages for guns became really practical.

Electronic-transducer gages

The concept of the electronic-transducer gage dates from about 1915, though reasonably accurate results with such gages were not achieved until about 20 years later. From the beginning, the most successful electronic-transducer gages have been of two types.

One of the early successful gages was of the strain-resistance type. In that type of gage, a thin wire is arranged in some way so that it will be stretched, more or less, in proportion to the pressure. Stretching of the wire increases its length, decreases its diameter, and increases its electrical resistance. By suitable circuitry, this change in resistance can be converted to an electrical signal that is fed into the cathode-ray tube, producing the familiar trace of a pressure-time curve. Such a gage was first described in the early 1920's. A very sophisticated strain-resistance gage was developed, and in use for measurement of pressure in small arms, by the U.S. Army Ballistic Research Laboratories, more than 50 years later. The strain-resistance gage developed by the Ballistic Research Laboratories produces excellent results, but it has so far been too expensive to produce, with the required precision, for routine use.

The other type of successful electronic-transducer gage employs a piezoelectric transducer element. This type of gage was suggested by Sir J. J. Thomson during World War I (1914-1918), but piezoelectric pressure-measuring systems that gave a useful degree of accuracy were not developed until about 1935. The piezoelectric gage depends upon the fact that certain mineral crystals, most importantly quartz and tourmaline, when cut in a certain way, have the property of generating an electrical charge when subjected to a mechanical force acting against opposite faces of the crystal. The charge generated is practically in direct proportion to the applied force, or at least it can be made so by proper design and construction of the transducer element. For measuring gun pressures, quartz crystals are generally used, because they have the mechanical strength to resist breakage under heavy loads, suddenly applied.

The early piezoelectric gages developed for use in small arms consisted of a piezoelectric transducer that was substituted directly for the crusher in a crusher-type system, between the piston connected with the chamber, and the anvil which normally supported the other end of the crusher cylinder. This type of gage had the advantage of being capable of calibration on a simple mechanical dead-load press, with a carefully calibrated mechanical force applied, much as crushers are calibrated. However, the piston that is required in such gages, to transmit the force from the powder gas to the transducer (or crusher), itself entails some disadvantages, and introduces some potential inaccuracies into the measurement. For that reason, the piezoelectric transducers now most commonly used are miniaturized, completely contained inside a relatively small threaded steel body or "plug," that is screwed into the chamber wall, and equipped with a diaphragm against which the powder gas acts directly, or through the medium of a short column of grease. The elimination of the piston is desirable, but it precludes calibrating the transducer on a simple mechanical press, and requires instead a calibrator that can develop nearly 100,000 psi of hydraulic pressure, with a high degree of accuracy. Such calibrators are relatively complicated and expensive. The initial calibration of the transducer is normally accomplished by the manufacturer, and furnished to the buyer. Some users, who did not have access to a hydraulic calibrator, have attempted to use the transducer throughout its life, with only the original calibration. As a matter of experience, however, the characteristics of transducers sometimes

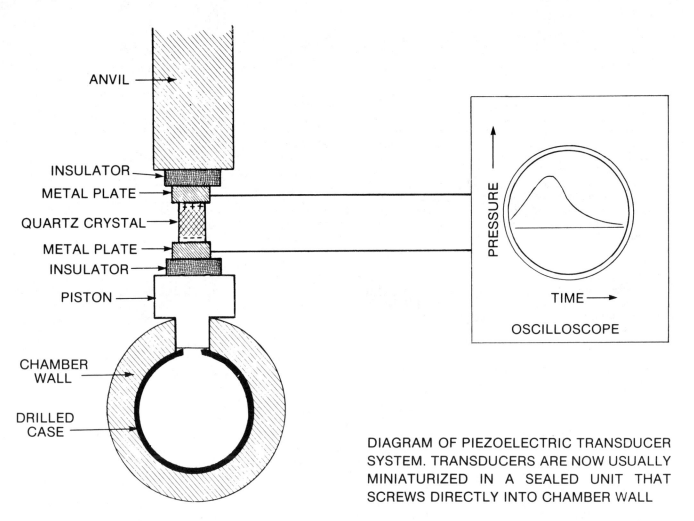

ANVIL

INSULATOR

METAL PLATE

QUARTZ CRYSTAL

METAL PLATE

INSULATOR

PISTON

CHAMBER WALL

DRILLED CASE

PRESSURE

TIME

OSCILLOSCOPE

DIAGRAM OF PIEZOELECTRIC TRANSDUCER SYSTEM. TRANSDUCERS ARE NOW USUALLY MINIATURIZED IN A SEALED UNIT THAT SCREWS DIRECTLY INTO CHAMBER WALL

change during use, and data taken without fairly frequent recalibration are not entirely reliable.

In summary, electronic-transducer pressure-measuring systems provide pressure-time data that are not available in any other way (though the usefulness of pressure-time data is limited to those skilled in its interpretation), and they are amenable to automation and automatic data processing. These are great advantages in many applications. On the debit side they are much more complicated than crusher-systems, more difficult to calibrate and more dependent on frequent calibration, and they are more susceptible to error in the hands of operators who do not fully appreciate the need, or have the facilities, for meeting their relatively sophisticated requirements in operation and maintenance. These disadvantages will undoubtedly be overcome, eventually, and electronic-transducer systems will probably replace crusher systems entirely for ballistic measurements in years ahead.

The types of gages described above, for use in small arms, are called "radial-type" gages. This is because they are located in a hole drilled into the chamber, along a radius of the chamber. In cannon, where the volume of the chamber is relatively very large, crusher-type gages are usually completely contained in a small sealed body or capsule,

that leaves only the face of the piston exposed through the outside wall of the capsule. The whole capsule is then loaded into the chamber, along with the propellant charge, and it remains there (usually) during and after firing. The capsule is then retrieved and disassembled, the crusher is removed and measured just as it is after compression in a radial-type gage. No modification of the gun is required for measurement of pressure by these means, which is of course a great advantage. Unfortunately, however, the method is not applicable to small arms, because it is not practicable to make a gage assembly small enough to fit inside the cartridge, and occupy only an insignificant part of the powder space. There is, however, a crusher-type gage for small arms that is used without drilling a hole through the barrel wall.

British base-crusher gage

The British have for many years used a gage commonly called the "base-pressure" or "base-crusher" gage. In a base-crusher system, the barrel is not drilled, but simply screwed into a special test action. In use, the cartridge head is supported by the front end of a freely moving steel cap having an axial hole through its center to permit passage of the firing pin. The steel cap is supported at its other end by a special copper

crusher, cylindrical or barrel-shaped, with an axial hole through its center for passage of the firing pin. The other end of the crusher is in turn supported solidly by a threaded breech-bolt, that screws into a supporting member in the body of the action. In preparation for firing, the cartridge is quite heavily oiled, so as to minimize friction between the case walls and the walls of the chamber. When the cartridge is fired, the case is thrust back against the steel cap which supports it, becoming in effect the pressure-piston of the gage. The floating steel cap, in turn, is thrust back and compresses the crusher by which it is supported, to a degree that depends on the peak chamber pressure. The crusher compression is then determined by measurement, and the pressure is determined by reference to a tarage table, taking account of the diameter (actually cross-sectional area) of the chamber. The pressures recorded by the base-crusher gage are typically less than those recorded by a radial-type crusher gage, usually by about 10 to 20 per cent. It is for this reason, incidentally, that British guns are often proof-marked with a pressure that seems surprisingly low to American shooters. A British-made .30-06, for example, may be marked "18 t.s.i.," meaning 18 tons per square inch. Since there are 2,240 pounds in a British long ton, this figure is, by direct conversion, 40,320 psi. That is, in fact, the specified maximum service pressure for British .30-06 ammunition, as tested in their standard base-crusher gage. The same ammunition that records 40,320 psi in the base-crusher gage would, however, approach 50,000 psi (c.u.p.) in an American radial-type crusher gage. The actual proof pressures for British small arms are typically about 30 to 45 per cent higher than those of the service ammunition, and British guns are proof-fired using oiled cases in the gun, which serves to increase the thrust on the bolt face, in comparison to that of dry cartridges. The relatively low pressures stamped on British guns does not, therefore, indicate that they are proofed to less stringent standards than those made in other countries. British proof, on the contrary, is highly respected throughout the world.

Laboratory practices reduce variables

There has been a trend among American shooters, in recent years, to disparage all chamber-pressure measurements made in ballistics laboratories, especially those made with crusher-type gages. This is due in part to the fact that chamber pressures quoted for the same cartridge, same powder charge and same bullet weight, coming from different laboratories, are usually found to be somewhat different. It is due also to the fact that the sources of certain inaccuracies in chamber-pressure measurements have been widely publicized, apparently to instill in hand-loaders a sensible measure of caution about using maximum loads. The effect, unfortunately, has not been as intended. Instead, respect for laboratory measurements of chamber pressure has been eroded, and it has even been suggested that subjective "pressure signs" such as the appearance of primers or the permanent expansion of cases were more trustworthy than laboratory pressure measurements. Nothing could be further from the truth. Some information on the controls imposed on pressure-measuring apparatus and procedures in professional laboratories will illustrate the point.

The variability of copper crushers, from piece to piece or lot to lot, has sometimes been put forth as a major source of error in crusher-gage measurements. Crushers are made from electrolytic copper, a material notable for its very high degree of freedom from impurities. In order to maintain this high degree of purity, the process for obtaining electrolytic copper is, in fact, so costly that used crushers are not normally sold as ordinary scrap from laboratories, but are segregated and returned to the manufacturer for recycling and production of new crushers.

The crushers are fully annealed after being formed, under the most critical controls. The object is to produce crushers that have extremely uniform hardness, and the careful controls achieve this to a remarkable degree. The dimensions of crushers are also controlled, to tolerances of a few ten-thousandths of an inch, and rigid dimensional inspections assure that the tolerance requirements are met. Finally, a large sample of crushers from each lot, usually at least 400, are compressed at various levels of force, for acceptance and for construction of the tarage table. The data from the compression testing is analyzed statistically for uniformity, and lots of crushers that do not meet the stringent requirements are rejected.

In contrast, cartridge cases are made of brass, usually containing about 70 per cent copper, 30 per cent zinc, with small amounts of impurities allowed. The object in manufacturing cartridge cases is to be quite sure that the various regions of the case are hard enough and strong enough to withstand the stresses of firing, but not so hard as to develop cracks in long-term storage, or upon firing. Within these limits, a case head harder than necessary is no detriment, and case heads may range in hardness from about 160 to 200 in terms of the Vickers DPN scale. These hardness limits correspond to yield strengths of roughly 70,000 to 90,000 psi. Since the chamber pressure at which a cartridge-case head undergoes permanent deformation is proportional (though not equal) to the yield strength of the material, it is clear that some cartridge cases might be deformed at pressures as much as 30 per cent lower than that required to cause permanent deformation of other case heads. It is obvious, therefore, that chamber-pressure comparisons inferred from such signs as expansion of case heads might be in error by 30 per cent or more. This kind of error is incomparably greater than the error in pressure measurements introduced by differences in hardness among copper crushers. Indeed, if chamber pressures could be determined with satisfactory accuracy by so simple a process as measuring the diameters of fired cases, the cost-conscious manufacturers of ammunition would long ago have abandoned the construction and use of expensive pressure barrels and copper crushers or electronic transducers.

It has also been stated, often and quite correctly, that there are differences among individual test barrels in respect to the pressures and velocities that they produce, with the same kind of ammunition. Less well known are the procedures developed and employed among professional laboratories to minimize the effect of barrel-to-barrel differences, and other

sources of error, in their ballistic testing. The procedures to be described are those in effect at Government laboratories, but they are substantially the same as those employed in commercial laboratories operating in accordance with approved practices of the Sporting Arms and Ammunition Manufacturers' Institute (SAAMI).

Pressure and velocity test barrels are manufactured to appreciably closer tolerances than those applied to military and commercial sporting weapons. The dimensions affecting chamber pressure (and incidentally velocity) are usually maintained within that part of the normal dimensional tolerance range that tends to produce the highest pressures. This is to assure, insofar as practicable, that the pressures developed in test barrels are at least as high as those likely to be encountered in any military or sporting weapon in the field, having barrel and chamber dimensions that meet the broader tolerances allowed in such weapons under military specifications or SAAMI agreements. In addition, each test barrel is subjected to a series of firing with reference ammunition when it is first put into service, and on each occasion of firing thereafter, throughout its life.

The subject of reference ammunition now requires some explanation. It consists of a single lot of ammunition, usually manufactured under special controls intended to produce the highest practicable degree of uniformity in its ballistic performance, and representing insofar as possible a velocity and pressure typical for that particular cartridge design. Having produced such a lot, the manufacturing agency (or a government laboratory) conducts an extensive test of the lot, both to determine its acceptability as reference ammunition, and to assess the velocity and pressure that are typical of its performance. Such a firing is called an "assessment," and the velocity and pressure determined from the test are called the "assessed velocity" and "assessed pressure."

An assessment firing usually consists of one 20-round series for velocity, another for pressure, in each of at least five different test barrels of each type, repeated on each of three different days. The results at the completion of the assessment are carefully analyzed, by statistical methods, and compared to very stringent requirements. If any of the five barrels shows too great a difference from the others, it is withdrawn from service, and the test is repeated with another barrel. If the ammunition shows too much variation from shot to shot (expressed in terms of standard deviation), or if its average ballistics deviate too much from the typical or specified ballistics for that type of ammunition, the lot is rejected for reference use, and another lot is loaded. When all of the requirements for acceptance have been met, the grand average of all the velocity measurements, and of all the pressure measurements, are established as the "assessed velocity" and "assessed pressure" of that particular reference lot. Quantities of the reference lot are then distributed to all of the participating laboratories, along with copies of the assessment results. The laboratory responsible for the reference lot then monitors its performance, by accumulating data on subsequent firings in its own tests, and sometimes from other participating laboratories as well, to assure that the initially assessed values are consistent with subsequent performance of the lot. If accumulated experience indicates the need to revise the assessment values, they are revised accordingly, and the new values are published.

The principal purpose of reference ammunition is to calibrate test barrels and the associated equipment, on each occasion of testing. Prior to firing any sample of test ammunition, the particular barrel to be used (and associated test equipment) is checked by firing a series of reference ammunition of the same caliber. In government practice, if the velocity obtained with reference ammunition differs from the assessed velocity by more than 35 fps, or the pressure differs by more than 3,500 psi, the system is considered to be out of the acceptable calibration range, and testing cannot proceed until the problem has been found and corrected. If the results with reference ammunition are acceptable, then they are recorded, and the firing of test ammunition proceeds, with exactly the same test set-up. The results of the reference firing are then used to establish calibration corrections (sometimes called "correction factors") to be applied to the results of the test firings.

For example, if a reference lot of .30-06 ammunition were assessed at 2,740 fps and 46,000 psi, but in a particular barrel, on a particular day, the results obtained were 2,750 fps and 45,000 psi, the correction factors would be respectively —10 fps (2,740-2,750 fps) and + 1,000 psi (46,000-45,000 psi), since these are the values that must be applied to the observed values to agree with the assessed values of the reference lot. If the values actually observed with a sample of test ammunition fired on the same occasion were 2,755 fps and 46,500 psi, for example, these uncorrected values would be corrected to 2,745 fps (2,755-10 fps) and 47,500 psi (46,500+1,000 psi) respectively. Insofar as practicable, these corrections compensate for small individual differences among test barrels (and other factors that might influence the results), and give a more truly representative account of the test-ammunition performance.

Subjective pressure signs — be careful

Notwithstanding the fact that subjective pressure signs are less reliable than laboratory pressure measurements, it is important that the handloader be familiar with the subjective pressure signs, and use them intelligently in making decisions about his loads.

Practically all reloading manuals, and the data published by the powder manufacturers themselves for Du Pont and Winchester-Western powders, warn that maximum charges should be reduced by about 10 per cent for initial trials, and then increased in small increments until either the listed maximum load is reached, **or until signs of excessive pressure appear.** This is sound advice, and should be scrupulously followed. It is particularly useful for strong bolt-action rifles, which can withstand without damage chamber pressures that produce obvious high-pressure symptoms in brass cases. These symptoms include hard extraction, leaking primer pockets, loose primers, primers extruded into the firing-pin hole in the bolt face, imprints of the ejector hole on the head of the case, and expanded case heads. These signs may appear singly, or in different combinations, depending upon the characteristics of the rifle in which the ammunition is fired. If any of them appear, it is prudent to reduce by at least five per cent the powder charge that produced that sign, and regard that charge as "maximum" in that particular rifle. It is possible for some of these symptoms to be caused by faults in the rifle rather than excessive chamber pressures in the loads. If that is suspected, it is good practice to fire a few factory loads for comparison. If the symptom still persists, the handloader should take the gun to a competent gunsmith for inspection, and repair if necessary.

Because these pressure signs are useful in working up to a published maximim charge, some handloaders by logical extension assume that it is permissible to increase charges **beyond** those listed as maximum in a reliable data source, on grounds that some rifles can accommodate heavier charges than others before case failure becomes imminent, and therefore that published maximum charges can be exceeded with impunity unless some signs of excessive pressure appear. Although this is a moot point among some authorities, most if not all professional ballistics laboratories consider it poor practice. It can be argued that, if pressure signs are used to establish a safe limit on charge weight below a published maximum, then the same criteria are acceptable for establishing charges above a published maximum. The difference is, however, that for charges below a published maxi-

mum, we have no choice. We must start somewhere, neither too high nor too low, because even too-light charges can be hazardous with some slow-burning powders. The best guidance available to us is the published information on maximum charges established in a reliable ballistics laboratory. In the great majority of cases, the maximum charges published in reliable data sources will be found quite safe and satisfactory. In the few instances where they are not, in some particular rifle, we have no alternative but to rely on the subjective pressure signs, notwithstanding that they are much less reliable than the results of properly done ballistics tests in a standard pressure barrel.

There are two important reasons that subjective pressure signs should not be used to justify extending loads upward beyond the maximum loads published in a reliable data source. First is the fact that cartridge cases may vary considerably in hardness and strength, as explained before. Though cases within the same lot are unlikely to vary as much as cases of different lots, the differences may nevertheless be quite appreciable. The second reason is that chamber pressures may vary considerably from shot to shot, even if the loading is carefully done. When powder charges are increased to the point where a few rounds show case-head expansion, and then reduced only slightly, the chances are that the small sample tested has not included the extreme combination of an unusually high chamber pressure in an unusually soft case. That combination will eventually be encountered, however, and the result might be an expanded head, a stuck case, and a disabled rifle, or even a serious gas leak.

Reliance on most of the pressure signs as a basis for establishing safe maximum loads is especially unwise when loading for handguns, or for rifles that might be damaged or fail catastrophically at chamber pressures below about 55,000 c.u.p. Case-head expansion is unlikely to occur at pressures lower than that, but many weapons might well be damaged at lower pressures. The only sign that might appear in these weapons is hard extraction, because that depends upon a relationship between the expansion of case walls, and the elastic recovery of the chamber and/or the locking members of the action, rather than the expansion of the solid case head. It is especially important to observe carefully any increase in extractive effort when working up loads for handguns, or any but the strongest rifles. If extraction is noticeably hard, the chamber pressure is probably too high, and the charge that produced it should be reduced by five per cent. When the charge weight reaches the published maximum, the handloader should stop there, and not test his luck.

EFFECTS OF COMPONENT SWITCHING ON BALLISTICS OF THE .30-06

By WM. C. DAVIS, JR.

THE practice of substituting one brand or type of bullet, primer or case for another specified in a published source of reloading data is often called *component switching*. Some years ago, the most commonly used reloading publications did not identify the specific brand or type of the metal components (bullet, primer and case) used to develop the loads they recommended. Bullets were commonly identified only by weight, and by type as jacketed or cast.

Most current sources of reloading data identify the metal components quite specifically, though some do not. Some publications specifically warn against component switching, and others do not.

The subject has not received the attention that it deserves, and many handloaders switch components very casually, unaware that the particular brand or type of primer, case, and bullet (of a specified weight) might have a significant effect on the velocity or pressure of the load. The subject has not been widely investigated on a systematic basis, and the data that have been published on it are not, in most instances, reported in sufficient detail to establish the significance of the results. There are, however, a few reports that give sufficient detail to warrant some conclusions.

The subject was examined systematically in two articles that appeared in *The American Rifleman*, one by William Dresser in February 1964, the other by the late M. D. Waite, longtime technical editor of *The American Rifleman*, in June 1955. Dresser described an extensive firing program with the .30-06 cartridge, involving 10 different brands of cases, 10 different brands or types of primers, and 21 brands or types of 150-grain jacketed bullets. Dresser's tests were designed to determine the effects of these various components on muzzle velocity, and pressure measurements were not made. Waite examined the effect of using 10 different brands and types of 150-grain jacketed bullets in the .30-06, all with the same combination of primer, case and powder charge. Waite's article included radial-copper chamber-pressure measurements as well as instrumental velocities. Much was learned in these investigations, and both articles were reprinted

in the previous edition of the NRA Handloader's Guide. The data developed by Dresser and Waite are summarized and further examined in this article.

A summary of Dresser's data is shown in Tables 1, 2, 3 and 4. Dresser used IMR-4064 propellant throughout his tests. Table 1 shows the effect of using entirely different brands of metal components (primer, case and bullet) with charges of 49.0 and 54.0 grains of IMR-4064 powder. It is interesting to note that there were not only significant differences in velocity at a given charge weight with the different combinations of metal components, but also that the charge-velocity relationship was not the same. The data for Table 1 were analyzed statistically, and the effect of using these two different combinations of metal components was found clearly significant.

Dresser's plan was to vary only one component at a time, all with the same charge of 49.0 grains of IMR-4064 powder and observe the effect of this on the instrumental velocities which he measured at 10 feet from the muzzle. Tables 2, 3 and 4 show his results and the captions below the tables are self-explanatory.

A statistician was engaged to analyze Dresser's results, and a summary of this analysis was given by Col. E. H. Harrison, then of the NRA Technical Staff. There were two important points in this analysis. One was that the analysis showed evidence of what statisticians call "interaction." This means that one of the variables (primer, case or

bullet) was found to alter the effect of the others on the instrumental velocities. The comparison of different primers, for example, was conducted using only military DEN 42 cases and military M2 ball bullets, and the ranking of primers from highest velocity to lowest velocity applies only to that particular combination of case and bullet (and powder charge as well). The existence of "interaction" implies, for example, that the ranking of primers might have been somewhat different had another combination of cases and bullets been used for the comparison.

Though the existence of such interaction is not implausible on engineering grounds, it is difficult to be very confident from statistical analysis alone about interaction effects in velocity and/or pressure tests, unless the test is specifically designed for that purpose, the sequence of testing is known, and reference ammunition is fired on each occasion of test firing. As a matter of experience in ballistic testing, it often happens that two samples from the same lot of reference ammunition, fired on consecutive days, will show differences between averages that cannot reasonably be ascribed to the random shot-to-shot variation observed on the two separate occasions of firing. This is due apparently to some systematic difference in test conditions that cannot be eliminated, even by the most diligent efforts to control the procedures, and has plagued investigators in ballistics laboratories for many years. One of its troublesome effects is that it may give the appearance

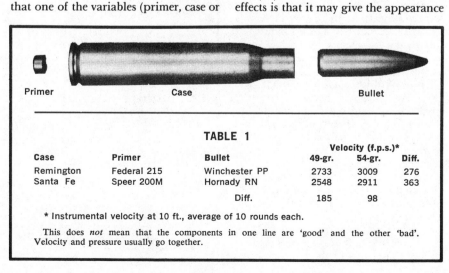

Primer   Case   Bullet

TABLE 1

Case	Primer	Bullet	Velocity (f.p.s.)*		
			49-gr.	54-gr.	Diff.
Remington	Federal 215	Winchester PP	2733	3009	276
Santa Fe	Speer 200M	Hornady RN	2548	2911	363
		Diff.	185	98	

* Instrumental velocity at 10 ft., average of 10 rounds each.

This does *not* mean that the components in one line are 'good' and the other 'bad'. Velocity and pressure usually go together.

133

of interaction when in fact there is none, or possibly obscure the effects of interaction when it really exists, if the data from several days of firing are analyzed for the effects of two or more variables at the same time. If interaction existed in Dresser's results, and it might well have, the reasons for it are not known, and cannot be determined from statistical analysis.

The second point of interest was that the random shot-to-shot variation in velocities was such that small differences between averages were not statistically significant. In general, differences of less than about 30 fps were not statistically significant. For example, although the Winchester Power Point bullet in Table 4 produced 2,724 fps and the Remington Core-Lokt bullet produced 2,697 fps, the 27-fps difference between them was not necessarily significant, nor was the difference between those bullets and any of the three other bullets between them in the ranking. If the test was repeated, the ranking among those five bullets (and others similarly close together in velocity) might change, simply as a manifestation of chance variations in the experiment.

A third and incidental point was that the statistician found in some series (marked with an asterisk in the tables) that there was one anomalous velocity or "flyer" that fell outside the range expected from the other nine shots.

The results of statistical analysis do not detract from the importance of this valuable investigation. They are included merely to warn the reader against unwarranted inferences. In particular, one cannot justifiably predict that one primer, for example, always produces higher velocities than another in the same load simply because it appears higher in the ranking, with this particular load, in this particular test. What is well demonstrated is that there are real differences in velocity to be expected in consequence of switching from one brand or type of metal component to another. Though chamber pressures were not measured in Dresser's test, it is virtually certain that the significant differences in velocity would have been accompanied by significant differences in pressure as well.

Waite's investigation, though less extensive, included pressure measurements. His results are summarized in Tables 5 and 6. Details of the load, and other significant particulars, are given in the note below Table 5. Table 6 gives the relative ranking of the 10 bullets tested, with respect to some characteristics of their design that might reasonably be expected to affect the velocity and pressure.

There is no clear correlation in Table 6 between the ranking of any of the four bullet characteristics and the observed

TABLE 2

Velocity effect of changing the cartridge case

Case Make	Cartridge Case Weight (grs.)		Velocity (f.p.s.)	
	Average	Range	Average	Range
Remington	202.4	6.3	*2672	129
Peters	214.1	6.6	2668	28
Winchester	190.6	7.1	*2663	122
FA 57 Match	199.4	5.0	2659	42
DEN 42	199.0	8.0	2655	56
Western	189.0	7.0	2645	49
Norma	189.8	1.7	2607.5	42
Canadian Ind.	195.2	4.5	2607.5	75
Herter	200.0	2.4	2574	65
Santa Fe	198.5	2.1	2570	39

* Ten-shot series contained one apparently erroneous velocity—see Editor's Note.

Remarks: Instrumental velocities at 10 ft. from the muzzle. Range temperature 65° to 69° F., relative humidity 70% to 75%. All loads fired in Model 1903 Springfield, SA 968676, with SA 5-33 issue barrel. Weights are of fired cases and include the fired primer. Federal #210 primer, lot AL 26293. Powder charges 49.0 grs. DuPont IMR 4064, lot 84, weighed to ± .1 gr. M2 Ball bullets. Ten such bullets averaged 151.1 grs., varied 150.4 to 151.6 grs. in weight and averaged .3078" in diameter. Over-all cartridge length 3.35".

TABLE 3

Velocity effect of changing the primer

Primer		Velocity (f.p.s.)	
Make	Lot	Average	Range
Federal #215	AL16175	2671	58
Federal #210	AL26293	2655	56
Winchester-Western #8½-120	TA81L26	*2654	167
RWS #2845	—	2649	84
CCI #250 Magnum	11 6	2640	56
CCI #200	1 556	2639	49
U. S. Military, cal. .30	WCC-11	2628	56
Canadian Ind. #8½	L3KFT56	2625	106
Remington #9½	505 5061	2619	42
U. S. Military, cal. .30	Speer Ctg. Works 200M	2601	54

* Ten-shot series contained one apparently erroneous velocity—see Editor's Note.

Remarks: Instrumental velocities at 10 ft. from the muzzle. Range temperature 65° to 67° F., relative humidity 65% to 72%. All loads fired in Model 1903 Springfield, SA 968676, with SA 5-33 issue barrel. DEN 42 cartridge cases. Ten such cases averaged 199.0 grs., varying from 202.8 to 194.8 grs. Powder charge 49.0 grs. DuPont IMR 4064, lot 84, weighed to ± .1 gr. M2 Ball bullets. Ten such bullets averaged 151.1 grs., varied 150.4 to 151.6 grs. and averaged .3078" in diameter. Over-all cartridge length 3.35".

TABLE 4

Velocity effect of changing the bullet

	Seat Depth (ins.)	Dia. (ins.)	Weight (grs.)		Velocity (f.p.s.)	
			Average	Range	Average	Range
Win. Power Point	.22	.3083	150.6	.6	2724	44
Win. Silvertip	.25	.3084	150.6	.9	2714	43
Norma FJBT	.24	.3082	151.4	1.4	2710	29
Speer spitzer SP	.20	.3083	150.8	1.1	2704	36
Rem. SP Core-Lokt	.21	.3080	149.6	1.2	*2697	119
Nosler	.26	.3079	150.1	.7	2689	43
Sierra spitzer	.21	.3080	149.5	.3	2685	43
Speer RNSP	.23	.3083	150.4	1.4	2683	36
Rem. Bronze Pt.	.23	.3081	149.4	1.0	2662	57
Rem. PSP Core-Lokt	.23	.3084	149.8	2.4	2661	58
M2 Ball	.23	.3078	151.1	1.2	2655	56
Hornady Spire-pt.	.23	.3079	150.2	.3	2647	56
CIL pt.-soft-pt.	.22	.3076	150.2	1.3	2643	71
Western open pt. ex.	.25	.3084	148.9	.8	*2639	129
Norma SPBT	.30	.3077	154.3	1.0	2638	77
Sierra flat-nose	.24	.3068	150.1	.4	2633	63
Herter semi-pt'd	.24	.3084	150.4	.5	2630	56
Norma SP flat-nose	.24	.3078	150.0	1.0	2630	70
Herter Wasp-Waist	.27	.3076	150.2	.4	2616	82
Speer WR soft pt.	.23	.3080	149.9	1.4	2596	68
Hornady round-nose	.25	.3076	149.8	.4	2583	26

* Ten-shot series contained one apparently erroneous velocity—see Editor's Note.

Remarks: Instrumental velocities taken at 10 ft. from the muzzle. Range temperatures 67° to 74° F., relative humidity 80% to 75%. All loads fired in M1903 Springfield, SA 968676, with SA 5-33 issue barrel. DEN 42 cases. Ten such cases averaged 199.0 grs., varied 202.8 to 194.8 grs. Powder charge 49.0 grs. DuPont IMR 4064, lot 84, weighed to ± .1 gr. Federal #210 primers, lot AL 26293.

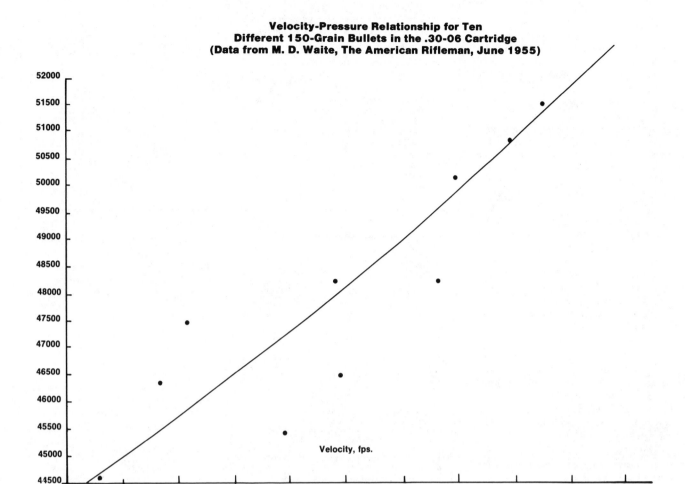

**Velocity-Pressure Relationship for Ten
Different 150-Grain Bullets in the .30-06 Cartridge
(Data from M. D. Waite, The American Rifleman, June 1955)**

Velocity, fps.

velocity or pressure. Possibly this is because the effects of one characteristic in a particular bullet obscures the effects of others, and possibly the characteristics interact among themselves. In any event, it is clear that none of the characteristics listed is, by itself, a reliable basis for predicting where the bullet will fall in the ranking of velocity or pressure. What is apparent from the rankings is that the velocity and pressure are closely correlated, and a statistical analysis of the data confirms this correlation at a high level of confidence.

The last column of Table 5 from Waite's original article lists the velocity /pressure ratio, which he calculated by dividing the velocity in feet per second by the pressure in thousands of pounds per square inch (kpsi). Though this provides a simple basis of comparison among the bullets, it is somewhat misleading, since it might imply that a change in the bullet producing a velocity difference of about 60 fps would correspond to a pressure change of only 1,000 psi, whereas that is not actually the case.

The more significant velocity-pressure relationship is indicated in the accompanying graph and in Table 7. The graph shows plotted points of the pressures and velocities from Waite's data in Table 5 and a curve fitted by

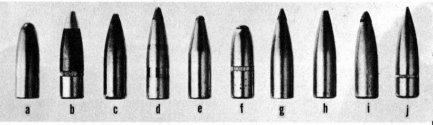

TABLE 5—150-Grain Bullet Comparison Table

Type	Length (inches)	Diameter (inches)	Core Weight (grains)	Jacket Weight (grains)	Bearing Length (inches)	Pressure (pounds per square inch)	Velocity (feet per second)	Velocity-pressure ratio (foot-seconds per 1000 pounds pressure per square inch)
(a) Speer Round-Nose Soft-Point	.92	.3085	111.0	39.0	.54	51,900	3037	58.5
(b) Winchester Silvertip	1.07	.3085	96.0	54.0	.56	50,740	3031	59.7
(c) Sierra Soft-Point	1.03	.308	93.2	57.0	.55	50,090	3021	60.3
(d) Nosler Partition Jacket	1.12	.308	100.2	50.0	.52	48,210	3018	62.6
(e) Hornady Spire-Point	1.00	.308	109.2	41.5	.57	48,200	2999	62.2
(f) Hornady Round-Nose	.89	.3085	108.0	42.0	.59	47,430	2972	62.7
(g) Speer Spitzer Soft-Point	1.08	.3085	107.0	43.5	.50	46,490	3000	64.5
(h) WTCW Open-Point	1.07	.308	95.5	56.0	.53	46,330	2967	64.0
(i) Barnes Soft-Point	1.05	.308	87.8	62.0	.52	45,430	2990	65.8
(j) U. S. M2 Full-Metal-Jacket	1.11	.308	113.5	36.5	.47	44,510	2956	66.4

Loading data: Seating depth, .34"; charge, 51.0 grs. IMR 3031 Lot #157; case, Western; primer, Federal #210. Note: 10-round samples fired.

Instrumental velocities taken at 20 ft. from the muzzle of the gun. Range temperature varied from 72° to 74° F; relative humidity 43% to 58%. All loads tested in Winchester pressure barrel 24" long, groove diameter .308", land diameter .300"; 4 grooves, right-hand twist, one turn in 10"

statistical methods to the ten plotted data points. The velocities and corresponding pressures in Table 7 are those that might be read from the graph, though they were actually obtained mathematically from the equation of the fitted curve, because greater accuracy can be attained this way. The curve is, in effect, a representation of Waite's velocity and pressure data, smoothed to remove the random scatter of individual data points. The column headed "Change, fps/kpsi" indicates the change in velocity corresponding to a change of 1,000 psi (1 kpsi) in chamber pressure. It is significant to note that a pressure increase of 1,000 psi corresponds to a gain in velocity of 14 fps at about 45,000 psi, whereas the same pressure increase corresponds to only 10 fps at about 52,000 psi. This illustrates that gains in velocity exhibited among the different bullets were made only at the expense of disproportionate increases in chamber pressure.

An interesting question now arising is whether, when changing to a different bullet that produces higher velocity than another, the powder charge might simply be reduced to produce the same velocity as before, and thus reduce the pressure to the same level as before. The answer is that it probably could not.

Though Waite's data do not include velocities and pressures obtained with different powder charges, it is expected from interior ballistic theory, and generally borne out by experience as well, that pressures are approximately proportional to the square of velocities, when brought about by changes in the powder charge. For small changes, this is practically equivalent to the statement that each change of 1 per cent in velocity is accompanied by a 2 per cent change in pressure when the powder charge is adjusted. Thus a reduction from 3,050 fps to 3,000 fps (about 1.6 per cent) produced by reducing the charge weight is expected to reduce the pressure by about 3.2 per cent, or about 1600 psi in the vicinity of 50,000 psi. Waite's data, however, indicate that an increase from 3,000 fps to 3,050 fps, when brought about by changing the bullet, produced a pressure increase of about 4,500 psi, or nearly three times as much as the change to be expected by adjusting the powder charge between the same velocity limits. The data thus indicate that the increase in pressure caused by changing bullets is so disproportionate to the gain in velocity that it cannot be compensated by adjusting the powder charge downward on the basis of velocity data. Reducing the velocity to the same level as before by adjusting the charge weight downward will not, in general, reduce the pressure to the same level as before.

Considering Waite's and Dresser's data together is also informative. If the velocity-pressure relationship of about

TABLE 6—Comparison of Factors (highest is 1)

For example, the Speer RN SP is ninth in length, or next to the shortest. It is fifth in bearing length, second in both core weight and core hardness, first (highest) in both pressure and velocity, and tenth (poorest) in ratio of velocity to pressure.

	Bullet Length	Bearing Length	Core Weight	Core Hardness	Pressure	Velocity	Velocity-Pressure Ratio
Speer Round-Nose Soft-Point	9	5	2	2	1	1	10
Winchester Silvertip	4	3	7	10	2	2	9
Sierra Soft-Point	7	4	9	6	3	3	8
Nosler Partition Jacket	1	8	6	4	4	4	6
Hornady Spire-Point	8	2	3	9	5	6	7
Hornady Round-Nose	10	1	4	3	6	8	5
Speer Spitzer Soft-Point	3	9	5	1	7	5	3
WTCW Open-Point	5	6	8	7	8	9	4
Barnes Soft-Point	6	7	10	8	9	7	2
U. S. M2 Full-Metal-Jacket	2	10	1	5	10	10	1

TABLE 7

Velocity, fps	Pressure, psi	Change fps/kpsi
2950	44,270	14.7
2960	44,960	14.3
2970	45,670	13.7
2980	46,420	13.1
2990	47,200	12.6
3000	48,010	12.1
3010	48,850	11.8
3020	49,710	11.4
3030	50,610	11.0
3040	51,530	10.7
3050	52,480	10.3

Pressures corresponding to different velocity levels obtained with different 150-grain bullets, using the same particular combination of primers, cases and powder charge, in the .30-06 cartridge.

10 to 14 fps per 1,000 psi, as established by Waite's data, are applied to the extreme velocity spread of 141 fps observed by Dresser among the 21 bullets that he tested, then the spread of pressures among Dresser's loads must have been about 10,000 psi. There is no way to tell from the available data whether the velocity-pressure relationship established by Waite in his tests of different bullets would also apply to changes in primers and cases, but if they were to apply, then the change of 185 fps reported by Dresser in Table 1 for the 49.0-grain charge of IMR-4064 would imply a pressure change of about 13,000 to 15,000 psi. This is certainly quite astonishing. Dresser's data seem to indicate that the effect of using different metal components is less at higher charge weights than at lower ones. The difference observed at the 54.0-grain charge weight of IMR-4064 was only 98 fps, implying a pressure difference of about 7,000 psi, but even that is quite enough to cause serious problems with a near-maximum load. It is about the same as Waite observed in his bullet tests with 51.0 grains of the faster-burning IMR-3031 powder.

It should be noted that the powder charges used by Dresser and Waite in these investigations are not necessarily recommended charges. Dresser's charge of 54.0 grains of IMR-4064 powder, and Waite's charge of 51.0 grains of IMR-3031, both exceed the charges currently

recommended by the powder manufacturer for a specified 150-grain bullet in the .30-06. In fact, Waite's data show that three of the ten bullets tested did exceed the industry-agreed 50,000-psi (now c.u.p.) pressure limit for the .30-06 cartridge with the 51.0-grain charge of IMR-3031. The charges were chosen for the purposes of the investigations, and not intended as necessarily recommended charges.

These investigations provide a useful insight into the effects of component switching on ballistics. They prove that the effect is real, and large enough to demand caution when near-maximum loads are being used. They do not, unfortunately, provide a simple set of rules by which the effects of component switching can be accurately predicted, even in the .30-06 cartridge which was used for the investigations. The complexity of the problem, as revealed by these investigations, indicates that there are no simple rules. A fair question is, "What should the handloader's position be on the practice of component switching?"

A safe and obvious answer is that the practice of component switching must be completely avoided, and that is undoubtedly the best course where it is practicable. The handloader is well advised to use exactly the same combination of primer, case, powder and bullet specified in his source of loading data when those particular components are available to him, and he has no compelling reason for substituting others. It often happens, however, that only a limited selection of component brands is marketed in certain areas, and other brands cannot be obtained by reasonable efforts, so the particular primer, bullet or case required for a recommended load is unavailable. It may also be that the handloader is loading for a gun with special requirements, such as the commercial versions of military semiautomatic rifles, which often function better with military cartridge cases than with some brands of commercial cases. It may be simply that a reloader has an abundant supply of good cases, but desires to use some loads for which there are no published loading data specifying the particular type of cases that he has. In such instances, the practice of component switching is undeniably widespread, notwithstanding warnings against it. It is best that the handloader under these circumstances be as well informed as possible, so that he can assess the risks and proceed with due caution as dictated by intelligent understanding. It is not the purpose of this article to recommend component switching, or to forbid it, but to provide the handloader with a basis of intelligent judgement on the subject.

The general rules that emerge are these:

1. Do not load maximum charges when moderate loads will suffice as well. With charges 10 per cent less than the maximum charges listed in reliable data sources, there is little danger that a change in the type of primer, bullet or case will raise the pressures excessively. For most purposes, loads 5 to 10 per cent below maximum are completely adequate, and may even be preferable to maximum loads.

2. When substituting any metal component (primer, bullet or case) for one of another brand or type in a near-maximum load, *always* reduce the charge weight by about 10 per cent, as is recommended by most powder manufacturers and reloading manuals. The one exception to this rule is in the use of certain powders such as Winchester-Western 296 in handguns or 785 in rifles, for which the manufacturer specifically warns that powder charges should neither be increased nor reduced from those recommended. Such powders, though excellent in their limited applications, should not be used with any components except those specifically recommended by the powder manufacturer.

3. If the reduced charge shows none of the characteristic signs of excessive chamber pressure, and it is desired to increase it, limit the increments of increase to about 1 per cent of the charge weight, and test-fire each incremental increase before proceeding to fire the next higher one.

4. If any sign of excessive pressure is encountered, such as hard extraction, loose or leaking primer pockets, cratered or perforated primers, or expansion of the solid case head, reduce the charge that produced the symptom by 5 per cent, and regard that as the maximum charge.

5. If no sign of excessive pressure is encountered before the charge weight has reached the maximum charge listed in a reliable source of reloading data, stop at the maximum charge listed. Subjective pressure signs are useful as the only alternative to measuring pressures when a pressure barrel is not available, but they are far less reliable than the pressure measurements usually made by the compilers of reloading data. When the compiler of the published data lists a charge as maximum, his information is most probably more reliable than that of the handloader who has no pressure barrel, and the published data should be heeded.

Handloaders should be aware that component switching is not without some risk, even if these rules are heeded, and it should not be done without some compelling reason. If it must be done, following these rules provides the best chance of avoiding any serious consequences.

SOME SIMPLIFIED INTERIOR BALLISTICS FOR HANDLOADERS

By WM. C. DAVIS, JR.

Small arms are least predictable

In all the science of gun ballistics, the interior ballistics of small arms is perhaps the part most difficult to deal with by calculations. The interior ballistics of cannon are much more reliably predictable from calculations, and most of the professional literature on interior ballistics deals almost exclusively with the ballistics of artillery gun/ammunition systems. The classic book on the subject in the English language, Corner's "Theory of the Interior Ballistics of Guns," devotes only one of its 434 pages to small arms. Corner gives several good technical reasons why the interior-ballistic problems of small arms are not amenable to solution by the usual mathematical methods, and concludes with the observation that: "Ballistic methods for small arms are accordingly more empirical . . .," which is to say that velocity and pressure tests, rather than calculations, are much the preferred way to obtain reliable ballistic data for small arms. That is good advice.

Nevertheless, there remains a need for some reasonably simple methods that serious handloaders can use to answer some of their questions on the subject. The purpose of this article is to present some methods of computation, that can be understood and employed by any handloader who is reasonably competent in algebra at the high-school level, and who has one of the common electronic calculators that can perform the square-root function.

It must be understood at the outset, however, that *calculations are not to be trusted to establish safe handloading data*. The best information on safe and satisfactory handloads is that based on actual pressure and velocity tests, which is published in the many excellent handloading manuals such as those of Hodgdon, Hornady, Nosler, Sierra and Speer, and the literature of DuPont, Hercules, Norma and Winchester-Western. Loads established on the basis of calculation should not be assumed to be safe loads. If possible, they should be checked against published data to see that the expected pressures will not exceed those of loads that have been found safe in actual firing tests. Where that is not possible, as in the case of wildcat cartridges for which such published data are not available, the handloader should have facilities for remote firing during load development, with effective protection against personal injury in the event of an unanticipated high-pressure malfunction. Experimenting with ammunition is not for the inexperienced handloader, or one who fails to learn from experience, or one inclined to the derring-do attitude toward thrilling new experiences. These points are made not just as perfunctory disclaimers, but should be taken very seriously.

The methods described here are, in general, applicable only to DuPont IMR powders fired in strong centerfire rifles, capable of withstanding loads that typically develop pressures on the order of 50,000 c.u.p. A few handguns also fall into that category. It is assumed that the experimenter who plans to reduce any of these calculations to practice is sufficiently well informed about the strength of his gun and cartridge cases, and about safe handloading and testing procedures, to avoid any hazardous practices in his loading and shooting.

The most important factors

The most important characteristics in determining the performance of a cartridge are the charge weight, the capacity of the powder chamber, the diameter and weight of the bullet, and the length of the barrel in which it will be fired. These basic characteristics are combined in various ways to derive some of the other terms commonly used in interior ballistics, such as loading density, expansion ratio, sectional density, and the ratio of charge weight to bullet weight.

It is widely believed that the shape of the cartridge case is also of great importance, and many wildcat cartridges are based on the supposition that some unusual configuration of the powder chamber will provide an over-riding advantage over all conventional configurations, and thus produce ballistic performance far transcending the ordinary. While there is some credible evidence that certain shapes of the case are better than others, for various reasons, the differences are relatively small in comparison to the fundamental characteristics mentioned above. This article does not deal with such esoteric refinements, but for those interested in the question, a very informative series of articles appeared in THE AMERICAN RIFLEMAN, issues of April through July in 1946. The author of those articles conducted a very carefully controlled series of experiments, in a professionally equipped laboratory, using cartridges identical in every way except for radically different shapes of powder chamber. He was unable, in those particular experiments, to distinguish the performance of one from another. It appears unlikely, therefore,

TABLE 1.

CARTRIDGE	FULL CASE CAPACITY GRAINS WATER	CASE LENGTH INCHES	CARTRIDGE MAXIMUM LENGTH INCHES	CARTRIDGE	FULL CASE CAPACITY GRAINS WATER	CASE LENGTH INCHES	CARTRIDGE MAXIMUM LENGTH INCHES
.17 REM	26	1.786	2.150	.300 SAV	52	1.861	2.600
.22 HORNET	14	1.393	1.723	.308 WIN	56	2.005	2.800
.218 BEE	18	1.335	1.680	7.62MM NATO	54	2.005	2.800
.221 FIREBALL	20	1.390	1.830	.30-06	69	2.484	3.340
.222 REM	27	1.690	2.130	.300 H&H MAG	86	2.835	3.600
.223 REM	31	1.750	2.260	.308 NORMA MAG	87	2.550	3.250
.222 REM MAG	32	1.840	2.280	.300 WIN MAG	88	2.610	3.340
.219 WASP	35	1.770	2.190	.300 WEATH MAG	98	2.815	3.562
.219 ZIPPER	34	1.930	2.260	7.65MM MAUS	57	2.096	2.970
.225 WIN	40	1.920	2.500	.303 BRITISH	57	2.212	3.075
.224 WEATH	38	1.913	2.312	7.7MM JAP	60	2.264	3.150
.22-250	45	1.902	2.350	.32-20	22	1.295	1.592
.220 SWIFT	48	2.195	2.680	.32-40	41	2.130	2.500
6 X 47MM	33	1.840	2.500	.32 SPECIAL	45	2.030	2.565
.243 WIN	54	2.035	2.710	.32 REM	46	2.040	2.525
6MM/.244 REM	55	2.223	2.825	8 X 57MM MAUS	60	2.230	3.250
.240 WEATH MAG	65	2.490	3.062	8MM-06	70	2.484	3.340
.256 WIN	22	1.271	1.590	8MM REM MAG	98	2.840	3.600
.25-20 WCF	19	1.320	1.592	.338 WIN MAG	85	2.490	3.340
.25-35	37	2.030	2.550	.340 WEATH MSG	96	2.815	3.562
.250 SAV	46	1.910	2.515	.348 WIN	75	2.245	2.795
.257 ROBERTS	55	2.223	2.775	.38 SPECIAL	24	1.145	1.550
.25-06 REM	66	2.484	3.250	.357 MAG	27	1.280	1.590
.257 WEATH MAG	84	2.540	3.250	.357 HERRETT	41	1.750	2.550
6.5 X 54MM M.S.	50	2.102	3.010	.35 REM	51	1.910	2.525
6.5MM JAP	48	1.974	2.890	.351 WIN S.L.	27	1.370	1.900
6.5 X 55MM	56	2.155	3.062	.358 WIN	57	2.005	2.780
6.5MM REM MAG	68	2.160	2.800	.35 WHELEN	70	2.484	3.340
.264 WIN MAG	82	2.490	3.340	.350 REM MAG	71	2.160	2.800
.270 WIN	68	2.530	3.340	.358 NORMA MAG	88	2.510	3.230
.270 WEATH MAG	82	2.540	3.250	.375 WIN	49	2.010	2.560
7 X 57MM MAUS	59	2.225	3.065	.375 H&H MAG	94	2.840	3.600
.284 WIN	66	2.160	2.800	.378 WEATH MAG	133	2.903	3.700
7MM EXP/.280 REM	68	2.530	3.330	.38-40 WCF	40	1.295	1.592
7MM-08 REM			2.800	.38-55	52	2.120	2.550
7 X 61MM S&H	75	2.392	3.190	.44 MAG	39	1.275	1.610
7MM WEATH MAG	82	2.540	3.250	.44-40 WCF	40	1.295	1.592
7MM REM MAG	84	2.490	3.290	.444 MARLIN	66	2.215	2.570
.30 CARBINE	20	1.280	1.680	.45-70	79	2.095	2.550
.30 HERRETT	35	1.604	2.300	.458 WIN MAG	93	2.490	3.340
.30-30	45	2.030	2.550	.460 WEATH MAG	138	2.913	3.700
.30-40	58	2.304	3.089				

that any particular chamber configuration can be relied upon to free the experimenter from the long-standing basic constraints of interior ballistics, which are based on the fundamental characteristics mentioned above.

Before any useful calculations can be done, reliable data must be obtained for input into the mathematical formulas. We must first consider, therefore, the methods by which the necessary data can be obtained.

Finding powder space by direct weighing

One of the most important characteristics in determining the interior-ballistic performance of a cartridge is the capacity of the powder chamber in the case. There is some confusion as to how that can best be determined and expressed. It is sometimes given as the capacity to the juncture of the neck and shoulder, but that is not always meaningful, since some bullets must be seated to intrude

below the base of the neck to maintain an acceptable overall length for the loaded cartridge, and others leave considerable unoccupied space in the case neck. For cases that are not bottle-necked, of course there is no shoulder to define the point of measurement. There are more meaningful ways to find and express the case capacity.

The important characteristic from the standpoint of interior ballistics is the amount of space available for the powder charge, when a bullet is seated to the desired depth in the case neck. This means that bullets having different seating depths will allow different amounts of powder capacity, when seated in the same cartridge case. The volume displaced when the bullet is seated must therefore be taken into account for a meaningful comparison among different loads and cartridges.

The most direct way to determine the volume of the powder space for any particular load is as follows: File a small groove lengthwise on the cylindrical

bearing surface of a bullet, so that water will have a path to escape when the bullet is seated in a water-filled case. Take a case that has been resized, and seat a fired primer in the pocket. Weigh the case and grooved bullet together on your powder scale. Fill the case to the mouth with water, seat the bullet carefully to the desired seating depth, dry the exterior of the case and bullet, and weigh the water-filled cartridge. The difference between the empty and full weights is obviously the capacity of the cartridge, with that particular bullet, in grains of water.

Calculating powder space from measurements

An alternate method of determining case capacity involves a little more computation, but it is often more convenient, especially if different bullets and/or different seating depths are involved. To begin, the cartridge case (with the primer pocket sealed by a

TABLE 2.

LIST OF VARIABLES

A = Mass ratio (charge weight/bullet weight)
B = Bullet length (inches)
C = Case length (inches)
D = Bullet diameter (inch)
E = Barrel length (inches)
F = Full water capacity of case (grains)
G = Bullet weight (grains)
H = Height (axial length) of boat-tail (inch)
I = Charge weight (grains)
J = Tail diameter (small end) of boattail (inch)
K = Displacement correction for boattail bullet (grains)
L = Cartridge overall length (inches)
LD = Density of loading (I / W ratio)
$M = 1 / \sqrt[3]{R}$
N = (1 - M)
P = Water displaced by seating flat-base bullet (grains)
Q = Effective bore volume (cubic inches)
R = Expansion ratio
S = Bullet seating depth (inch)
T = Bullet travel in barrel (inches)
U = Volume of cartridge powder chamber (cubic inch)
V = Muzzle velocity (ft/sec)
W = Water capacity of cartridge powder chamber (grains)
X = Powder-selection index
Y = (G + I / 3)
Z = Bullet sectional density (lb/in^2)

primer or otherwise) is first weighed empty, and then filled carefully to the mouth with water. Some care should be taken to fill the case level full, without either a concave or convex meniscus in the water surface at the mouth, and be sure that no air bubbles remain inside. The weight of water is obtained by subtraction as described before. This is the full case capacity, and should be recorded for future reference. The length of the cartridge case should also be carefully measured at this time, and recorded for future reference.

For those who want to compare cartridges for which they do not have specimens to weigh and measure, Table 1 gives the nominal full-case water capacity, case length and cartridge overall length of some common cartridge cases. The numbers in the table should be considered approximate, however, since cases of the same caliber, but different brands or different lots, may be found to have capacities differing by as much as about five percent.

It will be found convenient, as measurements are made, to record them by their descriptive names, and identify them also by the alphabetic variable names assigned in Table 2. These are not the variable names assigned in the

traditional literature on ballistics, but are used here to avoid the necessity of using Greek letters and subscripts, in the hope that the formulas will seem clearer and less formidable in this simpler notation.

The next step is to measure the length of the bullet, and establish the desired overall length of the loaded cartridge. From these measurements, the seating depth of the bullet is conveniently found, by adding together the length of the bullet and the length of the case, and subtracting from this sum the overall length of the loaded cartridge. The formula is:

$$S = C + B - L$$

where S = seating depth, inch
C = case length, inches
B = bullet length, inches
L = length overall of loaded cartridge, inches

The amount of water displaced by seating a flat-base bullet can now be found by the following formula:

$$P = 198 \times S \times D^2$$

where P = water displaced by bullet, grains
S = seating depth, inch
D = bullet diameter, inch

To find the water capacity of the powder chamber, with a flat-base bullet seated, the following formula may now be used:

$$W = F - P$$

where W = water capacity of the cartridge, grains
F = full water capacity of the case, grains
P = water displaced by seating the bullet, grains

If a boattail bullet is to be used, a small correction can be made to allow for the tapered rear end of the bullet. The correction is usually less than one grain, and hardly necessary, but the formula for the correction (K) is:

$$K = 66 \times H \times (2 \times D^2 - D \times J - J^2)$$

where K = correction for boattail, grains
H = height (axial length) of boattail, inch
D = bullet diameter, inch
J = tail diameter (small end) of boattail, inch

The correction (K) should be added in the formula for water capacity of the powder chamber (W), which then becomes (for boattail bullets):

$$W = F - P + K$$

where F, P and K are found as described above

Occasionally the handloader may wish to consider the use of a bullet of which he has no sample for measurement. A fair estimate of the bullet length can be made by measuring the illustration of the bullet in a handloading manual such as the Hornady, Nosler, Sierra or Speer, all of which depict the bullet at approximately actual size.

Finding the bullet travel

The next step in acquiring data for the calculations is to determine the distance that the base of the bullet must travel from its starting position until it clears the muzzle. This is most easily done by adding the length of the barrel (measured from the bolt face) to the seating depth of the bullet, and subtracting from this sum the case length determined as described above. In terms of a formula, the bullet travel is:

$$T = E + S - C$$

where T = bullet travel, inches
E = barrel length, inches
S = seating depth, inch
C = case length, inches

Finding the expansion ratio

The information is now available for determining the expansion ratio for the cartridge and barrel being considered. The expansion ratio in a gun is an important factor in determining ballistic performance. It is comparable to the compression ratio in internal-combustion engines. Increasing the expansion ratio by providing a longer barrel generally produces more energy from the same powder charge, just as increasing the compression ratio of an engine by increasing the piston stroke produces more energy from the same charge of fuel in the cylinder. The expansion ratio in a gun is the ratio of the volume of the bore plus the powder chamber, to the volume of the powder chamber alone. The volumes are commonly expressed in cubic inches.

The volume of the powder chamber is easily found by dividing the water capacity (in grains) by 252.4, which is the density of water at a normal room temperature of 70 degrees F. In terms of the previous formulas, the volume of the powder chamber (U) is:

$$U = W / 252.4$$

where U = volume of powder chamber, cubic inch
W = water capacity of powder chamber, grains

The effective volume of the bore can be calculated from the effective diameter of the bore, and the length of bullet travel. The effective diameter of the bore is somewhat less than the groove diameter, and somewhat more than the land (bore) diameter, and it depends on the actual height and width of the rifling lands in a particular barrel. In general, the lands are about .0025 to .0050-inch high, and are narrower than the grooves, and the necessary allowance for the lands is about 1½ per cent of the bore cross-sectional area.

This allowance has been made in the following formula, so the diameter of the bullet can be used. The formula for finding the effective bore volume is then:

$$Q = .773 \times T \times D^2$$

where Q = effective bore volume, cubic inches
T = bullet travel, inches
D = bullet diameter (barrel groove diameter), inch

The expansion ratio for the gun and cartridge can now be calculated from the following formula:

R = (Q + U) / U

where R = expansion ratio
Q = volume of bore
U = volume of powder chamber

Estimating the powder charge

Having now the essential data on the cartridge, bullet and barrel, we can proceed to consider the powder type and charge weight. The first problem is to identify a potentially suitable type (or types) of powders, and that requires some understanding of the properties to be considered in the powder selection.

Assuming that we wish to obtain the maximum practicable velocity with a particular cartridge case and bullet, it is obvious that we must try to maximize the energy we derive from the powder charge. There are two different limitations on the amount of powder that we can use in a cartridge. First is the amount that the cartridge case will conveniently hold, based on its cubic capacity. The second limitation is the amount of any particular powder that we can burn without producing excessive chamber pressure. What we seek, therefore, is a powder with which we can just conveniently fill the available powder space in the cartridge, with a charge weight that will closely approach, but not exceed, a safe working chamber pressure.

For the DuPont IMR powders, and some similar powders sold by Hodgdon, it will be found that the maximum charge weight which can be conveniently loaded into a cartridge case, without compressing the powder, is about 80 to 90 per cent of the weight of water required to fill the powder space. This concept is expressed in interior ballistics by the term "density of loading" (or "loading density") which is defined as the ratio of the weight of powder charge to the weight of water required to fill the available volume of the powder chamber. Some powders pack more densely than others, owing mostly to the size, shape and surface finish of the powder granules, and this characteristic is expressed by another term called "bulk density," or "gravimetric density." The bulk density of IMR-4227 and IMR-4198 is somewhat less than that of the other IMR canister powders, and for that reason, it will be found that a charge weight equal to about 80 per cent of the water capacity will nearly fill the available powder space. For the other IMR powders, a charge weight equal to about 86 per cent

of the water capacity can be accommodated, without quite filling the available powder space. The "ideal" charge weight will therefore be about 80 per cent of the water capacity for IMR-4227 and IMR-4198, and about 86 per cent of the water capacity for the other IMR canister powders. In terms of a formula, therefore, we can determine our estimated charge weight (I) as follows:

I = .86 x W (except for IMR 4227 and IMR 4198)
or I = .80 x W (for IMR 4227 and IMR 4198)
where I = charge weight, grains
W = water capacity of powder chamber, grains

Defining the powder characteristics

Having decided on the amount of powder, we must now consider the burning characteristics desired, so that the established charge will closely approach, but not exceed, the maximum safe working pressure in the gun. For powders of similar composition and grain form, such as the Du Pont IMR powders, the chamber pressure developed under given conditions of loading depends mostly on a characteristic called "relative quickness." When handloaders speak of "fast-burning" or "fast" powders, and "slow-burning" or "slow" powders, they are referring to this property that ballisticians call relative quickness. We will use the handloaders' terms "fast" and "slow" in that sense in this article, though some professional ballisticians might object to that usage, since it could be confused with terms referring to the linear burning rate of powder, which is an entirely different concept and one we will not describe here.

The relative quickness of the Du Pont powders is expressed on an arbitrary scale, on which IMR-4350 is assigned a value of 100. "Faster" powders have higher numbers, and "slower" powders have lower numbers. The IMR powders available to handloaders (called "canister powders"), rank as follows on the Du Pont scale of relative quickness:

Powder Type	Relative Quickness
IMR 4227	180
IMR 4198	160
IMR 3031	135
IMR 4064	120
IMR 4895	115
IMR 4320	110
IMR 4350	100
IMR 4831	95

Relative-quickness data are based on laboratory tests instead of on gun firings, and serve as a general guide for the expected performance in cartridges, but it is found that powders which are placed fairly close together in the relative-quickness range may change their

relative positions if ranked according to their performance in actual gun firings. This is particularly true of IMR-4064, IMR-4895 and IMR-4320, which rank in that order according to relative quickness, from "fastest" to "slowest." In actual firing, however, IMR-4064 is often found to allow higher charge weights, and produce higher velocities at acceptable pressure, than do either IMR-4895 or IMR-4320, both of which rank lower ("slower") on the relative-quickness scale. For that reason, it is impossible to say with certainty which of the powders in this group of three - IMR-4064, IMR-4895 or IMR-4320 - will be found most suitable in a particular load for which all three have reasonably suitable characteristics. The same is occasionally true of IMR-4350 and IMR-4831, which are separated by only five points on the relative quickness scale. The choice among powders within these groupings cannot be reliably predicted by calculation, but must be determined by actual firing tests in the cartridge under consideration. What we are seeking, in terms of relative quickness, is a powder "fast" enough to produce the maximum safe working pressure at the selected charge weight, but "slow" enough not to produce excessive pressure before the powder chamber in the case is nearly filled.

The degree of relative quickness required to meet our conditions depends most importantly on three factors: (1) the ratio of powder-charge weight to bullet weight, which is sometimes called the "mass ratio"; (2) the sectional density of the bullet; and (3) the maximum working chamber pressure we are prepared to accept. For purposes of the method described here, we will establish the maximum working pressure in the approximate range 45,000 c.u.p. to 50,000 c.u.p. We can now proceed to find the other factors that enter into the powder-selection decision.

The first step is to establish the charge weight. If it appears that a powder "slower" than IMR-4198 will be required, we can proceed on the assumption that the density of loading should be .86, as explained before. If it appears that a powder "faster" than IMR-3031 will be required, we can assume that the loading density should be .80. These rules will not select compressed charges, but will leave little free airspace in the cartridge case, and thus minimize the undesirable effects of shifting powder position from shot to shot. There is nothing inherently wrong about using compressed charges, and sometimes they are advantageous, but this simplified program does not cover their use.

The powder-selection index

Having found the estimated charge weight as described before, our next step is to find the ratio of charge weight to bullet weight, which is sometimes called the "mass ratio" for the load. The formula for the mass ratio (A) is:

$$A = I / G$$

where I = charge weight, grains
G = bullet weight, grains

The next step is to find the sectional density of the bullet. Most reloading manuals list this information, but it is also easily found from the following formula:

$$Z = G / (7000 \times D^2)$$

where Z = sectional density, lb/in²
G = bullet weight, grains
D = bullet diameter, inch

The next step in the procedure is to find a number that we will call the "powder-selection index," and assign to it the variable name X. It is not a term found in traditional ballistics. It has been empirically determined to yield numbers corresponding roughly to the Du Pont index of relative quickness, when the working chamber pressure is about 45,000 to 50,000 c.u.p. The correspondence with the Du Pont relative-quickness scale is not perfect, of course, partly because the behavior of powders in different cartridges and loads sometimes indicates a different ranking than that established by the relative-quickness numbers, as explained before. It should also be emphasized that the powder selected by calculation is an "ideal" IMR powder, which would yield pressures of 45,000 to 50,000 c.u.p. when loaded in a particular cartridge, at the assumed loading density of .86 (or .80) as described before. This "ideal" powder for any particular cartridge probably will not correspond exactly to any of the canister IMR powders actually available, since only eight powders could hardly be "ideal" for nearly 100 cartridges and perhaps a thousand different bullets that might be used. The best we can do, therefore, is to identify the selected powder as *similar* to one or more of the available IMR canister powders, recognizing that the final determination must be made on the basis of actual firing tests in the cartridge being considered. The formula for finding the powder-selection index (X) is then:

$$X = 20 + 12/(Z \times \sqrt{A})$$

where X = powder-selection index
A = mass ratio (charge weight/bullet weight)
Z = bullet sectional density (lb/in²)

Table 3 can now be used to identify the powder, or group of powders, which will most nearly correspond to the "ideal" IMR powder for the load in question.

The final step in the powder-selection process is to reexamine the choice of the loading density chosen to calculate the charge weight. If the charge weight was based on the loading density of .86,

assuming that a powder "slower" than IMR-4198 would be used, but the powder-selection index was found to indicate IMR-4198 or IMR-4227, then the charge weight should now be recalculated using a loading density of .80, as explained before. Conversely, if a loading density of .80 was assumed, but the powder-selection index was found to indicate IMR-3031 or a "slower" powder, then the charge weight should now be recalculated at a loading density of .86, as explained before.

Calculating the velocity performance

Having now established all the characteristics of the load, we can proceed to calculate the expected performance. In this part of the method, we are indebted to Homer S. Powley, for a key equation that he developed some years ago to predict the performance of rifle loads using the Du Pont IMR powders. The Powley Computer for Handloaders (available from Homer S. Powley, Petra Lane, RR 1, Eldridge, IA 52748) is an ingenious slide-rule device, having eleven scales on the front and five scales on the back, which can be used to select an IMR powder, estimate a charge weight, and predict the velocity expected, all on the basis of input measurements similar to those described in this article. Powley's equation is a semi-empirical one, which gives remarkably accurate results considering the complications of small-arms interior ballistics, and it has the great virtue of being simpler than any of the other methods so far devised. Even so, in its original form, the equation might appear formidable to those not accustomed to solving lengthy equations. We shall therefore break

down the equation into simpler steps for solution. We do this by introducing three additional variables, which we will define in terms of other variables that we have already found. They are as follows:

$$M = 1 / \sqrt[4]{R}$$
$$N = (1 - M)$$
$$Y = (G + I / 3)$$

In terms of these variables, Powley's equation for muzzle velocity (V) now becomes:

$$V = 8000 \times SQR (I - N / Y)$$

(SQR indicates "square root of")

A WORKED-OUT EXAMPLE

To illustrate the method, which takes much longer to explain than to perform, let us use the example of establishing a load for the .30-06, with a 180-grain boattail bullet. It would be much easier, of course, to find the load in a handloading manual, but our purpose is to illustrate the method on a cartridge for which we have tested data available to compare.

Suppose we do not have a .30-06 case available for taking weights or measurements, and so we consult Table 1 for typical values, finding:

Case Length, inches: C = 2.484
Full case capacity —
Grs water: F = 69

We next measure the 180-grain boattail bullet (or a life-size illustration of it) and find the following:

Bullet length, inches: B = 1.220
Length of boattail, inch: H = .150
Diameter of tail, inch: J = .200
Diameter of bullet, inch: D = .308
Weight of bullet, grains: G = 180

We decide to load the cartridge to an overall length of 3.30 inches:

Cartridge length, inches: L = 3.30

We now measure the length of the .30-06 barrel which we plan to use in our firing:

Barrel length, inches: E = 24

We are now ready to begin the calculations.

The seating depth of the bullet is:

$$S = C + B - L$$
$$= 2.484 + 1.220 - 3.30$$
$$= .404 \text{ inch}$$

The water displaced by seating a flat-base bullet would be:

$$P = 198 \times S \times D^2$$
$$= 198 \times .404 \times .308^2$$
$$= 7.59 \text{ grains}$$

The correction required for the boattail bullet is found as follows:

$$K = 66 \times H \times (2 \times D^2 - D \times J - J^2)$$
$$= 66 \times .150 \times (2 \times .308^2 - .308 \times .200 - .200^2)$$
$$= .87 \text{ grain}$$

The water capacity of the powder chamber in the cartridge, with the boattail bullet seated, is then:

W = F – P + K
  = 69 – 7.59 + .87
  = 62.3 grains

The bullet travel through the 24-inch barrel is:

T = E + S – C
  = 24 + .404 – 2.484
  = 21.9 inches

The cubic volume of the powder chamber is:

U = W / 252.4
  = 62.3 / 252.4
  = .247 cubic inch

The effective volume of the bore is:

$Q = .773 \times T \times D^2$
  $= .773 \times 21.9 \times .308^2$
  = 1.606 cubic inches

The expansion ratio is:

R = (Q + U) / U
  = (1.606 + .247) / .247
  = 7.50

The estimated charge weight is:

$I = .86 \times W$
  $= .86 \times 62.3$
  = 53.6 grains

The mass ratio (charge weight/bullet weight) is:

A = I / G
  = 53.6 / 180
  = .298

The sectional density of the bullet is:

$Z = G / (7000 \times D^2)$
  $= 180 / (7000 \times .308^2)$
  = .271

The powder-selection index is:

$X = 20 + 12/(Z \times \sqrt{A})$
  $= 20 + 12/(.271 \times \sqrt{.298})$
  = 101

Consulting Table 3, we find that the powder is similar to IMR-4831 and IMR-4350.

We solve now for the variable M. (The fourth root of a number is easily found by entering the number in the calculator, and pressing the square-root key twice.)

$M = 1/\sqrt[4]{R}$
  $= 1/\sqrt[4]{7.50}$
  = .604

We now find the variables N and Y:

N = (1 – M)
  = (1 – .604)
  = .396

Y = (G + I / 3)
  = (180 + 53.6 / 3)
  = 197.9

Powley's equation for velocity, in terms of these variables, is then:

$V = 8000 \times SQR (I \times N / Y)$
  $= 8000 \times SQR (53.6 \times .396/197.9)$
  = 2620 fps

Checking the results

Consulting some sources of handloading data, we see that 2620 fps is a very good estimate of the velocity to be expected from our estimated charge of 53.6 grains of a powder such as IMR-4350 or IMR-4831, in the .30-06 with 180-grain bullets. The following data for comparison were interpolated for a 53.6-grain charge, in the loading tables of the latest Sierra Bullets Reloading Manual and Speer Manual Number 10:

	Speer 22″ barrel	Sierra 26″ barrel
IMR-4350	2621	2672
IMR-4831	2537	2600

Calculating velocity vs barrel length

As might be expected, some knowledge of interior-ballistic calculations is useful, even for those who do not aspire to develop a new load or a wildcat cartridge from basic design principles. One particularly useful purpose is the prediction of the effects of small changes in barrel length, charge weight, or case capacity.

It should be clear that the effect of a change in barrel length can be calculated by means of the method previously described. Since the barrel length was one of the input parameters used to determine the expansion ratio, we need only go to that point in the calculations, and input a new barrel length, all other factors remaining the same, to calculate a new velocity. If that is done, using the previous example of the .30-06 cartridge with 180-grain bullet, the velocities indicated for various barrel lengths are as follows:

Barrel length, inches	Muzzle velocity, fps
20	2530
22	2577
24	2620
26	2657
28	2690

Effects of varying loading density

Understanding the concept of loading density is also useful, as that is an important factor in considering the effects of small changes in case volume and/or charge weight. Since the loading density is the ratio of charge weight to the capacity of the powder chamber expressed in grains of water, it is apparent that changing either of these factors will change the loading density. Higher loading density produces higher chamber pressure, and conversely lower loading density produces lower chamber pressure. For small changes, the chamber pressure is approximately proportional to the square of loading density.

Suppose for example, we are using a load in the .308 Winchester, developed in commercial cases that are found to have a powder-chamber water capacity (W) of 52.0 grains. The charge weight (I) is 45.0 grains, so the loading density is then

LD = I / W
   = 45.0 / 52.0
   = .865

This charge is listed as a maximum load, indicating that the pressure is probably about 52,000 c.u.p.

Suppose further that we have acquired some military 7.62mm cases that we wish to utilize, and we have determined that the water capacity of the powder chamber in these cases is 49.5 grains, using the same bullet and seating depth as before. We compute the loading density of the 45.0-grain charge in these cases as follows:

LD = I / W
   = 45.0 / 49.5
   = .909

Using the approximate rule that the chamber pressure is proportional to the square of the loading density, and assuming that the charge was developed at 52,000 c.u.p. in the commercial cases, we estimate the pressure in the military cases as follows:

$P = 52,000 \times .909^2 / .865^2$
  = 57,425 c.u.p.

That pressure would certainly be excessive, so a reduction in charge weight will clearly be required. To achieve the same pressure level as before (52,000 c.u.p.), the charge must be reduced so that the loading density is the same as before (.865). The loading-density equation is conveniently rearranged as follows:

LD = I / W
$I = W \times LD$

Since the water capacity of the powder chamber in the military cases is W = 49.5, and our desired loading density LD = .865, the charge weight can now be computed as follows:

$I = W \times LD$
  $= 49.5 \times .865$
  = 42.8 grains

This is then the charge weight to be used in the military cases if we wish to maintain the same safe pressure level as that of the 45.0-grain charge developed in the commercial cases of larger capacity. The velocity of the lower charge weight, in the case of smaller capacity, will generally be somewhat less than that of the former load, but not much less. In any event, the reduction is necessary in the interests of safety.

It should be said here again that calculation should not be used as the basis for adjusting charge weights upward, on grounds that one can supposedly tolerate somewhat higher pressure than that listed for a maximum load. Though the result might very well be as expected, the uncertainties of calculation should deter us from using them to justify any change that might result in an unexpected pressure increase which could be hazardous.

Calculating chamber pressure

A common and intriguing question among handloaders is whether the chamber pressure of a load can be calculated, based on characteristics of the cartridge that are known or easily measured. The answer is a qualified yes, provided the limitations of the method are fully understood.

One of the simplest and most useful methods is a semi-empirical one developed by Homer S. Powley (Petra Lane, RR1, Eldridge, IA 52748). It is the basis for the "Powley psi Calculator", an ingenious slide-rule device for calculating pressures of cartridges using the Du Pont IMR powders. The psi Calculator is available from the inventor, at the address above. The input parameters required to use the psi Calculator can be found by the procedures previously described in this article.

Though Powley's final equation for calculating chamber pressure is one of the simplest yet devised, it might in its original form appear too formidable to those unaccustomed to dealing with lengthy algebraic expressions. It can, however, be broken down into simpler steps, and solved quite easily by using a pocket calculator.

In addition to the parameters we have already found, the equation involves also an empirically determined factor which depends upon the expansion ratio (R) and the mass ratio (A). We will call this factor F2. It can be found from Table 4. The numbers in the body of Table 4 are the values of F2, corresponding to the values of R and A in the line and column in which they appear.

Finally, the muzzle velocity of the load (V) must be known. This is best found by actual measurement, using an accurate chronograph, rather than by previous calculation. That is because characteristics in the gun that affect chamber pressures of a specified load also tend to affect velocities, in the same direction. A chamber pressure based on the measured velocity is therefore likely to be more accurate than one based on a calculated velocity.

We can now define the three new variables, in terms of the parameters we have already found. We will call them K1, K2 and K3, defined as follows:

$$K1 = .0142 \times I \times F2 \times V$$
$$K2 = .53 \times (G/I) + .26$$
$$K3 = W \times (R - 1.0)$$

In terms of these variables, Powley's equation for chamber pressure (P), in psi as measured by the crusher-type gage, is this:

$$P = K1 \times K2/K3$$

A chamber-pressure example

For example, suppose that we wish to calculate the chamber pressure of the previously described load for the .30-06, using a 180-grain bullet and 53.6 grains of IMR powder similar to IMR 4350 or IMR 4831. Suppose also that we have measured the velocity of the load, and confirmed that the muzzle velocity is 2620 fps when fired from a 24-inch barrel. These, and the other parameters found as described before, are as follows:

$I = 53.6$ grains $R = 7.5$
$W = 62.3$ grains $A = .298$
$G = 180$ grains $V = 2620$ fps

Looking now for the value of F2 in Table 4, we find that A equals .298, or practically .30, and no interpolation is required. The expansion ratio R equals 7.5, however, so we must interpolate between 7.4 and 7.6 in the table. Making the proper interpolation, we find:

$$F2 = 1.74$$

Our three derived variables, K1, K2 and K3, can now be found:

$$K1 = .0142 \times I \times F2 \times V^2$$
$$= .0142 \times 53.6 \times 1.74 \times 2620^2$$
$$= 9,090,854$$
$$K2 = .53 \times (G/I) + .26$$
$$= .53 \times (180/53.6) + .26$$
$$= 2.040$$
$$K3 = W \times (R - 1.0)$$
$$= 62.3 \times (7.5 - 1.0) = 405$$

We can now calculate the pressure, P, as follows:

$$P = K1 \times K2/K3$$
$$= 9,090,854 \times 2.040/405$$
$$= 45,790 \text{ psi (copper crusher)}$$

The pressures calculated by this method are practically the same as those determined by the Powley psi Calculator. They are usefully accurate estimates, but their limitations must be understood. For a variety of reasons, the actual measured pressures may be somewhat different. A comparison was made between pressures calculated by this method, and pressures measured for the same loads as recorded in the DuPont Handloader's Guide for Smokeless Powders (1975-1976).

The results indicated that the calculated pressures for cartridges from about .25-caliber to .338-caliber were usually within about 10 per cent of the measured pressures, about equally divided above and below. For the smaller calibers, the calculated pressures were typically somewhat below the measured pressures, the average being about 4 per cent lower for the 6mm/.243 calibers, and about 8 per cent for the .22 calibers. For calibers larger than the .338, the calculated pressures were typically somewhat higher than the measured pressures, the average being about 7 per cent higher for the .35-caliber cartridges, and about 15 per cent higher for the .458 Winchester Magnum. The .375 H&H Magnum, in exception to the trend, gave calculated pressures in very good agreement with the measured pressures.

The reason for this apparent caliber-dependence of the difference between calculated and measured pressures is not known. It is not certain that it truly exists, since some of the details for the Du Pont test loads were not known, and typical values for the cartridges were used in the calculations. It is possible to improve the agreement between calculated and measured pressures, for these particular data, by introducing another factor into the equation for pressure calculations, but it is doubtful if the accuracy of the data warrant that refinement. Experimenters should be aware, however, that some such trend might exist, and treat their calculations accordingly.

It must be emphasized again that these calculations, like others in the interior ballistics of small arms, cannot be relied upon where matters of safety might be involved. Testing must be done only with appropriate safeguards against injury in the event of unanticipated excessive chamber pressures.

TABLE 4

EXPANSION RATIO (R)	MASS RATIO (CHARGE WEIGHT/BULLET WEIGHT) (A)								
	0.20	.30	.40	.50	.60	.70	.80	.90	1.00
5.0	1.27	1.26	1.25	1.24	1.22	1.21	1.19	1.18	1.17
5.2	1.31	1.30	1.29	1.28	1.26	1.25	1.23	1.22	1.20
5.4	1.35	1.34	1.33	1.32	1.30	1.28	1.26	1.25	1.24
5.6	1.39	1.38	1.36	1.35	1.33	1.31	1.30	1.28	1.27
5.8	1.43	1.42	1.40	1.39	1.37	1.35	1.34	1.32	1.31
6.0	1.47	1.46	1.44	1.43	1.41	1.39	1.38	1.36	1.35
6.2	1.50	1.49	1.48	1.46	1.45	1.43	1.41	1.39	1.38
6.4	1.54	1.53	1.52	1.50	1.48	1.46	1.45	1.43	1.41
6.6	1.58	1.57	1.55	1.53	1.52	1.50	1.48	1.46	1.45
6.8	1.62	1.60	1.59	1.57	1.56	1.54	1.52	1.50	1.48
7.0	1.66	1.64	1.63	1.61	1.59	1.57	1.56	1.54	1.52
7.2	1.70	1.68	1.66	1.64	1.63	1.61	1.59	1.57	1.55
7.4	1.73	1.72	1.70	1.69	1.67	1.65	1.62	1.60	1.59
7.6	1.77	1.76	1.74	1.72	1.70	1.68	1.66	1.64	1.62
7.8	1.81	1.79	1.77	1.76	1.74	1.72	1.70	1.67	1.65
8.0	1.85	1.83	1.81	1.79	1.77	1.75	1.73	1.71	1.69
8.2	1.88	1.86	1.85	1.83	1.81	1.79	1.76	1.74	1.72
8.4	1.92	1.90	1.88	1.86	1.84	1.82	1.80	1.78	1.75
8.6	1.96	1.94	1.92	1.90	1.88	1.86	1.83	1.81	1.79
8.8	1.99	1.97	1.95	1.93	1.91	1.89	1.87	1.84	1.82
9.0	2.03	2.01	1.99	1.97	1.94	1.92	1.90	1.87	1.85
9.2	2.07	2.05	2.02	2.00	1.98	1.96	1.94	1.91	1.88
9.4	2.10	2.08	2.06	2.04	2.02	2.00	1.97	1.94	1.92
9.6	2.14	2.12	2.09	2.07	2.05	2.03	2.00	1.97	1.95
9.8	2.17	2.15	2.13	2.11	2.08	2.06	2.04	2.01	1.98
10.0	2.21	2.18	2.16	2.14	2.12	2.10	2.07	2.04	2.02
10.2	2.25	2.22	2.20	2.17	2.15	2.13	2.10	2.07	2.05
10.4	2.28	2.25	2.23	2.21	2.18	2.16	2.14	2.11	2.08
10.6	2.32	2.29	2.27	2.25	2.22	2.19	2.17	2.14	2.11
10.8	2.35	2.33	2.30	2.27	2.25	2.23	2.20	2.17	2.14
11.0	2.39	2.36	2.33	2.30	2.28	2.25	2.23	2.20	2.17
11.5	2.47	2.44	2.42	2.39	2.36	2.33	2.31	2.28	2.25
12.0	2.56	2.53	2.50	2.47	2.44	2.41	2.39	2.36	2.33
13.0	2.73	2.70	2.66	2.63	2.60	2.57	2.54	2.52	2.48

RELOADING
DATA SECTION

Introduction to Reloading Data

Many of the loads listed in the following tables are considered "maximum", indicating that they approach the maximum acceptable chamber pressure for the cartridge involved. *With a few specific exceptions,* maximum loads should be reduced for initial trials, and increased in small increments as pressure indications permit, but not to exceed the maximum loads listed.

Winchester-Western advises that maximum loads of Ball powders should be reduced by 10 per cent for initial trials, *except* that loads of 296 pistol powder, or 785 rifle powder, and *all* loads listed for the 8x57mm Mauser and .338 Winchester Magnum cartridges, must be loaded exactly as specified.

Du Pont also advises a reduction of 10 per cent in charge weights for initial trials, while Sierra and Nosler recommend a reduction of five per cent. Other sources generally advise comparable reductions.

Charges reduced more than 10 per cent from maximum should not be used unless listed in a reliable data source. In particular, much reduced loads of some slow-burning powders have produced destructively excessive chamber pressures and such loads should be avoided. **Important: Whenever a load approaches factory ballistics levels, it is wise to reduce it 5 to 10 per cent, as suggested by the various data sources noted above.**

In the following tables of loading data, the charge weights and bullet weights are in grains, velocity is the approximate muzzle velocity in feet per second (fps), pressure is the approximate chamber pressure in copper units of pressure (c.u.p.), OAL indicates cartridge overall length in inches, and barrel length is given in inches. Where blank spaces appear in the tables, the information omitted was not available.

CAUTION

The loads listed in the following tables are believed to be safe and satisfactory loads when properly assembled, and fired in sound firearms of the appropriate types, in good mechanical condition. All technical data conveyed reflects the experience of persons using specific equipment and components under specific circumstances. However, because of unavoidable variations in handloading components used in various combinations, and the firearms in which the handloaded ammunition may be fired, neither the National Rifle Association of America, nor any of the manufacturers whose products are listed, or publishers whose data are quoted from original sources, can assume any responsibility for any consequence of using the information in the following tables. The data are furnished for the information and use of handloaders, entirely at the user's own risk, initiative and responsibility.

SYMBOLS AND ABBREVIATIONS USED:

ALC = ALCAN
BDOT = BLUE-DOT
BJ = BODY-JACKETED
BYE, BEYE = BULLSEYE
CAST = CAST LEAD-ALLOY
CCI = CCI (OMARK)
CIL = CANADIAN INDUSTRIES
DOM = DOMINION (CANADIAN)
DUP = DUPONT
FCB = FRANK C BARNES & DBI BOOKS
FED = FEDERAL
FJ = FULL-JACKETED (NON-EXPANDING)
FLN = FLAT-NOSE
FRO = FRONTIER (HORNADY)
GDOT = GREEN DOT
HDY = HORNADY
HER = HERCULES
HOD = HODGDON
HP = HOLLOW-POINT
LG = GASCHECK LEAD BULLET
LP = PLAIN-BASE LEAD BULLET
MIL = MILITARY
NOR = NORMA
NOS = NOSLER
NRA = NATIONAL RIFLE ASSOCIATION
PBT = POINTED BOATTAIL

PTD = POINTED (FLAT-BASE)
RDOT = RED DOT
REM = REMINGTON
RL7, RLR7 = RELODER 7
RNN = ROUND-NOSE
RWS = RWS (GERMANY)
SAK = SAKO (FINLAND)
SP = SOFT-POINT
SPD = SEMI-POINTED
SPR = SPEER
SRA = SIERRA
SUV = SUPER VEL
SWC = SEMI-WADCUTTER
TR100 = TRAP 100
UNIQ = UNIQUE
WC = WADCUTTER
WEA = WEATHERBY
WIN = WINCHESTER-WESTERN
ZER = ZERO
CHARGE WEIGHT IS IN GRAINS.
BULLET WEIGHT IS IN GRAINS.
VELOCITY IS IN FEET PER SECOND.
CHAMBER PRESSURE IS IN C.U.P.
OAL IS CARTRIDGE OVERALL LENGTH IN INCHES.
BARREL LENGTH IS IN INCHES.

RIFLE RELOADING DATA SECTION

.17 REMINGTON

The .17 Remington cartridge was introduced in 1971, evidently in response to widespread interest among wildcatters in cartridges using the small .17-caliber bullet. Its nominal muzzle velocity of 4,040 fps is impressive. Like the .220 Swift, which produced velocities of more than 4,000 fps about 40 years ago, the .17 Remington has the troublesome tendency to develop severe bore fouling, which seriously impairs accuracy. Some reduction in bore fouling is achieved by loading at more moderate velocities, but the effectiveness of the small 25-grain bullet is, of course, inferior to that of .22-caliber bullets weighing twice that much at similar velocities. Successful use of the .17 Remington with full charge loads requires frequent, careful and thorough cleaning of the bore.

The ballistic coefficient of the 25-grain .17-caliber bullet is equal to that of similarly shaped .22-caliber bullets weighing about 42 grains, and the energy of the 25-grain bullet is half that of a 50-grain bullet at the same striking velocity. The .17 Remington is suitable for hunting small varmints, and its impressively flat trajectory is advantageous. The striking energy is much less than that of the .222 Remington, at all ranges, and the .17 Remington should not be used on larger animals than those for which the .222 Remington is suitable.

Typical chamber pressure for the .17 Remington is about 52,000 c.u.p. The maximum product average for factory ammunition should not exceed 55,200 c.u.p.

Max. Case Length: 1.800″ **Trim-To Length:** 1.790″
Max. Overall Length: 2.150″ **Primer Size:** Small Rifle **Bullet Dia.:** .172″

RIFLE LOADS FOR THE .17 REMINGTON

LOAD NUMBER	BULLET				POWDER			VELOCITY FPS	PRESSURE CUP	CASE BRAND	PRIMER		CARTRIDGE OAL	BARREL LENGTH	DATA SOURCE
	WEIGHT	BRAND	SHAPE	TYPE	WEIGHT	BRAND	TYPE				BRAND	TYPE			
1	25	REM	PTD	HP	22.5	DUP	3031	4015	51700	REM	REM	7½	2.100	24	DUP
2	25	REM	PTD	HP	24.0	DUP	4064	4005	50700	REM	REM	7½	2.100	24	DUP
3	25	HDY	PTD	HP	27.7	WIN	760	4000		REM	REM	7½		24	HDY
4	25	HDY	PTD	HP	24.7	DUP	4320	4000		REM	REM	7½		24	HDY
5	25	HDY	PTD	HP	25.5	HOD	H414	3845		REM	REM	7½		24	HOD
6	25	HDY	PTD	HP	22.0	HOD	BL-C-(2)	3772		REM	REM	7½		24	HOD
7	25	HDY	PTD	HP	27.5	HOD	H450	3794		REM	REM	7½		24	HOD

.22 HORNET

The .22 Hornet is the progenitor of the dozens of .22-caliber high-velocity varmint cartridges that have been used since the 1930's. It began as a wildcat, produced by a group of experimenters that included the late Colonel Townsend Whelen, at the U.S. Army Springfield Armory. The early Hornet rifles were built using modified Springfield Model 1903 or Model 1922 rifles, with rechambered Model 1922 barrels originally made for .22 rimfire ammunition. Because these barrels had groove diameters of about .223-inch, Hornet bullets were originally of that diameter, and some of these bullets are still available. Rifle manufacturers later produced Hornet barrels of .224-inch groove diameter, so both types may be found in service. Though the .223- and .224-inch bullets can be used interchangeably with satisfactory results in both types of barrel, best accuracy is often achieved by using

the bullets that match the groove diameter of the barrel.

The Hornet is a remarkably versatile and useful cartridge, and it is regrettable that few modern handloaders are aware of its capabilities. With full-charge loads and well-shaped bullets, it is suitable for hunting woodchucks or smaller varmints at ranges up to 200 yards. It can be easily loaded to approximate the performance of the .22 Winchester Magnum Rimfire cartridge for hunting turkeys and other small game, with either jacketed or cast gas-check bullets, at less cost than .22 WMR ammunition. With light charges of powders such as PB or Unique, and lubricated lead bullets (cast or swaged), the performance of .22 short, long or long-rifle ammunition can be duplicated, with excellent accuracy.

The small powder capacity and long case neck of the

Hornet are advantages for lead-bullet loading. Lead-bullet loads in the Hornet need not have excessive airspace in the case, as they usually do in the larger rifle cartridges. Gas-check bullets made of linotype alloy do well in the Hornet with full-charge loads. Lead bullets are easily swaged, using dies such as those available from Corbin, and any weight desired can be made with the same die set. The cast-bullet handloader who has a good .22 Hornet can duplicate the performance of any .22 rimfire ammunition, and considerably exceed that of the .22 WMR cartridge at less cost. The Hornet is as versatile in the Contender pistol as in a rifle, and a good choice for the small-game and varmint hunter who seeks fine accuracy, mild report, and economical reloading.

Some Hornet barrels have 16-inch twist of rifling — a practice carried over from the use of .22 rimfire barrels in building the early Hornet rifles — and that is unfortunate. Such barrels are often limited to bullets weighing less than 50 grains for best accuracy. The 14-inch twist shoots the light bullets equally well, and allows use of cast or jacketed bullets up to 55 grains, so that should be chosen whenever possible.

Hornet cases last longer if not full-length resized too often. A neck-resizing die is worthwhile, but good results are also obtained by turning the full-length die a full turn away from contact with the shell holder, if the reloads are to be used in the same gun in which the cases were previously fired.

Typical chamber pressure for the .22 Hornet is about 43,000 c.u.p. The maximum product average for factory ammunition is not to exceed 47,000 c.u.p.

Max. Case Length: 1.403″ **Trim-To Length:** 1.393″ **Max. Overall Length:** 1.723″ **Primer Size:** Small Rifle **Bullet Dia:** .224″

RIFLE LOADS FOR THE .22 HORNET

LOAD NUMBER	BULLET				POWDER			VELOCITY FPS	PRESSURE CUP	CASE BRAND	PRIMER		CARTRIDGE OAL	BARREL LENGTH	DATA SOURCE
	WEIGHT	BRAND	SHAPE	TYPE	WEIGHT	BRAND	TYPE				BRAND	TYPE			
1	40	SPR	SPD	SP	9.0	HOD	H110	2551		WIN	WIN	6½-116		20	HOD
2	40	HDY	RNN	SP	11.1	HER	2400	2800		REM	REM	6½		22	HDY
3	40	SRA	RNN	SP	11.6	DUP	4227	2800		REM	REM	6½		26	SRA
4	40	SPR	SPD	SP	12.5	WIN	680	2784		WIN	CCI	400		24	SPR
5	45	HDY	PTD	SP	11.5	DUP	4227	2515	38900	REM	REM	6½	1.720	25	DUP
6	45	WIN	RNN	SP	11.8	WIN	680	2650	41000	WIN	WIN	6½-116		24	WIN
7	45	SRA	RNN	SP	10.0	HER	2400	2600		REM	REM	6½		26	SRA
8	45	SPR	SPD	SP	11.5	DUP	4198	2484		WIN	CCI	400		24	SPR
9	45	SPR	RNN	SP	9.0	HOD	H110	2504		WIN	WIN	6½-116		20	HOD
10	50	SRA	SPD	SP	11.5	DUP	4227	2600		REM	REM	6½		26	SRA
11	50	SPR	SPD	SP	11.5	WIN	680	2455		WIN	CCI	400		24	SPR
12	50	HDY	PTD	SP	10.7	HER	2400	2500		REM	REM	6½		22	HDY
13	45	SRA	RNN	SP	9.0	DUP	4227	2110		REM	CCI	400	1.720	25	NRA
14	46	CAST	FLN	LP	2.0	DUP	PB	1115		REM	CCI	400	1.720	25	NRA
15	46	CAST	FLN	LP	3.0	DUP	PB	1360		REM	CCI	400	1.720	25	NRA
16	46	CAST	FLN	LG	6.0	DUP	4227	1600		REM	CCI	400	1.720	25	NRA
17	46	CAST	FLN	LG	8.0	DUP	4227	2015		REM	CCI	400	1.720	25	NRA

.218 BEE

The .218 Bee was introduced by Winchester in 1938 for use in a modernized version of their Model 1892 lever-action rifle which they identified as the Model 65. The cartridge is based on a necked-down .25-20 W.C.F. case, and is somewhat more powerful than the .22 Hornet. The accuracy of the Model 65 lever-action rifle was not equal to that of the bolt-action rifles adapted to the contemporary .22 Hornet cartridge, so the .218 Bee did not achieve comparable popularity. Single-shot and bolt-action rifles chambered for the .218 Bee can give excellent accuracy, however, and the .218 Bee was used in many custom single-shots during the 1940's. Factory ammunition is still available for the .218 Bee, but its low and declining popularity might cause it to be discontinued in event the factories decide to reduce their lists of current calibers in the near future.

Typical chamber pressure for the .218 Bee is about 40,000 c.u.p. The maximum product average for factory ammunition should not exceed 44,000 c.u.p.

Max. Case Length: 1.345″ **Trim-To Length:** 1.335″ **Max. Overall Length:** 1.680″ **Primer Size:** Small Rifle **Bullet Dia.:** .224″

RIFLE LOADS FOR THE .218 BEE

LOAD NUMBER	BULLET				POWDER			VELOCITY FPS	PRESSURE CUP	CASE BRAND	PRIMER		CARTRIDGE OAL	BARREL LENGTH	DATA SOURCE
	WEIGHT	BRAND	SHAPE	TYPE	WEIGHT	BRAND	TYPE				BRAND	TYPE			
1	45	SPR	RNN	SP	14.0	HOD	H4198	2779		WIN	WIN	6½-116		26	HOD
2	45	HDY	PTD	SP	14.5	DUP	4198	2900		WIN	WIN	6½-116		24	HDY
3	45	SRA	SPD	SP	12.0	HER	2400	2800		REM	REM	6½		26	SRA
4	45	SRA	SPD	SP	13.0	DUP	4227	2800		REM	REM	6½		26	SRA
5	50	SPR	PTD	SP	13.5	HOD	H4198	2582		WIN	WIN	6½-116		26	HOD
6	50	HDY	PTD	SP	14.7	DUP	4198	2800		WIN	WIN	6½-116		24	HDY
7	50	SRA	SPD	SP	12.5	DUP	4227	2600		REM	REM	6½		26	SRA
8	50	SRA	SPD	SP	10.0	HER	2400	2310	38160	WIN	WIN	6½-116	1.680	23½	NRA
9	55	SRA	SPD	SP	14.0	DUP	4198	2474	37700	WIN	WIN	6½-116	1.680	23½	NRA
10	55	SPR	PTD	SP	13.5	HOD	H4198	2567		WIN	WIN	6½-116		26	HOD

.222 REMINGTON

The .222 Remington cartridge was an immediate success upon its introduction by Remington in 1950. Being based on a head size different from that of any previous cartridge, it is unusual in that its design is not claimed by any of the numerous "wildcatters" who have asserted their claims of priority on practically every other centerfire cartridge that has been introduced as a standard caliber. The .222 is justly popular. It is doubtful that any other cartridge has been used in so many of the superbly accurate benchrest rifles, or that any other has been so widely used by varmint hunters. It has the desirable characteristics of fine accuracy, mild report, reasonably flat trajectory, economical reloading, long barrel life and wide availability.

Though seldom used with cast bullets, the .222 can produce excellent accuracy with proper cast-bullet loads. It can also be used very satisfactorily with reduced loads to approximate the performance of the .22 Winchester Magnum Rimfire, and (with lubricated lead bullets) even the .22 short, long and long-rifle.

The .222 Remington has been the basis for innumerable wildcats, and the basic case design has been used in development of such standardized cartridges as the .17 Remington, .223 Remington (5.56mm) and .222 Remington Magnum. It is an excellent choice as either a target or varmint cartridge.

Typical chamber pressure for the .222 Remington is about 46,000 c.u.p. The maximum product average pressure for factory ammunition should not exceed 49,200 c.u.p.

Max. Case Length: 1.700" **Trim-To Length:** 1.690" **Max. Overall Length:** 2.130" **Primer Size:** Small Rifle **Bullet Dia.:** .224"

RIFLE LOADS FOR THE .222 REMINGTON

LOAD NUMBER	BULLET				POWDER			VELOCITY FPS	PRESSURE CUP	CASE BRAND	PRIMER		CARTRIDGE OAL	BARREL LENGTH	DATA SOURCE
	WEIGHT	BRAND	SHAPE	TYPE	WEIGHT	BRAND	TYPE				BRAND	TYPE			
1	40	SPR	SPD	SP	21.5	HOD	H4198	3566	48000	WIN	WIN	6½-116		26	HOD
2	40	SPR	SPD	SP	25.5	DUP	4320	3536	<46000	WIN	CCI	BR4		24	SPR
3	40	SRA	RNN	SP	22.3	HER	RL7	3400		REM	REM	7½		26	SRA
4	45	SPR	PTD	SP	20.0	HER	RL7	3250	46000	FED	FED	205	2.130	26	HER
5	45	SPR	PTD	SP	24.5	HOD	BL-C-(2)	3305	45900	WIN	WIN	6½-116		26	HOD
6	45	HDY	PTD	SP	21.5	DUP	4198	3315	45000	REM	REM	7½	2.130	25	DUP
7	45	WIN	RNN	SP	25.5	WIN	748	3210	41000	WIN	WIN	6½-116	2.130	24	WIN
8	45	SRA	PTD	SP	24.4	NOR	201	3300		REM	REM	7½		26	SRA
9	50	HDY	PTD	SP	20.5	DUP	4198	3130	44500	REM	REM	7½	2.130	25	DUP
10	50	HDY	PTD	SP	25.0	DUP	4895	3085	41300	REM	REM	7½	2.130	25	DUP
11	50	WIN	PTD	SP	24.0	WIN	748	2980	38000	WIN	WIN	6½-116	2.130	24	WIN
12	50	FED	PTD	SP	19.5	HER	RL7	3080	43000	REM	REM	7½	2.130	26	HER
13	50	SPR	PTD	SP	24.0	HOD	BL-C-(2)	3206	49600	WIN	WIN	6½-116		26	HOD
14	50	NOR	PTD	SP	21.0	NOR	200	3200	<46400	NOR	NOR	SR	2.110	24	NOR
15	50	SPR	PTD	SP	23.5	DUP	3031	3407	<46000	SPR	CCI	BR4		24	SPR
16	50	SRA	PTD	SP	26.4	HOD	H335	3200		REM	REM	7½		26	SRA
17	50	NOS	PBT	HP	22.5	HOD	H322	3195		REM	REM	7½		20	NOS
18	52	WIN	PTD	HP	22.6	WIN	748	2815	34500	WIN	WIN	6½-116	2.130	24	WIN

LOAD NUMBER	BULLET				POWDER			VELOCITY FPS	PRESSURE CUP	CASE BRAND	PRIMER		CARTRIDGE OAL	BARREL LENGTH	DATA SOURCE
	WEIGHT	BRAND	SHAPE	TYPE	WEIGHT	BRAND	TYPE				BRAND	TYPE			
19	52-53	SRA	PTD	HP	26.8	WIN	748	3200		REM	REM	7½		26	SRA
20	52	NOS	PBT	HP	24.5	DUP	4895	3100		REM	REM	7½		20	NOS
21	52	SPR	PTD	HP	19.5	DUP	4198	3161	<46000	SPR	CCI	BR4		24	SPR
22	52-53			HP	23.5	HOD	BL-C-(2)	3075	47600	WIN	WIN	6½-116		26	HOD
23	52-53			HP	22.0	HOD	H322	3059	48000	WIN	WIN	6½-116		26	HOD
24	53	HDY	PTD	HP	24.2	NOR	201	3300		REM	CCI	400		26	HDY
25	55	REM	PTD	SP	25.0	DUP	4895	3085	45900	REM	REM	7½		25	DUP
26	55	SPR	PTD	SP	19.0	HOD	H4198	3051	48500	WIN	WIN	6½-116		26	HOD
27	55	NOS	PBT	SP	22.0	DUP	3031	3041		REM	REM	7½		20	NOS
28	55	SRA	PTD	SP	20.6	HER	RL7	3100		REM	REM	7½		26	SRA
29	55	SPR	PTD	SP	24.0	HOD	H335	3283	<46000	SPR	CCI	450		24	SPR
30	55	HDY	PTD	SP	27.2	WIN	748	3200		REM	REM	7½	2.130	20	HDY
31	60	NOS	PBT	SP	24.5	WIN	748	2994		REM	REM	7½		20	NOS
32	60	HDY	PTD	SP-HP	23.3	DUP	4064	2800		REM	REM	7½	2.130	20	HDY
33	60-63			SP	22.0	HOD	BL-C-(2)	2856	45600	WIN	WIN	6½-116		26	HOD
34	60-63			SP	20.5	HOD	H322	2805	46900	WIN	WIN	6½-116		26	HOD
35	63	SRA	SPD		23.0	DUP	3031	2900		REM	REM	7½		26	SRA
36	63	SRA	SPD		24.0	DUP	4895	2900		REM	REM	7½		26	SRA
37	70	SPR	SPD	SP	21.5	DUP	4064	2775	<46000	SPR	CCI	BR4		24	SPR
38	70	SPR	SPD	SP	22.0	DUP	4895	2825		SPR	CCI	400		24	SPR
39	70	SPR	SPD	SP	21.0	HOD	BL-C-(2)	2623	44700	WIN	WIN	6½-116		26	HOD
40	70	SPR	SPD	SP	23.0	HOD	H380	2646	45300	WIN	WIN	6½-116		26	HOD
41	45	SPR	PTD	SP	7.0	DUP	4759	1540		SPR	CCI	BR4		24	SPR
42	45	SPR	PTD	SP	9.0	DUP	4759	1961		SPR	CCI	BR4		24	SPR
43	46	CAST	FLN	LG	3.0	HER	UNIQ	1260		REM	CCI	400	2.130	20	NRA
44	46	CAST	FLN	LG	5.0	HER	UNIQ	1635		REM	CCI	400	2.130	20	NRA
45	46	CAST	FLN	LG	14.0	DUP	4198	2350		REM	FED	205	2.130	26	NRA
46	46	CAST	FLN	LG	12.0	DUP	4759	2320		REM	FED	205	2.130	26	NRA
47	46	CAST	FLN	LG	12.0	HER	2400	2560		REM	FED	205	2.130	26	NRA
48	50	SPR	PTD	SP	7.5	DUP	4759	1584		SPR	CCI	BR4		24	SPR
49	50	SPR	PTD	SP	9.5	DUP	4759	1995		SPR	CCI	BR4		24	SPR
50	55	SPR	SPD	FJ	8.0	DUP	4759	1662		SPR	CCI	BR4		24	SPR
51	55	SPR	SPD	FJ	10.0	DUP	4759	2070		SPR	CCI	BR4		24	SPR
52	46	CAST	FLN	LP	1.0	HER	BYE	550		WIN	CCI	550	2.130	20	NRA

.222 REMINGTON MAGNUM

The .222 Remington Magnum is said to have originated as an experimental military cartridge developed by Remington under contract with the Army. Possibly that is true, though it is merely a slightly longer version of the basic .222 Remington case, having a slightly longer body and neck than the .223 Remington, so its "origin" is a moot point. The .222 Remington was well established when the .222 Remington Magnum was introduced in 1958, and the difference in performance was not sufficient to lure many prospective users away from the popular standard .222.

The adoption of the .223 as a military cartridge also occurred shortly after commercial introduction of the .222 Remington Magnum, and it produced practically identical ballistics. The .222 Remington Magnum never achieved popularity comparable to the .222 or the .223, and it now seems obsolescent. It is, nevertheless, a perfectly satisfactory cartridge, slightly more powerful than the .223 at the same levels of chamber pressure. In factory loads, the nominal ballistics for the .222 Magnum and .223 Remington are the same, but the chamber-pressure limit is 50,000 c.u.p. for the .222 Magnum and 52,000 c.u.p. for the .223.

Possibly more .222 Remington Magnum cartridge cases are now used in the semi-wildcat 6X47mm benchrest cartridge than in the .222 Magnum itself.

The maximum product average chamber pressure for .222 Remington Magnum factory ammuniton should not exceed 53,200 c.u.p.

Max. Case Length: 1.850″ **Trim-To Length:** 1.840″
Max. Overall Length: 2.280″ **Primer Size:** Small Rifle **Bullet Dia:** .224″

RIFLE LOADS FOR THE .222 REMINGTON MAGNUM

LOAD NUMBER	BULLET				POWDER			VELOCITY FPS	PRESSURE CUP	CASE BRAND	PRIMER		CARTRIDGE OAL	BARREL LENGTH	DATA SOURCE
	WEIGHT	BRAND	SHAPE	TYPE	WEIGHT	BRAND	TYPE				BRAND	TYPE			
1	50	HDY	PTD	SP	26.0	DUP	3031	3350	49000	REM	REM	7½	2.280	24	DUP
2	50	HDY	PTD	SP	27.0	DUP	4895	3310	49500	REM	REM	7½	2.280	24	DUP
3	50	SPR	PTD	SP	27.0	HOD	H335	3476	48200	REM	REM	6½		26	HOD
4	50	SRA	PTD	SP	23.0	HER	RL7	3310	49000	REM	REM			26	HER
5	50	SRA	PTD	SP	27.6	DUP	4320	3300		REM	REM	7½		24	SRA
6	50	SPR	PTD	SP	23.0	DUP	4198	3415		REM	CCI	400		24	SPR
7	55	REM	PTD	SP	25.5	DUP	3031	3215	49900	REM	REM	7½	2.280	24	DUP
8	55	REM	PTD	SP	26.5	DUP	4064	3180	50000	REM	REM	7½	2.280	24	DUP
9	55	SPR	PTD	SP	26.5	HOD	BL-C-(2)	3240	46800	REM	REM	6½		26	HOD
10	55	SRA	PTD	SP	22.0	HER	RL7	3100	48500	REM	REM				HER
11	55	HDY	PTD	SP	27.1	DUP	4320	3200		REM	CCI	400		26	HDY
12	55	SPR	PTD	SP	26.5	HOD	BL-C-(2)	3295		REM	CCI	450		24	SPR
13	55	SRA	PTD	SP	25.0	DUP	3031	3300		REM	REM	7½		24	SRA
14	55	WIN	PTD	SP	27.2	WIN	748	3215	42500	WIN	WIN	6½-116	2.280	24	WIN
15	55	NOS	PBT	SP	26.0	DUP	4895	3379		REM	REM	7½		25	NOS
16	60	HDY	PTD	SP-HP	25.0	DUP	3031	3200		REM	CCI	400		26	HDY
17	63	SRA	SPD	SP	25.6	HOD	335	3000		REM	REM	7½		24	SRA
18	60-63				26.0	HOD	BL-C-(2)	3078		REM	REM	6½		26	HOD
19	70	SPR	SPD	SP	26.5	DUP	4064	3043		REM	CCI	400		24	SPR
20	70	SPR	SPD	SP	29.0	HOD	H414	2864	47400	REM	REM	6½		26	HOD
21	50	SPR	PTD	SP	9.0	DUP	4759	1690		REM	CCI	400		24	SPR
22	50	SPR	PTD	SP	11.0	DUP	4759	2075		REM	CCI	400		24	SPR
23	70	SPR	SPD	SP	10.0	DUP	4759	1615		REM	CCI	400		24	SPR
24	70	SPR	SPD	SP	12.0	DUP	4759	1925		REM	CCI	400		24	SPR

.223 REMINGTON (5.56mm)

The .223 Remington cartridge was developed by Remington, in conjunction with Eugene Stoner, designer of the Armalite rifle known as the AR-15. When the military version of the AR-15 rifle was adopted for military use, and its ammunition was further developed by the Army, the official military nomenclature of the cartridge was assigned as "5.56mm." It is based essentially on a lengthened .222 Remington case, with a longer body and shorter neck. Commercial .223 Remington and military 5.56mm ammunition can be used interchangeably in most .223/5.56 rifles, but the 5.56mm M193 Ball military cartridge usually does not shoot well in rifles having a 14-inch twist of rifling, because the 55-grain pointed boattail bullet is not adequately stablized with a twist longer than 12 inches per turn.

A warning has also been issued by the Sporting Arms and Ammunition Manufacturers' Institute (SAAMI) to the effect that 5.56mm military ammunition may produce excessive chamber pressure if used in some commercial rifles chambered for the .223 Remington cartridge. This is said to be due to the fact that commercial .223 Remington chambers produced by some manufacturers differ significantly in dimensions from the prescribed 5.56mm military chambers. SAAMI therefore advises that only .223 Remington commercial ammunition is suitable for use in commercial .223 Remington rifles, and 5.56mm military ammunition should not be fired in such rifles. The user who is in doubt about the suitability of his particular rifle, or one that he proposes to purchase, for use with 5.56mm military ammunition, should consult the rifle manufacturer on that point.

Some handloaders consider the short neck of the .223 case less desirable than the longer necks of the .222 and .222 Magnum, and possibly that is a disadvantage, though the evidence is not conclusive for normal jacketed-bullet loads. For long cast gas-check bullets, in which it is desirable that the bullet base not intrude behind the base of the neck, a short-necked case is certainly undesirable.

The ballistics of the .223 Remington are considerably more impressive than those of the .222, in part because of the greater case capacity, but also because the upper limit of operating chamber pressure is about 52,000 c.u.p. for the .223 and only 46,000 c.u.p. for the .222.

When loading for semiautomatic rifles, it is desirable to use cannelured bullets, and crimp the case mouth into the cannelure. This helps to prevent pushing the bullet more deeply into the case as the cartridge is stripped from the magazine and fed into the chamber rapidly during the gun cycle. If case necks are correctly resized, and the expanding plug is not more than .223 inch in diameter, then uncrimped loads function quite satisfactorily in most .223 autoloaders, but Ruger specifically warns against their use in the Ruger Mini-14. Reduced loads do not function reliably in automatic or semi-automatic guns, though they can be fired by loading them manually into the chamber. Lead-bullet loads should be avoided in gas-operated autoloaders, because they may cause clogging of the gas system.

The maximum product average chamber pressure for the .223 Remington factory ammunition should not exceed 55,200 c.u.p.

Max. Case Length: 1.760″ **Trim-To Length:** 1.750″
Max. Overall Length: 2.260″ **Primer Size:** Small Rifle
Bullet Dia.: .224″

RIFLE LOADS FOR THE .223 REMINGTON (5.56 mm)

LOAD NUMBER	BULLET				POWDER			VELOCITY FPS	PRESSURE CUP	CASE BRAND	PRIMER		CARTRIDGE OAL	BARREL LENGTH	DATA SOURCE
	WEIGHT	BRAND	SHAPE	TYPE	WEIGHT	BRAND	TYPE				BRAND	TYPE			
1	40	SRA	RNN	SP	22.0	DUP	4198	3300		REM	REM	7½		20	SRA
2	40	SPR	PTD	SP	28.0	HOD	H335	3336		WIN	CCI	450		20	SPR
3	45	SRA	PTD	SP	22.0	DUP	4198	3360	50300	REM	REM	7½	2.19	24	DUP
4	45	SPR	PTD	SP	28.0	HOD	H335	3508	47600	REM	REM	6½		26	HOD
5	50	SRA	PTD	SP	25.5	DUP	3031	3225	45300	REM	REM	7½	2.26	24	DUP
6	50	WIN	PTD	SP	26.0	WIN	748	3200	40000	WIN	WIN	6½-116	2.120	24	WIN
7	50	SRA	PTD	SP	22.1	HER	RLR7	3200		REM	REM	7½		20	SRA
8	50	SPR	PTD	SP	28.0	HOD	BL-C-(2)	3428	47100	REM	REM	6½		26	HOD
9	52	SRA	PBT	HP	26.6	DUP	4895	3200		REM	REM	7½		20	SRA
10	52	SPR	PTD	HP	26.5	DUP	4895	3064		WIN	CCI	400		20	SPR
11	52	NOS	PBT	HP	26.5	WIN	748	3217		MIL	REM	7½		24	NOS
12	53	HDY	PTD	HP	25.4	DUP	3031	3100		REM	REM	6½		20	HDY
13	53	WIN	PTD	HP	26.0	WIN	748	3200	43500	WIN	WIN	6½-116	2.220	24	WIN
14	53	SRA	PTD	HP	22.5	HER	RLR7	3200		REM	REM	7½		20	SRA
15	53	SRA	PTD	HP	28.0	HOD	BL-C-(2)	3328	47600	REM	REM	6½		26	HOD
16	55	SPR	PTD	SP	25.0	DUP	3031	3050	45100	REM	REM	6½		20	NRA
17	55	SRA	PTD	SP	27.2	DUP	4320	3200		REM	REM	7½		20	SRA
18	55	HDY	PTD	SP	26.0	DUP	4895	3120	51100	REM	REM	7½	2.26	24	DUP
19	55	WIN	PTD	SP	26.3	WIN	748	3150	39000	WIN	WIN	6½-116	2.220	24	WIN
20	55	NOR	SPD	SP	25.9	NOR	201	3300	47000	NOR	NOR	SR	2.17	24	NOR
21	55	NOS	PBT	SP	25.0	HOD	H335	3142		MIL	REM	7½		24	NOS
22	55	SPR	PTD	SP	27.5	HOD	BL-C-(2)	3313	48500	REM	REM	6½		26	HOD
23	55	REM	PTD	SP	22.5	HER	RLR7	3070	49000	REM	REM			26	HER
24	60	HDY	PTD	HP	25.0	DUP	4895	3014	47860	REM	REM	7½	2.26	24	NRA
25	60	HDY	PTD	HP	27.0	WIN	748	3174	49400	REM	REM	7½	2.26	24	NRA
26	63	SRA	SPD	SP	25.0	DUP	4895	2979	48260	REM	REM	7½	2.23	24	NRA
27	63	SRA	SPD	SP	27.0	WIN	748	3137	50240	REM	REM	7½	2.23	24	NRA
28	70	SPR	SPD	SP	24.0	DUP	4064	2623		WIN	CCI	400		20	SPR
29	60	NOS	PBT	SP	24.0	DUP	3031	3065		MIL	REM	7½		24	NOS
30	45	SPR	PTD	SP	8.0	DUP	4759	1524		REM	CCI	400		24	SPR
31	45	SPR	PTD	SP	10.0	DUP	4759	1922		REM	CCI	400		24	SPR
32	50	SPR	PTD	SP	8.5	DUP	4759	1620		REM	CCI	400		24	SPR
33	50	SPR	PTD	SP	10.5	DUP	4759	2012		REM	CCI	400		24	SPR
34	55	SPR	SPD	FJ	8.5	DUP	4759	1597		REM	CCI	400		24	SPR
35	55	SPR	SPD	FJ	10.5	DUP	4759	1996		REM	CCI	400		24	SPR

.219 DONALDSON

The .219 Donaldson is also known as the .219 Wasp and .219 Donaldson Wasp. It is usually associated with the late Harvey Donaldson, though as with many wildcat cartridges that achieve substantial popularity, there are conflicting claims of priority on the design, and that accounts for the variety of names by which the cartridge is known. It is basically a rimmed case of the type used for the .30-30, .25-35, .219 Zipper, etc., shortened, necked to accept .22-caliber bullets, modified, to a 30 degree shoulder angle, and fire-formed to provide less body taper. Slightly different versions, having different neck lengths, are sometimes encountered. Donaldson's work with this type of cartridge began about 1935, and his design was finally established in the early 1940's. The modern revival of competitive benchrest shooting occurred during the 1940's, and the .219 Donaldson cartridge soon became the most popular of all cartridges with the benchrest shooters. It was also widely used as a varmint cartridge, and served very well in that role. Though some exaggerated claims for its qualities were made by its proponents, as is usually the case with wildcat cartridges, they were probably based on velocities achieved at the expense of excessive chamber pressures. Nevertheless, it is an excellent cartridge in all respects except the necessity of forming the cases by a somewhat laborious process. Case-forming dies are available from firms such as RCBS and these are effective and convenient to use. Necks usually require thinning if the cases are formed from .30-30 brass, now the type most commonly used.

The groups made by benchrest shooters using the .219 Wasp during the 1940's were probably as good as could be made with the bullets then available, and a .219 Wasp benchrest rifle made by one of the competent benchrest riflesmiths today would probably compare favorably with any modern benchrest rifle. The introduction of the .222 Remington in 1950, with readily available factory brass, at least equally good accuracy, and the endorsement of such a highly competent designer and benchrest shooter as Mike Walker of Remington, soon turned the tide of popularity to the .222 at the expense of the wildcat .219 Donaldson. The excellent Remington Model 722 action, to which the .222 cartridge was adapted but the .219 Donaldson was not, was another factor in the decline in relative popularity of the .219 Wasp. It is interesting to note that the recently introduced semi-wildcat .22 PPC, for which some benchrest shooters have abandoned their .222 Remington benchrest rifles, is very similar to the .219 Donaldson, except for the supposed advantage of the .175-inch instead of the .210-inch primer pocket.

Max Case Length: 1.750″ **Trim-To Length:** 1.740″
Max. Overall Length: 2.188″ **Primer Size:** Large Rifle
Bullet Dia.: .224″

RIFLE LOADS FOR THE .219 DONALDSON WASP

LOAD NUMBER	BULLET				POWDER			VELOCITY FPS	PRESSURE CUP	CASE BRAND	PRIMER		CARTRIDGE OAL	BARREL LENGTH	DATA SOURCE
	WEIGHT	BRAND	SHAPE	TYPE	WEIGHT	BRAND	TYPE				BRAND	TYPE			
1	50	SRA	PTD	SP	28.9	DUP	4064	3400		REM	REM	9½		26	SRA
2	50	SRA	PTD	SP	26.9	DUP	3031	3400		REM	REM	9½		26	SRA
3	52-53	SRA	PTD	HP	28.5	DUP	4064	3300		REM	REM	9½		26	SRA
4	52-53	SRA	PTD	HP	25.4	DUP	3031	3300		REM	REM	9½		26	SRA
5	55	HDY	PTD	SP	28.2	DUP	4064	3400		REM	FED	210		29	HDY
6	55	HDY	PTD	SP	26.6	DUP	3031	3400		REM	FED	210		29	HDY
7	55	HDY	PTD	SP	27.8	HOD	BL-C-(2)	3300		REM	FED	210		29	HDY
8	60	HDY	PTD	SP-HP	26.6	DUP	4064	3200		REM	FED	210		29	HDY
9	60	HDY	PTD	SP-HP	28.3	DUP	4320	3200		REM	FED	210		29	HDY
10	60	HDY	PTD	SP-HP	30.0	HOD	H380	3200		REM	FED	210		29	HDY
11	48	CAST	FLN	LG	2.0	HER	UNIQ	950		WIN	WIN	7-111		26	NRA
12	48	CAST	FLN	LG	3.0	HER	UNIQ	1165		WIN	WIN	7-111		26	NRA
13	48	CAST	FLN	LG	4.0	HER	UNIQ	1400		WIN	WIN	7-111		26	NRA

.219 ZIPPER

The .219 Zipper was a sort of "companion" cartridge to the .218 Bee, introduced by Winchester in 1937 for their modernized version of the Model 1894 rifle, which was identified as the Model 64. As with the .218 Bee, the cartridge was handicapped by the fact that the lever-action rifle to which it was adapted compared unfavorably with bolt-action rifles as to accuracy. It was further handicapped by the necessity of using blunt round-nose bullets because of the tubular magazine in the Model 64 rifle. The .219 Zipper never achieved much popularity, though some

very accurate varmint rifles were custom built on single-shot actions for it. Early users of the .219 Donaldson often used .219 Zipper brass as the basis for their case forming. The .219 Zipper cartridge is no longer manufactured, but cases can be formed from .30-30 brass using case-forming dies available from firms such as RCBS.

Max. Case Length: 1.875″ **Trim-To Length:** 1.865″
Max. Overall Length: 2.260″ **Primer Size:** Large Rifle
Bullet Dia.: .224″

RIFLE LOADS FOR THE .219 ZIPPER

LOAD NUMBER	BULLET				POWDER			VELOCITY FPS	PRESSURE CUP	CASE BRAND	PRIMER		CARTRIDGE OAL	BARREL LENGTH	DATA SOURCE
	WEIGHT	BRAND	SHAPE	TYPE	WEIGHT	BRAND	TYPE				BRAND	TYPE			
1	45	SRA	SPD	SP	24.3	DUP	3031	3300		WIN	WIN	8½-120	2.260	26	SRA
2	45	SRA	SPD	SP	26.5	DUP	4320	3300		WIN	WIN	8½-120	2.260	26	SRA
3	50	SRA	SPD	SP	24.3	DUP	4895	3200		WIN	WIN	8½-120	2.260	26	SRA
4	50	SRA	SPD	SP	27.0	HOD	H380	3300		WIN	WIN	8½-120	2.260	26	SRA
5	55	SRA	SPD	SP	24.0	DUP	4895	3000		WIN	WIN	8½-120	2.260	26	SRA
6	55	SRA	SPD	SP	26.0	HOD	H380	3100		WIN	WIN	8½-120	2.260	26	SRA

.224 WEATHERBY VARMINTMASTER

The .224 Weatherby Varmintmaster case resembles a miniature of the large Weatherby belted magnum cases. In case capacity, it is intermediate between the .222 Remington Magnum and the .22-250, being about seven grains more than the former and six grains less than the latter. The head diameter is larger than that of the cases based on the .222, and smaller than that of the cases such as the .22-250, so is not well suited to actions other than the Weatherby action made especially for it. Possibly for that reason, it has not been widely used in

custom rifles, and is not a very popular varmint cartridge. There is nothing inherently wrong with the design, however, and it performs as well as other .22 varmint cartridges having comparable capacity, loaded to comparable levels of chamber pressure.

Max. Case Length: 1.923″ **Trim-To Length:** 1.913″
Max. Overall Length: 2.312″ **Primer Size:** Large Rifle
Bullet Dia.: .224″

RIFLE LOADS FOR THE .224 WEATHERBY VARMINTMASTER

LOAD NUMBER	BULLET				POWDER			VELOCITY FPS	PRESSURE CUP	CASE BRAND	PRIMER		CARTRIDGE OAL	BARREL LENGTH	DATA SOURCE
	WEIGHT	BRAND	SHAPE	TYPE	WEIGHT	BRAND	TYPE				BRAND	TYPE			
1	50	HDY	PTD	SP	29.5	DUP	3031	3500	45700	WEA	FED	215	2.312	26	WEA
2	50	HDY	PTD	SP	30.5	DUP	3031	3620	50000	WEA	FED	215	2.312	26	WEA
3	50	HDY	PTD	SP	31.5	DUP	3031	3695	52600	WEA	FED	215	2.312	26	WEA
4	50	SRA	PTD	SP	32.0	DUP	4064	3700		WEA	REM	9½		26	SRA
5	52	SRA	PBT	HP	30.5	DUP	3031	3700		WEA	REM	9½		26	SRA
6	53	SRA	PTD	HP	31.5	NOR	201	3600		WEA	REM	9½		26	SRA
7	55	HDY	PTD	SP	29.0	DUP	3031	3390	46700	WEA	FED	215	2.312	26	WEA
8	55	HDY	PTD	SP	30.0	DUP	3031	3470	49100	WEA	FED	215	2.312	26	WEA
9	55	HDY	PTD	SP	30.5	DUP	3031	3525	53200	WEA	FED	215	2.312	26	WEA
10	55	SRA	PTD	SP	30.6	NOR	201	3500		WEA	REM	9½		26	SRA
11	60	HDY	PTD	HP	31.4	DUP	4064	3400		WEA	FED	210		24	HDY
12	63	SRA	SPD	SP	31.4	DUP	4064	3500		WEA	REM	9½		26	SRA
13	70	SPR	SPD	SP	31.0	HOD	H205	2974		WEA	CCI	250		23	HOD
14	70	SPR	SPD	SP	31.0	HOD	H414	2969		WEA	CCI	250		23	HOD

.225 WINCHESTER

The .225 Winchester cartridge is a semi-rimmed case, having practically the same diameter ahead of the rim as the old .219 Zipper case, and the same rim diameter as cases such as the .22-250 and .243. This peculiar design, like that of the .220 Swift, is undoubtedly to gain the convenience of interchangeability of bolt-face dimensions with the larger cartridges, while employing a slimmer body. Headspace control is accomplished by the shoulder, as it is for rimless cases. The .225 cartridge was, like some other Winchester cartridges, handicapped by the rifle with which it was introduced. The cartridge was introduced in 1964, concurrently with the first cost-reduced version of the Model 70 bolt-action rifles, which was an ugly and cheap-looking rifle in comparison to the handsome pre-1964 Model 70. The second blow to the popularity of the .225 Winchester came in 1965, when Remington "legitimized" the popular .22-250 wildcat, which was already well established among varmint hunters. Though subsequent improvements in the cost-reduced Model 70 Winchester rifle have regained a large part of its former popularity, the .225 Winchester cartridge did not survive the competition, and it is now obsolescent, though there is no fundamental flaw in its design.

Typical chamber pressure for the .225 Winchester is about 50,000 c.u.p. The maximum product average for the .225 Winchester factory ammunition should not exceed 53,200 c.u.p.

Max. Case Length: 1.930" **Trim-To Length:** 1.920"
Max. Overall Length: 2.500" **Primer Size:** Large Rifle **Bullet Dia.:** .224"

RIFLE LOADS FOR THE .225 WINCHESTER

LOAD NUMBER	BULLET				POWDER			VELOCITY FPS	PRESSURE CUP	CASE BRAND	PRIMER		CARTRIDGE OAL	BARREL LENGTH	DATA SOURCE
	WEIGHT	BRAND	SHAPE	TYPE	WEIGHT	BRAND	TYPE				BRAND	TYPE			
1	50	WIN	PTD	SP	36.0	WIN	760	3570	49000	WIN	WIN	8½-120	2.500	24	WIN
2	50	WIN	PTD	SP	22.0	HER	RL7	3130	44000	WIN	WIN	8½-120	2.450	26	HER
3	50	SRA	PTD	SP	33.0	DUP	4895	3600		WIN	WIN	8½-120		22	SRA
4	50	SPR	PTD	SP	33.5	DUP	4064	3641	<50000	WIN	CCI	200		24	SPR
5	50	HDY	PTD	SP	36.1	HOD	H380	3600		WIN	WIN	8½-120		24	HDY
6	55	WIN	PTD	SP	35.8	WIN	760	3410	49000	WIN	WIN	8½-120	2.500	24	WIN
7	55	WIN	PTD	SP	22.0	HER	RL7	3075	44500		WIN	8½-120	2.450		HER
8	55	SRA	PTD	SP	32.6	DUP	4895	3500		WIN	WIN	8½-120		22	SRA
9	55	SPR	PTD	SP	32.5	DUP	4064	3503	<50000	WIN	CCI	200		24	SPR
10	55	HDY	PTD	SP	35.2	HOD	H380	3500		WIN	WIN	8½-120		24	HDY
11	55	NOS	PBT	SP	37.0	DUP	4350	3337		WIN	CCI	BR2		22	NOS
12	55	SPR	PTD	SP	34.0	HOD	BL-C-(2)	3643	49400	WIN	WIN	8½-120		26	HOD

RIFLE LOADS FOR THE .225 WINCHESTER

LOAD NUMBER	BULLET				POWDER			VELOCITY FPS	PRESSURE CUP	CASE BRAND	PRIMER		CARTRIDGE OAL	BARREL LENGTH	DATA SOURCE
	WEIGHT	BRAND	SHAPE	TYPE	WEIGHT	BRAND	TYPE				BRAND	TYPE			
13	60	HDY	PTD	SP-HP	32.2	DUP	4895	3400		WIN	WIN	8½-120		24	HDY
14	63	SRA	SPD	SP	30.9	DUP	4064	3300		WIN	WIN	8½-120		22	SRA
15	60-63				32.0	HOD	4895	3396	49000	WIN	WIN	8½-120		26	HOD
16	60-63				35.0	HOD	H380	3387	48500	WIN	WIN	8½-120		26	HOD
17	70	SPR	SPD	SP	34.5	HOD	H205	3023	48000	WIN	WIN	8½-120		26	HOD
18	70	SPR	SPD	SP	33.5	HOD	H414	2940	47200	WIN	WIN	8½-120		26	HOD
19	45	SPR	PTD	SP	9.0	DUP	4759	1659		WIN	CCI	200		24	SPR
20	45	SPR	PTD	SP	11.0	DUP	4759	2039		WIN	CCI	200		24	SPR
21	55	SPR	PTD	SP	10.0	DUP	4759	1679		WIN	CCI	200		24	SPR
22	55	SPR	PTD	SP	12.0	DUP	4759	2009		WIN	CCI	200		24	SPR

.22-250 REMINGTON

The .22-250 is essentially a necked-down .250 Savage cartridge, hence the name. Many wildcat cartridges were made in the 1930's and 1940's by necking the .250 case to accept .22-caliber bullets, and some experts of the day considered the design superior to the .220 Swift which was introduced in 1935 by Winchester. The most popular version was probably that of gunsmith J. E. Gebby, which he called the ".22 Varminter." The .22-250 was one of the rare wildcats that stood the test of time for more than 30 years, until it was introduced as a factory load by Remington in 1965. It was, and it remains, deservedly popular. Usually loaded with 55-grain bullets at more moderate velocities than those of the 48-grain bullets which were standard in the .220 Swift, the .22-250 gave less problems of severe bore fouling than the .220 Swift. It produced excellent accuracy, and is one of very few cartridges which, as a wildcat, won out in competition with a very similar factory cartridge in the long run. The .220 Swift is obsolescent or obsolete, and the popularity of the .22-250 still continues.

Typical chamber pressure for the .22-250 should not exceed 53,000 c.u.p. The maximum product average chamber pressure for factory ammunition does not exceed 56,200 c.u.p.

Max. Case Length: 1.912″ **Trim-To Length:** 1.902″
Max. Overall Length: 2.350″ **Primer Size:** Large
Rifle **Bullet Dia.:** .224″

RIFLE LOADS FOR THE .22-250 REMINGTON

LOAD NUMBER	BULLET				POWDER			VELOCITY FPS	PRESSURE CUP	CASE BRAND	PRIMER		CARTRIDGE OAL	BARREL LENGTH	DATA SOURCE
	WEIGHT	BRAND	SHAPE	TYPE	WEIGHT	BRAND	TYPE				BRAND	TYPE			
1	50	SRA	PTD	SP	35.0	DUP	3031	3785	52700	REM	REM	9½	2.350	24	DUP
2	50	WIN	PTD	SP	39.5	WIN	760	3700	49200	WIN	WIN	8½-120	2.350	24	WIN
3	50	SRA	PTD	SP	30.0	HER	RL7	3710	52000	REM	REM			26	HER
4	50	HDY	PTD	SP	35.1	DUP	4895	3700	52000	FRO	FED	210	2.350	24	HDY
5	50	NOS	PBT	SP	40.0	DUP	4350	3796		WIN	CCI	250		24	NOS
6	50	SPR	PTD	SP	42.0	HOD	H380	3865	<53000	WIN	CCI	250		24	SPR
7	52-53	SRA	PTD	HP	35.7	DUP	4895	3700		REM	REM	9½		26	SRA
8	52	SPR	PTD	HP	41.0	HOD	H380	3788	<53000	WIN	CCI	250		24	SPR
9	52	NOS	PBT	HP	40.0	DUP	4350	3803		WIN	CCI	250		24	NOS
10	53	HDY	PTD	HP	35.1	DUP	4895	3700		REM	REM	9½		28	HDY
11	55	REM	PTD	SP	35.5	DUP	4895	3645	53000	REM	REM	9½		24	DUP
12	55	WIN	PTD	SP	39.0	WIN	760	3675	49000	WIN	WIN	8½-120	2.350	24	WIN
13	55	REM	PTD	SP	29.0	HER	RL7	3510	52500	REM	REM			26	HER
14	55	HDY	PTD	SP	36.3	DUP	4064	3700	52900	FRO	FED	210	2.350	24	HDY
15	55	NOS	PBT	SP	32.0	DUP	3031	3610		WIN	CCI	250		24	NOS
16	55	SRA	PTD	SP	36.7	HOD	H380	3600		REM	REM	9½		26	SRA
17	60	HDY	PTD	SP	28.5	HER	RL7	3360	52700	REM	REM			26	HER

RIFLE LOADS FOR THE .22-250 REMINGTON

| LOAD NUMBER | BULLET | | | | POWDER | | | VELOCITY FPS | PRESSURE CUP | CASE BRAND | PRIMER | | CARTRIDGE OAL | BARREL LENGTH | DATA SOURCE |
	WEIGHT	BRAND	SHAPE	TYPE	WEIGHT	BRAND	TYPE				BRAND	TYPE			
18	60	HDY	PTD	SP-HP	40.5	DUP	4350	3600		REM	REM	9½		28	HDY
19	60-63			SP	34.0	HOD	4895	3486	50400	WIN	WIN	8½-120		26	HOD
20	63	SRA	SPD	SP	34.7	DUP	4895	3500		REM	REM	9½		26	SRA
21	70	SPR	SPD	SP	38.0	DUP	4350	3379	<53000	WIN	CCI	200		24	SPR
22	70	SPR	SPD	SP	38.0	HOD	4831	3189	50300	WIN	WIN	8½-120		26	HOD
23	70	SPR	SPD	SP	35.0	HOD	H205	3172	51000	WIN	WIN	8½-120		26	HOD
24	60	NOS	PBT	SP	33.0	DUP	4064	3486		WIN	CCI	250		24	NOS
25	50	SPR	PTD	SP	10.0	DUP	4759	1650		WIN	CCI	200		24	SPR
26	50	SPR	PTD	SP	12.0	DUP	4759	1982		WIN	CCI	200		24	SPR
27	70	SPR	SPD	SP	13.0	DUP	4759	1711		WIN	CCI	200		24	SPR
28	70	SPR	SPD	SP	15.0	DUP	4759	1939		WIN	CCI	200		24	SPR
29	46	CAST	FLN	LG	1.0	HER	BYE	651		WIN	CCI	350		26	NRA

.220 SWIFT

The .220 Swift was a phenomenon of the 1930's, being introduced by Winchester in 1935 for use in their Model 54 bolt-action rifle, which was the progenitor of the famous Model 70. The originally-advertised velocity of 4,140 fps was far greater than that of any other cartridge at that time, and many tales were told about the phenomenal effectiveness of this ultra-high velocity cartridge on large game. In truth, the 48-grain bullet lacked the necessary penetration for reliable kills on animals as large as deer, though it did produce lightning-bolt effects when the shot was taken from an angle such that little depth of penetration was needed to reach the vital organs of the animal. Its failures on large game with rear-end or raking shots caused some experts to condemn the cartridge as resoundingly as others praised it, and as is usual in such partisan arguments, the truth of the matter was soon hopelessly obscured.

The .220 Swift was, and is in fact, a superb varmint cartridge, provided only that its few peculiarities are understood. Probably owing to its very high velocity, it was susceptible to excessive bore fouling unless the bore was thoroughly, carefully and frequently cleaned. The fouling was not easily seen by casual inspection, and not removed by infrequent or casual cleaning, and it was seriously detrimental to accuracy.

Many owners of Swifts undoubtedly replaced their barrels in the belief they were "shot out" after only a few hundred rounds, when a thorough cleaning would have restored the former accuracy. The Swift thus became infamous for short barrel life. The loads originally recommended developed very high chamber pressures, as indeed did the factory loads, and there was little margin of strength between legitimate maximum loads and those that expanded the primer pockets. The Swift thus acquired a largely undeserved reputation for "unpredictable" load behavior when some slight change in the load produced a blown primer.

Shooters were initially led to believe that the .220 Swift was an effective big-game cartridge by witnesses who had seen only a few quick kills result from atypical hits, and it inevitably gained the reputation of living on exaggerated claims when it failed in other circumstances. It was, in fact, a superb specialized varmint cartridge, and a phenomenal achievement in ballistics 45 years ago. It is regrettable that misunderstanding of its proper use and care has relegated it to obsolescence.

Typical .220 Swift loads should not exceed 53,000 c.u.p. and the maximum product average for factory ammunition does not exceed 57,000 c.u.p.

Max. Case Length: 2.205″ Trim-To Length: 2.195″
Max. Overall Length: 2.680″ Primer Size: Large Rifle
Bullet Dia.: .224″

RIFLE LOADS FOR THE .220 SWIFT

| LOAD NUMBER | BULLET | | | | POWDER | | | VELOCITY FPS | PRESSURE CUP | CASE BRAND | PRIMER | | CARTRIDGE OAL | BARREL LENGTH | DATA SOURCE |
	WEIGHT	BRAND	SHAPE	TYPE	WEIGHT	BRAND	TYPE				BRAND	TYPE			
1	45	SPR	PTD	SP	45.0	DUP	4350	4005	<53000	WIN	CCI	200		26	SPR
2	45	SRA	PTD	SP	39.5	DUP	4320	4100		REM	REM	9½		26	SRA
3	45	HDY	PTD	SP	36.7	DUP	3031	4000		REM	REM	9½		26	HDY
4	50	NOR	PTD	SP	39.3	NOR	202	3980	<53700	NOR	NOR	LR	2.620	24	NOR
5	50	SRA	PTD	SP	39.5	DUP	4064	3895	52500	REM	REM	9½	2.680	24	DUP
6	50	HDY	PTD	SP	39.5	DUP	4320	3900		REM	REM	9½		26	HDY

RIFLE LOADS FOR THE .220 SWIFT

LOAD NUMBER	BULLET WEIGHT	BULLET BRAND	BULLET SHAPE	BULLET TYPE	POWDER WEIGHT	POWDER BRAND	POWDER TYPE	VELOCITY FPS	PRESSURE CUP	CASE BRAND	PRIMER BRAND	PRIMER TYPE	CARTRIDGE OAL	BARREL LENGTH	DATA SOURCE
7	50	SPR	PTD	SP	44.0	DUP	4350	3868	<53000	WIN	CCI	250		26	SPR
8	50	NOS	PBT	SP	40.0	DUP	4350	3749		NOR	FED	210		26	NOS
9	55	SPR	PTD	SP	36.0	DUP	3031	3656		WIN	CCI	200		26	SPR
10	55	HDY	PTD	SP	38.5	DUP	4320	3800		REM	REM	9½		26	HDY
11	55	SRA	PTD	SP	39.0	DUP	4064	3900		REM	REM	9½		26	SRA
12	55	NOS	PBT	SP	44.0	DUP	4831	3873		NOR	FED	210		26	NOS
13	60	HDY	PTD	SP	42.5	DUP	4831	3555	53000	REM	REM	9½	2.680	24	DUP
14	63	SRA	SPD	SP	35.3	DUP	4064	3500		REM	REM	9½		26	SRA
15	60-63			SP	46.0	HOD	4831	3586	52000	WIN	WIN	8½-120		26	HOD
16	70	SPR	SPD	SP	43.0	NOR	MRP	3292	<53000	WIN	CCI	250		26	SPR
17	70	SPR	SPD	SP	42.0	HOD	4831	3359	52600	WIN	WIN	8½-120		26	HOD
18	70	SPR	SPD	SP	42.0	HOD	H450	3301	50300	WIN	WIN	8½-120		26	HOD
19	60	NOS	PBT	SP	39.0	DUP	4350	3569		NOR	FED	210		26	NOS
20	55	SPR	SPD	FJ	11.5	DUP	4759	1709		WIN	CCI	200		26	SPR
21	55	SPR	SPD	FJ	13.5	DUP	4759	2000		WIN	CCI	200		26	SPR

6 x 47mm

The 6x47mm cartridge might be called a semi-wildcat, because no factory ammunition of that caliber has ever been produced, although Remington has for many years chambered the factory-made Model 40XB-BR rifle for it. Its original purpose may have been to comply with rules restricting the caliber of benchrest rifles in certain classes of competition to those using 6mm or larger bullets, while still retaining the mild recoil, long barrel life and superb accuracy of cartridges such as the .222 Remington. Whatever its original purpose, it has proved to be fully as accurate as the famous .222 Remington in benchrest competition, when used with suitably accurate bullets, and it now stands on its own merits as one of the most popular calibers among benchrest shooters.

The cases are usually formed simply by expanding the necks of .222 Remington Magnum brass to accept .243-inch bullets. Recognizing the need for high-quality brass, Federal now provides excellent empty cases for handloaders, though no 6x47mm factory loads are offered. Most benchrest shooters neck-turn the cases to improve concentricity, and some custom chambers are dimensioned especially for neck-turned brass and should not be used with unmodified cases. A shooter who acquires a 6x47mm rifle should be sure of his chamber dimensions before handloading for it, making a chamber cast if necessary.

Max. Case Length: 1.850″ Trim-To Length: 1.840″
Max. Overall Length: Varies Primer Size: Small Rifle Magnum Bullet Dia.: .243″

RIFLE LOADS FOR THE 6x47 mm

LOAD NUMBER	BULLET WEIGHT	BULLET BRAND	BULLET SHAPE	BULLET TYPE	POWDER WEIGHT	POWDER BRAND	POWDER TYPE	VELOCITY FPS	PRESSURE CUP	CASE BRAND	PRIMER BRAND	PRIMER TYPE	CARTRIDGE OAL	BARREL LENGTH	DATA SOURCE
1	60	SRA	PTD	HP	30.5	HOD	BL-C-(2)	3233	45300	REM	REM	7½		23½	HOD
2	60	SRA	PTD	HP	28.0	HOD	H322	3222	44500	REM	REM	7½		23½	HOD
3	60	SRA	PTD	HP	26.7	DUP	3031	3300		REM	REM	7½		29	SRA
4	60	SRA	PTD	HP	28.7	WIN	748	3200		REM	REM	7½		29	SRA
5	70	SRA	PBT	HP	30.0	HOD	BL-C-(2)	3050	48000	REM	REM	7½		23½	HOD
6	70	SRA	PBT	HP	28.0	HOD	H322	3116	49800	REM	REM	7½		23½	HOD
7	70	SRA	PBT	HP	28.8	WIN	748	3100		REM	REM	7½		29	SRA
8	70	SRA	PBT	HP	24.3	DUP	4198	3200		REM	REM	7½		29	SRA
9	70	NOS	PBT	HP	25.0	HER	RL7	3242		REM	REM	7½		26	NOS
10	70	NOS	PBT	HP	29.5	HOD	H380	3011		REM	REM	7½		26	NOS
11	75	SPR	PTD	HP	27.5	HOD	4895	2911	47500	REM	REM	7½		23½	HOD
12	75	SPR	PTD	HP	29.0	HOD	H335	2953	46900	REM	REM	7½		23½	HOD
13	75	SRA	PTD	HP	25.7	DUP	3031	3100		REM	REM	7½		29	SRA
14	75	SRA	PTD	HP	29.0	WIN	748	3100		REM	REM	7½		29	SRA

LOAD NUMBER	BULLET				POWDER			VELOCITY FPS	PRESSURE CUP	CASE BRAND	PRIMER		CARTRIDGE OAL	BARREL LENGTH	DATA SOURCE
	WEIGHT	BRAND	SHAPE	TYPE	WEIGHT	BRAND	TYPE				BRAND	TYPE			
15	75	SPR	PTD	HP	26.0	HOD	H335	2987		FED	CCI	BR4		20	SPR
16	75	SPR	PTD	HP	24.0	HOD	H322	2682		FED	CCI	BR4		20	SPR
17	80	SPR	PTD	SP	28.0	HOD	H335	2946		REM	REM	7½		20	SPR
18	80	SPR	PTD	SP	29.0	HOD	BL-C-(2)	2935	48500	REM	REM	7½		23½	HOD
19	90	SPR	PTD	SP	25.5	HOD	4895	2627	48000	REM	REM	7½		23½	HOD
20	90	SPR	PTD	SP	25.0	HOD	H335	2623		REM	REM	7½		20	SPR
21	100	SRA	PBT	SP	26.0	HOD	BL-C-(2)	2571	49400	REM	REM	7½		23½	HOD
22	100	SRA	PBT	SP	25.0	HOD	4895	2485	50300	REM	REM	7½		23½	HOD
23	90	SPR	PTD	FJ	11.0	DUP	4759	1600		REM	REM	7½		20	SPR
24	90	SPR	PTD	FJ	13.0	DUP	4759	1902		REM	REM	7½		20	SPR

.243 WINCHESTER

The .243 Winchester was introduced in 1955, largely in consequence of the popularity of various 6mm wildcat cartridges publicized by authorities such as the late Warren Page. Some experts deplored Winchester's choice of the relatively long 20 degree shoulder, and the short neck of the case, whereas most of the popular 6mm wildcats had sharper shoulders and longer necks. The .243 case is essentially a necked-down .308 Winchester, though the .243 case is actually about .030 of an inch longer. Winchester envisioned the .243 as a dual-purpose cartridge, suitable for hunting both varmints and deer-size game, and indeed it is well suited to both those purposes. The 80-grain bullet of the factory load provides flat trajectory, and a high ballistic coefficient which allows much less wind deflection than do .22-caliber varmint bullets. The 100-grain factory load is suitable for deer-size game.

The fact that the cartridge is short enough to be accommodated in short-action rifles designed around the popular .308 Winchester cartridge, and in the long-popular Savage Model 99, has undoubtedly contributed to its popularity. Notwithstanding that the .243 has been condemned or given only faint praise by some authorities, it has become one of the most popular hunting cartridges, and seems destined for a long and prosperous life.

There is, however, some substance to the objection of the cartridge design. With an overall cartridge length limited to 2.71 inches by factory specifications, and a case length of about 2.04 inches, the maximum allowable bullet protrusion is then about .67 inch. Since the neck length measures only about .24 inch, any bullet longer than about .91 inch must protrude beyond the base of the case neck, into the powder chamber of the cartridge. Since most .243 bullets heavier than about 80 grains measure longer than .91

inch, they do intrude into the powder chamber. Though this condition is also true of many other successful cartridges, it is somewhat undesirable. The intrusion of the bullet reduces the available powder space somewhat. The resistance of the bullet to being pushed more deeply into the case during handling or feeding in the gun is reduced when the cylindrical bearing surface of the bullet must pass completely through the case neck. There is also some evidence, though perhaps not conclusive, that with certain powders and long bullets in the .243 cartridge the bullet base is expanded somewhat, before it leaves the case, and the necessity of swaging it back to original size as it passes the forcing cone in the barrel causes an increase in chamber pressure.

Since many rifles chambered for the .243 will accept cartridges longer than the standard 2.71 inches overall length, the handloader can seat the long bullets less deeply for such rifles, provided his chamber throat will accommodate the "long-loaded" rounds, and thereby avoid the problems of bullet intrusion into the powder chamber.

Loads for the .243 Winchester should typically not exceed 52,000 c.u.p. The maximum product average for factory ammunition does not exceed 55,200 c.u.p.

Max. Case Length: 2.045″ **Trim-To Length:** 2.035″
Max. Overall Length: 2.710″ **Primer Size:** Large Rifle **Bullet Dia.:** .243″

RIFLE LOADS FOR THE .243 WINCHESTER

LOAD NUMBER	BULLET				POWDER			VELOCITY FPS	PRESSURE CUP	CASE BRAND	PRIMER		CARTRIDGE OAL	BARREL LENGTH	DATA SOURCE
	WEIGHT	BRAND	SHAPE	TYPE	WEIGHT	BRAND	TYPE				BRAND	TYPE			
1	60	SRA	PTD	HP	49.0	WIN	760	3800		REM	REM	9½		26	SRA
2	70	SRA	PBT	HP	38.0	DUP	3031	3400		REM	REM	9½		26	SRA
3	70	SRA	PBT	HP	39.0	DUP	4895	3400		REM	REM	9½		26	SRA
4	70	HDY	PTD	SP	42.5	DUP	4064	3500	52000	FRO	FED	210	2.650	22	HDY
5	70	NOS	PBT	HP	47.0	DUP	4350	3612		REM	REM	9½		24	NOS
6	70	HDY	PTD	SP	47.5	HOD	H414	3613	49600	WIN	WIN	8½–120		26	HOD
7	75	SRA	PTD	HP	40.5	DUP	4320	3400		REM	REM	9½		26	SRA
8	75	WIN	PTD	HP	43.0	WIN	760	3320	49000	WIN	WIN	8½–120	2.710	24	WIN
9	75	HDY	PTD	HP	41.9	DUP	4064	3400	<52000	FRO	FED	210	2.640	22	HDY
10	75	SPR	PTD	HP	47.0	DUP	4350	3381	<52000	WIN	CCI	200		22	SPR
11	75	SPR	PTD	HP	47.0	HOD	H414	3534	49500	WIN	WIN	8½–120		26	HOD
12	80	WIN	PTD	SP	48.8	WIN	785	3365	49000	WIN	WIN	8½–120	2.710	24	WIN
13	80	REM	PTD	SP	42.5	DUP	4064	3360	52000	REM	REM	9½	2.640	22	DUP
14	80	SPR	PTD	SP	46.0	HOD	H414	3453	49200	WIN	WIN	8½–120		26	HOD
15	80	SPR	PTD	SP	45.5	DUP	4350	3288	<52000	WIN	CCI	200		22	SPR
16	85	SRA	PBT	HP	39.2	DUP	4320	3200		REM	REM	9½		26	SRA
17	85	SRA	PTD	SP	46.8	HOD	H450	3300		REM	REM	9½		26	SRA
18	85	NOS	PBT	SP	44.0	DUP	4350	3275		REM	REM	9½		24	NOS
19	85	SRA	PBT	SP	45.0	HOD	H414	3307	49200	WIN	WIN	8½–120		26	HOD
20	87	HDY	PTD	SP	42.7	DUP	4350	3200		WIN	FED	210		22	HDY
21	90	SPR	PTD	SP	46.0	DUP	4831	3171	<52000	WIN	CCI	200		22	SPR
22	95	NOS	PTD	SP	42.0	DUP	4350	3092		REM	REM	9½		24	NOS
23	100	WIN	PTD	SP	43.0	WIN	785	2930	49000	WIN	WIN	8½–120	2.710	24	WIN
24	100	REM	PTD	SP	46.0	DUP	4831	3010	51800	REM	REM	9½	2.710	22	DUP
25	100	SRA	PBT	SP	48.0	HOD	4831	3141	49500	WIN	WIN	8½–120		26	HOD
26	100	NOS	PBT	SP	42.0	DUP	4350	3078		REM	REM	9½		24	NOS
27	100	HDY	PTD	SP	38.2	DUP	4320	2900	52000	FRO	FED	210		22	HDY
28	100	SRA	PBT	SP	45.2	HOD	H450	3000		REM	REM	9½		26	SRA
29	100	NOR	PTD	SP	49.2	NOR	MRP	3199	<52200	NOR	NOR	LR	2.620	24	NOR
30	105	SPR	PTD	SP	42.0	DUP	4350	2995	<52500	WIN	CCI	200		22	SPR
31	85	CAST	RNN	LG	4.0	HER	UNIQ	1005		WIN	CCI	200	2.470	23	NRA
32	85	CAST	RNN	LG	6.0	HER	UNIQ	1295		WIN	CCI	200	2.470	23	NRA
33	85	CAST	RNN	LG	9.0	DUP	4759	1175		WIN	CCI	200	2.470	23	NRA
34	85	CAST	RNN	LG	12.0	DUP	4759	1510		WIN	CCI	200	2.470	23	NRA
35	90	SPR	SPD	FJ	17.0	DUP	4198	1766		WIN	CCI	200		22	SPR
36	90	SPR	SPD	FJ	19.0	DUP	4198	1990		WIN	CCI	200		22	SPR
37	96	CAST	RNN	LG	12.0	DUP	4759	1530		WIN	CCI	200	2.470	23	NRA

6mm/.244 REMINGTON

The 6mm and .244 Remington cartridges are technically two different types, though in fact they are merely different loads in the same cartridge cases. The .244 Remington was introduced in 1955, in the same year as the .243 Winchester, with which its ballistic similarity is obvious.

Numerous analyses have been written as to why the .243 far outstripped the .244 in popularity. The most popular theory is that the .244 was viewed only as a varmint rifle, because the 12-inch twist employed could not adequately stablize the pointed 100-grain bullets that were used in the game loads for the .243, which had a 10-inch twist. Some experts have disputed this theory, and the controversy is pointless except for the sake of argument. Whatever the reasons, the .243 continued to increase in popularity whereas the .244 did not. In the course of production, Remington changed the standard twist of .244 rifles from 12 to 10-inches per turn, thereby eliminating the problem of marginal stability with 100-grain bullets, but the unfavorable image of the .244 in comparison with the .243 was apparently not erased from the public mind. In 1963, Remington announced the 6mm Remington cartridge, which was in fact the .244 loaded with a 100-grain bullet, having a nominal muzzle velocity of 2,960 fps. The 6mm Remington rifles had barrels with 9-inch twist. The limit of acceptable chamber pressure was apparently increased from about 50,000 c.u.p. to 52,000 c.u.p., so that the ballistics of the 6mm could compare more favorably with those of the .243, which had a limit of 52,000 c.u.p. since its introduction. These changes apparently had the desired effect on acceptance of the cartridge, as the 6mm Remington has steadily improved its position relative to the .243 since the changes were made.

The 6mm cartridge is an excellent choice for a gun that may be used for hunting both varmints and deer-size game. It is preferred to the .243 by some handloaders, because of its sharper shoulder angle and longer case neck, though the ballistics of the two cartridges are not noticeably different in the field. The one advantage still enjoyed by the .243 over the 6mm Remington is that some short-action rifles such as the Savage Model 99 will accept the .243, but not the longer 6mm Remington cartridge.

The maximum product average chamber pressure of 6mm Remington factory ammunition will not exceed 55,200 c.u.p.
   Max. Case Length: 2.233″   **Trim-To Length:** 2.223″
Max. Overall Length: 2.825″   **Primer Size:** Large Rifle   **Bullet Dia.:** .243″

RIFLE LOADS FOR THE 6mm/.244 REMINGTON

LOAD NUMBER	BULLET				POWDER			VELOCITY FPS	PRESSURE CUP	CASE BRAND	PRIMER		CARTRIDGE OAL	BARREL LENGTH	DATA SOURCE
	WEIGHT	BRAND	SHAPE	TYPE	WEIGHT	BRAND	TYPE				BRAND	TYPE			
1	60	SRA	PTD	HP	43.4	DUP	4064	3700		REM	REM	9½		26	SRA
2	70	SRA	PBT	HP	39.9	DUP	3031	3400		REM	REM	9½		26	SRA
3	70	SRA	PBT	HP	41.0	DUP	4895	3400		REM	REM	9½		26	SRA
4	70	HDY	PTD	SP	48.9	DUP	4350	3600		REM	REM	9½		22	HDY
5	70	NOS	PBT	HP	43.0	DUP	4320	3594		NOR	REM	9½		22	NOS
6	70	HDY	PTD	SP	44.0	HOD	H380	3544	48700	REM	REM	9½		26	HOD
7	75	REM	PTD	SP	40.5	DUP	3031	3490	52000	REM	REM	9½	2.740	25	DUP
8	75	SRA	PTD	HP	42.8	DUP	4320	3400		REM	REM	9½		26	SRA
9	75	HDY	PTD	HP	47.5	DUP	4350	3500		REM	REM	9½		22	HDY
10	75	SPR	PTD	HP	48.0	DUP	4831	3310	<52000	WIN	CCI	200		22	SPR
11	75	SPR	PTD	HP	42.0	HOD	BL-C-(2)	3467	48400	REM	REM	9½		26	HOD
12	80	REM	PTD	SP	46.0	DUP	4350	3310	52000	REM	REM	9½	2.790	22	DUP
13	80	SPR	PTD	SP	46.0	HOD	H414	3416	51200	REM	REM	9½		26	HOD
14	80	SPR	PTD	SP	49.0	HOD	4831	3343	49600	REM	REM	9½		26	HOD
15	80	SPR	PTD	SP	48.0	DUP	4831	3356	<52000	WIN	CCI	200		22	SPR
16	85	SRA	PBT	HP	48.7	HOD	4831	3300		REM	REM	9½		26	SRA
17	85	SRA	PBT	HP	41.0	HOD	H380	3203	49200	REM	REM	9½		26	HOD
18	85	NOS	SPD	SP	45.0	DUP	4350	3288		NOR	REM	9½		22	NOS
19	85	NOS	PBT	SP	39.5	DUP	4320	3200		NOR	REM	9½		22	NOS
20	87	HDY	PTD	SP	45.8	DUP	4350	3300		REM	REM	9½		22	HDY
21	90	SPR	PTD	SP	47.0	DUP	4831	3225	<52000	WIN	CCI	200		22	SPR
22	95	NOS	PTD	SP	43.0	DUP	4350	3089		NOR	REM	9½		22	NOS
23	100	REM	PTD	SP	45.5	DUP	4831	3095	52000	REM	REM	9½	2.735	22	DUP
24	100	WIN	PTD	SP	46.5	WIN	785	3040	49000	WIN	WIN	8½-120	2.825	24	WIN
25	100	SRA	PTD	SP	46.0	HOD	4831	3074	49600	REM	REM	9½		26	HOD
26	100	NOS	PBT	SP	45.5	DUP	4831	3087		NOR	REM	9½		22	NOS
27	100	HDY	PTD	SP	42.7	DUP	4350	3000		REM	REM	9½		22	HDY
28	100	SRA	PBT	SP	46.7	HOD	4831	3000		REM	REM	9½		26	SRA
29	100	NOR	PTD	SP	48.2	NOR	MRP	3248	<52200	NOR	NOR	LR		24	NOR
30	105	SPR	PTD	SP	48.0	HOD	H450	3084	<52000	WIN	CCI	250		22	SPR
31	90	SPR	SPD	FJ	17.0	DUP	4198	1770		WIN	CCI	200		22	SPR
32	90	SPR	SPD	FJ	19.0	DUP	4198	1987		WIN	CCI	200		22	SPR

.240 WEATHERBY MAGNUM

The .240 Weatherby Magnum, introduced in 1968, is the largest of the 6mm factory cartridges standardized in the U.S. The case capacity is about 20 per cent greater than that of the 6mm Remington cartridge. The case is of belted type, and the shoulder is of typical Weatherby configuration, but the rim and belt diameter measures nominally .473 inch, the same as that of the head of the .30-06, .270, .243, etc., instead of about .531 inch as found on the larger magnum-type cases.

No commercial rifles except the Weatherby are factory-chambered for the .240 Weatherby cartridge, but custom rifles for it can be built on actions that accommodate the 8x57mm Mauser and similar cartridges. It is more powerful than either the .243 Winchester or .244 Remington cartridges, and therefore probably more suitable for use on larger game, though the difference in velocities is only about 100 fps at comparable chamber pressures.

Max. Case Length: 2.500″ **Trim-To Length:** 2.490″
Max. Overall Length: 3.062″ **Primer Size:** Large Rifle Magnum **Bullet Dia.:** .243″

RIFLE LOADS FOR THE .240 WEATHERBY MAGNUM

LOAD NUMBER	BULLET				POWDER			VELOCITY FPS	PRESSURE CUP	CASE BRAND	PRIMER		CARTRIDGE OAL	BARREL LENGTH	DATA SOURCE
	WEIGHT	BRAND	SHAPE	TYPE	WEIGHT	BRAND	TYPE				BRAND	TYPE			
1	70	HDY	PTD	SP	53.0	DUP	4350	3684	48530	WEA	FED	215	3.062	26	WEA
2	70	HDY	PTD	SP	55.0	DUP	4350	3780	52270	WEA	FED	215	3.062	26	WEA
3	70	SRA	PBT	HP	54.2	DUP	4831	3600		WEA	FED	215		26	SRA
4	70	HDY	PTD	SP	55.0	HOD	4831	3533	44680	WEA	FED	215		26	WEA
5	70	HDY	PTD	SP	57.0	HOD	4831	3708	52070	WEA	FED	215	3.062	26	WEA
6	70	HDY	PTD	SP	59.4	NOR	MRP	3838	53790	WEA	FED	215	3.062	26	WEA
7	75	HDY	PTD	HP	56.7	HOD	H450	3600		WEA	FED	210		24	HDY
8	75	SPR	PTD	HP	55.0	DUP	4831	3620	<55100	WEA	CCI	250		24	SPR
9	80	SPR	PTD	SP	57.0	HOD	H450	3553	<55100	WEA	CCI	250		24	SPR
10	85	SRA	PBT	HP	52.5	DUP	4831	3400		WEA	FED	215		26	SRA
11	87	HDY	PTD	SP	54.5	NOR	MRP	3497	53420	WEA	FED	215	3.062	26	WEA
12	90	SPR	PTD	SP	52.0	DUP	4831	3420	<55100	WEA	CCI	250		24	SPR
13	100	HDY	PTD	SP	50.0	DUP	4350	3308	53400	WEA	FED	215	3.062	26	WEA
14	100	HDY	PTD	SP	53.0	HOD	4831	3268	51760	WEA	FED	215	3.062	26	WEA
15	100	SRA	PBT	SP	50.6	DUP	4831	3200		WEA	FED	215		26	SRA
16	100	HDY	PTD	SP	53.2	HOD	4831	3200		WEA	FED	210		24	HDY
17	100	HDY	PTD	SP	54.0	NOR	MRP	3395	52900	WEA	FED	215	3.062	26	WEA
18	105	SPR	PTD	SP	49.5	DUP	4831	3154	<55100	WEA	CCI	250		24	SPR
19	90	SPR	SPD	FJ	18.0	DUP	4198	1776		WEA	CCI	250		24	SPR
20	90	SPR	SPD	FJ	20.0	DUP	4198	1982		WEA	CCI	250		24	SPR

.256 WINCHESTER

The .256 Winchester was developed as a revolver cartridge, in cooperation with a major handgun manufacturer. Owing to technical difficulties with the gun, however, the revolver for the .256 cartridge was never marketed. The cartridge was announced in 1960, nevertheless, and the lever-action Marlin Model 62 rifle was adapted to it in 1963. Ruger also made a single-shot pistol called the "Hawkeye" for the .256 Winchester cartridge. Both of these guns have now been discontinued, though some certainly remain in use. There are also some custom single-shot rifles built for the cartridge, and it is suitable in such guns as a cartridge for small game and varmints.

Typical chamber pressure for the .256 Winchester cartridge should be limited to about 42,000 c.u.p. and the maximum product average chamber pressure of factory loads will not exceed 46,300 c.u.p.

Max. Case Length: 1.281″ **Trim-To Length:** 1.275″
Max. Overall Length: 1.590″ **Primer Size:** Small Rifle **Bullet Dia.:** .257″

RIFLE LOADS FOR THE .256 WINCHESTER

LOAD NUMBER	BULLET				POWDER			VELOCITY FPS	PRESSURE CUP	CASE BRAND	PRIMER		CARTRIDGE OAL	BARREL LENGTH	DATA SOURCE
	WEIGHT	BRAND	SHAPE	TYPE	WEIGHT	BRAND	TYPE				BRAND	TYPE			
1	60	HDY	FLN	SP	14.5	HER	2400	2700		WIN	WIN	6½-116		24	HDY
2	60	HDY	FLN	SP	15.5	DUP	4227	2700		WIN	WIN	6½-116		24	HDY
3	60	HDY	FLN	SP	18.0	HOD	H4198	2794		WIN	WIN	6½-116		24	HOD
4	75	HDY	PTD	HP	15.8	DUP	4198	2300		WIN	WIN	6½-116		24	HDY
5	75	SRA	PTD	HP	14.3	DUP	4227	2300		WIN	REM	6½		24	SRA
6	87	SRA	PTD	SP	15.0	DUP	4198	2100		WIN	REM	6½		24	SRA
7	87	HDY	PTD	SP	12.9	DUP	4227	2100		WIN	WIN	6½-116		24	HDY
8	87	HDY	PTD	SP	15.0	HOD	H4198	2192		WIN	WIN	6½-116		24	HOD

.25-20 WINCHESTER CENTER FIRE (W.C.F.)

The .25-.20 W.C.F. was introduced in the mid-1890's for the Winchester Model 1892 rifle. It is essentially a necked-down version of the much older .32-20 (.32 W.C.F.) cartridge that had been used in the Winchester Model 1873 rifle. The original factory loads were similar in performance to the .25-20 Single-Shot cartridge, which was a popular small-game, target and varmint cartridge of its day. The .25-20 Single-Shot cartridge was too long for the Model 1892 action, so Winchester approximated its performance in the shorter .25-20 W.C.F. cartridge.

In the early 1930's, before the advent of the .22 Hornet, the .25-20 was a popular small varmint cartridge, commonly loaded with a 60-grain bullet in the high-velocity factory load, at a muzzle velocity of about 2,250 fps. Though outclassed by the .22 Hornet as a varmint cartridge, the .25-20 is actually quite a good small-game cartridge, performing well with cast bullets and moderate loads. A few bolt-action rifles have been chambered for the .25-20 W.C.F., and these give surprisingly good accuracy at moderate ranges. When loading for tubular-magazine rifles, flat-nose or blunt round-nose bullets must be used, and the case mouth must be crimped securely into a cannelure on the bullet.

Chamber pressure for the .25-20 Winchester is customarily limited to about 28,000 c.u.p. The maximum product average of factory ammunition should not exceed 31,200 c.u.p.

Max. Case Length: 1.330″ **Trim-To Length:** 1.320″
Max. Overall Length: 1.592″ **Primer Size:** Small Rifle **Bullet Dia.:** .257″

RIFLE LOADS FOR THE .25-20 WINCHESTER

LOAD NUMBER	BULLET				POWDER			VELOCITY FPS	PRESSURE CUP	CASE BRAND	PRIMER		CARTRIDGE OAL	BARREL LENGTH	DATA SOURCE
	WEIGHT	BRAND	SHAPE	TYPE	WEIGHT	BRAND	TYPE				BRAND	TYPE			
1	60	WIN	RNN	HP	13.0	WIN	680	2300	26000	WIN	WIN	6½-116		24	WIN
2	60	HDY	FLN	SP	10.6	HER	2400	2000		REM	WIN	6½-116		24	HDY
3	60	HDY	FLN	SP	11.9	DUP	4227	2100		REM	WIN	6½-116		24	HDY
4	60	HDY	FLN	SP	8.4	HOD	H110	1827	19500	WIN	WIN	6½-116		26	HOD
5	86	WIN	FLN	SP	11.0	WIN	680	1800	23500	WIN	WIN	6½-116		24	WIN
6	86	WIN	FLN	LP	11.1	WIN	680	1895	25500	WIN	WIN	6½-116	1.592	24	WIN
7	86	REM	FLN	SP	11.5	HER	RL7	1460	15000	REM	CCI	400	1.590	24	HER
8	86	REM	FLN	SP	8.0	HER	2400	1340	18300	REM	CCI	400	1.590	24	HER
9	86	WIN	FLN	SP	8.0	HOD	H110	1444			WIN	WIN	6½-116		20	HOD

.25-35 WINCHESTER (and .25 REMINGTON)

The .25-35 Winchester was introduced in 1895 for the Model 1894 Winchester rifle. With its 117-grain bullet at about 2,300 fps, it is adequate for deer-size game if the shots are reasonably well placed. The recoil is very moderate, the trajectory slightly flatter than that of the .30-30 with 170-grain bullets, and the .25-35 is altogether a very pleasant rifle to shoot. Before the introduction of the high-velocity .22-caliber cartridges, the .25-35 on a good single-shot action such as the Winchester high-wall, was a fairly popular target and varmint cartridge. Some such rifles could produce groups of about one inch at 100 yards, which was probably about the best accuracy obtainable from the bullets then available. The .25-35 is also a good cast-bullet cartridge, capable of excellent accuracy with proper loads. The cartridge has not been loaded in the U.S. for several years, but cases for it can be formed quite easily from .30-30 brass. In Europe, the cartridge is called the 6.5x52mmR, and is used in some single-shot and combination rifle/shotgun hunting arms.

The .25 Remington rimless cartridge is ballistically almost identical to the .25-35, though the cartridges are not interchangeable. Loading data for the .25-35 may also be used satisfactorily in the .25 Remington cartridge.

The typical working pressure for the .25-35 is about 37,000 c.u.p., and the maximum product average for factory ammunition should not exceed 40,200 c.u.p.

Max. Case Length: 2.040″ **Trim-To Length:** 2.030″
Max. Overall Length: 2.253″ **Primer Size:** Large Rifle
Bullet Dia.: .257″

RIFLE LOADS FOR THE .25-35 WINCHESTER

LOAD NUMBER	BULLET				POWDER			VELOCITY FPS	PRESSURE CUP	CASE BRAND	PRIMER		CARTRIDGE OAL	BARREL LENGTH	DATA SOURCE
	WEIGHT	BRAND	SHAPE	TYPE	WEIGHT	BRAND	TYPE				BRAND	TYPE			
1	60	HDY	FNN	SP	28.2	DUP	3031	2800		REM	WIN	8½-120		20	HDY
2	60	HDY	FNN	SP	32.3	DUP	4320	2900		REM	WIN	8½-120		20	HDY
3	117	HDY	RNN	SP	25.7	DUP	3031	2300		REM	WIN	8½-120		20	HDY
4	117	HDY	RNN	SP	27.0	HOD	4895	2207		WIN	WIN	8½-120		20	HOD
5	117	CIL		SP	19.0	HER	RL7	2000	36500	CIL	CIL			24	HER

.250 SAVAGE

Reportedly designed by Charles Newton, this cartridge was introduced by Savage in 1915, and originally named the .250-3000 because it developed a muzzle velocity of 3,000 fps with 87-grain bullets. It is still commonly called the .250-3000 Savage, though the name has been shortened for convenience by ammunition manufacturers.

The .250 Savage is an excellent choice for hunters who require minimum recoil from a rifle having adequate power for deer-size game. Full-charge loads with 100-grain bullets in an eight pound .250 Savage rifle produce only about 6.8 foot pounds of free-recoil energy, compared to 8.0 foot pounds for a .243 and 15.1 foot pounds for a .308 of the same weight, firing 100- and 150-grain bullets repectively.

The 100-grain bullet is the best choice for deer hunting with the .250 Savage, because the penetration is better on shots taken from unfavorable angles. If shots are carefully placed, however, the 87-grain bullet is adequate for deer hunting.

The .250 Savage is a very good varmint cartridge with bullets of 75 to 90 grains, and capable of excellent accuracy. If .25-caliber bullets of benchrest quality were available, the .250 Savage could be a benchrest cartridge fully competitive with the various 6mm cartridges commonly used by benchrest shooters. Though not of benchrest quality, the modern .25-caliber bullets are easily capable of accuracy better than one MOA, and entirely adequate for varmint or deer hunting.

The working pressure of the .250 Savage is normally limited to about 45,000 c.u.p., and the maximum product average for factory ammunition should not exceed 48,200 c.u.p.

Max. Case Length: 1.912″ **Trim-To Length:** 1.902″
Max. Overall Length: 2.515″ **Primer Size:** Large Rifle **Bullet Dia.:** .257″

LOAD NUMBER	BULLET				POWDER			VELOCITY FPS	PRESSURE CUP	CASE BRAND	PRIMER		CARTRIDGE OAL	BARREL LENGTH	DATA SOURCE
	WEIGHT	BRAND	SHAPE	TYPE	WEIGHT	BRAND	TYPE				BRAND	TYPE			
1	60	WIN	RNN	HP	40.8	WIN	748	3470	40500	WIN	WIN	8½-120		24	WIN
2	60	SPR	PTD	SP	36.5	DUP	3031	3380		WIN	CCI	200		24	SPR
3	60	HDY	FNN	SP	37.9	DUP	4064	3400		REM	FED	210		24	HDY
4	60	SPR	PTD	SP	37.0	HOD	4895	3409		WIN	WIN	8½-120		24	HOD
5	75	SRA	PTD	HP	34.5	DUP	3031	3300		REM	REM	9½		24	SRA
6	87	SRA	PTD	SP	35.5	DUP	4064	3075	45000	REM	REM	9½	2.515	24	DUP
7	87	WIN	PTD	SP	39.5	WIN	760	2985	43500	WIN	WIN	8½-120		24	WIN
8	87	SPR	PTD	SP	40.5	DUP	4350	2929	<45000	WIN	CCI	200		24	SPR
9	87	SRA	PTD	SP	33.5	DUP	3031	3100		REM	REM	9½		24	SRA
10	90	SRA	PTD	SP	33.5	DUP	3031	3100		REM	REM	9½		24	SRA
11	100	HDY	PTD	SP	34.5	DUP	4064	2875	44100	REM	REM	9½	2.515	24	DUP
12	100	WIN	SPD	SP	35.5	WIN	748	2820	43500	WIN	WIN	8½-120		24	WIN
13	100	SPR	PTD	SP	40.0	DUP	4831	2782	<45000	WIN	CCI	200		24	SPR
14	100	SRA	PTD	SP	32.9	DUP	3031	3000		REM	REM	9½		24	SRA
15	100	NOS	PBT	SP	35.0	DUP	4320	2788		WIN	CCI	200		24	NOS
16	117	NOS	SPD	SP	36.0	DUP	4350	2539		WIN	CCI	200		24	NOS
17	117	HDY	RNN	SP	31.5	DUP	4064	2600		REM	FED	210		24	HDY
18	117	SRA	PTD	SP	34.5	HOD	H380	2600		REM	REM	9½		24	SRA
19	120	SPR	PTD	SP	38.0	DUP	4831	2590		WIN	CCI	200		24	SPR
20	120	SPR	PTD	SP	39.5	HOD	H450	2516	43500	WIN	WIN	8½-120		26	HOD
21	60	SPR	PTD	SP	12.0	DUP	4759	1675		WIN	CCI	200		24	SPR
22	60	SPR	PTD	SP	14.0	DUP	4759	1960		WIN	CCI	200		24	SPR
23	100	SPR	PTD	SP	14.0	DUP	4759	1702		WIN	CCI	200		24	SPR
24	100	SPR	PTD	SP	16.0	DUP	4759	1994		WIN	CCI	200		24	SPR

.257 ROBERTS

The .257 Roberts was named for the late N. H. "Ned" Roberts in the 1930's, and was once a very popular long-range varmint cartridge. It is one of the earliest popular wildcats to be standardized by Remington (in 1934), just as the .22-250 and .25-06 were standardized during this generation. Before its standardization, the cartridge was known as the .25 Roberts, and the famous A. O. Neidner built beautiful classic target rifles chambered for it. They were among the first high-velocity rifles that could consistently average groups less than one MOA. With modern bullets, they would undoubtedly have done much better than that. The original .25 Roberts was based on a necked-down 7x57mm Mauser case, but the factory .257 Roberts has a slightly greater head-to-shoulder length, so the two are not interchangeable, though they are very similar.

The .257 was somewhat handicapped by some arbitrary constraints imposed when it was standardized. One was that the maximum working chamber pressure is 45,000 c.u.p., which restricted its velocity performance more severely than that of the contemporary .270 Winchester and the present 6mm Remington or .243 Winchester that operate at 52,000 to 54,000 c.u.p. Another handicap is that blunt-nose bullets were used, producing relatively poor ballistic coefficients, and the overall length of the cartridge was limited to 2.775 inches which allows only about .540-

inch bullet protrusion. Long pointed bullets must therefore be seated too deeply in the case for best results, if the cartridges are to be used in a magazine designed for the .257 Roberts factory loads. In rifles that can accommodate cartridges such as the .30-06, the overall cartridge length can be increased to as much as 3.34 inches, and more favorable ballistics can be achieved by the handloader.

The chamber-pressure limitation may have been established at 45,000 c.u.p. because there were custom .257 rifles built on the Mauser Model 1893 actions, and greater pressures were considered not entirely safe in those guns. In the stronger rifles commercially chambered for the .257, using magazines that accommodate the .30-06 and similar cartridges, loads could be developed for the .257 that would exceed the performance of the 6mm Remington and approach that of the .25-06. Even with the handicaps mentioned, the .257 Roberts is a very satisfactory dual-purpose cartridge for long-range varmint hunting and deer-size game.

The maximum product average chamber pressure for the .257 Roberts should not exceed 48,200 c.u.p.

Max. Case Length: 2.233" **Trim-To Length:** 2.223"
Max. Overall Length: 2.775" **Primer Size:** Large Rifle **Bullet Dia.:** .257"

RIFLE LOADS FOR THE .257 ROBERTS

LOAD NUMBER	BULLET				POWDER			VELOCITY FPS	PRESSURE CUP	CASE BRAND	PRIMER		CARTRIDGE OAL	BARREL LENGTH	DATA SOURCE
	WEIGHT	BRAND	SHAPE	TYPE	WEIGHT	BRAND	TYPE				BRAND	TYPE			
1	60	SPR	PTD	SP	54.0	HOD	H414	3818	43800	WIN	WIN	8½-120		26	HOD
2	60	SPR	PTD	SP	48.0	HOD	BL-C-(2)	3834	45900	WIN	WIN	8½-120		26	HOD
3	60	SPR	PTD	SP	46.0	HOD	4895	3805	45000	WIN	WIN	8½-120		26	HOD
4	60	SPR	PTD	SP	40.5	DUP	3031	3329		WIN	CCI	200		24	SPR
5	60	HDY	FNN	SP	44.2	DUP	4064	3700		REM	FED	210		24	HDY
6	75	SRA	PTD	HP	52.0	HOD	H414	3555	45300	WIN	WIN	8½-120		26	HOD
7	75	SRA	PTD	HP	46.0	HOD	BL-C-(2)	3531	46700	WIN	WIN	8½-120		26	HOD
8	75	SRA	PTD	HP	44.0	HOD	4895	3561	47300	WIN	WIN	8½-120		26	HOD
9	75	SRA	PTD	HP	44.0	DUP	4064	3500		REM	REM	9½		24	SRA
10	75	HDY	PTD	HP	44.2	DUP	4895	3500		REM	FED	210		24	HDY
11	87-90			SP	50.0	HOD	H414	3368	44400	WIN	WIN	8½-120		26	HOD
12	87-90			SP	42.0	HOD	4895	3372	47600	WIN	WIN	8½-120		26	HOD
13	87	HDY	PTD	SP	43.3	DUP	4320	3200		REM	FED	210		24	HDY
14	87	SPR	PTD	SP	46.0	HOD	H414	3052	<48000	WIN	CCI	250		24	SPR
15	87	SRA	PTD	SP	42.9	DUP	4064	3300		REM	REM	9½		24	SRA
16	90	SRA	PBT	HP	42.9	DUP	4064	3300		REM	REM	9½		24	SRA
17	100	SRA	PTD	SP	39.5	DUP	4064	2945	44800	REM	REM	9½	2.775	24	DUP
18	100	HDY	PTD	SP	44.4	NOR	204	3000		REM	FED	210		24	HDY
19	100	NOS	PTD	SP	45.5	DUP	4831	3092		WIN	WIN	8½-120		24	NOS
20	100	SPR	PTD	SP	50.0	HOD	H450	3040	<48000	WIN	CCI	250		24	SPR
21	115	NOS	PTD	SP	38.0	HOD	H380	2821		WIN	WIN	8½-120		24	NOS
22	117	HDY	RNN	SP	44.6	HOD	4831	2800		REM	FED	210		24	HDY
23	117	SRA	PBT	SP	35.9	DUP	4064	2600		REM	REM	9½		24	SRA
24	117-120			SP	46.0	HOD	H205	2851	47400	WIN	WIN	8½-120		26	HOD
25	117-120			SP	49.0	HOD	4831	2974	46800	WIN	WIN	8½-120		26	HOD
26	120	SRA	PBT	HP	44.0	DUP	4831	2810	45000	REM	REM	9½	2.775	24	DUP
27	120	HDY	PTD	HP	42.0	DUP	4350	2800		REM	FED	210		24	HDY
28	120	SPR	PTD	SP	47.5	HOD	H450	2825	<48000	WIN	CCI	250		24	SPR
29	87	SPR	PTD	SP	15.0	DUP	4759	1762		WIN	CCI	200		24	SPR
30	87	SPR	PTD	SP	17.0	DUP	4759	2008		WIN	CCI	200		24	SPR

.25-06 REMINGTON

The .25-06 Remington is another of the popular wildcats "legitimized" by Remington as a standard factory cartridge. A. O. Neidner built rifles for the wildcat .25-06 cartridge in the 1920's, and various "improved" versions of it have been developed during the past 45 years. The version standardized by Remington in 1969 is simply the .30-06 necked down to accept .25-caliber bullets, and that is probably as good as any of the variations.

The obvious similarity to the .270 Winchester cartridge invites comparison, and the .25-06 is less impressive from the standpoint of velocity with comparable bullet weights. This is due in part to the smaller bore diameter, which is less efficient from the interior ballistic standpoint, and in part to the fact that the pressure limit for the .270 is slightly greater than for the .25-06.

The .25-06 is, nevertheless, a very good long-range varmint cartridge, and suitable for deer-size game at long range with appropriate bullets. With well designed controlled-expansion bullets of 115 grains or more, the .25-06 is suitable for even larger animals. The 120-grain, .257-inch bullet has sectional density about equal to that of a 141-grain bullet in the .270 or a 172-grain bullet in the .30-06, so the penetration shoud be comparable, at comparable velocities, if controlled-expansion bullets are used.

The working pressure of the .25-06 cartridge is limited to about 53,000 c.u.p., and the maximum product average for factory ammunition should not exceed 56,200 c.u.p.

Max. Case Length: 2.494" **Trim-To Length:** 2.484"
Max. Overall Length: 3.250" **Primer Size:** Large Rifle **Bullet Dia.:** .257"

RIFLE LOADS FOR THE .25-06 REMINGTON

LOAD NUMBER	BULLET				POWDER			VELOCITY FPS	PRESSURE CUP	CASE BRAND	PRIMER		CARTRIDGE OAL	BARREL LENGTH	DATA SOURCE
	WEIGHT	BRAND	SHAPE	TYPE	WEIGHT	BRAND	TYPE				BRAND	TYPE			
1	75	SRA	PTD	HP	61.0	HOD	4831	3618	49300	WIN	WIN	8½-120		26	HOD
2	75	SRA	PTD	HP	54.0	HOD	H414	3672	48300	WIN	WIN	8½-120		26	HOD
3	75	HDY	PTD	HP	49.0	DUP	4064	3500		REM	REM	9½		24	HDY
4	75	SRA	PTD	HP	49.0	DUP	4895	3600		REM	WIN	8½-120		26	SRA
5	87	SRA	PTD	SP	59.0	DUP	4831	3560	52200	REM	REM	9½	3.100	24	DUP
6	87	SPR	PTD	SP	56.0	DUP	4350	3534	<53000	WIN	CCI	200		24	SPR
7	87	HDY	PTD	SP	55.9	HOD	4831	3400		REM	REM	9½		24	HDY
8	87-90			SP	54.0	HOD	H205	3393	50700	WIN	WIN	8½-120		26	HOD
9	90	SRA	PBT	HP	57.9	NOR	MRP	3500		REM	WIN	8½-120		26	SRA
10	100	SRA	PTD	SP	56.0	DUP	4831	3335	53000	REM	REM	9½	3.090	24	DUP
11	100	HDY	PTD	SP	53.3	DUP	4350	3300		REM	REM	9½		24	HDY
12	100	SPR	PTD	SP	47.0	DUP	4064	3281	<53000	WIN	CCI	200		24	SPR
13	100	NOS	PBT	SP	54.0	NOR	MRP	3345		WIN	REM	9½		26	NOS
14	100	SPR	PTD	SP	58.0	HOD	4831	3440	53400	WIN	WIN	8½-120		26	HOD
15	100	SPR	PTD	SP	49.0	HOD	H205	3268	51600	WIN	WIN	8½-120		26	HOD
16	100	SRA	PTD	SP	53.3	NOR	MRP	3300		REM	WIN	8½-120		26	SRA
17	115	NOS	PTD	SP	52.0	NOR	MRP	3170		WIN	REM	9½		26	NOS
18	117	NOS	SPD	SP	50.0	HOD	H450	3086		WIN	REM	9½		26	NOS
19	117	HDY	RNN	SP	54.7	HOD	4831	3000		REM	REM	9½		24	HDY
20	117	SRA	PBT	SP	49.0	NOR	MRP	3000		REM	WIN	8½-120		26	SRA
21	120	SRA	PBT	HP	48.5	DUP	4350	2950	51500	REM	REM	9½	3.100	24	DUP
22	120	HDY	PTD	SP	53.8	HOD	4831	3100		REM	REM	9½		24	HDY
23	120	SPR	PTD	SP	50.0	DUP	4831	2980	<53000	WIN	CCI	200		24	SPR
24	120	SPR	PTD	SP	64.0	HOD	H870	3204	48000	WIN	CCI	250		26	HOD
25	120	NOS	PBT	SP	50.0	HOD	H450	3080		WIN	REM	9½		26	NOS
26	87	SPR	PTD	SP	13.0	DUP	4759	1502		WIN	CCI	200		24	SPR
27	87	SPR	PTD	SP	17.0	DUP	4759	1933		WIN	CCI	200		24	SPR
28	100	SPR	PTD	SP	15.0	DUP	4759	1524		WIN	CCI	200		24	SPR
29	100	SPR	PTD	SP	19.0	DUP	4759	1892		WIN	CCI	200		24	SPR

.257 WEATHERBY MAGNUM

The .257 Weatherby Magnum is the largest of the .25-caliber factory cartridges, having a case capacity about 25 per cent greater than that of the .25-06. The velocities attainable at comparable chamber pressures are therefore greater in the .257 Weatherby, and the trajectories are correspondingly flatter. The cartridge is especially suitable for long-range shooting at animals such as antelope, where flatness of trajectory is an important advantage, and heavy bullets are not required.

The .257 Weatherby cartridge is based on a shortened and necked-down belted magnum case, having the same rim and belt diameter as the .375 and .300 H&H cases from which most of the modern magnums were derived. The overall cartridge length does not exceed 3.25 inches, making the cartridge suitable for use in actions that can accommodate the 8x57mm Mauser cartridge. In actions designed around the .30-06 cartridge, overall cartridge lengths up to 3.34 inches are acceptable.

Max. Case Length: 2.549″ **Trim-To Length:** 2.539″
Max. Overall Length: 3.250″ **Primer Size:** Large Rifle Magnum **Bullet Dia.:** .257″

RIFLE LOADS FOR THE .257 WEATHERBY MAGNUM

LOAD NUMBER	BULLET				POWDER			VELOCITY FPS	PRESSURE CUP	CASE BRAND	PRIMER		CARTRIDGE OAL	BARREL LENGTH	DATA SOURCE
	WEIGHT	BRAND	SHAPE	TYPE	WEIGHT	BRAND	TYPE				BRAND	TYPE			
1	75	SRA	PTD	HP	70.5	DUP	4350	4000		WEA	FED	215		26	SRA
2	75	HDY	PTD	HP	73.3	HOD	4831	3900		WEA	FED	215		26	HDY
3	87	HDY	PTD	SP	68.0	DUP	4350	3698	51790	WEA	FED	215	3.250	26	WEA
4	87	HDY	PTD	SP	69.0	DUP	4350	3715	53270	WEA	FED	215	3.250	26	WEA
5	87	HDY	PTD	SP	71.0	HOD	4831	3617	48140	WEA	FED	215	3.250	26	WEA
6	87	HDY	PTD	SP	73.0	HOD	4831	3751	52470	WEA	FED	215	3.250	26	WEA
7	87	HDY	PTD	SP	74.1	NOR	MRP	3815	50700	WEA	FED	215	3.250	26	WEA
8	90	SRA	PBT	HP	68.2	DUP	4350	3700		WEA	FED	215		26	SRA
9	100	NOS	PTD	SP	67.0	NOR	MRP	3504		WEA	FED	210		24	NOS
10	100	SPR	PTD	SP	68.0	DUP	4831	3361		WEA	CCI	250		24	SPR
11	100	SRA	PTD	SP	66.4	DUP	4350	3500		WEA	FED	215		26	SRA
12	100	HDY	PTD	SP	66.0	DUP	4350	3520	54860	WEA	FED	215	3.250	26	WEA
13	100	HDY	PTD	SP	66.0	HOD	4831	3315	43640	WEA	FED	215	3.250	26	WEA
14	100	HDY	PTD	SP	70.0	HOD	4831	3543	53410	WEA	FED	215	3.250	26	WEA
15	115	NOS	PTD	SP	64.0	DUP	4831	3279		WEA	FED	210		24	NOS
16	117	SRA	PBT	SP	61.8	DUP	4350	3200		WEA	FED	215		26	SRA
17	117	NOS	SPD	SP	63.0	NOR	MRP	3206		WEA	FED	210		24	NOS
18	117	HDY	RNN	SP	63.0	HOD	4831	3152	46650	WEA	FED	215	3.250	26	WEA
19	117	HDY	RNN	SP	67.0	HOD	4831	3326	53930	WEA	FED	215	3.250	26	WEA
20	120	SRA	PBT	HP	66.7	HOD	4831	3200		WEA	FED	215		26	SRA
21	120	SPR	PTD	SP	76.0	HOD	H870	3240	53200	WEA	CCI	250		26	HOD
22	120	SPR	PTD	SP	76.0	HOD	H570	3261	51200	WEA	CCI	250		26	HOD
23	120	NOS	PBT	SP	64.0	HOD	H450	3200		WEA	FED	210		24	NOS
24	87	SPR	PTD	SP	16.0	DUP	4759	1619		WEA	CCI	250		24	SPR
25	87	SPR	PTD	SP	20.0	DUP	4759	2030		WEA	CCI	250		24	SPR
26	100	SPR	PTD	SP	18.0	DUP	4759	1608		WEA	CCI	250		24	SPR
27	100	SPR	PTD	SP	22.0	DUP	4759	1975		WEA	CCI	250		24	SPR

6.5 x 54mm MANNLICHER-SCHOENAUER

The 6.5mm bullet was used in some of the earliest small-caliber cartridges designed for military use. A 6.5mm cartridge designed by the Steyr-Werke A. G. in Austria was adopted by Romania as their Model 1892 military cartridge, using a round-nose 160-grain bullet. Various modifications of the same basic cartridge were later adopted by the Netherlands, Portugal and Greece. Some of these were rimmed cartridges, and others were rimless.

The rimless 6.5x54mm Mannlicher-Schoenauer soon achieved some popularity as a sporting cartridge, and sporting rifles adapted to it have been made in Europe since the early 1900's. Sporting loads for the 6.5x54 Mannlicher-Schoenauer were produced before World War II in the United States, though production was not resumed after being interrupted during that period for military production.

The long 156-grain bullet commonly used in the 6.5x54mm Mannlicher-Schoenauer has a sectional density of about .320 (in the usual U.S. dimensions), equivalent to that of a .30-caliber bullet weighing about 212 grains. Consequently it gained a reputation as giving deep penetration for so small a caliber, and it was used with some success by African hunters on very large game, although the energy is not sufficient for such use except in the hands of a very careful shot, under ideal shooting conditions.

Loaded with modern 6.5mm bullets of 120 grains or more, it is entirely adequate for deer-size game. Cases are not readily formed from those of any commonly available type made in the U.S., but imported ammunition and Berdan primers suitable for reloading are available from suppliers such as Eastern Sports International, and possibly others. Military ammunition is also occasionally available from dealers in military surplus foreign ammunition, and the cases are reloadable if Berdan primers of the correct type can be found.

Max. Case Length: 2.110″ **Trim-To Length:** 2.100″
Max. Overall Length: 3.010″ **Primer Size:** Large Rifle **Bullet Dia.:** .264″

RIFLE LOADS FOR THE 6.5 x 54 mm MANNLICHER-SCHOENAUER

LOAD NUMBER	BULLET WEIGHT	BULLET BRAND	BULLET SHAPE	BULLET TYPE	POWDER WEIGHT	POWDER BRAND	POWDER TYPE	VELOCITY FPS	PRESSURE CUP	CASE BRAND	PRIMER BRAND	PRIMER TYPE	CARTRIDGE OAL	BARREL LENGTH	DATA SOURCE
1	85	SRA	PTD	HP	38.7	DUP	3031	3000		NOR	REM	9½		20	SRA
2	87	SPR	PTD	SP	40.8	DUP	3031	2901	44850	DOM	WIN	8½-120	2.745	18	NRA
3	87	SPR	PTD	SP	44.5	DUP	4320	2894	45250	DOM	WIN	8½-120	2.745	18	NRA
4	100	SRA	PTD	HP	36.7	DUP	3031	2800		NOR	REM	9½		20	SRA
5	120	SRA	PTD	SP	36.5	DUP	3031	2444	45240	NOR	WIN	8½-120	2.920	18	NRA
6	120	SRA	PTD	SP	35.9	DUP	3031	2600		NOR	REM	9½		20	SRA
7	129	HDY	PTD	SP	34.8	DUP	4064	2300		NOR	FED	210		18	HDY
8	140	SRA	PBT	SP	35.5	DUP	4064	2207	44330	DOM	WIN	8½-120	3.100	18	NRA
9	140	SRA	PBT	SP	35.1	DUP	4064	2300		NOR	REM	9½		20	SRA
10	140	HDY	PTD	SP	39.7	DUP	4350	2300		NOR	FED	210		18	HDY
11	160	HDY	RNN	SP	39.0	DUP	4350	2200		NOR	FED	210		18	HDY

6.5mm JAPANESE

The 6.5mm Japanese cartridge was employed in the Model 38 Arisaka Japanese rifle in 1905. Many of these rifles were captured and brought back to the U.S. by returning military personnel after World War II. Cases can be formed from .220 Swift brass, though the case body measures about .010 inch undersize at the rear, and the rims measure .013 inch undersize. The more satisfactory solution for acquiring cases is to buy imported ones from Norma. The performance of the cartridge is comparable to that of the .250 Savage or .257 Roberts, and it is suitable for hunting deer-size game. The Arisaka rifle does not make a very convenient sporter, however, and it is now little used for that purpose.

Some 6.5mm Arisaka rifles were rechambered by gunsmiths to accept .257 Roberts cases neck-expanded to accept 6.5mm bullets, because the .257 cases are more easily obtainable. The .257 case is considerably larger than the 6.5 Japanese case, and 6.5 Japanese ammunition should not be fired in a rechambered rifle. Not all gunsmiths remarked the rifle after rechambering, so it is well to make a chamber cast of any 6.5mm Arisaka rifle acquired, before firing it or reloading for it.

Max. Case Length: 1.984″ **Trim-To Length:** 1.974″
Max. Overall Length: 2.940″ **Primer Size:** Large
Rifle **Bullet Dia.:** .264″

FULL-CHARGE LOADS FOR THE 6.5 mm JAPANESE

LOAD NUMBER	BULLET WEIGHT	BULLET BRAND	BULLET SHAPE	BULLET TYPE	POWDER WEIGHT	POWDER BRAND	POWDER TYPE	VELOCITY FPS	PRESSURE CUP	CASE BRAND	PRIMER BRAND	PRIMER TYPE	CARTRIDGE OAL	BARREL LENGTH	DATA SOURCE
1	85	SRA	PTD	HP	39.6	DUP	4320	2800		NOR	REM	9½		19	SRA
2	100	SRA	PTD	HP	38.1	DUP	4320	2600		NOR	REM	9½		19	SRA
3	100	HDY	PTD	SP	39.9	DUP	4350	2800		NOR	FED	210		32	HDY
4	120	SRA	PTD	SP	39.1	DUP	4350	2400		NOR	REM	9½		19	SRA
5	129	HDY	PTD	SP	38.5	DUP	4350	2600		NOR	FED	210		32	HDY
6	139	NOR	SPD	SP	30.9	NOR	202	2270	<32200	NOR	NOR	LR	2.820	24	NOR
7	139	NOR	SPD	SP	37.7	NOR	MRP	2740	<37700	NOR	NOR	LR	2.810	24	NOR
8	139	NOR	PBT	SP	32.3	DUP	4064	2480	35100	NOR	NOR	LR	3.010	24	NRA
9	156	NOR	RNN	SP	29.3	DUP	4064	2149	37900	NOR	NOR	LR	2.890	24	NRA
10	156	NOR	RNN	SP	38.1	NOR	MRP	2310	<37700	NOR	NOR	LR	2.890	24	NOR
11	160	HDY	RNN	SP	37.3	HOD	4831	2300		NOR	FED	210		32	HDY

6.5mm CARCANO

The 6.5mm Carcano, also known as the 6.5mm Italian and 6.5mm Mannlicher-Carcano, was used as the Italian military cartridge in the Model 1891 rifle and rifle-caliber Italian machine guns. The nominal working chamber pressure was about 38,000 c.u.p., and it should not be exceeded in the Italian rifle. Many Italian service rifles of this caliber were imported after World War II, and sold at low prices by dealers in surplus arms. The case-head diameter is not the same as that of any readily available cartridge, and cases cannot readily be formed from any cases made by U.S. manufacturers. Imported ammunition is available from Norma, however, and the cases are reloadable.

Max. Case Length: 2.065″ **Trim-To Length:** 2.055″
Max. Overall Length: 2.900″ **Primer Size:** Large Rifle **Bullet Dia.:** .264″

RIFLE LOADS FOR THE 6.5 mm CARCANO

LOAD NUMBER	BULLET				POWDER			VELOCITY FPS	PRESSURE CUP	CASE BRAND	PRIMER		CARTRIDGE OAL	BARREL LENGTH	DATA SOURCE
	WEIGHT	BRAND	SHAPE	TYPE	WEIGHT	BRAND	TYPE				BRAND	TYPE			
1	77	NOR	PTD	SP	46.2	NOR	MRP	2965	<37700	NOR	NOR	LR	2.52	24	NOR
2	85	SRA	PTD	HP	38.8	DUP	4320	2700		NOR	REM	9½		21	SRA
3	100	HDY	PTD	SP	32.0	DUP	3031	2500		NOR	FED	210		21	HDY
4	100	SRA	PTD	HP	37.0	DUP	4320	2500		NOR	REM	9½		21	SRA
5	120	SRA	PTD	SP	33.0	DUP	3031	2587	35620	NOR			2.90	31	NRA
6	129	HDY	PTD	SP	32.9	DUP	4064	2300		NOR	FED	210		21	HDY
7	139	NOR	SPD	SP	43.2	NOR	MRP	2570	<37700	NOR	NOR	LR	2.85	24	NOR
8	140	HDY	RNN	SP	34.0	DUP	4064	2486	37350	NOR			2.97	31	NRA
9	156	NOR	RNN	SP	42.4	NOR	MRP	2435	<37700	NOR	NOR	LR	2.95	24	NOR
10	160	HDY	RNN	SP	38.5	DUP	4350	2200		NOR	FED	210		21	HDY

6.5 x 55mm

The 6.5x55mm cartridge was originally designed for military use in the Swedish Model 1894 Mauser carbine and the Norwegian 1894 Krag-Jorgensen rifle. Its military designation in the Scandinavian countries is the 6.5mm Model 94. It proved to be an excellent sporting cartridge, for hunting as well as target shooting, and its popularity in the Scandinavian countries is comparable to that of the .30-06 in the United States. Excellent match-type bullets are available in Norway and Sweden for the 6.5x55mm, and target shooters in those countries do excellent shooting with their 6.5x55 mm match rifles.

Cases for the 6.5x55mm can be formed from .30-06, .270 and similar brass, but the body diameter at the rear measures about .007 inch undersize in the reformed cases, and they will show a noticeable bulge upon firing. Though the NRA knows of no instance in which this expansion has resulted in a case split or other failure, the possibility obviously exists, so the best policy is to obtain new 6.5x55mm cases imported and sold by Norma. They accept standard U.S. primers, and are of good quality.

Max. Case Length: 2.160″ **Trim-To Length:** 2.150″
Max. Overall Length: 3.062″ **Primer Size:** Large Rifle **Bullet Dia.:** .264″

RIFLE LOADS FOR THE 6.5 x 55 mm

LOAD NUMBER	BULLET				POWDER			VELOCITY FPS	PRESSURE CUP	CASE BRAND	PRIMER		CARTRIDGE OAL	BARREL LENGTH	DATA SOURCE
	WEIGHT	BRAND	SHAPE	TYPE	WEIGHT	BRAND	TYPE				BRAND	TYPE			
1	77	NOR	PTD	SP	37.8	NOR	200	3115	<45000	NOR	NOR	LR	2.620	24	NOR
2	77	NOR	PTD	SP	43.0	DUP	3031	3144	44040	NOR	WIN	8½-120	2.610	17⅜	NRA
3	85	SRA	PTD	HP	42.1	DUP	3031	3000		NOR	REM	9½		18	SRA
4	87	SPR	PTD	SP	42.0	DUP	3031	3029	43670	NOR	WIN	8½-120	2.760	18	NRA
5	100	SRA	PTD	HP	42.0	DUP	4064	2843	44510	NOR	WIN	8½-120	2.840	17⅜	NRA
6	100	HDY	PTD	SP	41.8	DUP	4320	2800		NOR	REM	9½		18	HDY
7	100	SPR	PTD	HP	50.0	DUP	4350	2876		NOR	CCI	200		18	SPR
8	120	SRA	PTD	SP	40.0	DUP	4320	2558	44600	NOR	WIN	8½-120	3.00	17⅜	NRA
9	120	SPR	PTD	SP	48.0	DUP	4831	2714		NOR	CCI	200		18	SPR
10	129	HDY	RNN	SP	48.1	HOD	4831	2600		NOR	REM	9½		18	HDY
11	139	NOR	SPD	SP	49.4	NOR	MRP	2815	<49300	NOR	NOR	LR	2.990	24	NOR
12	139	NOR	PBT	FJ	43.0	DUP	4350	2388	43820	NOR	WIN	8½-120	3.020	17⅜	NRA
13	140	SRA	PBT	SP	38.2	DUP	4064	2400		NOR	REM	9½		18	SRA
14	140	HDY	PTD	SP	46.2	HOD	4831	2500		NOR	REM	9½		18	HDY
15	140	SPR	PTD	SP	45.0	DUP	4831	2480		NOR	CCI	200		18	SPR
16	156	NOR	RNN	SP	48.0	NOR	MRP	2645	<49300	NOR	NOR	LR	3.070	24	NOR
17	160	HDY	RNN	SP	39.0	DUP	4350	2121	42590	NOR	WIN	8½-120	3.010	17⅜	NRA
18	160	HDY	RNN	SP	44.5	HOD	4831	2400		NOR	REM	9½		18	HDY
19	160	HDY	RNN	SP	43.0	DUP	4350	2400		NOR	REM	9½		18	HDY
20	87	SPR	PTD	SP	13.0	DUP	4759	1611		NOR	CCI	200		18	SPR
21	87	SPR	PTD	SP	15.0	DUP	4759	1851		NOR	CCI	200		18	SPR
22	120	SPR	PTD	SP	15.0	DUP	4759	1673		NOR	CCI	200		18	SPR
23	120	SPR	PTD	SP	17.0	DUP	4759	1911		NOR	CCI	200		18	SPR

6.5mm REMINGTON MAGNUM

The 6.5mm Remington Magnum was introduced by Remington in 1966. The case capacity is intermediate between that of the 6.5x55mm Swedish and the .264 Winchester Magnum, and practically the same as that of the wildcat 6.5-06 or 6.5x63mm cartridge, if measured to the base of the case neck. Unfortunately, not all of this space is available for powder when the longer 6.5mm bullets are used, because the 2.80-inch maximum overall length of the cartridge allows only about .63 inch of bullet protrusion, and the case neck is only about .25 inch long, so any bullet longer than about .88 inch must intrude beyond the case neck into the powder space.

In custom rifles having magazines sufficiently long to accommodate cartridges longer than 2.80 inches, the problem can be alleviated by seating the bullets less deeply, and throating the barrel to accept the bullets so seated. However, the very short neck of the 6.5mm Remington Magnum case does not always hold the bullets very securely, especially when they are seated with more than the normal protrusion, and they may not withstand rough handling without loosening undesirably or being pushed deeper into the case.

The 6.5mm Remington Magnum cartridge was handicapped by the compromises in its mechanical design which were necessary to fit it into short-action guns that cannot accept cartridges more than 2.80 inches in overall length. It was further handicapped by the characteristics of the gun in which Remington chose to introduce it: the short-action Model 600 carbine with 18½-inch barrel. The short barrel was a disadvantage in achieving the velocities implied by the large powder capacity and small bore, and the Model 600 carbine was not a gun that attracted hunters seeking a first-class long-range hunting rifle. Though Remington later chambered the excellent Model 700 BDL for the 6.5mm Remington Magnum, that failed to redeem the unfavorable image of the cartridge, and it is no longer being offered in the Remington line of rifles. It appears to have been one of Remington's rare failures to judge correctly the conditions for public acceptance of a new cartridge.

The chamber pressure of the 6.5 mm Remington Magnum is normally limited to about 53,000 c.u.p., and the maximum product average for factory ammunition should not exceed 56,200 c.u.p.

Max. Case Length: 2.170″ **Trim-To Length:** 2.160″
Max. Overall Length: 2.800″ **Primer Size:** Large Rifle Magnum **Bullet Dia.:** .264″

RIFLE LOADS FOR THE 6.5 mm REMINGTON MAGNUM

LOAD NUMBER	BULLET				POWDER			VELOCITY FPS	PRESSURE CUP	CASE BRAND	PRIMER		CARTRIDGE OAL	BARREL LENGTH	DATA SOURCE
	WEIGHT	BRAND	SHAPE	TYPE	WEIGHT	BRAND	TYPE				BRAND	TYPE			
1	77	NOR	PTD	SP	52.0	DUP	3031	3559	49850	REM	REM	9½	2.700	20	NRA
2	85	SRA	PTD	HP	57.2	DUP	4350	3100		REM	REM	9½M		18½	SRA
3	87	SPR	PTD	SP	50.0	DUP	3031	3351	49420	REM	REM	9½	2.700	20	NRA
4	87	SPR	PTD	SP	57.0	DUP	4350	3437		REM	FED	215		24	SPR
5	87	SPR	PTD	SP	61.0	HOD	4831	3570	46700	REM	WIN	8½-120		26	HOD
6	100	SPR	PTD	HP	58.0	DUP	4831	3335	52300	REM	REM	9½M	2.800	24	DUP
7	100	SRA	PTD	HP	55.8	DUP	4350	3000		REM	REM	9½M		18½	SRA
8	100	HDY	PTD	SP	56.6	HOD	4831	3200		REM	ALC	LR		24	HDY
9	100	HDY	PTD	SP	55.0	HOD	H205	3310	49800	REM	WIN	8½-120		26	HOD
10	120	SPR	PTD	SP	54.0	DUP	4831	3060	52900	REM	REM	9½M	2.800	24	DUP
11	120	SRA	PTD	SP	51.2	DUP	4350	2700		REM	REM	9½M		18½	SRA
12	120	SPR	PTD	SP	59.0	HOD	4831	3286	51000	REM	WIN	8½-120		26	HOD
13	129	HDY	PTD	SP	54.2	HOD	4831	3000		REM	ALC	LR		24	HDY
14	140	HDY	PTD	SP	52.0	HOD	4831	2800		REM	ALC	LR		24	HDY
15	140	SPR	PTD	SP	52.0	DUP	4831	2755	<53000	REM	CCI	250		24	SPR
16	160	HDY	RNN	SP	50.2	HOD	4831	2600		REM	ALC	LR		24	HDY
17	87	SPR	PTD	SP	16.0	DUP	4759	1706		REM	FED	215		24	SPR
18	87	SPR	PTD	SP	18.0	DUP	4759	1915		REM	FED	215		24	SPR
19	120	SPR	PTD	SP	20.0	DUP	4759	1763		REM	CCI	250		24	SPR
20	120	SPR	PTD	SP	22.0	DUP	4759	1958		REM	CCI	250		24	SPR

.264 WINCHESTER MAGNUM

The .264 Winchester Magnum was introduced in 1960 for the popular and superb Model 70 rifle then in production. It was intended as a long-range hunting cartridge, and was designed with considerable sophistication for that specific purpose. One of the sophisticated features of the design was a 2-diameter 140-grain bullet, appreciably smaller in the front bearing section of the body than at the bore-sealing rear section.

Factory rifles were apparently throated for that bullet, and when conventionally shaped bullets were seated to the same overall cartridge length, they sometimes pre-engraved upon chambering, or the free run was so reduced as to raise chamber pressures significantly. Another difficulty was that the high sectional density of the small-caliber bullet, and the large capacity of the case, demanded a "slower" powder than any available to handloaders, and efforts to produce factory ballistics with handloads using canister powders resulted in excessive chamber pressures.

Unsatisfactory results obtained by handloaders with the .264 Winchester cartridge reflected unfavorably on its image. The introduction of the 7mm Remington Magnum in 1962, a cartridge intended for the same uses, was clearly a competitive contender that affected the acceptance of the .264 Winchester Magnum. For these and perhaps other reasons, the .264 Winchester Magnum has not achieved great popularity. Bullets designed specifically for the .264 Winchester Magnum are now available. If more suitable canister powders were available, its potential capabilities could be more nearly realized, and its popularity might increase. Even with its present limitations, it is a good long-range hunting cartridge, suitable for all but the largest North American game.

The normal maximum working pressure for the .264 Winchester Magnum is about 54,000 c.u.p. The maximum product average for factory ammunition should not exceed 57,200 c.u.p.

Max. Case Length: 2.500″ **Trim-To Length:** 2.490″
Max. Overall Length: 3.340″ **Primer Size:** Large Rifle, Large Rifle Magnum **Bullet Dia.:** .264″

RIFLE LOADS FOR THE .264 WINCHESTER MAGNUM

LOAD NUMBER	BULLET				POWDER			VELOCITY FPS	PRESSURE CUP	CASE BRAND	PRIMER		CARTRIDGE OAL	BARREL LENGTH	DATA SOURCE
	WEIGHT	BRAND	SHAPE	TYPE	WEIGHT	BRAND	TYPE				BRAND	TYPE			
1	85	SRA	PTD	HP	72.7	HOD	4831	3700		WIN	REM	9½M		24	SRA
2	87	SPR	PTD	HP	73.0	HOD	4831	3812	54100		CCI	250		26	HOD
3	87	SPR	PTD	HP	64.0	DUP	4831	3529		WIN	FED	215		24	SPR
4	100	SRA	PTD	HP	60.0	DUP	4350	3385	53900	REM	REM	9½M	3.100	24	DUP
5	100	SPR	PTD	HP	66.0	HOD	H450	3428		WIN	FED	215		24	SPR
6	100	HDY	PTD	SP	68.5	HOD	4831	3600		WIN	REM	9½		26	HDY
7	120	SRA	PTD	SP	60.3	DUP	4350	3300		WIN	REM	9½M		24	SRA
8	120	SPR	PTD	SP	59.0	DUP	4831	3082	<54000	WIN	CCI	250		24	SPR
9	120	SRA	PTD	SP	65.0	HOD	4831	3369	52100	WIN	CCI	250		26	HOD
10	125	NOS			63.0	NOR	MRP	3110		WIN	WIN	8½-120		24	NOS
11	129	HDY	RNN	SP	63.0	HOD	4831	3100		WIN	REM	9½		26	HDY
12	140	SRA	PBT	SP	54.5	DUP	4831	2875	53600	REM	REM	9½M	3.230	24	DUP
13	140	HDY	PTD	SP	60.2	HOD	4831	3000		WIN	REM	9½		26	HDY
14	140	HDY	PTD	SP	61.0	HOD	4831	3065	52000	WIN	CCI	250		26	HOD
15	140	NOS	PTD	SP	72.0	HOD	H870	3006		WIN	WIN	8½-120		24	NOS
16	140	HDY	PTD	SP	73.0	HOD	H870	3163	54200	WIN	CCI	250		26	HOD
17	140	SPR	PTD	SP	73.0	HOD	H870	3130	<54000	WIN	CCI	250		24	SPR
18	160	HDY	RNN	SP	55.6	HOD	4831	2600		WIN	REM	9½		26	HDY
19	120	SPR	PTD	SP	21.0	DUP	4198	1760		WIN	CCI	250		24	SPR
20	120	SPR	PTD	SP	23.0	DUP	4198	1932		WIN	CCI	250		24	SPR

.270 WINCHESTER

The .270 Winchester cartridge was introduced in 1925, simultaneously with the introduction of the Model 54 bolt-action rifle, which was chambered for the new cartridge as well as for the .30-06. The .270 was a success almost immediately, and it has remained popular for the 55 years since then. It is based on the .30-06 case, simply necked-down to accept .278-inch bullets, and left at a length of about 2.54 inches, which measures about .045 inch longer than the .30-06 case. Serviceable .270 cases can be formed simply by running .30-06 brass into a .270 full-length resizing die, though the reformed cases are of course somewhat shorter than factory .270 cases.

The original factory load for the .270 used a 130-grain bullet at a nominal muzzle velocity of 3,160 fps, impressively faster than the 150-grain factory load for the .30-06 which was then listed at 2,700 fps. The contrast was due largely to the fact that the .270 operated at a maximum working pressure of 54,000 c.u.p., whereas the limit for the .30-06 was 50,000 c.u.p., and the .30-06 load at 2,700 fps did not crowd that chamber pressure very closely. It was subsequently found that the 3,160 fps velocity advertized for the .270 load could not be consistently maintained at acceptable chamber pressures, and it was reduced first to 3,140 fps, and later to 3,110 fps where it remains today. Nevertheless, the .270 ballistics were impressive, and lightning-bolt kills on deer-size animals gained a very favorable reputation for the cartridge. The popularity of the .270 was further increased by the writing of the late Jack O'Connor, for whom it seemed to be the favorite cartridge.

The 130-grain bullets originally available were said by some users to expand too quickly for adequate penetration on animals larger than whitetail deer (though this was disputed by others), and in 1933 Winchester introduced a .270 load using 150-grain bullets at a nominal velocity of 2,850 fps. In 1937, a varmint load using 100-grain bullets was introduced.

With modern controlled-expansion bullets, the .270 is suitable for all but the largest North American game, and some loyal partisans would dispute even that limitation. It is, beyond reasonable question, an excellent hunting cartridge, well deserving the popularity that it has enjoyed for more than 50 years. It has probably also fueled more fiercely partisan arguments than any other cartridge in the last half century about its merits relative to those of all other big-game loads.

The maximum product average chamber pressure for .270 factory ammunition should not exceed 57,200 c.u.p.

Max. Case Length: 2.540″ **Trim-To Length:** 2.530″
Max. Overall Length: 3.340″ **Primer Size:** Large Rifle **Bullet Dia.:** .277″

LOAD NUMBER	BULLET				POWDER			VELOCITY FPS	PRESSURE CUP	CASE BRAND	PRIMER		CARTRIDGE OAL	BARREL LENGTH	DATA SOURCE
	WEIGHT	BRAND	SHAPE	TYPE	WEIGHT	BRAND	TYPE				BRAND	TYPE			
1	90	SRA	PTD	HP	55.9	HOD	H380	3600		WIN	WIN	8½-120		26	SRA
2	90	SRA	PTD	HP	60.9	DUP	4350	3500		WIN	WIN	8½-120		26	SRA
3	100	REM	PTD	SP	60.0	DUP	4350	3365	53900	REM	REM	9½	3.075	23	DUP
4	100	HDY	PTD	SP	60.0	DUP	4831	3200		FRO	WIN	8½-120	3.075	24	HDY
5	100	SPR	PTD	HP	61.0	DUP	4831	3303	<54000	WIN	CCI	200		22	SPR
6	100	WIN	PTD	SP	56.0	WIN	760	3335	48000	WIN	WIN	8½-120	3.340	24	WIN
7	110	SRA	PTD	SP	56.5	WIN	760	3300		REM	WIN	8½-120		26	SRA
8	110	HDY	PTD	HP	62.0	HOD	H450	3200		FRO	WIN	8½-120	3.305	24	HDY
9	130	REM	PTD	SP	59.0	DUP	4831	3110	53600	REM	REM	9½	3.250	23	DUP
10	130	WIN	PTD	SP	60.5	WIN	785	3100	51000	WIN	WIN	8½-120		24	WIN
11	130	SPR	PTD	SP	62.0	NOR	MRP	3071	<54000	WIN	CCI	200		22	SPR
12	130	HDY	PTD	SP	61.7	HOD	H450	3100		FRO	WIN	8½-120		24	HDY
13	130	SRA	PBT	SP	54.9	DUP	4350	3100		WIN	WIN	8½-120		26	SRA
14	130	NOS	PTD	SP	57.0	DUP	4831	3053		NOR	REM	9½		26	NOS
15	150	REM	RNN	SP	57.0	DUP	4831	2980	53900	REM	REM	9½	3.220	23	DUP
16	150	WIN	PTD	SP	58.0	WIN	785	2880	51000	WIN	WIN	8½-120		24	WIN
17	150	NOS	PTD	SP	55.0	DUP	4831	2904		NOR	REM	9½		26	NOS
18	150	SRA	PBT	SP	56.4	HOD	H450	2900		REM	WIN	8½-120		26	SRA
19	150	SPR	PTD	SP	55.0	DUP	4831	2827	<54000	WIN	CCI	200		22	SPR
20	150	HDY	PTD	SP	54.1	DUP	4350	2900		FRO	WIN	8½-120		24	HDY
21	150	NOR	PTD	SP	58.4	NOR	MRP	2969	<52200	NOR	NOR	LR	3.23	24	NOR
22	160	NOS	SPD	SP	54.0	DUP	4831	2806		NOR	REM	9½		26	NOS
23	100	NOS	PBT	SP	49.0	DUP	4320	3334		NOR	REM	9½		26	NOS
24	140	HDY	PBT	SP	59.1	HOD	H450	3000		FRO	FED	210		22	HDY
25	140	HDY	PBT	SP	55.7	DUP	4831	2900		FRO	FED	210		22	HDY
26	100	SPR	PTD	SP	16.0	DUP	4759	1548		WIN	CCI	200		22	SPR
27	100	SPR	PTD	SP	20.0	DUP	4759	1915		WIN	CCI	200		22	SPR
28	150	SPR	PTD	SP	20.0	DUP	4759	1651		WIN	CCI	200		22	SPR
29	150	SPR	PTD	SP	24.0	DUP	4759	1998		WIN	CCI	200		22	SPR

.270 WEATHERBY MAGNUM

The .270 Weatherby Magnum cartridge has about 25 per cent more powder capacity than has the .270 Winchester, and consequently can produce higher velocities with the same bullets at comparable chamber pressures. Whether this is an advantage has been disputed by some partisan defenders of the .270 Winchester, but it is unquestionably a fact. The Weatherby 150-grain factory load at 3,245 fps is 345 fps faster than the Winchester-Western .270 Winchester 150-grain factory load at 2,900 fps. The maximum operating chamber pressure for the Weatherby cartridge is 55,000 c.u.p., compared to 54,000 c.u.p. for the .270 Winchester.

The .270 Weatherby is an excellent long-range hunting cartridge, having extremely flat trajectory, and sufficient bullet weight for hunting practically any North American game, with bullets of proper construction.

Max. Case Length: 2.549" **Trim-To Length:** 2.539"
Max. Overall Length: 3.250" **Primer Size:** Large Rifle Magnum, Large Rifle **Bullet Dia.:** .277"

RIFLE LOADS FOR THE .270 WEATHERBY MAGNUM

LOAD NUMBER	BULLET				POWDER			VELOCITY FPS	PRESSURE CUP	CASE BRAND	PRIMER		CARTRIDGE OAL	BARREL LENGTH	DATA SOURCE
	WEIGHT	BRAND	SHAPE	TYPE	WEIGHT	BRAND	TYPE				BRAND	TYPE			
1	90	SRA	PTD	HP	77.5	HOD	4831	3700		WEA	FED	215		26	SRA
2	90	SRA	PTD	HP	74.9	DUP	4831	3700		WEA	FED	215		26	SRA
3	100	HDY	PTD	SP	70.0	DUP	4350	3636	49550	WEA	FED	215	3.250	26	WEA
4	100	HDY	PTD	SP	72.0	DUP	4350	3764	54540	WEA	FED	215	3.250	26	WEA

LOAD NUMBER	BULLET				POWDER			VELOCITY FPS	PRESSURE CUP	CASE BRAND	PRIMER		CARTRIDGE OAL	BARREL LENGTH	DATA SOURCE
	WEIGHT	BRAND	SHAPE	TYPE	WEIGHT	BRAND	TYPE				BRAND	TYPE			
5	100	HDY	PTD	SP	76.0	HOD	4831	3594	47790	WEA	FED	215	3.250	26	WEA
6	100	HDY	PTD	SP	78.0	HOD	4831	3705	52890	WEA	FED	215	3.250	26	WEA
7	100	HDY	PTD	SP	77.2	NOR	MRP	3760	51400	WEA	FED	215	3.250	26	WEA
8	110	SRA	PTD	SP	76.0	HOD	4831	3500		WEA	FED	215		26	SRA
9	110	SRA	PTD	SP	72.6	DUP	4831	3500		WEA	FED	215		26	SRA
10	130	SRA	PBT	SP	68.0	DUP	4831	3200		WEA	FED	215		26	SRA
11	130	HDY	PTD	SP	70.0	HOD	4831	3178	47600	WEA	FED	215	3.250	26	WEA
12	130	HDY	PTD	SP	72.0	HOD	4831	3301	52980	WEA	FED	215	3.250	26	WEA
13	150	HDY	PTD	SP	68.5	NOR	MRP	3245	51800	WEA	FED	215	3.250	26	WEA
14	170	SPR	SPD	SP	78.0	HOD	H870	2869		WEA	CCI	250		26	HOD

7mm-08 Remington

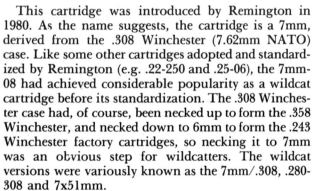

This cartridge was introduced by Remington in 1980. As the name suggests, the cartridge is a 7mm, derived from the .308 Winchester (7.62mm NATO) case. Like some other cartridges adopted and standardized by Remington (e.g. .22-250 and .25-06), the 7mm-08 had achieved considerable popularity as a wildcat cartridge before its standardization. The .308 Winchester case had, of course, been necked up to form the .358 Winchester, and necked down to 6mm to form the .243 Winchester factory cartridges, so necking it to 7mm was an obvious step for wildcatters. The wildcat versions were variously known as the 7mm/.308, .280-308 and 7x51mm.

It should be carefully noted that custom chambers intended for the wildcat versions of this cartridge may not be compatible with the standard factory version. In particular, the maximum length of the 7mm-08 factory case is 2.035 inches, or .020-inch more than that of the .308 Winchester. In custom chambers intended for use with necked-down .308 Winchester cases, the factory 7mm-08 cartridge case may be slightly too long. In those circumstances, chambering a standard 7mm-08 cartridge in the wildcat chamber can cause the case mouth to be jammed forcibly into the constricting shoulder at the chamber mouth. *That is a potentially hazardous condition.* The case mouth cannot expand normally to release the bullet, and chamber pressures might be increased to hazardous levels. Owners of custom rifles should have their chamber dimensions carefully checked, by a competent gunsmith, to determine whether the dimensions are compatible with the longer cases of 7mm-08 Remington factory loads, before using the 7mm-08 factory loads, or factory cases in handloads. If the dimensions of the custom chamber are not compatible with factory cases, rechambering with a standard 7mm-08 reamer will be required.

If 7mm-08 cases are obtained by reforming .308 Winchester or 7.62mm NATO military brass, it is im-

perative that the neck thickness be carefully checked, and the necks thinned by reaming or turning if necessary. The outside diameter of the neck of a loaded cartridge *must not exceed .315-inch,* if the weapon has a chamber meeting standard industry dimensions for the 7mm-08 cartridge. Custom chambers may have smaller neck diameters, and case necks must be thinned accordingly for use in such chambers. Cases formed from .308 or 7.62mm NATO brass will be slightly shorter than 7mm-08 factory cases, but that is not a hazardous condition.

Another obvious possibility is to form 7mm-08 cases by neck-expanding .243 Winchester brass. The .243 Winchester case has a maximum length of 2.045 inches, or .010-inch more than the 7mm-08 case. Thus, cases formed from .243 Winchester brass will normally require trimming, after forming, to the proper length for 7mm-08 cases, which is 2.035 inches - .020-inch.

The powder capacity of the 7mm-08 is nearly the same as that of the 7x57mm Mauser, and it is most probable that the ballistics of the two cartridges would be nearly the same, if the same limits of chamber pressure were applied to both. However, the 7x57mm has, in the United States, been limited to relatively low chamber pressures, probably in deference to the many old rifles of uncertain strength that might still be fired with 7x57 factory loads. The 7mm-08 is not subject to that limitation, and its factory ballistics are considerably more impressive than those of the 7x57 Mauser. A further advantage of the 7mm-08 is that its shorter overall length will permit its use in some short-action rifles which cannot accommodate the longer 7x57 mm Mauser cartridge.

The 7mm-08 had achieved considerable popularity in the sport of shooting metallic silhouettes, even before the cartridge was standardized, and it is anticipated that its popularity among silhouette shooters will now surge upward still further. The excellent Sierra 168-grain and Hornady 162-grain boattail match bullets are well adapted to target loads in the 7mm-08 cartridge. The wide variety of 7mm hunting bullets available to handloaders will make the 7mm-08 a very versatile hunting cartridge as well. It should serve very well for any purpose from long-range varmint shooting, to hunting practically any big

game found in the United States, if appropriate bullets are used.

Max. Case Length: 2.035″ **Trim-To Length:** 2.025″
Max. Overall Length: 2.800″ **Primer Size:** Large Rifle
Bullet Dia.: .284″

RIFLE LOADS FOR THE 7mm-08 REMINGTON

LOAD NUMBER	BULLET				POWDER			VELOCITY FPS	PRESSURE CUP	CASE BRAND	PRIMER		CARTRIDGE OAL	BARREL LENGTH	DATA SOURCE
	WEIGHT	BRAND	SHAPE	TYPE	WEIGHT	BRAND	TYPE				BRAND	TYPE			
1	120	HDY	PTD	SP	42.4	DUP	4320	2800		REM	REM	9½	2.730	18½	HDY
2	120	SRA	PTD	SP	41.5	DUP	3031	3000		REM	REM	9½	2.765	24	SRA
3	120				42.0	HOD	BL-C(2)	2799						18½	HOD
4	139	HDY	PTD	SP	40.5	DUP	3031	2830	51900	REM	REM	9½	2.800	24	DUP
5	139	HDY	PTD	SP	42.5	DUP	4064	2835	51300	REM	REM	9½	2.800	24	DUP
6	139	HDY	PTD	SP	40.5	DUP	4895	2790	51000	REM	REM	9½	2.800	24	DUP
7	139	HDY	PTD	SP	41.5	DUP	4320	2800	50400	REM	REM	9½	2.800	24	DUP
8	139	HDY	PTD	SP	46.0	DUP	4350	2750	44200	REM	REM	9½	2.800	24	DUP
9	140	SRA	PTD	SP	49.0	HOD	H205	2900		REM	REM	9½	2.780	24	SRA
10	140				45.0	HOD	H414	2646						18½	HOD
11	154	HDY	PTD	SP	39.7	DUP	4064	2500		REM	REM	9½	2.830	18½	HDY
12	154	HDY	PTD	SP	44.3	HOD	H205	2500		REM	REM	9½	2.830	18½	HDY
13	160	SRA	PBT	SP	46.3	DUP	4350	2700		REM	REM	9½	2.800	24	SRA
14	160	SRA	PBT	SP	45.6	HOD	H205	2700		REM	REM	9½	2.800	24	SRA
15	162	HDY	PBT	HP	37.7	DUP	4064	2400		REM	REM	9½	2.850	18½	HDY
16	162	HDY	PBT	HP	37.8	NOR	202	2400		REM	REM	9½	2.850	18½	HDY
17	162	HDY	PBT	HP	42.6	HOD	H205	2400		REM	REM	9½	2.850	18½	HDY
18	168	SRA	PBT	HP	37.0	DUP	3031	2515	50500	REM	REM	9½	2.800	24	DUP
19	168	SRA	PBT	HP	38.0	DUP	4064	2475	46000	REM	REM	9½	2.800	24	DUP
20	168	SRA	PBT	HP	38.0	DUP	4895	2535	51400	REM	REM	9½	2.800	24	DUP
21	168	SRA	PBT	HP	40.0	DUP	4320	2590	51800	REM	REM	9½	2.800	24	DUP
22	168	SRA	PBT	HP	40.0	DUP	4350	2365	39800	REM	REM	9½	2.800	24	DUP
23	168	SRA	PBT	HP	44.0	HOD	H205	2600		REM	REM	9½	2.800	24	SRA
24	168	SRA	PBT	HP	40.7	WIN	748	2600		REM	REM	9½	2.800	24	SRA
25	170	SRA	RNN	SP	44.7	DUP	4350	2500		REM	REM	9½	2.800	24	SRA
26	170	SRA	RNN	SP	48.3	NOR	MRP	2500		REM	REM	9½	2.800	24	SRA
27	175	SRA	PBT	SP	39.7	DUP	4064	2500		REM	REM	9½	2.800	24	SRA
28	175	SRA	PBT	SP	42.7	HOD	H205	2500		REM	REM	9½	2.800	24	SRA
29	175	HDY	PTD	SP	41.8	DUP	4350	2300		REM	REM	9½	2.810	18½	HDY
30	175	HDY	PTD	SP	37.8	WIN	748	2300		REM	REM	9½	2.810	18½	HDY

7 x 57mm MAUSER

The 7x57mm Mauser is among the oldest smokeless military cartridges, having been designed by Paul Mauser in 1892 and first offered in the Model 1892 Mauser military rifle. Spain was the first major power to adopt the cartridge, and its use against U.S. forces during the Spanish-American war undoubtedly influenced the American thinking that culminated in the Mauser-type Model 1903 rifle by the United States.

The chamber pressure of 7x57mm Mauser sporting ammunition made in the U.S. has always been quite conservative, probably in deference to the many old Model 1893 Mauser rifles chambered for it, which are intended for ammunition not exceeding about 45,000 c.u.p. For such rifles, the handloader should not

exceed the pressures of U.S. factory loads, which are limited to 46,000 c.u.p. European manufacturers, on the other hand, load 7x57mm sporting ammunition at somewhat higher pressures, up to about 49,300 c.u.p., as indicated by load number 11 which is recommended by Norma. In Mauser Model 98 rifles, and others having comparably strong actions, pressures up to 50,000 c.u.p. are not excessive and would show appreciable improvement over the performance of U.S. factory loads. Unfortunately, few such loads have been developed in pressure barrels, using American components, so the handloader incurs some risk in trying to develop them.

While calculation is not recommended as a basis for

establishing maximum loads without verification in a pressure barrel, there are some rules that can be useful in developing loads for strong 7x57mm rifles, based on pressure-tested data for loads that do not exceed 46,000 c.u.p. As a first approximation, chamber pressure is expected to increase about in proportion to the square of the charge weight, whereas velocity is expected to increase about in direct proportion to charge weight, if all other factors remain the same, On that basis, the increase in charge weight corresponding to a pressure increase from 46,000 to 50,000 c.u.p. would be about four per cent, and the corresponding velocity increase would also be about four per cent. Using load number nine as an example, it could be estimated that an increase in charge weight from 47.0 grains of IMR-4350 to 48.9 grains would increase the pressure from 46,000 c.u.p. to about 50,000 c.u.p., and the velocity from 2,650 fps to about 2,760 fps. No such load should be tried without working up in small increments from a charge weight 10 per cent lower, watching carefully for any signs of excessive pressure. In any event, the maximum charge weight based on this method of estimation should not be exceeded, even in the strongest rifles.

The maximum product average chamber pressure for the 7x57mm Mauser ammunition loaded by factories in the U.S. is 49,200 c.u.p.
Max. Case Length: 2.235″ **Trim-To Length:** 2.225″
Max. Overall Length: 3.065″ **Primer Size:** Large Rifle **Bullet Dia.:** .284″

RIFLE LOADS FOR THE 7 x 57 mm MAUSER

LOAD NUMBER	BULLET				POWDER			VELOCITY FPS	PRESSURE CUP	CASE BRAND	PRIMER		CARTRIDGE OAL	BARREL LENGTH	DATA SOURCE
	WEIGHT	BRAND	SHAPE	TYPE	WEIGHT	BRAND	TYPE				BRAND	TYPE			
1	115	SPR	PTD	HP	51.0	DUP	4350	2811	<46000	WIN	CCI	200		22	SPR
2	120	HDY	PTD	SP	49.1	DUP	4350	2800		REM	WIN	8½-120		24	HDY
3	120	SRA	PTD	SP	50.0	DUP	4831	2800		WIN	WIN	8½-120		29	SRA
4	125	WIN	PTD	SP	48.7	WIN	760	2885	43500	WIN	WIN	8½-120		24	WIN
5	130	SPR	PTD	SP	50.0	DUP	4831	2750	46000	REM	REM	9½	2.965	24	DUP
6	139	HDY	PTD	SP	37.5	DUP	3031	2609	45500	WIN	WIN	8½-120	3.000	24	NRA
7	140	NOS	PBT	SP	49.0	HOD	H414	2792		WIN	WIN	8½-120		24	NOS
8	140	SRA	PTD	SP	53.2	HOD	4831	2800		WIN	WIN	8½-120		29	SRA
9	145	SPR	PTD	SP	47.0	DUP	4350	2650	46000	REM	REM	9½	3.065	24	DUP
10	150	WIN	PTD	SP	46.5	WIN	760	2660	43500	WIN	WIN	8½-120		24	WIN
11	150	NOR	PBT	SP	44.0	NOR	202	2690	<49300	NOR	NOR	LR	3.050	24	NOR
12	150	NOS	PBT	SP	46.0	DUP	4350	2588		WIN	WIN	8½-120		24	NOS
13	154	HDY	RNN	SP	47.0	DUP	4350	2573	44940	WIN	WIN	8½-120	2.940	24	NRA
14	160	SPR	PTD	SP	47.5	DUP	4831	2540	45600	REM	REM	9½	3.065	24	DUP
15	160	SRA	PBT	SP	49.9	HOD	4831	2600		WIN	WIN	8½-120		29	SRA
16	160	NOS	PTD	SP	47.0	DUP	4831	2570		WIN	WIN	8½-120		24	NOS
17	162	HDY	PBT	HP	45.0	WIN	760	2500		REM	WIN	8½-120		24	HDY
18	168	SRA	PBT	HP	43.5	DUP	4350	2500		WIN	WIN	8½-120		29	SRA
19	170	SRA	RNN	SP	48.8	HOD	4831	2500		WIN	WIN	8½-120		29	SRA
20	175	HDY	RNN	SP	48.5	HOD	4831	2500		REM	WIN	8½-120		24	HDY
21	175	SPR	SPD	SP	48.0	DUP	4831	2578	<50000	WIN	CCI	200		22	SPR
22	175	NOS	SPD	SP	43.0	WIN	760	2456		WIN	WIN	8½-120		24	NOS
23	175	WIN	RNN	SP	44.0	WIN	760	2400	44500	WIN	WIN	8½-120		24	WIN
24	130	SPR	PTD	SP	18.0	DUP	4759	1658		WIN	CCI	200		22	SPR
25	130	SPR	PTD	SP	22.0	DUP	4759	2004		WIN	CCI	200		22	SPR
26	175	SPR	SPD	SP	22.0	DUP	4198	1633		WIN	CCI	200		22	SPR
27	175	SPR	SPD	SP	26.0	DUP	4198	1915		WIN	CCI	200		22	SPR

.284 WINCHESTER

The .284 Winchester was introduced in 1963, during that rather remarkable period from 1960 to 1966 that also saw the introduction of the .264 Winchester Magnum (1960), 7mm Remington Magnum (1962), 6mm Remington (1963) and 6.5mm Remington Magnum (1966). Perhaps it was inevitable that, among these five new cartridges competing for the market in the 6mm-to-7mm range, some were doomed to failure or only limited success. The .284 is one that enjoyed only limited success.

Its handicaps were in many ways similar to those that beset the 6.5mm Remington Magnum, in that its mechanical design was compromised by the need to fit it into short-action rifles that would not accept a cartridge longer than about 2.80 inches. The case length (2.17 inches) and overall cartridge length (2.80 inches) are identical to those of the 6.5mm Remington Magnum, and they imposed the same handicaps upon it. The case neck is only about .285-inch long, and bullets longer than about .91-inch must be seated so as to intrude into the powder space behind the junction of the neck and shoulder. For .284-inch pointed bullets of good ballistic shape, this includes practically any bullet weighing more than about 115 grains, and no effective 7mm game bullet weighs less than that.

Unlike the 6.5mm Remington Magnum, the .284 Winchester does not employ a belted-magnum case, but instead uses an unusual rebated-rim design. The rim diameter measures nominally .473 inch and therefore suited to the same bolt-face dimensions as the .308 Winchester, .243 and similar cases, while the body diameter just forward of the extractor groove is about .500 inch., or quite nearly the same as that of a typical belted-magnum case just forward of the belt. This design allows a case capacity nearly equal to that of the .270 or .30-06, within the length constraints of the short cartridge, while also permitting interchangeability of breech-bolt design with those of .308 and .243 rifles of the same type. This feature is unique among American cartridges, and has attracted many wildcatters to use the .284 case for innumerable necking-up or necking-down experiments.

The .284 Winchester was apparently designed to provide in the short-action Model 88 lever-operated rifle a cartridge having ballistics comparable to those of the popular .270 Winchester. It achieved that aim, providing 2,736 foot-pounds of muzzle energy from a 125-grain bullet at 3,140 fps, compared to 2,791 foot-pounds in the .270 from a 130-grain bullet at 3,110 fps. Some other short-action rifles, such as the Model 99 Savage lever-action were also chambered for the .284 briefly, but these chamberings are now discontinued, as is also the Winchester Model 88 rifle itself. Unless a new rifle chambered for the .284 appears on the market, the .284 cartridge now seems doomed to obsolescence.

The working maximum chamber pressure for the .284 Winchester cartridge is about 54,000 c.u.p., and the maximum product average for factory ammunition should not exceed 57,200 c.u.p.

Max. Case Length: 2.170″ **Trim-To Length:** 2.160″
Max. Overall Length: 2.800″ **Primer Size:** Large Rifle **Bullet Dia.:** .284″

RIFLE LOADS FOR THE .284 WINCHESTER

LOAD NUMBER	BULLET				POWDER			VELOCITY FPS	PRESSURE CUP	CASE BRAND	PRIMER		CARTRIDGE OAL	BARREL LENGTH	DATA SOURCE
	WEIGHT	BRAND	SHAPE	TYPE	WEIGHT	BRAND	TYPE				BRAND	TYPE			
1	115	SPR	PTD	HP	57.0	WIN	760	3122	<54000	WIN	CCI	250		22	SPR
2	120	SRA	PTD	SP	57.5	DUP	4350	3100		WIN	WIN	8½–120		22	SRA
3	120	HDY	PTD	SP	49.2	DUP	4064	3100		WIN	REM	9½		22	HDY
4	125	WIN	PTD	SP	57.0	WIN	760	3180	50000	WIN	WIN	8½–120		24	WIN
5	130	SPR	PTD	SP	57.0	DUP	4350	3130	53600	WIN	WIN	8½–120	2.800	24	DUP
6	139	HDY	PTD	SP	57.7	HOD	4831	3000		WIN	REM	9½		22	HDY
7	140	SRA	PTD	SP	48.7	DUP	4064	2900		WIN	WIN	8½–120		22	SRA
8	140	SRA	PTD	SP	48.0	HOD	BL-C-(2)	2914	47400	WIN	WIN	8½–120		26	HOD
9	145	SPR	PTD	SP	56.0	DUP	4350	2940	<54000	WIN	CCI	200		22	SPR
10	150	WIN	PTD	SP	54.0	WIN	760	2890	49000	WIN	WIN	8½–120		24	WIN
11	150	WIN	PTD	SP	56.0	DUP	4350	3008	46910	WIN	WIN	8½–120	2.790	26	NRA
12	154	HDY	PTD	SP	54.5	DUP	4350	2900		WIN	REM	9½		22	HDY
13	160	SPR	PTD	SP	47.0	DUP	4064	2760	53700	WIN	WIN	8½–120	2.800	24	DUP
14	160	SRA	PBT	SP	52.4	DUP	4350	2700		WIN	WIN	8½–120		22	SRA
15	168	SRA	PBT	HP	52.7	DUP	4350	2700		WIN	WIN	8½–120		22	SRA
16	170	SRA	RNN	SP	50.9	DUP	4350	2600		WIN	WIN	8½–120		22	SRA
17	175	HDY	RNN	SP	52.4	HOD	4831	2600		WIN	REM	9½		22	HDY
18	130	SPR	PTD	SP	20.0	DUP	4759	1694		WIN	CCI	200		22	SPR
19	130	SPR	PTD	SP	24.0	DUP	4759	2029		WIN	CCI	200		22	SPR

.280 REMINGTON/ 7mm EXPRESS REMINGTON

The .280 Remington cartridge was introduced in 1957, and initially was used in the Model 740 autoloading rifle. The object was apparently to provide in the Model 740 autoloader a cartridge having ballistics comparable to those of the .270 Winchester, but avoiding the relatively high chamber-pressure level of 54,000 c.u.p. which makes the .270 less than ideal in an autoloading sporting rifle. Probably by virtue of the slightly larger bullet diameter, the .280 Remington practically matched the .270 Winchester performance with a 150-grain bullet at 2,890 fps (compared to 2,900 fps in the .270 Winchester) within a chamber-pressure limit of 50,000 c.u.p.

The .280 Remington is a well-designed cartridge, having practically the same overall length as the .30-06, with adequate neck length (.34 inch) for long pointed bullets, and the general configuration of the well proven .30-06 and .270 cases. The only important difference between the .280 case and those of the .270 or .30-06, except the difference in neck diameters, is that the .280 case measures about .051 longer in head-to-shoulder length, a design precaution against the inadvertent firing of a .280 cartridge in a loosely chambered .270 rifle, in which it would produce excessive chamber pressure if it could be chambered and fired.

Notwithstanding its many excellent qualities, the .280 Remington did not achieve great popularity. Apparently following the example of their earlier success in the revival of the .244/6mm Remington cartridge in 1963, Remington in 1979 renamed the .280 the "7mm Express Remington," and improved the performance of the factory loads. The name of the new cartridge was originally announced as the "7mm-06," but was changed before significant quantities of guns or ammunition were shipped, to avoid possible confusion with any of the various wildcat cartridges by that name which have shorter head-to-shoulder length. Such cartridges would present a headspace problem if they were used in a rifle chambered for the Remington factory cartridge.

The new 7mm Express factory load produces a nominal muzzle velocity of 2,970 fps with a 150-grain bullet. The new cartridge was developed and standardized on the basis of chamber pressures measured in an electronic-transducer system, of a particular type that has been approved by U.S. manufacturers as an acceptable alternate to the long-standard copper-crusher system. The industry is extending the use of this electronic-transducer system, which will probably supersede the copper-crusher system completely in due time. Though this change has some advantages, as described in an article elsewhere in this book, it also poses some problems of interpretation, because the electronic-transducer pressures are not numerically the same as copper-crusher pressures. Furthermore, the pressures are not related by any simple universal factor or difference by means of which measurements of the one kind can be accurately converted to measurements of the other kind.

In the particular case of the 7mm Express cartridge, Remington has advised that the electronic-transducer pressure limit is equivalent to a maximum average working pressure limit of 50,900 c.u.p. as measured in the industry-standard copper-crusher system. The pressure is therefore only slightly higher than that of the .280 Remington cartridge, for which the maximum working pressure is 50,000 c.u.p. Remington has further advised that the 7mm Express factory loads will function reliably and safely in the Remington Model 742 auto-loading rifles chambered for the .280 Remington cartridge.

Analysis of the velocity and pressure data available for the .280 Remington cartridge indicates that handloaders, using available canister powders, will be unlikely to match the nominal performance of the 7mm Express cartridge within the average working pressure limit of 50,900 c.u.p. That is unfortunate for handloaders who use the bolt-action Remington Model 700 rifle or other manually operated arms of comparable strength, because the full potential of the new cartridge in such guns cannot be realized. It does appear, from analysis of published data for the .280 Remington cartridge, that the factory ballistics of the new 7mm Express could be achieved, with the most suitable canister powders, within an average working pressure of 52,000 c.u.p. It further seems likely that this limit, which is still substantially less than that of the .270 Winchester, would allow safe and satisfactory operation in the Model 700 bolt-action rifle, or other manually operated arms of comparable strength. The only obstacle to use of the slightly higher chamber-pressure limit would appear to be the possibility of less reliable functioning in the Remington Model 742 autoloader chambered for the .280 Remington cartridge.

In the interests of the many shooters who will undoubtedly be using the new 7mm Express cartridge in the Remington Model 700 and other bolt-action rifles, possibly the laboratories using the copper-crusher system of pressure measurement for handload development could advantageously adopt the 52,000-c.u.p. limit for loads to be fired in manually operated arms. With suitable powders, such as IMR-4831, Hodgdon 4831 and Norma MRP, a reduction of about three per cent in charge weight should then effect a reduction of chamber pressure to less than 50,000

c.u.p., which is more suitable for ammunition to be used in autoloading arms such as the Remington Model 742 rifle.

Max. Case Length: 2.540″ **Trim-To Length:** 2.530″
Max. Overall Length: 3.330″ **Primer Size:** Large Rifle **Bullet Dia.:** .284″

RIFLE LOADS FOR THE .280 REMINGTON/7mm EXPRESS

LOAD NUMBER	BULLET				POWDER			VELOCITY FPS	PRESSURE CUP	CASE BRAND	PRIMER		CARTRIDGE OAL	BARREL LENGTH	DATA SOURCE
	WEIGHT	BRAND	SHAPE	TYPE	WEIGHT	BRAND	TYPE				BRAND	TYPE			
1	115	SPR	PTD	HP	60.0	DUP	4831	3246	<50000	REM	CCI	200		24	SPR
2	120	NOS	PBT	SP	54.0	DUP	4350	2954		REM	REM	9½		22	NOS
3	120	HDY	PTD	SP	45.0	DUP	4064	2975	46970	REM	REM	9½	3.280	24	NRA
4	125	REM	PTD	SP	60.0	DUP	4831	3115	50000	REM	REM	9½	3.250	24	DUP
5	130	SPR	PTD	SP	58.0	DUP	4831	3077	<50000	REM	CCI	200		24	SPR
6	139	HDY	PTD	SP	46.0	DUP	4064	2835	46650	REM	REM	9½	3.320	24	NRA
7	139	HDY	PTD	SP	57.9	HOD	4831	2900		REM	REM	9½		22	HDY
8	140	NOS	PBT	SP	56.0	DUP	4831	2982		REM	REM	9½		22	NOS
9	140	SRA	PTD	SP	54.4	DUP	4350	2900		REM	REM	9½		22	SRA
10	145	SPR	PTD	SP	51.0	DUP	4350	2862	49390	REM	REM	9½	3.300	24	NRA
11	150	REM	PTD	SP	57.0	DUP	4831	2930	50000	REM	REM	9½	3.325	24	DUP
12	150	NOS	PTD	SP	55.5	NOR	MRP	2830		REM	REM	9½		22	NOS
13	154	HDY	PTD	SP	54.5	DUP	4350	2900		REM	REM	9½		22	HDY
14	160	SRA	PBT	SP	55.9	HOD	4831	2700		REM	REM	9½		22	SRA
15	160	SPR	PTD	SP	51.0	DUP	4350	2736	48790	REM	REM	9½	3.300	24	NRA
16	160	NOS	PTD	SP	54.0	DUP	4831	2812		REM	REM	9½		22	NOS
17	162	HDY	PBT	HP	53.6	DUP	4350	2800		REM	REM	9½		22	HDY
18	165	REM	PTD	SP	55.5	DUP	4831	2775	50000	REM	REM	9½	3.325	24	DUP
19	168	SRA	PBT	HP	53.8	DUP	4831	2700		REM	REM	9½		22	SRA
20	170	SRA	RNN	SP	50.7	DUP	4350	2600		REM	REM	9½		22	SRA
21	175	HDY	RNN	SP	54.6	HOD	4831	2600		REM	REM	9½		22	HDY
22	175	NOS	SPD	SP	52.5	DUP	4831	2678		REM	REM	9½		22	NOS
23	130	SPR	PTD	SP	20.0	DUP	4759	1680		REM	CCI	200		24	SPR
24	130	SPR	PTD	SP	24.0	DUP	4759	2024		REM	CCI	200		24	SPR
25	175	SPR	SPD	SP	21.0	DUP	4759	1490		REM	CCI	200		24	SPR
26	175	SPR	SPD	SP	25.0	DUP	4759	1753		REM	CCI	200		24	SPR

7 x 61mm SHARPE & HART (SUPER 7 x 61)

The 7x61mm Sharpe & Hart cartridge was originated as a "wildcat" in the early 1950s by Philip B. Sharpe, a popular gun writer from the 1930s to the 1950s, and Richard Hart (no kin of the famous Hart family of barrel makers and benchrest gunsmiths in Pennsylvania and New York). A commercial rifle chambered for the 7x61mm S&H cartridge was introduced by Schultz and Larsen, a European manufacturer, and imported for sale in the United States beginning about 1953.

Some exceedingly optimistic claims for the cartridge were made by some users of it, and it achieved some popularity as a long-range game cartridge, though some difficulties arose among handloaders using it with casually developed loads trying to match the claimed performance. Among the various custom rifles chambered for it, some apparently had free-bored throats, whereas others did not.

Loads developed on the basis of subjective pressure signs in free-bored rifles most probably developed excessive chamber pressures when fired in rifles having conventional throats. The rear-locking bolt of the

Schultz and Larsen action, though amply strong for safety, permits somewhat more elastic distortion than do guns with front-locking bolts under comparable chamber pressures, and this aggravates case-stretching with heavy loads. Because of that, case life was relatively short, circumferential ruptures occurring early if very heavy loads were used.

The production of factory ammunition adapted to 7x61 S&H rifles was begun in Europe by Norma. The cartridge case was said to have been redesigned, to provide somewhat greater internal volume, and it was renamed by Norma the "Super 7x61."

Handloaders who use this cartridge should proceed with due caution, because different throating configurations may produce markedly different chamber pressures with the same load. Loads developed in some rifles might be quite excessive in others chambered for the same cartridge.

Max. Case Length: 2.402″ **Trim-To Length:** 2.392″
Max. Overall Length: 3.190″ **Primer Size:** Large Rifle **Bullet Dia.:** .284″

RIFLE LOADS FOR THE 7 x 61 SHARPE & HART

LOAD NUMBER	BULLET				POWDER			VELOCITY FPS	PRESSURE CUP	CASE BRAND	PRIMER		CARTRIDGE OAL	BARREL LENGTH	DATA SOURCE
	WEIGHT	BRAND	SHAPE	TYPE	WEIGHT	BRAND	TYPE				BRAND	TYPE			
1	120	HDY	PTD	HP	64.2	DUP	4350	3300		NOR	FED	210		24	HDY
2	120	SRA	PTD	SP	55.8	DUP	4064	3200		NOR	REM	9½		24	SRA
3	139	HDY	PTD	SP	65.0	HOD	4831	3200		NOR	FED	210		24	HDY
4	140	SRA	PTD	SP	62.9	DUP	4350	3200		NOR	REM	9½		24	SRA
5	150	NOR	PBT	SP	58.5	NOR	204	2950	<55100	NOR	NOR	LR	3.190	24	NOR
6	150	NOR	PBT	FJ	67.4	NOR	MRP	3165	<55100	NOR	NOR	LR	3.190	24	NOR
7	154	HDY	PTD	SP	60.2	DUP	4350	3000		NOR	FED	210		24	HDY
8	160				66.5	NOR	MRP	3100	<55100	NOR	NOR	LR	3.190	24	NOR
9	160	SRA	PBT	SP	66.0	HOD	4831	3000		NOR	REM	9½		24	SRA
10	162	HDY	PBT	HP	58.1	DUP	4350	2900		NOR	FED	210		24	HDY
11	168	SRA	PBT	HP	66.5	HOD	4831	3000		NOR	REM	9½		24	SRA
12	170	SRA	RNN	SP	61.9	DUP	4831	2900		NOR	REM	9½		24	SRA
13	175	HDY	RNN	SP	62.5	HOD	4831	2900		NOR	FED	210		24	HDY
14	175				64.8	NOR	MRP	2904	<55100	NOR	NOR	LR	3.190	24	NOR

7mm WEATHERBY MAGNUM

The 7mm Weatherby Magnum was developed by Roy Weatherby in the 1940's, many years before the introduction of the 7mm Remington Magnum. Unlike most Weatherby magnum cartridges, the case capacity of the 7mm Weatherby Magnum is slightly less than that of the comparable cartridge produced by a major U.S. ammunition manufacturer. Like the 7mm Remington Magnum, the Weatherby cartridge is based on a case shorter than those of the .300 H.&H. or .300 Weatherby Magnum, and can be used in actions that were designed for cartridges such as the .30-06. The 7mm Weatherby Magnum provides velocities generally within about 100 fps of those produced by the 7mm Remington Magnum at similar chamber pressure. The preformance of the two cartridges is so similar that any differences would likely go unnoticed in the field.

Some shooters who compete in matches at the "Original Pennsylvania 1,000-Yard Benchrest Club" have experimented extensively with a wildcat cartridge based on the full-length .300 Weatherby Magnum necked down to accept 7mm bullets. This wildcat is usually called the 7mm-300 Weatherby Magnum, and should not be confused with the 7mm Weatherby Magnum factory cartridge.

Max. Case Length: 2.549″ **Trim-To Length:** 2.539″
Max. Overall Length: 3.250″ **Primer Size:** Large Rifle Magnum **Bullet Dia.:** .284″

LOAD NUMBER	BULLET				POWDER			VELOCITY FPS	PRESSURE CUP	CASE BRAND	PRIMER		CARTRIDGE OAL	BARREL LENGTH	DATA SOURCE
	WEIGHT	BRAND	SHAPE	TYPE	WEIGHT	BRAND	TYPE				BRAND	TYPE			
1	120	HDY	PTD	SP	74.7	HOD	4831	3500		WEA	FED	215		24	HDY
2	120	SRA	PTD	SP	76.2	HOD	4831	3500		WEA	FED	215		26	SRA
3	139	HDY	PTD	SP	69.0	DUP	4350	3308	54310	WEA	FED	215	3.250	26	WEA
4	139	HDY	PTD	SP	73.0	HOD	4831	3233	49700	WEA	FED	215	3.250	26	WEA
5	139	HDY	PTD	SP	75.0	HOD	4831	3328	53520	WEA	FED	215	3.250	26	WEA
6	139	HDY	PTD	SP	74.1	NOR	MRP	3300	50300	WEA	FED	215	3.250	26	WEA
7	150	NOS	PTD	SP	69.0	NOR	MRP	3160		WEA	REM	9½M		26	NOS
8	154	HDY	PTD	SP	67.0	DUP	4350	3141	54500	WEA	FED	215	3.250	26	WEA
9	154	HDY	PTD	SP	71.0	HOD	4831	3066	49160	WEA	FED	215	3.250	26	WEA
10	154	HDY	PTD	SP	73.0	HOD	4831	3183	54910	WEA	FED	215	3.250	26	WEA
11	154	HDY	PTD	SP	71.0	NOR	MRP	3160	51250	WEA	FED	215	3.250	26	WEA
12	160	NOS	PTD	SP	66.0	DUP	4831	3075		WEA	REM	9½M		26	NOS
13	160	NOS	PTD	SP	71.8	NOR	MRP	3150	53700	WEA	FED	215	3.250	26	WEA
14	175	HDY	RNN	SP	71.0	NOR	MRP	3070	53350	WEA	FED	215	3.250	26	WEA
15	175	HDY	RNN	SP	65.0	DUP	4350	2946	53830	WEA	FED	215	3.250	26	WEA
16	175	HDY	RNN	SP	70.0	HOD	4831	2924	52680	WEA	FED	215	3.250	26	WEA
17	175	NOS	SPD	SP	78.0	HOD	H870	2988		WEA	REM	9½M		26	NOS
18	120	NOS	PBT	SP	72.0	DUP	4831	3542		WEA	REM	9½M		26	NOS

7mm
REMINGTON
MAGNUM

The 7mm Remington Magnum was introduced in 1962. It is based on a shortened, necked-down, reduced-taper, belted-magnum case of the type that originated with the .375 and .300 Holland & Holland Magnum cartridges. It has enjoyed well deserved popularity ever since its introduction. Having a cartridge overall length of 3.29 inches, it can be used in actions designed to accommodate the .30-06 and similar cartridges. The case capacity and bore diameter seem to represent a very favorable balance between piezometric and thermodynamic efficiency, producing adequate velocities for long-range shooting, at acceptable pressures, without requiring disproportionately heavy powder charges.

The variety of excellent 7mm bullets now available provides a suitable bullet for practically every purpose. The excellent accuracy and aerodynamic design of the 162-grain Hornady and 168-grain Sierra boattail match bullets make them especially suitable for target shooting with the 7mm Remington Magnum cartridge, and 10-shot groups in less than one minute-of-angle have been made with them by benchrest shooters at a range of 1,000 yards. The controlled-expansion bullets weighing more than about 160 grains are adequate for hunting the largest North American game.

The problem most commonly encountered by handloaders with the 7mm Remington Magnum, and with other belted-magnum cartridges, is short case life. This is usually attributable to stretching of cases in the lower body area, resulting in circumferential ruptures after a number of reloads. It is usually corrected by adjusting the resizing die in the press, so that the shoulder is not pushed back during resizing any farther than is necessary for easy chambering in the rifle. If that practice is carefully followed, the case is headspaced on the shoulder, rather than on the belt as originally intended in the belted-case design and case stretching is thereby minimized. For cases having a long gently sloping shoulder such as the .300 H.&H. Magnum, the belt is essential for headspace control, but for sharp-shouldered cases, such as the 7mm Remington Magnum, that function is performed more effectively by the shoulder, as it is done for rimless cases, and the belt is unnecessary. The belt seems to have been retained in the design of sharp-shouldered magnum cases principally for cosmetic reasons, and the supposed extra appeal to consumers. The belt controls headspace adequately for the first firing on new cases, however, and is no detriment to handloaders who do not depend on it for that purpose in subsequent reloads.

The maximum working pressure for the 7mm Remington Magnum is usually limited to 52,000 c.u.p. The maximum product average for factory ammunition should not exceed 55,200 c.u.p.

Max. Case Length: 2.500″ **Trim-To Length:** 2.490″
Max. Overall Length: 3.290″ **Primer Size:** Large Rifle
Magnum **Bullet Dia.:** .284″

RIFLE LOADS FOR THE 7mm REMINGTON MAGNUM

LOAD NUMBER	BULLET				POWDER			VELOCITY FPS	PRESSURE CUP	CASE BRAND	PRIMER		CARTRIDGE OAL	BARREL LENGTH	DATA SOURCE
	WEIGHT	BRAND	SHAPE	TYPE	WEIGHT	BRAND	TYPE				BRAND	TYPE			
1	115	SPR	PTD	HP	66.0	DUP	4350	3330	<52000	WIN	CCI	250		24	SPR
2	120	HDY	PTD	SP	68.5	DUP	4831	3335	51400	REM	REM	9½M	3.290	24	DUP
3	120	NOS	PBT	SP	59.0	DUP	4320	3257		WIN	REM	9½M		25	NOS
4	130	SPR	PTD	SP	62.0	DUP	4350	3224	51240	REM	REM	9½	3.240	26	NRA
5	139	HDY	PTD	SP	64.0	DUP	4350	3156	50240	REM	REM	9½	3.290	26	NRA
6	140	NOS	PTD	SP	62.0	DUP	4350	3139	50630	REM	REM	9½	3.290	26	NRA
7	140	SRA	PTD	SP	67.5	HOD	4831	3100		REM	REM	9½M		26	SRA
8	145	SPR	PTD	SP	59.0	DUP	4350	3027	51200	REM	REM	9½	3.290	26	NRA
9	150	REM	PTD	SP	66.5	DUP	4831	3055	52000	REM	REM	9½M	3.290	24	DUP
10	150	NOS	PBT	SP	63.0	DUP	4350	3230		WIN	REM	9½M		24	NOS
11	150	NOR	PBT	SP	71.4	NOR	MRP	3250	<55100	NOR	NOR	LR	3.250	24	NOR
12	154	HDY	PTD	SP	65.4	DUP	4831	3000	<52000	FRO	REM	9½M	3.290	24	HDY
13	160	SRA	PBT	SP	76.5	HOD	H870	3000		REM	REM	9½M		26	SRA
14	160	NOS	PTD	SP	60.0	DUP	4350	3003		WIN	REM	9½M		25	NOS
15	160	SPR	PTD	SP	60.0	DUP	4831	2978	<52000	WIN	CCI	250		24	SPR
16	162	HDY	PBT	HP	56.6	DUP	4350	2800	49800	FRO	REM	9½M		24	HDY
17	168	SRA	PBT	HP	63.5	HOD	4831	2900		REM	REM	9½M		26	SRA
18	170	SRA	RNN	SP	62.4	NOR	MRP	2900		REM	REM	9½M		26	SRA
19	175	SRA	PBT	SP	62.8	DUP	4831	2900		REM	REM	9½M		26	SRA
20	175	REM	PTD	SP	59.5	DUP	4350	2765	51800	REM	REM	9½M	3.290	24	DUP
21	175	NOS	SPD	SP	64.0	NOR	MRP	2958		WIN	REM	9½M		25	NOS
22	130	SPR	PTD	SP	22.0	DUP	4759	1721		WIN	CCI	250		24	SPR
23	130	SPR	PTD	SP	26.0	DUP	4759	2028		WIN	CCI	250		24	SPR
24	175	SPR	SPD	SP	28.0	DUP	4759	1793		WIN	CCI	250		24	SPR
25	175	SPR	SPD	SP	32.0	DUP	4759	2045		WIN	CCI	250		24	SPR

7.35mm CARCANO

The 7.35mm Carcano cartridge, sometimes called the 7.35mm Mannlicher-Carcano, was adopted by Italy in the late 1930's as a replacement for the earlier 6.5mm Carcano that had been in use since 1891. The logistic problems of World War II prevented the general deployment of the new cartridge, however, and the 6.5mm cartridge continued in use throughout that war. When Italy became a NATO partner after World War II, the Italian armed forces adopted the standard 7.62mm NATO cartridge, and the 7.35mm Carcano was never widely deployed. Large quantities of surplus 7.35mm arms and ammunition were sold in the U.S. at low prices, however, and many of the rifles and carbines are still in use.

The 7.35mm Carcano cartridge is comparable in performance to the .30-30, but requires a special bullet measuring about .300-inch diameter, and should not be loaded with any standard .308-inch bullet. Cases cannot readily be formed from any standard U.S. cartridge case, but can be formed from 6.5x54mm Mannlicher-Schoenauer brass. Dealers in surplus ammunition occasionally have supplies of military ammunition, but Berdan primers suitable for reloading the cases may be hard to find. Custom loaders can form the cases from .220 Swift brass by lathe-turning the rim and extractor groove, and cases made that way are easily reloadable.

Max. Case Length: 2.015″ **Trim-To Length:** 2.005″
Max. Overall Length: 2.755″ **Primer Size:** Large Rifle **Bullet Dia.:** .300″

RIFLE LOADS FOR THE 7.35 mm CARCANO

LOAD NUMBER	BULLET				POWDER			VELOCITY FPS	PRESSURE CUP	CASE BRAND	PRIMER		CARTRIDGE OAL	BARREL LENGTH	DATA SOURCE
	WEIGHT	BRAND	SHAPE	TYPE	WEIGHT	BRAND	TYPE				BRAND	TYPE			
1	128	HDY	PTD	SP	38.0	DUP	3031	2588	37170	NOR	WIN	8½-120	2.750	21	NRA
2	128	HDY	PTD	SP	41.0	DUP	4064	2600		NOR	FED	210		21	HDY
3	150	SPR	SPD	SP	36.0	DUP	3031	2384	37010	NOR	WIN	8½-120	2.780	21	NRA

7.5mm SCHMIDT-RUBIN (SWISS)

A 7.5mm cartridge was adopted by Switzerland for military use in 1889, and originally loaded with a paper-patched, steel-capped bullet and a compressed charge of semi-smokeless powder. A smokeless-powder version using a conventional jacketed bullet was later adopted for the Model 1899 rifle, developing a maximum chamber pressure of about 37,000 c.u.p. with a 190-grain bullet at about 2,050 fps. The diameter of the bullet measured .3075 inch (maximum), though the groove diameter of the Model 1889 rifle was nominally only .304 inch. The loads listed here, using .308-inch bullets and developing chamber pressures that exceed 40,000 c.u.p., **should not be used in the old Model 1889 Swiss rifles.**

The 7.5mm Swiss cartridge was modernized in 1911, and identified as the Model 1911 cartridge. The arms adapted to it were also identified as Model 1911 or as Model 1896/11, and the groove diameter of the barrel was increased to .3087 inch (maximum). It is for these arms that the loads listed here are intended.

The 7.5mm Swiss cartridge measures about .020 inch larger than the .30-06, .270, 8x57mm, etc., at the head, and cannot be formed readily from any available American case. Dealers in surplus ammunition sometimes have 7.5mm Swiss cartridges, which are usually Berdan-primed. The Berdan 217B primer was used in the Hornady loads listed here.

Max. Case Length: 2.180″   Trim-To Length: 2.170″
Max. Overall Length: 3.060″   Primer Size: Large Rifle   Bullet Dia.: .308″

RIFLE LOADS FOR THE 7.5mm SCHMIDT-RUBIN (SWISS)
(Only for Model 96/11 and 11 Rifles, and Model 11 and 31 Carbines)

LOAD NUMBER	BULLET				POWDER			VELOCITY FPS	PRESSURE CUP	CASE BRAND	PRIMER		CARTRIDGE OAL	BARREL LENGTH	DATA SOURCE
	WEIGHT	BRAND	SHAPE	TYPE	WEIGHT	BRAND	TYPE				BRAND	TYPE			
1	130	HDY	PTD	SP	43.0	DUP	3031	2900		(1)	(1)	(1)		31	HDY
2	150	SRA	PTD	SP	45.0	DUP	3031	2822	44020	(2)	WIN	8½-120	2.96	31	NRA
3	165	HDY	PTD	SP	43.2	DUP	4064	2600		(1)	(1)	(1)		31	HDY
4	180	HDY	PTD	SP	45.0	DUP	4064	2569	44070	(2)	WIN	8½-120	2.85	31	NRA
5	180	HDY	PTD	SP	39.0	HOD	4895	2296		NOR	WIN	8½-120		31	HOD

NOTE (1): Hornady loads assembled in imported Swiss cases, with Berdan 217B primers.
NOTE (2): NRA loads assembled in Japanese Toyo cases.

7.5mm FRENCH MAS

The 7.5mm French MAS cartridge is of modern design, producing ballistics comparable to those of the 7.62mm NATO cartridge. Though .308-inch bullets can be used, the bore diameter of the French barrels may be considerably less than the .300-inch used for most .30-caliber American barrels, and loads using .308-inch bullets should be approached cautiously from well below the maximum charge. The load listed is believed to be safe, with proper cases, in rifles that are in good mechanical condition, but pressure data are unavailable. It approximates the performance of the French military load.

The cases cannot readily be formed from any commonly available American cases, so Berdan-primed imported ammunition is practically the only source of cases for reloading.

FULL-CHARGE LOADS FOR THE 7.5 x 54 FRENCH MAS

LOAD NUMBER	BULLET				POWDER			VELOCITY FPS	PRESSURE CUP	CASE BRAND	PRIMER		CARTRIDGE OAL	BARREL LENGTH	DATA SOURCE
	WEIGHT	BRAND	SHAPE	TYPE	WEIGHT	BRAND	TYPE				BRAND	TYPE			
1	150				54.0	HOD	4831	2680							FCB
2	149		(Military Factory Load)		—	—		2674							FCB

Note (1): Data from "Cartridges of the World," courtesy of Frank C. Barnes and DBI, Inc.

.30 M1 CARBINE

Designed by Winchester and standardized for U.S. military use in 1941, the .30 Carbine cartridge saw much use during World War II. Many M1 carbines were sold as surplus after World War II, and the cartridge became popular among civilian shooters. Carbines similar to the military models were manufactured soon after the supplies of surplus weapons were exhausted, and these continue to be made in various configurations.

The M1 carbine was intended as a more effective replacement for the Caliber .45 Model 1911A1 pistol, and indeed it is far more effective in the hands of troops than is any handgun. As a military weapon, it served its intended purpose. Because it is a shoulder weapon, however, it was often compared with the M1 rifle, and in that comparison, the carbine came out badly. Possibly in consequence of that, it was not popular among troops who were called upon to function as riflemen and tried to employ the carbine in that role. Because it is more cumbersome than the pistol to carry, it was not popular among troops who were required to carry it instead of a pistol, but never had occasion to fire it in combat. Though not universally popular as a military weapon, the M1 Carbine is light, well balanced, without any unpleasant recoil, and appeals to many civilian shooters.

With only about 930 foot-pounds of energy at the muzzle and a 110-grain bullet, the .30 Carbine is not powerful enough for hunting deer-size game. Although many deer have certainly been killed by the .30 Carbine, it is too likely to wound without producing a quick and humane kill on such animals, and it should not be used for deer hunting. It is popular among jackrabbit hunters, and those who enjoy informal target shooting with autoloading arms. It has also enjoyed some popularity with law-enforcement agencies, and unfortunately with some of their adversaries as well.

Military specifications for the .30 Carbine ammunition require a maximum average chamber pressure not to exceed 40,000 p.s.i. (copper), corresponding to 40,000 c.u.p., which is also the normal working pressure for the sporting load. The maximum product average for non-military factory ammunition is 43,200 c.u.p.

Max. Case Length: 1.290″ **Trim-To Length:** 1.285″
Max. Overall Length: 1.680″ **Primer Size:** Small Rifle **Bullet Dia.:** .308″

RIFLE LOADS FOR THE .30 M1 CARBINE

LOAD NUMBER	BULLET				POWDER			VELOCITY FPS	PRESSURE CUP	CASE BRAND	PRIMER		CARTRIDGE OAL	BARREL LENGTH	DATA SOURCE
	WEIGHT	BRAND	SHAPE	TYPE	WEIGHT	BRAND	TYPE				BRAND	TYPE			
1	77	NOR			17.0	HOD	H110	2382		WIN	WIN	6½-116		18	HOD
2	85	NOR			16.0	HOD	H110	2356		WIN	WIN	6½-116		18	HOD
3	93	NOR			15.5	HOD	H110	2221		WIN	WIN	6½-116		18	HOD
4	100	SPR	RNN	SP	16.5	WIN	680	1862	<40000	MIL	CCI	400		18	SPR
5	100	SPR	RNN	SP	12.0	WIN	630	1733	<40000	MIL	CCI	400		18	SPR
6	100	SPR	RNN	SP	15.5	WIN	296	2010		MIL	CCI	400		18	SPR
7	100	HDY	RNN	SP	15.1	HER	2400	2100		MIL	REM	6½		18	HDY
8	100	HDY	RNN	SP	14.9	HOD	H110	2000		MIL	REM	6½		18	HDY
9	100	HDY	RNN	SP	16.2	DUP	4227	2100		MIL	REM	6½		18	HDY
10	109	LYM	RNN	LP	15.0	DUP	4227	1938	39080	MIL	REM	6½	1.670	18	NRA
11	110	HDY	RNN	SP	15.0	DUP	4227	1873	37960	MIL	REM	6½	1.670	18	NRA
12	110	HDY	RNN	SP	14.0	HOD	H110	1906	32400	WIN	WIN	6½-116		18	HOD
13	110	HDY	RNN	SP	11.0	DUP	4759	1545	26100	REM	REM	6½	1.680	18	DUP
14	110	HDY	RNN	SP	15.0	DUP	4227	1900	40000	REM	REM	6½	1.680	18	DUP
15	110	HDY	RNN	SP	14.5	DUP	4198	1495	20900	REM	REM	6½	1.680	18	DUP
16	110	SPR	FLN	HP	16.0	WIN	680	1805	<40000	MIL	CCI	400		18	SPR
17	110	SPR	FLN	HP	15.0	WIN	296	1945	<40000	MIL	CCI	400		18	SPR
18	110	SPR	FLN	HP	12.0	HER	2400	1745	<40000	MIL	CCI	400		18	SPR
19	110	WIN	RNN	HP	16.0	WIN	680	1970	37500	WIN	WIN	6½-116	1.680	20	WIN
20	110	WIN	RNN	HP	15.0	WIN	296	1980	36000	WIN	WIN	6½-116	1.680	20	WIN
21	110	WIN	RNN	HP	11.5	WIN	630	1725	34000	WIN	WIN	6½-116	1.680	20	WIN
22	112	CAST	FLN	LG	9.8	HER	BDOT	1495	34300	REM	CCI	400	1.625	18	HER
23	112	CAST	FLN	LG	10.3	HER	2400	1590	35700	REM	CCI	400	1.625	18	HER

7.62 x 39mm RUSSIAN (M1943)

The 7.62x39mm cartridge is a Russian design for military use in assault rifles and light machineguns. It is somewhat less powerful than the .30-30, but more powerful than the .30 M1 Carbine. Its sporting uses are limited both by the power of the cartridge and by the types of weapons in which it is used. The Kalashnikov AK-47 and more recent AKM rifle are most commonly associated with the 7.62x39mm cartridge, but few such rifles are legally owned by civilians in the U.S., because they are subject to the restrictions of the BATF on ownership of automatic weapons. The semiautomatic Simonov SKS carbine is not subject to those restrictions, and is therefore more common among U.S. handloaders.

Cases for the 7.62x39mm cartridge cannot readily be formed from any commonly available American brass, so imported cases offer practically the only source. A few of these accept standard boxer-type primers, but most do not. Substantial quantities of 7.62x39mm ammunition were produced by the Lake City Army Ammunition Plant for use in weapons captured in Southeast Asia during the war there, but very few of these cases found their way into civilian hands. Most of the Russian military ammunition, and that manufactured in the other Communist countries, employs steel cases.

Max. Case Length: 1.525″ **Trim-To Length:** 1.520″
Max. Overall Length: 2.200″ **Primer Size:** Small Rifle **Bullet Dia.:** .308″ and .311″

RIFLE LOADS FOR THE 7.62 x 39 mm RUSSIAN (M1943)

LOAD NUMBER	BULLET				POWDER			VELOCITY FPS	PRESSURE CUP	CASE BRAND	PRIMER		CARTRIDGE OAL	BARREL LENGTH	DATA SOURCE
	WEIGHT	BRAND	SHAPE	TYPE	WEIGHT	BRAND	TYPE				BRAND	TYPE			
1	110	SPR	FLN	HP	27.0	DUP	3031	2405		MIL	CCI	200		24	SPR
2	110	SPR	FLN	HP	25.0	DUP	4198	2667		MIL	CCI	200		24	SPR
3	110	SPR	FLN	HP	24.0	DUP	4227	2605		MIL	CCI	200		24	SPR
4	110	SRA	RNN	HP	25.3	WIN	680	2600		SAK	CCI	200		24	SRA
5	110	SRA	RNN	HP	30.8	NOR	200	2600		SAK	CCI	200		24	SRA
6	125	SRA	PTD	SP	24.3	DUP	4227	2500		SAK	CCI	200		24	SRA
7	125	SRA	PTD	SP	24.7	WIN	680	2500		SAK	CCI	200		24	SRA
8	125	SRA	PTD	SP	26.3	DUP	4198	2400		SAK	CCI	200		24	SRA
9	130	SPR	PTD	HP	25.0	DUP	4198	2470		MIL	CCI	200		24	SPR
10	130	SPR	PTD	HP	27.0	DUP	3031	2255		MIL	CCI	200		24	SPR
11	130	SPR	PTD	HP	27.0	NOR	200	2435		MIL	CCI	200		24	SPR
12	150	SRA	PTD	SP	22.5	WIN	680	2200		SAK	CCI	200		24	SRA
13	150	SRA	PTD	SP	24.6	DUP	4198	2200		SAK	CCI	200		24	SRA

.30-30 WINCHESTER (and .30 REMINGTON)

The .30-30 cartridge was introduced in 1895, especially for the Model 1894 Winchester rifle. It was one of the first sporting cartridges specifically designed for smokeless powder, and the nomenclature is a carry-over from the custom of naming black-powder cartridges with the caliber of the bullet followed by the customary weight of the powder charge in grains. The name thus implies a .30-caliber bullet, and a nominal charge of 30 grains of (smokeless) powder.

It was soon recognized that different types of smokeless powder might require substantially different charge weights, and the practice of using the charge weight in the cartridge identification was abandoned early in the era of smokeless powder. It persists only in a few early smokeless cartridges such as the .30-30, .30-40 and .25-35. It should not be taken literally, of course, since the actual charge weight depends upon the particular type of powder, weight of bullet, and other factors that affect performance of modern ammunition.

Though there are partisans who deprecate and those who extol the virtues of the .30-30 with more emotion than reason, it is in fact an adequate deer cartridge for moderate ranges, and has enjoyed great popularity for more than 80 years. Though not often associated with highly accurate shooting, the .30-30 does produce excellent accuracy in well made bolt-action and single-shot rifles, and some of the old lever-action repeating rifles having heavy octagon barrels shot surprisingly well. It is an excellent cartridge for handloaders interested in target shooting with cast bullets, because the case capacity is well suited to the powder charges that produce best results in cast-bullet loads.

The Marlin Micro-Groove barrels, though entirely satisfactory for use with jacketed bullets, are not suitable for cast-bullet loads. For cartridges to be used in tubular magazines, flat-nose bullets are best in the interests of safety, and pointed bullets should never be used. Crimping the case mouth into a groove or cannelure of the bullet is also required for use in tubular magazines.

The .30 Remington cartridge, designed for use in the Remington Model 8 autoloader and Model 14 slide-action rifles, is ballistically nearly the same as the .30-30, though the .30 Remington is a rimless cartridge and not interchangeable with the .30-30. Loading data for the .30-30 may also be used satisfactorily for the .30 Remington cartridge.

Normal maximum working pressure for .30-30 cartridges is about 38,000 c.u.p. The maximum product average for factory ammunition should not exceed 41,200 c.u.p.

Max. Case Length: 2.039″ **Trim-To Length:** 2.029″
Max. Overall Length: 2.550″ **Primer Size:** Large Rifle **Bullet Dia.:** .308″

RIFLE LOADS FOR THE .30-30 WINCHESTER

LOAD NUMBER	BULLET				POWDER			VELOCITY FPS	PRESSURE CUP	CASE BRAND	PRIMER		CARTRIDGE OAL	BARREL LENGTH	DATA SOURCE
	WEIGHT	BRAND	SHAPE	TYPE	WEIGHT	BRAND	TYPE				BRAND	TYPE			
1	100	SPR	RNN	SP	37.5	DUP	4064	2681	<38000	WIN	CCI	200		20	SPR
2	100	HDY	RNN	SP	35.3	DUP	3031	2600	<38000	FRO	FRD	210	2.435	20	HDY
3	110	SRA	SPD	HP	35.0	DUP	3031	2672	38100	WIN	WIN	8½-120	2.550	24	NRA
4	110	HDY	RNN	SP	36.4	DUP	4064	2500	<35600	FRO	FED	210	2.490	20	HDY
5	110	SPR	FLN	HP	37.0	WIN	748	2504	<38000	WIN	CCI	250		20	SPR
6	125	SRA	FLN	HP	35.4	DUP	3031	2600		WIN	WIN	8½-120		20	SRA
7	125	SRA	FLN	HP	37.8	DUP	4895	2600		WIN	WIN	8½-120		20	SRA
8	130	SPR	FLN	SP	35.5	WIN	748	2448	<38000	WIN	CCI	250		20	SPR
9	130	SPR	FLN	SP	31.0	HER	RL7	2424	<38000	WIN	CCI	200		20	SPR
10	150	SRA	FLN	SP	27.2	HER	RL7	2300		WIN	WIN	8½-120		26	SRA
11	150	SPR	FLN	SP	33.0	HOD	H335	2304		WIN	CCI	200		20	SPR
12	150	HDY	RNN	SP	35.5	DUP	3031	2370	37700	REM	REM	9½	2.550	20	DUP
13	150	WIN	FLN	SP	34.5	WIN	748	2310	36000	WIN	WIN	8½-120		24	WIN
14	170	WIN	FLN	SP	32.0	WIN	748	2145	36000	WIN	WIN	8½-120		24	WIN
15	170	REM	RNN	SP	34.0	DUP	4064	2130	38000	REM	REM	9½	2.520	20	DUP
16	170	HDY	FLN	SP	30.0	DUP	3031	2177	38660	WIN	WIN	8½-120	2.550	24	NRA
17	170	SPR	FLN	SP	31.0	HOD	H335	2120		WIN	CCI	250		20	SPR
18	170	SRA	FLN	SP	25.5	HER	RL7	2100		WIN	WIN	8½-120		26	SRA
19	150	SPR	FLN	SP	17.0	DUP	4759	1522		WIN	CCI	200		20	SPR
20	108	CAST	FLN	LP	4.0	HER	UNIQ	970		FED	CCI	200	2.400	26	NRA
21	108	CAST	FLN	LP	6.0	HER	UNIQ	1295		FED	CCI	200	2.400	26	NRA
22	115	CAST	FLN	LG	12.0	DUP	4759	1345		FED	CCI	200	2.400	26	NRA
23	115	CAST	FLN	LG	15.0	DUP	4759	1645		FED	CCI	200	2.400	26	NRA
24	155	CAST	SPD	LG	12.0	DUP	4759	1300		FED	CCI	200	2.585	26	NRA
25	155	CAST	SPD	LG	15.0	DUP	4759	1565		FED	CCI	200	2.585	26	NRA
26	180	CAST	RNN	LG	12.0	DUP	4759	1270		FED	CCI	200	2.600	26	NRA
27	180	CAST	RNN	LG	15.0	DUP	4759	1530		FED	CCI	200	2.600	26	NRA
28	180	CAST	RNN	LG	21.0	HER	RL7	1790		FED	CCI	200	2.600	26	NRA

.303 SAVAGE

The .303 Savage cartridge is a contemporary of the .30-30, having been designed during the 1890's for use in the Savage Model 1895 military rifle, which with minor modifications became the famous lever-action Savage Model 1899. The cartridge and Savage rifle were not accepted for military use, though a few Model 1899 rifles were purchased by various elements of the National Guard in the early 1900's.

The .303 Savage is very similar in performance to the .30-30, although it has always been factory-loaded with heavier bullets. The .303 Savage case is about .020 inch larger at the head than the .30-30 case measures, and the two cartridges are not interchangeable. Factory loads for the .303 Savage originally used a 190-grain bullet and Winchester-Western factory loads still use that weight, but Remington-Peters has for years loaded 180-grain bullets in the .303 Savage. There have been conflicting reports about whether the .303 Savage bullet is actually larger than the normal .30-caliber

bullets. The nominal groove diameter of .303 Savage barrels is listed in several sources as .308 inch, and an ammunition list in a Winchester catalog for 1896 lists the cartridge as the ".30 Savage" rather than .303 Savage. However, the factory loads for .303 Savage generally use bullets of about .309- to .310-inch diameter, and industry standards allow bullets up to .311 of an inch in diameter.

Probably there is considerable variation among .303 Savage barrels, and the handloader is well advised to slug his barrel to determine whether .308- or .311-inch bullets give the better fit. In many .303 Savage rifles, normal .308-inch bullets give good results. The operating pressure for the .303 Savage was about 34,000 c.u.p., which is less than that for the .30-30.

Max. Case Length: 2.015″ **Trim-To Length:** 2.010″
Max. Overall Length: 2.520″ **Primer Size:** Large Rifle **Bullet Dia.:** .308″

RIFLE LOADS FOR THE .303 SAVAGE

LOAD NUMBER	BULLET				POWDER			VELOCITY FPS	PRESSURE CUP	CASE BRAND	PRIMER		CARTRIDGE OAL	BARREL LENGTH	DATA SOURCE
	WEIGHT	BRAND	SHAPE	TYPE	WEIGHT	BRAND	TYPE				BRAND	TYPE			
1	150	SPR	FLN	SP	31.0	DUP	4895	2220	<34000	WIN	WIN	8½-120	2.520	26	NRA
2	170	SPR	FLN	SP	29.0	DUP	4895	1990	<34000	WIN	WIN	8½-120	2.520	26	NRA
3	180	SPR	RNN	SP	29.0	DUP	4895	1940	<34000	WIN	WIN	8½-120	2.520	26	NRA

.30-40 KRAG

The .30-40 Krag cartridge was developed for military use in the Krag-Jorgensen rifle, Model of 1892. The ammunition originally employed a 230-grain bullet of .309-inch diameter, but old records of Frankford Arsenal show that the bullet was changed to 220-grain weight and .308-inch diameter in 1893. The ammunition produced an instrumental velocity of about 1,970 fps at 53 feet from the muzzle.

Many Krag rifles were sold by the DCM during the 1920's and 1930's, and the cartridge was once a very popular one for sporting use. The case capacity of the .30-40 is practically the same as that of the .308 Winchester, but the ballistics of the .308 Winchester cannot be duplicated within the chamber-pressure limit of 40,000 c.u.p. established for the .30-40 cartridge. The .30-40 gives good results with a wide variety of full-charge and reduced loads, including cast-bullet loads to which the long-necked case is very well suited. The long throat in Krag rifles, designed

for the 220-grain round-nose bullet, does not usually allow the best accuracy with spitzer bullets. The 150-grain and 170-grain round-nose bullets intended for use in the .30-30, seated in .30-40 cases to give an overall cartridge length of 3.089 inches, usually give excellent accuracy in good Krag rifles. The 170-grain .30-30 bullet, with full-charge loads in the .30-40 Krag, is a very effective cartridge on whitetail deer.

The maximum average chamber pressure for the .30-40 factory ammunition should not exceed 43,200 c.u.p.

Max. Case Length: 2.314″ **Trim-To Length:** 2.304″
Max. Overall Length: 3.089″ **Primer Size:** Large Rifle **Bullet Dia.:** .308″

RIFLE LOADS FOR THE .30-40 KRAG

LOAD NUMBER	BULLET				POWDER			VELOCITY FPS	PRESSURE CUP	CASE BRAND	PRIMER		CARTRIDGE OAL	BARREL LENGTH	DATA SOURCE
	WEIGHT	BRAND	SHAPE	TYPE	WEIGHT	BRAND	TYPE				BRAND	TYPE			
1	100	SPR	RNN	SP	48.0	DUP	4320	2952	<40000	WIN	CCI	200		21	SPR
2	100	HDY	RNN	SP	47.6	DUP	4064	3000		REM	FED	210		30	HDY
3	110	SRA	SPD	HP	44.2	DUP	3031	2800		REM	REM	9½		22	SRA
4	110	HDY	PTD	SP	46.5	DUP	4064	3000		REM	FED	210		30	HDY
5	110	SPR	FLN	HP	45.0	DUP	4064	2667	<40000	WIN	CCI	200		21	SPR
6	125	SRA	PTD	SP	41.8	DUP	3031	2600		REM	REM	9½		22	SRA
7	130	SPR	PTD	HP	46.0	DUP	4064	2647	<40000	WIN	CCI	200		21	SPR
8	130	HDY	PTD	SP	42.7	DUP	3031	2900		REM	FED	210		30	HDY
9	150	SPR	PTD	SP	42.0	DUP	3031	2695	39600	WIN	WIN	8½-120	3.000	25½	DUP
10	150	NOS	PTD	SP	48.0	DUP	4350	2580	34380	REM	WIN	8½-120	3.150	28	NRA
11	150	HDY	PTD	SP	40.1	DUP	3031	2700		REM	FED	210		30	HDY
12	150	SRA	PTD	SP	44.7	DUP	4064	2500		REM	REM	9½		22	SRA
13	165	SPR	PTD	SP	42.0	DUP	4064	2542	38770	REM	WIN	8½-120	3.150	28	NRA
14	165	HDY	PTD	SP	47.3	DUP	4350	2500		REM	FED	210		30	HDY
15	165	SRA	PBT	SP	50.0	DUP	4831	2300		REM	REM	9½		22	SRA
16	180	SRA	PTD	SP	45.0	DUP	4350	2354	32940	REM	WIN	8½-120	3.150	28	NRA
17	180	SPR	PTD	SP	38.0	DUP	4064	2112	<40000	WIN	CCI	200		21	SPR
18	180	HDY	PTD	SP	38.0	DUP	3031	2400		REM	FED	210		30	HDY
19	180	REM	RNN	SP	49.0	DUP	4831	2425	35900	WIN	WIN	8½-120	3.000	25½	DUP
20	200	SPR	PTD	SP	44.0	DUP	4350	2018	<40000	WIN	CCI	200		21	SPR
21	220	SRA	RNN	SP	44.4	DUP	4831	2000		REM	REM	9½		22	SRA
22	220	HDY	RNN	SP	42.0	DUP	4350	2100		REM	FED	210		30	HDY
23	220	REM	RNN	SP	37.5	DUP	4064	2155	39400	WIN	WIN	8½-120	3.080	25½	DUP
24	100	SPR	BJ	SP	16.0	DUP	4759	1571		WIN	CCI	200		21	SPR
25	100	SPR	BJ	SP	20.0	DUP	4759	1941		WIN	CCI	200		21	SPR
26	165	SPR	PTD	SP	22.0	DUP	4759	1639		WIN	CCI	200		21	SPR
27	165	SPR	PTD	SP	24.0	DUP	4759	1805		WIN	CCI	200		21	SPR

.300 SAVAGE

The .300 Savage cartridge was introduced in 1921, especially for use in the Savage Model 99 lever-action and Model 20 bolt-action rifles. It was intended by Savage to produce the same ballistics as the .30-06, in a cartridge adaptable to their short-action rifles, and was advertised as doing so upon its introduction. Experience has proved, however, that the originally advertised ballistics of a 150-grain bullet at 2,700 fps muzzle velocity cannot consistently be achieved at acceptable chamber pressures, and the velocity of the 150-grain bullet is now listed as 2,630 fps in factory loads.

The neck of the .300 Savage case measures only about .20 inch long, so most bullets must be loaded with the base intruding into the powder space. The short neck does not provide a secure grip on the bullet unless it fits quite tightly, and crimping the case mouth into a bullet cannelure is desirable for hunting ammunition in this caliber. Uncannelured bullets can be used, of course, but the expanding plug should be not larger than about .307 inch when loading with .308-inch bullets. The .300 Savage is a very satisfactory cartridge for hunting, but not the best choice for a handloader. The .308 Winchester cartridge is now available in the excellent Model 99 Savage rifle, and the superior characteristics of the .308 have made the .300 Savage obsolescent. No factory arms are currently chambered for the .300 Savage, but many older rifles chambered for it continue in use.

Working chamber pressures for the .300 Savage are limited to about 46,000 c.u.p. The maximum product average for factory ammunition should not exceed 49,200 c.u.p.

Max. Case Length: 1.871″ **Trim-To Length:** 1.866″
Max. Overall Length: 2.600″ **Primer Size:** Large Rifle **Bullet Dia.:** .308″

RIFLE LOADS FOR THE .300 SAVAGE

LOAD NUMBER	BULLET				POWDER			VELOCITY FPS	PRESSURE CUP	CASE BRAND	PRIMER		CARTRIDGE OAL	BARREL LENGTH	DATA SOURCE
	WEIGHT	BRAND	SHAPE	TYPE	WEIGHT	BRAND	TYPE				BRAND	TYPE			
1	100	SPR	RNN	SP	45.0	DUP	4064	2849	<46000	WIN	CCI	200		20	SPR
2	100	HDY	RNN	SP	43.0	DUP	3031	3100		REM	FED	210		24	HDY
3	110	HDY	PTD	SP	43.0	DUP	3031	3049	44680	WIN	WIN	8½-120	2.500	24	NRA
4	110	SPR	PTD	SP	45.0	DUP	4064	2849	<46000	WIN	CCI	200		20	SPR
5	110	SRA	SPD	HP	46.7	DUP	4320	3000		REM	REM	9½		22	SRA
6	110	WIN	RNN	SP	45.2	WIN	748	2930	41500	WIN	WIN	8½-120		24	WIN
7	125	SRA	PTD	SP	42.0	DUP	3031	2929	46270	WIN	WIN	8½-120	2.550	24	NRA
8	130	SPR	PTD	HP	43.0	DUP	4064	2717	<46000	WIN	CCI	200		20	SPR
9	130	HDY	PTD	SP	41.7	DUP	3031	2900		REM	FED	210		24	HDY
10	150	SPR	PTD	SP	38.5	DUP	3031	2575	44500	REM	REM	9½	2.600	24	DUP
11	150	WIN	PTD	SP	42.0	WIN	748	2600	41000	WIN	WIN	8½-120		24	WIN
12	150	SRA	PTD	SP	42.0	DUP	4064	2638	44190	WIN	WIN	8½-120	2.740	24	NRA
13	150	HDY	PTD	SP	39.5	DUP	3031	2664	45370	WIN	WIN	8½-120	2.675	24	NRA
14	150	NOS	PBT	SP	39.0	DUP	4895	2583		WIN	WIN	8½-120		24	NOS
15	165	SRA	PBT	SP	38.0	DUP	3031	2500		REM	REM	9½		22	SRA
16	165	HDY	PTD	SP	39.9	DUP	4064	2500		REM	FED	210		24	HDY
17	165	SPR	PTD	SP	41.0	WIN	748	2421	<46000	WIN	CCI	250		20	SPR
18	165	NOS	PBT	SP	37.0	DUP	4895	2415		WIN	WIN	8½-120		24	NOS
19	180	SPR	RNN	SP	40.0	DUP	4320	2390	46000	REM	REM	9½	2.600	24	DUP
20	180	SRA	PTD	SP	37.0	DUP	3031	2420	45420	WIN	WIN	8½-120	2.670	24	NRA
21	180	HDY	PTD	SP	37.3	DUP	3031	2400		REM	FED	210		24	HDY
22	180	WIN	PTD	SP	44.5	WIN	760	2410	41000	WIN	WIN	8½-120		24	WIN
23	180	NOS	PBT	SP	36.0	DUP	4064	2274		WIN	WIN	8½-120		24	NOS
24	200	SPR	PTD	SP	41.0	WIN	760	2128	<46000	WIN	CCI	250		20	SPR
25	200	NOS	RNN	SP	34.0	DUP	4064	2103		WIN	WIN	8½-120		24	NOS
26	100	SPR	BJ	SP	16.0	DUP	4759	1675		WIN	CCI	200		20	SPR
27	100	SPR	BJ	SP	18.0	DUP	4759	1897		WIN	CCI	200		20	SPR
28	150	SPR	PTD	SP	17.0	DUP	4759	1523		WIN	CCI	200		20	SPR
29	150	SPR	PTD	SP	21.0	DUP	4759	1873		WIN	CCI	200		20	SPR

7.62 x 54mmR RUSSIAN

The 7.62x54mmR cartridge was adopted by Russia in 1891 for use in the Model 1891 Mosin-Nagant military rifle. Many of these rifles were manufactured in the United States by Winchester, Remington and New England Westinghouse under contracts with the Imperial Russian government. After the Bolshevik revolution in 1917, these rifles were undeliverable, and the U.S. government acquired those on hand, amounting to about 280,000 rifles. Many of these were later sold to NRA members through the Director of Civilian Marksmanship, and 7.62mm Russian sporting ammunition consequently became quite popular in America. It was loaded for many years by Remington, but discontinued in about 1950.

The 7.62x54mm rimmed Russian cartridge is comparable in performance to the .30-06. The Mosin-Nagant rifles are adequately strong for such a load, though clumsy in handling and appearance, and awkward in operation. Some of the rifles were crudely converted to fire .30-06 ammunition by simply running a .30-06 chambering reamer into the original barrel, and sold as .30-06 sporting rifles. This is a hazardous conversion, however, because the 7.62x54mmR chamber is usually about .020 of an inch larger than the .30-06 case at the rear, and .30-06 cases may not expand that much without splitting. A split case may release high-pressure gas rearward, injuring the shooter. Rifles so converted should not be fired.

Max. Case Length: 2.114″ **Trim-To Length:** 2.104″
Max. Overall Length: 3.037″ **Primer Size:** Large Rifle **Bullet Dia.:** .308″

RIFLE LOADS FOR THE 7.62 x 54mmR RUSSIAN

LOAD NUMBER	BULLET				POWDER			VELOCITY FPS	PRESSURE CUP	CASE BRAND	PRIMER		CARTRIDGE OAL	BARREL LENGTH	DATA SOURCE
	WEIGHT	BRAND	SHAPE	TYPE	WEIGHT	BRAND	TYPE				BRAND	TYPE			
1	110	HDY	PTD	SP	48.0	DUP	3031	3000		NOR	FED	210		31	HDY
2	110	SRA	SPD	HP	58.1	HOD	H380	3000		NOR	REM	9½		24	SRA
3	125	SRA	PTD	SP	53.7	DUP	4320	3000		NOR	REM	9½		24	SRA
4	130	HDY	PTD	SP	49.4	DUP	3031	3000		NOR	FED	210		31	HDY
5	130	NOR	SPD	SP	51.4	NOR	201	3100	<47900	NOR	NOR	LR	2.660	24	NOR
6	150	NOR	SPD	SP	47.8	NOR	201	2800	<47900	NOR	NOR	LR	2.750	24	NOR
7	150	HDY	PTD	SP	53.2	HOD	H380	2900		NOR	FED	210		31	HDY
8	150	SRA	PTD	SP	49.1	DUP	4064	2800		NOR	REM	9½		24	SRA
9	165	SRA	PBT	SP	48.1	DUP	4064	2700		NOR	REM	9½		24	SRA
10	165	HDY	PTD	SP	49.6	HOD	H380	2700		NOR	FED	210		31	HDY
11	168	HDY	PBT	HP	49.8	HOD	H380	2700		NOR	FED	210		31	HDY
12	180	NOR	SPD	SP	47.2	NOR	202	2595		NOR	NOR	LR	2.820	24	NOR
13	180	SRA	PTD	SP	53.6	DUP	4350	2600		NOR	REM	9½		24	SRA
14	180	HDY	PTD	SP	51.5	HOD	H380	2700		NOR	FED	210		31	HDY
15	190	HDY	PBT	HP	53.5	NOR	204	2500		NOR	FED	210		31	HDY
16	220	HDY	RNN	SP	52.9	NOR	204	2400		NOR	FED	210		31	HDY

.308 WINCHESTER (7.62mm NATO)

This cartridge, also called the 7.62x51mm NATO, was developed by the Ordnance Department of the U.S. Army during the late 1940's and early 1950's. It was adopted by the NATO nations as the first standard NATO cartridge, after extensive competitive trials carried out under NATO auspices at the United Kingdom Pendine Experimental Establishment in Wales during 1953. When development of the military cartridge was nearly completed, Winchester requested and was granted permission by the Ordnance Department to introduce the cartridge (then called the "Caliber .30 Light-Rifle" or "Caliber .30 T65") under the Winchester name as a sporting load. The .308 Winchester was thus introduced in 1952, and the cartridge has achieved great popularity worldwide, in both military and sporting versions.

The object of this military development was to provide a cartridge not less effective than the .30-06, in a length at least ½-inch shorter than the .30-06. In military automatic weapons, it is generally possible to shorten the gun receiver by an amount equal to twice the shortening of the cartridge, so a cartridge shortened by ½-inch allows a reduction of about one inch in length of the receiver, with the attendant benefits of reduced weight and more compact configuration.

The ballistics of the 7.62mm NATO general-purpose military load, the M80 Ball cartridge, provide a 149-grain boattail bullet at a nominal instrumental velocity of 2,750 fps at 78 feet, corresponding to a muzzle velocity of about 2,808 fps. This practically duplicates the performance of the Caliber .30 M2 Ball (.30-06) military cartridge, which uses a 150-grain flat-base bullet at a nominal instrumental velocity of 2,740 fps at 78 feet, corresponding to a muzzle velocity of about 2,803 fps.

Because the boattail 7.62mm bullet is aerodynamically more efficient than the flat-base caliber .30 bullet, the downrange velocities are higher for the 7.62mm than for the caliber .30. The maximum range of the 7.62mm M80 bullet, fired at an elevation of about 30 degrees, is approximately 4,200 yards, whereas that of the caliber .30 M2 Ball bullet is only about 3,500 yards. To achieve the same muzzle velocity, with the same bullet weight, in the 7.62mm NATO as in the .30-06 requires higher chamber pressures in the smaller cartridge, but that is quite acceptable, since the ballistics of the Caliber .30 M2 Ball cartridge are typically achieved with a chamber pressure substantially below the maximum limit allowed.

The principal complication in handloading for the .308 Winchester is that there is a great difference in capacity of the various commercial and military cases. Winchester-Western commercial cases are usually lightest of all, weighing only about 155 grains, and consequently these have the greatest powder capacity. Military cases are designed for use in a variety of automatic weapons, some of which do not function well (if at all) with light thin-walled cartridge cases. The military cases are therefore made with thicker walls and head, and usually weigh about 180 grains. This difference of 25 grains in weight corresponds to a difference of about three grains in water capacity, which has a very significant effect on the interior ballistics of the loads. The NRA found that a full-charge load developed in Winchester-Western commercial cases increased by as much as 12,000 c.u.p. in chamber pressure when assembled in Lake City military cases, with no other change in components. To avoid problems due to differences in case capacity, it is necessary to reduce the powder charge when changing from cases of greater capacity to cases of less capacity. A satisfactory rule of thumb is to decrease the charge weight in the heavier cases by 12 per cent of the difference in case weights.

It will be found that the quasi-military rifles, such as the Springfield Armory M1A, function more reliably with the military cases than with thin-walled commercial cases, and military or thick-walled commercial cases should be used in such weapons. Sporting autoloaders such as the Remington Model 742 and Winchester Model 100 usually require the use of small-base resizing dies in reloading for reliable functioning, and some lever-action rifles also require the use of small-base dies for easy chambering of reloaded cartridges.

The maximum average chamber pressure for the 7.62 mm NATO military loads must not exceed 50,000 p.s.i., measured in the military pressure barrel for copper-crusher pressures. The commercial .308 Winchester cartridge is normally limited to a working pressure of about 52,000 c.u.p., and the maximum product average for commercial ammunition should not exceed 55,200 c.u.p.

Max. Case Length: 2.015″ **Trim-To Length:** 2.005″
Max. Overall Length: 2.800″ **Primer Size:** Large Rifle **Bullet Dia.:** .308″

RIFLE LOADS FOR THE .308 WINCHESTER

LOAD NUMBER	BULLET				POWDER			VELOCITY FPS	PRESSURE CUP	CASE BRAND	PRIMER		CARTRIDGE OAL	BARREL LENGTH	DATA SOURCE
	WEIGHT	BRAND	SHAPE	TYPE	WEIGHT	BRAND	TYPE				BRAND	TYPE			
1	100	SPR	RNN	SP	54.0	WIN	748	3288	<52000	WIN	CCI	250		22	SPR
2	100	HDY	RNN	SP	46.8	DUP	3031	3100		WIN	FED	210		22	HDY
3	110	HDY	PTD	SP	47.5	DUP	3031	3182	47620	WIN	WIN	8½-120	2.640	24	NRA
4	110	SRA	SPD	HP	50.0	DUP	4064	3147	46760	WIN	WIN	8½-120	2.570	24	NRA
5	110	SPR	PTD	SP	52.5	WIN	748	3208	46160	WIN	WIN	8½-120	2.560	24	NRA
6	125	SRA	PTD	SP	49.0	DUP	4064	3027	47740	WIN	WIN	8½-120	2.630	24	NRA
7	130	HDY	PTD	SP	46.0	DUP	4895	2962	48040	WIN	WIN	8½-120	2.620	24	NRA
8	130	SPR	PTD	HP	47.0	DUP	4320	2908	47960	WIN	WIN	8½-120	2.580	24	NRA
9	130	NOR	SPD	SP	40.1	NOR	200	2900	<52200	NOR	NOR	LR	2.620	24	NOR
10	150	HDY	PTD	SP	54.0	WIN	760	2843	46620	WIN	WIN	8½-120	2.710	24	NRA
11	150	SRA	PTD	SP	43.0	DUP	3031	2804	46930	WIN	WIN	8½-120	2.750	24	NRA
12	150	SPR	PTD	SP	46.0	DUP	4064	2858	47560	WIN	WIN	8½-120	2.710	24	NRA
13	150	REM	PTD	SP	46.0	DUP	4064	2800	51500	REM	REM	9½	2.700	23	DUP
14	150	WIN	PTD	SP	48.5	WIN	748	2865	48000	WIN	WIN	8½-120		24	WIN
15	150	NOR	SPD	SP	45.5	NOR	201	2860	<52500	NOR	NOR	LR	2.650	24	NOR
16	150	NOS	PTD	SP	46.0	DUP	4064	2852		WIN	REM	9½		22	NOS
17	165	SRA	PBT	HP	41.0	DUP	3031	2673	47260	WIN	WIN	8½-120	2.710	24	NRA
18	165	SPR	PTD	SP	42.0	HOD	BL-C-(2)	2612	<52000	WIN	CCI	250		22	SPR
19	165	HDY	PTD	SP	46.0	HOD	BL-C-(2)	2703	49900	WIN	WIN	8½-120		22	HOD
20	165	NOS	PTD	SP	44.0	DUP	4064	2680		WIN	REM	9½		22	NOS
21	165	HDY	PTD	SP	45.8	WIN	748	2700	49300	FRO	FED	210	2.750	22	HDY
22	168	HDY	PBT	HP	43.5	DUP	4064	2666	47180	WIN	WIN	8½-120	2.800	24	NRA
23	168	NOS	PBT	HP	45.0	HOD	BL-C-(2)	2679		WIN	REM	9½		22	NOS
24	168	SRA	PBT	HP	42.0	DUP	4895	2608	47770	WIN	WIN	8½-120	2.800	24	NRA
25	168	SRA	PBT	HP	46.0	WIN	748	2693	47060	WIN	WIN	8½-120	2.800	24	NRA
26	180	SRA	PBT	HP	41.5	DUP	4320	2521	47300	WIN	WIN	8½-120	2.800	24	NRA
27	180	SRA	PBT	SP	49.5	DUP	4350	2657	48350	WIN	WIN	8½-120	2.800	24	NRA
28	180	REM	PTD	SP	42.5	DUP	4895	2540	50900	REM	REM	9½	2.725	23	DUP
29	180	HDY	PTD	SP	49.0	DUP	4350	2590	48520	WIN	WIN	8½-120	2.800	24	NRA
30	180	SPR	PTD	SP	42.0	HOD	H335	2469	<52000	WIN	CCI	250		22	SPR
31	180	NOS	PTD	SP	43.0	DUP	4064	2605	46650	WIN	WIN	8½-120	2.800	24	NRA
32	180	NOR	SPD	SP	42.1	NOR	202	2525	<52200	NOR	NOR	LR	2.700	24	NOR
33	190	HDY	PBT	HP	39.5	DUP	4895	2400	47880	WIN	WIN	8½-120	2.800	24	NRA
34	190	WIN	PBT	HP	42.0	WIN	748	2445	49000	WIN	WIN	8½-120	2.800	24	WIN
35	190	SRA	PBT	HP	47.5	WIN	760	2568	47260	WIN	WIN	8½-120	2.800	24	NRA
36	190	SRA	PBT	HP	48.2	DUP	4350	2500		REM	REM	9½		26	SRA
37	200	NOS	RNN	SP	47.5	DUP	4350	2443	46250	WIN	WIN	8½-120	2.800	24	NRA
38	200	SPR	PTD	SP	48.0	HOD	H414	2454	<52000	WIN	CCI	250		22	SPR
39	200	SRA	PBT	SP	48.5	HOD	H205	2450		REM	REM	9½		26	SRA
40	200	WIN	SPD	SP	45.7	WIN	760	2430	46500	WIN	WIN	8½-120		24	WIN
41	100	SPR	RNN	SP	15.0	DUP	4759	1516		WIN	CCI	200		22	SPR
42	100	SPR	RNN	SP	19.0	DUP	4759	1925		WIN	CCI	200		22	SPR

LOAD NUMBER	BULLET				POWDER			VELOCITY FPS	PRESSURE CUP	CASE BRAND	PRIMER		CARTRIDGE OAL	BARREL LENGTH	DATA SOURCE
	WEIGHT	BRAND	SHAPE	TYPE	WEIGHT	BRAND	TYPE				BRAND	TYPE			
43	150	SPR	PTD	SP	19.0	DUP	4759	1654		WIN	CCI	200		22	SPR
44	150	SPR	PTD	SP	23.0	DUP	4759	1988		WIN	CCI	200		22	SPR
45	165	SPR	RNN	SP	19.0	DUP	4759	1593		WIN	CCI	200		22	SPR
46	165	SPR	RNN	SP	23.0	DUP	4759	1918		WIN	CCI	200		22	SPR
47	108	CAST	FLN	LP	4.0	HER	UNIQ	905		MIL	CCI	200	2.310	22	NRA
48	108	CAST	FLN	LP	6.0	HER	UNIQ	1225		MIL	CCI	200	2.310	22	NRA
49	115	CAST	FLN	LG	12.0	DUP	4759	1230		MIL	CCI	200	2.310	22	NRA
50	115	CAST	FLN	LG	16.0	DUP	4759	1625		MIL	CCI	200	2.310	22	NRA
51	155	CAST	SPD	LG	14.0	DUP	4759	1365		MIL	CCI	200	2.510	22	NRA
52	155	CAST	SPD	LG	20.0	DUP	4759	1815		MIL	CCI	200	2.510	22	NRA
53	180	CAST	RNN	LG	14.0	DUP	4759	1345		MIL	CCI	200	2.510	22	NRA
54	180	CAST	RNN	LG	20.0	DUP	4759	1780		MIL	CCI	200	2.510	22	NRA

.30-06 SPRINGFIELD

The .30-06 cartridge was adopted for U.S. military use in 1906, and is a modification of the earlier caliber .30 Model 1903 cartridge which was adopted concurrently with the Model 1903 Springfield rifle. The .30-06 has had a distinguished career as a military cartridge, serving U.S. forces well in World War I, World War II and the Korean conflict. It has also been widely used by military allies and other countries friendly to the United States, and it is popular worldwide as a sporting cartridge.

The .30-06 suffers somewhat in comparison to similar cartridges such as the .270 Winchester because the normal chamber pressure is 50,000 c.u.p. for the .30-06, whereas the others operate at 52,000 to 54,000 c.u.p. The 150-grain bullet at a muzzle velocity of 2,910 fps is, nevertheless, a very good flat-trajectory long-range hunting load, and the 200-grain bullets at 2,550 fps or the 220-grain at 2,410 fps are adequate for any North American game. The selection of bullets available to the handloader is extremely wide, and includes some superbly accurate match-type bullets for target shooting.

Though arguments are endless about what constitutes the most desirable all-around centerfire rifle cartridge, the .30-06 certainly has many of the desired characteristics. It performs well with bullets from 110 to 220 grains, jacketed or cast, in full-charge or reduced loads. Bullets of 125 to 130 grains in an accurate .30-06

give creditable performance in varmint hunting, and bullets from 150 to 220 grains are suitable for all types of North American big game. Cast-bullet loads provide inexpensive practice, and loading them for maximum accuracy has its own peculiar fascination for experimentally inclined handloaders.

The maximum product average for commercial .30-06 factory ammunition should not exceed 53,200 c.u.p. in chamber pressure.

Max. Case Length: 2.494" **Trim-To Length:** 2.484"
Max. Overall Length: 3.340" **Primer Size:** Large Rifle **Bullet Dia.:** .308"

RIFLE LOADS FOR THE .30-06

LOAD NUMBER	BULLET				POWDER			VELOCITY FPS	PRESSURE CUP	CASE BRAND	PRIMER		CARTRIDGE OAL	BARREL LENGTH	DATA SOURCE
	WEIGHT	BRAND	SHAPE	TYPE	WEIGHT	BRAND	TYPE				BRAND	TYPE			
1	110	HDY	PTD	SP	56.0	DUP	3031	3365	49300	REM	REM	9½	3.130	23	DUP
2	110	SPR	PTD	SP	57.0	DUP	4320	3237	41690	WIN	WIN	8½-120	3.140	24	NRA
3	110	SRA	SPD	HP	56.4	HOD	H380	3300		WIN	WIN	8½-120		26	SRA
4	110	WIN	PTD	SP	52.7	WIN	748	3230	47000	WIN	WIN	8½-120		24	WIN
5	125	WIN	PTD	SP	57.8	WIN	760	3125	45000	WIN	WIN	8½-120		24	WIN
6	125	SRA	PTD	SP	55.0	DUP	4320	3132	43570	WIN	WIN	8½-120	3.210	24	NRA
7	130	SPR	PTD	HP	50.0	DUP	3031	3122	48340	WIN	WIN	8½-120	3.100	24	NRA
8	130	HDY	PTD	SP	54.0	DUP	4064	3158	49210	WIN	WIN	8½-120	3.100	24	NRA
9	130	NOR	SPD	SP	56.3	NOR	202	3205	<50800	NOR	NOR	LR	3.110	24	NOR
10	150	HDY	PTD	SP	48.0	DUP	3031	2906	48080	WIN	WIN	8½-120	3.200	24	NRA
11	150	SRA	PTD	SP	50.0	DUP	4064	2815	41820	WIN	WIN	8½-120	3.320	24	NRA
12	150	SRA	PTD	SP	52.8	DUP	4064	3000		WIN	WIN	8½-120		26	SRA
13	150	SPR	PTD	SP	59.0	DUP	4350	2955	<50000	WIN	CCI	200		22	SPR
14	150	NOS	PBT	HP	54.0	WIN	760	2821		REM	REM	9½		22	NOS
15	150	NOR	SPD	SP	52.5	NOR	202	2955	<50800	NOR	NOR	LR	3.130	24	NOR
16	150	WIN	PTD	SP	54.0	WIN	760	2900	48000	WIN	WIN	8½-120		24	WIN
17	150	REM	PTD	SP	52.0	DUP	4064	2885	50000	REM	REM	9½	3.200	23	DUP
18	165	NOS	PTD	SP	57.0	DUP	4350	2832		REM	REM	9½		22	NOS
19	165	HDY	PTD	SP	59.0	DUP	4350	2874	45670	WIN	WIN	8½-120	3.300	24	NRA
20	165	SPR	PTD	SP	47.0	DUP	3031	2790	49500	WIN	WIN	8½-120	3.200	24	NRA
21	165	SRA	PBT	SP	59.9	HOD	4831	2800		WIN	WIN	8½-120		26	SRA
22	168	SRA	PBT	HP	49.0	DUP	4064	2780	47310	WIN	WIN	8½-120	3.300	24	NRA
23	168	SRA	PBT	HP	47.4	DUP	4895	2700		WIN	WIN	8½-120		26	SRA
24	168	HDY	PBT	HP	56.0	DUP	4350	2826	47410	WIN	WIN	8½-120	3.280	24	NRA
25	168	HDY	PBT	HP	46.0	DUP	4064	2674	46810	WIN	WIN	8½-120	3.280	24	NRA
26	168	NOS	PBT	HP	52.0	WIN	760	2642		REM	REM	9½		22	NOS
27	180	REM	PTD	SP	57.0	DUP	4350	2750	49700	REM	REM	9½	3.200	23	DUP
28	180	WIN	PTD	SP	53.0	WIN	760	2725	50000	WIN	WIN	8½-120		24	WIN
29	180	NOR	SPD	SP	56.3	NOR	204	2700	<50800	NOR	NOR	LR	3.150	24	NOR
30	180	HDY	PTD	SP	47.0	DUP	4064	2646	49090	WIN	WIN	8½-120	3.300	24	NRA
31	180	SPR	PTD	SP	56.0	DUP	4350	2750	48720	WIN	WIN	8½-120	3.300	24	NRA
32	180	SRA	PBT	SP	49.0	DUP	4064	2721	48920	WIN	WIN	8½-120	3.320	24	NRA
33	180	NOS	PTD	SP	57.0	HOD	H205	2821		REM	REM	9½		22	NOS
34	180	SRA	PBT	HP	56.0	DUP	4350	2800		WIN	WIN	8½-120		26	SRA
35	180	SRA	PBT	HP	48.8	DUP	4064	2700		WIN	WIN	8½-120		26	SRA
36	180	SRA	PBT	HP	50.4	HOD	H380	2700		WIN	WIN	8½-120		26	SRA
37	190	SRA	PBT	HP	55.0	DUP	4350	2723	49260	WIN	WIN	8½-120	3.300	24	NRA
38	190	SRA	PBT	HP	58.5	HOD	4831	2700		WIN	WIN	8½-120		26	SRA
39	190	HDY	PBT	HP	55.0	DUP	4350	2685	46780	WIN	WIN	8½-120	3.300	24	NRA
40	190	HDY	PBT	HP	58.2	HOD	H450	2700		MIL	FED	210		24	HDY
41	200	SRA	PBT	SP	57.6	HOD	4831	2600		WIN	WIN	8½-120		26	SRA
42	200	SRA	PBT	HP	54.0	DUP	4350	2600	46730	WIN	WIN	8½-120	3.300	24	NRA
43	200	WIN	SPD	SP	49.0	WIN	760	2470	46000	WIN	WIN	8½-120		24	WIN
44	200	SPR	PTD	SP	52.0	DUP	4350	2508	45320	WIN	WIN	8½-120	3.340	24	NRA
45	200	NOS	RNN	SP	55.0	HOD	205	2680		REM	REM	9½		22	NOS
46	220	WIN	RNN	SP	49.0	WIN	760	2370	48000	WIN	WIN	8½-120		24	WIN
47	220	HDY	RNN	SP	56.0	DUP	4831	2490	49500	REM	REM	9½	3.185	23	DUP
48	220	SRA	RNN	SP	55.5	NOR	MRP	2500		REM	WIN	8½-120		26	SRA
49	220	SRA	PBT	HP	53.0	DUP	4350	2500		WIN	WIN	8½-120		26	SRA
50	220	SRA	PBT	HP	55.7	HOD	4831	2500		WIN	WIN	8½-120		26	SRA
51	110	SPR	PTD	SP	17.0	DUP	4759	1590		WIN	CCI	200		22	SPR
52	110	SPR	PTD	SP	21.0	DUP	4759	1980		WIN	CCI	200		22	SPR
53	108	CAST	FLN	LP	4.0	HER	UNIQ	865		REM	REM	9½	2.750	24	NRA
54	108	CAST	FLN	LP	6.0	HER	UNIQ	1150		REM	REM	9½	2.750	24	NRA
55	115	CAST	FLN	LG	12.0	DUP	4759	1185		REM	REM	9½	2.750	24	NRA
56	115	CAST	FLN	LG	16.0	DUP	4759	1475		REM	REM	9½	2.750	24	NRA
57	155	CAST	SPD	LG	14.0	DUP	4759	1245		REM	REM	9½	3.000	24	NRA
58	155	CAST	SPD	LG	20.0	DUP	4759	1715		REM	REM	9½	3.000	24	NRA
59	180	CAST	RNN	LG	14.0	DUP	4759	1265		REM	REM	9½	3.000	24	NRA
60	180	CAST	RNN	LG	20.0	DUP	4759	1680		REM	REM	9½	3.000	24	NRA
61	210	CAST	FLN	LG	16.0	DUP	4759	1325		REM	REM	9½	3.225	24	NRA
62	210	CAST	FLN	LG	20.0	DUP	4759	1575		REM	REM	9½	3.225	24	NRA

.300 HOLLAND & HOLLAND MAGNUM

The .300 H.&H. Magnum was introduced by the venerable British gunmaking firm of Holland & Holland during the 1920's, and in England is known as "Holland's Super .30." It was used by NRA shooter Ben Comfort in 1935 to win the famous Wimbledon Cup Match at Camp Perry, and the attendant publicity did much to popularize the .300 H.&H. Magnum in the U.S. Both Winchester and Remington have chambered rifles for it, and many custom guns have been built for it by both hunters and target shooters.

Because the maximum overall length of the cartridge exceeds the length that can be accommodated by many rifles designed for cartridges such as the .30-06, there are few actions suitable for building a custom magazine rifle for the .300 H.&H. Magnum. The .300 Winchester Magnum produces comparable ballistics in a shorter cartridge, and its increasing popularity has been largely at the expense of the .300 H.&H. Magnum. No factory rifles are now chambered for the .300 H.&H. Magnum by U.S. manufacturers, and it is not often chosen for a custom rifle nowadays, though many rifles of this caliber are still in use. It is still a good choice for large North American game, or for medium game at long ranges.

The maximum working pressure for the .300 H&H is limited to about 54,000 c.u.p., and the maximum product average for factory ammunition should not exceed 57,200 c.u.p.

Max. Case Length: 2.850" **Trim-To Length:** 2.840"
Max. Overall Length: 3.655" **Primer Size:** Large Rifle **Bullet Dia.:** .308"

RIFLE LOADS FOR THE .300 H&H MAGNUM

LOAD NUMBER	BULLET				POWDER			VELOCITY FPS	PRESSURE CUP	CASE BRAND	PRIMER		CARTRIDGE OAL	BARREL LENGTH	DATA SOURCE
	WEIGHT	BRAND	SHAPE	TYPE	WEIGHT	BRAND	TYPE				BRAND	TYPE			
1	110	SPR	PTD	SP	75.0	DUP	4350	3636	<54000	WIN	CCI	200		26	SPR
2	110	HDY	PTD	SP	62.0	DUP	3031	3600		WIN	WIN	8½-120		26	HDY
3	110	SRA	SPD	HP	67.9	DUP	4064	3700		WIN	WIN	8½-120		26	SRA
4	125	SRA	PTD	SP	76.4	DUP	4350	3600		WIN	WIN	8½-120		26	SRA
5	130	SPR	PTD	HP	75.0	DUP	4350	3449	51000	WIN	WIN	8½-120	3.400	26	NRA
6	130	HDY	PTD	SP	65.0	DUP	4064	3370	50520	WIN	WIN	8½-120	3.400	26	NRA
7	150	REM	PTD	SP	73.0	DUP	4350	3215	53600	REM	REM	9½M	3.550	24	DUP
8	150	SRA	PTD	SP	63.4	DUP	4064	3200		WIN	WIN	8½-120		26	SRA
9	150	HDY	PTD	SP	71.0	DUP	4350	3223	50920	WIN	WIN	8½-120	3.500	26	NRA
10	150	SPR	PTD	SP	73.0	DUP	4831	3322	<54000	WIN	CCI	200		26	SPR
11	150	NOS	PBT	SP	75.0	NOR	MRP	3296		REM	CCI	250		26	NOS
12	165	SRA	PBT	SP	67.9	HOD	H380	3100		WIN	WIN	8½-120		26	SRA
13	165	HDY	PTD	SP	74.2	HOD	4831	3200		WIN	WIN	8½-120		26	HDY
14	165	SPR	PTD	SP	71.0	DUP	4831	3185	<54000	WIN	CCI	200		26	SPR
15	165	NOS	PTD	SP	72.0	NOR	MRP	3130		REM	CCI	250		26	NOS
16	168	SRA	PBT	HP	69.0	DUP	4350	3093	51750	WIN	WIN	8½-120		26	NRA
17	180	REM	PTD	SP	73.0	DUP	4831	3035	53500	REM	REM	9½M	3.520	24	DUP
18	180	HDY	PTD	SP	69.8	HOD	4831	3000		WIN	WIN	8½-120		26	HDY
19	180	SPR	PTD	SP	68.0	DUP	4350	3086	<54000	WIN	CCI	200		26	SPR
20	180	SRA	PBT	SP	59.1	DUP	4064	2900		WIN	WIN	8½-120		26	SRA
21	180	NOS	PTD	SP	70.0	NOR	MRP	2941		REM	CCI	250		26	NOS
22	190	SRA	PBT	HP	66.0	DUP	4350	2894	51790	WIN	WIN	8½-120	3.600	26	NRA
23	200	SPR	PTD	SP	66.0	DUP	4350	2915	<54000	WIN	CCI	200		26	SPR
24	200	SRA	PBT	SP	67.7	DUP	4831	2800		WIN	WIN	8½-120		26	SRA
25	200	SRA	PBT	HP	65.0	DUP	4350	2804	52040	WIN	WIN	8½-120	3.600	26	NRA
26	200	NOS	RNN	SP	67.0	NOR	MRP	2811		REM	CCI	250		26	NOS
27	220	REM	RNN	SP	67.0	DUP	4831	2710	54000	REM	REM	9½M	3.575	24	DUP
28	220	SRA	RNN	SP	63.2	DUP	4350	2700		WIN	WIN	8½-120		26	SRA
29	220	HDY	RNN	SP	80.0	HOD	H870	2700		WIN	WIN	8½-120		26	HDY
30	220	SRA	PBT	HP	68.8	HOD	4831	2700		WIN	WIN	8½-120		26	SRA

.308 NORMA MAGNUM

The .308 Norma Magnum was introduced in 1961 by the Swedish firm of AB Norma Projektilfabrik. It is based on the shortened reduced-taper belted-magnum case, and the overall cartridge length does not exceed that of the 8x57mm Mauser, so it is particularly suitable for conversion of .30-06 rifles to magnum chambering. Many surplus .30-06 Model 1903 and 1903A3 rifles were converted to .308 Norma Magnum by gunsmiths during the 1960's. It would probably have achieved greater popularity in the U.S. if Norma cases and ammunition had been more widely available, and had it not been for the introduction of the similar .300 Winchester Magnum cartridge in 1963.

Some handloaders consider the .308 Norma Magnum superior in design to the .300 Winchester Magnum because its neck length measures about .32 inch, compared to a length of about .26 inch for the Winchester cartridge. The marksmanship units of the U.S. armed forces have generally built their custom long-range bolt-action rifles for the wildcat .30-338 cartridge, which closely resembles the .308 Norma

Magnum, in preference to the standard .300 Winchester Magnum. On the other hand, the shorter neck of the .300 Winchester Magnum allows a longer case body, within the same constraints of overall cartridge length, and thus provides somewhat greater powder capacity.

A precaution that must be taken into account by handloaders who use the .308 Norma Magnum is the comparatively great difference in throat configuration among different rifles chambered for the cartridge. Some rifles were deliberately chambered with very long throats, sometimes called "freeboring," and loads developed in barrels of that type may prove excessive in normally throated barrels. It is therefore especially necessary that the handloader develop charges carefully, starting well below the maximum charges listed, and working up in small increments while watching carefully for signs of excessive pressure.

Max. Case Length: 2.559″ **Trim-To Length:** 2.549″
Max. Overall Length: 3.250″ **Primer Size:** Large
Rifle Magnum **Bullet Dia.:** .308″

RIFLE LOADS FOR THE .308 NORMA MAGNUM

LOAD NUMBER	BULLET WEIGHT	BULLET BRAND	BULLET SHAPE	BULLET TYPE	POWDER WEIGHT	POWDER BRAND	POWDER TYPE	VELOCITY FPS	PRESSURE CUP	CASE BRAND	PRIMER BRAND	PRIMER TYPE	CARTRIDGE OAL	BARREL LENGTH	DATA SOURCE
1	110	SPR	PTD	SP	78.0	DUP	4831	3521		NOR	CCI	250		24½	SPR
2	110	HDY	PTD	SP	69.0	HOD	H380	3500		NOR	WIN	8½-120		24	HDY
3	110	SRA	SPD	HP	77.4	DUP	4350	3500		NOR	FED	215		24	SRA
4	110	SPR	PTD	SP	80.0	HOD	4831	3563	50100	NOR	CCI	250		26	HOD
5	110	SPR	PTD	SP	71.0	HOD	H380	3609	51100	NOR	CCI	250		26	HOD
6	125	SRA	PTD	SP	81.0	HOD	H450	3300		NOR	FED	215		24	SRA
7	130	SPR	PTD	HP	80.0	HOD	H450	3429	54100	NOR	CCI	250		26	HOD
8	130	SPR	PTD	HP	70.0	HOD	H380	3415	50900	NOR	CCI	250		26	HOD
9	130	NOR	SPD	SP	78.4	NOR	204	3545	<55100	NOR	NOR	LR	3.170	24	NOR
10	130	SPR	PTD	HP	79.0	HOD	H450	3296		NOR	CCI	250		24½	SPR
11	150	NOR	SPD	SP	76.7	NOR	204	3330	<55100	NOR	NOR	LR	3.210	24	NOR
12	150	SRA	PTD	SP	72.4	DUP	4350	3200		NOR	FED	215		24	SRA
13	150	HDY	PTD	SP	76.4	HOD	H450	3200		NOR	WIN	8½-120		24	HDY
14	150	SPR	PTD	SP	75.0	DUP	4831	3188		NOR	CCI	250		24½	SPR
15	150	NOS	PTD	SP	74.0	DUP	4831	3193		NOR	REM	9½M		25	NOS
16	150	SPR	PTD	SP	76.0	HOD	4831	3258	51900	NOR	CCI	250		26	HOD
17	150	SPR	PTD	SP	77.0	HOD	H450	3241	54400	NOR	CCI	250		26	HOD
18	165	SPR	PTD	SP	75.0	HOD	4831	3140	52300	NOR	CCI	250		26	HOD
19	165	SPR	PTD	SP	75.0	HOD	H450	3122	53200	NOR	CCI	250		26	HOD
20	165	SPR	PTD	SP	67.0	HOD	H380	3079	52100	NOR	CCI	250		26	HOD
21	165	SPR	PTD	SP	65.0	HOD	H205	2952		NOR	CCI	250		24½	SPR
22	165	HDY	PTD	SP	73.2	HOD	4831	3100		NOR	WIN	8½-120		24	HDY
23	165	NOS	PBT	SP	72.0	DUP	4831	3085		NOR	REM	9½M		25	NOS
24	165	SRA	PBT	SP	71.0	DUP	4350	3100		NOR	FED	215		24	SRA
25	168	HDY	PBT	HP	68.9	DUP	4350	3100		NOR	WIN	8½-120		24	HDY
26	180	SPR	PTD	SP	73.0	HOD	4831	3022	52300	NOR	CCI	250		26	HOD
27	180	SPR	PTD	SP	71.0	HOD	H450	3013	53600	NOR	CCI	250		26	HOD
28	180	SRA	PBT	HP	71.2	DUP	4831	2900		NOR	FED	215		24	SRA

LOAD NUMBER	BULLET				POWDER			VELOCITY FPS	PRESSURE CUP	CASE BRAND	PRIMER		CARTRIDGE OAL	BARREL LENGTH	DATA SOURCE
	WEIGHT	BRAND	SHAPE	TYPE	WEIGHT	BRAND	TYPE				BRAND	TYPE			
29	180	HDY			72.0	HOD	4831	2900		NOR	WIN	8½-120		24	HDY
30	180	SPR			71.0	HOD	H450	2859		NOR	CCI	250		24½	SPR
31	180	NOS	PTD	SP	71.0	DUP	4831	2971		NOR	REM	9½M		25	NOS
32	180	NOR	SPD	SP	74.3	NOR	MRP	3020	<55100	NOR	NOR	LR	3.250	24	NOR
33	190	HDY	PBT	HP	65.8	DUP	4350	2900		NOR	WIN	8½-120		24	HDY
34	200	SPR	PTD	SP	70.0	HOD	4831	2889	52700	NOR	CCI	250		26	HOD
35	200	SPR	PTD	SP	70.0	HOD	H450	2810	53400	NOR	CCI	250		26	HOD
36	200	SPR	PTD	SP	64.0	HOD	H205	2747	53500	NOR	CCI	250		26	HOD
37	200	SPR	PTD	SP	70.0	HOD	H450	2833		NOR	CCI	250		24½	SPR
38	200	SRA	PBT	HP	69.0	DUP	4831	2700		NOR	FED	215		24	SRA
39	200	NOS	RNN	SP	69.0	DUP	4831	2763		NOR	REM	9½M		25	NOS
40	220	HDY	RNN	SP	68.0	HOD	4831	2697	52700	NOR	CCI	250		26	HOD
41	220	HDY	RNN	SP	70.0	HOD	450	2712	53600	NOR	CCI	250		26	HOD
42	220	SRA	PBT	HP	68.6	DUP	4831	2700		NOR	FED	215		24	SRA
43	220	HDY	RNN	SP	66.8	HOD	4831	2600		NOR	WIN	8½-120		24	HDY

.300 WINCHESTER MAGNUM

The .300 Winchester Magnum was introduced in 1963. It is based on a shortened reduced-taper belted magnum case, and the overall cartridge length of 3.34 inches is the same as that of the .30-06, allowing it to be used in medium-length actions. It is designed to have the maximum practicable powder capacity attainable in a cartridge of this length based on the standard magnum case. The neck length is minimized to achieve the longest possible body (and thus the greatest powder capacity), and the neck is therefore only about .26 inch in length. This is only marginally sufficient to hold the bullet securely in the case, so that it will not be driven back into the case during handling or feeding in the rifle. Loaded cartridges should be tested by pressing the bullet nose firmly against a solid surface while holding onto the case. If the bullets are pushed farther into the case, a smaller expanding plug must be used, or the case mouth crimped into a bullet cannelure, or a different bullet must be selected.

The maximum allowable bullet protrusion, determined by the difference between case length and overall cartridge length measures about .72 inch or 2.34 calibers. Any bullet having an axial length of ogive greater than 2.34 calibers, such as many match-type .308-inch bullets have, will have the cylindrical bearing surface below the case mouth when seated to the nominal overall length of 3.34 inches, and therefore will have less support even than the short case neck otherwise would provide. Such bullets are not suitable for use in the .300 Winchester Magnum unless they can be "long-loaded" to exceed the industry-established limits for overall cartridge length.

This is not a problem for most hunting bullets, because they generally have shorter ogival length. However, any bullet having an overall length greater than about .98 inch (or 3.19 calibers) will intrude below the case neck, into the powder space, when seated to the maximum cartridge overall length of 3.34 inches. Most pointed .308-inch bullets weighing 150 grains or greater are longer than .98 inch, and they will therefore intrude into the powder space, more or less according to their weights, when seated in the .300 Winchester Magnum cartridge.

Despite the compromises made in its design, the .300 Winchester Magnum is a very powerful and satisfactory hunting cartridge, suitable for the largest North American game. In match rifles that are single-loaded, the nominal overall cartridge length can be exceeded for handloading, and the cartridge is then a suitable one for long-range target shooting.

The working pressure for the .300 Winchester Magnum cartridge is normally limited to about 54,000 c.u.p. The maximum product average for factory ammunition should not exceed 57,200 c.u.p.

Max. Case Length: 2.620″ **Trim-To Length:** 2.610″
Max. Overall Length: 3.340″ **Primer Size:** Large Rifle **Bullet Dia.:** .308″

RIFLE LOADS FOR THE .300 WINCHESTER MAGNUM

LOAD NUMBER	BULLET				POWDER			VELOCITY FPS	PRESSURE CUP	CASE BRAND	PRIMER		CARTRIDGE OAL	BARREL LENGTH	DATA SOURCE
	WEIGHT	BRAND	SHAPE	TYPE	WEIGHT	BRAND	TYPE				BRAND	TYPE			
1	110	WIN	PTD	SP	81.8	WIN	785	3500	46500	WIN	WIN	8½-120		24	WIN
2	110	HDY	PTD	SP	79.9	DUP	4350	3600		WIN	CCI	250		24	HDY
3	110	SRA	SPD	HP	80.4	HOD	205	3600		WIN	WIN	8½-120		24	SRA
4	110	SPR	PTD	SP	80.0	DUP	4350	3616	<54000	WIN	CCI	250		24	SPR
5	125	SRA	PTD	SP	80.0	HOD	205	3500		WIN	WIN	8½-120		24	SRA
6	125	WIN	PTP	SP	81.8	WIN	785	3405	49000	WIN	WIN	8½-120		24	WIN
7	130	SPR	PTD	HP	80.0	DUP	4831	3448	<54000	WIN	CCI	250		24	SPR
8	130	HDY	PTD	SP	75.0	DUP	4350	3524	52090	WIN	WIN	8½-120	3.340	26	NRA
9	150	WIN	PTD	SP	76.0	WIN	785	3150	51000	WIN	WIN	8½-120		24	WIN
10	150	REM	PTD	SP	80.0	DUP	4831	3365	54000	REM	REM	9½M	3.250	24	DUP
11	150	SPR	PTD	SP	73.0	DUP	4350	3333	52350	WIN	WIN	8½-120	3.340	26	NRA
12	150	HDY	PTD	SP	78.0	DUP	4831	3311		WIN	CCI	250		24	HDY
13	150	SRA	PTD	SP	75.7	HOD	H205	3300		WIN	WIN	8½-120		24	SRA
14	150	NOS	PBT	SP	74.0	DUP	4350	3416		WIN	REM	9½M		26	NOS
15	165	SPR	PTD	SP	72.0	DUP	4350	3217	53490	WIN	WIN	8½-120	3.340	26	NRA
16	165	NOS	PTD	SP	74.0	HOD	H205	3261		WIN	REM	9½M		26	NOS
17	165	HDY	PTD	SP	79.0	HOD	4831	3200		WIN	CCI	250		24	HDY
18	165	SRA	PBT	SP	77.4	DUP	4831	3200		WIN	WIN	8½-120		24	SRA
19	168	HDY	PBT	HP	77.8	HOD	4831	3100		WIN	CCI	250		24	HDY
20	180	WIN	PTD	SP	72.0	WIN	785	2880	51000	WIN	WIN	8½-120		24	WIN
21	180	REM	PTD	SP	75.5	DUP	4831	3105	53700	WIN	WIN	8½-120	3.250	24	DUP
22	180	SRA	PBT	SP	71.0	DUP	4350	3124	53750	WIN	WIN	8½-120	3.340	26	NRA
23	180	HDY	PTD	SP	68.0	DUP	4350	3015	52110	WIN	WIN	8½-120	3.340	26	NRA
24	180	SPR	PTD	SP	73.0	DUP	4831	2996	<54000	WIN	CCI	250		24	SPR
25	180	NOS	PTD	SP	71.0	HOD	H205	3092		WIN	REM	9½M		26	NOS
26	190	SRA	PBT	HP	72.4	DUP	4831	2900		WIN	WIN	8½-120		24	SRA
27	190	HDY	PBT	HP	69.0	DUP	4350	2999	52300	WIN	WIN	8½-120	3.340	26	NRA
28	200	SRA	PBT	HP	73.6	HOD	4831	2800		WIN	WIN	8½-120		24	SRA
29	200	SPR	PTD	SP	66.0	DUP	4350	2845	52830	WIN	WIN	8½-120	3.340	26	NRA
30	200	NOS	RNN	SP	66.0	DUP	4350	2885		WIN	REM	9½M		26	NOS
31	220	REM	RNN	SP	70.0	DUP	4831	2730	53100	WIN	WIN	8½-120	3.250	24	DUP

.300 WEATHERBY MAGNUM

The .300 Weatherby Magnum is among the earliest of the Weatherby cartridges, and was developed in the early 1940's. It is based on a full-length .300 H.&H. Magnum case, expanded to greatly reduced body taper, and having the peculiar Weatherby shoulder configuration consisting of relatively long, blended radii at the junctures of the shoulder with the body and the neck. The cartridge was widely used as a "semi-wildcat" before factory-made cases were available for it, and the cases were fire-formed simply by firing .300 H.&H. Magnum cartridges in the Weatherby chamber. The fire-formed cases were then reloaded with powder charges heavier than those which the .300 H.&H. Magnum cartridge could accommodate.

Some rifles chambered for the .300 Weatherby cartridge have "free-bored" throats, a device intended to permit the use of heavier powder charges than would be permissible with conventional throating, and the handloader must be cautious not to use loads developed in a "free-bored" chamber if the chamber in his particular rifle has conventional throating.

The powder capacity of the .300 Weatherby Magnum exceeds that of the .300 Winchester Magnum by at least 10 per cent, and by more than that if long heavy bullets are seated to standard overall cartridge length in the short-necked Winchester case. The .300 Weatherby is, therefore, a more powerful cartridge, capable of generating more than 4,000 foot-pounds of muzzle energy with maximum loads, compared to about 3,600 foot-pounds for the .300 Winchester Magnum.

The .300 Weatherby Magnum is probably the most

popular of all the Weatherby Magnum cartridges, and deservedly so. It is unequalled in muzzle energy by any other standard U.S. cartridge firing .30-caliber bullets, and more than adequate for the largest North American game. It has also been used successfully on thin-skinned African game, and undoubtedly serves that purpose well when properly constructed bullets are used.

Max. Case Length: 2.825″ **Trim-To Length:** 2.815″
Max. Overall Length: 3.562″ **Primer Size:** Large Rifle Magnum **Bullet Dia.:** .308″

RIFLE LOADS FOR THE .300 WEATHERBY MAGNUM

LOAD NUMBER	BULLET				POWDER			VELOCITY FPS	PRESSURE CUP	CASE BRAND	PRIMER		CARTRIDGE OAL	BARREL LENGTH	DATA SOURCE
	WEIGHT	BRAND	SHAPE	TYPE	WEIGHT	BRAND	TYPE				BRAND	TYPE			
1	110	HDY	PTD	SP	90.0	DUP	4350	3863	53460	WEA	FED	215	3.562	26	WEA
2	110	HDY	PTD	SP	81.0	NOR	203	3900	53050	WEA	FED	215	3.562	26	WEA
3	110	SRA	SPD	HP	78.7	DUP	4064	3800		WEA	FED	215		26	SRA
4	110	SPR	PTD	SP	88.0	DUP	4831	3788		WEA	CCI	250		26	SPR
5	125	SRA	PTD	SP	85.2	DUP	4350	3600		WEA	FED	215		26	SRA
6	130	HDY	PTD	SP	84.0	DUP	4350	3567	52570	WEA	FED	215	3.562	26	WEA
7	130	SPR	PTD	HP	86.0	DUP	4831	3660		WEA	CCI	250		26	SPR
8	150	HDY	PTD	SP	82.0	DUP	4350	3458	52380	WEA	FED	215	3.562	26	WEA
9	150	HDY	PTD	SP	88.0	HOD	4831	3470	54570	WEA	FED	215	3.562	26	WEA
10	150	HDY	PTD	SP	88.0	NOR	MRP	3545	53490	WEA	FED	215	3.562	26	WEA
11	165	SPR	PTD	SP	82.0	DUP	4831	3235		WEA	CCI	250		26	SPR
12	165	SRA	PBT	SP	78.2	DUP	4350	3200		WEA	FED	215		26	SRA
13	165	NOS	PTD	SP	74.0	HOD	H205	3162		WEA	FED	215		24	NOS
14	180	HDY	SPD	SP	79.0	DUP	4350	3145	53610	WEA	FED	215	3.562	26	WEA
15	180	HDY	SPD	SP	82.0	HOD	4831	3145	54310	WEA	FED	215	3.562	26	WEA
16	180	SPR	SPD	SP	79.0	DUP	4831	3064		WEA	CCI	250		26	SPR
17	180	SRA	PBT	SP	77.1	DUP	4350	3100		WEA	FED	215		26	SRA
18	180	NOS	PTD	SP	76.0	NOR	MRP	3010		WEA	FED	215		24	NOS
19	200	SRA	PBT	HP	75.8	DUP	4350	3000		WEA	FED	215		26	SRA
20	200	NOS	RNN	SP	77.2	NOR	MRP	3000	49000	WEA	FED	215	3.562	26	WEA
21	200	NOS	RNN	SP	80.0	HOD	4831	3029	54690	WEA	FED	215	3.562	26	WEA
22	200	NOS	RNN	SP	78.0	HOD	4831	2926	50620	WEA	FED	215	3.562	26	WEA
23	200	SPR	PTD	SP	75.0	DUP	4350	2917		WEA	CCI	250		26	SPR
24	220	SRA	PBT	HP	72.8	DUP	4350	2800		WEA	FED	215		26	SRA
25	220	SRA	PTD	SP	73.6	DUP	4831	2700		WEA	FED	215		26	SRA
26	220	HDY	RNN	SP	73.0	DUP	4350	2878	54890	WEA	FED	215	3.562	26	WEA
27	220	HDY	RNN	SP	76.0	HOD	4831	2800	51060	WEA	FED	215	3.562	26	WEA
28	220	HDY	RNN	SP	77.2	NOR	MRP	2905	52850	WEA	FED	215	3.562	26	WEA

7.65 x 53mm MAUSER

The 7.65x53mm Mauser was originally designed for use in the Belgian Model 1889 Mauser rifle, and it is sometimes called the "7.65mm Belgian Mauser." It has also been used as a military cartridge by Spain, Turkey, Argentina, Bolivia, Colombia, Ecuador, Paraguay and Peru. It enjoyed some popularity as a sporting cartridge in the U.S. years ago. The Remington Model 30S, Winchester Model 54, and a few Winchester Model 70 rifles were chambered for it, and sporting ammunition of this caliber was made by U.S. factories until about 1936. A revival of interest in the cartridge was begun when a large number of Argentine Model 1891 Mauser rifles, many in excellent condition, were imported and sold in the U.S. during the 1950's and 1960's. Other types of military rifles adapted to this cartridge have also been imported in considerable quantities.

Cases for the 7.65x53mm Mauser are easily formed from .30-06, 8x57mm or similar brass simply by running the cases into a 7.65x53mm full-length resizing die (from which the decapper/expander assembly has been removed) and cutting and/or trimming the cases to 2.11 inches in length. The nominal bore and groove diameters of 7.65x53mm barrels are .301 and .311 of an inch respectively, and .311- or .312-inch bullets are the best choice for reloading.

Max. Case Length: 2.105″ **Trim-To Length:** 2.100″
Max. Overall Length: 2.970″ **Primer Size:** Large Rifle **Bullet Dia.:** .311″

RIFLE LOADS FOR THE 7.65 x 53 mm MAUSER

LOAD NUMBER	BULLET				POWDER			VELOCITY FPS	PRESSURE CUP	CASE BRAND	PRIMER		CARTRIDGE OAL	BARREL LENGTH	DATA SOURCE
	WEIGHT	BRAND	SHAPE	TYPE	WEIGHT	BRAND	TYPE				BRAND	TYPE			
1	100	SPR	RNN	SP	49.0	DUP	4064	2763		NOR	CCI	200		29	SPR
2	150	SPR	PTD	SP	42.0	DUP	3031	2577		NOR	CCI	200		29	SPR
3	150	HDY	PTD	SP	44.1	DUP	4064	2700		NOR	FED	210		29	HDY
4	150	SRA	PTD	SP	44.0	DUP	4895	2600		NOR	REM	9½		29	SRA
5	150	NOR	SPD	SP	47.8	NOR	201	2920	<49300	NOR	NOR	LR	2.850	24	NOR
6	174	HDY	RNN	SP	47.7	DUP	4350	2500		NOR	FED	210		29	HDY
7	175	SPR	RNN	SP	48.0	DUP	4831	2356		NOR	CCI	200		29	SPR
8	180	SRA	PTD	SP	41.0	DUP	4064	2440	38140	WIN	WIN	8½-120	2.960	29	NRA
9	180	SPR	RNN	SP	48.0	DUP	4831	2356		NOR	CCI	200		29	SPR

.303 BRITISH

The .303 British cartridge was adopted by Great Britain in 1888. In the countries of the former British Empire, the .303 British cartridge achieved popularity comparable to that of the .30-06 in the United States. Originally loaded with a compressed blackpowder charge and a 215-grain jacketed roundnose bullet, the cartridge was converted in 1892 to a smokeless load using the famous British cordite propellant. The round-nose 215-grain bullet was replaced by a 174-grain pointed bullet in the general-purpose military round about 1914, and this load continued in use until the cartridge became obsolete with the adoption of the 7.62mm NATO cartridge by British forces in the 1960's. A great variety of special-purpose military loads was also used, including one containing a pointed boattail bullet and single-base smokeless powder similar to the Du Pont IMR types. This cartridge, called the Mark VIIIZ, was intended especially for machine guns, in which the boattail bullet provided improved long-range effectiveness, and the single-base powder produced less erosion than did the British cordite in the machinegun barrels.

The working chamber pressure of the .303 British cartridge is about 45,000 c.u.p., in equivalent U.S. units, and it therefore produces more energy than the contemporary .30-40 Krag which is limited to about 40,000 c.u.p. Jacketed bullets for the .303 British should be of .311 to .312 of an inch in diameter.

The maximum product average chamber pressure for the .303 British cartridge, as loaded for sporting use by U.S. manufacturers, should not exceed 48,200 c.u.p.

Max. Case Length: 2.222″ **Trim-To Length:** 2.212″
Max. Overall Length: 3.075″ **Primer Size:** Large Rifle **Bullet Dia.:** .311″

RIFLE LOADS FOR THE .303 BRITISH

LOAD NUMBER	BULLET				POWDER			VELOCITY FPS	PRESSURE CUP	CASE BRAND	PRIMER		CARTRIDGE OAL	BARREL LENGTH	DATA SOURCE
	WEIGHT	BRAND	SHAPE	TYPE	WEIGHT	BRAND	TYPE				BRAND	TYPE			
1	100	SPR	RNN	SP	44.0	DUP	3031	2933		CIL	CCI	200		25	SPR
2	150	HDY	PTD	SP	44.0	DUP	3031	2787	44990	REM	WIN	8½-120	2.840	26	NRA
3	150	SRA	PTD	SP	48.5	DUP	4320	2808	43830	REM	WIN	8½-120	2.945	26	NRA
4	150	NOR	SPD	SP	44.6	NOR	201	2720	<46400	NOR	NOR	LR	2.950	24	NOR
5	150	SPR	PTD	SP	50.0	DUP	4350	2584		CIL	CCI	200		25	SPR
6	174	HDY	RNN	SP	46.5	DUP	4350	2400		REM	FED	210		25	HDY
7	180	SPR	RNN	SP	47.0	DUP	4831	2421		CIL	CCI	200		25	SPR
8	180	SRA	PTD	SP	42.0	DUP	3031	2533	44220	REM	WIN	8½-120	3.075	26	NRA
9	180	NOR	SPD	SP	43.0	NOR	202	2540	<46400	NOR	NOR	LR	2.970	24	NOR
10	215	REM	RNN	SP	49.5	DUP	4350	2432	44630	REM	WIN	8½-120	3.075	26	NRA

7.7mm JAPANESE ARISAKA

The 7.7mm Arisaka cartridge was adopted to replace the 6.5mm Arisaka military cartridge by Japan in 1939, though both cartridges continued in use throughout World War II. It is comparable in power to the .303 British cartridge. Popularity of the 7.7mm Arisaka in the U.S. is due to the acquisition of large numbers of the Japanese Model 99 Arisaka rifle by returning U.S. military personnel after World War II. The 7.7mm Arisaka cartridge has been loaded by Norma and imported for sale in the U.S. for many years, and the Norma cases are adapted to standard .210-inch American rifle primers. Satisfactory cases can also be formed from .30-06 brass, using only the regular 7.7mm Arisaka full-length resizing die, and trimming to a length of 2.26 inches. Bullets of .311-inch diameter are most suitable for loading the 7.7mm Arisaka

cartridge. The Model 99 Arisaka rifle is clumsy, and many were crudely manufactured, but it is a strong rifle and very serviceable. Many were "sporterized" during the late 1940's and 1950's, although they do not make very handome or convenient sporters owing to the configuration of the action and the inconvenient operation of the safety.

Another 7.7mm Japanese cartridge exists, the Type 92, designed for use in machineguns. It is of semi-rimless configuration, and is not interchangeable with the 7.7mm Arisaka cartridge.

Max. Case Length: 2.270″ **Trim-To Length:** 2.260″
Max. Overall Length: 3.150″ **Primer Size:** Large
Rifle **Bullet Dia.:** .311″

RIFLE LOADS FOR THE 7.7 JAPANESE ARISAKA

LOAD NUMBER	BULLET				POWDER			VELOCITY FPS	PRESSURE CUP	CASE BRAND	PRIMER		CARTRIDGE OAL	BARREL LENGTH	DATA SOURCE
	WEIGHT	BRAND	SHAPE	TYPE	WEIGHT	BRAND	TYPE				BRAND	TYPE			
1	100	SPR	RNN	SP	48.0	DUP	3031	2621		NOR	CCI	200		26	SPR
2	130	NOR	SPD	SP	51.7	NOR	202	3005	<39200	NOR	NOR	LR	2.840	24	NOR
3	130	NOR	SPD	SP	47.0	DUP	3031	3018	40500	NOR	NOR	LR			NRA
4	150	NOR	SPD	SP	50.0	DUP	4064	2888	41600	NOR	NOR	LR			NRA
5	150	SRA	PTD	SP	48.8	DUP	4320	2700		NOR	REM	9½		25	SRA
6	150	SPR	PTD	SP	53.0	DUP	4350	2586		NOR	CCI	200		26	SPR
7	150	HDY	PTD	SP	54.8	HOD	4831	2500		NOR	FED	210		25½	HDY
8	174	HDY	RNN	SP	42.8	DUP	4064	2400		NOR	FED	210		25½	HDY
9	180	NOR	SPD	SP	46.0	NOR	202	2515	<39200	NOR	NOR	LR	3.030	24	NOR
10	180	NOR	SPD	SP	46.0	DUP	4064	2559	38800	NOR	NOR	LR			NRA
11	180	SRA	PTD	SP	50.5	DUP	4350	2500		NOR	REM	9½		25	SRA
12	215	NOR	RNN	SP	43.5	DUP	4064	2313	38100	NOR	NOR	LR			NRA

.32-20 (.32 W.C.F.)

Introduced by Winchester in about 1882 for use in their Model 1873 rifle, the .32-20 was soon chambered in the Colt single-action revolvers. Colt and Smith & Wesson double-action revolvers were later chambered for it, and some foreign revolvers imported years ago into the U.S. also use this cartridge. After the introduction of the Winchester Model 1892 rifle chambered for the .32-20, a special high-velocity factory load was introduced especially for the Model 1892 and other rifles of comparable strength. The chamber-pressure limit for these high-velocity loads was about 26,000 c.u.p., compared to about 16,000

c.u.p. for the standard-velocity load. Notices printed on the ammunition box warned against using these high-velocity loads in the old Model 1873 rifle, or in any handgun, because of the greatly increased pressure. Some old handloading data were developed for these high-velocity rifle loads, and handloaders must exercise due care against using such data for handgun loads.

The .32-20 is not a particularly difficult cartridge to load for a handgun. Because it is slightly bottle-necked, chambers and cartridges should be kept free of excessive oil or grease to prevent "set-back" which can otherwise cause the cylinder to bind instead of rotating freely. Cases must be trimmed to uniform length for uniform crimping, and care must be exercised to avoid excessive force in crimping, since the cases are relatively thin, and may crumple at the shoulder if crimped with excessive force.

Pressure-tested loading data are unfortunately very scarce for the .32-20. Hercules formerly listed extensive data for it, using Bullseye and Unique powders which are still available. They now warn against using those data, however, owing to changes in cartridge cases and other components since the data were developed. Winchester-Western has, however, provided data for their 630 powder, suitable for use in both rifle and handgun loads. A fairly strong crimp is required for proper ignition and burning of 630 in .32-20 handguns.

Hercules Unique has been used for many years in .32-20 handloads, and been found very satisfactory. The loads listed here using Unique have not been pressure-tested, but they are substantially less than the maximum loads formerly listed by Hercules, and are believed to produce pressures not exceeding the 16,000-c.u.p. limit now established for the cartridge. Long use of these loads in .32-20 revolvers has been entirely satisfactory.

Some of .32-20 cases are of balloon-head type, and should not be used for handloading. Cases of recent manufacture are of the much stronger solid-head type.

The maximum product average chamber pressure for the .32-20 cartridge is now established at 17,700 c.u.p.

Max. Case Length: 1.315″ **Trim-To Length:** 1.310″
Max. Overall Length: 1.592″ **Primer Size:** Small Rifle **Bullet Dia.:** .310″

RIFLE LOADS FOR THE .32-20

LOAD NUMBER	BULLET				POWDER			VELOCITY FPS	PRESSURE CUP	CASE BRAND	PRIMER		CARTRIDGE OAL	BARREL LENGTH	DATA SOURCE
	WEIGHT	BRAND	SHAPE	TYPE	WEIGHT	BRAND	TYPE				BRAND	TYPE			
1	100	WIN	FLN	LP	7.2	WIN	630	1210	<16000	WIN	WIN	6½-116	1.590	26	WIN
2	100	WIN	FLN	SP	7.5	WIN	630	1210	<16000	WIN	WIN	6½-116	1.590	26	WIN
3	100	CAST	FLN	LP	4.1	HER	UNIQ	1210		WIN	WIN	6½-116	1.590	26	NRA
4	115	CAST	FLN	LP	4.3	HER	UNIQ	1200		WIN	WIN	6½-116	1.590	26	NRA

.32-40 (Ballard, Marlin & Winchester)

This .32-40 cartridge was introduced about 1884, primarily as a target cartridge. It was loaded with blackpowder and lead bullets, at a velocity of about 1,400 fps. Originally used in single-shot target rifles such as the Ballard, Stevens and Winchester, it was soon adopted for use in the Marlin Models 1881 and 1893 lever-action repeating rifles.

The famous Winchester Model 1894 rifle was designed for the new smokeless-powder ammunition then under development, but Winchester's ammunition development had fallen behind the development of the rifle, so no suitable smokeless-powder cartridge was available when the rifle was scheduled for introduction in 1894. The first Model 1894 Winchester rifles were therefore chambered for the .32-40 and .38-55 cartridges. The Savage Model 1899 was also offered later in .32-40 chambering. The .32-40 cartridge achieved considerable popularity as a hunting cartridge (though it is marginal by modern standards for deer-size game), and it was widely used by deer hunters until the 1930's.

The greatest popularity of the .32-40 was, however, as a target cartridge, in the days of blackpowder shooting. It is said to have been the favorite cartridge of Harry M. Pope, the famed barrel-maker and Scheutzen rifleman, and Pope fitted many .32-40 barrels to Ballard, Stevens and Winchester single-shot rifles. Though no factory rifles have been chambered for the .32-40 in the past 40 years, the cartridge still enjoys well deserved popularity among the present shooters of single-shot cast-bullet match rifles. It should be noted, incidentally, that there were in the late 19th century at least two other cartridges having the same numerical designation, the .32-40 Remington and .32-40 Bullard, which are not interchangeable with the .32-40 Ballard, Marlin and Winchester.

As with some other blackpowder cartridges that existed during the transition to smokeless powder, the .32-40 was for some time produced in a special "high-velocity" smokeless load, developing substantially more chamber pressure than the blackpowder load. Such loads were intended for use only in the stronger guns, such as the Winchester 1894, Marlin 1893, Savage 1899, Winchester Single-Shot and Stevens 44½. They should not be used in the weaker blackpowder guns such as the Ballard or Stevens Model 44 single-shots. The normal working pressure for .32-40 ammunition, when it was last loaded by U.S. factories, was about 30,000 c.u.p. That is undoubtedly satisfactory for the stronger actions mentioned above, but for the old Ballards and similar actions, it would be inadvisable to exceed the ballistics of blackpowder loads. Loads 4 through 8 in the accompanying table

should be safe in the older .32-40 rifles if they are in sound mechanical condition.

Max. Case Length: 2.130″ **Trim-To Length:** 2.120″
Max. Overall Length: 2.500″ **Primer Size:** Large Rifle
Bullet Dia.: .322″

RIFLE LOADS FOR THE .32-40

LOAD NUMBER	BULLET				POWDER			VELOCITY FPS	PRESSURE CUP	CASE BRAND	PRIMER		CARTRIDGE OAL	BARREL LENGTH	DATA SOURCE
	WEIGHT	BRAND	SHAPE	TYPE	WEIGHT	BRAND	TYPE				BRAND	TYPE			
1	165	REM	FLN	SP	26.0	HER	RL7	2025	25000	CIL	REM 9½		2.590	26	HER
2	170	REM	FLN	SP	25.5	HER	RL7	1930	25900	CIL	REM 9½		2.590	26	HER
3	165	WIN	FLN	SP	12.2	WIN	630	1420	<30000	WIN	WIN	8½-120	2.500	24	WIN
4	125	CAST	FLN	LP	7.0	HER	UNIQ	1425		WIN	WIN	8½-120		26	NRA
5	165	CAST	FLN	LP	6.0	HER	UNIQ	1110		WIN	WIN	8½-120		26	NRA
6	165	CAST	FLN	LP	12.6	HER	2400	1440		WIN	WIN	8½-120		26	NRA
7	175	CAST	FLN	LP	14.0	DUP	4227	1375		WIN	WIN	8½-120		26	NRA
8	175	CAST	FLN	LP	13.5	DUP	4759	1400		WIN	WIN	8½-120		26	NRA

.32 WINCHESTER SPECIAL (and .32 REMINGTON)

The .32 Special cartridge was introduced by Winchester in 1895 for use in the Model 1894 Winchester lever-action rifle. Its ballistics are practically identical to those of the .30-30. It is said to have been designed as a compromise for use with either smokeless or blackpowder. The credibility of this explanation is strengthened by the fact that the .32 Special can be used with the same bullets used in the older .32-40, for which many handloaders of the 1890's probably had bullet molds. The twist of rifling in the .32 Special is 16 inches per turn, the same as that of most .32-40 rifles, which was considered superior to the 12-inch twist of the .30-30 for lead-bullet blackpowder loads. A point hotly argued years ago was whether the .32 Special was more effective on game than the contemporary .30-30 cartridge, but the very close similarity of ballistics indicates that there could hardly be any noticeable difference between the two cartridges in that respect. The .32 Special never achieved popularity comparable to that of the .30-30, but many fine old Model 1894 rifles chambered for it are still in use. It was also a standard chambering in the lever-action Marlin Model 1893, and briefly in the successor Marlin Model 336.

The .32 Remington was a rimless cartridge introduced by Remington for use in their Model 8

autoloader and Model 14 slide-action repeater. It is ballistically nearly the same as the .32 Special, though the cartridges are not interchangeable. The .32 Remington is now obsolete, but some rifles of that caliber are still in use. The loads listed for the .32 Special can also be used satisfactorily in the .32 Remington cartridge.

The working pressure for the .32 Special cartridge should be limited to about 38,000 c.u.p. The maximum product average for factory ammunition should not exceed 41,200 c.u.p.

Max. Case Length: 2.040″ **Trim-To Length:** 2.035″
Max. Overall Length: 2.565″ **Primer Size:** Large Rifle **Bullet Dia.:** .320-.321″

LOAD NUMBER	BULLET				POWDER			VELOCITY FPS	PRESSURE CUP	CASE BRAND	PRIMER		CARTRIDGE OAL	BARREL LENGTH	DATA SOURCE
	WEIGHT	BRAND	SHAPE	TYPE	WEIGHT	BRAND	TYPE				BRAND	TYPE			
1	170	WIN	FLN	SP	36.2	WIN	748	2240	32500	WIN	WIN	8½-120		24	WIN
2	170	SPR	FLN	SP	35.0	DUP	4895	2205		WIN	CCI	200		20	SPR
3	170	SPR	FLN	SP	34.0	DUP	3031	2201		WIN	CCI	200		20	SPR
4	170	HDY	FLN	SP	35.2	DUP	4064	2200		REM	FED	210		20	HDY
5	170	HDY	FLN	SP	36.9	DUP	4320	2200		REM	FED	210		20	HDY
6	170	REM	FLN	SP	31.0	HER	RL7	2240	34500	REM	REM			24	HER
7	170	SPR	FLN	SP	27.0	HOD	H4198	2168		WIN	WIN	8½-120		20	HOD

8 x 57mm MAUSER

The 8x57mm Mauser was designed as a military cartridge for use in the Model 1888 Commission rifle. It is commercially identified in Europe as the 8x57mmJ or 8x57mmJS, the two different designations applying to the original cartridge and a later variation of it respectively. The 8x57mm Mauser was the most widely used of the several Mauser cartridges, and its worldwide popularity rivals that of the .30-06.

As originally introduced, the 8x57mmJ cartridge used a bullet of about .318-inch diameter, and was loaded to a chamber-pressure level not exceeding about 45,000 c.u.p. The rifles chambered for the original cartridge had a nominal groove diameter of about .320 of an inch, though many commercial rifles had groove diameters less than that.

In 1903, German military designers modified the cartridge specifications to employ a spitzer bullet of about .323-inch diameter, and the suffix "S" was added to the nomenclature (8x57mmJS) to indicate the larger bullet. Rifles made for the modified cartridge had correspondingly larger groove diameter. The operating chamber pressure of the 8x57mmJS cartridge was established at the higher level of about 49,800 c.u.p.

This change in the 8x57mm Mauser cartridge has caused much confusion about its suitability for use in various weapons. The 8x57mmJS cartridge can be chambered and fired in weapons designed for use with the earlier 8x57J cartridge, but *that practice is not safe.* The higher chamber pressure to which the 8x57mmJS cartridge is normally loaded in Europe is aggravated by the fact that the .323-inch bullet fired in a barrel having about .320-inch or smaller groove diameter further increases the chamber pressure. The older rifles, such as the 1888 Commission model, were designed for pressures not exceeding that of the original 8x57J cartridge (about 45,000 c.u.p.), whereas 8x57JS ammunition fired in them may develop chamber pressures considerably in excess of 50,000 c.u.p.

In Europe, the difference between the 8x57J and 8x57JS cartridges is generally understood, and each type is used in the appropriate rifle. In America, however, the difference is less well understood, and many users are inclined to fire "8mm Mauser"

ammunition, of whatever type, in the weapon that they happen to have in hand. The response of U.S. manufacturers to this potentially hazardous practice was to design the 8mm Mauser commercial cartridge with a .323-inch bullet, as is necessary for acceptable accuracy in S-bore barrels, but loaded to a chamber pressure not exceeding about 37,000 c.u.p., in the hope that the chamber pressure would not then be raised to hazardous level if the ammunition were fired in a rifle intended for use with the original 8x57J cartridge. This arrangement seems generally to have worked as intended, since many rounds of American-made 8mm Mauser commercial ammunition have undoubtedly been fired in weapons designed for the old 8x57mmJ cartridge, and few if any have been blown up. Nevertheless, U.S. manufacturers do *not* recommend the use of their 8mm Mauser ammuniton in the old weapons intended for use with 8x57J ammunition. The undesirable but unavoidable other consequence is, however, that U.S.-made 8mm Mauser commercial ammuniton produces ballistics considerably inferior to those produced by 8x57mm JS sporting ammunition loaded in Europe, and the greater potential effectiveness of strong 8mm Mauser rifles having S-bore barrels is not achieved with U.S.-made 8mm Mauser factory loads.

For the handloader, the best way out of this confusing dilemma is probably as follows:

— If in doubt about whether his 8x57mm rifle has the J-bore or S-bore barrel, he should measure the groove diameter using a lead slug or a cast, or have a gunsmith do this for him.

— If the groove diameter is less than .320 inch, he should use only the .318-inch jacketed bullets imported by firms such as Eastern Sports International, and loads not exceeding 40,000 c.u.p.

— If the groove diameter is .320 inch or greater, the .321-inch bullets intended for use in the .32 Special can be used, with powder charges not exceeding the 37,000 c.u.p. limit established for U. S. sporting ammunition.

— If the groove diameter is .322 inch or greater, standard .323-inch bullets can be used. If the rifle is a Model 98 Mauser, or another type having a comparably strong action, loads developing up to 50,000 c.u.p. are acceptable. However, some rifles of the 1888 Commission pattern have been fitted with barrels having the nominal .323-inch groove diameter, and chamber pressures in those rifles should be limited to about 40,000 c.u.p. for safety.

The maximum product average chamber pressure for the 8x57 mm Mauser factory ammunition for sporting use in the U.S. should not exceed 40,200 c.u.p.

Max. Case Length: 2.240″ **Trim-To Length:** 2.235″
Max. Overall Length: 3.250″ **Primer Size:** Large Rifle **Bullet Dia.:** .323″

RIFLE LOADS FOR THE 8 x 57 mm MAUSER

LOAD NUMBER	BULLET WEIGHT	BRAND	SHAPE	TYPE	POWDER WEIGHT	BRAND	TYPE	VELOCITY FPS	PRESSURE CUP	CASE BRAND	PRIMER BRAND	TYPE	CARTRIDGE OAL	BARREL LENGTH	DATA SOURCE
1	125	HDY	PTD	SP	46.0	HOD	BL-C-(2)	2614		WIN	WIN	8½-120		23	HOD
2	125	HDY	PTD	SP	47.0	HOD	H335	2637		WIN	WIN	8½-120		23	HOD
3	150	SPR	PTD	SP	34.5	DUP	3031	2335	37000	WIN	WIN	8½-120	2.945	25	DUP
4	150	SPR	PTD	SP	47.0	DUP	4831	2325	36800	WIN	WIN	8½-120	2.945	25	DUP
5	150	SPR	PTD	SP	43.0	DUP	4350	2315	36800	WIN	WIN	8½-120	2.945	25	DUP
6	150	SPR	PTD	SP	36.0	DUP	4895	2310	37000	WIN	WIN	8½-120	2.945	25	DUP
7	150	SPR	PTD	SP	46.0	HOD	BL-C-(2)	2553	33500	WIN	WIN	8½-120		26	HOD
8	150	SPR	PTD	SP	53.0	HOD	H450	2285	35900	WIN	WIN	8½-120		26	HOD
9	170	HDY	RNN	SP	46.0	DUP	4831	2255	37000	WIN	WIN	8½-120	2.840	25	DUP
10	170	HDY	RNN	SP	42.0	DUP	4350	2180	37000	WIN	WIN	8½-120	2.840	25	DUP
11	170	HDY	RNN	SP	35.0	DUP	4064	2175	36900	WIN	WIN	8½-120	2.840	25	DUP
12	170	SPR	SPD	SP	49.0	HOD	H450	2138	36500	WIN	WIN	8½-120		26	HOD
13*	170	WIN	PTD	SP	46.0	WIN	748	2410	37000	WIN	WIN	8½-120		24	WIN
14*	170	WIN	PTD	SP	48.0	WIN	760	2240	32000	WIN	WIN	8½-120		24	WIN
15	125	HDY	PTD	SP	49.2	DUP	3031	3100		REM	REM	9½		23	HDY
16	150	HDY	PTD	SP	53.5	DUP	4320	2900		REM	REM	9½		23	HDY
17	150	SRA	PTD	SP	52.7	DUP	4064	2900		WIN	REM	9½		23	SRA
18	150	SPR	PTD	SP	50.0	HOD	H335	2771	<50000	FED	CCI	250		24	SPR
19	170	SPR	SPD	SP	49.0	DUP	4064	2723	<50000	FED	CCI	200		24	SPR
20	170	SPR	SPD	SP	55.0	DUP	4350	2632	<50000	FED	CCI	200		24	SPR
21	170	SPR	SPD	SP	46.0	DUP	4895	2640	<50000	FED	CCI	200		24	SPR
22	175	SRA	PTD	SP	56.0	DUP	4350	2746	40750	REM	REM	9½	3.050	24	NRA
23	196	NOR	RNN	SP	48.3	NOR	202	2485	<49300	NOR	NOR	LR	2.970	24	NOR
24	200	SPR	PTD	SP	55.0	HOD	H205	2509	<50000	FED	CCI	200		24	SPR
25	200	SPR	PTD	SP	53.0	DUP	4350	2432	<50000	FED	CCI	200		24	SPR
26	200	SPR	PTD	SP	46.0	DUP	4064	2434	<50000	FED	CCI	200		24	SPR
27	220	SRA	PBT	SP	41.1	DUP	4064	2200		WIN	REM	9½		23	SRA

*Loads 13 and 14 should not be increased or decreased, but loaded exactly as specified, according to Winchester.

8mm-06

The 8mm-06 is a wildcat cartridge made simply by expanding the neck of the .30-06 case to accept .323-inch bullets. It was probably originated by some unknown gunsmith to "magnumize" the 8x57mmJS Model 98 military rifles that were cheap and plentiful during the years following World War II. The conversion requires only rechambering the 8x57mmJS rifle with the 8mm-06 reamer, and it becomes what would be, in typical European nomenclature, an 8x63mm, with considerably increased powder capacity, and the ability to use the .30-06 military brass that was also cheap and plentiful a few years ago.

Because the larger diameter of the 8mm bullet gives it a lower sectional density than a .308-inch bullet of the same weight, the chamber pressure in the 8mm-06

is somewhat lower than it would be with the same powder charge and bullet weight fired in a .30-06. The muzzle velocity obtainable in the 8mm-06 is therefore somewhat higher than it would be in a .30-06, using a bullet of the same weight, at the same level of acceptable chamber pressure. Aside from the conveniences afforded by the inexpensive modification, the 8mm-06 is a powerful and very satisfactory cartridge, easily exceeding the performance of the standard 8x57mmJS round.

Max. Case Length: 2.494″ **Trim-To Length:** 2.484″
Max. Overall Length: 3.250″ **Primer Size:** Large Rifle **Bullet Dia.:** .323″

RIFLE LOADS FOR THE 8mm-06

LOAD NUMBER	BULLET				POWDER			VELOCITY FPS	PRESSURE CUP	CASE BRAND	PRIMER		CARTRIDGE OAL	BARREL LENGTH	DATA SOURCE
	WEIGHT	BRAND	SHAPE	TYPE	WEIGHT	BRAND	TYPE				BRAND	TYPE			
1	125	HDY	PTD	SP	54.0	DUP	3031	3200		MIL	WIN	8½-120		23½	HDY
2	125	SPR	PTD	SP	55.0	DUP	4064	3190		WIN	CCI	200		24	SPR
3	150	SPR	PTD	SP	55.0	DUP	4064	2881		WIN	CCI	200		24	SPR
4	150	SRA	PTD	SP	59.2	HOD	H380	3000		MIL	WIN	8½-120		24	SRA
5	150	HDY	PTD	SP	62.2	WIN	760	3000		MIL	WIN	8½-120		23½	HDY
6	170	HDY	RNN	SP	60.6	DUP	4350	2800		MIL	WIN	8½-120		23½	HDY
7	170	SPR	SPD	SP	54.0	DUP	4064	2675		WIN	CCI	200		24	SPR
8	175	SRA	PTD	SP	66.0	NOR	MRP	2800		MIL	WIN	8½-120		24	SRA
9	175	SRA	PTD	SP	59.3	WIN	760	2800		MIL	WIN	8½-120		24	SRA
10	175	SRA	PTD	SP	56.8	HOD	H380	2800		MIL	WIN	8½-120		24	SRA
11	220	SRA	PBT	SP	55.8	HOD	4831	2400		MIL	WIN	8½-120		24	SRA
12	220	SRA	PBT	SP	54.2	DUP	4831	2400		MIL	WIN	8½-120		24	SRA
13	200	SPR	PTD	SP	53.0	DUP	4064	2647		WIN	CCI	200		24	SPR
14	200	SPR	PTD	SP	58.0	DUP	4350	2580		WIN	CCI	200		24	SPR

8mm REMINGTON MAGNUM

The 8mm Remington Magnum was introduced in 1977. It is based on a full-length belted .375 or .300 H.&H. Magnum case, necked to accept .323-inch bullets, with a reduced-taper case body and 25 degree shoulder angle. The case body is as long as practicable, leaving a neck length measuring about .32 inch. The overall cartridge length of 3.600 inches is the same as that of the .300 H.&H. Magnum, and the maximum allowable bullet protrusion is only about .75 inch. Bullets longer than about 1.07 inches will intrude into the powder space behind the case neck. The case capacity is about 20 per cent greater than that of the .338 Winchester Magnum or the .375 H.&H. Magnum.

The 8mm bullets available to handloaders when the 8mm Remington Magnum was introduced were designed for the substantially lower velocities obtained in the 8x57mm Mauser cartridge, and would not enable the handloader to take advantage of the penetration that the big magnum could provide on very large game. The 185-grain and 220-grain bullets used by Remington in their 8mm magnum factory loads are, of course, designed for the proper degree of expansion at the higher velocities obtained in that cartridge. Bullet makers who produce bullets primarily for handloading can be expected to make an increasing number of bullets available, designed specifically for this high-velocity 8mm cartridge. With a muzzle energy of nearly 4,000 foot-pounds, the 8mm Remington Magnum is certainly adequate for the largest North American game. The relatively flat trajectory makes the cartridge especially suitable for hunting where long-range shots must occasionally be taken at large animals.

The working chamber pressure for the 8 mm Remington Magnum is comparable to that of other very powerful magnum loads such as the .338 Winchester, at about 54,000 c.u.p. The maximum product average for factory ammunition should not exceed 57,200 c.u.p.

Max. Case Length: 2.850″ **Trim-To Length:** 2.840″
Max. Overall Length: 3.600″ **Primer Size:** Large Rifle Magnum **Bullet Dia.:** .323″

RIFLE LOADS FOR THE 8mm REMINGTON MAGNUM

LOAD NUMBER	BULLET				POWDER			VELOCITY FPS	PRESSURE CUP	CASE BRAND	PRIMER		CARTRIDGE OAL	BARREL LENGTH	DATA SOURCE
	WEIGHT	BRAND	SHAPE	TYPE	WEIGHT	BRAND	TYPE				BRAND	TYPE			
1	150	SRA	PTD	SP	84.8	DUP	4350	3450		REM	REM	9½M		24	SRA
2	150	SRA	PTD	SP	86.0	NOR	204	3450		REM	REM	9½M		24	SRA
3	150	SPR	PTD	SP	86.0	DUP	4831	3436	<54000	REM	CCI	250		24	SPR
4	150	SPR	PTD	SP	92.0	NOR	MRP	3433	<54000	REM	CCI	250		24	SPR

RIFLE LOADS FOR THE 8 mm REMINGTON MAGNUM

LOAD NUMBER	BULLET				POWDER			VELOCITY FPS	PRESSURE CUP	CASE BRAND	PRIMER		CARTRIDGE OAL	BARREL LENGTH	DATA SOURCE
	WEIGHT	BRAND	SHAPE	TYPE	WEIGHT	BRAND	TYPE				BRAND	TYPE			
5	170	SPR	SPD	SP	80.0	DUP	4831	3114	<54000	REM	CCI	250		24	SPR
6	170	SPR	SPD	SP	76.0	HOD	H205	3039	<54000	REM	CCI	250		24	SPR
7	175	SRA	PTD	SP	80.3	DUP	4350	3200		REM	REM	9½M		24	SRA
8	175	SRA	PTD	SP	85.7	HOD	4831	3200		REM	REM	9½M		24	SRA
9	185	REM	PTD	SP	66.5	DUP	4064	2975	54000	REM	REM	9½M	3.560	24	DUP
10	185	REM	PTD	SP	77.5	DUP	4350	3090	53100	REM	REM	9½M	3.560	24	DUP
11	185	REM	PTD	SP	79.5	DUP	4831	3095	52900	REM	REM	9½M	3.560	24	DUP
12	200	SPR	PTD	SP	78.0	DUP	4831	2996	<54000	REM	CCI	250		24	SPR
13	200	SPR	PTD	SP	74.0	DUP	4350	2936	<54000	REM	CCI	250		24	SPR
14	220	REM	PTD	SP	62.5	DUP	4064	2700	53800	REM	REM	9½M	3.560	24	DUP
15	220	REM	PTD	SP	72.0	DUP	4350	2795	53000	REM	REM	9½M	3.560	24	DUP
16	220	REM	PTD	SP	76.0	DUP	4831	2845	53800	REM	REM	9½M	3.560	24	DUP
17	220	HDY	PTD	SP	79.3	NOR	MRP	2900		REM	REM	9½M	3.600	24	HDY
18	220	HDY	PTD	SP	80.3	HOD	4831	2900		REM	REM	9½M	3.600	24	HDY
19	220	HDY	PTD	SP	82.1	HOD	H450	2900		REM	REM	9½M	3.600	24	HDY
20	220	SRA	PBT	SP	76.9	DUP	4831	2900		REM	REM	9½M		24	SRA
21	220	SRA	PBT	SP	80.0	HOD	4831	2900		REM	REM	9½M		24	SRA
22	220	SRA	PBT	SP	79.6	HOD	H450	2850		REM	REM	9½M		24	SRA
23	150	SPR	PTD	SP	28.0	DUP	4198	1763		REM	CCI	250		24	SPR
24	150	SPR	PTD	SP	32.0	DUP	4198	2002		REM	CCI	250		24	SPR
25	170	SPR	PTD	SP	30.0	DUP	4198	1790		REM	CCI	250		24	SPR
26	170	SPR	PTD	SP	34.0	DUP	4198	2042		REM	CCI	250		24	SPR

.33 WINCHESTER

The .33 Winchester cartridge was introduced in 1902, for use in the Model 1886 Winchester lever-action rifle. Though not a very widely used cartridge, it was highly regarded for its performance on game as large as elk.

Factory ammunition has not been loaded for the .33 Winchester since World War II. However, the case is based on the .45-70, and excellent .33 Winchester cases can be formed from new .45-70 brass. Case-forming dies for that purpose are available from RCBS. Hornady manufactures a 200-grain soft-point bullet that duplicates the original 200-grain factory bullet. Owners of the fine old Model 1886 Winchester or Model 1895 Marlin rifles chambered for the .33 Winchester cartridge, can thus load ammunition equivalent to the original factory loads, in this cartridge which has not been manufactured for nearly 40 years. It is a credit to firms such as Hornady and

RCBS that they make available the components and tools necessary to handload obsolete cartridges such as the .33 Winchester, especially since the sales volume is almost certainly too low to produce substantial profit. One of the important advantages of handloading is the ability to make use of some fine old rifles such as the .33 Winchester long after factory loads have become obsolete and unavailable.

Max. Case Length: 2.105" **Trim-To Length:** 2.100"
Max. Overall Length: 2.795" **Primer Size:** Large Rifle **Bullet Dia.:** .338"

RIFLE LOADS FOR THE .33 WINCHESTER

LOAD NUMBER	BULLET				POWDER			VELOCITY FPS	PRESSURE CUP	CASE BRAND	PRIMER		CARTRIDGE OAL	BARREL LENGTH	DATA SOURCE
	WEIGHT	BRAND	SHAPE	TYPE	WEIGHT	BRAND	TYPE				BRAND	TYPE			
1	200	HDY	FLN	SP	40.0	DUP	3031	2100		REM	WIN	8½-120		24	HDY
2	200	HDY	FLN	SP	41.2	DUP	4064	2000		REM	WIN	8½-120		24	HDY
3	200	HDY	FLN	SP	43.1	DUP	4895	2100		REM	WIN	8½-120		24	HDY
4	200	HDY	FLN	SP	43.2	WIN	748	2100		REM	WIN	8½-120		24	HDY

.338 WINCHESTER MAGNUM

The .338 Winchester Magnum cartridge was introduced in 1959. It is one of the "short-magnum" cartridges having an overall length not greater than that of the .30-06, and it is therefore suitable for use in standard-length actions originally designed around the .30-06 cartridge. The neck length measures about .33 inch, and the maximum allowable bullet protrusion is about .84 inch, so bullets longer than about 1.17 inches will intrude into the powder space behind the case neck. The case is well designed, and has been much used by wildcatters for the .30-338 cartridge, which many prefer to the longer-bodied .300 Winchester Magnum.

The capacity of the .338 Winchester Magnum case is only about two per cent less than that of the .375 H.&H. Magnum case, despite the fact that the .375 H.&H. cartridge is a "long magnum" with an overall length of 3.60 inches. Originally announced with a 200-grain bullet at 3,000 fps and 250-grain bullet at 2,700 fps, these factory loads are now listed at 2,960 fps and 2,660 fps respectively, and a 300-grain bullet has been added at a muzzle velocity of 2,430 fps. The handloader can duplicate the performance of factory loads in this magnum cartridge with available canister powders, a condition unfortunately not true of all magnum cartridges. With muzzle energy of nearly 4,000 foot-pounds, the .338 Winchester is amply powerful for any North American game, and would undoubtedly perform satisfactorily on most African game as well.

The working chamber pressure for the .338 Winchester Magnum cartridge is about 54,000 c.u.p. The maximum product average for factory ammunition should not exceed 57,200 c.u.p.

Max. Case Length: 2.500″ **Trim-To Length:** 2.490″
Max. Overall Length: 3.340″ **Primer Size:** Large Rifle Magnum **Bullet Dia.:** .338″

RIFLE LOADS FOR THE .338 WINCHESTER MAGNUM

LOAD NUMBER	BULLET				POWDER			VELOCITY FPS	PRESSURE CUP	CASE BRAND	PRIMER		CARTRIDGE OAL	BARREL LENGTH	DATA SOURCE
	WEIGHT	BRAND	SHAPE	TYPE	WEIGHT	BRAND	TYPE				BRAND	TYPE			
1	200	WIN	PTD	SP	70.0*	WIN	760	2900	51000	WIN	WIN	8½-120		24	WIN
2	200	WIN	PTD	SP	73.0	DUP	4350	3030	53900	WIN	WIN	8½-120	3.330	25	DUP
3	200	HDY	PTD	SP	75.0	DUP	4350	2931	51380	WIN	WIN	8½-120	3.300	25	NRA
4	200	SPR	PTD	SP	63.0	DUP	4320	2826	52050	WIN	WIN	8½-120	3.260	25	NRA
5	200	SPR	PTD	SP	77.0	HOD	H450	2947	51500	WIN	CCI	250		26	HOD
6	210	NOS	PTD	SP	74.0	DUP	4350	2924	52250	WIN	WIN	8½-120	3.310	25	NRA
7	210	NOS	PTD	SP	75.0	DUP	H450	2864		WIN	REM	9½-M		24	NOS
8	225	HDY	PTD	SP	72.0	DUP	4350	2864	53320	WIN	WIN	8½-120	3.340	25	NRA
9	225	HDY	PTD	SP	74.0	HOD	4831	2900		WIN	WIN	8½-120		25	HDY
10	250	WIN	SPD	SP	73.8*	WIN	785	2645	50500	WIN	WIN	8½-120		24	WIN
11	250	WIN	SPD	SP	63.2*	WIN	760	2545	50500	WIN	WIN	8½-120		24	WIN
12	250	HDY	RNN	SP	70.0	DUP	4350	2666	51370	WIN	WIN	8½-120	3.300	25	NRA
13	250	NOS	RNN	SP	70.0	DUP	4350	2661	52720	WIN	WIN	8½-120	3.340	25	NRA
14	250	SRA	PBT	SP	74.8	HOD	4831	2700		WIN	REM	9½M		24	SRA
15	250	SPR	SPD	SP	69.0	DUP	4350	2719	<54000	WIN	CCI	250		24	SPR
16	275	SPR	SPD	SP	70.0	HOD	H450	2544	51400	WIN	CCI	250		26	HOD
17	275	SPR	SPD	SP	74.0	NOR	MRP	2614	<54000	WIN	CCI	250		24	SPR
18	300	WIN	RNN	SP	68.5*	WIN	785	2375	50000	WIN	WIN	8½-120		24	WIN
19	300	WIN	RNN	SP	68.5	DUP	4831	2480	54000	WIN	WIN	8½-120	3.330	25	DUP

*Loads 1, 10, 11 and 18 should be neither increased nor decreased, but loaded exactly as specified, according to Winchester.

.340 WEATHERBY MAGNUM

The .340 Weatherby Magnum was announced in 1962. It uses the same .338-inch bullets as the .338 Winchester Magnum, but is based on a full-length belted-magnum case, giving the cartridge a powder capacity about 12 per cent greater than that of the .338 Winchester cartridge. Velocities attainable in the .340 Weatherby Magnum are about 150 to 200 fps higher than those obtained in the .338 Winchester Magnum. Producing muzzle energies up to about 4,500 foot-pounds with its heavy bullets, the .340 Weatherby Magnum is an exceedingly powerful cartridge. It somewhat exceeds the performance of the .375 H.&H.

Magnum, which has been used successfully for many years in taking the largest species of game in the world. With bullets of proper construction, the .340 Weatherby Magnum should have greater penetration than the .375 H.&H. Magnum, because the .338-inch bullets have sectional density about 23 per cent greater than that of .375-inch bullets of the same weight.

Max. Case Length: 2.825″ **Trim-To Length:** 2.815″
Max. Overall Length: 3.562″ **Primer Size:** Large Rifle Magnum **Bullet Dia.:** .338″

RIFLE LOADS FOR THE .340 WEATHERBY MAGNUM

LOAD NUMBER	BULLET				POWDER			VELOCITY FPS	PRESSURE CUP	CASE BRAND	PRIMER		CARTRIDGE OAL	BARREL LENGTH	DATA SOURCE
	WEIGHT	BRAND	SHAPE	TYPE	WEIGHT	BRAND	TYPE				BRAND	TYPE			
1	200	HDY	PTD	SP	80.0	DUP	4350	3075	48290	WEA	FED	215	3.562	26	WEA
2	200	HDY	PTD	SP	84.0	DUP	4350	3210	54970	WEA	FED	215	3.562	26	WEA
3	200	HDY	PTD	SP	86.0	HOD	4831	3004	45940	WEA	FED	215	3.562	26	WEA
4	200	HDY	PTD	SP	90.0	HOD	4831	3137	52700	WEA	FED	215	3.562	26	WEA
5	200	SPR	PTD	SP	83.0	DUP	4831	2976		WEA	CCI	250		26	SPR
6	210	NOS	PTD	SP	92.0	NOR	MRP	3180	51290	WEA	FED	215	3.562	26	WEA
7	210	NOS	PTD	SP	84.0	DUP	4350	3115	51450	WEA	FED	215	3.562	26	WEA
8	250	HDY	RNN	SP	76.0	DUP	4350	2800	51370	WEA	FED	215	3.562	26	WEA
9	250	HDY	RNN	SP	82.0	HOD	4831	2764	49180	WEA	FED	215	3.562	26	WEA
10	250	HDY	RNN	SP	85.0	HOD	4831	2860	54400	WEA	FED	215	3.562	26	WEA
11	250	HDY	RNN	SP	84.9	NOR	MRP	2850	49600	WEA	FED	215	3.562	26	WEA
12	250	SRA	PBT	SP	84.2	HOD	H450	2800		WEA	FED	215		26	SRA
13	250	SRA	PBT	SP	80.2	DUP	4831	2800		WEA	FED	215		26	SRA
14	250	SPR	SPD	SP	81.0	DUP	4831	2896		WEA	CCI	250		26	SPR
15	275	SPR	SPD	SP	78.0	DUP	4831	2677		WEA	CCI	250		26	SPR

.348 WINCHESTER

The .348 Winchester cartridge was introduced in 1936, in conjunction with the lever-action Model 71 Winchester rifle. The Model 71 rifle was a modernized version of the popular Winchester Model 1886, and the .348 Winchester cartridge was a more powerful successor to the .33 Winchester cartridge that was chambered in the Model 1886 rifle. Originally announced with a 150-grain bullet at a muzzle velocity of 2,920 fps and a 200-grain bullet at 2,535 fps, the .348 cartridge rivaled the performance of the .30-06, and was easily the most powerful lever-action rifle made since discontinuance of the lever-action Winchester

Model 1895. The Model 71 Winchester rifle was well designed and superbly crafted, fine workmanship being about at its peak among American arms manufacturers in the late 1930's when the Model 71 was introduced.

The high-velocity 150-grain bullet was not a very popular load, because neither the rifle nor the cartridge were suitable for long-range shooting, despite their many excellent qualities. A load using 250-grain bullets at a muzzle velocity of 2,350 fps was later introduced for the .348, and the velocities of the 150-grain and 200-grain bullets were reduced to 2,890 fps and 2,530 fps respectively. As the cartdrige became obsolescent, after production of the Model 71 rifle was discontinued, the 150-grain and 250-grain bullets were dropped from production, and only the 200-grain load now remains.

The .348 cartridge was based on the huge .50-110 Winchester blackpowder cartridge that had been chambered in the Model 1886 rifle, and the body diameter at the head measures about .548 inch. It is therefore suitable for forming some of the very large cases used in other rifles for which ammunition is no longer available. The .348 case has been much used by wildcatters, who fire-formed it to use in the old blackpowder rifles, or necked it up or down to suit their ideas for powerful smokeless-powder wildcats.

The maximum working pressure for the .348 Winchester cartridge is about 40,000 c.u.p. The maximum product average for factory ammunition is not to exceed 43,200 c.u.p.

Max. Case Length: 2.255″ **Trim-To Length:** 2.245″ **Max. Overall Length:** 2.795″ **Primer Size:** Large Rifle **Bullet Dia.:** .348″

RIFLE LOADS FOR THE .348 WINCHESTER

LOAD NUMBER	BULLET				POWDER			VELOCITY FPS	PRESSURE CUP	CASE BRAND	PRIMER		CARTRIDGE OAL	BARREL LENGTH	DATA SOURCE
	WEIGHT	BRAND	SHAPE	TYPE	WEIGHT	BRAND	TYPE				BRAND	TYPE			
1	200	HDY	FLN	SP	42.6	DUP	3031	2200		WIN	FED	210		24	HDY
2	200	HDY	FLN	SP	49.2	DUP	3031	2500		WIN	FED	210		24	HDY
3	200	HDY	FLN	SP	59.1	WIN	760	2500		WIN	FED	210		24	HDY
4	200	HDY	FLN	SP	66.1	NOR	204	2500		WIN	FED	210		24	HDY
5	200				62.0	HOD	H450	2319	32800					26	HOD
6	220				57.0	HOD	H450	2214	33500					26	HOD

.357 MAGNUM (RIFLE)

The .357 Magnum revolver cartridge was first used in rifles built by custom gunsmiths, usually on the Winchester Model 1892 action. It is really quite a versatile rifle cartridge, performing well with the mild .38 Special loads on small game, and adequate for hunting deer in the hands of a careful hunter who limits the range to about 100 yards and places his shots very carefully. With a muzzle energy limited to about 1200 foot-pounds, however, it cannot be recommended for general use as a deer-hunting cartridge. For use on deer, bullets weighing at least 140 grains should be chosen.

It is sometimes implied that heavier loads may be used in rifles chambered for the .357 Magnum than in handguns, but that practice should not be recommended for most rifles adapted to the .357 Magnum.

Most such rifles, including the Model 92 Winchester, were designed for cartridges operating at chamber pressures substantially less than the limit of about 42,500 c.u.p. that applies to .357 Magnum handgun loads. Such rifles should not be subjected to still higher chamber pressure by exceeding the charges recommended for .357 Magnum loads in handguns.

The most satisfactory working pressures for the .357 Magnum are below about 40,000 c.u.p., but the maximum product average established for the cartridge is 46,000 c.u.p.

Max. Case Length: 1.290″ **Trim-To Length:** 1.285″ **Max. Overall Length:** 1.590″ **Primer Size:** Small Pistol **Bullet Dia.:** .357″

RIFLE LOADS FOR THE .357 MAGNUM

LOAD NUMBER	BULLET				POWDER			VELOCITY FPS	PRESSURE CUP	CASE BRAND	PRIMER		CARTRIDGE OAL	BARREL LENGTH	DATA SOURCE
	WEIGHT	BRAND	SHAPE	TYPE	WEIGHT	BRAND	TYPE				BRAND	TYPE			
1	110	SPR	FLN	HP	16.5	HER	BDOT	2347	<46000	SPR	CCI	500		18½	SPR
2	110	SPR	FLN	HP	20.0	HER	2400	2299	<46000	SPR	CCI	550		18½	SPR
3	110	SPR	FLN	HP	9.0	HER	UNIQ	1817	<46000	SPR	CCI	550		18½	SPR
4	125	SPR	FLN	HP	21.6	HOD	H110	2272	<46000	SPR	CCI	550		18½	SPR
5	125	SPR	FLN	HP	20.1	DUP	4227	2072	<46000	SPR	CCI	550		18½	SPR
6	125	SPR	FLN	HP	15.0	WIN	630	2200	<46000	SPR	CCI	500		18½	SPR

RIFLE LOADS FOR THE .357 MAGNUM

LOAD NUMBER	BULLET				POWDER			VELOCITY FPS	PRESSURE CUP	CASE BRAND	PRIMER		CARTRIDGE OAL	BARREL LENGTH	DATA SOURCE
	WEIGHT	BRAND	SHAPE	TYPE	WEIGHT	BRAND	TYPE				BRAND	TYPE			
8	125	HDY	FLN	HP	16.1	HER	2400	1950		WIN	ALC	SP		23	HDY
9	140	SPR	FLN	HP	19.2	DUP	4227	1909	<46000	SPR	CCI	550		18½	SPR
10	140	SPR	FLN	HP	19.5	HOD	H110	2093	<46000	SPR	CCI	550		18½	SPR
11	140	SPR	FLN	HP	17.5	HER	2400	2039	<46000	SPR	CCI	550		18½	SPR
12	140	SPR	FLN	HP	13.0	HER	BDOT	1825	<46000	SPR	CCI	500		18½	SPR
13	140	SPR	FLN	HP	8.8	HER	UNIQ	1638	<46000	SPR	CCI	500		18½	SPR
14	140	SPR	FLN	HP	6.8	HER	UNIQ	1265	<46000	SPR	CCI	500		18½	SPR
15	158	HDY	FLN	HP	14.5	HER	2400	1650		WIN	ALC	SP		23	HDY
16	158	HDY	FLN	HP	13.7	WIN	630	1650		WIN	ALC	SP		23	HDY
17	158	SPR	FLN	SP	13.0	HER	BDOT	1825	<46000	SPR	CCI	500		18½	SPR
18	158	SPR	FLN	SP	15.9	HER	2400	1824	<46000	SPR	CCI	550		18½	SPR
19	158	SPR	FLN	SP	16.5	DUP	4227	1718	<46000	SPR	CCI	550		18½	SPR
20	200	CAST	FLN	LG	12.0	HER	2400	1315		FED	CCI	550	1.800	22	NRA
21	200	CAST	FLN	LG	16.0	HER	RL7	1310		FED	CCI	500	1.800	22	NRA

.35 REMINGTON

The .35 Remington cartridge was introduced in 1908. It is one of the series of rimless cartridges introduced by Remington for their Model 8 autoloader rifle, and later used in the Model 14 Remington slide-action rifle. These rifles were later updated, and identified as the Models 81 and 141, and continued in production until Remington replaced them with the Model 740 autoloader and Model 760 slide-action rifles, which are chambered for more powerful cartridges. The other cartridges in this Remington series are the .25, .30 and .32 Remington, all using the same basic rimless case having a body diameter at the head of about .421 of an inch, whereas the .35 Remington has a larger case body of about .457-inch diameter at the head. The smaller cartridges became obsolescent when the Models 81 and 141 rifles were discontinued, and only the .30 Remington cartridge is still manufactured. The .35 Remington is used in some other popular rifles, however, such as the Marlin Model 336 lever-action, and it did not become obsolescent with the passing of the rifles in which it was originally employed.

The .35 Remington has a good reputation as a short-range deer-hunting cartridge. With muzzle energy of about 1,900 foot-pounds, it is comparable in that respect to the .30-30, but the heavier 200-grain bullet in the .35 Remington is believed by some hunters to have superior "stopping power." The .35 Remington is also supposed to be a superior "brush-bucker," though the idea that any bullet can "buck" much brush and continue on its original course is very questionable.

The deer hunter who occasionally uses his .35 Remington for hunting varmints at short and moderate ranges will find that the .357-inch handgun bullets do well in handloads. The .35 Remington cartridge has also achieved some popularity among shooters on the Long-Range Pistol metallic-silhouette course, who use it in the Thompson-Center handgun.

The working pressure of the .35 Remington cartridge is commonly limited to about 35,000 c.u.p. The maximum product average established for factory ammunition is 38,200 c.u.p.

Max. Case Length: 1.920" **Trim-To Length:** 1.910"
Max. Overall Length: 2.525" **Primer Size:** Large Rifle **Bullet Dia.:** .358"

RIFLE LOADS FOR THE .35 REMINGTON

LOAD NUMBER	BULLET				POWDER			VELOCITY FPS	PRESSURE CUP	CASE BRAND	PRIMER		CARTRIDGE OAL	BARREL LENGTH	DATA SOURCE
	WEIGHT	BRAND	SHAPE	TYPE	WEIGHT	BRAND	TYPE				BRAND	TYPE			
1	125	HDY	FLN	HP	27.1	HER	2400	2400		REM	FED	210		20	HDY
2	125	SPR	FLN	HP	43.0	HER	RL7	2734	<35000	WIN	CCI	200		20	SPR
3	140	SPR	FLN	HP	40.0	HER	RL7	2539	<35000	WIN	CCI	200		20	SPR
4	150	REM	PTD	SP	42.0	DUP	3031	2390	34200	REM	REM	9½	2.500	23	DUP
5	150	REM	PTD	SP	42.5	DUP	4895	2340	34600	REM	REM	9½	2.500	23	DUP
6	158	HDY	FLN	SP	37.0	DUP	3031	2200		REM	FED	210		20	HDY
7	158	SPR	FLN	SP	39.0	DUP	4895	2185	<35000	WIN	CCI	200		20	SPR
8	180	SPR	FLN	SP	38.0	HOD	H335	2224	<35000	WIN	CCI	250		20	SPR
9	180	SPR	FLN	SP	37.0	DUP	4895	2055	<35000	WIN	CCI	200		20	SPR

LOAD NUMBER	BULLET				POWDER			VELOCITY FPS	PRESSURE CUP	CASE BRAND	PRIMER		CARTRIDGE OAL	BARREL LENGTH	DATA SOURCE
	WEIGHT	BRAND	SHAPE	TYPE	WEIGHT	BRAND	TYPE				BRAND	TYPE			
10	200	WIN	RNN	SP	39.0	WIN	748	2130	33000	WIN	WIN	8½-120		24	WIN
11	200	REM		SP	34.0	HER	RL7	2200	32000	REM	REM			22	HER
12	200	HDY	RNN	SP	37.5	DUP	3031	2110	34700	REM	REM	9½	2.500	23	DUP
13	200	HDY	RNN	SP	39.5	DUP	4064	2080	34200	REM	REM	9½	2.500	23	DUP
14	200	SRA	RNN	SP	40.0	HOD	BL-C-(2)	2050		REM	REM	9½		20	SRA
15	200	SRA	RNN	SP	42.0	HOD	H380	2000		REM	REM	9½		20	SRA
16	180	SPR	FLN	SP	18.0	DUP	4759	1499		WIN	CCI	200		20	SPR
17	180	SPR	FLN	SP	20.0	DUP	4759	1653		WIN	CCI	200		20	SPR

.358 WINCHESTER

The .358 Winchester cartridge was introduced in 1955, initially for use in the Model 70 bolt-action rifle. It is one of the family of cartridges based on the 7.62mm NATO case, which includes also the .243 and .308 Winchester. The .358 Winchester has also been chambered in other rifles, such as the lever-action Winchester Model 88 and the famous Savage Model 99. It is much more powerful than the .35 Remington, partly because of greater case capacity, but also because the chamber-pressure limit for the .358 Winchester is about 52,000 c.u.p., compared to only about 35,000 c.u.p. for the .35 Remington. With a muzzle energy of about 2,750 foot-pounds, and bullets weighing up to 250 grains, it is suitable for all but the largest North American game.

The .358 Winchester has not achieved popularity comparable to that of the .243 or .308 Winchester cartridges, possibly because it has no particular advantages over those cartridges for hunting animals such as whitetail deer, its trajectory is less flat, its recoil is heavier, and it is much less suitable as a dual-purpose varmint and deer cartridge. Its forte is for hunting game larger than whitetail deer, where its heavy 200- and 250-grain bullets are advantageous. With its 250-grain bullet at a muzzle velocity of 2,230 fps, the .358 Winchester slightly exceeds the performance of the old .35 Winchester cartridge chambered in the Model 1895 rifle, which propelled a 250-grain bullet at 2,195 fps, and was considered in its day an excellent cartridge for large North American game such as elk and moose.

The maximum product average chamber pressure established for the .358 Winchester factory load is 55,200 c.u.p.

Max. Case Length: 2.015″ **Trim-To Length:** 2.005″
Max. Overall Length: 2.780″ **Primer Size:** Large Rifle **Bullet Dia.:** .358″

RIFLE LOADS FOR THE .358 WINCHESTER

LOAD NUMBER	BULLET				POWDER			VELOCITY FPS	PRESSURE CUP	CASE BRAND	PRIMER		CARTRIDGE OAL	BARREL LENGTH	DATA SOURCE
	WEIGHT	BRAND	SHAPE	TYPE	WEIGHT	BRAND	TYPE				BRAND	TYPE			
1	200	WIN	SPD	SP	49.0	DUP	3031	2630	51800	WIN	WIN	8½-120	2.765	25	DUP
2	200	WIN	SPD	SP	49.0	DUP	4895	2565	50800	WIN	WIN	8½-120	2.765	25	DUP
3	200	WIN	SPD	SP	50.6	WIN	748	2500	50000	WIN	WIN	8½-120		24	WIN
4	200	HDY	RNN	SP	48.2	HOD	BL-C-(2)	2400		WIN	WIN	8½-120		22	HDY
5	200	HDY	RNN	SP	50.7	WIN	748	2400		WIN	WIN	8½-120		22	HDY
6	200	SRA	RNN	SP	49.1	DUP	4064	2500		WIN	CCI	200		22	SRA
7	200	SRA	RNN	SP	50.7	DUP	4320	2500		WIN	CCI	200		22	SRA
8	250	WIN	SPD	SP	44.0	DUP	4064	2270	52000	WIN	WIN	8½-120	2.780	25	DUP
9	250	WIN	SPD	SP	46.2	WIN	748	2250	50500	WIN	WIN	8½-120		24	WIN
10	250	HDY	PTD	SP	41.5	DUP	3031	2200		WIN	WIN	8½-120		22	HDY
11	250	HDY	PTD	SP	46.1	HOD	BL-C-(2)	2200		WIN	WIN	8½-120		22	HDY
12	250	HDY	PTD	SP	45.4	HOD	H335	2200		WIN	WIN	8½-120		22	HDY
13	250	SPR	PTD	SP	43.0	HOD	H322	2289	<52000	WIN	CCI	200		22	SPR
14	250	SPR	PTD	SP	37.0	HER	RL7	2169	<52000	WIN	CCI	200		22	SPR

.35 WHELEN

The .35 Whelen was developed in 1922 by James V. Howe, later of the famous Griffin & Howe gunsmithing firm, when he was employed at the Army's Frankford Arsenal. Howe named the new wildcat for the late Colonel Townsend Whelen, who was then stationed at Frankford Arsenal and collaborated with Howe on much of the experimental work that he did there. The cartridge is based on the standard .30-06 case, merely necked-up to accept .35-caliber bullets. Because the shoulder of the case is rather narrow when the neck is expanded to .35 caliber, some variants of this wildcat cartridge are formed with a shoulder angle steeper than that of the .30-06 (which is about 17 degrees) to provide more positive headspace control. Though not truly necessary for a closely chambered rifle with carefully resized cases, the steeper shoulder is probably a worthwhile improvement. It has little effect on the ballistic performance of the cartridge.

The .35 Whelen has been a moderately popular wildcat for more than 55 years, and justly so. Its popularity would probably be greater still if there were a demand for such powerful big-bore cartridges comparable to the demand for varmint and deer hunters' cartridges. It performs well with bullet weights from 200 to 300 grains, though .35-caliber bullets heavier than 250 grains are no longer widely available.

Max. Case Length: 2.494″ **Trim-To Length:** 2.489″
Max. Overall Length: Varies **Primer Size:** Large Rifle **Bullet Dia.:** .358″

RIFLE LOADS FOR THE .35 WHELEN

LOAD NUMBER	BULLET WEIGHT	BULLET BRAND	BULLET SHAPE	BULLET TYPE	POWDER WEIGHT	POWDER BRAND	POWDER TYPE	VELOCITY FPS	PRESSURE CUP	CASE BRAND	PRIMER BRAND	PRIMER TYPE	CARTRIDGE OAL	BARREL LENGTH	DATA SOURCE
1	200	HDY	RNN	SP	58.4	DUP	4320	2700		MIL	FED	210		22½	HDY
2	200	HDY	RNN	SP	58.6	HOD	H380	2600		MIL	FED	210		22½	HDY
3	200	REM	RNN	SP	53.0	DUP	4064	2473	32010					26	NRA
4	250	SPR	PTD	SP	52.5	DUP	4064	2487	48420					26	NRA
5	250	HDY	PTD	SP	59.9	DUP	4350	2400		MIL	FED	210		22½	HDY
6	250	HDY	PTD	SP	55.6	HOD	H380	2400		MIL	FED	210		22½	HDY

.350 REMINGTON MAGNUM

The .350 Remington Magnum cartridge was introduced in 1965, in conjunction with the Remington Model 600 bolt-action carbine which was chambered for it. The Model 600 carbine is a short-action gun, limiting the length of cartridges used in it to about 2.80 inches. This design constraint handicaps the cartridge performance to some degree. The maximum bullet protrusion allowed is only about .63 inch, and the neck length is only about .35 inch. This limits the suitable bullets to those having an ogival length that does not exceed .63 inch or about 1.76 calibers, and bullets longer than those about .98 inch will intrude into the powder space behind the case neck. All of the bullets listed in the accompanying data are so designed that they can be loaded to the correct overall cartridge length of 2.80 inches, but the ones weighing more than 200 grains will intrude more or less into the powder space. The 250-grain Speer spitzer bullet, as one example, will intrude about .25 inch behind the base of the case neck, reducing the effective case capacity by about 10 per cent. This by no means precludes the use of pointed 250-grain bullets in the .350 Remington Magnum, but it limits the charge weight, and therefore affects the ballistics that can be obtained with such bullets in this short cartridge.

The working pressure for the .350 Remington Magnum cartridge is limited to about 53,000 c.u.p. The maximum product average established for the cartridge is 56,200 c.u.p.

Max. Case Length: 2.170″ **Trim-To Length:** 2.160″
Max. Overall Length: 2.800″ **Primer Size:** Large Rifle **Bullet Dia.:** .358″

FULL-CHARGE LOADS FOR THE .350 REMINGTON MAGNUM

LOAD NUMBER	BULLET				POWDER			VELOCITY FPS	PRESSURE CUP	CASE BRAND	PRIMER		CARTRIDGE OAL	BARREL LENGTH	DATA SOURCE
	WEIGHT	BRAND	SHAPE	TYPE	WEIGHT	BRAND	TYPE				BRAND	TYPE			
1	125	SPR	FLN	HP	60.0	DUP	4895	2849	<53000	REM	CCI	200		22	SPR
2	140	SPR	FLN	HP	62.0	DUP	4064	2882	<53000	REM	CCI	200		22	SPR
3	158	SPR	FLN	SP	62.0	DUP	4064	2841	<53000	REM	CCI	200		22	SPR
4	180	SPR	FLN	SP	62.0	DUP	4064	2914	<53000	REM	CCI	200		22	SPR
5	180	SPR	FLN	SP	61.0	HOD	4895	3015	52300	REM	REM	9½		26	HOD
6	180	SPR	FLN	SP	62.0	HOD	H335	3006	50600	REM	REM	9½		26	HOD
7	200	SRA	RNN	SP	62.6	HOD	H380	2700		REM	REM	9½		18½	SRA
8	200	HDY	RNN	SP	64.8	WIN	760	2600		REM	FED	210		18½	HDY
9	200	REM	RNN	SP	60.0	DUP	3031	2835	50700	REM	REM	9½M	2.765	20	DUP
10	200	REM	RNN	SP	64.5	DUP	4320	2820	52100	REM	REM	9½M	2.765	20	DUP
11	200	REM	RNN	SP	62.0	DUP	4895	2815	52300	REM	REM	9½M	2.765	20	DUP
12	250	REM	PTD	SP	56.0	DUP	4895	2485	52500	REM	REM	9½M	2.730	20	DUP
13	250	REM	PTD	SP	53.0	DUP	3031	2410	47800	REM	REM	9½M	2.730	20	DUP
14	250	SPR	PTD	SP	55.0	DUP	4064	2348	<53000	REM	CCI	200		22	SPR
15	250	SPR	PTD	SP	52.0	HOD	BL-C-(2)	2257	<53000	REM	CCI	250		22	SPR
16	250	HDY	PTD	SP	54.9	DUP	4320	2400		REM	FED	210		18½	HDY
17	250	HDY	PTD	SP	58.3	WIN	760	2300		REM	FED	210		18½	HDY

.358 NORMA MAGNUM

The .358 Norma Magnum cartridge was designed by the A B Norma Projektilfabrik of Amotfors, Sweden, and introduced in the U.S. in 1959. Designed for medium-length actions that can accommodate the 8x57mm Mauser cartridge, the .358 Norma Magnum is not so severely limited in length as is the .350 Remington Magnum. Though loaded by Norma with a maximum overall cartridge length of 3.23 inches (approximately the maximum length of 8x57mm Mauser cartridges) it can be loaded to a length of about 3.33 inches in actions designed around the .30-06 cartridge. The maximum bullet protrusion is about .72 inch with the 3.23-inch cartridge length, and about .82 inch with the longer 3.33-inch cartridge length. The case neck is only about .30 of an inch long, however, which is less than that of the .350 Remington Magnum, and bullets longer than about 1.02 inches will intrude somewhat into the powder space if loaded to the 3.23-inch overall cartridge length prescribed by Norma. With a cartridge length of 3.33 inches, bullets as long as 1.12 inches do not intrude behind the case neck, and 250-grain pointed bullets intrude only about .10 inch, which reduces the effective powder capacity by only about three per cent. With a muzzle energy of more than 4,000 foot-pounds, the .358 Norma Magnum is suitable for the largest North American game.

Max. Case Length: 2.515″ **Trim-To Length:** 2.505″
Max. Overall Length: 3.270″ **Primer Size:** Large Rifle Magnum **Bullet Dia.:** .358″

RIFLE LOADS FOR THE .358 NORMA MAGNUM

LOAD NUMBER	BULLET				POWDER			VELOCITY FPS	PRESSURE CUP	CASE BRAND	PRIMER		CARTRIDGE OAL	BARREL LENGTH	DATA SOURCE
	WEIGHT	BRAND	SHAPE	TYPE	WEIGHT	BRAND	TYPE				BRAND	TYPE			
1	180	SPR	FLN	SP	78.0	DUP	4350	2948		NOR	CCI	250		24	SPR
2	200	HDY	RNN	SP	74.4	DUP	4350	2900		NOR	RWS	LR		25½	HDY
3	250	SPR	PTD	SP	76.0	DUP	4350	2732		NOR	CCI	250		24	SPR
4	250	NOR	SPD	SP	66.3	NOR	202	2710	<53400	NOR	NOR	LR	3.230	24	NOR
5	250	SPR	PTD	SP	78.0	HOD	H205	2680		NOR	CCI	250		24	SPR
6	250	HDY	PTD	SP	76.7	HOD	H450	2700		NOR	RWS	LR		25½	HDY

.375 WINCHESTER

Introduced in 1978 in conjunction with the lever-action Model 94 Big Bore rifle, the .375 Winchester cartridge closely resembles the much older .38-55, though the cartridges are not interchangeable. The .375 Winchester was announced as having a normal working chamber pressure of 50,000 c.u.p., whereas that for the .38-55 is 30,000 c.u.p. Though the .375 Winchester cartridge chambers easily and can be fired in .38-55 rifles, to do so is dangerous because of the much higher chamber pressure developed by the .375 cartridge. Neither should any .38-55 ammunition ever be chambered and fired in a .375 Winchester rifle, because the .38-55 case is sufficiently longer than the .375 case that it extends past the chamber mouth, constricting the case mouth so that the bullet is not properly released, and that condition can produce excessive chamber pressure.

Bullets for the .375 Winchester are about .376-inch in diameter, smaller by only about .001 inch than .38-55 factory bullets, and .38-55 bullets should not be used in handloading for the .375 Winchester. It is probable, however, that bullets designed for the .375 Winchester might perform satisfactorily in a .38-55 handload, which would be a welcome coincidence for handloaders who have for some years been unable to obtain .38-55 jacketed bullets from the major bullet manufacturers. Limited trials of the bullets pulled from .375 Winchester factory loads, loaded in .38-55 cases, and fired in a usually accurate .38-55 Winchester high-wall single-shot rifle, produced only mediocre accuracy, however. Possibly this was due to the undersize bullets, since the groove diameter of this .38-55 barrel is about .378 inch, and quite possibly due in part to the 16-inch twist in the .38-55 whereas the .375 Winchester bullets were designed for the 12-inch twist of the .375 Winchester barrel.

The .375 Winchester provides about 11 per cent more striking energy at 100 yards than that of the .30-30. The .375 Winchester factory load with 200-grain bullets produces about 11 per cent more muzzle energy than that of the .35 Remington cartridge with the same weight of bullet. It is therefore appreciably more powerful than either of these other popular lever-action cartridges. The muzzle energy is, however, only about 75 per cent as great as that of the .358 Winchester cartridge with bullets of the same weight, and about 70 per cent as great as that of the 240-grain bullet in the .444 Marlin lever-action rifle.

The maximum product average chamber pressure for the .375 Winchester cartridge is established at 55,200 c.u.p., the same as that of the .308 and .358 Winchester cartridges, suggesting that the working pressure may be comparable to that of these other cartridges at about 50,000 to 52,000 c.u.p.

Max. Case Length: 2.020″ **Trim-To Length:** 2.010″ **Max. Overall Length:** 2.560″ **Primer Size:** Large Rifle **Bullet Dia.:** .375″

RIFLE LOADS FOR THE .375 WINCHESTER

LOAD NUMBER	BULLET				POWDER			VELOCITY FPS	PRESSURE CUP	CASE BRAND	PRIMER		CARTRIDGE OAL	BARREL LENGTH	DATA SOURCE
	WEIGHT	BRAND	SHAPE	TYPE	WEIGHT	BRAND	TYPE				BRAND	TYPE			
1	200	WIN	FLN	SP	39.0	HOD	H4895	1893		WIN	WIN	8½-120		20	HOD
2	200	WIN	FLN	SP	41.0	HOD	H4895	2044		WIN	WIN	8½-120		20	HOD
3	200	WIN	FLN	SP	42.0	HOD	BL-C-(2)	1825		WIN	WIN	8½-120		20	HOD
4	200	WIN	FLN	SP	44.0	HOD	BL-C-(2)	2018		WIN	WIN	8½-120		20	HOD
5	200	WIN	FLN	SP	30.0	HOD	H4198	1894		WIN	WIN	8½-120		20	HOD
6	200	WIN	FLN	SP	33.0	HOD	H4198	2137		WIN	WIN	8½-120		20	HOD
7	250	WIN	FLN	SP	35.0	HOD	H4895	1713		WIN	WIN	8½-120		20	HOD
8	250	WIN	FLN	SP	37.0	HOD	H4895	1845		WIN	WIN	8½-120		20	HOD
9	250	WIN	FLN	SP	38.0	HOD	BL-C-(2)	1693		WIN	WIN	8½-120		20	HOD
10	250	WIN	FLN	SP	40.0	HOD	BL-C-(2)	1820		WIN	WIN	8½-120		20	HOD
11	250	WIN	FLN	SP	28.0	HOD	H4198	1737		WIN	WIN	8½-120		20	HOD
12	250	WIN	FLN	SP	30.0	HOD	H4198	1858		WIN	WIN	8½-120		20	HOD
13	220	HDY	FLN	SP	32.2	DUP	4198	2000		WIN	WIN	8½-120	2.560	20	HDY
14	220	HDY	FLN	SP	28.0	DUP	4198	1800		WIN	WIN	8½-120	2.560	20	HDY
15	220	HDY	FLN	SP	36.0	NOR	200	2100		WIN	WIN	8½-120	2.560	20	HDY
16	220	HDY	FLN	SP	38.0	HER	RL7	2200		WIN	WIN	8½-120	2.560	20	HDY
17	220	HDY	FLN	SP	32.8	HER	RL7	1900		WIN	WIN	8½-120	2.560	20	HDY
18	220	HDY	FLN	SP	35.2	DUP	3031	1900		WIN	WIN	8½-120	2.560	20	HDY
19	220	HDY	FLN	SP	38.6	HOD	H322	2000		WIN	WIN	8½-120	2.560	20	HDY
20	220	HDY	FLN	SP	34.8	HOD	H322	1800		WIN	WIN	8½-120	2.560	20	HDY
21	235	SPR	SPD	SP	30.0	DUP	4198	1851		WIN	CCI	200		22	SPR
22	235	SPR	SPD	SP	33.0	HER	RL7	1837		WIN	CCI	200		22	SPR
23	235	SPR	SPD	SP	35.0	HOD	H322	1823		WIN	CCI	200		22	SPR

NOTE: Use only flat-nose cannelured bullets in tubular magazines.

.375 HOLLAND & HOLLAND MAGNUM

Since its introduction in 1912 by the venerable English firm of Holland & Holland, the .375 H.&H. Magnum has achieved worldwide popularity as a big-game cartridge, suitable for all but the largest of African game. It has in fact been used on the largest game by experienced African hunters who placed their shots carefully and used non-expanding bullets (called "solids") of proper construction. Though unnecessarily powerful for most North American game, it would be a good choice if one rifle were to be used on all game from deer to moose or large bear. Handloads using the 235-grain Speer bullet can develop nearly 2,900 fps, and the trajectory is then flat enough for effective long-range shooting. With 300-grain bullets at a velocity of 2,500 fps, the muzzle energy is more than 4,100 foot-pounds, and certainly adequate for the largest North American game.

Having an overall cartridge length of 3.60 inches, the .375 H.&H. rifle must be built on a longer action than that required for the .30-06 or the so-called "short" magnum cartridges. Excellent accuracy can also be obtained with suitable reduced loads in the .375

H.&H. Magnum, so the handloader can prepare hunting loads that are more suitable than the full-charge loads for hunting deer or other medium-size game.

The working pressure for the .375 H&H Magnum cartridge is about 53,000 c.u.p. and the established maximum product average for factory ammunition is 56,200 c.u.p.

Max. Case Length: 2.850" **Trim-To Length:** 2.840"
Max. Overall Length: 3.600" **Primer Size:** Large Rifle Magnum **Bullet Dia.:** .375"

RIFLE LOADS FOR THE .375 H&H MAGNUM

LOAD NUMBER	BULLET				POWDER			VELOCITY FPS	PRESSURE CUP	CASE BRAND	PRIMER		CARTRIDGE OAL	BARREL LENGTH	DATA SOURCE
	WEIGHT	BRAND	SHAPE	TYPE	WEIGHT	BRAND	TYPE				BRAND	TYPE			
1	235	SPR	SPD	SP	85.0	DUP	4831	2809	<53000	WIN	CCI	200		24	SPR
2	235	SPR	SPD	SP	85.0	DUP	4350	2898	<53000	WIN	CCI	200		24	SPR
3	270	REM	SPD	SP	78.5	DUP	4350	2710	53000	WIN	WIN	8½-120	3.600	25	DUP
4	270	REM	SPD	SP	69.0	DUP	4064	2655	52500	WIN	WIN	8½-120	3.600	25	DUP
5	270	WIN	SPD	SP	77.5	WIN	760	2660	51000	WIN	WIN	8½-120		24	WIN
6	270	NOS	RNN	SP	78.0	HOD	H205	2652		WIN	REM	9½M		24	NOS
7	270	HDY	PTD	SP	77.7	DUP	4350	2600		WIN	WIN	8½-120		25	HDY
8	300	WIN	SPD	SP	78.0	DUP	4350	2620	52700	WIN	WIN	8½-120	3.600	25	DUP
9	300	WIN	SPD	FJ	77.5	WIN	760	2560	51500	WIN	WIN	8½-120		24	WIN
10	300	HDY	RNN	SP	84.8	HOD	4831	2600		WIN	WIN	8½-120		25	HDY
11	300	HDY	RNN	SP	76.4	DUP	4350	2500		WIN	WIN	8½-120		25	HDY
12	300	SRA	PBT	SP	77.0	DUP	4350	2550		WIN	FED	215M		25	SRA
13	300	SRA	PBT	SP	76.8	HOD	H205	2550		WIN	FED	215M		25	SRA
14	300	SRA	PBT	SP	81.1	NOR	MRP	2550		WIN	FED	215M		25	SRA
15	300	NOS	RNN	SP	76.0	HOD	H450	2472		WIN	REM	9½M		24	NOS
16	300	NOS	RNN	SP	78.0	DUP	4831	2503		WIN	REM	9½M		24	NOS
17	285	SPR	SPD	SP	85.0	DUP	4831	2696	<53000	WIN	CCI	200		24	SPR
18	285	SPR	SPD	SP	84.0	DUP	4350	2756	<53000	WIN	CCI	200		24	SPR
19	285	SPR	SPD	SP	86.0	HOD	H450	2660	<53000	WIN	CCI	250		24	SPR
20	235	SPR	SPD	SP	26.0	DUP	4759	1500		WIN	CCI	200		24	SPR
21	235	SPR	SPD	SP	30.0	DUP	4759	1701		WIN	CCI	200		24	SPR
22	285	SPR	SPD	SP	31.0	DUP	4759	1448		WIN	CCI	200		24	SPR
23	285	SPR	SPD	SP	35.0	DUP	4759	1671		WIN	CCI	200		24	SPR

.378 WEATHERBY MAGNUM

The .378 Weatherby Magnum cartridge was introduced in 1953, as a high-velocity heavy-bullet cartridge suitable for the largest game. It uses a belted case considerably larger in diameter than the H.&H. magnum cartridges, approximating the dimensions of the famous British .416 Rigby rimless case. Because of the very large cartridge case, rifles designed around cartridges such as the .30-06 or the standard H.&H. magnum cartridges are not readily convertible to use the .378 Weatherby Magnum cartridge. With muzzle energy of nearly 6,000 foot pounds, the .378 Weatherby is more powerful than any other American factory cartridge except the huge .460 Weatherby Magnum. It is unnecessarily powerful for North American game, and capable of taking the largest game found anywhere in the world, if properly constructed bullets are used.

The recoil of a full-charge .378 Weatherby Magnum cartridge using the 300-grain bullet is practically the same as that of the .458 Winchester Magnum full-charge load with 500-grain bullet, in rifles of the same weight.

Max. Case Length: 2.913″ **Trim-To Length:** 2.903″
Max. Overall Length: 3.690″ **Primer Size:** Large Rifle **Bullet Dia.:** .375″

RIFLE LOADS FOR THE .378 WEATHERBY MAGNUM

LOAD NUMBER	BULLET				POWDER			VELOCITY FPS	PRESSURE CUP	CASE BRAND	PRIMER		CARTRIDGE OAL	BARREL LENGTH	DATA SOURCE
	WEIGHT	BRAND	SHAPE	TYPE	WEIGHT	BRAND	TYPE				BRAND	TYPE			
1	270	HDY	PTD	SP	106	DUP	4350	3015	44800	WEA	FED	215	3.687	26	WEA
2	270	HDY	PTD	SP	108	DUP	4350	3112	54620	WEA	FED	215	3.687	26	WEA
3	270	HDY	PTD	SP	118	HOD	4831	3128	51930	WEA	FED	215	3.687	26	WEA
4	270	NOS	RNN	SP	107	HOD	H450	3088		WEA	REM	9½M		26	NOS
5	270	HDY	RNN	SP	118	NOR	MRP	3180	52800	WEA	FED	215	3.687	26	WEA
6	300	SRA	PBT	SP	111.4	HOD	4831	2900		WEA	FED	215		26	SRA
7	300	HDY	RNN	SP	101	DUP	4350	2831	49500	WEA	FED	215	3.687	26	WEA
8	300	HDY	RNN	SP	103	DUP	4350	2922	54300	WEA	FED	215	3.687	26	WEA
9	300	HDY	RNN	SP	110	HOD	4831	2897	51050	WEA	FED	215	3.687	26	WEA
10	300	HDY	RNN	SP	112	HOD	4831	2958	53410	WEA	FED	215	3.687	26	WEA
11	300	NOS	RNN	SP	103	HOD	H450	2847		WEA	REM	9½M		26	NOS
12	300	HDY	RNN	SP	112.6	NOR	MRP	2925	52800	WEA	FED	215	3.687	26	WEA

.38-40 (.38 W.C.F.)

Introduced by Winchester in 1874 for use in their Model 1873 rifle, the .38-40 cartridge was soon adopted by Colt for use in the Colt single-action revolver. The idea of a rifle and revolver firing the same ammunition was appealing to frontiersmen, and the .38-40, along with the .44-40 and .32-20, provided this capability. Originally a blackpowder cartridge, the .38-40 made the transition to smokeless powder successfully. Like the .32-20 and .44-40, the .38-40 was for some years factory-loaded with a high-velocity smokeless load intended only for use in the Winchester Model 1892 rifle and other rifles of comparable strength. These high-velocity loads should not be fired in any handgun.

Loading data for the .38-40, using modern components, are very scarce. Hercules formerly listed many pressure-tested loads, but now warn against the use of the old data, because of changes in cases and other components. The loads listed have not been tested for chamber pressure, but are believed not to exceed industry limits for this cartridge.

Colt single-action revolvers having serial numbers below 160,000 were intended only for use with blackpowder, and were proof-tested accordingly. Those guns should not be fired with any smokeless load.

Some old .38-40 cases are of balloon-head construction, and are not suitable for handloading. Cases of recent manufacture are of modern solid-head construction.

The maximum product average chamber pressure of the .38-40 cartridge is now established at 14,000 c.u.p.

Max. Case Length: 1.305″ **Trim-To Length:** 1.300″
Max. Overall Length: 1.592″ **Primer Size:** Large Pistol **Bullet Dia.:** .400″

RIFLE LOADS FOR THE .38-40

LOAD NUMBER	BULLET				POWDER			VELOCITY FPS	PRESSURE CUP	CASE BRAND	PRIMER		CARTRIDGE OAL	BARREL LENGTH	DATA SOURCE
	WEIGHT	BRAND	SHAPE	TYPE	WEIGHT	BRAND	TYPE				BRAND	TYPE			
1	180	WIN	FLN	SP	12.0	WIN	630	1150		WIN	WIN	7-111	1.590	24	NRA
2	180	CAST	FLN	LP	8.0	HER	UNIQ	1330		WIN	WIN	7-111	1.590	24	NRA
3	180	CAST	FLN	LP	15.0	HER	2400	1330		WIN	WIN	7-111	1.590	24	NRA
4	180	CAST	FLN	LP	16.0	DUP	4759	1330		WIN	WIN	7-111	1.590	24	NRA
5	180	CAST	FLN	LP	16.2	DUP	4227	1330		WIN	WIN	7-111	1.590	24	NRA

.38-55

Like the .32-40 Ballard, Marlin and Winchester cartridge, the .38-55 was introduced about 1884, for use in the Ballard single-shot rifle. Also like the .32-40, the .38-55 was soon adopted as a hunting cartridge in some repeating rifles such as the Marlin Model 1893, Winchester Model 1894 and Savage Model 1899.

In single-shot match rifles, the .38-55 was the principal rival of the .32-40 cartridge among target shooters of the blackpowder era. Because of its heavier bullets, the .38-55 was often preferred to the .32-40 for ranges of 200 yards or longer. The .38-55 also weathered the transition to smokeless powder, and was for some time factory-loaded in a "high-velocity" version, intended for use only in the stronger rifles such as the Winchester Model 1894, Marlin Model 1893 and Savage Model 1899. The .38-55 earned a reputation as a good hunting cartridge for deer-size animals in the blackpowder era, and some modern devotees of cast-bullet shooting have found that it is indeed a good choice for hunting deer with cast-bullet loads.

The original blackpowder load for the .38-55 produced about 1,320 fps, with a 255-grain lead bullet, as did the standard-velocity smokeless load. The "high-velocity" factory load produced about 1590 fps, with a jacketed softpoint bullet, and should not be used in old blackpowder rifles with the weaker actions, such as the Ballards. Manufacture of the .38-55 factory load was discontinued about 1970, but resumed several years later, when Winchester produced a special version of the Model 1894 rifle that appeals particularly to those interested in arms that were prominent in history. Current factory loads use a 255-grain softpoint bullet, at the original velocity of 1,320 fps. The current maximum working pressure for the .38-55 is about 33,200 c.u.p., which is suitable for the stronger arms such as the Winchester Model 1894, but perhaps more than the weaker guns such as the Ballard could withstand without possible damage.

It should be noted that the modern .375 Winchester cartridge can be chambered and fired in .38-55 rifles.

That practice can be hazardous, however, and should be scrupulously avoided. The chamber pressure of the .375 Winchester factory cartridge is far greater than that of the .38-55. It is possible for handloaders to use .375 Winchester cases in loading for the .38-55, though the .375 Winchester case is shorter by about .110-inch, and crimping the case mouth cannot normally be accomplished in the .38-55 seating die. Because the powder capacity of .375 Winchester cases is less than that of .38-55 cases, full-charge loads developed in the .38-55 cases should be reduced by 10 percent if .375 Winchester cases are used instead. It is sometimes feasible to seat the bullets less deeply in the .375 Winchester cases, so that the overall length of the loaded cartridge is the same as that of the normal .38-55 load. In that event, the normal .38-55 load need be reduced by only 5 percent, to accommodate the thicker head and case walls of the .375 Winchester cases. Accuracy may also be improved by this "long-seating" of bullets, when .375 Winchester cases must be used in the .38-55.

Max. Case Length: 2.128″ **Trim-To Length:** 2.118″
Max. Overall Length: 2.550″ **Primer Size:** Large Rifle
Bullet Dia.: .379″

LOAD NUMBER	BULLET				POWDER			VELOCITY FPS	PRESSURE CUP	CASE BRAND	PRIMER		CARTRIDGE OAL	BARREL LENGTH	DATA SOURCE
	WEIGHT	BRAND	SHAPE	TYPE	WEIGHT	BRAND	TYPE				BRAND	TYPE			
1	255	CIL	FLN	SP	26.5	HER	RL7	1725	26000	CIL	CCI 200		2.530	24	HER
2	255	WIN	FLN	SP	19.5	DUP	4198	1300	<30000	WIN	WIN	8½-120	2.550	24	NRA
3	245	CAST	FLN	LP	18.0	DUP	4759	1350			WIN	WIN	8½-120	2.550	30	NRA
4	245	CAST	FLN	LP	9.5	HER	UNIQ	1320			WIN	WIN	8½-120	2.550	30	NRA
5	245	CAST	FLN	LP	20.0	DUP	4198	1300			WIN	WIN	8½-120	2.550	30	NRA

.44-40 (.44 W.C.F.)

The .44-40 was first introduced by Winchester in 1873, for the now-famous Model 1873 lever-action rifle. Colt soon adopted it for their single-action revolver, and a great many other arms have been chambered for the .44-40 during the century since its introduction. It was probably the most widely used cartridge by those frontiersmen who wanted a rifle and handgun using the same ammunition. Originally using a 200-grain lead bullet and 40 grains of blackpowder, the .44-40 developed a velocity of about 1200 fps in a rifle. Early smokeless loads produced practically the same ballistics. Like the .32-20 and .38-40, the .44-40 was factory loaded for some years with a special high-velocity load, intended only for use with the Winchester Model 1892 rifle and other rifles of comparable strength. These loads should not be fired in any handgun.

The .44-40 is still listed as a factory load, with ballistics nearly the same as those of the original blackpowder load. Chamber pressure is limited to a moderate 13,000 c.u.p., in deference to the relatively weak old guns in which the ammunition might be used. Colt single-action revolvers having serial numbers below 160,000 were not intended for use with any smokeless loads. One load listed here was furnished by Winchester-Western, and is consistent with their factory loading practice.

Some old .44-40 cases were of balloon-head construction, and should not be used for handloading. Unless the handloader can recognize balloon-head cases, he should use only those known to be of recent manufacture.

The maximum product average chamber pressure for the .44-40 cartridge is now established at 13,700 c.u.p.
Max. Case Length: 1.305″ **Trim-To Length:** 1.300″
Max. Overall Length: 1.592″ **Primer Size:** Large Pistol **Bullet Dia.:** .425″ - .429″

RIFLE LOADS FOR THE .44-40

LOAD NUMBER	BULLET				POWDER			VELOCITY FPS	PRESSURE CUP	CASE BRAND	PRIMER		CARTRIDGE OAL	BARREL LENGTH	DATA SOURCE
	WEIGHT	BRAND	SHAPE	TYPE	WEIGHT	BRAND	TYPE				BRAND	TYPE			
1	200	WIN	FLN	SP	13.0	WIN	630	1175	<13000	WIN	WIN	7-111	1.590	24	WIN
2	200	CAST	FLN	LP	8.1	HER	UNIQ	1200			WIN	WIN	7-111	1.590	24	NRA
3	200	CAST	FLN	LP	16.0	DUP	4759	1200			WIN	WIN	7-111	1.590	24	NRA
4	200	CAST	FLN	LP	17.5	DUP	4227	1200			WIN	WIN	7-111	1.590	24	NRA
5	200	CAST	FLN	LP	16.5	HER	2400	1200			WIN	WIN	7-111	1.590	24	NRA

.44 MAGNUM (RIFLE)

The .44 Magnum cartridge was announced by Remington in 1956, in conjunction with the Smith & Wesson .44 Magnum revolver. It was quite sensational as a handgun cartridge, far out-performing any other handgun cartridge then available. Possibly because the .44 Magnum is obviously reminiscent of the .44-40 Winchester cartridge developed more than 80 years

earlier for use in the famous Winchester Model 1873 rifle, gunsmiths soon began to rebarrel Model 1892 Winchester lever-action rifles for the new handgun cartridge. Though the .44 Magnum cartridge has a maximum working chamber-pressure limit of 40,000 c.u.p., whereas the comparable .38-40 and .44-40 cartridges for which the Model 92 Winchester rifle was designed were limited to about 20,000 c.u.p., even in the high-velocity smokeless loads that were once factory-produced for such rifles, no serious trouble seems to have arisen with the Model 1892 rifles rebarreled for the .44 Magnum unless a handloader incautiously tried to exceed the performance of factory loads. Even in those instances, the consequences were more often a swelled chamber rather than a failure of the action, indicating that John M. Browning designed the Model 92 to withstand pressures considerably higher than those developed by the cartridges to which it was adapted. The Ruger autoloading carbine chambered for the .44 Magnum cartridge was introduced in 1961, and soon found favor with hunters who wanted a light, compact gun for hunting game up to the size of deer in thick cover, where long shots were not required. Other rifles and carbines were subsequently offered in .44 Magnum chambering, including the lever-action Marlin 1894 and Winchester 94, and the cartridge is now well established as suitable for shoulder arms as well as handguns.

The .44 Magnum factory load produces about 1,650 foot-pounds of muzzle energy when fired from a rifle, nearly as much as the .250 Savage or .257 Roberts, and it is adequate for hunting deer-size game at short and moderate ranges. Handloaders are sometimes advised that .44 Magnum ammunition intended for use in rifles can be loaded safely to pressures exceeding those of maximum loads for handguns, but that is poor advice. The 40,000-c.u.p. pressure limit imposed on factory loads applies equally to the loads intended primarily for rifle use and those intended for handgun use, and it ought to be respected by handloaders as well.

The handloader may find that the soft swaged lead bullets intended for handguns do not shoot well in .44 Magnum rifles, and the Micro-Groove rifling used in the barrels of Marlin Model 1894 carbines does not allow good shooting with any unjacketed bullets, either cast or swaged. For use in tubular-magazine rifles, cases should always be crimped securely into a bullet cannelure to prevent them from being driven into the case under the forces of recoil while in the magazine.

Another precaution that must be scrupulously observed for safety is to avoid use of any bullet except those having flat noses in a tubular-magazine gun. Round-nose bullets have been known to impinge on the primer of the cartridge ahead in a tubular magazine when the gun was fired, firing that cartridge, and in turn exploding all of the cartridges in the magazine practically simultaneously. The shooter in one such incident suffered serious injury, and handloaders must heed that example or risk serious consequences.

The maximum product average chamber pressure established for .44 Magnum factory ammunition is 43,500 c.u.p.

Max. Case Length: 1.285″ **Trim-To Length:** 1.280″ **Max. Overall Length:** 1.610″ **Primer Size:** Large Pistol **Bullet Dia.:** .429″

RIFLE LOADS FOR THE .44 MAGNUM

LOAD NUMBER	BULLET				POWDER			VELOCITY FPS	PRESSURE CUP	CASE BRAND	PRIMER		CARTRIDGE OAL	BARREL LENGTH	DATA SOURCE
	WEIGHT	BRAND	SHAPE	TYPE	WEIGHT	BRAND	TYPE				BRAND	TYPE			
1	180	SRA	FLN	HP	28.4	HOD	H110	2100		REM	CCI	350		20	SRA
2	180	SRA	FLN	HP	26.5	HER	2400	2000		REM	CCI	350		20	SRA
3	200	HDY	FLN	HP	22.0	WIN	630	1800		REM	FED	150		18	HDY
4	200	SPR	FLN	HP	27.0	HOD	H110	1942	<43500	SPR	CCI	350		18½	SPR
5	200	SPR	FLN	HP	24.8	HER	2400	1965	<43500	SPR	CCI	350		18½	SPR
6	225	SPR	FLN	HP	17.5	HER	BDOT	1706	<43500	SPR	CCI	350		18½	SPR
7	240	REM	FLN	SP	23.5	DUP	4227	1680	39500	REM	REM	2½	1.610	22	DUP
8	240	REM	FLN	SP	21.0	DUP	4759	1630	38500	REM	REM	2½	1.610	22	DUP
9	240	HDY	FLN	HP	22.6	HOD	H110	1700		REM	FED	150		18	HDY
10	240	SPR	FLN	SP	24.7	WIN	296	1778	<43500	SPR	CCI	350		18½	SPR
11	240	SRA	FLN	HP	22.6	HER	2400	1700		REM	CCI	350		20	SRA

.444 MARLIN

The .444 Marlin cartridge was announced in 1964 by Remington, in conjunction with the announcement by Marlin of their new lever-action rifle chambered for it. The bullet used is apparently the same 240-grain soft-point that is used in the .44 Magnum cartridge, but the cartridge case is much longer and has more than twice the powder capacity of the .44 Magnum case. The muzzle velocity is nominally 2,350 fps, with an impressive 2,942 foot-pounds of muzzle energy. While the load is certainly ample for hunting deer-size animals, its potential effectiveness on larger game is not realized with the 240-grain bullet used in factory loads. With a sectional density of only .186, equal to that of a .30-caliber bullet weighing about 123 grains, the 240-grain .44-caliber bullet lacks the penetration required for effective use on animals much larger than whitetail deer.

Fortunately, the handloader can improve considerably on factory-load performance for larger animals by using the 265-grain Hornady bullet designed especially for the .444 Marlin cartridge. In 1979 Remington introduced a 265-grain factory load for the .444. Both by being heavier than the handgun bullet, and being designed for properly controlled expansion at the higher velocities achieved in the .444 Marlin cartridge, the 265-grain Hornaday or Remington bullets are far better suited to the cartridge than is the 240-grain factory bullet. An even heavier bullet might be better still, but calculations indicate that bullets much heavier than 265 grains would not be adequately

stabilized in the long 38-inch twist of the Marlin barrel.

As with the .44 Magnum, bullets must be securely crimped in the .444 Marlin case for use in the tubular magazine, and *only flat-point bullets must be used in the interests of safety*. Owing to the Micro-Groove rifling, the Marlin .444 rifle is not suitable for use with cast-bullet loads.

The maximum working pressure for the .444 Marlin is about 44,000 c.u.p. The established maximum product average for factory ammunition is 47,200 c.u.p.

Max. Case Length: 2.225″ Trim-To Length: 2.220″
Max. Overall Length: 2.570″ Primer Size: Large Rifle Bullet Dia.: .429″

RIFLE LOADS FOR THE .444 MARLIN

LOAD NUMBER	BULLET				POWDER			VELOCITY FPS	PRESSURE CUP	CASE BRAND	PRIMER		CARTRIDGE OAL	BARREL LENGTH	DATA SOURCE
	WEIGHT	BRAND	SHAPE	TYPE	WEIGHT	BRAND	TYPE				BRAND	TYPE			
1	180	SRA	FLN	HP	51.0	DUP	4198	2500		REM	WIN	8½-120		24	SRA
2	225	SPR	FLN	HP	50.0	HOD	H4198	2480	37800	REM	REM	9½		24	HOD
3	225	SPR	FLN	HP	61.0	HOD	BL-C-(2)	2358	33600	REM	REM	9½		24	HOD
4	225	SPR	FLN	HP	56.0	HOD	4895	2301	33000	REM	REM	9½		24	HOD
5	240	REM	FLN	SP	47.0	DUP	4198	2335	44000	REM	REM	9½	2.570	25	DUP
6	240	SPR	FLN	SP	60.0	HOD	H335	2309	31400	REM	REM	9½		24	HOD
7	240	SPR	FLN	SP	49.0	HOD	H4198	2407	38400	REM	REM	9½		24	HOD
8	240	SRA	FLN	HP	55.0	DUP	3031	2200		REM	WIN	8½-120		24	SRA
9	240	SPR	FLN	SP	57.0	DUP	4320	2123	<44000	REM	CCI	200		24	SPR
10	240	HDY	FLN	HP	45.0	DUP	4198	2200		REM	ALC	LR		24	HDY
11	240	REM	FLN	SP	33.0	DUP	4759	2055	43600	REM	REM	9½		25	DUP
12	240	REM	FLN	SP	56.0	DUP	4895	2200	38600	REM	REM	9½		25	DUP
13	240	REM	FLN	SP	54.5	DUP	3031	2175	35900	REM	REM	9½		25	DUP
14	240	REM	FLN	SP	56.0	DUP	4320	2125	37200	REM	REM	9½		25	DUP
15	265	HDY	FLN	SP	45.3	DUP	4198	2200		REM	ALC	LR		24	HDY
16	265	HDY	FLN	SP	54.0	HOD	H322	2248	35300	REM	REM	9½		24	HOD
17	265	HDY	FLN	SP	46.0	HOD	H4198	2242	37200	REM	REM	9½		24	HOD

.45-70 GOVERNMENT

The .45-70 cartridge was designed for military use in the Springfield Model 1873 rifle. It was originally called the .45-70-405, indicating a .45-caliber bullet, a 70-grain charge of blackpowder, and a bullet weight of 405 grains. The cartridge was later loaded with a 500-grain lead bullet, and accordingly called the .45-70-500, though the official nomenclature was "Rifle Ball Cartridge, Caliber .45, Reloading, Model 1881." The "Reloading" in the nomenclature signified that the cartridge cases were by then equipped with a replaceable primer similar to those in use today, whereas it had originally been loaded in a cartridge case resembling present rimfire cases, with an "inside primer" held in place for central firing by a supporting structure crimped in place inside the case. The "reloading" case was a logistic improvement, as it

was then common practice for the Army to return fired cases to Frankford Arsenal for reloading and reissue. A still later development was a cartridge loaded with 55 grains of blackpowder and a 405-grain bullet to reduce the heavy recoil produced when the full-charge rifle load was fired in the relatively light military carbine. That cartridge was sometimes known as the .45-55-405, though the case was the same, and it was interchangeable with the .45-70-500 rifle load.

The .45-70 cartridge did not survive the transition to smokeless powder as a military load, and was replaced by the smokeless .30-40 Krag in 1892. It survived and prospered as a sporting cartridge, however, and many sporting rifles were chambered for it. Now, more than 100 years after its introduction, the .45-70 has undergone a remarkable resurgence of popularity, for reasons that are not entirely clear. Several modern rifles are chambered for it, and its popularity seems still to be increasing.

The loading data given here are in three categories, representing three different levels of chamber pressure that are appropriate for rifles having different degrees of strength. **It is imperative for reasons of safety that the handloader understand the need to load his ammunition only with charges appropriate to the strength of his rifle.**

Loads one through 10 develop chamber pressures not exceeding about 18,000 c.u.p., and may be used in Springfield "trap-door" rifles that are properly fitted and in sound mechanical condition, or in other rifles of at least comparable strength. This includes some modern replicas of the "trap-door" Springfield, and other rifles originally intended only for blackpowder loads. If any uncertainty about the strength of an old weapon exists, it should be examined by a competent gunsmith **before firing with any ammunition.** Some authorities advocate the use of blackpowder exclusively in old .45-70 rifles, even in apparently good condition, and that is the prudent course unless the user is quite sure of the rifle's safety with at least mild charges of smokeless powder.

Loads 11 through 20 develop chamber pressures comparable to those of modern smokeless factory loads, for which the limit is about 28,000 c.u.p. They are generally suitable for use in rifles such as the Model 1886 Winchester, original Model 1895 Marlin, and modern .45-70 rifles for which factory ammunition is recommended. Though many smokeless factory loads have undoubtedly been fired in "trap-door" Springfields without untoward results, the practice cannot be recommended because of some uncertainty

about the strength of individual specimens. The modern Marlin Model 1895 is recommended for use with factory loads, and with handloads that are appropriate for the Model 1886 Winchester. Though some users have fired heavier loads in the modern Model 1895 Marlin rifle, it is prudent to heed the advice of the rifle manufacturer and limit the loads to those in the category of Loads 11 through 20. The modern Marlin Model 1895 is advertised as having "modified Micro-Groove" rifling that is suitable for use with both jacketed and cast bullets, but some users have reported unsatisfactory results with cast-bullet loads that shoot well in other .45-70 rifles, so it appears that the Marlin barrels are somewhat less suitable for cast-bullet loads than are barrels having conventional rifling.

Loads 21 through 26 develop chamber pressures exceeding that of .45-70 factory loads, and should be used only in the strongest rifles, such as the Ruger single-shot, custom rifles built on sound Mauser-type bolt actions, or other rifles that are comparably strong.

The .45-70 achieved a reputation as an effective big-game rifle in the last century, despite the rather moderate muzzle energy of about 1600 foot-pounds. The big bullet transfers energy effectively to the target even with only moderate expansion, and its great weight insures adequate penetration even at relatively low velocities. While it does not often produce the lightning-bolt killing effect of powerful high-velocity loads, it performs reliably, and well hit game seldom escapes wounded after being shot with the .45-70.

Max. Case Length: 2.105″ Trim-To Length: 2.100″
Max. Overall Length: 2.550″ Primer Size: Large Rifle Bullet Dia.: .458″

RIFLE LOADS FOR THE .45-70

LOAD NUMBER	BULLET				POWDER			VELOCITY FPS	PRESSURE CUP	CASE BRAND	PRIMER		CARTRIDGE OAL	BARREL LENGTH	DATA SOURCE
	WEIGHT	BRAND	SHAPE	TYPE	WEIGHT	BRAND	TYPE				BRAND	TYPE			
1	300	HDY	FLN	HP	33.7	DUP	4227	1800	<28000	WIN	FED	210	2.550	29½	HDY
2	300	SRA	FLN	SP	34.8	DUP	4198	1600		REM	REM	9½		32½	SRA
3	300	HDY	FLN	HP	33.0	HOD	H4198	1542		WIN	WIN	8½-120		32½	HOD
4	300	HDY	FLN	HP	34.0	HER	RL7	1450	16400	REM	REM	9½	2.475	24	HER
5	350	HDY	RNN	SP	32.0	HOD	H4198	1387		WIN	WIN	8½-120		32½	HOD
6	350	HDY	RNN	SP	32.8	DUP	4198	1400		REM	FED	210	2.550	26	HDY
7	405	WIN	FLN	SP	41.0	HOD	BL-C-(2)	1354	16400	WIN	WIN	8½-120		26	HOD
8	405	REM	FLN	SP	56.0	DUP	4831	1390	17800	WIN	WIN	8½-120	2.560	25	DUP
9	405	WIN	FLN	SP	20.5	WIN	630	1310	18000	WIN	WIN	8½-120		24	WIN
10	500	HDY	RNN	SP	28.0	DUP	4198	1100		REM	FED	210	2.925	26	HDY
11	300	HDY	FLN	HP	34.6	DUP	4227	1700		REM	FED	210	2.550	26	HDY
12	300	SRA	FLN	SP	41.0	DUP	4198	1800		REM	REM	9½		26	SRA
15	350	HDY	RNN	SP	50.6	DUP	4895	1600		REM	FED	210	2.550	26	HDY
16	400	SPR	FLN	SP	52.0	DUP	3031	1763	<28000	WIN	CCI	200		22	SPR
17	405	REM	FLN	SP	40.0	HER	RL7	1580	24900	REM	REM	9½	2.540	24	HER
18	405	REM	FLN	SP	51.5	DUP	3031	1795	27000	WIN	WIN	8½-120	2.560	25	DUP
19	405	REM	FLN	SP	52.5	DUP	4895	1785	26900	WIN	WIN	8½-120	2.560	25	DUP
20	500	HDY	RNN	SP	46.9	DUP	4895	1400		REM	FED	210		26	HDY
21	300	SRA	FLN	SP	51.8	DUP	4198	2150		REM	WIN	8½-120		22	SRA
22	300	HDY	FLN	HP	54.7	DUP	4198	2300		REM	ALC	LR		22	HDY
23	350	HDY	RNN	SP	53.3	DUP	4198	2200	49800	WIN	FED	210		22	HDY
24	350	HDY	RNN	SP	56.9	DUP	4895	1900	35800	WIN	FED	210		22	HDY
25	400	SPR	FLN	SP	64.0	DUP	4064	1964	<35000	WIN	CCI	200	2.735	22	SPR
26	500	HDY	RNN	SP	53.2	DUP	4895	1700	44000	WIN	FED	210	2.925	22	HDY

.458 WINCHESTER MAGNUM

The .458 Winchester Magnum was introduced in 1956, for the Model 70 Winchester rifle. It has achieved an enviable reputation worldwide among the hunters of the largest African game. It is more than adequate for any game native to North America. Its success on the largest African game is due at least in part to the excellent steel-jacketed "solid" or non-expanding bullet developed for it by Winchester. For thin-skinned large game, the 510-grain soft-point bullet, with more than 4,600 foot-pounds of muzzle energy, is most effective.

Many owners of .458 Magnum rifles desire to use their rifles more frequently than they can afford to go on African safaris. Practice loads, and hunting loads suitable for use on the more common big-game species, can be assembled by the handloader using bullets intended primarily for the .45-70 cartridge.

Such loads do not have the great recoil of full-charge factory ammunition, and they are much less expensive. Some of the loads listed are in that category, and if those are too powerful for the purpose, loading data for the .45-70 cartridge can safely be utilized, though velocities will be somewhat less than in the .45-70 because of the lower loading density in the larger .458 Magnum case.

The working chamber pressure for the .458 Winchester Magnum cartridge is commonly limited to about 53,000 c.u.p. The established maximum product average for factory ammunition is 56,200 c.u.p.

Max. Case Length: 2.500" **Trim-To Length:** 2.495"
Max. Overall Length: 3.340" **Primer Size:** Large Rifle **Bullet Dia.:** .458"

RIFLE LOADS FOR THE .458 WINCHESTER MAGNUM

LOAD NUMBER	BULLET				POWDER			VELOCITY FPS	PRESSURE CUP	CASE BRAND	PRIMER		CARTRIDGE OAL	BARREL LENGTH	DATA SOURCE
	WEIGHT	BRAND	SHAPE	TYPE	WEIGHT	BRAND	TYPE				BRAND	TYPE			
1	300	SRA	FLN	SP	63.7	DUP	4198	2500		WIN	WIN	8½-120		26	SRA
2	300	SRA	FLN	SP	72.9	DUP	3031	2500		WIN	WIN	8½-120		26	SRA
3	350	HDY	RNN	SP	75.1	DUP	3031	2400		WIN	WIN	8½-120		25	HDY
4	400	SPR	FLN	SP	75.0	DUP	4895	2261	<53000	WIN	CCI	200		24	SPR
5	500	HDY	RNN	SP	73.1	DUP	4895	2050		WIN	WIN	8½-120		25	HDY
6	500	WIN	RNN	FJ	73.0	WIN	748	2040	39000	WIN	WIN	8½-120		24	WIN
7	500	HDY	RNN	SP	77.0	HOD	BL-C-(2)	2117	43800	WIN	WIN	8½-120		26	HOD
8	510	WIN	RNN	SP	72.5	DUP	4895	2100	53000	WIN	WIN	8½-120	3.340	25	DUP
9	510	WIN.	RNN	SP	69.0	DUP	3031	2030	43900	WIN	WIN	8½-120	3.340	25	DUP
10	510	WIN	RNN	SP	75.0	WIN	748	2065	41000	WIN	WIN	8½-120		24	WIN
11	400	SPR	FLN	SP	26.0	DUP	4759	1262		WIN	CCI	200		24	SPR
12	400	SPR	FLN	SP	28.0	DUP	4759	1338		WIN	CCI	200		24	SPR
13	400	SPR	FLN	SP	30.0	DUP	4759	1445		WIN	CCI	200		24	SPR

.460 WEATHERBY MAGNUM

The .460 Weatherby Magnum cartridge was introduced in 1958. With more than 8,000 foot-pounds of muzzle energy, it is the most powerful factory cartridge adapted to sporting weapons. It is based on the same large belted case as the .378 Weatherby Magnum, though it develops about 40 per cent greater muzzle

energy. The free-recoil energy of the full-charge load in the 10½-pound Weatherby rifle is about 102 foot-pounds, and firing one is a memorable experience. By way of comparison, the free-recoil energy of an 8½-pound .300 Winchester Magnum with 180-grain factory loads is about 26 foot-pounds, or one-fourth that of the .460 Weatherby. The .458 Winchester Magnum fired in a 10½-pound rifle produces about 56 foot-pounds of free-recoil energy, barely more than half that of the .460 Weatherby fired in a rifle of the same weight. The largest British rifle and cartridge designed and used for African hunting, the .600 Nitro-Express, fires a 900-grain bullet at about 1,950 fps, developing muzzle energy of about 7,600 foot-pounds, or slightly less than that of the .460 Weatherby Magnum. The .600 Nitro-Express was generally fired in double-barrel rifles weighing not less than 16 pounds, in which it developed free-recoil energy of about 95 foot-pounds, or slightly less than that developed by the 10½-pound .460 Weatherby rifle.

The .460 Weatherby Magnum is a most impressive cartridge though its limited usefulness certainly restricts its popularity to those who can afford an African safari, or can afford to indulge an inclination to own the most powerful factory rifle made anywhere in the world.

Max. Case Length: 2.913″ **Trim-To Length:** 2.903″
Max. Overall Length: 3.750″ **Primer size:** Large Rifle Magnum **Bullet Dia.:** .458″

RIFLE LOADS FOR THE .460 WEATHERBY MAGNUM

LOAD NUMBER	BULLET				POWDER			VELOCITY FPS	PRESSURE CUP	CASE BRAND	PRIMER		CARTRIDGE OAL	BARREL LENGTH	DATA SOURCE
	WEIGHT	BRAND	SHAPE	TYPE	WEIGHT	BRAND	TYPE				BRAND	TYPE			
1	350	HDY	RNN	SP	111.0	DUP	4064	2900		WEA	FED	215		26	HDY
2	350	HDY	RNN	SP	124.8	DUP	4350	2800		WEA	FED	215		26	HDY
3	500	HDY	RNN	SP	115.0	DUP	4350	2513	44400	WEA	FED	215	3.750	26	WEA
4	500	HDY	RNN	SP	122.0	DUP	4350	2632	50370	WEA	FED	215	3.750	26	WEA
5	500	HDY	RNN	SP	124.0	DUP	4350	2678	52980	WEA	FED	215	3.750	26	WEA
6	500	HDY	RNN	SP	102.0	DUP	4064	2486	49000	WEA	FED	215	3.750	26	WEA
7	500	HDY	RNN	SP	106.0	DUP	4064	2553	53280	WEA	FED	215	3.750	26	WEA
8	500	HDY	RNN	SP	92.0	DUP	3031	2405	49530	WEA	FED	215	3.750	26	WEA
9	500	HDY	RNN	SP	96.0	DUP	3031	2470	53560	WEA	FED	215	3.750	26	WEA

SHELL HOLDER CHART
(Rifle Cartridges)

Cartridge	RCBS	Pacific	Lyman	Bonanza	Redding	C-H	Texan	Herter
.17 Remington	10	16	26	6	10	15	15	5
.22 Hornet	12	3	4	8	14			4
.218 Bee	1	7	10	10	3	3	3	11
.219 Donaldson	2	2	6	4	2	2	2	2
.219 Zipper	2	2	6	4	2	2	2	2
.222 Remington	10	16	26	6	10	15	15	5
.223 Remington	10	16	26	6	10	15	15	5
.222 Remington Magnum	10	16	26	6	10	15	15	5
.224 Weatherby Magnum	27	17	3	28				28
.225 Winchester	11	18	5	7	4	1	1	26
.22-250 Remington	3	1	2	1	1	1	1	1
.220 Swift	11	4	5	7	4	4	4	26
6x47mm	10	16	26	6	10	15	15	5
.243 Winchester	3	1	2	1	1	1	1	1
6mm/.244 Remington	3	1	2	1	1	1	1	1
.240 Weatherby Magnum	3	1	2	1	1	1	1	1
.256 Winchester	6	6	1	3	12	12	12	6
25-35	2	2	6	4	2	2	2	2
.250/3000 Savage	3	1	2	1	1	1	1	1
.257 Roberts	11	1	2 or 8	1	1	1	1	1
.25/06 Remington	3	1	2	1	1	1	1	1
.257 Weatherby Magnum	4	5	13	2	6	6	6	8
6.5mm Japanese	15	34	5	4	4	4	4	
6.5x54mm Mannlicher-Schoenauer	9	20	28	14	12	2	14	
6.5x52mm Mannlicher-Carcano	9	21	28	14	12	2	14	
6.5x55mm Swedish	2	2	27	4	1	13	13	21
6.5 Remington Magnum	4	5	13	2	6	6	6	8
.264 Winchester Magnum	4	5	13	2	6	6	6	8
.270 Winchester	3	1	2	1	1	1	1	1
.270 Weatherby Magnum	4	5	13	2	6	6	6	8
7x57mm Mauser	3 or 11	1	2	1	1	1	1	1
7mm-08	3	1	2	1	1	1	1	1
.284 Winchester	3	1	2	1	1	1	1	1
.280 Remington/7mm Exp.	3	1	2	1	1	1	1	1
7x61 Sharpe & Hart	4	5	13	2	6	6	6	8
7mm Remington Magnum	4	5	13	2	6	6	6	8
7mm Weatherby Magnum	4	5	13	2	6	6	6	8
7.35 Carcano	9	20	28	14	12	2	14	
7.5 Schmidt Rubin	2	30	7	4	8	8	2	22
.30 M1 Carbine	17	22	19	5	22		.30 M1	15
7.62x39mm Russian	9	20	28	14	12	2	14	
.30 Herrett	2	2	6	4	2	2	2	2
.30-30 Winchester	2	2	6	4	2	2	2	2
.303 Savage	21	33	7		21			22
.30/40 Krag	7	11	7	11	8	8	8	
.300 Savage	3	1	2	1	1	1	1	1
7.62 Russian	13	23	17	15	15			7
.308 Winchester	3	1	2	1	1	1	1	1
.30/06	3	1	2	1	1	1	1	1
.300 H&H Magnum	4	5	13	2	6	6	6	8
.30-.338	4	5	13	2	6	6	6	8
.300 Winchester Magnum	4	5	13	2	6	6	6	8
.308 Norma Magnum	4	5	13	2	6	6	6	8
.300 Weatherby Magnum	4	5	13	2	6	6	6	8
.303 British	7	11	7	11	8	8	8	3
7.65 Mauser	3	1	2	1	1	1	1	1
7.7 Japanese	3	1	2	4 or 1	1	1	1	1
32 Win. Spl.	2	2	6	4	2	2	2	2
8mm Mauser	3	1	2	1	1	1	1	1
8mm/06	3	1	2	1	1	1	1	1
8mm Remington Magnum	4	5	13	2	6	6	6	8
33 Winchester	14	14	17	16	18			7
.338 Winchester Magnum	4	5	13	2	6	6	6	8
.340 Weatherby Magnum	4	5	13	2	6	6	6	8
.348 Winchester	5	25	18		6	348		12
.35 Remington	9	26	2 or 8	14	1	14	14	1
.357 Magnum	6	6	1	3	12	12	12	6
.358 Winchester	3	1	2	1	1	1	1	1
.35 Whelen	3	1	2	1	1	1	1	1
.350 Remington Magnum	4	5	13	2	6	6	6	8
.358 Norma Mag.	4	5	13	2	6	6	6	8
.375 H&H Magnum	4	5	13	2	6	6	6	8
.375 Winchester	2	2	6	4	2	2	2	2
.378 Weatherby Magnum	14	14	17	16	18			7
.44 Remington Magnum	18	30	7	9	8	8	8	22
.444 Marlin	28	27	14B	27	19		8	28
.45-70 Government	14	14	17	16	18			7
.458 Winchester Magnum	4	5	13	2	6	6	6	8
.460 Weatherby Magnum	14	14	17	16	18			7

SHELL HOLDER CHART
(Pistol Cartridges)

Cartridge	RCBS	Pacific	Lyman	Bonanza	Redding	C-H	Texan	Herter
.22 Hornet	12	3	4	8	14			4
.22 Remington Jet	6	6	1	3	12	12	12	6
.221 Rem. Fireball	10	16	26	6	10	15	15	5
.222 Remington	10	16	26	6	10	15	15	5
.25 ACP	29	37						
.256 Win. Mag.	6	6	1	3	12	12	12	6
.25-35	2	2	6	4	2	2	2	2
.30 Luger	16	8	12	18	13	LG	11	19
.30 Carbine	17	22	19	5	22		.30 M1	15
.30 Herrett	2	2	6	4	2	2	2	2
.30-32	2	2	6	4	2	2		2
.32 ACP	17	22	23	5	10	.30 M1		5
.32 S&W	23	36	9	24	10	10	10	25
.32 Short Colt	23		1	6	10	10	10	25
.32 Long Colt	23		1	6	10	10	10	25
.32 S&W Long	23	36	9	24	10	10	10	25
.32-20	1	7	10	10	10	3	3	25
.380 ACP	10	16	26	6	10	15	15	25
9mm Luger	16	8	12	18	13	LG	16	19
.38 ACP	1	8	12	10	13	3	11	25
.38 Super Auto	1	8	12	10	13	3	11	25
.38 S&W	6	28	21	3	12	12	12	6
.38 Special	6	6	1	3	12	12	12	6
.357 Magnum	6	6	1	3	12	12	12	6
.357 Herrett	2	2	6	4	2	2	2	2
.35 Remington	9	26	2 or 8	14	1	14	14	1
.38-40	26 or 28	9	14B	27	9	9	9	23
.41 Magnum	30	29	30	4	21	41M	17	27
.44 Special	18	30	7	9	8	8	8	22
.44 Magnum	18	30	7	9	8	8	8	22
.44-40	26 or 28	9	14B	27	9	8B	9	23
.45 ACP	3	1	2	1	1	1	1	1
.45 Auto Rim	8	31	14A		17		18	24
.45 Colt	20	32	11	21	19	45LC		23
.45 Win. Mag.	3	1	2	1	1	1	1	1

HANDGUN RELOADING DATA SECTION

.22 HORNET

The .22 Hornet is a very versatile cartridge in the Thompson-Center Contender pistol. Because of its small powder capacity, the expansion ratio is quite favorable, even in the 10-inch barrel, and the velocity difference between rifle and handgun is consequently less for the Hornet than for most other rifle cartridges that are used in the Contender. Factory loads recently tested in a rifle with 25-inch barrel, and in a 10-inch Contender, produced 2,560 fps in the rifle, and 2,220 fps in the handgun, for a difference of 340 fps. By comparison, full-charge loads in a .222 Remington rifle and 10-inch Contender produced 3,150 fps and 2,630 fps respectively, for a loss of 520 fps. Because the charge used in the Hornet is only about half that used in a .222, the muzzle blast of the Hornet in the handgun is much less severe. The .22 Hornet is altogether a much pleasanter load than the .222 to shoot in the handgun, though, of course, it cannot match the performance of the larger cartridge if the maximum possible velocity is desired.

The .22 Hornet can be loaded with cast or swaged lead bullets to approximate the performance of any of the .22-caliber rimfire cartridges, and these loads can produce excellent accuracy. For the handgun hunter who wants a cartridge capable of good performance on small game such as rabbits and squirrels, and varmints up to the size of woodchucks at moderate ranges, the .22 Hornet in the Contender pistol is an excellent choice. The 40-grain and 45-grain jacketed bullets should be used on varmints, because they are designed to expand properly at the moderate velocity levels attainable in the small cartridge.

Typical chamber pressure for the .22 Hornet is about 43,000 c.u.p. The maximum product average for factory ammunition is not to exceed 47,000 c.u.p.
Max. Case Length: 1.403" **Trim-To Length:** 1.393"
Max. Overall Length: 1.723" **Primer Size:** Small Rifle **Bullet Dia:** .224"

HANDGUN LOADS FOR THE .22 HORNET T/C CONTENDER

LOAD NUMBER	BULLET				POWDER			VELOCITY FPS	PRESSURE CUP	CASE BRAND	PRIMER		CARTRIDGE OAL	BARREL LENGTH	DATA SOURCE
	WEIGHT	BRAND	SHAPE	TYPE	WEIGHT	BRAND	TYPE				BRAND	TYPE			
1	40	SRA	RNN	SP	11.5	DUP	4227	2335		REM	CCI	400	1.725	10	NRA
2	45	HDY	PTD	SP	11.5	DUP	4227	2307		REM	CCI	400	1.840	10	NRA
3	45	HDY	PTD	SP	10.0	HER	2400	2228		REM	CCI	400	1.840	10	NRA
4	50	SRA	SPD	SP	11.5	DUP	4227	2153		REM	CCI	400	1.840	10	NRA
5	50	SRA	SPD	SP	9.5	HER	2400	2063		REM	CCI	400	1.840	10	NRA
6	55	SRA	SPD	SP	10.0	DUP	4227	1991		REM	CCI	400	1.870	10	NRA
7	55	SRA	SPD	SP	8.0	DUP	4227	1632		REM	CCI	400	1.870	10	NRA
8	55	SRA	SPD	SP	8.0	HER	2400	1655		REM	CCI	400	1.870	10	NRA
9	38	CAST	RNN	LG	2.0	DUP	PB	1145		REM	CCI	400		10	NRA
10	46	CAST	FLN	LG	3.0	DUP	PB	1400		REM	CCI	400		10	NRA
11	46	CAST	FLN	LG	3.5	DUP	PB	1517		REM	CCI	400		10	NRA
12	46	CAST	FLN	LG	8.0	DUP	4227	1852		REM	CCI	400		10	NRA
13	46	CAST	FLN	LG	10.0	DUP	4227	2071		REM	CCI	400		10	NRA

.22 REMINGTON JET

The .22 Remington Jet was announced by Remington in 1961, in conjunction with the Smith & Wesson Model 53 revolver chambered for it. The very long gentle slope of the case shoulder was evidently intended to minimize the problem of "set-back" that is characteristic of bottle-necked cartridges used in

revolvers. The problem is brought about by the fact that bottle-necked cartridges tend to stretch in head-to-shoulder length during the interval of high chamber pressures, and do not fully recover their original dimensions when the chamber pressure drops.

In consequence, the case head is pressed hard against

the breech face after the cartridge has been fired. In rifles, this generally presents no problem, because the mechanism for opening the breech operates with a strong mechanical advantage through some system of cams or levers, and the friction between the case head and breech face is easily overcome. In a revolver, however, the friction must be overcome by cocking the hammer, or pulling the trigger to rotate the cylinder, and the mechanical advantage is much less. The revolver may therefore "lock-up" and the cylinder refuse to rotate.

The long gentle taper of the shoulder is a sound mechanical approach to solution of the problem, because the elastic recovery of the cartridge case diametrically results in greater axial or lengthwise clearance than would otherwise be provided after the chamber pressure has dropped. The remedy is not always sufficient, however, especially if there is any lubricant on the case or chamber walls, which tends to aggravate the head-to-shoulder stretching of the case. The Model 53 revolver suffered from this problem, and it was never extremely popular. It has now been discontinued.

Users of the .22 Jet in the Model 53 revolver will minimize the problem by using moderate loads, and thoroughly degreasing the chamber walls and cartridge cases before loading the gun.

The .22 Jet is also one of the many cartridges for which the Thompson-Center Contender pistol is available, and in that handgun it performs very well.

The maximum product average chamber pressure for this cartridge is limited to 42,100 c.u.p.

Max. Case Length: 1.288″ **Trim-To Length:** 1.283″
Max. Overall Length: 1.659″ **Primer Size:** Small Rifle **Bullet Dia.:** .223″

HANDGUN LOADS FOR THE .22 REMINGTON JET

LOAD NUMBER	BULLET				POWDER			VELOCITY FPS	PRESSURE CUP	CASE BRAND	PRIMER		CARTRIDGE OAL	BARREL LENGTH	DATA SOURCE
	WEIGHT	BRAND	SHAPE	TYPE	WEIGHT	BRAND	TYPE				BRAND	TYPE			
1	40	REM	SPD	SP	6.7	DUP	4756	1925	31200	REM	REM	6½	1.645	10*	DUP
2	40	REM	SPD	SP	13.5	DUP	4227	2290	32900	REM	REM	6½	1.645	10*	DUP
3	40	SPR	PTD	SP	10.2	HER	2400	1755		REM	REM	5½		6	SPR
4	40	SPR	PTD	SP	8.2	HER	BDOT	1782		REM	REM	5½		6	SPR
5	40	SPR	PTD	SP	11.0	HOD	H110	2019		REM	REM	6½		8¾	HOD
6	40	REM	SPD	SP	4.7	DUP	700X	1755	32000	REM	REM	6½		10*	DUP
7	40	REM	SPD	SP	5.1	DUP	PB	1690	32200	REM	REM	6½		10*	DUP
8	40	REM	SPD	SP	5.3	DUP	7625	1745	31200	REM	REM	6½		10*	DUP
9	45	SPR	PTD	SP	10.0	HER	2400	1687		REM	REM	5½		6	SPR

*Velocity in unvented test barrel; lower velocities expected in revolver.

.221 REMINGTON FIREBALL

The .221 Fireball was announced by Remington in 1962, in conjunction with the Remington Model XP-100 bolt-action pistol. The cartridge-case body and head diameter are practically the same as those of the .222 Remington, but the case is much shorter than the .222 Remington case.

The case capacity is appropriate for the 10½-inch barrel of the XP-100 pistol, and the factory loads produce a nominal velocity of 2,650 fps with a 50-grain bullet. That is easily the highest velocity developed by any factory cartridge designed specifically for handgun use. The XP-100 pistol more nearly resembles a bolt-action rifle than a pistol in the mechanical characteristics of its design, and readily accommodates chamber pressures up to 52,000 c.u.p.

The .221 Fireball cartridge fired in the XP-100 pistol also has the distinction of producing consistently better accuracy than any other factory cartridge and handgun. Benchrest shooters frequently can produce groups of 1-inch or less at 100 yards with the XP-100, and the gun and cartridge have recently undergone a spurt of popularity among shooters of metallic silhouettes. Some custom rifles have been built for the .221 Fireball cartridge, by shooters who desired a less powerful .22 centerfire cartridge than the .222 Remington, and the Thompson-Center Contender pistol is also available in this caliber.

Working pressure for the .221 Fireball is about 52,000 c.u.p. and the maximum product average for factory ammunition is not to exceed 55,500 c.u.p.

Max. Case Length: 1.400″ **Trim-To Length:** 1.395″
Max. Overall Length: 1.830″ **Primer Size:** Small Rifle **Bullet Dia.:** .224″

HANDGUN LOADS FOR THE .221 REMINGTON FIREBALL

LOAD NUMBER	BULLET				POWDER			VELOCITY FPS	PRESSURE CUP	CASE BRAND	PRIMER		CARTRIDGE OAL	BARREL LENGTH	DATA SOURCE
	WEIGHT	BRAND	SHAPE	TYPE	WEIGHT	BRAND	TYPE				BRAND	TYPE			
1	40	SRA	RNN	SP	18.0	DUP	4198	2588	35800	REM	REM	6½	1.680	10½	NRA
2	40	SPR	PTD	SP	17.0	DUP	4227	2843	50760	REM	REM	6½	1.700	10½	NRA
3	40	SPR	PTD	SP	15.5	HOD	H4227	2925		REM	REM	6½		10¾	HOD
4	45	CAST	FLN	LG	4.5	HOD	HS 6	1374		REM	REM	6½		10¾	HOD
5	45	SRA	PTD	SP	18.0	DUP	4198	2538	36850	REM	REM	6½	1.820	10½	NRA
6	45	SRA	PTD	SP	16.5	DUP	4227	2689	48080	REM	REM	6½	1.820	10½	NRA
7	45	SPR	PTD	SP	15.0	HER	2400	2782	<55500	REM	CCI	400		10¾	SPR
8	45	SPR	PTD	SP	14.0	HOD	H110	2757	<55500	REM	CCI	450		10¾	SPR
9	45	HDY	PTD	SP	16.3	DUP	4227	2700		REM	REM	7½	1.840	10¾	HDY
10	50	REM	PTD	SP	15.5	DUP	4227	2520	51000	REM	REM	7½	1.825	12	DUP
11	50	REM	PTD	SP	18.5	DUP	4198	2665	48900	REM	REM	7½	1.825	12	DUP
12	50	HDY	PTD	SP	23.0	HOD	BL-C-(2)	2600		REM	REM	7½	1.840	10¾	HDY
13	50	SPR	PTD	SP	13.5	HER	2400	2521	<55500	REM	CCI	400		10¾	SPR
14	50	SRA	PTD	SP	13.1	HOD	H110	2600		REM	REM	7½		10½	SRA
15	52	SPR	PTD	HP	17.0	DUP	4198	2527	<55500	REM	CCI	400		10¾	SPR
16	52	SRA	PBT	HP	13.9	HER	2400	2500		REM	REM	7½		10½	SRA
17	52	SRA	PBT	HP	12.9	HOD	H110	2600		REM	REM	7½		10½	SRA
18	53	HDY	PTD	HP	22.0	HOD	BL-C-(2)	2500		REM	REM	7½	1.840	10¾	HDY
19	53	HDY	PTD	HP	18.3	DUP	4198	2700		REM	REM	7½	1.840	10¾	HDY
20	55	HDY	PTD	SP	21.8	HOD	BL-C-(2)	2500		REM	REM	7½	1.840	10¾	HDY
21	55	SPR	PTD	SP	16.7	DUP	4198	2502	<55500	REM	CCI	400		10¾	SPR
22	60	HDY	PTD	SP	20.6	HOD	BL-C-(2)	2400		REM	REM	7½	1.840	10¾	HDY
23	63	SRA	SPD	SP	14.5	DUP	4227	2225	52000	REM	REM	7½ BR	1.825	10¾	DUP
24	63	SRA	SPD	SP	15.5	DUP	4198	2125	40600	REM	REM	7½ BR	1.825	10¾	DUP
25	63	SRA	SPD	SP	11.5	DUP	4759	1855	37200	REM	REM	7½ BR	1.825	10¾	DUP
26	70	SPR	SPD	SP	13.6	DUP	4227	2035	51500	REM	REM	7½ BR	1.770	10¾	DUP
27	70	SPR	SPD	SP	14.5	DUP	4198	1965	39300	REM	REM	7½ BR	1.770	10¾	DUP
28	70	SPR	SPD	SP	10.5	DUP	4759	1645	36300	REM	REM	7½ BR	1.770	10¾	DUP

.222 REMINGTON

The .222 Remington is, of course, primarily a rifle cartridge. It has been adopted by Thompson/Center for use in the Contender pistol, however, and is well liked by some varmint hunters who use it in the handgun. The industry-agreed chamber pressure limit for the .222 is 46,000 c.u.p., and that limit was observed in developing the loads listed here. Owing to the higher pressure limit of 52,000 c.u.p. allowed in the .221 Remington Fireball pistol cartridge, it can produce practically the same ballistics as the .222 Remington if both cartridges are fired in handguns having barrels of comparable length.

In general, factory loads and comparable loads that have been found safe and satisfactory in rifles can also be used satisfactorily in the .222 Contender handgun. Some handloaders suppose that faster-burning powders should be used when loading for the .222 handgun, but that is not the case. Powders such as IMR-4198 give the highest velocity at acceptable pressure in both the .222 handgun and the .222 rifle. The tables given here illustrate that even IMR-4227, among the slowest-burning powders commonly used for handgun loads, is too fast-burning for maximum velocity at acceptable pressure in the .222 Contender.

The loads listed here were developed in the Du Pont ballistics laboratories, using Thompson/Center barrels from ordinary production, modified only as required to make pressure measurements by the copper-crusher method. In accordance with sound handloading practice, charge weights should be reduced by 10 per cent for initial trials, and increased as pressure indications permit.

It will be found that .222 loads approximating factory-load performance will produce about 500 fps less velocity in the 10-inch Contender barrel than in a rifle.

The maximum product average chamber pressure for .222 Remington factory ammunition should not exceed 49,200 c.u.p.
Max. Case Length: 1.700″ Trim-To Length: 1.690″
Max. Overall Length: 2.130″ Primer Size: Small Rifle Bullet Dia.: .224″

HANDGUN LOADS FOR THE .222 REM (T/C CONTENDER)

LOAD NUMBER	BULLET				POWDER			VELOCITY FPS	PRESSURE CUP	CASE BRAND	PRIMER		CARTRIDGE OAL	BARREL LENGTH	DATA SOURCE
	WEIGHT	BRAND	SHAPE	TYPE	WEIGHT	BRAND	TYPE				BRAND	TYPE			
1	45	SRA	PTD	SP	17.1	DUP	4227	2500	45200	REM	REM	7½ BR	2.130	10	DUP
2	45	SRA	PTD	SP	21.1	DUP	4198	2640	45800	REM	REM	7½ BR	2.130	10	DUP
3	45	SRA	PTD	SP	24.2c	DUP	4895	2380	37400	REM	REM	7½ BR	2.130	10	DUP
4	50	REM	PTD	SP	16.1	DUP	4227	2365	45800	REM	REM	7½ BR	2.130	10	DUP
5	50	REM	PTD	SP	20.0	DUP	4198	2510	45600	REM	REM	7½ BR	2.130	10	DUP
6	50	REM	PTD	SP	24.2c	DUP	4895	2365	39300	REM	REM	7½ BR	2.130	10	DUP
7	52	SRA	PBT	HP	15.8	DUP	4227	2300	45600	REM	REM	7½ BR	2.190	10	DUP
8	52	SRA	PBT	HP	19.8	DUP	4198	2455	45800	REM	REM	7½ BR	2.190	10	DUP
9	52	SRA	PBT	HP	23.8c	DUP	4895	2325	40500	REM	REM	7½ BR	2.190	10	DUP
10	55	SPR	SPD	FJ	19.0	DUP	4198	2375	45200	REM	REM	7½ BR	2.085	10	DUP
11	55	SPR	SPD	FJ	21.5c	DUP	3031	2225	37800	REM	REM	7½ BR	2.085	10	DUP
12	55	SPR	SPD	FJ	23.0c	DUP	4895	2275	41200	REM	REM	7½ BR	2.085	10	DUP
13	60	HDY	PTD	HP	14.7	DUP	4227	2105	45000	REM	REM	7½ BR	2.245	10	DUP
14	60	HDY	PTD	HP	19.1	DUP	4198	2330	45800	REM	REM	7½ BR	2.245	10	DUP
15	60	HDY	PTD	HP	23.0c	DUP	4895	2235	42400	REM	REM	7½ BR	2.245	10	DUP
16	70	SPR	SPD	SP	17.9	DUP	4198	2145	45700	REM	REM	7½ BR	2.060	10	DUP
17	70	SPR	SPD	SP	20.5c	DUP	3031	2000	34900	REM	REM	7½ BR	2.060	10	DUP
18	70	SPR	SPD	SP	21.5c	DUP	4895	2050	37900	REM	REM	7½ BR	2.060	10	DUP

.25 ACP (6.35mm BROWNING)

The .25 A.C.P., usually known in Europe as the 6.35 mm Browning, was introduced in 1902 in conjunction with a small Colt automatic pistol. It is the smallest commonly produced centerfire cartridge, using a 50-grain full-metal-jacketed bullet in the factory load, at a nominal velocity of 810 fps when fired from a 2-inch barrel. Whether the .25 A.C.P. is more effective than the .22 long-rifle rimfire cartridge in a small pistol with 2-inch barrel has often been debated, but limited NRA testing indicates that the .25 A.C.P. is more effective in these small short-barreled guns.

The bullet diameter of the .25 A.C.P. is only about .251 inch, not .257 as is common for .25-caliber rifle bullets. The 50-grain FMJ factory bullet is available from Remington as a reloading component, but must generally be specially ordered, because the demand is not sufficient for most dealers to maintain retail stocks of the bullet. Molds for casting bullets are available, but bullet-sizing dies of the correct .251 of an inch diameter are not available from the manufacturers of sizer-lubricators. Fortunately, dies to fit the RCBS and

Lyman sizer-lubricators are available from Huntington Die Service, P.O. Box 991, Oroville, CA 95965.

Another means of obtaining bullets for the .25 A.C.P. is to swage them in dies that are available from Corbin Mfg. and Supply, Inc., P.O. Box 758, Phoenix, OR 97535. Swaging allows the handloader to make a variety of bullets not otherwise available for the .25 A.C.P.

Hornady has recently announced the availability of a 50-grain FMJ bullet specifically for the .25 ACP, and provided some of the handloads listed here. This should be good news from Hornady for those handloaders who have experienced difficulty in obtaining bullets for the .25 ACP.

The maximum product average chamber pressure for this cartridge has been established at 19,900 c.u.p.

Max. Case Length: .615″ **Trim-To Length:** .610″
Max. Overall Length: .910″ **Primer Size:** Small Pistol **Bullet Dia.:** .251″

HANDGUN LOADS FOR THE .25 A.C.P.

LOAD NUMBER	BULLET				POWDER			VELOCITY FPS	PRESSURE CUP	CASE BRAND	PRIMER		CARTRIDGE OAL	BARREL LENGTH	DATA SOURCE
	WEIGHT	BRAND	SHAPE	TYPE	WEIGHT	BRAND	TYPE				BRAND	TYPE			
1	50	REM	RNN	FJ	1.3	HER	BEYE	760	15000				.875		HER
2	50	REM	RNN	FJ	1.7	HER	UNIQ	760	14800				.875		HER
3	50	HDY	RNN	FJ	1.0	NOR	R-1	800		FRO	FED	100	.900	2	HDY

HANDGUN LOADS FOR THE .25 A.C.P.

LOAD NUMBER	BULLET				POWDER			VELOCITY FPS	PRESSURE CUP	CASE BRAND	PRIMER		CARTRIDGE OAL	BARREL LENGTH	DATA SOURCE
	WEIGHT	BRAND	SHAPE	TYPE	WEIGHT	BRAND	TYPE				BRAND	TYPE			
4	50	HDY	RNN	FJ	0.8	DUP	700X	650		FRO	FED	100	.900	2	HDY
5	50	HDY	RNN	FJ	1.0	DUP	700X	800		FRO	FED	100	.900	2	HDY
6	50	HDY	RNN	FJ	0.8	HER	RDOT	650		FRO	FED	100	.900	2	HDY
7	50	HDY	RNN	FJ	1.2	HER	RDOT	800		FRO	FED	100	.900	2	HDY
8	50	HDY	RNN	FJ	1.0	HER	BEYE	650		FRO	FED	100	.900	2	HDY
9	50	HDY	RNN	FJ	1.2	HER	BEYE	800		FRO	FED	100	.900	2	HDY
10	50	HDY	RNN	FJ	1.0	HOD	HP-38	650		FRO	FED	100	.900	2	HDY
11	50	HDY	RNN	FJ	1.3	HOD	HP-38	850		FRO	FED	100	.900	2	HDY
12	50	HDY	RNN	FJ	1.2	WIN	231	650		FRO	FED	100	.900	2	HDY
13	50	HDY	RNN	FJ	1.6	WIN	231	850		FRO	FED	100	.900	2	HDY

.256 WINCHESTER MAGNUM

The .256 Winchester Magnum cartridge was designed for use in revolvers, but no revolver has ever been commercially available for it. Though considerable development work was done by at least one of the major arms companies, the effort to develop a successful revolver for this cartridge was abandoned, largely because of the "set-back" problems described in conjunction with the .22 Remington Jet cartridge.

Winchester announced the cartridge in 1960, though there was then no arm adapted to its use. The Ruger "Hawkeye" single-shot pistol for the .256 cartridge was announced about two years after introduction of the cartridge, and was the only handgun of that caliber until Thompson-Center offered the Contender pistol for it some years later. The Ruger "Hawkeye" has been discontinued, and the T/C Contender is now the only handgun available for the .256 Winchester Magnum cartridge.

Marlin chambered their Model 62 lever-action rifle for this cartridge during the 1960's, but that model has since been discontinued. The .256 Winchester Magnum performs very well in the Contender pistol, and is a good choice for varmint hunting with that gun.

Max. Case Length: 1.281" **Trim-To Length:** 1.276"
Max. Overall Length: 1.590" **Primer Size:** Small Rifle **Bullet Dia.:** .257"

HANDGUN LOADS FOR THE .256 WINCHESTER

LOAD NUMBER	BULLET				POWDER			VELOCITY FPS	PRESSURE CUP	CASE BRAND	PRIMER		CARTRIDGE OAL	BARREL LENGTH	DATA SOURCE
	WEIGHT	BRAND	SHAPE	TYPE	WEIGHT	BRAND	TYPE				BRAND	TYPE			
1	60	WIN	RNN	HP	16.7	WIN	680	2195	41000	WIN	WIN	6½-116	1.590	8½	WIN
2	60	WIN	RNN	HP	14.0	HER	2400	2143	40440	WIN	WIN	6½-116	1.570	8¾	NRA
3	60	WIN	RNN	HP	16.0	DUP	4227	2196	40000	WIN	WIN	6½-116	1.570	8¾	NRA
4	60	WIN	RNN	HP	18.0	DUP	4198	2154	37070	WIN	WIN	6½-116	1.570	8¾	NRA
5	60	HDY	FLN	SP	16.0	DUP	4227	2300		WIN	WIN	6½-116	1.670	8½	HDY
6	60	SPR	PTD	SP	16.0	HOD	H110	2361		WIN	CCI	400		10	SPR
7	60	SPR	PTD	SP	16.7	WIN	680	2193		WIN	CCI	400		10	SPR
8	60	SPR	PTD	SP	16.0	DUP	4227	2343		WIN	CCI	400		10	SPR
9	60	SPR	PTD	SP	18.0	HOD	H4198	1704		WIN	WIN	6½-116		10	HOD
10	75	HDY	PTD	HP	12.5	HER	2400	1900		WIN	WIN	6½-116	1.740	8½	HDY
11	75	HDY	PTD	HP	13.2	DUP	4227	1900		WIN	WIN	6½-116	1.740	8½	HDY
12	75	HDY	PTD	HP	11.1	HOD	H110	1900		WIN	WIN	6½-116	1.740	8½	HDY
13	87	SPR	PTD	SP	15.0	DUP	4198	1786		WIN	CCI	400		10	SPR

The Thompson/Center Contender pistol is the only currently manufactured U.S. firearm chambered for the .25-35 cartridge. The data listed here were developed in the DuPont ballistics laboratories, using a 10-inch Thompson/Center barrel of ordinary production type, modified only as necessary to measure chamber pressures by the copper-crusher method.

The .25-35 suffers in performance in a barrel as short as 10 inches, because the relatively large case capacity and small bore do not afford a favorable expansion ratio in so short a barrel. Nevertheless, the data illustrate in an interesting way the fallacy of the common argument that fast-burning powders should be used for obtaining maximum velocities in short barrels. It is especially interesting to note that IMR-4350, among the slowest-burning rifle powders, produced the highest velocity at acceptable chamber pressure with the 100-grain .25-caliber bullet in the 10-inch barrel of the .25-35 Contender.

With muzzle energy limited to about 800 foot-pounds at acceptable chamber pressures, the .25-35 would be less effective as a deer-hunting cartridge than some of the larger calibers in the Contender. It should, however, be quite satisfactory as a varmint cartridge, especially with the lighter bullets. The expansion of the heavier .25-caliber bullets might be marginal when fired from the .25-35 Contender, since the bullets were designed for proper expansion at substantially higher velocities obtained in modern .25-caliber rifles.

The typical working pressure for the .25-35 is about 37,000 c.u.p., and the maximum product average for factory ammunition should not exceed 40,200 c.u.p.

Max. Case Length: 2.040″ **Trim-To Length:** 2.030″
Max. Overall Length: 2.253″ **Primer Size:** Large Rifle
Bullet Dia.: .257″

HANDGUN LOADS FOR THE .25-35 (T/C CONTENDER)

LOAD NUMBER	BULLET				POWDER			VELOCITY FPS	PRESSURE CUP	CASE BRAND	PRIMER		CARTRIDGE OAL	BARREL LENGTH	DATA SOURCE
	WEIGHT	BRAND	SHAPE	TYPE	WEIGHT	BRAND	TYPE				BRAND	TYPE			
1	60	SPR	PTD	SP	28.3	DUP	3031	2325	36900	REM	FED	210BR	2.390	10	DUP
2	60	SPR	PTD	SP	30.5c	DUP	4064	2285	36000	REM	FED	210BR	2.390	10	DUP
3	60	SPR	PTD	SP	27.4	DUP	4320	2240	37000	REM	FED	210BR	2.390	10	DUP
4	87	HDY	PTD	SP	23.4	DUP	3031	1965	36800	REM	FED	210BR	2.690	10	DUP
5	87	HDY	PTD	SP	25.7	DUP	4064	1960	36500	REM	FED	210BR	2.690	10	DUP
6	87	HDY	PTD	SP	25.3	DUP	4320	1950	37000	REM	FED	210BR	2.690	10	DUP
7	100	SPR	PTD	SP	22.1	DUP	3031	1845	36500	REM	FED	210BR	2.700	10	DUP
8	100	SPR	PTD	SP	25.2	DUP	4064	1875	37000	REM	FED	210BR	2.700	10	DUP
9	100	SPR	PTD	SP	31.0c	DUP	4350	1900	36400	REM	FED	210BR	2.700	10	DUP
10	117	SRA	PBT	SP	21.5	DUP	3031	1760	36700	REM	FED	210BR	2.700	10	DUP
11	117	SRA	PBT	SP	22.2	DUP	4895	1750	37000	REM	FED	210BR	2.700	10	DUP
12	117	SRA	PBT	SP	28.3c	DUP	4350	1760	35900	REM	FED	210BR	2.700	10	DUP

7.62mm RUSSIAN TOKAREV

This cartridge is practically identical in dimensions to the 7.63mm Mauser pistol cartridge, and 7.63mm Mauser ammunition is sometimes fired in the Tokarev pistol. Either 7.62mm Tokarev or 7.63mm Mauser cases are suitable for reloading, but will generally require the use of imported Berdan-type primers.

The cartridge case is not easily formed from available American brass, but it can be done. Nonte's

Cartridge Conversions suggests using .38 Special cases, lathe-turned in the head region to remove the rim and cut an extractor groove for a rimless configuration. With some .38 Special brass, however, the solid web in the case head is quite thin, and cutting an extractor groove might unduly weaken the case in that region.

It should be possible to die-form .222 Remington or similar rifle cases to the 7.62mm Tokarev configuration, and trim them to the correct length (.97 of an inch), but neck-turning or reaming would probably be required to reduce the case-neck thickness, which should not exceed .012 inches. Recently, Boxer-primed ammunition and cases have been made in the U.S., and are available from Midway Arms, Inc., Rt. 5, Box 298, Columbia, Mo. 65201.

Max. Case Length: .975″ **Trim-To Length:** .970″
Max. Overall Length: Varies **Primer Size:** Berdan
Bullet Dia.: .309″

HANDGUN LOADS FOR THE 7.62 mm RUSSIAN TOKAREV

LOAD NUMBER	BULLET				POWDER			VELOCITY FPS	PRESSURE CUP	CASE BRAND	PRIMER		CARTRIDGE OAL	BARREL LENGTH	DATA SOURCE
	WEIGHT	BRAND	SHAPE	TYPE	WEIGHT	BRAND	TYPE				BRAND	TYPE			
1	86		RNN	FJ	5.0	HER	BEYE	1390							FCB
2	100	SPR	RNN	BJ	4.6	HER	BEYE	1200							FCB

7.63mm (.30) MAUSER

The 7.63mm Mauser pistol cartridge was originally intended for use in the Model 1896 Mauser pistol, sometimes called the "broom-handle" model, because of the odd appearance of the pistol grip. Those guns were sufficiently common in the United States to warrant the factory loading of the ammunition, known here as the .30 Mauser, prior to World War II. The Winchester load of the 1930's was listed as having an 86-grain bullet, at a muzzle velocity of 1,397 fps, the highest velocity of any handgun cartridge then manufactured in the U.S. Practically the same round now survives in the current 7.62mm Tokarev ammunition for the Russian military pistol, but weapons adapted to it are not common in the United States.

Imported ammunition for the 7.63mm Mauser is occasionally advertised by dealers in foreign military cartridges, and, as in the case of the 7.62mm Tokarev, new Boxer-primed ammunition and cases are made by and available from Midway Arms, Inc., Rt. 5, Box 298, Columbia, Mo. 65201.

Max. Case Length: .990″ **Trim-To Length:** .985″
Max. Overall Length: 1.381″ **Primer Size:** Small
Pistol **Bullet Dia.:** .311″

HANDGUN LOADS FOR THE .30 (7.63 mm) MAUSER

LOAD NUMBER	BULLET				POWDER			VELOCITY FPS	PRESSURE CUP	CASE BRAND	PRIMER		CARTRIDGE OAL	BARREL LENGTH	DATA SOURCE
	WEIGHT	BRAND	SHAPE	TYPE	WEIGHT	BRAND	TYPE				BRAND	TYPE			
1	86			FJ	5.2	HER	BEYE	1410							FCB
2	93	NOR	RNN	SP	5.3	HER	UNIQ	1345							FCB

7.65mm FRENCH MAS

This cartridge was used in the French Model 1935 autoloading military pistol, and a few other French arms, but was little known outside of France until after World War II, when a considerable number of Model 1935 pistols were imported and sold in the U.S. as military surplus.

Whether by intention or coincidence, the cartridge is practically identical to that developed in the U.S. for use in the Pedersen device, a weapon designed and produced in great secrecy during World War I, and officially known by the deceptive title of "Automatic Pistol, Caliber .30, Model of 1918."

The Pedersen device was actually an automatic gun mechanism, so designed that it could be substituted for the bolt in a slightly modified Model 1903 Springfield Rifle (known as the "Model 1903, Mark I") converting the rifle in effect to a full-automatic submachine gun. Though about 65,000 Pedersen devices were manufactured, none were deployed in the field before World War I ended in November 1918, and practically all of those were subsequently destroyed by the Army. The device is now a highly prized collectors' item, as is also the .30 Pedersen cartridge, so those cartridges are not much used for shooting in the French Model 1935 pistol.

The French 7.65 MAS cartridge cannot readily be formed from any available American brass. Imported ammunition is also rather scarce, though occasionally it can be found. A few custom reloaders can furnish loaded ammunition, from which the cases can be saved for reloading.

HANDGUN LOADS FOR THE 7.65 FRENCH MAS

LOAD NUMBER	BULLET				POWDER			VELOCITY FPS	PRESSURE CUP	CASE BRAND	PRIMER		CARTRIDGE OAL	BARREL LENGTH	DATA SOURCE
	WEIGHT	BRAND	SHAPE	TYPE	WEIGHT	BRAND	TYPE				BRAND	TYPE			
1	77				3.6	HER	UNIQ	1100							FCB
2	100	SPR	RNN	BJ	3.1	HER	UNIQ	1030							FCB

.30 LUGER (7.65mm PARABELLUM)

This was the original cartridge for the Luger pistol, and was introduced in Germany about 1900. A few other handguns have also been chambered for it. Some superb Luger pistols chambered for this cartridge were imported by Stoeger between World War I and World War II, some with long barrels and detachable shoulder stocks.

The .30 Luger cartridge was loaded for many years by U.S. manufacturers, with 93-grain bullets of both full-jacketed and soft-point types. The soft-point bullets were about .309 inch to .310 inch in diameter, and performed very well as a handloading component in .30-40 Krag and .30-06 Enfield rifles, which often have barrels with oversize groove diameters. The factory soft-point .30 Luger bullets were sometimes marginal in expansion at the velocities attainable in the Luger pistol, but expanded violently at the velocities attainable in .30-40 or .30-06 varmint loads.

U.S. manufacturers still list the .30 Luger cartridge, but only with the round-nose full-jacketed bullet. The effectiveness of the .30 Luger cartridge could undoubtedly be improved by use of a properly constructed soft-point and/or hollow-point bullet, which would expand at the attainable velocities of about 1,200 fps. Swaging dies for such a bullet could probably be obtained from Corbin, by handloaders who wished to form the bullets themselves.

The maximum product average chamber pressure for commercial U.S. ammunition in this caliber has been established at 30,700 c.u.p.

Max. Case Length: .850″ Trim-To Length: .845″
Max. Overall Length: 1.175″ Primer Size: Small Pistol Bullet Dia.: .309″

HANDGUN LOADS FOR THE .30 (7.65 mm) LUGER

LOAD NUMBER	BULLET				POWDER			VELOCITY FPS	PRESSURE CUP	CASE BRAND	PRIMER		CARTRIDGE OAL	BARREL LENGTH	DATA SOURCE
	WEIGHT	BRAND	SHAPE	TYPE	WEIGHT	BRAND	TYPE				BRAND	TYPE			
1	93				5.0	HER	UNIQ	1240							FCB
2	100	SPR	RNN	BJ	4.8	HER	UNIQ	1210							FCB
3	93	WIN	RNN	FJ	4.2	WIN	231	1085	25500	WIN	WIN	1½-108	1.175	4½	WIN
4	93	WIN	RNN	FJ	8.4	WIN	630	1140	26000	WIN	WIN	1½-108	1.175	4½	WIN

.30 CARBINE

Introduced as a military cartridge for the .30 M1 Carbine in 1941, the .30 Carbine has not acheived the popularity it deserves as a handgun cartridge. Some experimental handguns chambered for it were proposed for military use, but none was satisfactory. Ruger introduced the single-action Blackhawk revolver chambered for the .30 Carbine in 1967, and a few imported single-action revolvers have also been adapted to the .30 Carbine cartridge, but it has not achieved much popularity among handgunners.

Though comparable in dimensions to the much older .32-20, the .30 Carbine is designed for much higher pressures, and therefore provides much more effective ballistic performance. Because of the rimless case design, it is not easily adapted to use in double-action revolvers that depend upon the case rim for extractor engagement, and that is probably one factor which has limited its popularity as a handgun cartridge. Another is that it produces a very sharp and unpleasant report when fired in a handgun, though not more so than most of the magnum handgun cartridges using high-velocity loads.

The .30 Carbine is a very good choice for the handloader who hunts varmints and small game. Low-velocity loads can duplicate the performance of the .32-20, an excellent small-game cartridge, and full-charge loads produce good accuracy, moderate recoil and relatively flat trajectory for varmint hunting.

Military specifications for the .30 Carbine ammunition require a maximum average chamber pressure not to exceed 40,000 p.s.i. (copper), corresponding to 40,000 c.u.p., which is also the normal working pressure for the sporting load. The maximum product average for non-military factory ammunition is 43,200 c.u.p.

Max. Case Length: 1.290″ **Trim-To Length:** 1.285″
Max. Overall Length: 1.680″ **Primer Size:** Small Rifle **Bullet Dia.:** .308″

HANDGUN LOADS FOR THE .30 CARBINE

LOAD NUMBER	BULLET				POWDER			VELOCITY FPS	PRESSURE CUP	CASE BRAND	PRIMER		CARTRIDGE OAL	BARREL LENGTH	DATA SOURCE
	WEIGHT	BRAND	SHAPE	TYPE	WEIGHT	BRAND	TYPE				BRAND	TYPE			
1	100	SPR	RNN	BJ	5.5	HER	UNIQ	1142	<40000	WIN	CCI	400		7½	SPR
2	100	SPR	RNN	BJ	14.5	DUP	4227	1417	<40000	WIN	CCI	400		7½	SPR
3	100	SPR	RNN	BJ	16.5	WIN	680	1385	<40000	WIN	CCI	450		7½	SPR
4	110	SPR	FLN	HP	14.5	DUP	4227	1387	<40000	WIN	CCI	400		7½	SPR
5	110	SPR	FLN	HP	14.7	WIN	296	1358	<40000	WIN	CCI	450		7½	SPR
6	110	SPR	FLN	HP	16.5	WIN	680	1252	<40000	WIN	CCI	450		7½	SPR
7	110	HDY	RNN	SP	13.7	HER	2400	1400	<40000	MIL	WIN	6½-116	1.680	7½	HDY
8	110	SRA	RNN	SP	13.8	HOD	H110	1400		MIL	REM	6½		7½	SRA

.30 HERRETT

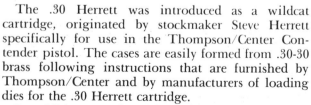

The .30 Herrett was introduced as a wildcat cartridge, originated by stockmaker Steve Herrett specifically for use in the Thompson/Center Contender pistol. The cases are easily formed from .30-30 brass following instructions that are furnished by Thompson/Center and by manufacturers of loading dies for the .30 Herrett cartridge.

In addition to reforming and trimming the case, however, *handloaders should be aware that neck-reaming or neck-turning may be required to thin the case necks.* There are some differences in the wall thickness of the various .30-30 cases from which .30 Herrett cases might be formed, and also some differences in the neck diameters of .30 Herrett chambers.

The safest practice is to make a chamber cast to obtain the diameter of the chamber neck. The neck diameter of the cartridge, with bullet seated, must be at least .001 inch less than the measured neck diameter of the chamber. A neck clearance of .002 inch is advisable to allow for possible inaccuracies in the measurements, and as much as .005 inch of clearance is not detrimental to performance. *Failure to allow adequate neck clearance, in this or any other cartridge, can cause dangerously excessive chamber pressures.*

The full-charge loads listed here were developed in the DuPont ballistics laboratories, using barrels from ordinary production, modified only as required to make chamber-pressure measurements by the copper crusher method. Ordinary production barrels are not necessarily produced to the very restricted dimensional tolerances normally employed for laboratory test barrels. For this and other good reasons, the charge weights listed should be reduced by 10 per cent for initial trials, and increased only as pressure indications permit.

Another important point of difference among .30 Herrett barrels is that some are free-bored whereas others are not. Using the 150-grain Sierra spitzer bullet, for example, and a cartridge overall length of 2.300 inches, different .30 Herret Contender barrels have been encountered having free run as little as .035 inch and as great as .385 inch. The length of free run before the bullet engages the rifling significantly affects both velocity and chamber pressure for any given load.

The barrels used in the DuPont laboratories to develop the .30 Herrett full-charge loads listed here were not free-bored. Free-bored barrels will probably produce somewhat lower velocities than those listed, with the charge weights listed. Free-bored barrels very probably could accommodate somewhat heavier powder charges, within the same chamber-pressure

limits. If the powder charge were increased in a free-bored barrel so as to achieve the listed velocity, the chamber pressure might be somewhat less than that listed for the lighter charge, fired in the conventionally throated barrel, but that is by no means certain. The safest course, therefore, is not to exceed the listed charge weights, even though the velocities obtained in a particular barrel are found to be somewhat less than the velocities listed for that bullet and powder type.

Notwithstanding the special precautions that must be observed in handloading it, the .30 Herrett cartridge is an excellent choice in the Contender pistol. With appropriate loads, it can develop ballistics comparable to the .32-20, an excellent small-game cartridge, or powerful loads exceeding 1,000 foot-pounds of muzzle energy, which is more than that of full-charge .44 Magnum loads fired in a revolver. The .30 Herrett is capable of excellent accuracy with a wide range of loads, and is therefore an excellent cartridge for the versatile Contender pistol.

Max. Case Length: 1.605″ **Trim-To Length:** 1.600″
Max. Overall Length: Varies **Primer Size:** Large Rifle **Bullet Dia.:** .308″

HANDGUN LOADS FOR .30 HERRETT (T/C CONTENDER)
CASES: REMINGTON PRIMERS: FEDERAL 210 BR

LOAD NUMBER	BULLET				POWDER			PRESSURE CUP	VELOCITY		CARTRIDGE OAL	DATA SOURCE
	WEIGHT	BRAND	SHAPE	TYPE	WEIGHT	BRAND	TYPE		10" BRL	14" BRL		
1	110	HDY	RNN	FJ	18.8	DUP	4227	44600	1910	2035	2.020	DUP
2	110	HDY	RNN	FJ	24.3	DUP	4198	44600	2075	2210	2.020	DUP
3	110	HDY	RNN	FJ	28.0C	DUP	3031	36000	1940	2070	2.020	DUP
4	130	HDY	PTD	SP	18.0	DUP	4227	44800	1775	1885	2.175	DUP
5	130	HDY	PTD	SP	22.5	DUP	4198	44400	1895	2015	2.175	DUP
6	130	HDY	PTD	SP	26.0C	DUP	3031	36300	1765	1875	2.175	DUP
7	150	SRA	PTD	SP	21.3	DUP	4198	44200	1760	1870	2.300	DUP
8	150	SRA	PTD	SP	25.5C	DUP	3031	36700	1680	1785	2.300	DUP
9	150	SRA	PTD	SP	27.0C	DUP	4895	40700	1735	1845	2.300	DUP
10	170	REM	RNN	SP	19.2	DUP	4198	44600	1575	1670	2.165	DUP
11	170	REM	RNN	SP	24.5C	DUP	3031	37800	1590	1690	2.165	DUP
12	170	REM	RNN	SP	26.0C	DUP	4895	41200	1625	1725	2.165	DUP
13	115	CAST	FLN	LG	12.0	DUP	4759		1035		2.040	NRA
14	115	CAST	FLN	LG	14.0	DUP	4759		1150		2.040	NRA
15	115	CAST	FLN	LG	16.0	DUP	4759		1325		2.040	NRA
16	150	CAST	SPD	LG	16.0	DUP	4198		1054		2.280	NRA
17	150	CAST	SPD	LG	18.0	DUP	4198		1190		2.280	NRA

.30-30

The .30-30 is not normally considered a handgun cartridge, but it has achieved some popularity in the Thompson/Center Contender pistol. It is especially suitable for the long-range silhouette course, fired at full-size metallic silhouette targets, at ranges up to 200 meters. It is also among the best choices for those who want to hunt deer-size game with the Contender pistol.

The loads listed here were developed in the DuPont ballistic laboratories, using Thompson/Center Con-

tender barrels, specially modified for the measurement of chamber pressures by the standard copper-crusher method. The chamber-pressure limits used by DuPont are consistent with the industry-standard limit for .30-30 factory loads, which is 38,000 c.u.p. It will be noted that the powders chosen by DuPont are the same as those found most suitable for .30-30 rifle loads. The DuPont tests showed that even IMR-4198, which is slower-burning than any powder commonly used in other handgun cartridges, is too fast-burning to produce favorable velocities at acceptable pressures in the .30-30 Contender. Even with 110-grain bullets, IMR-3031 produced higher velocity at acceptable pressure in the .30-30 than did any faster-burning powder. The widespread idea that faster-burning powders should be used when the .30-30 is handloaded for use in the Contender, is mistaken, and can lead to excessive chamber pressure if full-charge loads are being attempted.

There are reportedly some differences in the throat configuration among .30-30 Contender barrels, some allowing very little free run before bullet engraving, and others allowing considerably more. Those differences can affect velocities and pressures obtained with a given load. Full-charge loads listed should always be reduced by 10 per cent for initial trials.

Normal maximum working pressure for .30-30 cartridges is about 38,000 c.u.p. The maximum product average for factory ammunition should not exceed 41,200 c.u.p.

Max. Case Length: 2.039″ **Trim-To Length:** 2.029″ **Max. Overall Length:** 2.550″ **Primer Size:** Large Rifle **Bullet Dia.:** .308″

HANDGUN LOADS FOR .30-30 (T/C CONTENDER)
CASES: REMINGTON   PRIMERS: FEDERAL 210 BR

LOAD NUMBER	BULLET				POWDER			PRESSURE CUP	VELOCITY		CARTRIDGE OAL	DATA SOURCE
	WEIGHT	BRAND	SHAPE	TYPE	WEIGHT	BRAND	TYPE		10″ BRL	14″ BRL		
1	110	HDY	RNN	FJ	36.0C	DUP	3031	34000	2110	2265	2.450	DUP
2	110	HDY	RNN	FJ	34.6	DUP	4895	37800	2080	2235	2.450	DUP
3	110	HDY	RNN	FJ	36.5C	DUP	4064	33200	2020	2170	2.450	DUP
4	130	HDY	PTD	SP	36.0C	DUP	3031	37000	2025	2175	2.725	DUP
5	130	HDY	PTD	SP	36.5C	DUP	4064	36500	1965	2110	2.725	DUP
6	130	HDY	PTD	SP	31.0	DUP	4320	37600	1850	1990	2.725	DUP
7	150	SRA	PTD	SP	33.0	DUP	3031	37500	1895	2035	2.855	DUP
8	150	SRA	PTD	SP	34.4	DUP	4064	37400	1855	1995	2.855	DUP
9	150	SRA	PTD	SP	30.2	DUP	4320	37400	1770	1900	2.855	DUP
10	170	REM	RNN	SP	27.4	DUP	3031	37600	1660	1780	2.700	DUP
11	170	REM	RNN	SP	32.8	DUP	4064	37900	1750	1875	2.700	DUP
12	170	REM	RNN	SP	30.3	DUP	4320	37900	1650	1770	2.700	DUP

.32 A.C.P.

The .32 A.C.P. cartridge was introduced about 1899, for use in the Browning-designed autoloading pocket pistol manufactured by Fabrique Nationale in Belgium. It is commonly known in Europe as the 7.65 mm Browning. A great variety of small handguns has since been produced for use with this cartridge, both in the U.S. and abroad. Its principal virtue is that it can be used in a very compact autoloading pistol.

The round-nose full-jacketed bullet is relatively ineffective in a gun for defensive use, and there is little likelihood of effecting much improvement by use of an expanding-type bullet, because the attainable velocity is too low to assure reliable expansion. Some improvement in effectiveness might be achieved by using a bullet of wadcutter configuration, but that would probably entail feeding problems in the small autoloading pistols commonly adapted to this cartridge. In effectiveness, it ranks between the .25 A.C.P. and the .380 A.C.P., a better choice than the former, but poorer choice than the latter, for defensive use.

The maximum product average chamber pressure for this cartridge has been established at 16,900 c.u.p.

Max. Case Length: .680″ **Trim-To Length:** .675″ **Max. Overall Length:** .984″ **Primer Size:** Small Pistol **Bullet Dia.:** .309″

HANDGUN LOADS FOR THE .32 A.C.P.

LOAD NUMBER	BULLET				POWDER			VELOCITY FPS	PRESSURE CUP	CASE BRAND	PRIMER			CARTRIDGE OAL	BARREL LENGTH	DATA SOURCE
	WEIGHT	BRAND	SHAPE	TYPE	WEIGHT	BRAND	TYPE				BRAND	TYPE				
1	71		RNN	FJ	2.2	HER	BEYE	835	12500					.984		HER
2	71		RNN	FJ	2.4	HER	RDOT	850	12800					.984		HER
3	71		RNN	FJ	2.5	HER	UNIQ	820	11200					.984		HER
4	71		RNN	FJ	2.3	HOD	TR100	877		WIN	WIN	1½			3¾	HOD

.32 SMITH & WESSON

The .32 S.&W. cartridge is an old one, having been introduced about 1878. It has been used in a great variety of small inexpensive pocket pistols and revolvers. Some of these are of very uncertain strength, and their use cannot be recommended.

Originally a blackpowder cartridge containing only nine grains of powder and an 85-grain lead bullet at about 630 fps, it developed relatively low chamber pressure, and could be fired with reasonable safety in the weak revolvers adapted to it. Current factory loads are smokeless, with lead bullets of 85 to 88 grains,

developing about 680 fps. This performance is approximated with the handloads listed here, which should be used only in good-quality guns that are in sound condition.

The maximum product average chamber pressure for this cartridge is established at 13,900 c.u.p.

Max. Case Length: .605″ **Trim-To Length:** .600″
Max. Overall Length: .930″ **Primer Size:** Small
Pistol **Bullet Dia.:** .310″, .311″

HANDGUN LOADS FOR THE .32 S&W

LOAD NUMBER	BULLET				POWDER			VELOCITY FPS	PRESSURE CUP	CASE BRAND	PRIMER		CARTRIDGE OAL	BARREL LENGTH	DATA SOURCE
	WEIGHT	BRAND	SHAPE	TYPE	WEIGHT	BRAND	TYPE				BRAND	TYPE			
1	85	CAST	RNN	LP	1.2	HER	BEYE	500		WIN	WIN	1½-108	.930	3	NRA
2	85	WIN	RNN	LP	3.3	WIN	630	675	11000	WIN	WIN	1½-108	.930	3	WIN

.32 SHORT COLT

Introduced about 1875 as a blackpowder cartridge, the .32 Short Colt was originally assembled with a heel-loaded bullet, crimped in the case only by a rearward projection of reduced diameter, similar to .22 short, long and long-rifle rimfire ammunition. Because the bullets loaded in that way required the bullet lubricant to be exposed, they were not very suitable for carrying loose in the pocket, or in a pocket pistol, since the lubricant attracted particles of dirt. The ammunition was later changed to the so-called "inside-lubricated" design, in which the lubricated bearing surface of the bullet is within the case. This necessitated reducing the bullet diameter, of course, so it could fit within the case, but it then fit loosely in the barrel, and accuracy was impaired.

The .32 Short Colt factory load is still made, and fires an 80-grain lead bullet at a nominal velocity of 745 fps. Guns adapted to this cartridge are not common, and it is surprising that the cartridge

remains on the list of U.S. manufacturers. The handloader who expects to load this round long in the future would probably be well advised to acquire a supply of cases for his future requirements, in event it is discontinued soon.

According to Barnes' *Cartridges of the World*, .32 Short Colt ammunition can also be used satisfactorily in foreign guns chambered for the .320 Revolver cartridge, a round of British origin that has not been produced in the U.S. for about 50 years.

The maximum product average chamber pressure for this cartridge should not exceed 14,900 c.u.p.

Max. Case Length: .650″ **Trim-To Length:** .645″
Max. Overall Length: 1.015″ **Primer Size:** Small
Pistol **Bullet Dia.:** .310″ - .312″

HANDGUN LOADS FOR THE .32 SHORT COLT

LOAD NUMBER	BULLET				POWDER			VELOCITY FPS	PRESSURE CUP	CASE BRAND	PRIMER		CARTRIDGE OAL	BARREL LENGTH	DATA SOURCE
	WEIGHT	BRAND	SHAPE	TYPE	WEIGHT	BRAND	TYPE				BRAND	TYPE			
1	82	CAST	RNN	LP	1.9	HER	BEYE	810	8000				1.05	6	NRA
2	82	CAST	RNN	LP	7.7	BLACK	FFFg	810					1.05	6	NRA

.32 LONG COLT

The .32 Long Colt differs from the .32 Short Colt principally in case length. Guns chambered for the .32 Long Colt can fire the .32 Short Colt cartridge as well, just as .22 shorts can be fired in guns chambered for .22 long or .22 long-rifle cartridges. The .32 Long Colt is still factory-loaded in the U.S., with an 82-grain bullet at a nominal velocity of 755 fps. It suffered in the transition from heel-loaded to inside-lubricated bullets, just as did the .32 Short Colt cartridge (see preceding page), and old guns chambered for it are not very accurate with inside-lubricated ammunition.

The maximum product average chamber pressure for this cartridge is the same as that for the .32 Short Colt, at 14,900 c.u.p.

Max. Case Length: .916″ **Trim-To Length:** .911″
Max. Overall Length: 1.216″ **Primer Size:** Small Pistol **Bullet Dia.:** .310″ - .312″

HANDGUN LOADS FOR THE .32 LONG COLT

LOAD NUMBER	BULLET				POWDER			VELOCITY FPS	PRESSURE CUP	CASE BRAND	PRIMER		CARTRIDGE OAL	BARREL LENGTH	DATA SOURCE
	WEIGHT	BRAND	SHAPE	TYPE	WEIGHT	BRAND	TYPE				BRAND	TYPE			
1	80	CAST	RNN	LP	2.1	HER	BEYE	770	8000				1.26	4	NRA
2	80	CAST	RNN	LP	10.0	BLACK	FFFg	770					1.26	4	NRA

.32 SMITH & WESSON LONG (.32 COLT NEW POLICE)

This cartridge, introduced about 1903, was originally designed for the Smith & Wesson First Model solid-frame revolver. An interchangeable cartridge, practically identical except for the shape of bullet, is the .32 Colt New Police. The S.&W. cartridge has a round-nose bullet, whereas the Colt cartridge has a flat-nose bullet. Both are still listed as factory loads, both using 98-grain lead bullets. The velocity of the S.&W. cartridge is listed at 705 fps, and that of the Colt cartridge at 680 fps.

The .32 S.&W. Long is now considered only marginally effective for police use, though in the past it was used fairly commonly for compact revolvers intended for concealed carrying. It is also an excellent target cartridge. In both of those roles, however, it has been overshadowed by the intensive development of the .38 Special cartridge, and specialized .38 Special handguns.

Factory ammunition for the .32 S.&W. Long does not compare favorably in accuracy with the .38 Special target loads. By careful handloading, however, the accuracy obtainable with the .32 S.&W. Long compares favorably with that of .38 Special target loads.

The light recoil of the .32 S.&W. Long cartridge makes it very pleasant to shoot as a target cartridge.

An interesting target handgun chambered for this cartridge is the German Walther GSP-C, a highly specialized autoloading target pistol that uses only the .32 S.&W. Long cartridge with flush-seated wadcutter bullets. Wadcutter ammunition in this caliber is factory-loaded in Europe, but not in the United States, so handloading is required for U.S. users of the Walther GSP-C, unless they can obtain imported wadcutter factory ammunition from abroad.

The maximum product average chamber pressure for this cartridge should not exceed 13,900 c.u.p.

Max. Case Length: .920″ **Trim-To Length:** .915″
Max. Overall Length: 1.280″ **Primer Size:** Small Pistol **Bullet Dia.:** .310 - .313″

HANDGUN LOADS FOR THE .32 S&W LONG

LOAD NUMBER	BULLET				POWDER			VELOCITY FPS	PRESSURE CUP	CASE BRAND	PRIMER		CARTRIDGE OAL	BARREL LENGTH	DATA SOURCE
	WEIGHT	BRAND	SHAPE	TYPE	WEIGHT	BRAND	TYPE				BRAND	TYPE			
1	95		SWC	LP	2.2	HER	BEYE	771		REM	CCI	500		4	SPR
2	95		SWC	LP	3.5	HER	UNIQ	898		REM	CCI	500		4	SPR
3	98	WIN	RNN	LP	2.4	WIN	231	765	11000	WIN	WIN	1½-108	1.280	4	WIN
4	98	WIN	RNN	LP	4.9	WIN	630	775	10000	WIN	WIN	1½-108	1.280	4	WIN
5	98		RNN	LP	2.2	HER	BEYE	820		REM	CCI	500		4	SPR
6	98		RNN	LP	3.2	HER	UNIQ	850		REM	CCI	500		4	SPR

.32-20 (.32 W.C.F.)

Introduced by Winchester in about 1882 for use in their Model 1873 rifle, the .32-20 was soon chambered in the Colt single-action revolvers. Colt and Smith & Wesson double-action revolvers were later chambered for it, and some foreign revolvers imported years ago into the U.S. also use this cartridge. After the introduction of the Winchester Model 1892 rifle chambered for the .32-20, a special high-velocity factory load was introduced especially for the Model 1892 and other rifles of comparable strength. The chamber-pressure limit for these high-velocity loads was about 26,000 c.u.p., compared to about 16,000 c.u.p. for the standard-velocity load. Notices printed on the ammunition box warned against using these high-velocity loads in the old Model 1873 rifle, or in any handgun, because of the greatly increased pressure. Some old handloading data were developed for these high-velocity rifle loads, and handloaders must exercise due care against using such data for handgun loads.

The .32-20 is not a particularly difficult cartridge to load for a handgun. Because it is slightly bottle-necked, chambers and cartridges should be kept free of excessive oil or grease to prevent "set-back" which can otherwise cause the cylinder to bind instead of rotating freely. Cases must be trimmed to uniform length for uniform crimping, and care must be exercised to avoid excessive force in crimping, since the cases are relatively thin, and may crumple at the shoulder if crimped with excessive force.

Pressure-tested loading data are unfortunately very scarce for the .32-20. Hercules formerly listed extensive data for it, using Bullseye and Unique powders which are still available. They now warn against using those data, however, owing to changes in cartridge cases and other components since the data were developed. Winchester-Western has, however, provided data for their 630 powder, suitable for use in both rifle and handgun loads. A fairly strong crimp is required for proper ignition and burning of 630 in .32-20 handguns.

Hercules Unique has been used for many years in .32-20 handloads, and been found very satisfactory. The loads listed here using Unique have not been pressure-tested, but they are substantially less than the maximum loads formerly listed by Hercules, and are believed to produce pressures not exceeding the 16,000-c.u.p. limit now established for the cartridge. Long use of these loads in .32-20 revolvers has been entirely satisfactory.

Some of .32-20 cases are of balloon-head type, and should not be used for handloading. Cases of recent manufacture are of the much stronger solid-head type.

The maximum product average chamber pressure for the .32-20 cartridge is now established at 17,700 c.u.p.

Max. Case Length: 1.315" **Trim-To Length:** 1.310"
Max. Overall Length: 1.592" **Primer Size:** Small Rifle **Bullet Dia.:** .310"

HANDGUN LOADS FOR THE .32-20

LOAD NUMBER	BULLET				POWDER			VELOCITY FPS	PRESSURE CUP	CASE BRAND	PRIMER		CARTRIDGE OAL	BARREL LENGTH	DATA SOURCE
	WEIGHT	BRAND	SHAPE	TYPE	WEIGHT	BRAND	TYPE				BRAND	TYPE			
1	100	CAST	FLN	LP	2.8	HER	BYE	750		WIN	WIN	6½-116	1.590	6	NRA
2	100	CAST	FLN	LP	4.1	HER	UNIQ	950		WIN	WIN	6½-116	1.590	6	NRA
3	100	CAST	FLN	LP	7.2	WIN	630	925		WIN	WIN	6½-116	1.590	6	NRA
4	115	CAST	FLN	LP	2.5	HER	BYE	715		WIN	WIN	6½-116	1.590	6	NRA
5	115	CAST	FLN	LP	4.3	HER	UNIQ	950		WIN	WIN	6½-116	1.590	6	NRA

.380 A.C.P. (9mm BROWNING SHORT)

Introduced in about 1912 for a Browning-designed autoloading pistol produced by Fabrique Nationale in Belgium, the .380 A.C.P. has since been used in a great variety of other pistols. Because it is not too powerful for use in simple blowback-operated handguns of small size and light weight, it has been especially popular in such guns, which are designed for convenient carrying and defensive use. It is the most powerful cartridge that is very suitable for use in such guns, and superior in effectiveness to such cartridges as the .32 A.C.P. and .25 A.C.P. Larger handguns adapted to this cartridge are widely used by uniformed police in Europe, though seldom so used in the U.S.

The original round-nose full-jacketed bullet is not of the most effective design for defensive purposes, and major bullet-makers have recently developed more effective bullets of expanding type. The velocities attainable at acceptable pressure and recoil impulse (which is important in blowback-operated guns) are only marginally sufficient for reliable bullet expansion, however, and the .380 is therefore less effective than cartridges such as the .38 Special fired in steel-frame revolvers that can withstand the pressure of higher-velocity loads. The .380 is nevertheless a good choice in a compact pocket pistol of autoloading type.

The maximum product average chamber pressure for factory ammunition of this caliber in the U.S. should not exceed 18,900 c.u.p.

Max. Case Length: .680″ Trim-To Length: .677″
Max. Overall Length: .984″ Primer Size: Small Pistol Bullet Dia.: .355″

HANDGUN LOADS FOR THE .380 A.C.P.

LOAD NUMBER	BULLET				POWDER			VELOCITY FPS	PRESSURE CUP	CASE BRAND	PRIMER		CARTRIDGE OAL	BARREL LENGTH	DATA SOURCE
	WEIGHT	BRAND	SHAPE	TYPE	WEIGHT	BRAND	TYPE				BRAND	TYPE			
1	88	SPR	FLN	HP	4.9	HOD	HS5	1060	<18900	REM	CCI	550		4½	SPR
2	90	SRA	FLN	HP	4.6	HER	UNIQ	1000		REM	CCI	500		3¼	SRA
3	90	SRA	FLN	HP	4.2	DUP	7625	1000		REM	CCI	500		3¼	SRA
4	95	WIN	RNN	FJ	3.2	WIN	231	860	15000	WIN	WIN	1½-108	.984	3¾	WIN
5	95	WIN	RNN	FJ	6:7	WIN	630	895	15000	WIN	WIN	1½-108	.984	3¾	WIN
6	100	SPR	FLN	HP	2.6	DUP	700X	918	<18900	WIN	CCI	500		4½	SPR
7	100	SPR	FLN	HP	3.7	HER	UNIQ	946	<18900	WIN	CCI	500		4½	SPR
8	100	SPR	FLN	HP	4.5	HOD	HS5	962	<18900	WIN	CCI	500		4½	SPR
9	100	SPR	FLN	HP	3.3	WIN	231	928	<18900	WIN	CCI	500		4½	SPR
10	115	SRA	FLN	HP	3.5	HER	UNIQ	850		REM	CCI	500		3¼	SRA
11	115	SRA	FLN	HP	3.4	DUP	7625	900		REM	CCI	500		3¼	SRA
12	115	SRA	FLN	HP	2.6	DUP	700X	850		REM	CCI	500		3¼	SRA
13	95	CAST		LP	3.2	HOD	TR100	944		WIN	WIN	1½-108		3¾	HOD
14	95	CAST		LP	3.2	HOD	HP38	904		WIN	WIN	1½-108		3¾	HOD

9mm LUGER (PARABELLUM)

This cartridge was introduced about 1902, for use in the Luger autoloading pistol. It was adopted shortly thereafter as the standard military handgun cartridge by Germany, and has since then become the most widely used handgun cartridge in the world by military and police establishments. It has been adopted as a NATO standard cartridge for use in handguns and submachine guns, although the U.S. did not participate actively in that standardization agreement, deciding to keep in service the .45 A.C.P. instead.

That 1955 decision was not based on technical

performance, however, but on logistic considerations, including the existence of large stocks of caliber .45 weapons and ammunition, and the fact that handguns were then felt to be of relatively minor importance in warfare. Current logistic and performance considerations have led the joint services to again consider possible adoption of a 9mm handgun as an eventual replacement for the .45 pistol. Trials are underway, as of this writing, which could lead to development of a specification for a future service pistol. Existing stocks of M1911A1 pistols are said to be reaching the end of their maintainable life, and critics of the .45 cartridge contend that it lacks penetration against known body armor.

The modern science of wound ballistics has established beyond reasonable doubt that the 9mm cartridge is highly effective. A study reported in 1975, done by the U.S. Army Ballistic Research Laboratory at Aberdeen Proving Ground for the U.S. Department of Justice, ranks the Remington 9mm Luger factory load with 115-grain JHP bullets 17th among 142 cartridges tested, whereas the classic .45 A.C.P. "hardball" load with its 230-grain bullet ranked 110th in the same list. Nevertheless, the 9mm is less appealing to some handgun enthusiasts than is the bellowing, hard-kicking .45 A.C.P., firing bullets twice as heavy. The 9mm is often disparaged in comparison to the .45, by those who prefer their own criteria of defensive handgun effectivenss to the modern science of wound ballistics. Only if the target were a very large animal, requiring deep penetration of the bullet to reach vital regions of the body, is the 9mm JHP load likely to be inferior to the .45 A.C.P. with its heavy full-jacketed bullet.

As with all cartridges to be used in autoloading pistols, the 9mm must be loaded to approximate the ballistics of factory loads fairly closely for reliable functioning of the gun.

The maximum product average chamber pressure for this cartridge in the U.S. non-military loads is 35,700 c.u.p.

Max. Case Length: .754″ Trim-To Length: .751″
Max. Overall Length: 1.169″ Primer Size: Small Pistol Bullet Dia.: .354″ - .356″

HANDGUN LOADS FOR THE 9 mm LUGER (PARABELLUM)

LOAD NUMBER	BULLET				POWDER			VELOCITY FPS	PRESSURE CUP	CASE BRAND	PRIMER		CARTRIDGE OAL	BARREL LENGTH	DATA SOURCE
	WEIGHT	BRAND	SHAPE	TYPE	WEIGHT	BRAND	TYPE				BRAND	TYPE			
1	90	SRA	FLN	HP	5.0	HER	BEYE	1287	28950	REM	REM	1½	1.010	4	NRA
2	90	SRA	FLN	HP	6.0	HER	UNIQ	1350		SUV	CCI	500		5	SRA
3	90	SRA	FLN	HP	5.8	DUP	7625	1350		SUV	CCI	500		5	SRA
4	100	HDY	RNN	FJ	5.7	HER	UNIQ	1235	30370	REM	REM	1½	1.090	4	NRA
5	100	HDY	RNN	FJ	6.6	HER	HERCO	1232	29200	REM	REM	1½	1.090	4	NRA
6	100	SPR	FLN	HP	10.2	HER	BDOT	1438	<35700	SPR	CCI	500		4	SPR
7	100	SPR	FLN	HP	4.8	HER	BEYE	1191	29150	REM	REM	1½	1.090	4	NRA
8	100	SPR	FLN	HP	5.3	DUP	7625	1178	28240	REM	REM	1½	1.090	4	NRA
9	100	WIN	RNN	SP	5.6	WIN	231	1220	31000	WIN	WIN	1½-108	1.169	4	WIN
10	100	WIN	RNN	SP	10.9	WIN	630	1210	28000	WIN	WIN	1½-108	1.169	4	WIN
11	108		FLN	SP	7.1	HOD	HS6	1272		WIN	WIN	1½-108		4	HOD
12	110	ZER	FLN	HP	4.1	DUP	700X	1096	29690	REM	REM	1½	1.030	4	NRA
13	110	ZER	FLN	HP	4.6	HER	RDOT	1131	29720	REM	REM	1½	1.030	4	NRA
14	112	SUV	FLN	HP	4.5	HER	BEYE	1121	29250	REM	REM	1½	1.060	4	NRA
15	115	HDY	FLN	HP	4.4	HER	BEYE	1100	<33000	FRO	FED	100	1.105	4	HDY
16	115	WIN	RNN	FJ	5.1	WIN	231	1125	30500	WIN	WIN	1½-108	1.169	4	WIN
17	115	WIN	RNN	FJ	10.3	WIN	630	1125	31000	WIN	WIN	1½-108	1.169	4	WIN
18	115	REM	FLN	HP	5.4	HER	UNIQ	1118	28260	REM	REM	1½	1.110	4	NRA
19	115	SRA	FLN	HP	4.5	HER	RDOT	1118	30630	REM	REM	1½	1.020	4	NRA
20	124	REM	RNN	FJ	6.1	DUP	4756	1092	28480	REM	REM	1½	1.150	4	NRA
21	125	SPR	RNN	SP	5.2	HER	UNIQ	1064	29880	REM	REM	1½	1.140	4	NRA
22	125	SPR	RNN	SP	4.5	HER	RDOT	1051	30280	REM	REM	1½	1.140	4	NRA
23	125	SPR	RNN	SP	6.0	HER	HERCO	1085	29290	REM	REM	1½	1.140	4	NRA
24	105	CAST	SWC	LP	5.5	HER	UNIQ	1276	28210	REM	REM	1½	1.010	4	NRA
25	105	CAST	SWC	LP	4.6	HER	BEYE	1263	27550	REM	REM	1½	1.010	4	NRA
26	111	CAST	RNN	LP	4.6	HER	RDOT	1197	29730	REM	REM	1½	1.030	4	NRA
27	117	CAST	RNN	LP	4.3	HER	BEYE	1177	29620	REM	REM	1½	1.030	4	NRA
28	125	CAST	RNN	LP	4.2	HER	BEYE	1118	28590	REM	REM	1½	1.090	4	NRA
29	125	SPR	RNN	LP	4.5	HER	UNIQ	1007	<35700	SPR	CCI	500		4	SPR

.38 A.C.P.

This cartridge was introduced about 1900, for use in a Browning-designed autoloading pistol. The factory load employs a 130-grain bullet at a velocity of 1,040 fps. It is, unfortunately, dimensionally the same as the .38 Super Auto, which fires a 130-grain bullet at 1,280 fps, and develops much higher chamber pressure than is permissible in guns intended for the .38 A.C.P. Users of a .38 A.C.P. pistol must be aware of this difference, and so must handloaders, *to assure that .38 Super Auto ammunition is not fired in a weapon intended only for use with the .38 A.C.P. round.*

The 130-grain round-nose factory bullet is not of the most effective design, and performance of this cartridge as a defensive load is undoubtedly improved by handloading with the lighter expanding-type bullets, which can safely be driven at sufficient velocity to produce reliable expansion.

The maximum product average chamber pressure for this cartridge should not exceed 25,700 c.u.p.
Max. Case Length: .900″ **Trim-To Length:** .895″
Max. Overall Length: 1.280″ **Primer Size:** Small Pistol, Small Pistol Magnum **Bullet Dia.:** .355″

HANDGUN LOADS FOR THE .38 A.C.P.

LOAD NUMBER	BULLET				POWDER			VELOCITY FPS	PRESSURE CUP	CASE BRAND	PRIMER		CARTRIDGE OAL	BARREL LENGTH	DATA SOURCE
	WEIGHT	BRAND	SHAPE	TYPE	WEIGHT	BRAND	TYPE				BRAND	TYPE			
1	110	HDY	FLN	HP	4.8	HER	BEYE	1150		WIN	ALC	SP	1.100	6	HDY
2	110	HDY	FLN	HP	4.4	DUP	700X	1150		WIN	ALC	SP	1.100	6	HDY
3	115	HDY	FLN	HP	4.7	HER	BEYE	1100		WIN	ALC	SP	1.115	6	HDY
4	115	HDY	FLN	HP	4.6	HER	RDOT	1100		WIN	ALC	SP	1.115	6	HDY
5	125	HDY	FLN	HP	4.5	HER	RDOT	1050		WIN	ALC	SP	1.060	6	HDY
6	125	HDY	FLN	HP	5.9	HER	HERCO	1050		WIN	ALC	SP	1.060	6	HDY
7	130	WIN	RNN	FJ	4.4	WIN	231	875	20000	WIN	WIN	1½-108		5	WIN
8	130	WIN	RNN	FJ	8.7	WIN	630	960	21500	WIN	WIN	1½-108		5	WIN

.38 SUPER AUTO COLT

This cartridge is dimensionally interchangeable with the .38 A.C.P. cartridge, but it is loaded to higher velocities and pressures, and intended only for use in the Colt .38 Super handgun or weapons of comparable strength. No harm is done by firing .38 A.C.P. ammunition in a Colt .38 Super Auto handgun, but functioning may not be very reliable. *The .38 Super Auto cartridge should not be fired in guns intended for use only with .38 A.C.P. ammunition.* The headstamp on modern .38 Super Auto ammunition now includes the "+P" marking, which is familiar to users of .38 Special loads, and this is a useful aid in making the necessary distinction between .38 Super and .38 A.C.P. ammunition. However, .38 Super loads produced years ago did not have the distinguishing "+P" in the headstamp, though the same precautions must apply to their use.

At the time of its introduction in 1929 by Colt, the .38 Super Auto was a very impressive handgun cartridge, with its muzzle velocity of 1,280 fps. The modern magnum revolver cartridges later surpassed its performance, but it still remains a very powerful handgun cartridge. The addtion of a 115-grain jacketed hollow-point bullet at 1,300 fps in factory loads has greatly increased the effectiveness of the cartridge for defensive purposes.

Unlike the rimless .45 A.C.P. which headspaces on the case mouth, the .38 Super is a semi-rimless cartridge, intended to headspace on the narrow rim, against a surface at the breech face of the barrel. Owing to the very narrow rim, and to diametral tolerances allowed for cartridges and chambers, there are instances in which the rim does not firmly engage the surface intended to support it, and headspace control is therefore erratic. Probably for this reason, ignition may also be erratic, and accuracy may be disappointing. The .38 Super Auto has never achieved a reputation for accuracy as a target arm, though it is mechanically nearly identical to the Colt .45 Automatic which is highly regarded among target shooters. Some custom gunsmiths have modified .38 Super Auto handguns so as to headspace on the case mouth, as the .45 A.C.P. does, and reported very substantial improvements in accuracy.

The maximum product average chamber pressure for this cartridge should not exceed 35,700 c.u.p.

Max. Case Length: .900″ **Trim-To Length:** .895″
Max. Overall Length: 1.280″ **Primer Size:** Small Pistol **Bullet Dia.:** .355″

HANDGUN LOADS FOR THE .38 SUPER AUTO

LOAD NUMBER	BULLET				POWDER			VELOCITY FPS	PRESSURE CUP	CASE BRAND	PRIMER		CARTRIDGE OAL	BARREL LENGTH	DATA SOURCE
	WEIGHT	BRAND	SHAPE	TYPE	WEIGHT	BRAND	TYPE				BRAND	TYPE			
1	90	SRA	FLN	HP	6.7	HER	BEYE	1500		REM	CCI	500		5	SRA
2	90	SRA	FLN	HP	7.4	DUP	PB	1450		REM	CCI	500		5	SRA
3	100	SPR	FLN	HP	10.8	HER	BDOT	1428	<35700	SUV	CCI	500		5	SPR
4	100	SPR	FLN	HP	6.5	HER	UNIQ	1335	<35700	SUV	CCI	500		5	SPR
5	110	HDY	FLN	HP	6.0	HER	BEYE	1350		WIN	ALC	SP	1.100	5	HDY
6	110	HDY	FLN	HP	5.4	DUP	700X	1350		WIN	ALC	SP	1.100	5	HDY
7	115	HDY	FLN	HP	5.8	HER	BEYE	1300		WIN	ALC	SP	1.115	5	HDY
8	115	HDY	FLN	HP	6.9	HER	UNIQ	1300		WIN	ALC	SP	1.115	5	HDY
9	115	SRA	FLN	HP	8.8	DUP	4756	1350		REM	CCI	500		5	SRA
10	115	SRA	FLN	HP	14.6	HOD	H110	1350		REM	CCI	500		5	SRA
11	125	SPR	RNN	SP	9.8	HER	BDOT	1295	<35700	SUV	CCI	500		5	SPR
12	125	SPR	RNN	SP	13.8	DUP	4227	1195	<35700	SUV	CCI	550		5	SPR
13	125	WIN	FLN	HP	5.8	WIN	231	1125	31000	WIN	WIN	1½-108	1.280	5	WIN
14	125	WIN	FLN	HP	10.9	WIN	630	1185	30500	WIN	WIN	1½-108	1.280	5	WIN
15	130	WIN	RNN	FJ	5.4	WIN	231	1075	30500	WIN	WIN	1½-108	1.280	5	WIN
16	130	WIN	RNN	FJ	10.0	WIN	630	1160	31000	WIN	WIN	1½-108	1.280	5	WIN
17	125			LP	6.8	HOD	HS6	1286		WIN	WIN	1½-108		4⅞	HOD
18	125			LP	6.0	HOD	HS5	1042		WIN	WIN	1½-108		4⅞	HOD
19	125			LP	5.0	HOD	HP38	1014		WIN	WIN	1½-108		4⅞	HOD
20	125	SPR	RNN	LP	5.8	WIN	231	1229	<35700	SUV	CCI	500		5	SPR
21	125	SPR	RNN	LP	5.7	HER	UNIQ	1191	<35700	SUV	CCI	500		5	SPR
22	125	SPR	RNN	LP	7.0	HER	HERCO	1266	<35700	SUV	CCI	500		5	SPR

.38 SMITH & WESSON (.38 COLT NEW POLICE)

Introduced about 1877 by Smith & Wesson, this cartridge was originally loaded with blackpowder, but successfully made the transition to smokeless with undiminished popularity. Several variants have been loaded during the many years of its existence. The original smokeless load used a 146-grain round-nose bullet at about 730 fps. The .38 Colt New Police was practically identical, but used a 150-grain flat-nose bullet at about 710 fps. A version commercially loaded by Western Cartridge Company for many years used a 200-grain, blunt, round-nose bullet at about 610 fps, and was called the .38 S.&W. Super Police load. In England, the cartridge is loaded with a 200-grain bullet, and is commonly called the .380/200. The .380/200 was the official military handgun cartridge in England for some years prior to the adoption of the 9mm Parabellum. The current U.S. commercial load uses a 145-grain or 146-grain bullet, at a muzzle velocity of 685 fps. There are many old guns of uncertain strength adapted to this cartridge, which may explain the very conservative loads now produced in the U.S. for the .38 S.&W.

The .38 S.&W. is much less popular than it was in the early 1900's, when a variety of pocket pistols were chambered for it. The small .38 Special revolvers and .380 A.C.P. autoloaders have practically displaced the .38 S.&W. as pocket guns, but some of these remain in use, in addition to some military weapons formerly made for British forces and later sold as military surplus in the U.S.

Max. Case Length: .775″ **Trim-To Length:** .770″
Max. Overall Length: 1.180″ **Primer Size:** Small Pistol **Bullet Dia.:** .360″

HANDGUN LOADS FOR THE .38 S&W (.38 COLT N.P.)

LOAD NUMBER	BULLET				POWDER			VELOCITY FPS	PRESSURE CUP	CASE BRAND	PRIMER		CARTRIDGE OAL	BARREL LENGTH	DATA SOURCE
	WEIGHT	BRAND	SHAPE	TYPE	WEIGHT	BRAND	TYPE				BRAND	TYPE			
1	110	SPR	FLN	HP	3.0	HER	BEYE	894		WIN	CCI	500		4	SPR
2	110	SPR	FLN	HP	3.2	HER	RDOT	852		WIN	CCI	500		4	SPR
3	125	SPR	FLN	HP	2.8	HER	BEYE	742		WIN	CCI	500		4	SPR
4	125	SPR	FLN	HP	3.0	HER	RDOT	773		WIN	CCI	500		4	SPR
5	145	WIN	RNN	LP	2.6	WIN	231	675	11500	WIN	WIN	1½-108	1.180	4	WIN
6	145	WIN	RNN	LP	5.1	WIN	630	700	12000	WIN	WIN	1½-108	1.180	4	WIN
7	145	WIN	RNN	LP	2.4	HER	BEYE	680							HER
8	145	WIN	RNN	LP	2.5	HER	RDOT	725							HER
9	145	WIN	RNN	LP	3.2	HER	UNIQ	700							HER
10	148	SPR	WC	LP	2.5	HER	BEYE	701		WIN	CCI	500	*	4	SPR
11	148	SPR	WC	LP	2.7	HER	RDOT	698		WIN	CCI	500	*	4	SPR
12	158	SPR	SW	LP	2.2	HER	BEYE	629		WIN	CCI	500		4	SPR
13	158	SPR	SW	LP	2.4	HER	RDOT	667		WIN	CCI	500		4	SPR

*Crimp in top lubrication groove for this bullet.

.38 SPECIAL

The .38 Special has been variously known as the .38 Smith & Wesson Special, .38 Colt Special, and .38-44. Originated by Smith & Wesson about 1902 with a round-nose 158-grain lead bullet, it was later announced as the .38 Colt Special, with a 158-grain flat-nose bullet. The .38-44 was a high-velocity version of the 1930's, comparable to modern +P ammunition, and intended for use only in heavy-frame revolvers. Such revolvers were then identified as being built on ".44 frames," hence the .38-44 cartridge designation. The .38 Special is undoubtedly the most widely used centerfire revolver cartridge in the U.S. today, and it is offered in a great variety of factory loads, with bullets from 95 to 200 grains.

A question often asked is why the .38 Special is so designated when the bullet is actually .357 inch in diameter, being therefore about .36 caliber instead of .38. The name for this, and some other .38 caliber handgun cartridges, appears to have been established many years ago, when the custom was to use heel-loaded outside-lubricated bullets, which were of practically the same diameter as the cartridge case. The diameter of the .38 Special cartridge case is indeed about .38 inch. But when the designs evolved toward inside-lubricated bullets, the bullet diameter was reduced to approximately .36 inch, to fit in the .38

case, but the custom of calling them .38 caliber cartridges persisted until the introduction of the .357 Magnum in the 1930's, which was named according to its actual bullet diameter.

The .38 Special loads listed here are in three categories. Loads 1 through 15 are jacketed-bullet loads supposed not to exceed the chamber-pressure limit of 17,000 c.u.p. that is generally applied to standard-velocity .38 Special loads. These loads should be safe in any sound .38 Special revolver. **Loads 16 through 30 are comparable to factory +P loads, and should be used only in revolvers specifically approved by their manufacturers for use with +P factory ammunition.** Chamber pressures of loads 16 through 30 may approach 20,000 c.u.p. Loads 31 through 50 are lead-bullet loads, believed to fall within the chamber-pressure limits established for standard-velocity .38 Special ammunition.

Maximum product average chamber pressures for the .38 Special are established at 18,900 c.u.p. for standard loads, and 22,400 c.u.p. for +P loads.
Max. Case Length: 1.155" Trim-To Length: 1.150"
Max. Overall Length: 1.550" Primer Size: Small Pistol Bullet Dia.: .357"

HANDGUN LOADS FOR THE .38 SPECIAL

LOAD NUMBER	BULLET				POWDER			VELOCITY FPS	PRESSURE CUP	CASE BRAND	PRIMER		CARTRIDGE OAL	BARREL LENGTH	DATA SOURCE
	WEIGHT	BRAND	SHAPE	TYPE	WEIGHT	BRAND	TYPE				BRAND	TYPE			
1	90		FLN	HP	10.0	HOD	HS6	1405	15000	WIN	WIN	1½-108		*7½	HOD
2	95	REM	BJ	HP	4.5	DUP	700X	1060	16000	REM	FED	100	1.465	6	DUP
3	95	REM	BJ	HP	6.5	DUP	4756	1130	16000	REM	FED	100	1.465	6	DUP
4	110	SRA	FLN	HP	5.5	DUP	7625	1115	15900	REM	FED	100	1.465	6	DUP
5	110	HDY	FLN	HP	5.4	HER	GDOT	1095							HER
6	110	SPR	FLN	HP	7.6	HER	BDOT	992	<18900	SPR	CCI	500		6	SPR

HANDGUN LOADS FOR THE .38 SPECIAL

LOAD NUMBER	BULLET				POWDER			VELOCITY FPS	PRESSURE CUP	CASE BRAND	PRIMER		CARTRIDGE OAL	BARREL LENGTH	DATA SOURCE
	WEIGHT	BRAND	SHAPE	TYPE	WEIGHT	BRAND	TYPE				BRAND	TYPE			
7	125	REM	FLN	HP	5.8	DUP	4756	985	15800	REM	REM	1½	1.525	6	DUP
8	125	HDY	FLN	HP	4.4	HER	BEYE	1035							HER
9	125	SRA	FLN	SP	8.9	HER	BDOT	1000		SUV	CCI	550		6	SRA
10	140	SPR	FLN	HP	7.0	HER	BDOT	879	<18900	SPR	CCI	500		6	SPR
11	146	SPR	BJ	HP	7.0	HER	BDOT	903	<18900	SPR	CCI	500		6	SPR
12	158	HDY	FLN	HP	8.6	WIN	630	850	<18000	FRO	FED	100	1.455	4	HDY
13	158	SPR	FLN	SP	7.3	HOD	HS7	828	<18900	SPR	CCI	550		6	SPR
14	158	SRA	FLN	SP	5.0	HER	UNIQ	750		SUV	CCI	500		6	SRA
15	160	SPR	BJ	SP	6.7	HER	BDOT	822	<18900	SPR	CCI	550		6	SPR
16	110	HDY	FLN	HP	6.5	HER	UNIQ	1241	18460	WIN	WIN	1½-108	1.450	*7¾	NRA
17	110	WIN	FLN	HP	9.1	WIN	630	1220	19000	WIN	WIN	1½-108	1.445	*6	WIN
18	110	SRA	FLN	HP	11.3	HER	BDOT	1350		SUV	CCI	500		6	SRA
19	110	SPR	FLN	HP	12.7	HOD	H110	1146	<22400	SPR	CCI	550		6	SPR
20	125	SRA	FLN	SP	4.8	HER	BEYE	1095	18300	WIN	WIN	1½-108	1.440	*7¾	NRA
21	125	ZER	FLN	HP	6.0	HER	UNIQ	1133	17170	WIN	WIN	1½-108	1.470	*7¾	NRA
22	125	WIN	FLN	HP	8.7	WIN	630	1150	19000	WIN	WIN	1½-108	1.445	*6	WIN
23	125	HDY	FLN	HP	4.5	HER	BEYE	950	<20000	FRO	FED	100	1.455	4	HDY
24	140	SPR	FLN	HP	5.5	HER	UNIQ	1020	18010	WIN	WIN	1½-108	1.450	*7¾	NRA
25	140	SPR	FLN	HP	8.4	HER	BDOT	1024	<22400	SPR	CCI	550		6	SPR
26	150	SRA	FLN	HP	7.8	HER	BDOT	900		SUV	CCI	550		6	SRA
27	158	SRA	FLN	SP	7.4	HER	BDOT	800		SUV	CCI	550		6	SRA
28	158	HDY	FLN	HP	3.9	HER	BEYE	880	17200	WIN	WIN	1½-108	1.450	*7¾	NRA
29	158	SPR	FLN	SP	5.0	HER	UNIQ	933	16800	WIN	WIN	1½-108	1.450	*7¾	NRA
30	158	HDY	FLN	HP	9.9	HER	2400	900		FRO	FED	100	1.455	4	HDY
31	148	SPR	WC	LP	3.9	HER	BEYE	813	<18900	SPR	CCI	500		6	SPR
32	148	SPR	WC	LHB	2.8	HER	BEYE	741	<18900	SPR	CCI	500		6	SPR
33	148	SPR	WC	LP	5.1	HER	UNIQ	981	<18900	SPR	CCI	500		6	SPR
34	148	HDY	WC	LP	2.7	HER	RDOT	750	<17000	FRO	FED	100		4	HDY
35	148	HDY	WC	LP	3.4	HER	UNIQ	750	<17000	FRO	FED	100		4	HDY
36	148	REM	WC	LP	2.5	DUP	700X	755	10200	REM	REM	1½	1.195	6	DUP
37	148	REM	WC	LP	2.8	DUP	PB	770	11100	REM	REM	1½	1.195	6	DUP
38	148	WIN	WC	LP	3.1	WIN	231	800	11000	WIN	WIN	1½-108	1.185	6	WIN
39	148	WIN	WC	LP	6.9	WIN	630	925	15000	WIN	WIN	1½-108	1.185	6	WIN
40	148	SPR	WC	LP	2.8	HOD	HP38	802	10400	WIN	WIN	1½-108		*7½	HOD
41	158	WIN	SWC	LP	8.1	WIN	630	900	15500	WIN	WIN	1½-108	1.445	6	WIN
42	158	REM	RNN	LP	5.3	DUP	4756	875	15400	REM	REM	1½	1.550	6	DUP
43	158		RN	LP	6.5	HOD	HS6	986	14400	WIN	WIN	1½-108		*7½	HOD
44	158	SPR	SWC	LP	6.3	HER	BDOT	868	<18900	SPR	CCI	500		6	SPR
45	158	HDY	SWC	LP	4.8	HER	UNIQ	900	<17000	FRO	FED	100		6	HDY
46	200	REM	RNN	LP	4.3	DUP	4756	785	15600	REM	REM	1½	1.550	6	DUP
47	200	REM	RNN	LP	8.9	DUP	4227	855	15600	REM	REM	1½	1.550	6	DUP
48	200	WIN	RNN	LP	3.8	WIN	231	770	15500	WIN	WIN	1½-108	1.520	6	WIN
49	200	WIN	RNN	LP	7.2	WIN	630	780	15500	WIN	WIN	1½-108	1.520	6	WIN
50	200	WIN	RNN	LP	8.5	HOD	4227	842	15900	WIN	WIN	1½-108		*7½	HOD

*Unvented test barrel; lower velocities are expected in revolvers.

.357 MAGNUM

Introduced by Smith & Wesson in 1935, this cartridge was quite sensational at that time. The late Philip B. Sharpe, a gun writer of considerable accomplishment and popularity from the 1930's to 1950's, was said to have had considerable influence in its development. It is based on the .38 Special case, but lengthened by about 1/10 of an inch to prevent the chambering and firing of the powerful .357 Magnum in .38 Special revolvers not designed to withstand the high chamber pressures of the magnum round.

Revolvers chambered for the .357 Magnum may be used with .38 Special ammunition, however, and frequently are so used.

The .357 Magnum develops velocities about 60 per cent higher than those of standard .38 Special loads, and energy about 2½ times greater, with bullets of the same weight. This is accomplished largely at the expense of chamber pressure levels about 2½ times higher in the .357 than in the standard .38 Special. The attempt to duplicate .357 Magnum ballistics in .38 Special guns is a constant temptation to handloaders, and yielding to it has caused the ruin of many fine, .38 Special revolvers. Each cartridge has its range of usefulness with safety, and safe handloaders must recognize that .357 loads are safe only when correctly assembled in .357 cases, and fired only in .357 guns. **Most .357 guns perform very well with .38 Special loads, but the .357 loads must never be assembled in .38 Special cases, or fired in .38 Special guns.**

The .357 Magnum is an excellent cartridge for law-enforcement use, and it is used in some jurisdictions for that purpose. In the social climate of the 1960's and 1970's, however, limiting the capacity of law-enforcement officers to use force against criminal suspects has become a subject of debate along ideological and political lines, and the .357 Magnum has been forbidden in some political jurisdictions on grounds that it is unnecessarily effective.

The .357 is a very versatile cartridge for sporting use, performing well on the target range with mild wadcutter loads, in the field with moderate small-game loads, and even on deer-size animals, with full-charge loads, in the hands of a good hunter and careful shot. It has also achieved some popularity as a short-range rifle cartridge of moderate power.

Max. Case Length: 1.290″ **Trim-To Length:** 1.285″
Max. Overall Length: 1.590″ **Primer Size:** Small Pistol **Bullet Dia.:** .357″

HANDGUN LOADS FOR THE .357 MAGNUM

LOAD NUMBER	BULLET				POWDER			VELOCITY FPS	PRESSURE CUP	CASE BRAND	PRIMER		CARTRIDGE OAL	BARREL LENGTH	DATA SOURCE
	WEIGHT	BRAND	SHAPE	TYPE	WEIGHT	BRAND	TYPE				BRAND	TYPE			
1	90		FLN	HP	11.5	HOD	HS6	1855	32400	WIN	WIN	1½-108		*7½	HOD
2	110	SRA	FLN	HP	10.0	HER	UNIQ	1655	34000	WIN	WIN	1½-108	1.545	*8⅜	HER
3	110	HDY	FLN	HP	18.5	WIN	630	1650	<45000	FRO	FED	200	1.590	8⅜	HDY
4	110	SRA	FLN	HP	10.0	HER	UNIQ	1400		SPR	CCI	550		6	SRA
5	110	SPR	FLN	HP	21.0	HER	2400	1735	<46000	SPR	CCI	550		6	SPR
6	125	SPR	FLN	HP	12.0	HER	BDOT	1720	39900	SPR	CCI	500	1.570	6	HER
7	125	HDY	FLN	HP	18.2	HER	2400	1500	<45000	FRO	FED	200		8⅜	HDY
8	125	SRA	FLN	SP	15.3	WIN	630	1300		SPR	CCI	550		6	SRA
9	125	WIN	FLN	SP	15.4	WIN	630	1710	42500	WIN	WIN	1½-108	1.580	*8⅜	WIN
10	140	SPR	FLN	HP	19.2	DUP	4227	1306		SPR	CCI	550		6	SPR
11	150	SRA	FLN	HP	16.0	HER	2400	1300		SPR	CCI	550		6	SRA
12	158	SRA	FLN	SP	16.6	WIN	296	1150		SPR	CCI	550		6	SRA
13	158	WIN	FLN	SP	16.6	WIN	296	1610	39500	WIN	WIN	1½-108	1.560	*8⅜	WIN
14	158	HDY	FLN	HP	14.8	HER	2400	1250	<45000	FRO	FED	200	1.590	8⅜	HDY
15	158	SPR	FLN	SP	17.8	HOD	H110	1330	<46000	SPR	CCI	550		6	SPR
16	160	SPR	BJ	SP	15.7	HER	2400	1341	<46000	SPR	CCI	550		6	SPR
17	170	SRA	RNN	FJ	10.0	HER	BDOT	1345	39700	SPR	CCI	550	1.550	6	HER
18	148	SPR	WC	LHB	3.0	HER	RDOT	750	<46000	SPR	CCI	500		6	SPR
19	158	SPR	SWC	LP	4.5	DUP	700X	904	<46000	SPR	CCI	500		6	SPR
20	158	SPR	SWC	LP	6.0	HER	UNIQ	1034	<46000	SPR	CCI	550		6	SPR
21	158	HDY	RNN	LP	5.1	DUP	4756	900	<45000	WIN	ALC	SP	1.590	8	HDY
22	158	HDY	RNN	LP	6.7	DUP	4756	1100	<45000	WIN	ALC	SP	1.590	8	HDY
23	158	REM	SWC	LG	9.3	DUP	4756	1315	36000	REM	REM	5½	1.590	6½	DUP
24	158	REM	SWC	LG	15.0	DUP	4227	1355	35300	REM	REM	5½	1.590	6½	DUP
25	200	REM	RNN	LP	7.2	DUP	4756	1085	35200	REM	REM	5½	1.590	6½	DUP
26	200	REM	RNN	LP	12.2	DUP	4227	1105	34200	REM	REM	5½	1.590	6½	DUP

*Unvented test barrel. Lower velocities expected in revolvers.

.357 HERRETT

This cartridge is a wildcat, originated by stockmaker Steve Herrett for use in the Thompson-Center Contender pistol. It is based on a shortened and reformed .30-30 case. The cases are easily formed in a .357 Herrett full-length resizing die, after which they are trimmed to proper length, and fire-formed in the gun.

The loads listed here were developed in the ballistics laboratories of Du Pont, using Thompson-Center Contender barrels, modified to permit measuring chamber pressure by the standard copper-crusher method. Some experimenters have used much heavier loads than those listed here, but that is not recommended. A chamber-pressure limit of 45,000 c.u.p. was agreed by Thomspon-Center for the development of these loads, and that limit was respected by DuPont. Within this limitation, the cartridge can develop muzzle energy up to about 1,500 foot-pounds, which should be sufficient for any purpose that a handgun might reasonably be expected to serve.

Max. Case Length: 1.760" **Trim-To Length:** 1.750"
Max. Overall Length: Varies **Primer Size:** Large Rifle Magnum **Bullet Dia.:** .357"

HANDGUN LOADS FOR .357 HERRETT (T/C CONTENDER)
CASES: WINCHESTER   **PRIMERS: FEDERAL 210 BR**

LOAD NUMBER	BULLET				POWDER			PRESSURE CUP	VELOCITY		CARTRIDGE OAL	DATA SOURCE
	WEIGHT	BRAND	SHAPE	TYPE	WEIGHT	BRAND	TYPE		10" BRL	14" BRL		
1	110	HDY	FLN	HP	24.5C	DUP	4759	35600	1950	2070	2.080	DUP
2	110	HDY	FLN	HP	23.8	DUP	4227	44500	2095	2225	2.080	DUP
3	110	HDY	FLN	HP	32.0C	DUP	4198	33900	2070	2200	2.080	DUP
4	125	HDY	FLN	HP	24.0C	DUP	4759	38400	1880	1990	2.080	DUP
5	125	HDY	FLN	HP	22.3	DUP	4227	44900	1955	2070	2.080	DUP
6	125	HDY	FLN	HP	31.0C	DUP	4198	38100	2015	2135	2.080	DUP
7	158	HDY	FLN	SP	23.0C	DUP	4759	42000	1705	1810	2.150	DUP
8	158	HDY	FLN	SP	20.2	DUP	4227	44900	1710	1815	2.150	DUP
9	158	HDY	FLN	SP	29.9C	DUP	4198	44900	1925	2045	2.150	DUP
10	170	SRA	RNN	FJ	23.0C	DUP	4759	41400	1655	1750	2.230	DUP
11	170	SRA	RNN	FJ	20.1	DUP	4227	45000	1640	1735	2.230	DUP
12	170	SRA	RNN	FJ	30.0C	DUP	4198	44600	1835	1940	2.230	DUP
13	200	HDY	PTD	SP	23.0C	DUP	4759	44100	1575	1675	2.540	DUP
14	200	HDY	PTD	SP	28.2	DUP	4198	45000	1715	1820	2.540	DUP
15	200	HDY	PTD	SP	31.0C	DUP	3031	32400	1540	1635	2.540	DUP
16	200	HDY	PTD	SP	34.0C	DUP	4895	38300	1605	1705	2.540	DUP

.35 REMINGTON

The .35 Remington in the Thompson/Center Contender pistol is potentially much more powerful than the .357 Herrett, but this potential is not realized in the loads listed here, because of the difference in acceptable pressure limits imposed on the two cartridges. The industry-agreed limit of 35,000 c.u.p. for the .35 Remington cartridge is less by 10,000 c.u.p. than the limit imposed on the .357 Herrett. Under that handicap for the .35 Remington, the velocities achieved are nearly the same as those obtained in the .357 Herrett, with the same bullets and barrel length.

The .35 Remington is nevertheless a very powerful cartridge in the Contender, suitable for hunting deer and game of similar size, provided the user can shoot well with a gun producing very heavy recoil. The availability of factory ammunition and cartridge cases is a point of advantage for the .35 Remington over the .357 Herrett, though it is not a great advantage for the handloader.

Limited testing of factory loads using 200-grain bullets in both a 22-inch rifle barrel and a 14-inch Contender barrel showed a velocity difference of about 200 fps between rifle and handgun with the .35 Remington cartridge.

The working pressure of the .35 Remington cartridge is commonly limited to about 35,000 c.u.p. The maximum product average established for factory ammunition is 38,200 c.u.p.

Max. Case Length: 1.920" **Trim-To Length:** 1.910"
Max. Overall Length: 2.525" **Primer Size:** Large Rifle **Bullet Dia.:** .358"

HANDGUN LOADS FOR THE .35 REMINGTON (T/C CONTENDER)

LOAD NUMBER	BULLET				POWDER			VELOCITY FPS	PRESSURE CUP	CASE BRAND	PRIMER		CARTRIDGE OAL	BARREL LENGTH	DATA SOURCE
	WEIGHT	BRAND	SHAPE	TYPE	WEIGHT	BRAND	TYPE				BRAND	TYPE			
1	158	HDY	FLN	SP	38.4C	DUP	3031	2030	34500	REM	FED	210BR	2.300	14	DUP
2	158	HDY	FLN	SP	37.8	DUP	4895	1975	34700	REM	FED	210BR	2.300	14	DUP
3	158	HDY	FLN	SP	39.5C	DUP	4064	1925	32600	REM	FED	210BR	2.300	14	DUP
4	170	SRA	RNN	FJ	38.5C	DUP	3031	1985	33700	REM	FED	210BR	2.405	14	DUP
5	170	SRA	RNN	FJ	37.8	DUP	4895	1920	34100	REM	FED	210BR	2.405	14	DUP

HANDGUN LOADS FOR THE .35 REMINGTON (T/C CONTENDER)

LOAD NUMBER	BULLET				POWDER			VELOCITY FPS	PRESSURE CUP	CASE BRAND	PRIMER		CARTRIDGE OAL	BARREL LENGTH	DATA SOURCE
	WEIGHT	BRAND	SHAPE	TYPE	WEIGHT	BRAND	TYPE				BRAND	TYPE			
6	170	SRA	RNN	FJ	39.5C	DUP	4064	1885	32900	REM	FED	210BR	2.405	14	DUP
7	200	HDY	PTD	SP	36.0	DUP	3031	1870	35000	REM	FED	210BR	2.685	14	DUP
8	200	HDY	PTD	SP	38.1	DUP	4064	1850	35000	REM	FED	210BR	2.685	14	DUP
9	200	HDY	PTD	SP	34.0	DUP	4320	1730	34600	REM	FED	210BR	2.685	14	DUP
10	250	SPR	PTD	SP	31.0	DUP	3031	1620	35000	REM	FED	210BR	2.800	14	DUP
11	250	SPR	PTD	SP	33.0	DUP	4064	1610	34800	REM	FED	210BR	2.800	14	DUP
12	250	SPR	PTD	SP	31.9	DUP	4320	1570	35800	REM	FED	210BR	2.800	14	DUP

.38-40 (.38 W.C.F.)

Introduced by Winchester in 1874 for use in their Model 1873 rifle, the .38-40 cartridge was soon adopted by Colt for use in the Colt single-action revolver. The idea of a rifle and revolver firing the same ammunition was appealing to frontiersmen, and the .38-40, along with the .44-40 and .32-20, provided this capability. Originally a blackpowder cartridge, the .38-40 made the transition to smokeless powder successfully. Like the .32-20 and .44-40, the .38-40 was for some years factory-loaded with a high-velocity smokeless load intended only for use in the Winchester Model 1892 rifle and other rifles of comparable strength. These high-velocity loads should not be fired in any handgun.

Loading data for the .38-40, using modern components, are very scarce. Hercules formerly listed many pressure-tested loads, but now warn against the use of the old data, because of changes in cases and other components. Fortunately, Winchester-Western agreed to furnish one load quoted here, which is consistent with their factory loading practice.

Colt single-action revolvers having serial numbers below 160,000 were intended only for use with blackpowder, and were proof-tested accordingly. Those guns should not be fired with any smokeless load.

Some old .38-40 cases are of balloon-head construction, and are not suitable for handloading. Cases of recent manufacture are of modern solid-head construction.

The maximum product average chamber pressure of the .38-40 cartridge is now established at 14,000 c.u.p.

Max. Case Length: 1.305″   **Trim-To Length:** 1.300″
Max. Overall Length: 1.592″   **Primer Size:** Large Pistol **Bullet Dia.:** .400″

HANDGUN LOADS FOR THE .38-40

LOAD NUMBER	BULLET				POWDER			VELOCITY FPS	PRESSURE CUP	CASE BRAND	PRIMER		CARTRIDGE OAL	BARREL LENGTH	DATA SOURCE
	WEIGHT	BRAND	SHAPE	TYPE	WEIGHT	BRAND	TYPE				BRAND	TYPE			
1	180	WIN	FLN	SP	12.0	WIN	630	975	<14000	WIN	WIN	7-111	1.590	*5	WIN
2	180	CAST	FLN	LP	4.0	HER	BEYE	750		WIN	WIN	7-111	1.590	7½	NRA
3	180	CAST	FLN	LP	8.0	HER	UNIQ	930		WIN	WIN	7-111	1.590	7½	NRA
4	180	CAST	FLN	LP	12.0	WIN	630	930		WIN	WIN	7-111	1.590	7½	NRA

.41 MAGNUM

Introduced by Remington in 1964, concurrently with the Smith & Wesson Model 57 revolver, the .41 Magnum was intended to provide a cartridge intermediate in power between the .357 and .44 Magnum cartridges. It is said that Elmer Keith, veteran gun writer and handgunner, was influential in the decision by Smith & Wesson to introduce a .41-caliber revolver. The .41 Magnum has had from its beginning not only a full-charge factory load with jacketed bullet, but also a lead-bullet reduced load available from the factory. The full-charge factory load with 210-grain jacketed bullet is currently listed at 1,300 fps, and the reduced load with lead bullet is listed at 965 fps.

The .41 Magnum has not achieved popularity comparable to that of the .357 or .44 Magnum, but is nevertheless well liked by most handgunners who have used it extensively. Unlike the .357 Magnum which can be fired with .38 Special ammunition, or the .44 Magnum which can be fired with .44 Special ammunition, no cartridge except the .41 Magnum can be fired in the .41 Magnum revolver, which possibly accounts for the availability of a factory reduced load

in this caliber. Many handloaders fire more reduced loads than full-charge loads in their .41 and .44 Magnum guns, since they serve well for practice, and are pleasanter to shoot.

The maximum product average chamber pressure for the .41 Magnum is not to exceed 43,500 c.u.p.
   Max. Case Length: 1.290″ **Trim-To Length:** 1.285″
Max. Overall Length: 1.590″ **Primer Size:** Large Pistol **Bullet Dia.:** .410″

HANDGUN LOADS FOR THE .41 MAGNUM

LOAD NUMBER	BULLET				POWDER			VELOCITY FPS	PRESSURE CUP	CASE BRAND	PRIMER		CARTRIDGE OAL	BARREL LENGTH	DATA SOURCE
	WEIGHT	BRAND	SHAPE	TYPE	WEIGHT	BRAND	TYPE				BRAND	TYPE			
1	170	SRA	FLN	HP	22.0	HER	2400	1500		REM	CCI	300		6	SRA
2	170	SRA	FLN	HP	18.2	WIN	630	1300		REM	CCI	300		6	SRA
3	170	SRA	FLN	HP	22.5	DUP	4227	1200		REM	CCI	300		6	SRA
4	200	SPR	BJ	HP	18.5	HER	2400	1384	<43500	WIN	CCI	350		6	SPR
5	200	SPR	BJ	HP	21.0	HOD	H110	1324	<43500	WIN	CCI	350		6	SPR
6	200	SPR	BJ	HP	14.2	HER	BDOT	1361	<43500	REM	CCI	350		6	SPR
7	210	WIN	FLN	SP	17.6	WIN	630	1460	38000	WIN	WIN	7-111	1.590	*10	WIN
8	210	WIN	FLN	SP	20.4	WIN	296	1460	24000	WIN	WIN	7-111	1.590	*10	WIN
9	210	HDY	FLN	HP	20.0	HER	2400	1350		REM	FED	150	1.580	6	HDY
10	210	SRA	FLN	HP	20.6	HOD	H110	1300		REM	CCI	300		6	SRA
11	210	REM	FLN	SP	22.0	DUP	4227	1570	39800	REM	REM	2½	1.590	*10	DUP
12	220	SPR	BJ	SP	20.0	HOD	H110	1305	<43500	REM	CCI	350		6	SPR
13	210	WIN	FLN	LP	7.4	WIN	231	1125	28000	WIN	WIN	7-111	1.590	*10	WIN
14	210	REM	FLN	LP	7.5	DUP	700X	1230	39900	REM	REM	2½	1.590	*10	DUP
15	210	REM	FLN	LP	12.5	DUP	4756	1450	39600	REM	REM	2½	1.590	*10	DUP
16	210	CAST	FLN	LP	9.0	DUP	4756	1050		REM	REM	2½	1.590	4	NRA
17	210	CAST	FLN	LP	8.8	HER	UNIQ	1050		REM	REM	2½	1.590	4	NRA

.44 SPECIAL

The .44 Special was introduced about 1907 by Smith & Wesson, to provide a more powerful .44-caliber cartridge than their famous .44 Russian, which had been popular since the 1870's. Heavy-frame S.&W. revolvers chambered for the .44 Special were widely used with "souped-up" handloads prior to the introduction of the .44 Magnum. Though this practice is certainly not without its hazards, it may well have influenced Smith & Wesson to introduce the .44 Magnum in 1956, as "souped-up" .38 Special loads in heavy-frame revolvers had influenced the development of the .357 Magnum cartridge 20 years earlier.

Owing to the existence of old .44 Special revolvers, some of foreign origin and uncertain strength, the chamber pressure of .44 Special factory loads has been maintained at the very moderate pressure level of 14,000 c.u.p. That limit should not be exceeded in old guns, or in the light-frame guns currently manufactured for the .44 Special cartridge. Although somewhat higher levels are safe in heavy-frame revolvers of high quality, there is no longer any excuse for overloading

the .44 Special cartridge, since the .44 Magnum easily and safely exceeds the performance of the heaviest loads that can safely be fired in a .44 Special.

Some old .44 Special cases are of balloon-head construction, and it is best to avoid their use. All cases of recent manufacture are of modern solid-head construction.

The maximum product average chamber pressure for the .44 Special has been established at 18,000 c.u.p.
   Max. Case Length: 1.160″ **Trim-To Length:** 1.155″
Max. Overall Length: 1.615″ **Primer Size:** Large Pistol **Bullet Dia.:** .429″

HANDGUN LOADS FOR THE .44 SPECIAL

LOAD NUMBER	BULLET				POWDER			VELOCITY FPS	PRESSURE CUP	CASE BRAND	PRIMER		CARTRIDGE OAL	BARREL LENGTH	DATA SOURCE
	WEIGHT	BRAND	SHAPE	TYPE	WEIGHT	BRAND	TYPE				BRAND	TYPE			
1	180	SRA	FLN	HP	16.0	HER	2400	900		WIN	CCI	300		4	SRA
2	180	SRA	FLN	HP	18.5	DUP	4227	900		WIN	CCI	300		4	SRA
3	200	SPR	FLN	HP	6.2	WIN	231	806	<15900	WIN	CCI	300		4	SPR
4	200	SPR	FLN	HP	13.0	HER	2400	911	<15900	WIN	CCI	350		4	SPR
5	225	SPR	BJ	HP	6.7	HER	UNIQ	782	<15900	WIN	CCI	300		4	SPR
6	240	SPR	FLN	SP	7.5	HOD	HS5	775	<15900	WIN	CCI	350		4	SPR
7	240	SPR	BJ	SP	11.5	HER	2400	739	<15900	WIN	CCI	350		4	SPR
8	240	SRA	FLN	HP	17.2	HOD	H110	950		WIN	CCI	300		4	SRA
9	240	SRA	FLN	HP	17.3	DUP	4227	900		WIN	CCI	300		4	SRA
10	185	CAST	WC	LP	4.5	HER	BEYE	830	4200	WIN	WIN	7-111		6½	NRA
11	185	CAST	WC	LP	6.0	HER	BEYE	1031	12840	WIN	WIN	7-111		6½	NRA
12	215	CAST	SWC	LP	5.0	HER	BEYE	804	8480	WIN	WIN	7-111		6½	NRA
13	240	HDY	SWC	LP	7.3	DUP	4756	1000	<14000	WIN	FED	150	1.500	*8¼	HDY
14	240	SPR	SWC	LP	7.5	HOD	HS5	804	<15900	WIN	CCI	350		4	SPR
15	246	WIN	RNN	LP	5.4	WIN	231	795	12500	WIN	WIN	7-111	1.615	*6½	WIN
16	246	REM	RNN	LP	18.5	DUP	4227	945	13500	REM	REM	2½	1.615	6½	DUP
17	250	CAST	SWC	LP	7.5	HER	UNIQ	928	11250	WIN	WIN	7-111		6½	NRA
18	250	CAST	SWC	LP	5.0	HER	BEYE	823	10370	WIN	WIN	7-111		6½	NRA
19	120	SPR	BALL	L	2.3	HER	BEYE	504		WIN	CCI	300		4	SPR
20	120	SPR	BALL	L	2.6	DUP	700X	509		WIN	CCI	300		4	SPR
21	120	SPR	BALL	L	2.8	WIN	231	488		WIN	CCI	300		4	SPR

.44 MAGNUM

Introduced by Remington, in collaboration with Smith & Wesson, in 1956, the .44 Magnum was by far the most powerful standard handgun cartridge at that time. It is still the most powerful standard revolver cartridge, and its popularity seems to be undiminishing nearly 25 years after its introduction.

Development of the .44 Magnum seems to have been a logical step in the progression of Smith & Wesson through several generations of successively more powerful large-bore handgun cartridges. The .44 S.&W. American cartridge, which was probably in use before 1870, was succeeded by the more powerful .44 Russian on the civilian market about 1878. The .44 Russian was in turn succeeded by the .44 Special in about 1907, and the .44 Special was succeeded by the .44 Magnum nearly 50 years later.

The .44 Magnum is capable of fine accuracy, though the recoil is so severe that many handgunners cannot shoot the gun well for many shots using full-charge loads. More moderate loads are far more pleasant for most handgunners to use, and Remington now has introduced a reduced load using a lead bullet, available as a factory load. With a 240-grain bullet developing up to 1,350 fps in a revolver, the .44 Magnum full-charge load is very impressive. It is undoubtedly the best choice for a handgunner who hunts big game with a revolver, provided, of course, that he can shoot it well in the field.

The maximum product average chamber pressure established for .44 Magnum factory ammunition is 43,500 c.u.p.

Max. Case Length: 1.285″ **Trim-To Length:** 1.280″
Max. Overall Length: 1.610″ **Primer Size:** Large Pistol **Bullet Dia.:** .429″

HANDGUN LOADS FOR THE .44 MAGNUM

LOAD NUMBER	BULLET				POWDER			VELOCITY FPS	PRESSURE CUP	CASE BRAND	PRIMER		CARTRIDGE OAL	BARREL LENGTH	DATA SOURCE
	WEIGHT	BRAND	SHAPE	TYPE	WEIGHT	BRAND	TYPE				BRAND	TYPE			
1	180	SRA	FLN	HP	12.6	HER	UNIQ	1400		SUV	CCI	350		7½	SRA
2	180	SRA	FLN	HP	14.8	DUP	4756	1500		SUV	CCI	350		7½	SRA
3	180	SRA	FLN	HP	22.9	WIN	630	1550		SUV	CCI	350		7½	SRA
4	180	SRA	FLN	HP	29.0	HOD	H110	1600		SUV	CCI	350		7½	SRA
5	200	SPR	FLN	HP	19.0	HER	BDOT	1556	<43500	SPR	CCI	350		7½	SPR
6	200	SPR	FLN	HP	27.0	DUP	4227	1492	<43500	SPR	CCI	350		7½	SPR

HANDGUN LOADS FOR THE .44 MAGNUM

LOAD NUMBER	BULLET				POWDER			VELOCITY FPS	PRESSURE CUP	CASE BRAND	PRIMER		CARTRIDGE OAL	BARREL LENGTH	DATA SOURCE
	WEIGHT	BRAND	SHAPE	TYPE	WEIGHT	BRAND	TYPE				BRAND	TYPE			
7	200	SPR	FLN	HP	12.3	HER	UNIQ	1403	<43500	SPR	CCI	350		7½	SPR
8	200	HDY	FLN	HP	15.0	DUP	4756	1400	<40000	REM	FED	150	1.590	7½	HDY
9	200	HDY	FLN	HP	24.5	HER	2400	1450	<40000	FRO	WIN	7M-111F	1.590	7½	HDY
10	200	HDY	FLN	HP	11.8	HER	UNIQ	1250	<40000	FRO	WIN	7M-111F	1.590	7½	HDY
11	225	SPR	FLN	BJHP	17.9	HER	BDOT	1488	<43500	SPR	CCI	350		7½	SPR
12	225	SPR	FLN	BJHP	25.0	DUP	4227	1471	<43500	SPR	CCI	350		7½	SPR
13	225	SPR	FLN	BJHP	11.9	HER	UNIQ	1350	<43500	SPR	CCI	350		7½	SPR
14	240	SPR	FLN	SP	24.0	DUP	4227	1312	<43500	SPR	CCI	350		7½	SPR
15	240	SPR	FLN	HP	24.4	HOD	H110	1416	<43500	SPR	CCI	350		7½	SPR
16	240	HDY	FLN	HP	20.9	WIN	630	1300	<40000	FRO	FED	150	1.590	7½	HDY
17	240	SRA	FLN	HP	18.3	HER	BDOT	1400		SUV	CCI	350		7½	SRA
18	240	SRA	FLN	HP	24.7	WIN	296	1400		SUV	CCI	350		7½	SRA
19	120	SPR	BALL	L	2.9	HER	BEYE	549		SPR	CCI	300		7½	SPR
20	184	CAST	WC	LP	5.0	HER	UNIQ	745		REM	REM	2½		*8¼	NRA
21	215	CAST		LG	8.0	HER	RDOT	1070		SPR	CCI	300		7½	SPR
22	215	CAST		LG	23.0	DUP	4227	1341		SPR	CCI	350		7½	SPR
23	240	SPR	SWC	LP	7.0	HER	UNIQ	906		SPR	CCI	300		7½	SPR
24	240	SPR	SWC	LP	8.5	HOD	HS5	932		SPR	CCI	300		7½	SPR
25	240	REM	SWC	LG	15.6	DUP	4756	1420	40000	REM	REM	2½	1.610	*8	DUP
26	240	REM	SWC	LG	25.0	DUP	4227	1530	39900	REM	REM	2½	1.610	*8	DUP
27	240	WIN	SWC	LP	19.5	WIN	630	1425	37000	WIN	WIN	7-111	1.610	*6½	WIN
28	240	WIN	SWC	LP	25.0	WIN	296	1560	37500	WIN	WIN	7-111	1.610	*6½	WIN
29	248	CAST	SWC	LP	22.0	HER	2400	1372	26700	REM	REM	2½	1.700	*8¼	NRA
30	250	CAST	SWC	LG	24.0	HOD	H110	1596	39200	WIN	CCI	350		7½	HOD

.44-40 (.44 W.C.F.)

The .44-40 was first introduced by Winchester in 1873, for the now-famous Model 1873 lever-action rifle. Colt soon adopted it for their single-action revolver, and a great many other arms have been chambered for the .44-40 during the century since its introduction. It was probably the most widely used cartridge by those frontiersmen who wanted a rifle and handgun using the same ammunition. Originally using a 200-grain lead bullet and 40 grains of blackpowder, the .44-40 developed a velocity of about 1,200 fps in a rifle. Early smokeless loads produced practically the same ballistics. Like the .32-20 and .38-40, the .44-40 was factory loaded for some years with a special high-velocity load, intended only for use with the Winchester Model 1892 rifle and other rifles of comparable strength. These loads would not be fired in any handgun.

The .44-40 is still listed as a factory load, with ballistics nearly the same as those of the original blackpowder load. Chamber pressure is limited to a moderate 13,000 c.u.p., in deference to the relatively weak old guns in which the ammunition might be used. Colt single-action revolvers having serial numbers below 160,000 were not intended for use with any smokeless loads. One load listed here was furnished by Winchester-Western, and is consistent with their factory loading practice.

Some old .44-40 cases were of balloon-head construction, and should not be used for handloading. Unless the handloader can recognize balloon-head cases, he should use only those known to be of recent manufacture.

The maximum product average chamber pressure for the .44-40 cartridge is now established at 13,700 c.u.p.

Max. Case Length: 1.305″ **Trim-To Length:** 1.300″
Max. Overall Length: 1.592″ **Primer Size:** Large Pistol **Bullet Dia.:** .425″ - .429″

HANDGUN LOADS FOR THE .44-40

LOAD NUMBER	BULLET				POWDER			VELOCITY FPS	PRESSURE CUP	CASE BRAND	PRIMER		CARTRIDGE OAL	BARREL LENGTH	DATA SOURCE
	WEIGHT	BRAND	SHAPE	TYPE	WEIGHT	BRAND	TYPE				BRAND	TYPE			
1	200	WIN	FLN	SP	13.0	WIN	630	975	<13000	WIN	WIN	7-111	1.590	*7½	WIN
2	200	CAST	FLN	LP	5.0	HER	BEYE	750		WIN	WIN	7-111	1.590	7½	NRA
3	200	CAST	FLN	LP	8.1	HER	UNIQ	850		WIN	WIN	7-111	1.590	7½	NRA
4	200	CAST	FLN	LP	12.0	WIN	630	850		WIN	WIN	7-111	1.590	7½	NRA
5	200	CAST	FLN	LP	17.5	DUP	4227	800		WIN	WIN	7-111	1.590	7½	NRA

*Unvented test barrel. Lower velocities expected in revolvers.

.45 A.C.P.

The cartridge commercially known as the .45 A.C.P. is, in military nomenclature, "Cartridge, Caliber .45, Ball, M 1911," and it has been in use since 1911 by the armed forces of the U.S. This military load uses a round-nose, full-jacket, 230-grain bullet, and the specified average velocity is 855 ± 25 fps, instrumental at 25.5 feet from the muzzle. The maximum average chamber pressure must not exceed 19,000 psi, as measured by the copper-crusher method, according to military specifications. The most common commercial .45 A.C.P. load is practically identical to the military load, except that the nominal muzzle velocity is 810 fps. This type of ammunition is usually called "hardball," distinguishing it from the wadcutter match loads and other loads employing various different bullets.

The .45 A.C.P. hardball load has been for years regarded by many handgunners as the ultimate defensive load for autoloading pistols. It is indeed a powerful cartridge, and its heavy bullet has been widely cited as accounting for its supposedly extraordinary effectiveness.

Various criteria have been devised for ranking handgun loads with respect to relative effectiveness or "stopping power," and the .45 A.C.P. usually stands near the top in those rankings. In general, however, it appears that the criteria have often been devised and manipulated to lend the appearance of quantitative authenticity to preconceived intuitive opinions, rather than to reflect any scientific basis in fact. The science of wound ballistics has progressed greatly since World War II, though that fact is little appreciated outside the scientific community. There are now objective effectiveness criteria, based on sophisticated research techniques that involve high-speed X-ray photography, biophysical evaluation of wound-ballistic data by professional medical experts, statistical probability analysis, and computer models which can combine and evaluate these factors. Studies using these techniques have been conducted by military research laboratories for many years, but the results (and descriptions of the techniques themselves) have been deliberately limited in distribution, for very good reasons. One such study was done in the early 1970's, by the U.S. Army Ballistic Research Laboratory, for the Law Enforcement Assistance Administration of the U.S. Department of Justice. It involved 142 different handgun loads, of various calibers, that might be employed for defensive purposes by law-enforcement officers. The results were summarized in a report issued in August 1975, and distribution was not limited. Curiously, this milestone report has received little publicity among non-professional handgun enthusiasts, though the results have not been systematically challenged or contradicted.

In these studies, the two .45 A.C.P. commercial hardball loads ranked 110th and 113th among the 142 cartridges tested. Among five different .45 A.C.P. loads

tested, the 230-grain "hardball" loads ranked last, far behind the 185-grain jacketed hollow-point load (34th) and considerably behind the two 185-grain wadcutter target loads (55th and 95th). The "macho" image of the .45 A.C.P. hardball load still persists, however, especially among enthusiasts in some combat-style competitive shooting events, where the rules sometimes penalize the competitor who uses a supposedly less effective cartridge.

The .45 Model 1911, or M1911A1, or "Colt's Government Model" in civilian nomenclature, is a remarkable gun, noted in its original form as a highly reliable military pistol under adverse environmental conditions, and in its accurized form as a superb target pistol. The venerable 230-grain hardball load, however, has little merit except that it feeds very reliably, even in the roughest military pistols. It has long been known that the wadcutter target bullets produced better accuracy, and it is now clearly established that they are more effective defense loads, even at the reduced velocities of target loads. At the higher velocities made possible by reduced bullet weight, either wadcutters or expanding bullets in the .45 A.C.P. are far superior to the round-nose 230-grain hardball load for defensive use.

The maximum product average chamber pressure for commercial .45 ACP ammunition is 19,900 c.u.p.

Max. Case Length: .898″ **Trim-To Length:** .895″
Max. Overall Length: 1.275″ **Primer Size:** Large Pistol **Bullet Dia.:** .450″ - .453″

HANDGUN LOADS FOR THE .45 ACP

LOAD NUMBER	BULLET				POWDER			VELOCITY FPS	PRESSURE CUP	CASE BRAND	PRIMER		CARTRIDGE OAL	BARREL LENGTH	DATA SOURCE
	WEIGHT	BRAND	SHAPE	TYPE	WEIGHT	BRAND	TYPE				BRAND	TYPE			
1	185	REM	SWC	FJ	4.0	DUP	700X	760	10100	REM	REM	2½	1.180	5	DUP
2	185	REM	SWC	FJ	5.5	DUP	700X	1030	17100	REM	REM	2½	1.180	5	DUP
3	185	REM	FLN	HP	5.5	DUP	700X	925	17700	REM	REM	2½	1.275	5	DUP
4	185	REM	FLN	HP	8.4	DUP	4756	1010	18000	REM	REM	2½	1.275	5	DUP
5	185	WIN	SWC	FJ	5.1	WIN	231	765	11500	WIN	WIN	7-111	1.170	5	WIN
6	185	SRA	FLN	HP	4.2	HER	BEYE	750		REM	CCI	300		5	SRA
7	185	HDY	FLN	HP	5.0	HOD	HP38	762	12000	WIN	WIN	7-111		7	HOD
8	185	SRA	FLN	HP	7.3	HER	UNIQ	950		REM	CCI	300		5	SRA
9	185	HDY	FLN	HP	5.7	HER	BEYE	900	<18000	REM	FED	150	1.230	5	HDY
10	200	SPR	FLN	HP	9.0	HER	BDOT	890	15200	SPR	CCI	300	1.150	5	HER
11	225	SPR	FLN	HP	7.2	HER	UNIQ	940	<19900	SPR	CCI	300		5	SPR
12	230	WIN	RNN	FJ	5.6	WIN	231	795	17000	WIN	WIN	7-111	1.275	5	WIN
13	230	REM	RNN	FJ	4.8	HER	BEYE	795							HER
14	230	REM	RNN	FJ	5.2	DUP	700X	850	17600	REM	REM	2½	1.275	5	DUP
15	230	WIN	RNN	FJ	5.3	HOD	HP38	832	16800	WIN	WIN	7-111		7	HOD
16	240	SRA	FLN	HP	9.1	HER	BDOT	850		REM	CCI	300		5	SRA
17	260	SPR	FLN	HP	6.4	DUP	4756	830	<19900	SPR	CCI	300		5	SPR
18	200	SPR	SWC	LP	4.2	HER	BEYE	744		SPR	CCI	300		5	SPR
19	200	SPR	SWC	LP	4.6	HER	BEYE	807		SPR	CCI	300		5	SPR
20	200	SPR	SWC	LP	3.8	DUP	700X	715		SPR	CCI	300		5	SPR
21	200	SPR	SWC	LP	4.2	DUP	700X	790		SPR	CCI	300		5	SPR
22	200	SPR	SWC	LP	4.6	WIN	231	739		SPR	CCI	300		5	SPR
23	200	SPR	SWC	LP	5.0	WIN	231	803		SPR	CCI	300		5	SPR
24	200	SPR	SWC	LP	6.7	HOD	HS5	721		SPR	CCI	300		5	SPR
25	225	CAST	RNN	LP	6.5	HER	UNIQ	820		MIL	CCI	300		5	NRA
26	225	CAST	RNN	LP	5.9	DUP	7625	820		MIL	CCI	300		5	NRA
27	225	CAST	RNN	LP	5.6	WIN	231	820		MIL	CCI	300		5	NRA
28	230	SPR	RNN	LP	7.6	HOD	HS5	831		SPR	CCI	300		5	SPR
29	230	SPR	RNN	LP	6.4	HER	HERCO	845		SPR	CCI	300		5	SPR
30	230	SPR	RNN	LP	4.7	DUP	700X	838		SPR	CCI	300		5	SPR

.45 AUTO RIM

This cartridge was designed and introduced shortly after World War I, by the Peters Cartridge Company. It was designed specifically for use in the Model 1917 military revolvers, manufactured by both Colt and Smith & Wesson during World War I, which were chambered for the .45 Model 1911 (.45 A.C.P.) cartridge.

The Model 1917 revolvers were ingenious adaptations of non-military revolvers in the Colt and S.&W. lines, enabling them to use the same rimless cartridge employed in the Model 1911 autoloading service pistol. This was accomplished by use of the so-called "half-moon" clips, flat steel devices of roughly semicircular configuration, each of which could be snap-assembled into three cartridges by engaging the extractor grooves. Two clips were loaded into the six-shot cylinder of the gun. During ejection, the clip was engaged by the ejector, since the cartridges had no rim to be engaged in the normal manner. The clips

provided ammunition interchangeability between the Model 1917 revolvers and Model 1911 pistol, and worked very well, but the necessity of using them is a nuisance for non-military users of the revolvers. To avoid this nuisance, Peters designed a special cartridge, having the body configuration of the .45 A.C.P., but a narrow rim, of sufficient thickness to occupy the space left by omission of the half-moon clips in the Model 1917 revolvers. These rimmed cartridges are, of course, engaged by the revolver extractor in the normal manner.

The use of .45 Auto Rim cases is not required in Model 1917 revolvers, but they afford a useful measure of convenience. They may also be used in the S.&W. .45 revolvers such as the Model 1950 and 1950 Target, and the Model 1955 Target which is also called the Model 25. Most Model 1917 revolvers can, in fact, be fired with .45 A.C.P. ammunition without the half-moon clip, since they are chambered so as to control headspace on the case mouth as it is done in the Model 1911 pistol, but the extractor does not then function, and cases must be individually extracted by other means. In a few early Model 1917 revolvers, the chamber is not designed to control headspace, and the .45 Auto Rim cartridge is then the only alternative to the use of half-moon clips.

Because the cylinder walls are rather thin, and the steels used were not as strong as those used in modern revolvers, the Model 1917 revolvers are less tolerant of excessive pressure than is the Model 1911 pistol. Handloaders should therefore be especially cautious, and select only conservative loads in the .45 Auto Rim

cartridge, or in .45 A.C.P. ammunition to be fired in the Model 1917 revolver.

The maximum product average chamber pressure for the .45 Auto Rim cartridge is established at 16,900 c.u.p. This is less by 3,000 c.u.p. than the limit imposed on the .45 ACP, which should emphasize the advisability of loading conservatively for the old Model 1917 revolvers.

Max. Case Length: .898″ Trim-To Length: .895″
Max. Overall Length: 1.275″ Primer Size: Large Pistol Bullet Dia.: .450″ - .452″

HANDGUN LOADS FOR THE .45 AUTO RIM

LOAD NUMBER	BULLET				POWDER			VELOCITY FPS	PRESSURE CUP	CASE BRAND	PRIMER		CARTRIDGE OAL	BARREL LENGTH	DATA SOURCE
	WEIGHT	BRAND	SHAPE	TYPE	WEIGHT	BRAND	TYPE				BRAND	TYPE			
1	185	HDY	FLN	HP	6.5	HER	RDOT	950		REM	FED	150	1.220	5½	HDY
2	185	SRA	FLN	HP	7.6	HER	UNIQ	1000		REM	CCI	300		5½	SRA
3	200	SPR	FLN	HP	8.2	HOD	HS5	923	<16900	REM	CCI	300		6½	SPR
4	225	SPR	FLN	HP	6.9	HER	UNIQ	900	<16900	REM	CCI	300		6½	SPR
5	240	SRA	FLN	HP	5.4	HER	BDOT	750		REM	CCI	300		5½	SRA
6	200	SPR	SWC	LP	4.3	DUP	700X	743	<16900	REM	CCI	300		6½	SPR
7	200	SPR	SWC	LP	4.5	HER	RDOT	717	<16900	REM	CCI	300		6½	SPR
8	250	SPR	SWC	LP	8.6	HER	BDOT	840	14400	WIN	WIN	111	1.200		NRA
9	255	CAST	SWC	LP	8.4	HER	BDOT	849	14400	WIN	WIN	111	1.210		NRA
10	300	CAST	FLN	LP	7.1	HER	BDOT	740	13300	WIN	WIN	111	1.265		NRA
11	141	SPR	BALL	L	3.0	HER	BEYE	592		REM	CCI	300		6½	SPR
12	141	SPR	BALL	L	3.0	DUP	700X	587		REM	CCI	300		6½	SPR
13	141	SPR	BALL	L	3.5	WIN	231	580		REM	CCI	300		6½	SPR
14	141	SPR	BALL	L	3.5	HOD	HP38	631		REM	CCI	300		6½	SPR

.45 COLT

Introduced in 1873 as an original cartridge for the famous Colt single-action "Peacemaker" revolver, the .45 Colt has been justly famous for more than a century. The late General J. S. Hatcher wrote during 1934, in his classic book *Pistols and Revolvers,* that the Remington blackpowder load in the .45 Colt used a 250-grain bullet and 40 grains of powder to produce "a velocity of 910 foot-seconds and a muzzle energy of 460 foot-pounds, which is the highest muzzle energy of any revolver or pistol cartridge now sold." That was, of course, more than 40 years into the era of smokeless powder, and just one year before the introduction of the "modern" .357 Magnum. This blackpowder factory load was more powerful than the smokeless load for the .45 Colt at that time, and is so even today, since the standard factory load now uses a 255-grain bullet at 860 fps, for about 420 foot-pounds of muzzle energy.

Loading for the .45 Colt requires special caution on the part of handloaders. Because guns for it have been made for more than 100 years, there are great differences in strength among them. The Colt single-action revolvers having serial numbers below 160,000 were made during the blackpowder era, and most authorities agree that they should not be fired with any smokeless loads whatsoever. Subsequent production of Colts were proofed for smokeless powder, and in sound condition they should be safe with current smokeless factory loads, and comparable handloads, developing pressures that do not exceed 14,000 c.u.p. Some modern guns chambered for the .45 Colt are much stronger, and can safely withstand considerably higher chamber pressures. These modern and stronger guns include, most notably, the Ruger Blackhawk revolver and the Thompson-Center Contender single-shot pistol.

The loads listed here are in three categories. Loads 1 through 8 are jacketed-bullet loads that are supposed to develop pressures not exceeding the limit established for factory loads. Loads 9 through 16 are lead-bullet loads in the same pressure category. Loads 1 through 16 should therefore be safe to fire in guns that are safe with modern smokeless factory loads. It may be found, however, that modern jacketed bullets give poor accuracy in some of the old .45 Colt revolvers because the guns may have groove diameters up to about .455 of an inch, whereas the bullets are normally .451 to .452 of an inch in diameter. In those old guns, lead-bullet loads generally shoot more accurately. If cast, the bullets should be sized to the groove diameter of the barrel. Swaged lead factory bullets are soft enough to expand upon firing, and generally give satisfactory accuracy even if they are somewhat undersize for the barrel. The .45 Colt barrels of more recent production (generally since World War II) usually have groove diameters of .451 to .452 inch, and shoot well with either lead or jacketed bullets.

Loads 17 through load 23 develop pressures generally exceeding the 14,000-c.u.p. limit for factory loads, and must not be used in any gun except the Ruger Blackhawk or Thompson-Center Contender, or other guns known to be of comparable strength. During its long existence, the .45 Colt has sometimes been handloaded to pressures far in excess of the factory-load limit, and these heavy loads have been fired in Colt and other revolvers, *usually* without blowing them up. Nevertheless, such loads may seriously damage those guns, and their use cannot be recommended, even though they may be found in some articles or old books on handloading.

Old .45 Colt cases are also suspect. Some are of the balloon-head type, rather than the modern solid-head type, and such cases are not suitable for handloading. Unless the handloader can make the distinction between these types of cases, he should use only cases known to be of recent manufacture.

The maximum product average chamber pressure for the .45 Colt factory ammunition is not to exceed 15,900 c.u.p., which implies a working pressure of about 14,000 c.u.p. for this cartridge.

Max. Case Length: 1.285″ **Trim-To Length:** 1.280″
Max. Overall Length: 1.600″ **Primer Size:** Large Pistol **Bullet Dia.:** .450″ - .454″

HANDGUN LOADS FOR THE .45 COLT

LOAD NUMBER	BULLET				POWDER			VELOCITY FPS	PRESSURE CUP	CASE BRAND	PRIMER		CARTRIDGE OAL	BARREL LENGTH	DATA SOURCE
	WEIGHT	BRAND	SHAPE	TYPE	WEIGHT	BRAND	TYPE				BRAND	TYPE			
1	185	HDY	FLN	HP	10.5	HER	UNIQ	1000		WIN	FED	150		4¾	HDY
2	185	SRA	FLN	HP	22.2	DUP	4227	1100		WIN	CCI	300		5½	SRA
3	200	SPR	FLN	HP	10.0	HER	HERCO	1020	<15900	WIN	CCI	300		5½	SPR
4	225	SPR	FLN	HP	17.7	DUP	4227	945	<15900	WIN	CCI	350		5½	SPR
5	240	SRA	FLN	HP	7.5	HER	BEYE	900		WIN	CCI	300		5½	SRA
6	250	HDY	FLN	HP	14.5	WIN	630	900		WIN	FED	150	1.595	4¾	HDY
7	260	SPR	FLN	HP	16.5	DUP	4227	864	<15900	WIN	CCI	350		5½	SPR
8	260	SPR	FLN	HP	8.5	HER	UNIQ	874	<15900	WIN	CCI	300		5½	SPR
9	200	SPR	SWC	LP	9.5	HER	UNIQ	1054	<15900	WIN	CCI	300		5½	SPR
10	235	CAST	WC	LP	5.5	HER	BEYE	850	11500	REM	REM	2½	1.550	7½	NRA
11	250	SPR	SWC	LP	8.5	HER	UNIQ	898	<15900	WIN	CCI	350		5½	SPR
12	250	REM	FLN	LP	8.5	DUP	PB	880	13400	REM	REM	2½	1.600	5½	DUP
13	250	REM	FLN	LP	12.5	DUP	4756	930	13500	REM	REM	2½	1.600	5½	DUP
14	250	REM	FLN	LP	23.0	DUP	4227	980	13500	REM	REM	2½	1.600	5½	DUP
15	255	WIN	FLN	LP	7.1	WIN	231	875	13000	WIN	WIN	7-111	1.600	5½	WIN
16	255	CAST	SWC	LP	8.5	HER	UNIQ	930	12600	REM	REM	2½	1.640	7½	NRA
17	200	SPR	FLN	HP	16.5	HER	BDOT	1356	<25000	WIN	CCI	350		7½	SPR
18	225	SPR	FLN	HP	19.5	HER	2400	1223	<25000	WIN	CCI	350		7½	SPR
19	240	SRA	FLN	HP	19.2	WIN	630	1200		WIN	CCI	350		7½	SRA
20	250	HDY	FLN	HP	16.4	WIN	630	950		WIN	FED	150	1.595	4¾	HDY
21	260	SPR	FLN	HP	19.0	HER	2400	1168	<25000	WIN	CCI	350		7½	SPR
22	260	SPR	FLN	HP	20.0	HOD	H110	1151	<25000	WIN	CCI	350		7½	SPR
23	260	SPR	FLN	HP	14.8	HER	BDOT	1115	<25000	WIN	CCI	350		7½	SPR

.45 Winchester Magnum

This powerful handgun cartridge was introduced by Winchester-Western in 1978. It was intended specifically for use in the Wildey autoloading pistol, to be manufactured by the Wildey Firearms Company of Cheshire, Connecticut. Owing to some unexpected delays in preparations to produce the Wildey pistol, the .45 Winchester Magnum cartridge was, at the time of its introduction, without any production firearm in which it could be used. Thompson-Center soon chambered their versatile Contender pistol for the new cartridge, and the Contender remains, in mid-1980, the only production gun adapted to this cartridge. The difficulties in producing the Wildey have now reportedly been overcome, and initial production of the gun for the .45 Magnum cartridge is scheduled for October 1980. The Wildey pistol is also to be offered for the 9mm Winchester Magnum cartridge, specifically designed for this handgun, and initial quantities of the 9mm guns are scheduled for production in late 1980. Though the 9mm Winchester Magnum cartridge has been announced by Winchester-Western, the ammunition has not yet been introduced to the market, and loading data for it are not available.

The Wildey pistol is a locked-breech gas-operated gun, capable of using ammunition that develops chamber pressures higher than those which other production autoloading pistols can accommodate. The nominal working chamber pressure for the .45 Magnum is reported to be about 40,000 c.u.p. (That of the 9mm Magnum is about 45,000 c.u.p.) The Winchester-Western factory load for the .45 Magnum is listed at a muzzle velocity of 1400 fps, with a 230-grain full-jacketed bullet, developed in a 5-inch test barrel. The muzzle energy of this factory load is listed at 1,001 foot-pounds, exceeding that of any other factory load listed for handguns by Winchester-Western. Higher velocity and energy are achieved when the cartridge is fired in the 10-inch or 14-inch barrels of the Contender pistol.

Max. Case Length: 1.198″ **Trim-To Length:** 1.193″
Max. Overall Length: 1.575″ **Primer Size:** Large Pistol
Bullet Dia.: .452″

HANDGUN LOADS FOR THE .45 WINCHESTER MAGNUM

LOAD NUMBER	BULLET				POWDER			VELOCITY FPS	PRESSURE CUP	CASE BRAND	PRIMER		CARTRIDGE OAL	BARREL LENGTH	DATA SOURCE
	WEIGHT	BRAND	SHAPE	TYPE	WEIGHT	BRAND	TYPE				BRAND	TYPE			
1	185	HDY	FLN	HP	21.3	HER	BDOT	1900		WIN	WIN	7M-111F	1.510	14	HDY
2	185	HDY	FLN	HP	21.8	HOD	HS7	1850		WIN	WIN	7M-111F	1.510	14	HDY
3	200	SPR	FLN	HP	19.0	HER	BDOT	1640		WIN	CCI	350		10	SPR
4	200	SPR	FLN	HP	32.0	WIN	680	1547		WIN	CCI	350		10	SPR
5	200	SPR	FLN	HP	26.5	DUP	4227	1539		WIN	CCI	350		10	SPR
6	225	SPR	FLN	HP	17.5	HER	BDOT	1514		WIN	CCI	350		10	SPR
7	225	SPR	FLN	HP	23.5	HOD	H110	1524		WIN	CCI	350		10	SPR
8	225	SPR	FLN	HP	23.0	DUP	4759	1409		WIN	CCI	350		10	SPR
9	230	HDY	FLN	FJ	18.0	HER	BDOT	1650		WIN	WIN	7M-111F	1.500	14	HDY
10	230	HDY	FLN	FJ	21.8	HER	2400	1550		WIN	WIN	7M-111F	1.500	14	HDY
11	230	HDY	FLN	FJ	25.0	DUP	4227	1500		WIN	WIN	7M-111F	1.500	14	HDY
12	230	HDY	FLN	FJ	18.0	HOD	HS7	1500		WIN	WIN	7M-111F	1.500	14	HDY
13	250	HDY	FLN	HP	16.8	HER	BDOT	1550		WIN	WIN	7M-111F	1.480	14	HDY
14	250	HDY	FLN	HP	24.2	DUP	4227	1500		WIN	WIN	7M-111F	1.480	14	HDY
15	250	HDY	FLN	HP	20.1	HER	2400	1450		WIN	WIN	7M-111F	1.480	14	HDY
16	250	HDY	FLN	HP	17.3	HOD	HS7	1450		WIN	WIN	7M-111F	1.480	14	HDY
17	260	SPR	FLN	HP	29.0	WIN	680	1435		WIN	CCI	350		10	SPR
18	260	SPR	FLN	HP	24.0	DUP	4227	1397		WIN	CCI	350		10	SPR
19	260	SPR	FLN	HP	16.0	HER	BDOT	1362		WIN	CCI	350		10	SPR
20	260	SPR	FLN	HP	22.0	HOD	H110	1319		WIN	CCI	350		10	SPR

REFERENCE SECTION

Standard Cartridge and Chamber Dimensions

Unlike some industrialized countries, the United States has no national laws governing critical dimensions and performance characteristics of ammunition or proof standards for firearms. Instead, through the establishment of recommendations by the Sporting Arms and Ammunition Manufacturers' Institute (SAAMI), a trade association representing nearly all major U.S. arms and ammunition manufacturers, a body of voluntary recommended practices and procedures has been generated by the American industry that generally serves to provide the standards that are imposed by law in other countries.

The SAAMI recommendations are in a virtually constant state of review, improvement and modernization. This process began in 1926 for civilian arms and ammunition, with roots dating to 1913 for military arms and ammunition. Major portions of the SAAMI recommendations have been accepted as voluntary industry consensus standards in accordance with recognized procedures of the American National Standards Institute and have been adopted and published as ANSI Standards. By supplying critical dimensions and certain performance criteria, these standards provide assurance of functional interchangeability of ammunition from various manufacturers in arms of designated calibers comparable to the assurance derived from practices established under law in other nations.

The following drawings are based on SAAMI material, some of it also found in ANSI Standards Z299.1, Z299.2, and Z299.3, reproduced here by permission in the interest of greater safety for handloaders. **This permission was granted by SAAMI to the National Rifle Association for use in this specific book, which is copyright material of the NRA, and does not include permission for further reproduction, which is therefore prohibited.** As a service to gunsmiths, handloaders and others in the firearms field, however, SAAMI will furnish on request official copies of the standard cartridge and chamber drawings from which the drawings here were adapted. Requests for information on current price and availability should be made, in writing to SAAMI, P.O. Box 218, Wallingford, CT. 06492.

The SAAMI practice for many years was to show only maximum cartridge dimensions, and only minimum chamber dimensions, on SAAMI drawings; tolerances were not specified. Current practice is to specify tolerances, as indicated on these drawings. The user should be aware of two important points concerning interpretation of these drawings, however.

First, they *do not* necessarily represent the manufacturing tolerances of any particular manufacturer of arms and/or ammunition. As a matter of practice, the manufacturing tolerances used by any particular producer are most likely to be less than the allowable tolerances shown on the SAAMI drawings. It is in the manufacturer's own interest to maintain the strictest dimensional control that is practicable for him, because this obviously can affect the quality of his products, and therefore his competitive position in respect to other manufacturers. Understandably, therefore, the manufacturing tolerances in use by any particular manufacturer are usually regarded as proprietary information, and are not publicly disclosed. The SAAMI tolerances can be regarded, in the practical interpretation, as limits that are very unlikely to be exceeded in the products of any manufacturer.

The second point is that some dimensions and tolerances shown on cartridge and/or chamber drawings are inseparably related to the design of the gages with which the measurements are made. The head-to-shoulder-cone length of a rimless cartridge, for example, is a case in point. It is impossible, in the normal processes by which cartridge cases are made, to form the case shoulder in the geometrically perfect frustrum of a cone, as it is necessarily depicted in a drawing. Since the important functional purpose of the shoulder is to control the headspace relationship between cartridge and chamber in the gun, the gage used to inspect cartridges for this characteristic is functionally designed to simulate the chamber in a gun. The handloader who attempts to measure the head-to-shoulder-cone length of a factory cartridge, without an accurate gage specifically designed for the purpose, might well find that his measurement does not fall within the tolerances listed on the drawing. In that case, the disparity is far more likely to be due to the method of measurement than to non-compliance of the cartridge with the drawing dimensions.

Probably the most important cartridge dimensions for the handloader, because they can affect the safety of reloaded ammunition, are the neck diameter, case length, and head-to-shoulder-cone length of the cartridge. Because case necks can thicken with repeated firing and reloading, the neck diameter of reloaded cartridges should be checked frequently, using an accurate micrometer or dial caliper, and checked against the drawing dimension. If the neck diameter exceeds that shown on the drawing, the cartridge might develop excessive chamber pressure, and should not be fired. Neck-reaming or neck-turning is then required if the case is to be used safely again. Similarly, case necks may lengthen with repeated reloading, and must be trimmed so as not to exceed the maximum drawing length, for safe use. The head-to-shoulder-cone length can be shortened by resizing, in some instances, with a particular combination of die and shell holder. It can also be shortened by firing loads developing very low chamber pressure. Further details on these subjects will be found elsewhere in the articles

in this book. It is good practice, however, for the handloader to obtain and use, for rimless cartridges, the specially designed case gages which have "GO" and "NO-GO" steps to indicate both head-to-shoulder-cone length and overall case length. Such gages are available from Forster Products, Inc., 82 E. Lanark Ave., Lanark, IL 61046, and from L. E. Wilson, Inc., P.O. Box 324, Cashmere, WA 98815, and perhaps from other manufacturers. Reference to cartridge drawings are not required for the use of these "GO/NO-GO" gages, and they provide virtually the only reliable way for a handloader to inspect his cartridges or cases for this important head-to-shoulder-cone dimension.

William C. Davis, Jr

WCD, Jr.

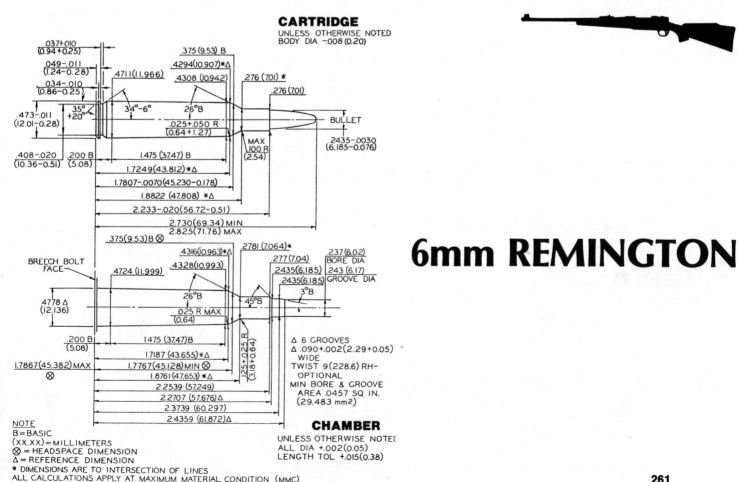

6mm REMINGTON

6.5mm REMINGTON MAGNUM

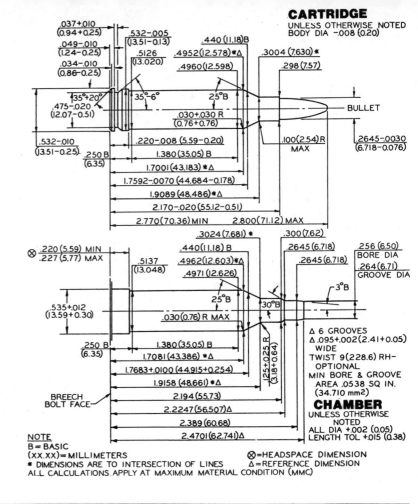

CARTRIDGE
UNLESS OTHERWISE NOTED
BODY DIA -.008 (0.20)

.037+.010
(0.94+0.25)
.049-.010
(1.24-0.25)
.034-.010
(0.86-0.25)
.532-.005
(13.51-0.13)
.5126
(13.020)
.475-.020
(12.07-0.51)
35°±20°
35°-6°
.440 (11.18)B
.4952(12.578)*Δ
.4960(12.598)
25°B
.030+.030 R
(0.76+0.76)
.3004 (7.630)*
.298 (7.57)
BULLET
.2645-.0030
(6.718-0.076)
.100(2.54)R
MAX
.532-.010
(13.51-0.25)
.250 B
(6.35)
.220-.008 (5.59-0.20)
1.380 (35.05) B
1.7001(43.183)*Δ
1.7592-.0070 (44.684-0.178)
1.9089 (48.486)*Δ
2.170-.020 (55.12-0.51)
2.770 (70.36) MIN   2.800 (71.12) MAX

⊗ .220 (5.59) MIN
.227 (5.77) MAX
.535+.012
(13.59+0.30)
.5137
(13.048)
.250 B
(6.35)
.3024(7.681)*
.440(11.18) B
.4962(12.603)*Δ
.4971 (12.626)
25°B
.030(0.76) R MAX
30°B
.125+.025 R
(3.18+0.64)
.300 (7.62)
.2645 (6.718)
.2645 (6.718)
3°B
.256 (6.50)
BORE DIA
.264 (6.71)
GROOVE DIA

BREECH
BOLT FACE
1.380 (35.05) B
1.7081(43.386)*Δ
1.7683+.0100 (44.915+0.254)
1.9158 (48.661)*Δ
2.194 (55.73)
2.2247 (56.507)Δ
2.389 (60.68)
2.4701 (62.741)Δ

Δ 6 GROOVES
Δ .095+.002(2.41+0.05)
WIDE
TWIST 9(228.6) RH-
OPTIONAL
MIN BORE & GROOVE
AREA .0538 SQ IN.
(34.710 mm2)

CHAMBER
UNLESS OTHERWISE
NOTED
ALL DIA +.002 (0.05)
LENGTH TOL +.015 (0.38)

NOTE
B = BASIC
(XX.XX) = MILLIMETERS
* DIMENSIONS ARE TO INTERSECTION OF LINES
ALL CALCULATIONS APPLY AT MAXIMUM MATERIAL CONDITION (MMC)
⊗ = HEADSPACE DIMENSION
Δ = REFERENCE DIMENSION

7mm-08 Remington

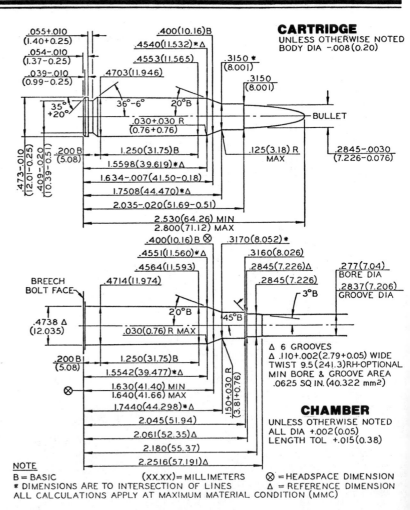

CARTRIDGE
UNLESS OTHERWISE NOTED
BODY DIA -.008 (0.20)

.055+.010
(1.40+0.25)
.054-.010
(1.37-0.25)
.039-.010
(0.99-0.25)
.4703(11.946)
35°
+20°
36°-6°
.400 (10.16)B
.4540(11.532)*Δ
.4553 (11.565)
20°B
.030+.030 R
(0.76+0.76)
.3150 *
(8.001)
.3150
(8.001)
BULLET
.2845-.0030
(7.226-0.076)
.125(3.18) R
MAX
.473-.010
(12.01-0.25)
.409-.020
(10.39-0.51)
.200 B
(5.08)
1.250 (31.75)B
1.5598(39.619)*Δ
1.634-.007 (41.50-0.18)
1.7508 (44.470)*Δ
2.035-.020 (51.69-0.51)
2.530 (64.26) MIN
2.800 (71.12) MAX

BREECH
BOLT FACE
.4738 Δ
(12.035)
.4714(11.974)
.400 (10.16)B ⊗
.4551(11.560)*Δ
.4564 (11.593)
20°B
.030(0.76) R MAX
45°B
.150+.030 R
(3.81+0.76)
.3170(8.052)*
.3160(8.026)
.2845(7.226)Δ
.2845(7.226)
3°B
.277(7.04)
BORE DIA
.2837(7.206)
GROOVE DIA
.200 B
(5.08)
⊗
1.250 (31.75)B
1.5542(39.477)*Δ
1.630(41.40) MIN
1.640(41.66) MAX
1.7440 (44.298)*Δ
2.045 (51.94)
2.061 (52.35)Δ
2.180 (55.37)
2.2516 (57.191)Δ

Δ 6 GROOVES
Δ .110+.002(2.79+0.05) WIDE
TWIST 9.5(241.3)RH-OPTIONAL
MIN BORE & GROOVE AREA
.0625 SQ IN. (40.322 mm2)

CHAMBER
UNLESS OTHERWISE NOTED
ALL DIA +.002(0.05)
LENGTH TOL +.015(0.38)

NOTE
B = BASIC   (XX.XX) = MILLIMETERS   ⊗ = HEADSPACE DIMENSION
* DIMENSIONS ARE TO INTERSECTION OF LINES   Δ = REFERENCE DIMENSION
ALL CALCULATIONS APPLY AT MAXIMUM MATERIAL CONDITION (MMC)

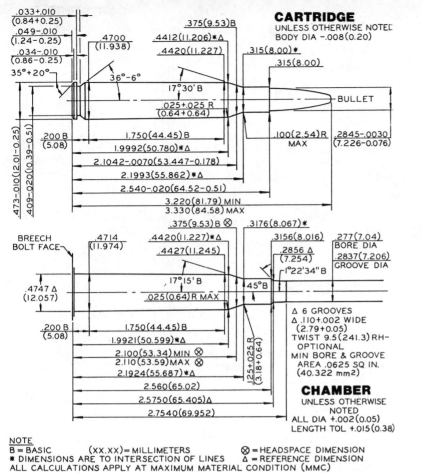

CARTRIDGE
UNLESS OTHERWISE NOTED
BODY DIA -.008(0.20)

.033+.010
(0.84+0.25)
.049-.010
(1.24-0.25)
.034-.010
(0.86-0.25)
35°+20°
.4700
(11.938)
36°-6°
.375(9.53)B
.4412(11.206)*Δ
.4420(11.227)
17°30'B
.025+.025 R
(0.64+0.64)
.315(8.00)*
.315(8.00)
BULLET
.100(2.54)R
MAX
.2845-.0030
(7.226-0.076)
.473-.010(12.01-0.25)
.409-.020(10.39-0.51)
.200 B
(5.08)
1.750(44.45)B
1.9992(50.780)*Δ
2.1042-.0070(53.447-0.178)
2.1993(55.862)*Δ
2.540-.020(64.52-0.51)
3.220(81.79) MIN
3.330(84.58) MAX

BREECH
BOLT FACE
.4714
(11.974)
.375(9.53)B ⊗
.4420(11.227)*Δ
.4427(11.245)
17°15'B
45°B
.3176(8.067)*
3156(8.016)
.2856 Δ
(7.254)
1°22'34"B
277(7.04)
BORE DIA
.2837(7.206)
GROOVE DIA
.4747 Δ
(12.057)
.025(0.64)R MAX
.200 B
(5.08)
1.750(44.45)B
1.9921(50.599)*Δ
2.100(53.34)MIN ⊗
2.110(53.59)MAX ⊗
2.1924(55.687)*Δ
2.560(65.02)
2.5750(65.405)Δ
2.7540(69.952)
.125+.025 R
(3.18+.64)

Δ 6 GROOVES
Δ .110+.002 WIDE
(2.79+0.05)
TWIST 9.5(241.3) RH-
OPTIONAL
MIN BORE & GROOVE
AREA .0625 SQ IN.
(40.322 mm2)

CHAMBER
UNLESS OTHERWISE
NOTED
ALL DIA +.002(0.05)
LENGTH TOL +.015(0.38)

NOTE
B = BASIC   (XX.XX)= MILLIMETERS   ⊗ = HEADSPACE DIMENSION
* DIMENSIONS ARE TO INTERSECTION OF LINES   Δ = REFERENCE DIMENSION
ALL CALCULATIONS APPLY AT MAXIMUM MATERIAL CONDITION (MMC)

7mm EXPRESS REMINGTON

CARTRIDGE
UNLESS OTHERWISE NOTED
BODY DIA -.008 (0.20)

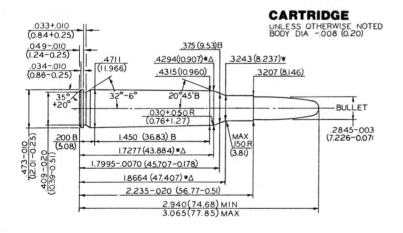

.033+.010
(0.84+0.25)
.049-.010
(1.24-0.25)
.034-.010
(0.86-0.25)
.4711
(11.966)
35°+20°
32°-6°
.375(9.53)B
.4294(10.907)*Δ
.4315(10.960)
20°45'B
.030+.050R
(0.76+1.27)
.3243(8.237)*
.3207(8.146)
BULLET
MAX
150 R
(3.81)
.2845-003
(7.226-0.07)
.473-.010(12.01-0.25)
.409-.020(10.39-0.51)
.200 B
(5.08)
1.450 (36.83) B
1.7277(43.884)*Δ
1.7995-.0070(45.707-0.178)
1.8664(47.407)*Δ
2.235-.020 (56.77-0.51)
2.940(74.68) MIN
3.065(77.85) MAX

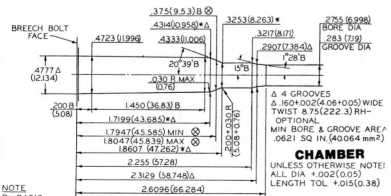

BREECH BOLT
FACE
.4723 (11.996)
.375(9.53)B ⊗
.4314(10.958)*Δ
.4333(11.006)
20°39'B
15°B
.030 R MAX
(0.76)
.3253(8.263)*
.3217(8.171)
.2907(7.384)Δ
1°28'B
2755(6.998)
BORE DIA
.283 (7.19)
GROOVE DIA
.4777 Δ
(12.134)
.200 B
(5.08)
1.450 (36.83) B
1.7199(43.685)*Δ
1.7947(45.585) MIN ⊗
1.8047(45.839) MAX ⊗
1.8607 (47.262)*Δ
2.255 (57.28)
2.3129 (58.748)Δ
2.6096(66.284)
.200+.030 R
(5.08+0.76)

Δ 4 GROOVES
Δ .160+.002(4.06+0.05) WIDE
TWIST 8.75(222.3) RH-
OPTIONAL
MIN BORE & GROOVE AREA
.0621 SQ IN.(40.064 mm2)

CHAMBER
UNLESS OTHERWISE NOTED
ALL DIA +.002(0.05)
LENGTH TOL +.015(0.38)

NOTE
B= BASIC
(XX.XX)= MILLIMETERS
* DIMENSIONS ARE TO INTERSECTION OF LINES
⊗ = HEADSPACE DIMENSION
Δ = REFERENCE DIMENSION
ALL CALCULATIONS APPLY AT MAXIMUM MATERIAL CONDITION (MMC)

7mm MAUSER (7x57)

7mm REMINGTON MAGNUM

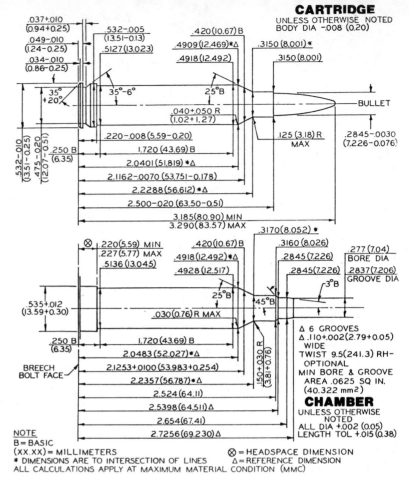

CARTRIDGE
UNLESS OTHERWISE NOTED
BODY DIA -.008 (0.20)

.037+.010 (0.94+0.25)
.049-.010 (1.24-0.25)
.034-.010 (0.86-0.25)
.532-.005 (13.51-0.13)
.5127 (13.023)
.420 (10.67) B
.4909 (12.469)*△
.4918 (12.492)
.3150 (8.001)
.3150 (8.001)
BULLET
35° +20°
35°-6°
25°B
.040+.050 R (1.02+1.27)
.125 (3.18) R MAX
.2845-.0030 (7.226-0.076)
.532-.010 (13.51-0.25)
.475-.020 (12.07-0.51)
.250 B (6.35)
.220-.008 (5.59-0.20)
1.720 (43.69) B
2.0401 (51.819) *△
2.1162-.0070 (53.751-0.178)
2.2288 (56.612) *△
2.500-.020 (63.50-0.51)
3.185 (80.90) MIN
3.290 (83.57) MAX

⊗ .220 (5.59) MIN
.227 (5.77) MAX
.5136 (13.045)
.420 (10.67) B
.4918 (12.492)*△
.4928 (12.517)
.3170 (8.052) *
.3160 (8.026)
.2845 (7.226)
.2845 (7.226)
.277 (7.04) BORE DIA
.2837 (7.206) GROOVE DIA
.535+.012 (13.59+0.30)
25°B
.030 (0.76) R MAX
45°B
3°B
.250 B (6.35)
BREECH BOLT FACE
1.720 (43.69) B
2.0483 (52.027)*△
2.1253+.0100 (53.983+0.254)
2.2357 (56.787)*△
.150+.030 R (3.81+0.76)
2.524 (64.11)
2.5398 (64.511)△
2.654 (67.41)
2.7256 (69.230)△

△ 6 GROOVES
△ .110+.002 (2.79+0.05) WIDE
TWIST 9.5 (241.3) RH-OPTIONAL
MIN BORE & GROOVE AREA .0625 SQ IN. (40.322 mm2)

CHAMBER
UNLESS OTHERWISE NOTED
ALL DIA +.002 (0.05)
LENGTH TOL +.015 (0.38)

NOTE
B = BASIC
(XX.XX) = MILLIMETERS
* DIMENSIONS ARE TO INTERSECTION OF LINES
ALL CALCULATIONS APPLY AT MAXIMUM MATERIAL CONDITION (MMC)
⊗ = HEADSPACE DIMENSION
△ = REFERENCE DIMENSION

8mm MAUSER (8x57)

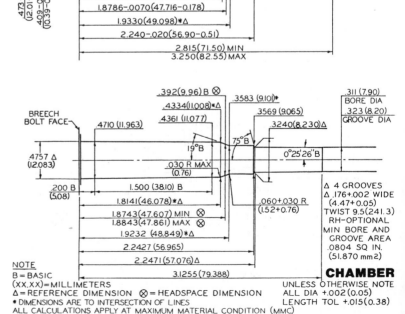

CARTRIDGE
UNLESS OTHERWISE NOTED
BODY DIA -.008 (0.20)

.033+.010 (0.84+0.25)
.049-.010 (1.24-0.25)
.034-.010 (0.86-0.25)
.4698 (11.933)
.392 (9.96) B
.4310 (10.947)*△
.4340 (11.024)
.3507 (8.908) *
.3493 (8.872)
BULLET
35° +20°
36°-6°
20°48'B
.045+.045 R (1.14+1.14)
.3230-.0030 (8.204-0.076)
.473-.010 (12.01-0.25)
.409-.020 (10.39-0.51)
.200 B (5.08)
1.500 (38.10) B
1.8273 (46.413) *△
1.8786-.0070 (47.716-0.178)
1.9330 (49.098) *△
2.240-.020 (56.90-0.51)
.050 (1.27) R MAX
2.815 (71.50) MIN
3.250 (82.55) MAX

BREECH BOLT FACE
.392 (9.96) B ⊗
.4334 (11.008)*△
.4361 (11.077)
.3583 (9.101)*
.3569 (9.065)
.3240 (8.230)△
.311 (7.90) BORE DIA
.323 (8.20) GROOVE DIA
.4710 (11.963)
19°B
75°B
0°25'26"B
.4757 △ (12.083)
.030 R MAX (0.76)
.200 B (5.08)
1.500 (38.10) B
1.8141 (46.078) *△
1.8743 (47.607) MIN ⊗
1.8843 (47.861) MAX ⊗
1.9232 (48.849) *△
.060+.030 R (1.52+0.76)
2.2427 (56.965)
2.2471 (57.076)△
3.1255 (79.388)

△ 4 GROOVES
△ .176+.002 WIDE (4.47+0.05)
TWIST 9.5 (241.3) RH-OPTIONAL
MIN BORE AND GROOVE AREA .0804 SQ IN. (51.870 mm2)

CHAMBER
UNLESS OTHERWISE NOTE
ALL DIA +.002 (0.05)
LENGTH TOL +.015 (0.38)

NOTE
B = BASIC
(XX.XX) = MILLIMETERS
△ = REFERENCE DIMENSION   ⊗ = HEADSPACE DIMENSION
* DIMENSIONS ARE TO INTERSECTION OF LINES
ALL CALCULATIONS APPLY AT MAXIMUM MATERIAL CONDITION (MMC)

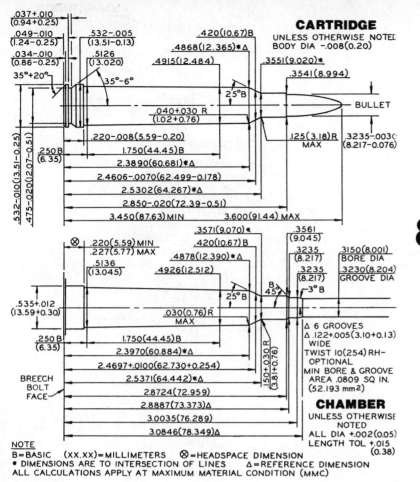

8mm REMINGTON MAGNUM

CARTRIDGE
UNLESS OTHERWISE NOTED
BODY DIA -.008(0.20)

.037+.010
(0.94+0.25)
.049-.010
(1.24-0.25)
.034-.010
(0.86-0.25)
35°+20°
.532-.005
(13.51-0.13)
.5126
(13.020)
35°-6°
.420(10.67)B
.4868(12.365)*Δ
.4915(12.484)
.3551(9.020)*
.3541(8.994)
25°B
BULLET
.040+.030 R
(1.02+0.76)
.125(3.18)R
MAX
.3235-.0030
(8.217-0.076)
.220-.008(5.59-0.20)
1.750(44.45)B
2.3890(60.681)*Δ
2.4606-.0070(62.499-0.178)
2.5302(64.267)*Δ
2.850-.020(72.39-0.51)
3.450(87.63)MIN
3.600(91.44) MAX
.532-.010(13.51-0.25)
.475-.020(12.07-0.51)
.250B (6.35)

.220(5.59) MIN
.227(5.77) MAX
.5136 (13.045)
.3571(9.070)*
.420(10.67)B
.4878(12.390)*Δ
.4926(12.512)
.3561 (9.045)
.3235 (8.217)
.3235 (8.217)
.3150(8.001) BORE DIA
.3230(8.204) GROOVE DIA
25°B
B 45°
3°B
.535+.012 (13.59+0.30)
.030(0.76)R MAX
.250 B (6.35)
BREECH BOLT FACE
1.750(44.45)B
2.3970(60.884)*Δ
2.4697+.0100(62.730+0.254)
2.5371(64.442)*Δ
2.8724(72.959)
2.8887(73.373)Δ
3.0035(76.289)
3.0846(78.349)Δ
.150+.030 R (3.81+0.76)

Δ 6 GROOVES
Δ .122+.005(3.10+0.13) WIDE
TWIST 10(254) RH-OPTIONAL
MIN BORE & GROOVE AREA .0809 SQ IN. (52.193 mm2)

CHAMBER
UNLESS OTHERWISE NOTED
ALL DIA +.002(0.05)
LENGTH TOL +.015 (0.38)

NOTE
B=BASIC   (XX.XX)=MILLIMETERS   ⊗=HEADSPACE DIMENSION
* DIMENSIONS ARE TO INTERSECTION OF LINES   Δ=REFERENCE DIMENSION
ALL CALCULATIONS APPLY AT MAXIMUM MATERIAL CONDITION (MMC)

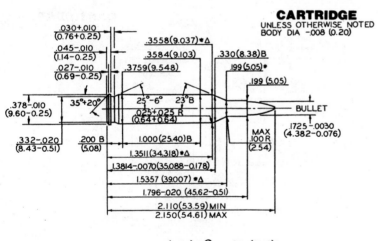

CARTRIDGE
UNLESS OTHERWISE NOTED
BODY DIA -.008 (0.20)

.17 REMINGTON

.030+.010
(0.76+0.25)
.045-.010
(1.14-0.25)
.027-.010
(0.69-0.25)
.378-.010 (9.60-0.25)
35°+20°
.3558(9.037)*Δ
.3584(9.103)
.3759(9.548)
.330(8.38)B
.199(5.05)*
.199 (5.05)
25°-6°
23°B
.025+.025 R (0.64+0.64)
BULLET
MAX .100 R (2.54)
.1725-.0030 (4.382-0.076)
.332-.020 (8.43-0.51)
.200 B (5.08)
1.000(25.40)B
1.3511(34.318)*Δ
1.3814-.0070(35.088-0.178)
1.5357 (39.007) *Δ
1.796-.020 (45.62-0.51)
2.110(53.59) MIN
2.150(54.61) MAX

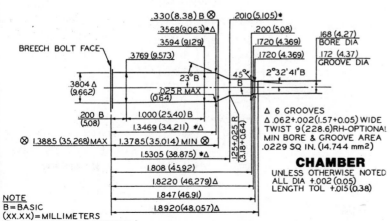

.330(8.38) B ⊗
.3568(9.063)*Δ
.3594 (9129)
.3769 (9.573)
.2010(5.105)*
.200 (5.08)
.1720 (4.369)
.1720 (4.369)
.168 (4.27) BORE DIA
.172 (4.37) GROOVE DIA
BREECH BOLT FACE
23°B
B
45°
2°32'41"B
.025 R MAX (0.64)
.3804 Δ (9.662)
.200 B (5.08)
1.000(25.40)B
1.3469 (34.211) *Δ
.125+.025 R (3.18+0.64)
⊗ 1.3885 (35.268)MAX
1.3785(35.014) MIN ⊗
1.5305 (38.875) *Δ
1.808 (45.92)
1.8220 (46.279)Δ
1.847 (46.91)
1.8920(48.057)Δ

Δ 6 GROOVES
Δ .062+.002(1.57+0.05) WIDE
TWIST 9 (228.6)RH-OPTIONAL
MIN BORE & GROOVE AREA .0229 SQ IN. (14.744 mm2)

CHAMBER
UNLESS OTHERWISE NOTED
ALL DIA +.002 (0.05)
LENGTH TOL +.015(0.38)

NOTE
B=BASIC
(XX.XX)=MILLIMETERS
⊗ = HEADSPACE DIMENSION
* DIMENSIONS ARE TO INTERSECTION OF LINES   Δ=REFERENCE DIMENSION
ALL CALCULATIONS APPLY AT MAXIMUM MATERIAL CONDITION (MMC)

.218 BEE

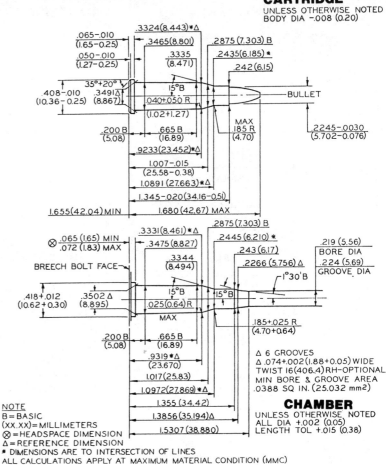

.3324(8.443)*Δ
.3465(8.801)
.065-.010 (1.65-0.25)
.050-.010 (1.27-0.25)
.3335 (8.471)
.2875 (7.303) B
.2435 (6.185) *
.242 (6.15)
35°+20°
15°B
.408-.010 (10.36-0.25)
.3491 Δ (8.867)
BULLET
.040+.050 R (1.02+1.27)
MAX .185 R (4.70)
.2245-.0030 (5.702-0.076)
.200 B (5.08)
.665 B (16.89)
.9233(23.452)*Δ
1.007-.015 (25.58-0.38)
1.0891(27.663)*Δ
1.345-.020(34.16-0.51)
1.655(42.04) MIN
1.680 (42.67) MAX

.2875 (7.303) B
.3331(8.461)*Δ
.3475(8.827)
.2445 (6.210) *
.243 (6.17)
.219 (5.56) BORE DIA
.224 (5.69) GROOVE DIA
⊗ .065 (1.65) MIN .072 (1.83) MAX
.3344 (8.494)
.2266 (5.756) Δ
1°30'B
BREECH BOLT FACE
.418+.012 (10.62+0.30)
.3502 Δ (8.895)
15°B
15°B
.025(0.64)R MAX
.185+.025 R (4.70+0.64)
.200 B (5.08)
.665 B (16.89)
.9319*Δ (23.670)
1.017(25.83)
1.0972(27.869)*Δ
1.355 (34.42)
1.3856(35.194)Δ
1.5307(38.880)

Δ 6 GROOVES
Δ .074+.002(1.88+0.05) WIDE
TWIST 16(406.4)RH-OPTIONAL
MIN BORE & GROOVE AREA
.0388 SQ IN. (25.032 mm2)

CHAMBER
UNLESS OTHERWISE NOTED
ALL DIA +.002 (0.05)
LENGTH TOL +.015 (0.38)

NOTE
B = BASIC
(XX.XX) = MILLIMETERS
⊗ = HEADSPACE DIMENSION
Δ = REFERENCE DIMENSION
* DIMENSIONS ARE TO INTERSECTION OF LINES
ALL CALCULATIONS APPLY AT MAXIMUM MATERIAL CONDITION (MMC)

.22 HORNET

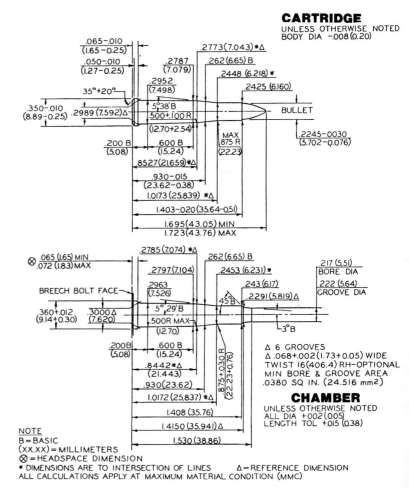

.065-.010 (1.65-0.25)
.050-.010 (1.27-0.25)
.2773(7.043)*Δ
.2787 (7.079)
.262 (6.65) B
.2448 (6.218) *
.2952 (7.498)
.2425 (6.160)
35°+20°
5°38'B
.350-.010 (8.89-0.25)
.2989 (7.592)Δ
.500+.100 R (12.70+2.54)
BULLET
MAX .875 R (22.23)
.2245-.0030 (5.702-0.076)
.200 B (5.08)
.600 B (15.24)
.8527(21.659)*Δ
.930-.015 (23.62-0.38)
1.0173 (25.839) *Δ
1.403-.020(35.64-0.51)
1.695(43.05) MIN
1.723(43.76) MAX

.2785 (7.074) *Δ
.262 (6.65) B
.217 (5.51) BORE DIA
⊗ .065 (1.65) MIN .072 (1.83)MAX
.2797 (7.104)
.2453 (6.231) *
.222 (564) GROOVE DIA
.2963 (7.526)
.243 (6.17)
BREECH BOLT FACE
5°29'B
45°B
.2291(5.819)Δ
.360+.012 (9.14+0.30)
.3000 Δ (7.620)
.500R MAX (12.70)
-3°B
.200B (5.08)
.600 B (15.24)
.875+.030R (22.23+0.76)
.8442*Δ (21.443)
.930(23.62)
1.0172(25.837)*Δ
1.408 (35.76)
1.4150(35.941)Δ
1.530 (38.86)

Δ 6 GROOVES
Δ .068+.002(1.73+0.05) WIDE
TWIST 16(406.4) RH-OPTIONAL
MIN BORE & GROOVE AREA
.0380 SQ IN. (24.516 mm2)

CHAMBER
UNLESS OTHERWISE NOTED
ALL DIA +.002 (0.05)
LENGTH TOL +.015 (0.38)

NOTE
B = BASIC
(XX.XX) = MILLIMETERS
⊗ = HEADSPACE DIMENSION
* DIMENSIONS ARE TO INTERSECTION OF LINES   Δ = REFERENCE DIMENSION
ALL CALCULATIONS APPLY AT MAXIMUM MATERIAL CONDITION (MMC)

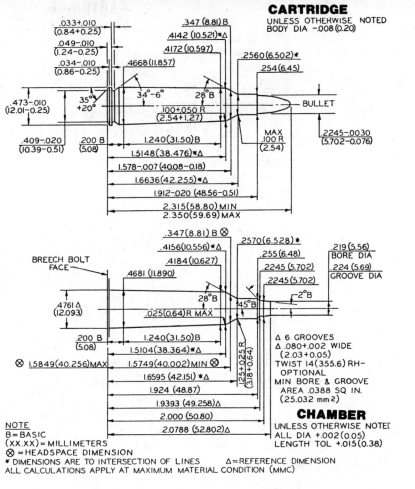

CARTRIDGE
UNLESS OTHERWISE NOTED
BODY DIA -.008 (0.20)

.033+.010
(0.84+0.25)
.049-.010
(1.24-0.25)
.034-.010
(0.86-0.25)
.473-.010
(12.01-0.25)
35° +20°
34°-6°
28° B
.4668 (11.857)
.347 (8.81) B
.4142 (10.521)*Δ
.4172 (10.597)
.2560 (6.502)*
.254 (6.45)
.100+.050 R
(2.54+1.27)
BULLET
MAX .100 R (2.54)
.2245-.0030
(5.702-0.076)
.409-.020
(10.39-0.51)
.200 B
(5.08)
1.240 (31.50) B
1.5148 (38.476)*Δ
1.578-.007 (40.08-0.18)
1.6636 (42.255)*Δ
1.912-.020 (48.56-0.51)
2.315 (58.80) MIN
2.350 (59.69) MAX

BREECH BOLT FACE
.4761 Δ
(12.093)
.347 (8.81) B ⊗
.4156 (10.556)*Δ
.4184 (10.627)
.4681 (11.890)
.2570 (6.528)*
.255 (6.48)
.2245 (5.702)
.2245 (5.702)
.219 (5.56) BORE DIA
.224 (5.69) GROOVE DIA
28° B
45° B
-2° B
.025 (0.64) R MAX
.125+.025 R (3.18+0.64)
⊗ 1.5849 (40.256) MAX
.200 B (5.08)
1.240 (31.50) B
1.5104 (38.364)*Δ
1.5749 (40.002) MIN ⊗
1.6595 (42.151)*Δ
1.924 (48.87)
1.9393 (49.258) Δ
2.000 (50.80)
2.0788 (52.802) Δ

Δ 6 GROOVES
Δ .080+.002 WIDE (2.03+0.05)
TWIST 14 (355.6) RH-OPTIONAL
MIN BORE & GROOVE AREA .0388 SQ IN. (25.032 mm2)

CHAMBER
UNLESS OTHERWISE NOTED
ALL DIA +.002 (0.05)
LENGTH TOL +.015 (0.38)

NOTE
B=BASIC
(XX.XX) = MILLIMETERS
⊗ = HEADSPACE DIMENSION
* DIMENSIONS ARE TO INTERSECTION OF LINES   Δ=REFERENCE DIMENSION
ALL CALCULATIONS APPLY AT MAXIMUM MATERIAL CONDITION (MMC)

.22-250 REMINGTON

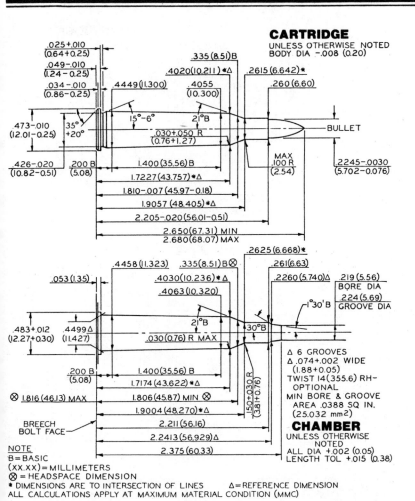

CARTRIDGE
UNLESS OTHERWISE NOTED
BODY DIA -.008 (0.20)

.025+.010
(0.64+0.25)
.049-.010
(1.24-0.25)
.034-.010
(0.86-0.25)
.473-.010
(12.01-0.25)
35° +20°
15°-6°
21° B
.4449 (11.300)
.335 (8.51) B
.4020 (10.211)*Δ
.4055 (10.300)
.2615 (6.642)*
.260 (6.60)
.030+.050 R (0.76+1.27)
BULLET
MAX .100 R (2.54)
.2245-.0030
(5.702-0.076)
.426-.020
(10.82-0.51)
.200 B (5.08)
1.400 (35.56) B
1.7227 (43.757)*Δ
1.810-.007 (45.97-0.18)
1.9057 (48.405)*Δ
2.205-.020 (56.01-0.51)
2.650 (67.31) MIN
2.680 (68.07) MAX

.053 (1.35)
.483+.012
(12.27+0.30)
.4499 Δ
(11.427)
.4458 (11.323)
.335 (8.51) B ⊗
.4030 (10.236)*Δ
.4063 (10.320)
.2625 (6.668)*
.261 (6.63)
.2260 (5.740) Δ
.219 (5.56) BORE DIA
.224 (5.69) GROOVE DIA
21° B
30° B
1°30' B
.030 (0.76) R MAX
.150+.030 R (3.81+0.76)
⊗ 1.816 (46.13) MAX
.200 B (5.08)
1.400 (35.56) B
1.7174 (43.622)*Δ
1.806 (45.87) MIN ⊗
1.9004 (48.270)*Δ
2.211 (56.16)
2.2413 (56.929) Δ
2.375 (60.33)
BREECH BOLT FACE

Δ 6 GROOVES
Δ .074+.002 WIDE (1.88+0.05)
TWIST 14 (355.6) RH-OPTIONAL
MIN BORE & GROOVE AREA .0388 SQ IN. (25.032 mm2)

CHAMBER
UNLESS OTHERWISE NOTED
ALL DIA +.002 (0.05)
LENGTH TOL +.015 (0.38)

NOTE
B=BASIC
(XX.XX) = MILLIMETERS
⊗ = HEADSPACE DIMENSION
* DIMENSIONS ARE TO INTERSECTION OF LINES   Δ=REFERENCE DIMENSION
ALL CALCULATIONS APPLY AT MAXIMUM MATERIAL CONDITION (MMC)

.220 SWIFT

.222 REMINGTON

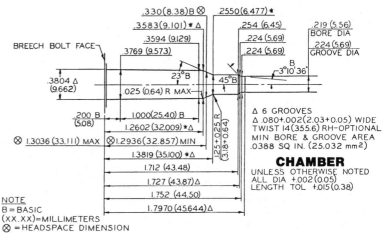

CARTRIDGE
UNLESS OTHERWISE NOTED
BODY DIA -.008 (0.20)

.025+.015 (0.64+0.38)
.045-.010 (1.14-0.25)
.027-.010 (0.69-0.25)
.378-.010 (9.60-0.25)
35° +20°
.332-.020 (8.43-0.51)
.200 B (5.08)
.330 (8.38) B
.3573 (9.075)*△
.3584 (9.103)
.3759 (9.548)
25°-6°   23°B
.025+.050 R (0.64+1.27)
.253 (6.43)*
.253 (6.43)
BULLET
MAX .100 R (2.54)
.2245-.0030 (5.702-0.076)
1.000 (25.40) B
1.2645 (32.118)*△
1.2966-.0070 (32.934-0.178)
1.3873 (35.237)*△
1.700-.020 (43.18-0.51)
2.040 (51.82) MIN
2.130 (54.10) MAX

BREECH BOLT FACE
.330 (8.38) B ⊗
.3583 (9.101)*△
.3594 (9.129)
.3769 (9.573)
23°B
.3804 △ (9.662)
.025 (0.64) R MAX
45°B
.2550 (6.477)*
.254 (6.45)
.224 (5.69)
.224 (5.69)
3°10'36"
.219 (5.56) BORE DIA
.224 (5.69) GROOVE DIA
.200 B (5.08)
1.000 (25.40) B
1.2602 (32.009)*△
⊗ 1.3036 (33.111) MAX   ⊗1.2936 (32.857) MIN
.125+.025 R (3.18+0.64)
1.3819 (35.100)*△
1.712 (43.48)
1.727 (43.87)△
1.752 (44.50)
1.7970 (45.644)△

△ 6 GROOVES
△ .080+.002 (2.03+0.05) WIDE
TWIST 14 (355.6) RH-OPTIONAL
MIN BORE & GROOVE AREA
.0388 SQ IN. (25.032 mm²)

CHAMBER
UNLESS OTHERWISE NOTED
ALL DIA +.002 (0.05)
LENGTH TOL +.015 (0.38)

NOTE
B=BASIC
(XX.XX)=MILLIMETERS
⊗ = HEADSPACE DIMENSION
* DIMENSIONS ARE TO INTERSECTION OF LINES   △=REFERENCE DIMENSION
ALL CALCULATIONS APPLY AT MAXIMUM MATERIAL CONDITION (MMC)

.222 REMINGTON MAGNUM

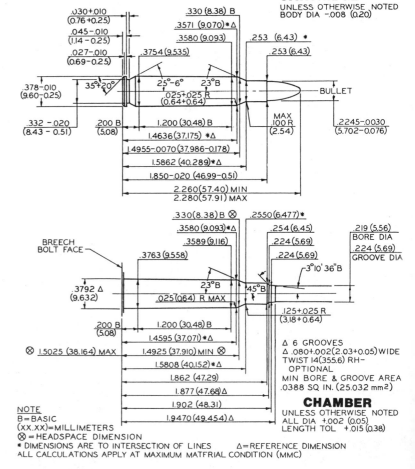

CARTRIDGE
UNLESS OTHERWISE NOTED
BODY DIA -.008 (0.20)

.030+.010 (0.76+0.25)
.045-.010 (1.14-0.25)
.027-.010 (0.69-0.25)
.378-.010 (9.60-0.25)
35°+20°
.332-.020 (8.43-0.51)
.200 B (5.08)
.330 (8.38) B
.3571 (9.070)*△
.3580 (9.093)
.3754 (9.535)
25°-6°   23°B
.025+.025 R (0.64+0.64)
.253 (6.43)*
.253 (6.43)
BULLET
MAX .100 R (2.54)
.2245-.0030 (5.702-0.076)
1.200 (30.48) B
1.4636 (37.175)*△
1.4955-.0070 (37.986-0.178)
1.5862 (40.289)*△
1.850-.020 (46.99-0.51)
2.260 (57.40) MIN
2.280 (57.91) MAX

BREECH BOLT FACE
.330 (8.38) B ⊗
.3580 (9.093)*△
.3589 (9.116)
.3763 (9.558)
23°B
.3792 △ (9.632)
.025 (0.64) R MAX
45°B
.2550 (6.477)*
.254 (6.45)
.224 (5.69)
.224 (5.69)
3°10'36"B
.219 (5.56) BORE DIA
.224 (5.69) GROOVE DIA
.200 B (5.08)
1.200 (30.48) B
1.4595 (37.071)*△
⊗ 1.5025 (38.164) MAX   1.4925 (37.910) MIN ⊗
.125+.025 R (3.18+0.64)
1.5808 (40.152)*△
1.862 (47.29)
1.877 (47.68)△
1.902 (48.31)
1.9470 (49.454)△

△ 6 GROOVES
△ .080+.002 (2.03+0.05) WIDE
TWIST 14 (355.6) RH-OPTIONAL
MIN BORE & GROOVE AREA
.0388 SQ IN. (25.032 mm²)

CHAMBER
UNLESS OTHERWISE NOTED
ALL DIA +.002 (0.05)
LENGTH TOL +.015 (0.38)

NOTE
B=BASIC
(XX.XX)=MILLIMETERS
⊗ = HEADSPACE DIMENSION
* DIMENSIONS ARE TO INTERSECTION OF LINES   △=REFERENCE DIMENSION
ALL CALCULATIONS APPLY AT MAXIMUM MATERIAL CONDITION (MMC)

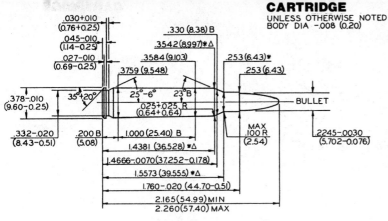

CARTRIDGE
UNLESS OTHERWISE NOTED
BODY DIA -.008 (0.20)

.030+010
(0.76+0.25)
.045-010
(1.14-0.25)
.027-010
(0.69-0.25)
.330 (8.38) B
.3542 (8.997) *Δ
.3584 (9.103)
.3759 (9.548)
.253 (6.43) *
.253 (6.43)
.378-.010
(9.60-0.25)
35°+20°
25°-6°
23° B
.025+.025 R
(0.64+0.64)
BULLET
MAX
.100 R
(2.54)
.332-.020
(8.43-0.51)
.200 B
(5.08)
1.000 (25.40) B
.2245-.0030
(5.702-0.076)
1.4381 (36.528) *Δ
1.4666-.0070 (37.252-0.178)
1.5573 (39.555) *Δ
1.760-.020 (44.70-0.51)
2.165 (54.99) MIN
2.260 (57.40) MAX

.223 REMINGTON

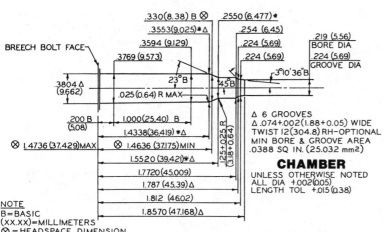

BREECH BOLT FACE

.330 (8.38) B ⊗
.3553 (9.025) *Δ
.3594 (9.129)
.3769 (9.573)
.2550 (6.477) *
.254 (6.45)
.224 (5.69)
.224 (5.69)
.219 (5.56)
BORE DIA
.224 (5.69)
GROOVE DIA
.3804 Δ
(9.662)
23° B
.025 (0.64) R MAX
45° B
3° 10' 36" B
.200 B
(5.08)
1.000 (25.40) B
⊗ 1.4736 (37.429) MAX
⊗ 1.4636 (37.175) MIN
1.5520 (39.421) *Δ
1.7720 (45.009)
1.787 (45.39) Δ
1.812 (46.02)
1.8570 (47.168) Δ
.125+.025 R
(3.18+0.64)

Δ 6 GROOVES
Δ .074+.002 (1.88+0.05) WIDE
TWIST 12 (304.8) RH-OPTIONAL
MIN BORE & GROOVE AREA
.0388 SQ IN. (25.032 mm2)

CHAMBER
UNLESS OTHERWISE NOTED
ALL DIA +.002 (0.05)
LENGTH TOL +.015 (0.38)

NOTE
B=BASIC
(XX.XX)=MILLIMETERS
⊗ =HEADSPACE DIMENSION
* DIMENSIONS ARE TO INTERSECTION OF LINES   Δ=REFERENCE DIMENSION
ALL CALCULATIONS APPLY AT MAXIMUM MATERIAL CONDITION (MMC)

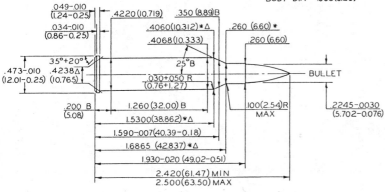

CARTRIDGE
UNLESS OTHERWISE NOTED
BODY DIA -.008 (0.20)

.049-010
(1.24-0.25)
.034-010
(0.86-0.25)
.4220 (10.719)
.350 (8.89) B
.4060 (10.312) *Δ
.4068 (10.333)
.260 (6.60) *
.260 (6.60)
.473-.010
(12.01-0.25)
35°+20°
.4238 Δ
(10.765)
25° B
.030+.050 R
(0.76+1.27)
BULLET
.200 B
(5.08)
1.260 (32.00) B
.100 (2.54) R
MAX
.2245-.0030
(5.702-0.076)
1.5300 (38.862) *Δ
1.590-.007 (40.39-0.18)
1.6865 (42.837) *Δ
1.930-.020 (49.02-0.51)
2.420 (61.47) MIN
2.500 (63.50) MAX

.225 WINCHESTER

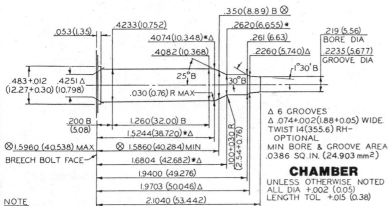

.053 (1.35)
.4233 (10.752)
.350 (8.89) B ⊗
.2620 (6.655) *
.4074 (10.348) *Δ
.4082 (10.368)
.261 (6.63)
.2260 (5.740) Δ
.219 (5.56)
BORE DIA
.2235 (5.677)
GROOVE DIA
.483+.012
(12.27+0.30)
.4251 Δ
(10.798)
25° B
30° B
1° 30' B
.030 (0.76) R MAX
.200 B
(5.08)
1.260 (32.00) B
1.5244 (38.720) *Δ
⊗1.5960 (40.538) MAX
⊗ 1.5860 (40.284) MIN
BREECH BOLT FACE
1.6804 (42.682) *Δ
1.9400 (49.276)
1.9703 (50.046) Δ
2.1040 (53.442)
.100+.030 R
(2.54+0.76)

Δ 6 GROOVES
Δ .074+.002 (1.88+0.05) WIDE
TWIST 14 (355.6) RH-
OPTIONAL
MIN BORE & GROOVE AREA
.0386 SQ IN. (24.903 mm2)

CHAMBER
UNLESS OTHERWISE NOTED
ALL DIA +.002 (0.05)
LENGTH TOL +.015 (0.38)

NOTE
B=BASIC
(XX.XX)=MILLIMETERS
⊗ = HEADSPACE DIMENSION
* DIMENSIONS ARE TO INTERSECTION OF LINES   Δ=REFERENCE DIMENSION
ALL CALCULATIONS APPLY AT MAXIMUM MATERIAL CONDITION (MMC)

.243 WINCHESTER

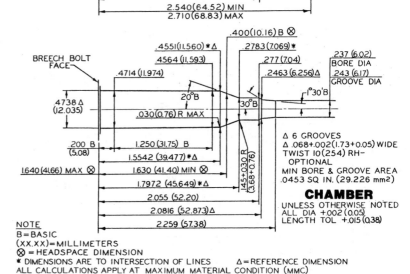

CARTRIDGE
UNLESS OTHERWISE NOTED
BODY DIA -.008 (0.20)

.055+.010 (1.40+0.25)
.054-.010 (1.37-0.25)
.039-.010 (0.99-0.25)
.473-.010 (12.01-0.25)
35° +20°
.4703 (11.946)
36°-6°
.400 (10.16) B
.4540 (11.532) *Δ
.4553 (11.565)
20° B
.030+.050 R (0.76+1.27)
.276 (7.01) *
.276 (7.01)
BULLET
.125 R MAX (3.18)
.2430-.0030 (6.172-0.076)
.409-.020 (10.39-0.51)
.200 B (5.08)
1.250 (31.75) B
1.5598 (39.619) *Δ
1.634-.007 (41.50-0.18)
1.8043 (45.829) *Δ
2.045-.020 (51.94-0.51)
2.540 (64.52) MIN
2.710 (68.83) MAX

BREECH BOLT FACE
.4551 (11.560) *Δ
.4564 (11.593)
.4714 (11.974)
.4738 Δ (12.035)
20° B
.030 (0.76) R MAX
.400 (10.16) B ⊗
.2783 (7.069) *
277 (7.04)
.2463 (6.256) Δ
1°30' B
30° B
.237 (6.02) BORE DIA
.243 (6.17) GROOVE DIA
.200 B (5.08)
1.250 (31.75) B
1.5542 (39.477) *Δ
1.640 (41.66) MAX ⊗
1.630 (41.40) MIN ⊗
1.7972 (45.649) *Δ
.145+.030 R (3.68+0.76)
2.055 (52.20)
2.0816 (52.873) Δ
2.259 (57.38)

Δ 6 GROOVES
Δ .068+.002 (1.73+0.05) WIDE
TWIST 10 (254) RH-
OPTIONAL
MIN BORE & GROOVE AREA
.0453 SQ IN. (29.226 mm2)

CHAMBER
UNLESS OTHERWISE NOTED
ALL DIA +.002 (0.05)
LENGTH TOL +.015 (0.38)

NOTE
B=BASIC
(XX.XX)=MILLIMETERS
⊗ = HEADSPACE DIMENSION
* DIMENSIONS ARE TO INTERSECTION OF LINES   Δ=REFERENCE DIMENSION
ALL CALCULATIONS APPLY AT MAXIMUM MATERIAL CONDITION (MMC)

.25-06 REMINGTON

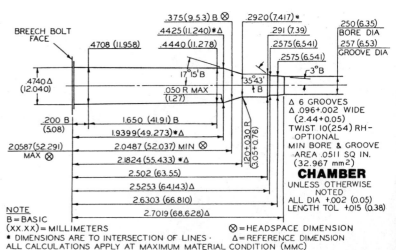

CARTRIDGE
UNLESS OTHERWISE NOTED
BODY DIA -.008 (0.20)

.033+.010 (0.84+0.25)
.049-.010 (1.24-0.25)
.034-.010 (0.86-0.25)
.473-.010 (12.01-0.25)
.409-.020 (10.39-0.51)
35° +20°
.4698 (11.933)
36°-6°
.375 (9.53) B
.440 (11.201) *Δ
.4426 (11.242)
17°30' B
.050+.050 R (1.27+1.27)
.2910 (7.391) *
.290 (7.37)
BULLET
MAX 100 R (2.54)
.2575-.0030 (6.541-0.076)
.200 B (5.08)
1.650 (41.91) B
1.9480 (49.479) *Δ
2.0526-.0070 (52.136-0.178)
2.1858 (55.519) *Δ
2.494-.020 (63.35-0.51)
3.010 (76.45) MIN
3.250 (82.55) MAX

BREECH BOLT FACE
.4708 (11.958)
.4740 Δ (12.040)
.375 (9.53) B ⊗
.4425 (11.240) *Δ
.4440 (11.278)
17°15' B
.050 R MAX (1.27)
.2920 (7.417) *
.291 (7.39)
.2575 (6.541)
.2575 (6.541)
35°43' B
3° B
.250 (6.35) BORE DIA
.257 (6.53) GROOVE DIA
.200 B (5.08)
1.650 (41.91) B
1.9399 (49.273) *Δ
2.0587 (52.291) MAX ⊗
2.0487 (52.037) MIN ⊗
.120+.030 R (3.05+0.76)
2.1824 (55.433) *Δ
2.502 (63.55)
2.5253 (64.143) Δ
2.6303 (66.810)
2.7019 (68.628) Δ

Δ 6 GROOVES
Δ .096+.002 WIDE (2.44+0.05)
TWIST 10 (254) RH-
OPTIONAL
MIN BORE & GROOVE AREA .0511 SQ IN. (32.967 mm2)

CHAMBER
UNLESS OTHERWISE NOTED
ALL DIA +.002 (0.05)
LENGTH TOL +.015 (0.38)

NOTE
B=BASIC
(XX.XX)=MILLIMETERS
⊗ = HEADSPACE DIMENSION
* DIMENSIONS ARE TO INTERSECTION OF LINES ·   Δ=REFERENCE DIMENSION
ALL CALCULATIONS APPLY AT MAXIMUM MATERIAL CONDITION (MMC)

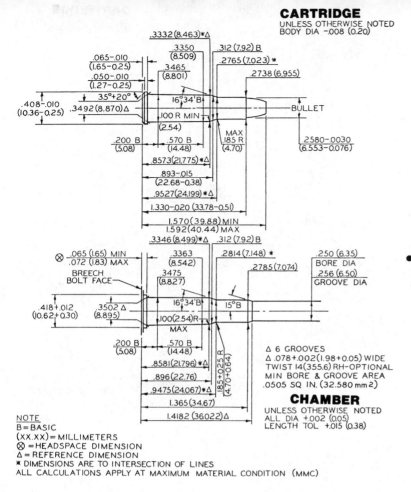

.25-20 WINCHESTER

Δ 6 GROOVES
Δ .078+.002(1.98+0.05) WIDE
TWIST 14(355.6) RH-OPTIONAL
MIN BORE & GROOVE AREA
.0505 SQ IN. (32.580 mm2)

CHAMBER
UNLESS OTHERWISE NOTED
ALL DIA +.002 (0.05)
LENGTH TOL +.015 (0.38)

NOTE
B=BASIC
(XX.XX)=MILLIMETERS
⊗ =HEADSPACE DIMENSION
Δ =REFERENCE DIMENSION
✱ DIMENSIONS ARE TO INTERSECTION OF LINES
ALL CALCULATIONS APPLY AT MAXIMUM MATERIAL CONDITION (MMC)

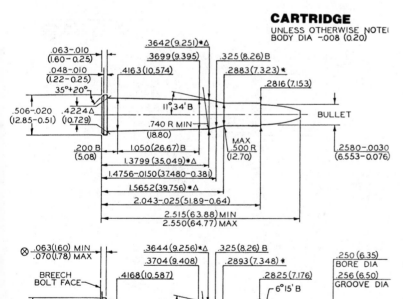

CARTRIDGE
UNLESS OTHERWISE NOTED
BODY DIA -.008 (0.20)

.25-35 WINCHESTER

Δ 6 GROOVES
Δ .0786+.0020 WIDE
(1.996+0.051)
TWIST 8(203.2) RH-
OPTIONAL
MIN BORE & GROOVE AREA
.0505 SQ IN. (32.580 mm2)

CHAMBER
UNLESS OTHERWISE NOTED
ALL DIA +.002 (0.05)
LENGTH TOL +.015 (0.38)

NOTE
B=BASIC
(XX.XX)=MILLIMETERS
⊗ =HEADSPACE DIMENSION
Δ =REFERENCE DIMENSION
✱ DIMENSIONS ARE TO INTERSECTION OF LINES
ALL CALCULATIONS APPLY AT MAXIMUM MATERIAL CONDITION (MMC)

271

.250 SAVAGE

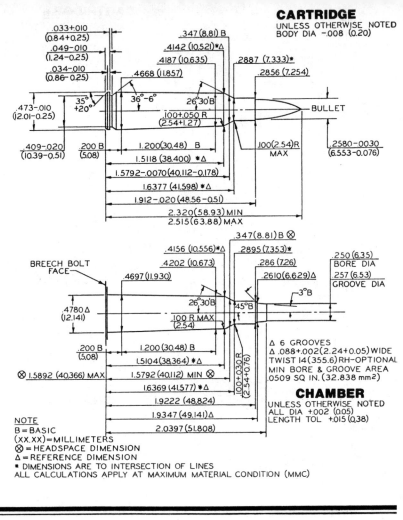

.256 WINCHESTER MAGNUM

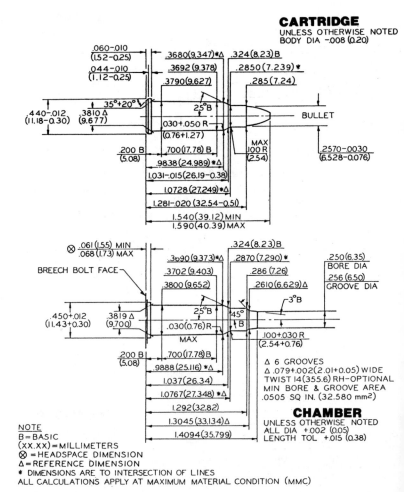

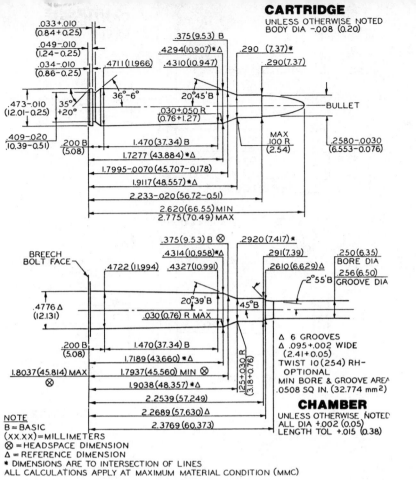

CARTRIDGE
UNLESS OTHERWISE NOTED
BODY DIA -.008 (0.20)

.033+.010
(0.84+0.25)
.049-.010
(1.24-0.25)
.034-.010
(0.86-0.25)
.4711 (11.966)
.375 (9.53) B
.4294 (10.907) *Δ
.4310 (10.947)
.290 (7.37) *
.290 (7.37)
.473-.010
(12.01-0.25)
35° +20°
36°-6°
20°45'B
.030+.050 R
(0.76+1.27)
BULLET
.409-.020
(10.39-0.51)
.200 B
(5.08)
MAX
.100 R
(2.54)
.2580-.0030
(6.553-0.076)
1.470 (37.34) B
1.7277 (43.884) *Δ
1.7995-.0070 (45.707-0.178)
1.9117 (48.557) *Δ
2.233-.020 (56.72-0.51)
2.620 (66.55) MIN
2.775 (70.49) MAX

.375 (9.53) B ⊗
.4314 (10.958) *Δ
.4327 (10.991)
.2920 (7.417) *
.291 (7.39)
.2610 (6.629) Δ
2°55'B
.250 (6.35) BORE DIA
.256 (6.50) GROOVE DIA
BREECH BOLT FACE
.4722 (11.994)
.4776 Δ
(12.131)
20°39'B
45°B
.030 (0.76) R MAX
.200 B
(5.08)
1.8037 (45.814) MAX ⊗
1.470 (37.34) B
1.7189 (43.660) *Δ
1.7937 (45.560) MIN ⊗
.125+.030 R
(3.18+0.76)
1.9038 (48.357) *Δ
2.2539 (57.249)
2.2689 (57.630) Δ
2.3769 (60.373)

Δ 6 GROOVES
Δ .095+.002 WIDE
(2.41+0.05)
TWIST 10 (254) RH-
OPTIONAL
MIN BORE & GROOVE AREA
.0508 SQ IN. (32.774 mm²)

CHAMBER
UNLESS OTHERWISE NOTED
ALL DIA +.002 (0.05)
LENGTH TOL +.015 (0.38)

NOTE
B = BASIC
(XX.XX) = MILLIMETERS
⊗ = HEADSPACE DIMENSION
Δ = REFERENCE DIMENSION
* DIMENSIONS ARE TO INTERSECTION OF LINES
ALL CALCULATIONS APPLY AT MAXIMUM MATERIAL CONDITION (MMC)

.257 ROBERTS

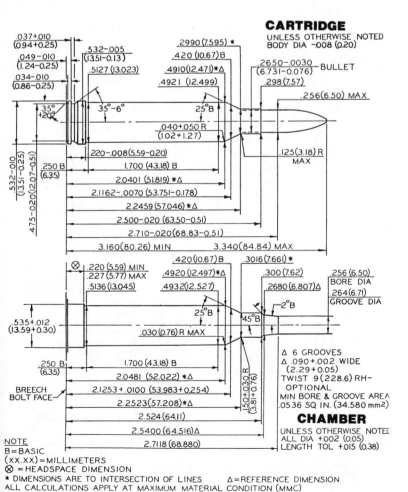

CARTRIDGE
UNLESS OTHERWISE NOTED
BODY DIA -.008 (0.20)

.037+.010
(0.94+0.25)
.049-.010
(1.24-0.25)
.034-.010
(0.86-0.25)
.532-.005
(13.51-0.13)
.5127 (13.023)
.2990 (7.595) *
.420 (10.67) B
.4910 (12.471) *Δ
.4921 (12.499)
.2650-.0030
(6.731-0.076) BULLET
.298 (7.57)
.256 (6.50) MAX
35° +20°
35°-6°
25°B
.040+.050 R
(1.02+1.27)
.125 (3.18) R MAX
.532-.010
(13.51-0.25)
.475-.020 (12.07-0.5)
.250 B
(6.35)
.220-.008 (5.59-0.20)
1.700 (43.18) B
2.0401 (51.819) *Δ
2.1162-.0070 (53.751-0.178)
2.2459 (57.046) *Δ
2.500-.020 (63.50-0.51)
2.710-.020 (68.83-0.51)
3.160 (80.26) MIN
3.340 (84.84) MAX

.220 (5.59) MIN ⊗
.227 (5.77) MAX
.5136 (13.045)
.420 (10.67) B
.4920 (12.497) *Δ
.4932 (12.527)
.3016 (7.661) *
.300 (7.62)
.2680 (6.807) Δ
.256 (6.50) BORE DIA
.264 (6.71) GROOVE DIA
2°B
.535+.012
(13.59+0.30)
25°B
45°B
.030 (0.76) R MAX
.250 B
(6.35)
1.700 (43.18) B
2.0481 (52.022) *Δ
2.1253+.0100 (53.983+0.254)
2.2523 (57.208) *Δ
.150+.030 R
(3.81+0.76)
2.524 (64.11)
2.5400 (64.516) Δ
2.7118 (68.880)
BREECH BOLT FACE

Δ 6 GROOVES
Δ .090+.002 WIDE
(2.29+0.05)
TWIST 9 (228.6) RH-
OPTIONAL
MIN BORE & GROOVE AREA
.0536 SQ IN. (34.580 mm²)

CHAMBER
UNLESS OTHERWISE NOTED
ALL DIA +.002 (0.05)
LENGTH TOL +.015 (0.38)

.264 WINCHESTER MAGNUM

NOTE
B = BASIC
(XX.XX) = MILLIMETERS
⊗ = HEADSPACE DIMENSION
* DIMENSIONS ARE TO INTERSECTION OF LINES   Δ = REFERENCE DIMENSION
ALL CALCULATIONS APPLY AT MAXIMUM MATERIAL CONDITION (MMC)

273

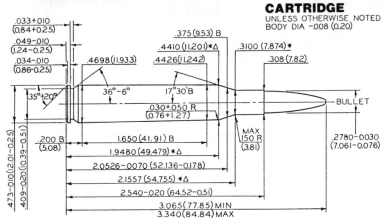

.270 WINCHESTER

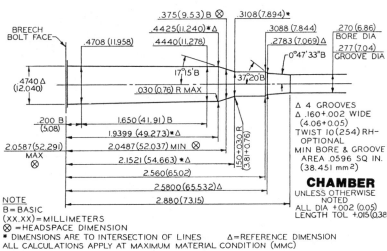

NOTE
B=BASIC
(XX.XX)=MILLIMETERS
⊗ =HEADSPACE DIMENSION
* DIMENSIONS ARE TO INTERSECTION OF LINES   Δ=REFERENCE DIMENSION
ALL CALCULATIONS APPLY AT MAXIMUM MATERIAL CONDITION (MMC)

CARTRIDGE
UNLESS OTHERWISE NOTED
BODY DIA −.008 (0.20)

Δ 4 GROOVES
Δ .160+.002 WIDE
(4.06+0.05)
TWIST 10(254) RH-
OPTIONAL
MIN BORE & GROOVE
AREA .0596 SQ IN.
(38.451 mm2)

CHAMBER
UNLESS OTHERWISE
NOTED
ALL DIA +.002 (0.05)
LENGTH TOL +.015 (0.38)

.280 REMINGTON

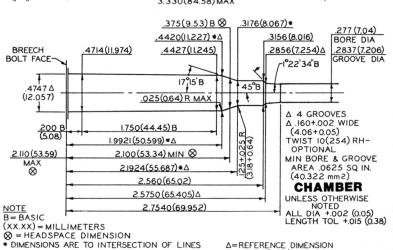

NOTE
B=BASIC
(XX.XX)=MILLIMETERS
⊗ =HEADSPACE DIMENSION
* DIMENSIONS ARE TO INTERSECTION OF LINES   Δ=REFERENCE DIMENSION
ALL CALCULATIONS APPLY AT MAXIMUM MATERIAL CONDITION (MMC)

CARTRIDGE
UNLESS OTHERWISE NOTED
BODY DIA −.008 (0.20)

Δ 4 GROOVES
Δ .160+.002 WIDE
(4.06+0.05)
TWIST 10(254) RH-
OPTIONAL
MIN BORE & GROOVE
AREA .0625 SQ IN.
(40.322 mm2)

CHAMBER
UNLESS OTHERWISE
NOTED
ALL DIA +.002 (0.05)
LENGTH TOL +.015 (0.38)

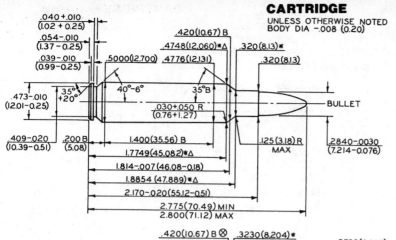

CARTRIDGE

UNLESS OTHERWISE NOTED
BODY DIA −.008 (0.20)

.040 +.010
(1.02 +0.25)
.054 −.010
(1.37 −0.25)
.039 −.010
(0.99 −0.25)
.473 −.010
(12.01 −0.25)
.5000 (12.700)
35° +20°
40° −6°
35° B
.420 (10.67) B
.4748 (12.060) *Δ
.4776 (12.131)
.320 (8.13) *
.320 (8.13)
.030 +.050 R
(0.76 +1.27)
BULLET
.409 −.020
(10.39 −0.51)
.200 B
(5.08)
1.400 (35.56) B
1.7749 (45.082) *Δ
1.814 −.007 (46.08 −0.18)
1.8854 (47.889) *Δ
2.170 −.020 (55.12 −0.51)
2.775 (70.49) MIN
2.800 (71.12) MAX
.125 (3.18) R
MAX
.2840 −.0030
(7.214 −0.076)

.284 WINCHESTER

BREECH
BOLT FACE
.420 (10.67) B ⊗
.4759 (12.088) *Δ
.4786 (12.156)
.5010 (12.725)
.3230 (8.204) *
.322 (8.18)
.2900 (7.366) Δ
0°47'33" B
.2755 (6.998)
BORE DIA
.283 (7.19)
GROOVE DIA
.5042 Δ
(12.807)
35° B
45° B
.030 (0.76) R MAX
.200 B
(5.08)
1.400 (35.56) B
1.7701 (44.961) *Δ
1.810 (45.97) MIN ⊗
1.8793 (47.734) *Δ
2.180 (55.37)
2.1960 (55.778) Δ
2.7201 (69.091)
1.820 (46.23) MAX
⊗
.125 +.030 R
(3.18 +0.76)

Δ 6 GROOVES
Δ .110 +.002 WIDE
(2.79 +0.05)
TWIST 10 (254) RH−
OPTIONAL
MIN BORE & GROOVE
AREA .0621 SQ IN.
(40.064 mm²)

CHAMBER
UNLESS OTHERWISE
NOTED
ALL DIA +.002 (0.05)
LENGTH TOL +.015
(0.38)

NOTE
B = BASIC
(XX.XX) = MILLIMETERS
⊗ = HEADSPACE DIMENSION
* DIMENSIONS ARE TO INTERSECTION OF LINES   Δ = REFERENCE DIMENSION
ALL CALCULATIONS APPLY AT MAXIMUM MATERIAL CONDITION (MMC)

CARTRIDGE
UNLESS OTHERWISE NOTED
BODY DIA −.008 (0.20)

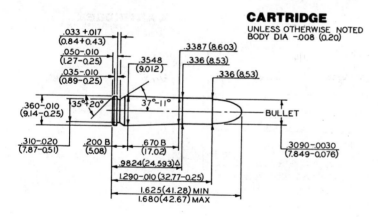

.033 +.017
(0.84 +0.43)
.050 −.010
(1.27 −0.25)
.035 −.010
(0.89 −0.25)
.360 −.010
(9.14 −0.25)
35° +20°
.3548
(9.012)
37° −11°
.3387 (8.603)
.336 (8.53)
.336 (8.53)
BULLET
.310 −.020
(7.87 −0.51)
.200 B
(5.08)
.670 B
(17.02)
.9824 (24.593) Δ
1.290 −.010 (32.77 −0.25)
1.625 (41.28) MIN
1.680 (42.67) MAX
.3090 −.0030
(7.849 −0.076)

.30 CARBINE

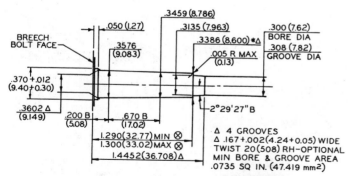

BREECH
BOLT FACE
.050 (1.27)
.3576
(9.083)
.3459 (8.786)
.3135 (7.963)
.3386 (8.600) *Δ
.005 R MAX
(0.13)
.300 (7.62)
BORE DIA
.308 (7.82)
GROOVE DIA
.370 +.012
(9.40 +0.30)
.3602 Δ
(9.149)
.200 B
(5.08)
.670 B
(17.02)
2°29'27" B
1.290 (32.77) MIN ⊗
1.300 (33.02) MAX ⊗
1.4452 (36.708) Δ

Δ 4 GROOVES
Δ .167 +.002 (4.24 +0.05) WIDE
TWIST 20 (508) RH−OPTIONAL
MIN BORE & GROOVE AREA
.0735 SQ IN. (47.419 mm²)

CHAMBER
UNLESS OTHERWISE NOTED
ALL DIA +.002 (0.05)
LENGTH TOL +.015 (0.38)

NOTE
B = BASIC
(XX.XX) = MILLIMETERS
⊗ = HEADSPACE DIMENSION
Δ = REFERENCE DIMENSION
* DIMENSIONS ARE TO INTERSECTION OF LINES
ALL CALCULATIONS APPLY AT MAXIMUM MATERIAL CONDITION (MMC)

.30 REMINGTON

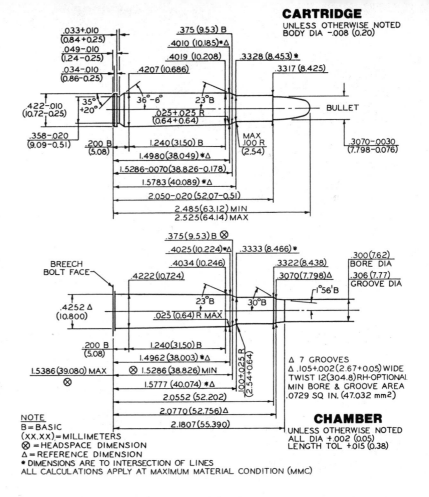

CARTRIDGE
UNLESS OTHERWISE NOTED
BODY DIA -.008 (0.20)

.033+.010
(0.84+0.25)
.049-.010
(1.24-0.25)
.034-.010
(0.86-0.25)
.4207 (10.686)
.375 (9.53) B
.4010 (10.185)*△
.4019 (10.208)
.3328 (8.453) *
.3317 (8.425)

.422-.010
(10.72-0.25)
35°+20°
36°-6°
23°B
.025+.025 R
(0.64+0.64)
BULLET

.358-.020
(9.09-0.51)
.200 B
(5.08)
MAX
.100 R
(2.54)
.3070-.0030
(7.798-0.076)

1.240 (31.50) B
1.4980 (38.049) *△
1.5286-.0070 (38.826-0.178)
1.5783 (40.089) *△
2.050-.020 (52.07-0.51)
2.485 (63.12) MIN
2.525 (64.14) MAX

.375 (9.53) B ⊗
.4025 (10.224) *△
.4034 (10.246)
.4222 (10.724)
.3333 (8.466) *
.3322 (8.438)
.3070 (7.798)△
.300 (7.62) BORE DIA
.306 (7.77) GROOVE DIA

BREECH
BOLT FACE
.4252 △
(10.800)
23°B
.025 (0.64) R MAX
30°B
1°56'B

.200 B
(5.08)
1.240 (31.50) B
1.4962 (38.003) *△
.100+.025 R
(2.54+0.64)

1.5386 (39.080) MAX
⊗
⊗ 1.5286 (38.826) MIN
1.5777 (40.074) *△
2.0552 (52.202)
2.0770 (52.756)△
2.1807 (55.390)

△ 7 GROOVES
△ .105+.002 (2.67+0.05) WIDE
TWIST 12 (304.8) RH-OPTIONAL
MIN BORE & GROOVE AREA
.0729 SQ IN. (47.032 mm2)

CHAMBER
UNLESS OTHERWISE NOTED
ALL DIA +.002 (0.05)
LENGTH TOL +.015 (0.38)

NOTE
B=BASIC
(XX.XX)=MILLIMETERS
⊗ =HEADSPACE DIMENSION
△ =REFERENCE DIMENSION
* DIMENSIONS ARE TO INTERSECTION OF LINES
ALL CALCULATIONS APPLY AT MAXIMUM MATERIAL CONDITION (MMC)

.30-06 SPRINGFIELD

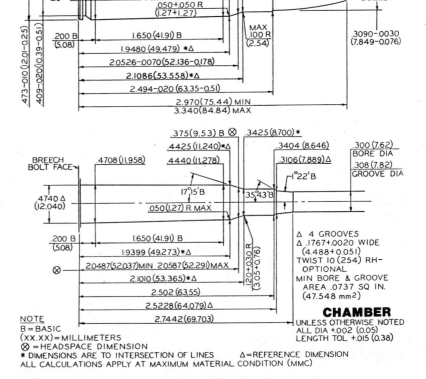

CARTRIDGE
UNLESS OTHERWISE NOTED
BODY DIA -.008 (0.20)

.033+.010
(0.84+0.25)
.049-.010
(1.24-0.25)
.034-.010
(0.86-0.25)
.4698 (11.933)
.469
.375 (9.53) B
.4435 .4410 (11.201) *△
.4426 (11.242)
.4450
.3397 (8.628) *
.3435
.3397 (8.628)
.3417

.473-.010 (12.01-0.25)
.409-.020 (10.39-0.51)
35°+20°
36°-6°
17°30'B
.050+.050 R
(1.27+1.27)
BULLET

.200 B
(5.08)
MAX
.100 R
(2.54)
.3090-.0030
(7.849-0.076)

1.650 (41.91) B
1.9480 (49.479) *△
2.0526-.0070 (52.136-0.178)
2.1086 (53.558) *△
2.494-.020 (63.35-0.51)
2.970 (75.44) MIN
3.340 (84.84) MAX

.375 (9.53) B ⊗
.4425 (11.240) *△
.4440 (11.278)
.4708 (11.958)
.3425 (8.700) *
.3404 (8.646)
.3106 (7.889)△
.300 (7.62) BORE DIA
.308 (7.82) GROOVE DIA

BREECH
BOLT FACE
.4740 △
(12.040)
17°15'B
.050 (1.27) R MAX
35°43'B
1°22'B

.200 B
(5.08)
1.650 (41.91) B
1.9399 (49.273) *△
.120+.030 R
(3.05+0.76)

⊗
2.0487 (52.037) MIN 2.0587 (52.291) MAX
2.1010 (53.365) *△
2.502 (63.55)
2.5228 (64.079)△
2.7442 (69.703)

△ 4 GROOVES
△ .1767+.0020 WIDE
(4.488+0.051)
TWIST 10 (254) RH-
OPTIONAL
MIN BORE & GROOVE
AREA .0737 SQ IN.
(47.548 mm2)

CHAMBER
UNLESS OTHERWISE NOTED
ALL DIA +.002 (0.05)
LENGTH TOL +.015 (0.38)

NOTE
B=BASIC
(XX.XX)=MILLIMETERS
⊗ =HEADSPACE DIMENSION
* DIMENSIONS ARE TO INTERSECTION OF LINES   △=REFERENCE DIMENSION
ALL CALCULATIONS APPLY AT MAXIMUM MATERIAL CONDITION (MMC)

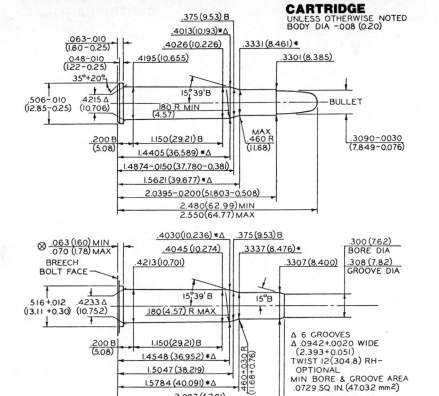

CARTRIDGE
UNLESS OTHERWISE NOTED
BODY DIA -.008 (0.20)

.063-.010 (1.60-0.25)
.048-.010 (1.22-0.25)
35°+20°
.506-.010 (12.85-0.25)
.4215 Δ (10.706)
.4195 (10.655)
.4026 (10.226)
.4013 (10.193)*Δ
.375 (9.53) B
.3331 (8.461)*
.3301 (8.385)
15°39'B
180 R MIN (4.57)
BULLET
.200 B (5.08)
1.150 (29.21) B
1.4405 (36.589)*Δ
1.4874 -.0150 (37.780-0.381)
1.5621 (39.677)*Δ
MAX .460 R (11.68)
.3090-.0030 (7.849-0.076)
2.0395 -.0200 (51.803-0.508)
2.480 (62.99) MIN
2.550 (64.77) MAX

⊗ .063 (1.60) MIN / .070 (1.78) MAX
BREECH BOLT FACE
.516+.012 (13.11+0.30)
.4233 Δ (10.752)
.4213 (10.701)
.4045 (10.274)
.4030 (10.236)*Δ
.375 (9.53) B
.3337 (8.476)*
.3307 (8.400)
.300 (7.62) BORE DIA
.308 (7.82) GROOVE DIA
15°39'B
15°B
180 (4.57) R MAX
.200 B (5.08)
1.150 (29.21) B
1.4548 (36.952)*Δ
1.5047 (38.219)
1.5784 (40.091)*Δ
460+.030 R (11.68+0.76)
2.083 (52.91)
2.1403 (54.364) Δ

Δ 6 GROOVES
Δ .0942+.0020 WIDE (2.393+0.051)
TWIST 12 (304.8) RH- OPTIONAL
MIN BORE & GROOVE AREA
.0729 SQ IN. (47.032 mm2)

CHAMBER
UNLESS OTHERWISE NOTED
ALL DIA +.002 (0.05)
LENGTH TOL +.015 (0.38)

NOTE
B = BASIC
(XX.XX) = MILLIMETERS
⊗ = HEADSPACE DIMENSION
Δ = REFERENCE DIMENSION
* DIMENSIONS ARE TO INTERSECTION OF LINES
ALL CALCULATIONS APPLY AT MAXIMUM MATERIAL CONDITION (MMC)

.30-30 WINCHESTER

CARTRIDGE
UNLESS OTHERWISE NOTED
BODY DIA -.008 (0.20)

.064-.010 (1.63-0.25)
.049-.010 (1.24-0.25)
40°+25°
.545-.010 (13.84-0.25)
.4611 Δ (11.712)
.4577 (11.626)
.4222 (10.724)
.4190 (10.643)*Δ
.375 (9.53) B
.3389 (8.608)*
.338 (8.59)
21°6'B
.155+.050 R (3.94+1.27)
BULLET
.200 B (5.08)
1.400 (35.56) B
1.7251 (43.818)*Δ
1.7821 -.0150 (45.265-0.381)
1.8289 (46.454)*Δ
.160 (4.06) R MAX
.3090-.0030 (7.849-0.076)
2.314 -.020 (58.78-0.51)
2.965 (75.31) MIN
3.089 (78.46) MAX

⊗ .064 (1.63) MIN / .071 (1.80) MAX
BREECH BOLT FACE
.555+.012 (14.10+0.30)
.4624 Δ (11.745)
.4590 (11.659)
.4235 (10.757)
.4202 (10.673)*Δ
.375 (9.53) B
.3396 (8.626)*
.3388 (8.606)
.3108 (7.894) Δ
.300 (7.62) BORE DIA
.308 (7.82) GROOVE DIA
21°6'B
12°B
1°10'B
.155 (3.94) R MAX
.200 B (5.08)
1.400 (35.56) B
1.7284 (43901)*Δ
1.787 (45.39)
1.8329 (46.556)*Δ
180+.030 R (4.57+0.76)
2.322 (58.98)
2.3879 (60.653) Δ
2.6529 (67.384)

Δ 6 GROOVES
Δ .094+.002 WIDE (2.39+0.05)
TWIST 10 (254) RH- OPTIONAL
MIN BORE & GROOVE AREA .0729 SQ IN. (47.032 mm2)

CHAMBER
UNLESS OTHERWISE NOTED
ALL DIA +.002 (0.05)
LENGTH TOL +.015 (0.38)

.30-40 KRAG

NOTE
B = BASIC
(XX.XX) = MILLIMETERS
⊗ = HEADSPACE DIMENSION
* DIMENSIONS ARE TO INTERSECTION OF LINES   Δ = REFERENCE DIMENSION
ALL CALCULATIONS APPLY AT MAXIMUM MATERIAL CONDITION (MMC)

.300 H&H MAGNUM

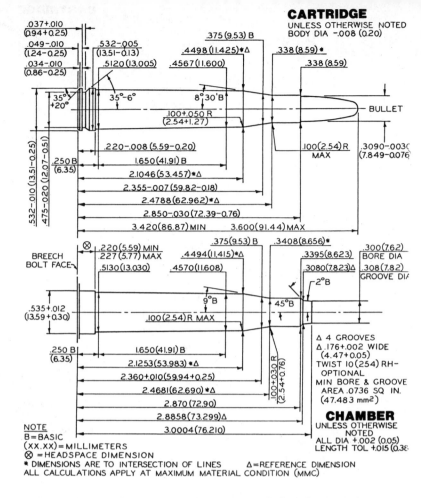

CARTRIDGE
UNLESS OTHERWISE NOTED
BODY DIA -.008 (0.20)

.037+.010
(0.94+0.25)
.049-.010
(1.24-0.25)
.034-.010
(0.86-0.25)
.532-.005
(13.51-0.13)
.5120 (13.005)
.375 (9.53) B
.4498 (11.425)*Δ
.4567 (11.600)
.338 (8.59) *
.338 (8.59)
BULLET
35°
+20°
35°-6°
8°30'B
.100+.050 R
(2.54+1.27)
.100 (2.54) R
MAX
.3090-.0030
(7.849-0.076)
.532-.010
(13.51-0.25)
.475-.020
(12.07-0.51)
.250 B
(6.35)
.220-.008 (5.59-0.20)
1.650 (41.91) B
2.1046 (53.457)*Δ
2.355-.007 (59.82-0.18)
2.4788 (62.962)*Δ
2.850-.030 (72.39-0.76)
3.420 (86.87) MIN
3.600 (91.44) MAX

BREECH
BOLT FACE
.220 (5.59) MIN
.227 (5.77) MAX
.5130 (13.030)
.375 (9.53) B
.4494 (11.415)*Δ
.4570 (11.608)
.3408 (8.656)*
.3395 (8.623)
.3080 (7.823)Δ
.300 (7.62)
BORE DIA
.308 (7.82)
GROOVE DIA
.535+.012
(13.59+0.30)
9°B
45°B
2°B
.100 (2.54) R MAX
.250 B
(6.35)
1.650 (41.91) B
2.1253 (53.983)*Δ
2.360+.010 (59.94+0.25)
2.4681 (62.690)*Δ
2.870 (72.90)
2.8858 (73.299)Δ
3.0004 (76.210)
.100+.030 R
(2.54+0.76)

Δ 4 GROOVES
Δ .176+.002 WIDE
(4.47+0.05)
TWIST 10 (254) RH-
OPTIONAL
MIN BORE & GROOVE
AREA .0736 SQ IN.
(47.483 mm2)

CHAMBER
UNLESS OTHERWISE
NOTED
ALL DIA +.002 (0.05)
LENGTH TOL +.015 (0.38

NOTE
B=BASIC
(XX.XX)=MILLIMETERS
⊗ =HEADSPACE DIMENSION
* DIMENSIONS ARE TO INTERSECTION OF LINES   Δ=REFERENCE DIMENSION
ALL CALCULATIONS APPLY AT MAXIMUM MATERIAL CONDITION (MMC)

.300 SAVAGE

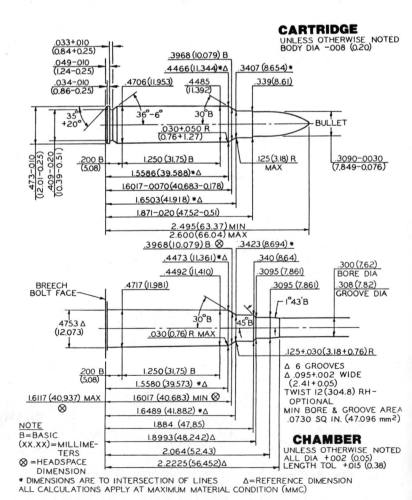

CARTRIDGE
UNLESS OTHERWISE NOTED
BODY DIA -.008 (0.20)

.033+.010
(0.84+0.25)
.049-.010
(1.24-0.25)
.034-.010
(0.86-0.25)
.3968 (10.079) B
.4466 (11.344)*Δ
.4485 (11.392)
.4706 (11.953)
.3407 (8.654)*
.339 (8.61)
35°
+20°
36°-6°
30°B
BULLET
.030+.050 R
(0.76+1.27)
.125 (3.18) R
MAX
.3090-.0030
(7.849-0.076)
.473-.010
(12.01-0.25)
.409-.020
(10.39-0.51)
.200 B
(5.08)
1.250 (31.75) B
1.5586 (39.588)*Δ
1.6017-.0070 (40.683-0.178)
1.6503 (41.918)*Δ
1.871-.020 (47.52-0.51)
2.495 (63.37) MIN
2.600 (66.04) MAX

BREECH
BOLT FACE
.3968 (10.079) B ⊗
.4473 (11.361)*Δ
.4492 (11.410)
.4717 (11.981)
.3423 (8.694)*
.340 (8.64)
.3095 (7.861)
.3095 (7.861)
.300 (7.62)
BORE DIA
.308 (7.82)
GROOVE DIA
30°B
45°B
1°43'B
.4753 Δ
(12.073)
.030 (0.76) R MAX
.125+.030 (3.18+0.76) R
.200 B
(5.08)
1.250 (31.75) B
1.5580 (39.573) *Δ
1.6117 (40.937) MAX
⊗
1.6017 (40.683) MIN ⊗
1.6489 (41.882) *Δ
1.884 (47.85)
1.8993 (48.242) Δ
2.064 (52.43)
2.2225 (56.452) Δ

Δ 6 GROOVES
Δ .095+.002 WIDE
(2.41+0.05)
TWIST 12 (304.8) RH-
OPTIONAL
MIN BORE & GROOVE AREA
.0730 SQ IN. (47.096 mm2)

CHAMBER
UNLESS OTHERWISE NOTED
ALL DIA +.002 (0.05)
LENGTH TOL +.015 (0.38)

NOTE
B=BASIC
(XX.XX)=MILLIME-
TERS
⊗ =HEADSPACE
DIMENSION
* DIMENSIONS ARE TO INTERSECTION OF LINES   Δ=REFERENCE DIMENSION
ALL CALCULATIONS APPLY AT MAXIMUM MATERIAL CONDITION (MMC)

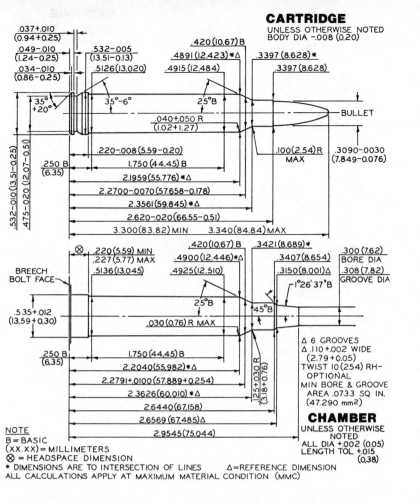

CARTRIDGE
UNLESS OTHERWISE NOTED
BODY DIA −.008 (0.20)

.037+.010
(0.94+0.25)

.049−.010
(1.24−0.25)

.034−.010
(0.86−0.25)

.532−.005
(13.51−0.13)

.5126(13.020)

.420(10.67) B

.4891(12.423) *△

.4915(12.484)

.3397(8.628) *

.3397(8.628)

35°+20°

35°−6°

25°B

BULLET

.040+.050 R
(1.02+1.27)

.100(2.54)R
MAX

.3090−.0030
(7.849−0.076)

.220−.008(5.59−0.20)

1.750(44.45) B

2.1959(55.776) *△

2.2700−.0070(57.658−0.178)

2.3561(59.845) *△

2.620−.020(66.55−0.51)

3.300(83.82) MIN   3.340(84.84)MAX

.250 B
(6.35)

.532−.010(13.51−0.25)
.475−.020(12.07−0.5)

.300 WINCHESTER MAGNUM

BREECH
BOLT FACE

.220(5.59) MIN
.227(5.77) MAX

.5136(13.045)

.420(10.67) B

.4900(12.446) *△

.4925(12.510)

.3421(8.689) *

.3407(8.654)

.3150(8.001)△

.300(7.62)
BORE DIA
.308(7.82)
GROOVE DIA

.535+.012
(13.59+0.30)

25°B

45°B

1°26'37"B

.030(0.76) R MAX

.250 B
(6.35)

1.750(44.45) B

2.2040(55.982) *△

2.2791+.0100(57.889+0.254)

2.3626(60.010) *△

2.6440(67.158)

2.6569(67.485)△

2.9545(75.044)

.125+.030 R
(3.18+0.76)

△ 6 GROOVES
△ .110+.002 WIDE
(2.79+0.05)
TWIST 10(254) RH−
OPTIONAL
MIN BORE & GROOVE
AREA .0733 SQ IN.
(47.290 mm²)

CHAMBER
UNLESS OTHERWISE
NOTED
ALL DIA +.002 (0.05)
LENGTH TOL +.015
(0.38)

NOTE
B = BASIC
(XX.XX) = MILLIMETERS
⊗ = HEADSPACE DIMENSION
* DIMENSIONS ARE TO INTERSECTION OF LINES   △=REFERENCE DIMENSION
ALL CALCULATIONS APPLY AT MAXIMUM MATERIAL CONDITION (MMC)

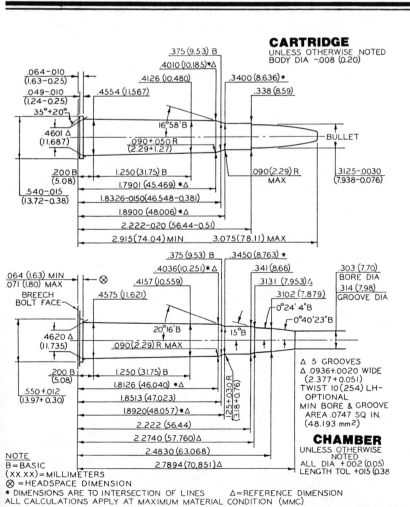

CARTRIDGE
UNLESS OTHERWISE NOTED
BODY DIA −.008 (0.20)

.064−.010
(1.63−0.25)

.049−.010
(1.24−0.25)

35°+20°

.4554(11.567)

.375(9.53) B

.4010(10.185)*△

.4126(10.480)

.3400(8.636) *

.338(8.59)

.4601 △
(11.687)

16°58'B

.090+.050 R
(2.29+1.27)

BULLET

.200 B
(5.08)

1.250(31.75) B

1.7901(45.469) *△

1.8326−.0150(46.548−0.381)

1.8900(48.006) *△

2.222−.020(56.44−0.51)

.090(2.29) R
MAX

.3125−.0030
(7.938−0.076)

.540−.015
(13.72−0.38)

2.915(74.04) MIN   3.075(78.11) MAX

.303 BRITISH

.064(1.63) MIN
.071(1.80) MAX

BREECH
BOLT FACE

.4575(11.621)

.375(9.53) B

.4036(10.251)*△

.4157(10.559)

.3450(8.763) *

.341(8.66)

.3131(7.953)△

.3102(7.879)

.303(7.70)
BORE DIA
.314(7.98)
GROOVE DIA

.4620 △
(11.735)

20°16'B

15°B

0°24'4"B

0°40'23"B

.090(2.29) R MAX

.200 B
(5.08)

1.250(31.75) B

1.8126(46.040) *△

1.8513(47.023)

1.8920(48.057) *△

2.222(56.44)

2.2740(57.760)△

2.4830(63.068)

2.7894(70.851)△

.550+.012
(13.97+0.30)

.125+.030 R
(3.18+0.76)

△ 5 GROOVES
△ .0936+.0020 WIDE
(2.377+0.051)
TWIST 10(254) LH−
OPTIONAL
MIN BORE & GROOVE
AREA .0747 SQ IN.
(48.193 mm²)

CHAMBER
UNLESS OTHERWISE
NOTED
ALL DIA +.002 (0.05)
LENGTH TOL +.015 (0.38)

NOTE
B = BASIC
(XX.XX) = MILLIMETERS
⊗ = HEADSPACE DIMENSION
* DIMENSIONS ARE TO INTERSECTION OF LINES   △=REFERENCE DIMENSION
ALL CALCULATIONS APPLY AT MAXIMUM MATERIAL CONDITION (MMC)

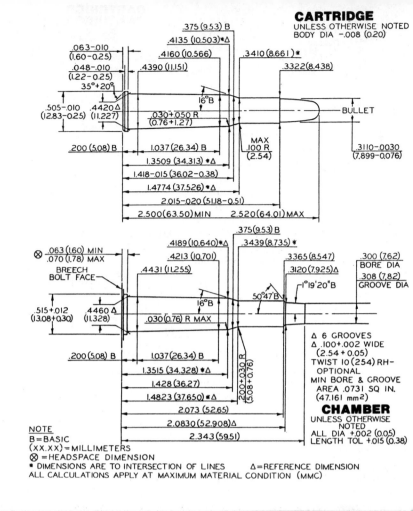

.303 SAVAGE

.063-.010 (1.60-0.25)
.048-.010 (1.22-0.25)
35°+20°
.505-.010 (12.83-0.25)
.4420 △ (11.227)
.200 (5.08) B
.375 (9.53) B
.4135 (10.503)*△
.4160 (10.566)
.4390 (11.151)
16°B
.030+.050 R (0.76+1.27)
1.037 (26.34) B
1.3509 (34.313)*△
1.418-.015 (36.02-0.38)
1.4774 (37.526)*△
2.015-.020 (51.18-0.51)
2.500 (63.50) MIN
.3410 (8.661)*
.3322 (8.438)
BULLET
MAX .100 R (2.54)
.3110-.0030 (7.899-0.076)
2.520 (64.01) MAX

⊗ .063 (1.60) MIN
.070 (1.78) MAX
BREECH BOLT FACE
.515+.012 (13.08+0.30)
.4460 △ (11.328)
.200 (5.08) B
.4189 (10.640)*△
.4213 (10.701)
.4431 (11.255)
16°B
.030 (0.76) R MAX
1.037 (26.34) B
1.3515 (34.328)*△
1.428 (36.27)
1.4823 (37.650)*△
2.073 (52.65)
2.0830 (52.908)△
2.343 (59.51)
.375 (9.53) B
.3439 (8.735)*
50°47'B
.200+.030 R (5.08+0.76)
.3365 (8.547)
.3120 (7.925)△
-1°19'20"B
.300 (7.62) BORE DIA
.308 (7.82) GROOVE DIA

△ 6 GROOVES
△ .100+.002 WIDE (2.54+0.05)
TWIST 10 (254) RH-OPTIONAL
MIN BORE & GROOVE AREA .0731 SQ IN. (47.161 mm2)

CHAMBER
UNLESS OTHERWISE NOTED
ALL DIA +.002 (0.05)
LENGTH TOL +.015 (0.38)

NOTE
B = BASIC
(XX.XX) = MILLIMETERS
⊗ = HEADSPACE DIMENSION
* DIMENSIONS ARE TO INTERSECTION OF LINES   △ = REFERENCE DIMENSION
ALL CALCULATIONS APPLY AT MAXIMUM MATERIAL CONDITION (MMC)

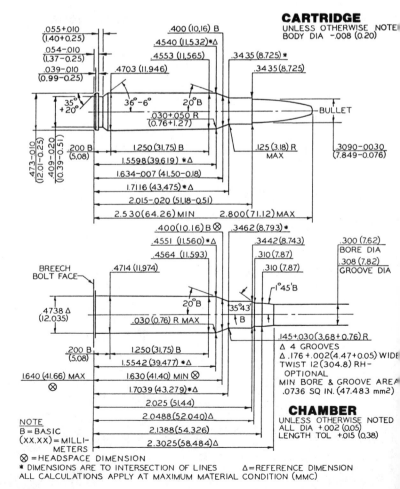

.308 WINCHESTER

.055+.010 (1.40+0.25)
.054-.010 (1.37-0.25)
.039-.010 (0.99-0.25)
.4703 (11.946)
35° +20°
36°-6°
20°B
.030+.050 R (0.76+1.27)
.473-.010 (12.01-0.25)
.409-.020 (10.39-0.51)
.200 B (5.08)
1.250 (31.75) B
1.5598 (39.619)*△
1.634-.007 (41.50-0.18)
1.7116 (43.475)*△
2.015-.020 (51.18-0.51)
2.530 (64.26) MIN
.400 (10.16) B
.4540 (11.532)*△
.4553 (11.565)
.3435 (8.725)*
.3435 (8.725)
.125 (3.18) R MAX
BULLET
.3090-.0030 (7.849-0.076)
2.800 (71.12) MAX

BREECH BOLT FACE
.4738 △ (12.035)
.200 B (5.08)
.4714 (11.974)
20°B
.030 (0.76) R MAX
1.640 (41.66) MAX ⊗
1.250 (31.75) B
1.5542 (39.477)*△
1.630 (41.40) MIN ⊗
1.7039 (43.279)*△
2.025 (51.44)
2.0488 (52.040)△
2.1388 (54.326)
2.3025 (58.484)△
.400 (10.16) B ⊗
.4551 (11.560)*△
.4564 (11.593)
.3462 (8.793)*
.3442 (8.743)
.310 (7.87)
.310 (7.87)
35°43'
B
-1°45'B
.300 (7.62) BORE DIA
.308 (7.82) GROOVE DIA
.145+.030 (3.68+0.76) R

△ 4 GROOVES
△ .176+.002 (4.47+0.05) WIDE
TWIST 12 (304.8) RH-OPTIONAL
MIN BORE & GROOVE AREA .0736 SQ IN. (47.483 mm2)

CHAMBER
UNLESS OTHERWISE NOTED
ALL DIA +.002 (0.05)
LENGTH TOL +.015 (0.38)

NOTE
B = BASIC
(XX.XX) = MILLIMETERS
⊗ = HEADSPACE DIMENSION
* DIMENSIONS ARE TO INTERSECTION OF LINES   △ = REFERENCE DIMENSION
ALL CALCULATIONS APPLY AT MAXIMUM MATERIAL CONDITION (MMC)

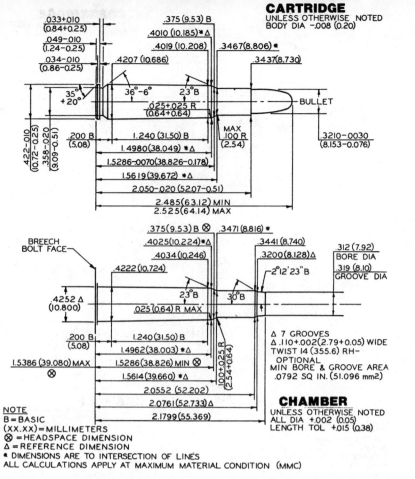

.32 REMINGTON

CARTRIDGE
UNLESS OTHERWISE NOTED
BODY DIA -.008 (0.20)

.033+.010
(0.84+0.25)
.049-.010
(1.24-0.25)
.034-.010
(0.86-0.25)
.4207 (10.686)
.375 (9.53) B
.4010 (10.185) *△
.4019 (10.208)
.3467 (8.806) *
.3437 (8.730)
BULLET
35°+20°
36°-6°
23°B
.025+.025 R
(0.64+0.64)
.422-.010
(10.72-0.25)
.358-.020
(9.09-0.51)
.200 B
(5.08)
1.240 (31.50) B
MAX .100 R
(2.54)
.3210-.0030
(8.153-0.076)
1.4980 (38.049) *△
1.5286-.0070 (38.826-0.178)
1.5619 (39.672) *△
2.050-.020 (52.07-0.51)
2.485 (63.12) MIN
2.525 (64.14) MAX

BREECH
BOLT FACE
.375 (9.53) B ⊗
.3471 (8.816) *
.4025 (10.224) *△
.4034 (10.246)
.3441 (8.740)
.3200 (8.128) △
.312 (7.92)
BORE DIA
.319 (8.10)
GROOVE DIA
.4222 (10.724)
2°12'23" B
.4252 △
(10.800)
23° B
30° B
.025 (0.64) R MAX
.200 B
(5.08)
1.240 (31.50) B
.100+.025 R
(2.54+0.64)
1.5386 (39.080) MAX ⊗
1.4962 (38.003) *△
1.5286 (38.826) MIN ⊗
1.5614 (39.660) *△
2.0552 (52.202)
2.0761 (52.733) △
2.1799 (55.369)

△ 7 GROOVES
△ .110+.002 (2.79+0.05) WIDE
TWIST 14 (355.6) RH-
OPTIONAL
MIN BORE & GROOVE AREA
.0792 SQ IN. (51.096 mm2)

CHAMBER
UNLESS OTHERWISE NOTED
ALL DIA +.002 (0.05)
LENGTH TOL +.015 (0.38)

NOTE
B = BASIC
(XX.XX) = MILLIMETERS
⊗ = HEADSPACE DIMENSION
△ = REFERENCE DIMENSION
* DIMENSIONS ARE TO INTERSECTION OF LINES
ALL CALCULATIONS APPLY AT MAXIMUM MATERIAL CONDITION (MMC)

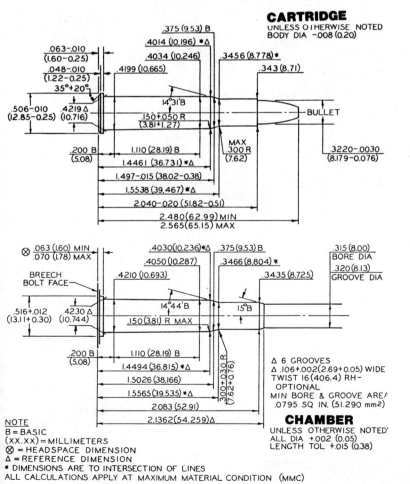

.32 WINCHESTER SPECIAL

CARTRIDGE
UNLESS OTHERWISE NOTED
BODY DIA -.008 (0.20)

.063-.010
(1.60-0.25)
.048-.010
(1.22-0.25)
.375 (9.53) B
.4014 (10.196) *△
.4034 (10.246)
.3456 (8.778) *
.343 (8.71)
.4199 (10.665)
BULLET
35°+20°
14°31' B
.150+.050 R
(3.81+1.27)
.506-.010
(12.85-0.25)
.4219 △
(10.716)
MAX .300 R
(7.62)
.3220-.0030
(8.179-0.076)
.200 B
(5.08)
1.110 (28.19) B
1.4461 (36.731) *△
1.497-.015 (38.02-0.38)
1.5538 (39.467) *△
2.040-.020 (51.82-0.51)
2.480 (62.99) MIN
2.565 (65.15) MAX

⊗ .063 (1.60) MIN
.070 (1.78) MAX
.4030 (10.236) *△
.375 (9.53) B
.315 (8.00)
BORE DIA
.320 (8.13)
GROOVE DIA
BREECH
BOLT FACE
.4050 (10.287)
.3466 (8.804) *
.4210 (10.693)
.3435 (8.725)
14°44' B
15° B
.516+.012
(13.11+0.30)
.4230 △
(10.744)
.150 (3.81) R MAX
.200 B
(5.08)
1.110 (28.19) B
.300+.030 R
(7.62+0.76)
1.4494 (36.815) *△
1.5026 (38.166)
1.5565 (39.535) *△
2.083 (52.91)
2.1362 (54.259) △

△ 6 GROOVES
△ .106+.002 (2.69+0.05) WIDE
TWIST 16 (406.4) RH-
OPTIONAL
MIN BORE & GROOVE AREA
.0795 SQ IN. (51.290 mm2)

CHAMBER
UNLESS OTHERWISE NOTED
ALL DIA +.002 (0.05)
LENGTH TOL +.015 (0.38)

NOTE
B = BASIC
(XX.XX) = MILLIMETERS
⊗ = HEADSPACE DIMENSION
△ = REFERENCE DIMENSION
* DIMENSIONS ARE TO INTERSECTION OF LINES
ALL CALCULATIONS APPLY AT MAXIMUM MATERIAL CONDITION (MMC)

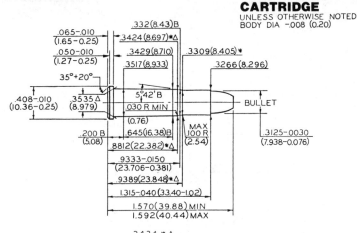

.32-20 WINCHESTER

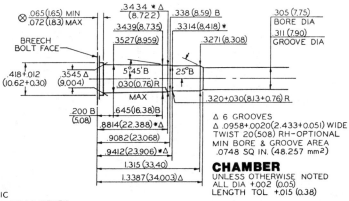

.338 WINCHESTER MAGNUM

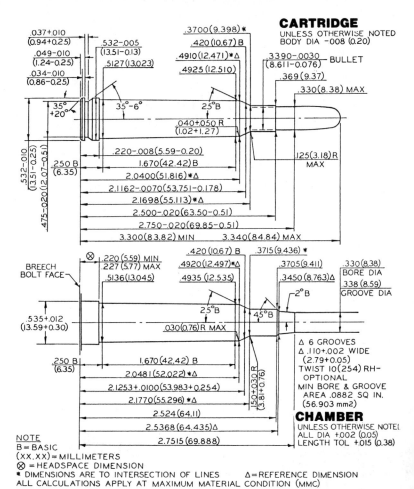

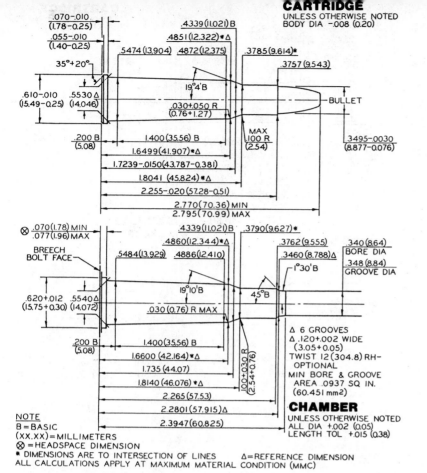

CARTRIDGE

UNLESS OTHERWISE NOTED
BODY DIA -.008 (0.20)

.070-.010
(1.78-0.25)
.055-.010
(1.40-0.25)
35°+20°
.610-.010
(15.49-0.25)
.5530 Δ
(14.046)
.200 B
(5.08)

.4339 (11.021) B
.4851 (12.322)*Δ
.5474 (13.904) .4872 (12.375)
19°4'B
.030+.050 R
(0.76+1.27)
.3785 (9.614)*
.3757 (9.543)
BULLET
MAX
.100 R
(2.54)
.3495-.0030
(8.877-0.076)
1.400 (35.56) B
1.6499 (41.907)*Δ
1.7239-.0150 (43.787-0.381)
1.8041 (45.824)*Δ
2.255-.020 (57.28-0.51)
2.770 (70.36) MIN
2.795 (70.99) MAX

⊗ .070 (1.78) MIN
.077 (1.96) MAX
BREECH
BOLT FACE
.620+.012 .5540 Δ
(15.75+0.30) (14.072)
.200 B
(5.08)

.4339 (11.021) B
.4860 (12.344)*Δ
.5484 (13.929) .4886 (12.410)
19°10'B
.030 (0.76) R MAX
.3790 (9.627)*
.3762 (9.555)
.3460 (8.788) Δ
1°30'B
45°B
.340 (8.64)
BORE DIA
.348 (8.84)
GROOVE DIA
1.400 (35.56) B
1.6600 (42.164)*Δ
1.735 (44.07)
1.8140 (46.076)*Δ
2.265 (57.53)
2.2801 (57.915) Δ
2.3947 (60.825)
.100+.030 R
(2.54+0.76)

Δ 6 GROOVES
Δ .120+.002 WIDE
(3.05+0.05)
TWIST 12 (304.8) RH-
OPTIONAL
MIN BORE & GROOVE
AREA .0937 SQ IN.
(60.451 mm2)

CHAMBER

UNLESS OTHERWISE NOTED
ALL DIA +.002 (0.05)
LENGTH TOL +.015 (0.38)

NOTE
B = BASIC
(XX.XX) = MILLIMETERS
⊗ = HEADSPACE DIMENSION
* DIMENSIONS ARE TO INTERSECTION OF LINES   Δ=REFERENCE DIMENSION
ALL CALCULATIONS APPLY AT MAXIMUM MATERIAL CONDITION (MMC)

.348 WINCHESTER

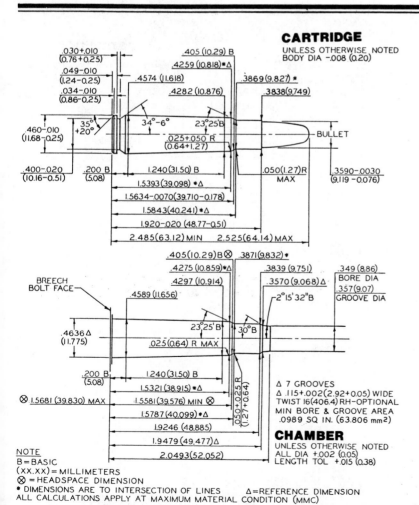

CARTRIDGE

UNLESS OTHERWISE NOTED
BODY DIA -.008 (0.20)

.030+.010
(0.76+0.25)
.049-.010
(1.24-0.25)
.034-.010
(0.86-0.25)
35°+20°
.460-.010
(11.68-0.25)
34°-6°
.400-.020
(10.16-0.51)
.200 B
(5.08)

.405 (10.29) B
.4259 (10.818)*Δ
.4574 (11.618) .4282 (10.876)
.025+.050 R
(0.64+1.27)
23°25'B
.3869 (9.827) *
.3838 (9.749)
BULLET
.050 (1.27) R
MAX
.3590-.0030
(9.119-0.076)
1.240 (31.50) B
1.5393 (39.098)*Δ
1.5634-.0070 (39.710-0.178)
1.5843 (40.241)*Δ
1.920-.020 (48.77-0.51)
2.485 (63.12) MIN   2.525 (64.14) MAX

BREECH
BOLT FACE
.4636 Δ
(11.775)
.200 B
(5.08)
⊗ 1.5681 (39.830) MAX

.405 (10.29) B ⊗ .3871 (9.832)*
.4275 (10.859)*Δ
.4297 (10.914) .3839 (9.751)
.4589 (11.656) .3570 (9.068) Δ
2°15'32"B
23°25'B 30°B
.025 (0.64) R MAX
.349 (8.86)
BORE DIA
.357 (9.07)
GROOVE DIA
1.240 (31.50) B
1.5321 (38.915)*Δ
1.5581 (39.576) MIN ⊗
1.5787 (40.099)*Δ
1.9246 (48.885)
1.9479 (49.477) Δ
2.0493 (52.052)
.050+.025 R
(1.27+0.64)

Δ 7 GROOVES
Δ .115+.002 (2.92+0.05) WIDE
TWIST 16 (406.4) RH-OPTIONAL
MIN BORE & GROOVE AREA
.0989 SQ IN. (63.806 mm2)

CHAMBER

UNLESS OTHERWISE NOTED
ALL DIA +.002 (0.05)
LENGTH TOL +.015 (0.38)

.35 REMINGTON

NOTE
B = BASIC
(XX.XX) = MILLIMETERS
⊗ = HEADSPACE DIMENSION
* DIMENSIONS ARE TO INTERSECTION OF LINES   Δ=REFERENCE DIMENSION
ALL CALCULATIONS APPLY AT MAXIMUM MATERIAL CONDITION (MMC)

.350 REMINGTON MAGNUM

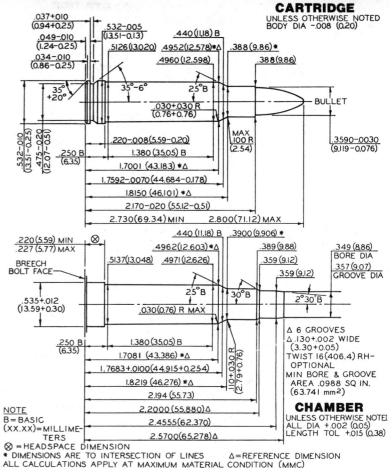

CARTRIDGE
UNLESS OTHERWISE NOTED
BODY DIA -.008 (0.20)

.037+.010
(0.94+0.25)
.049-.010
(1.24-0.25)
.034-.010
(0.86-0.25)
.532-.005
(13.51-0.13)
.5126(13.020)
.440 (11.18) B
.4952(12.578)*△
.4960 (12.598)
.388(9.86)*
.388 (9.86)
35°
+20°
35°-6°
25°B
BULLET
.030+.030 R
(0.76+0.76)
MAX
.100 R
(2.54)
.3590-.0030
(9.119-0.076)
.532-.010
(13.51-0.25)
.475-.020
(12.07-0.51)
.220-.008(5.59-0.20)
.250 B
(6.35)
1.380 (35.05) B
1.7001 (43.183) *△
1.7592-.0070(44.684-0.178)
1.8150 (46.101) *△
2.170-.020 (55.12-0.51)
2.730(69.34) MIN   2.800(71.12) MAX

.220(5.59) MIN
.227 (5.77) MAX
⊗
.440 (11.18) B
.3900 (9.906) *
.389 (9.88)
.359 (9.12)
.349 (8.86)
BORE DIA
.357 (9.07)
GROOVE DIA
BREECH
BOLT FACE
.5137(13.048)
.4962(12.603)*△
.4971(12.626)
.359 (9.12)
.535+.012
(13.59+0.30)
25°B
30°B
2°30'B
.030(0.76) R MAX
.250 B
(6.35)
1.380 (35.05) B
1.7081 (43.386) *△
1.7683+.0100(44.915+0.254)
1.8219 (46.276) *△
2.194 (55.73)
.110+.030 R
(2.79+0.76)
2.2000 (55.880) △
2.4555 (62.370)
2.5700 (65.278) △

△ 6 GROOVES
△ .130+.002 WIDE
(3.30+0.05)
TWIST 16(406.4) RH-
OPTIONAL
MIN BORE & GROOVE
AREA .0988 SQ IN.
(63.741 mm2)

CHAMBER
UNLESS OTHERWISE NOTED
ALL DIA +.002 (0.05)
LENGTH TOL +.015 (0.38)

NOTE
B = BASIC
(XX.XX) = MILLIME-
TERS
⊗ = HEADSPACE DIMENSION
* DIMENSIONS ARE TO INTERSECTION OF LINES   △ = REFERENCE DIMENSION
ALL CALCULATIONS APPLY AT MAXIMUM MATERIAL CONDITION (MMC)

CARTRIDGE
UNLESS OTHERWISE NOTED
BODY DIA -.008 (0.20)

.025+.010
(0.64+0.25)
.050-.010
(1.27-0.25)
.035-.010
(0.89-0.25)
.3805(9.665)△
.3804(9.662)
.3775(9.589)
.3770 (9.576) △
35°+20°
10°-3°
BULLET
.410-.010
(10.41-0.25)
.355-.020
(9.02-0.51)
.3520-.0030
(8.941-0.076)
.1523 (3.868)
.200 (5.08) B
1.000 (25.40) B
1.380-.020 (35.05-0.51)
1.875(47.63) MIN
1.900(48.26) MAX

.351 WINCHESTER SELF LOADING

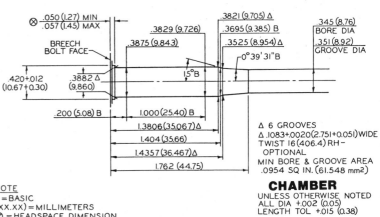

⊗ .050 (1.27) MIN
.057 (1.45) MAX
.3829 (9.726)
.3875 (9.843)
.3821 (9.705) △
.3695 (9.385) B
.3525 (8.954) △
.345 (8.76)
BORE DIA
.351 (8.92)
GROOVE DIA
BREECH
BOLT FACE
0°39'31"B
.420+.012
(10.67+0.30)
.3882 △
(9.860)
15°B
.200 (5.08) B
1.000 (25.40) B
1.3806(35.067)△
1.404 (35.66)
1.4357 (36.467)△
1.762 (44.75)

△ 6 GROOVES
△ .1083+.0020(2.751+0.051)WIDE
TWIST 16(406.4) RH-
OPTIONAL
MIN BORE & GROOVE AREA
.0954 SQ IN. (61.548 mm2)

CHAMBER
UNLESS OTHERWISE NOTED
ALL DIA +.002 (0.05)
LENGTH TOL +.015 (0.38)

NOTE
B = BASIC
(XX.XX) = MILLIMETERS
⊗ = HEADSPACE DIMENSION
△ = REFERENCE DIMENSION
* DIMENSIONS ARE TO INTERSECTION OF LINES
ALL CALCULATIONS APPLY AT MAXIMUM MATERIAL CONDITION (MMC)

.358 WINCHESTER

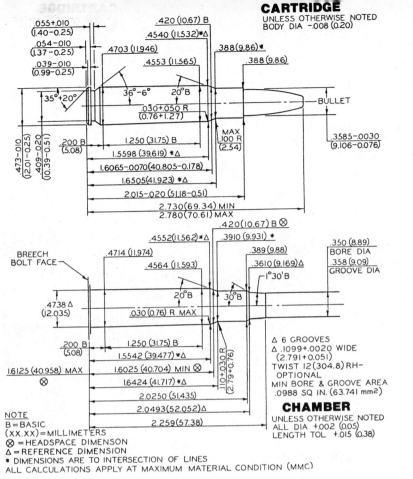

.055+.010 (1.40-0.25)
.054-.010 (1.37-0.25)
.039-.010 (0.99-0.25)
.4703 (11.946)
.4540 (11.532)*△
.420 (10.67) B
.4553 (11.565)
.388 (9.86) *
35°+20°
36°-6°
20°B
.030+.050 R (0.76+1.27)
BULLET
.473-.010 (12.01-0.25)
.409-.020 (10.39-0.51)
.200 B (5.08)
1.250 (31.75) B
MAX .100 R (2.54)
.3585-.0030 (9.106-0.076)
1.5598 (39.619) *△
1.6065-.0070 (40.805-0.178)
1.6505 (41.923) *△
2.015-.020 (51.18-0.51)
2.730 (69.34) MIN
2.780 (70.61) MAX

BREECH BOLT FACE
.4714 (11.974)
.4552 (11.562) *△
.4564 (11.593)
.420 (10.67) B ⊗
.3910 (9.931) *
.350 (8.89) BORE DIA
.389 (9.88)
.358 (9.09) GROOVE DIA
.3610 (9.169) △
1°30' B
.4738 △ (12.035)
20°B
30°B
.030 (0.76) R MAX
.200 B (5.08)
1.250 (31.75) B
1.6125 (40.958) MAX ⊗
1.5542 (39.477) *△
1.6025 (40.704) MIN ⊗
.110+.030 R (2.79+0.76)
1.6424 (41.717) *△
2.0250 (51.435)
2.0493 (52.052) △
2.259 (57.38)

△ 6 GROOVES
△ .1099+.0020 WIDE (2.791+0.051)
TWIST 12 (304.8) RH- OPTIONAL
MIN BORE & GROOVE AREA .0988 SQ IN. (63.741 mm²)

CHAMBER
UNLESS OTHERWISE NOTED
ALL DIA +.002 (0.05)
LENGTH TOL +.015 (0.38)

NOTE
B = BASIC
(XX.XX) = MILLIMETERS
⊗ = HEADSPACE DIMENSON
△ = REFERENCE DIMENSION
* DIMENSIONS ARE TO INTERSECTION OF LINES
ALL CALCULATIONS APPLY AT MAXIMUM MATERIAL CONDITION (MMC)

.375 H&H MAGNUM

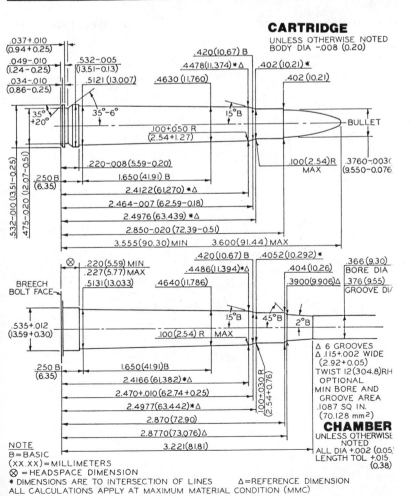

.037+.010 (0.94+0.25)
.049-.010 (1.24-0.25)
.034-.010 (0.86-0.25)
.532-.005 (13.51-0.13)
.5121 (13.007)
.4478 (11.374) *△
.4630 (11.760)
.420 (10.67) B
.402 (10.21) *
.402 (10.21)
35°+20°
35°-6°
15°B
BULLET
.100+.050 R (2.54+1.27)
.532-.010 (13.51-0.25)
.475-.020 (12.07-0.51)
.250 B (6.35)
.220-.008 (5.59-0.20)
1.650 (41.91) B
.100 (2.54) R MAX
.3760-.0030 (9.550-0.076)
2.4122 (61.270) *△
2.464-.007 (62.59-0.18)
2.4976 (63.439) *△
2.850-.020 (72.39-0.51)
3.555 (90.30) MIN
3.600 (91.44) MAX

BREECH BOLT FACE
⊗ .220 (5.59) MIN
.227 (5.77) MAX
.5131 (13.033)
.420 (10.67) B
.4486 (11.394) *△
.4640 (11.786)
.4052 (10.292) *
.404 (10.26)
.366 (9.30) BORE DIA
.3900 (9.906) △
.376 (9.55) GROOVE DIA
.535+.012 (13.59+0.30)
15°B
45°B
2°B
.100 (2.54) R MAX
.250 B (6.35)
1.650 (41.91) B
.100+.030 R (2.54+0.76)
2.4166 (61.382) *△
2.470+.010 (62.74+0.25)
2.4977 (63.442) *△
2.870 (72.90)
2.8770 (73.076) △
3.221 (81.81)

△ 6 GROOVES
△ .115+.002 WIDE (2.92+0.05)
TWIST 12 (304.8) RH OPTIONAL
MIN BORE AND GROOVE AREA .1087 SQ IN. (70.128 mm²)

CHAMBER
UNLESS OTHERWISE NOTED
ALL DIA +.002 (0.05)
LENGTH TOL +.015 (0.38)

NOTE
B = BASIC
(XX.XX) = MILLIMETERS
⊗ = HEADSPACE DIMENSION
△ = REFERENCE DIMENSION
* DIMENSIONS ARE TO INTERSECTION OF LINES
ALL CALCULATIONS APPLY AT MAXIMUM MATERIAL CONDITION (MMC)

285

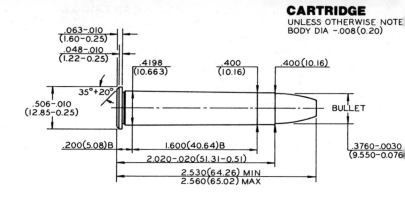

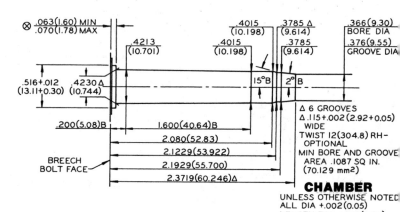

.375 WINCHESTER

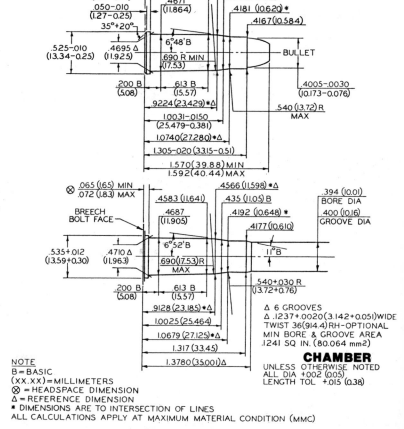

.38-40 WINCHESTER

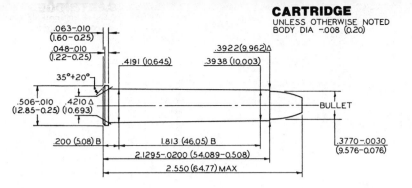

CARTRIDGE
UNLESS OTHERWISE NOTED
BODY DIA -.008 (0.20)

.063-.010
(1.60-0.25)

.048-.010
(1.22-0.25)

.4191 (10.645)

.3922 (9.962) Δ

.3938 (10.003)

35°±20°

.506-.010
(12.85-0.25)

.4210 Δ
(10.693)

BULLET

.200 (5.08) B

1.813 (46.05) B

.3770 -.0030
(9.576-0.076)

2.1295-.0200 (54.089-0.508)

2.550 (64.77) MAX

.38-55 WINCHESTER

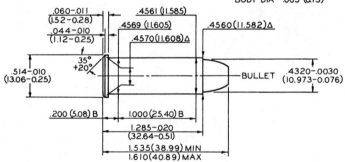

BREECH
BOLT FACE

.063 (1.60) MIN
.070 (1.78) MAX ⊗

.3934 (9.992) Δ

.385 (9.78) B

.373 (9.47)
BORE DIA

.4207 (10.686)

.3949 (10.030)

.379 (9.63)
GROOVE DIA

.516+.012
(13.11+0.30)

.4226 Δ
(10.734)

6°B

.200 (5.08) B

1.813 (46.05) B

2.1182 (53.802) Δ

2.1582 (54.818)

2.2153 (56.269) Δ

Δ 6 GROOVES
Δ .1171+.0020 WIDE
(2.974+0.051)
TWIST 18 (457.2) RH-
OPTIONAL
MIN BORE AND GROOVE
AREA .1114 SQ IN.
(71.871 mm²)

CHAMBER
UNLESS OTHERWISE NOTED
ALL DIA +.002 (0.05)
LENGTH TOL +.015 (0.38)

NOTE
B= BASIC
(XX.XX) = MILLIMETERS
⊗ = HEADSPACE DIMENSION
✱ DIMENSIONS ARE TO INTERSECTION OF LINES   Δ = REFERENCE DIMENSION
ALL CALCULATIONS APPLY AT MAXIMUM MATERIAL CONDITION (MMC)

CARTRIDGE
UNLESS OTHERWISE NOTED
BODY DIA -.005 (0.13)

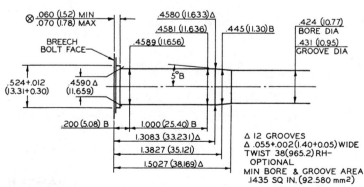

.060-.011
(1.52-0.28)

.4561 (11.585)

.4569 (11.605)

.4560 (11.582) Δ

.044-.010
(1.12-0.25)

.4570 (11.608) Δ

35°
+20°

.514-.010
(13.06-0.25)

BULLET

.4320-.0030
(10.973-0.076)

.200 (5.08) B

1.000 (25.40) B

1.285-.020
(32.64-0.51)

1.535 (38.99) MIN

1.610 (40.89) MAX

.44 REMINGTON MAGNUM

.060 (1.52) MIN ⊗
.070 (1.78) MAX

.4580 (11.633) Δ

.4581 (11.636)

.445 (11.30) B

.424 (10.77)
BORE DIA

BREECH
BOLT FACE

.4589 (11.656)

.431 (10.95)
GROOVE DIA

.524+.012
(13.31+0.30)

.4590 Δ
(11.659)

5°B

.200 (5.08) B

1.000 (25.40) B

1.3083 (33.231) Δ

1.3827 (35.121)

1.5027 (38.169) Δ

Δ 12 GROOVES
Δ .055+.002 (1.40+0.05) WIDE
TWIST 38 (965.2) RH-
OPTIONAL
MIN BORE & GROOVE AREA
.1435 SQ IN. (92.580 mm²)

CHAMBER
UNLESS OTHERWISE NOTED
ALL DIA +.004 (0.10)
LENGTH TOL +.015 (0.38)

NOTE
B= BASIC
(XX.XX) = MILLIMETERS
⊗ = HEADSPACE DIMENSION
Δ = REFERENCE DIMENSION
✱ DIMENSIONS ARE TO INTERSECTION OF LINES
ALL CALCULATIONS APPLY AT MAXIMUM MATERIAL CONDITION (MMC)

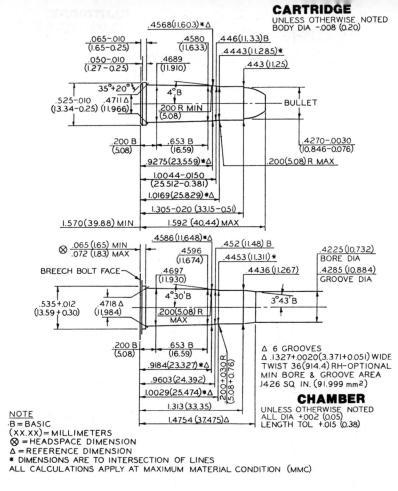

.44-40 WINCHESTER

NOTE
-B = BASIC
(XX.XX) = MILLIMETERS
⊗ = HEADSPACE DIMENSION
Δ = REFERENCE DIMENSION
* DIMENSIONS ARE TO INTERSECTION OF LINES
ALL CALCULATIONS APPLY AT MAXIMUM MATERIAL CONDITION (MMC)

.444 MARLIN

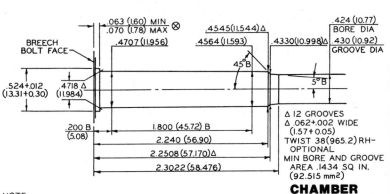

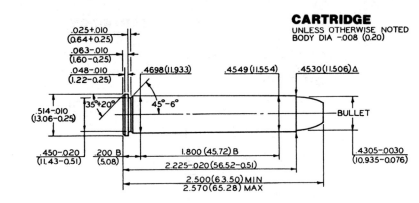

NOTE
B = BASIC
(XX.XX) = MILLIMETERS
⊗ = HEADSPACE DIMENSION
Δ = REFERENCE DIMENSION
* DIMENSIONS ARE TO INTERSECTION OF LINES
ALL CALCULATIONS APPLY AT MAXIMUM MATERIAL CONDITION (MMC)

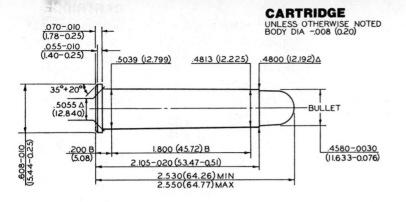

CARTRIDGE
UNLESS OTHERWISE NOTED
BODY DIA -.008 (0.20)

.070-.010
(1.78-0.25)

.055-.010
(1.40-0.25)

.5039 (12.799)

.4813 (12.225)

.4800 (12.192)△

35°+20°

.5055 △
(12.840)

BULLET

.608-.010
(15.44-0.25)

.200 B
(5.08)

1.800 (45.72) B

.4580-.0030
(11.633-0.076)

2.105-.020 (53.47-0.51)

2.530 (64.26) MIN
2.550 (64.77) MAX

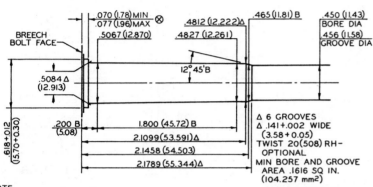

.070 (1.78) MIN
.077 (1.96) MAX ⊗

.5067 (12.870)

.4812 (12.222)△
.4827 (12.261)

.465 (11.81) B

.450 (11.43)
BORE DIA
.456 (11.58)
GROOVE DIA

BREECH
BOLT FACE

.5084 △
(12.913)

12° 45' B

.618+.012
(15.70+0.30)

.200 B
(5.08)

1.800 (45.72) B

2.1099 (53.591)△

2.1458 (54.503)

2.1789 (55.344)△

△ 6 GROOVES
△ .141+.002 WIDE
(3.58+0.05)
TWIST 20 (508) RH-
OPTIONAL
MIN BORE AND GROOVE
AREA .1616 SQ IN.
(104.257 mm2)

CHAMBER
UNLESS OTHERWISE NOTED
ALL DIA +.002 (0.05)
LENGTH TOL +.015 (0.38)

NOTE
B=BASIC
(XX.XX)=MILLIMETERS
⊗ = HEADSPACE DIMENSION
△ = REFERENCE DIMENSION
* DIMENSIONS ARE TO INTERSECTION OF LINES
ALL CALCULATIONS APPLY AT MAXIMUM MATERIAL CONDITION (MMC)

.45-70
GOVERNMENT

CARTRIDGE
UNLESS OTHERWISE NOTED
BODY DIA -.008 (0.20)

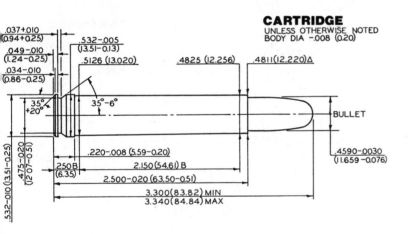

.037+.010
(0.94+0.25)

.049-.010
(1.24-0.25)

.034-.010
(0.86-0.25)

.532-.005
(13.51-0.13)

.5126 (13.020)

.4825 (12.256)

.4811 (12.220)△

35°
+20°

35°-6°

BULLET

.532-.010
(13.51-0.25)

.475-.020
(12.07-0.51)

.250 B
(6.35)

.220-.008 (5.59-0.20)

2.150 (54.61) B

.4590-.0030
(11.659-0.076)

2.500-.020 (63.50-0.51)

3.300 (83.82) MIN
3.340 (84.84) MAX

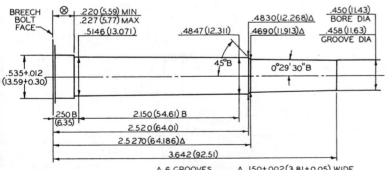

⊗ .220 (5.59) MIN
.227 (5.77) MAX

.5146 (13.071)

.4847 (12.311)

.4830 (12.268)△
.4690 (11.913)△

.450 (11.43)
BORE DIA
.458 (11.63)
GROOVE DIA

BREECH
BOLT
FACE

.535+.012
(13.59+0.30)

45° B

0° 29' 30" B

.250 B
(6.35)

2.150 (54.61) B

2.520 (64.01)

2.5270 (64.186)△

3.642 (92.51)

△ 6 GROOVES   △ .150+.002 (3.81+0.05) WIDE
TWIST 14 (355.6) RH-OPTIONAL
MIN BORE & GROOVE AREA .1627 SQ IN. (104.967 mm2)

CHAMBER
UNLESS OTHERWISE NOTED
ALL DIA +.002 (0.05)   LENGTH TOL +.015 (0.38)

.458 WINCHESTER
MAGNUM

NOTE
B=BASIC
(XX.XX)=MILLIMETERS
⊗ = HEADSPACE DIMENSION
△ = REFERENCE DIMENSION
* DIMENSIONS ARE TO INTERSECTION OF LINES
ALL CALCULATIONS APPLY AT MAXIMUM MATERIAL CONDITION (MMC)

9mm LUGER

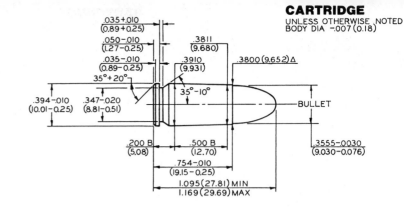

CARTRIDGE
UNLESS OTHERWISE NOTED
BODY DIA -.007(0.18)

.035+.010
(0.89+0.25)
.050-.010
(1.27-0.25)
.035-.010
(0.89-0.25)
35°+20°
35°-10°
.3811
(9.680)
.3910
(9.931)
.3800(9.652)△
BULLET
.394-.010
(10.01-0.25)
.347-.020
(8.81-0.51)
.200 B
(5.08)
.500 B
(12.70)
.3555-.0030
(9.030-0.076)
.754-.010
(19.15-0.25)
1.095(27.81) MIN
1.169(29.69) MAX

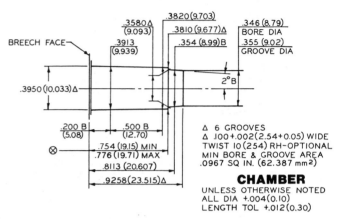

BREECH FACE
.3580△
(9.093)
.3913
(9.939)
.3820(9.703)
.3810(9.677)△
.354(8.99)B
.346(8.79)
BORE DIA
.355(9.02)
GROOVE DIA
.3950(10.033)△
2°B
.200 B
(5.08)
.500 B
(12.70)
⊗
.754(19.15) MIN
.776(19.71) MAX
.8113(20.607)
.9258(23.515)△

△ 6 GROOVES
△ .100+.002(2.54+0.05) WIDE
TWIST 10(254) RH-OPTIONAL
MIN BORE & GROOVE AREA
.0967 SQ IN. (62.387 mm²)

CHAMBER
UNLESS OTHERWISE NOTED
ALL DIA +.004(0.10)
LENGTH TOL +.012(0.30)

NOTE
B = BASIC
(XX.XX) = MILLIMETERS   ⊗ = HEADSPACE DIMENSION
✱ DIMENSIONS ARE TO INTERSECTION OF LINES   △ = REFERENCE DIMENSIONS
ALL CALCULATIONS APPLY AT MAXIMUM MATERIAL CONDITION (MMC)

9mm WINCHESTER MAGNUM

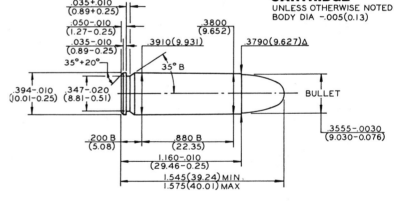

CARTRIDGE
UNLESS OTHERWISE NOTED
BODY DIA -.005(0.13)

.035+.010
(0.89+0.25)
.050-.010
(1.27-0.25)
.035-.010
(0.89-0.25)
35°+20°
.3910(9.931)
35° B
.3800
(9.652)
.3790(9.627)△
BULLET
.394-.010
(10.01-0.25)
.347-.020
(8.81-0.51)
.200 B
(5.08)
.880 B
(22.35)
.3555-.0030
(9.030-0.076)
1.160-.010
(29.46-0.25)
1.545(39.24) MIN
1.575(40.01) MAX

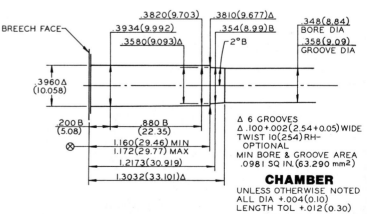

BREECH FACE
.3820(9.703)
.3934(9.992)
.3580(9.093)△
.3810(9.677)△
.354(8.99)B
2°B
.348(8.84)
BORE DIA
.358(9.09)
GROOVE DIA
.3960△
(10.058)
.200 B
(5.08)
.880 B
(22.35)
⊗
1.160(29.46) MIN
1.172(29.77) MAX
1.2173(30.919)
1.3032(33.101)△

△ 6 GROOVES
△ .100+.002(2.54+0.05) WIDE
TWIST 10(254) RH-
OPTIONAL
MIN BORE & GROOVE AREA
.0981 SQ IN. (63.290 mm²)

CHAMBER
UNLESS OTHERWISE NOTED
ALL DIA +.004(0.10)
LENGTH TOL +.012(0.30)

NOTE
B = BASIC   (XX.XX) = MILLIMETERS   ⊗ = HEADSPACE DIMENSION
✱ DIMENSIONS ARE TO INTERSECTION OF LINES   △ = REFERENCE DIMENSION
ALL CALCULATIONS APPLY AT MAXIMUM MATERIAL CONDITION (MMC)

.22 REMINGTON JET MAGNUM

CARTRIDGE
UNLESS OTHERWISE NOTED
BODY DIA -.008 (0.20)

.059-.010 (1.50-0.25)
.044-.010 (1.12-0.25)
.3682 (9.352)
.3759 (9.548)
.3657 (9.289)*Δ
.300 (7.62) B
2510 (6.375)*
.251 (6.38)
35°+20°
.440-.012 (11.18-0.30)
6°40'30" B
BULLET
MAX .100 R (2.54)
.200 B (5.08)
.300 B (7.62)
.030+.030 R (0.76+0.76)
.2225-.0060 (5.652-0.152)
.5984 (15.199)*Δ
.879-.015 (22.33-0.38)
UNDERCUT AHEAD OF RIM IS OPTIONAL
1.0883 (27.643)*Δ
1.288-.020 (32.72-0.51)
1.630 (41.40) MIN   1.659 (42.14) MAX

⊗ .060 (1.52) MIN   .070 (1.78) MAX
BREECH FACE
.3661 (9.299)*Δ
.3687 (9.365)
.3764 (9.561)
.2530* (6.426)
.300 B (7.62)
.252 (6.40)
.2245 (5.702)Δ
.2245 (5.702)
.219 (5.56) BORE DIA
.2225 (5.652) GROOVE DIA
CYLINDER FACE
.444+.012 (11.28+0.30)
.3800 Δ (9.652)
MAX .030 R (0.76)
6°40'30" B
45° B
BARREL FACE
.200 B (5.08)
.300 B (7.62)
.6007 (15.258)*Δ
.125+.030 R (3.18+0.76)
.8832 (22.433)
NOT ALL MANUFACTURERS USE A RECESS IN THE CYLINDER
1.0840 (27.534)*Δ
1.298 (32.97)
1.3118 (33.320)Δ

Δ 6 GROOVES
Δ .071+.002 (1.80+0.05) WIDE
TWIST 15(381) RH-OPTIONAL
MIN BORE & GROOVE AREA
.0384 SQ IN. (24.774 mm2)

CHAMBER
UNLESS OTHERWISE NOTED
ALL DIA +.002 (0.05)
LENGTH TOL +.015 (0.38)

NOTE
B = BASIC
(XX.XX) = MILLIMETERS   ⊗ = HEADSPACE DIMENSION
* DIMENSIONS ARE TO INTERSECTION OF LINES   Δ = REFERENCE DIMENSION
ALL CALCULATIONS APPLY AT MAXIMUM MATERIAL CONDITION (MMC)

.221 REMINGTON FIREBALL

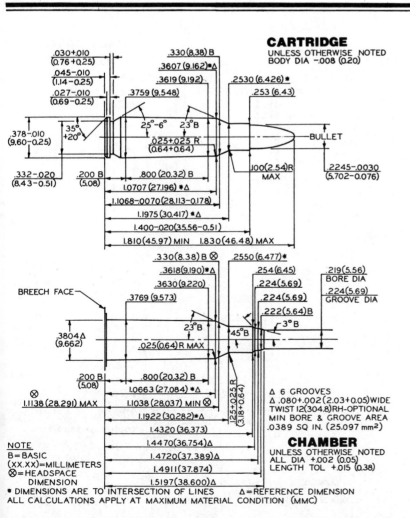

CARTRIDGE
UNLESS OTHERWISE NOTED
BODY DIA -.008 (0.20)

.030+.010 (0.76+0.25)
.045-.010 (1.14-0.25)
.027-.010 (0.69-0.25)
.330 (8.38) B
.3607 (9.162)*Δ
.3619 (9.192)
.3759 (9.548)
.2530 (6.426)*
.253 (6.43)
.378-.010 (9.60-0.25)
35° +20°
25°-6°
23° B
.025+.025 R (0.64+0.64)
BULLET
.100 (2.54)R MAX
.2245-.0030 (5.702-0.076)
.332-.020 (8.43-0.51)
.200 B (5.08)
.800 (20.32) B
1.0707 (27.196)*Δ
1.1068-.0070 (28.113-0.178)
1.1975 (30.417)*Δ
1.400-.020 (35.56-0.51)
1.810 (45.97) MIN   1.830 (46.48) MAX

BREECH FACE
.330 (8.38) B ⊗
.3618 (9.190)*Δ
.3630 (9.220)
.3769 (9.573)
.2550 (6.477)*
.254 (6.45)
.224 (5.69)
.224 (5.69)
.222 (5.64) B
.219 (5.56) BORE DIA
.224 (5.69) GROOVE DIA
.3804 Δ (9.662)
23° B
45° B
3° B
.025 (0.64) R MAX
.200 B (5.08)
.800 (20.32) B
1.0663 (27.084)*Δ
.125+.025 R (3.18+0.64)
1.1038 (28.037) MIN ⊗
⊗ 1.1138 (28.291) MAX
1.1922 (30.282)*Δ
1.4320 (36.373)
1.4470 (36.754)Δ
1.4720 (37.389)Δ
1.4911 (37.874)
1.5197 (38.600)Δ

Δ 6 GROOVES
Δ .080+.002 (2.03+0.05) WIDE
TWIST 12(304.8) RH-OPTIONAL
MIN BORE & GROOVE AREA
.0389 SQ IN. (25.097 mm2)

CHAMBER
UNLESS OTHERWISE NOTED
ALL DIA +.002 (0.05)
LENGTH TOL +.015 (0.38)

NOTE
B = BASIC
(XX.XX) = MILLIMETERS
⊗ = HEADSPACE DIMENSION
* DIMENSIONS ARE TO INTERSECTION OF LINES   Δ = REFERENCE DIMENSION
ALL CALCULATIONS APPLY AT MAXIMUM MATERIAL CONDITION (MMC)

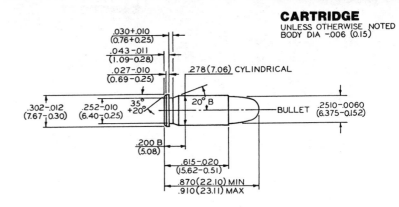

CARTRIDGE
UNLESS OTHERWISE NOTED
BODY DIA -.006 (0.15)

.25 AUTOMATIC

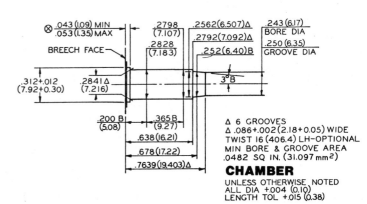

Δ 6 GROOVES
Δ .086+.002(2.18+0.05) WIDE
TWIST 16 (406.4) LH-OPTIONAL
MIN BORE & GROOVE AREA
.0482 SQ IN. (31.097 mm2)

CHAMBER
UNLESS OTHERWISE NOTED
ALL DIA +.004 (0.10)
LENGTH TOL +.015 (0.38)

NOTE
B = BASIC
(XX.XX) = MILLIMETERS   ⊗ = HEADSPACE DIMENSION
* DIMENSIONS ARE TO INTERSECTION OF LINES   Δ = REFERENCE DIMENSION
ALL CALCULATIONS APPLY AT MAXIMUM MATERIAL CONDITION (MMC)

CARTRIDGE
UNLESS OTHERWISE NOTED
BODY DIA -.008 (0.20)

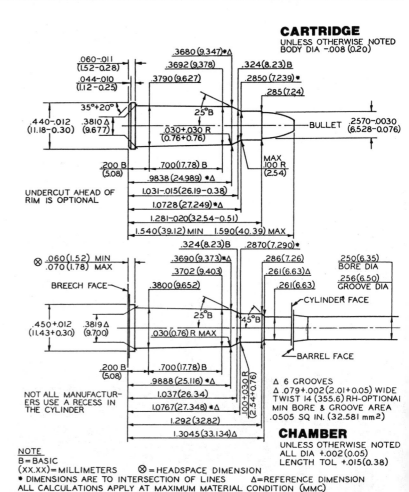

.256 WINCHESTER
MAGNUM

Δ 6 GROOVES
Δ .079+.002(2.01+0.05) WIDE
TWIST 14 (355.6) RH-OPTIONAL
MIN BORE & GROOVE AREA
.0505 SQ IN. (32.581 mm2)

CHAMBER
UNLESS OTHERWISE NOTED
ALL DIA +.002 (0.05)
LENGTH TOL +.015 (0.38)

NOTE
B = BASIC
(XX.XX) = MILLIMETERS   ⊗ = HEADSPACE DIMENSION
* DIMENSIONS ARE TO INTERSECTION OF LINES   Δ = REFERENCE DIMENSION
ALL CALCULATIONS APPLY AT MAXIMUM MATERIAL CONDITION (MMC)

.30 LUGER (7.65mm)

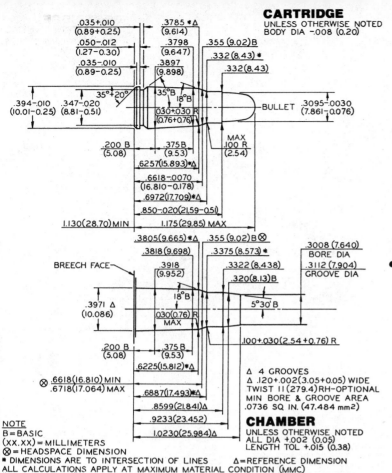

.035+.010 (0.89+0.25)
.050-.012 (1.27-0.30)
.035-.010 (0.89-0.25)
.3785 *Δ (9.614)
.3798 (9.647)
.3897 (9.898)
.355 (9.02)B
.332 (8.43) *
.332 (8.43)
35°+20°
35°B 18°B
BULLET
.3095-.0030 (7.861-0.076)
.394-.010 (10.01-0.25)
.347-.020 (8.81-0.51)
.030+.030 R (0.76+0.76)
.200 B (5.08)
.375B (9.53)
MAX .100 R (2.54)
.6257 (15.893) *Δ
.6618-.0070 (16.810-0.178)
.6972 (17.709) *Δ
.850-.020 (21.59-0.51)
1.130 (28.70) MIN
1.175 (29.85) MAX

.3805 (9.665) *Δ
.3818 (9.698)
.3918 (9.952)
.355 (9.02)B ⊗
.3375 (8.573) *
.3322 (8.438)
.320 (8.13)B
.3008 (7.640) BORE DIA
.3112 (7.904) GROOVE DIA
BREECH FACE
18°B
5°30'B
.3971 Δ (10.086)
.030 (0.76) R MAX
.100+.030 (2.54+0.76) R
.200 B (5.08)
.375 B (9.53)
⊗ .6618 (16.810) MIN
.6718 (17.064) MAX
.6225 (15.812) *Δ
.6887 (17.493) *Δ
.8599 (21.841) Δ
.9233 (23.452)
1.0230 (25.984) Δ

Δ 4 GROOVES
Δ .120+.002 (3.05+0.05) WIDE
TWIST 11 (279.4) RH-OPTIONAL
MIN BORE & GROOVE AREA
.0736 SQ IN. (47.484 mm2)

CHAMBER
UNLESS OTHERWISE NOTED
ALL DIA +.002 (0.05)
LENGTH TOL +.015 (0.38)

.32 AUTOMATIC

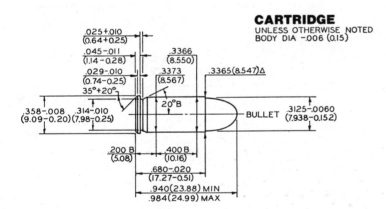

CARTRIDGE
UNLESS OTHERWISE NOTED
BODY DIA -.006 (0.15)

.025+.010 (0.64+0.25)
.045-.011 (1.14-0.28)
.029-.010 (0.74-0.25)
35°+20°
.3366 (8.550)
.3373 (8.567)
.3365 (8.547) Δ
20°B
.358-.008 (9.09-0.20)
.314-.010 (7.98-0.25)
BULLET
.3125-.0060 (7.938-0.152)
.200 B (5.08)
.400 B (10.16)
.680-.020 (17.27-0.51)
.940 (23.88) MIN
.984 (24.99) MAX

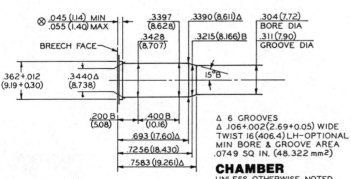

⊗ .045 (1.14) MIN
.055 (1.40) MAX
.3397 (8.628)
.3428 (8.707)
.3390 (8.611) Δ
.3215 (8.166) B
.304 (7.72) BORE DIA
.311 (7.90) GROOVE DIA
BREECH FACE
15°B
.362+.012 (9.19+0.30)
.3440 Δ (8.738)
.200 B (5.08)
.400 B (10.16)
.693 (17.60) Δ
.7256 (18.430) Δ
.7583 (19.261) Δ

Δ 6 GROOVES
Δ .106+.002 (2.69+0.05) WIDE
TWIST 16 (406.4) LH-OPTIONAL
MIN BORE & GROOVE AREA
.0749 SQ IN. (48.322 mm2)

CHAMBER
UNLESS OTHERWISE NOTED
ALL DIA +.004 (0.10)
LENGTH TOL +.015 (0.38)

.32 COLT NEW POLICE (.32 SMITH & WESSON LONG)

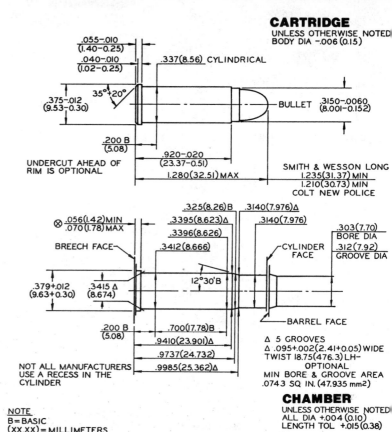

.055-.010
(1.40-0.25)
.040-.010
(1.02-0.25)
.337(8.56) CYLINDRICAL
35°+20°
.375-.012
(9.53-0.30)
BULLET
.3150-.0060
(8.001-0.152)
.200 B
(5.08)
UNDERCUT AHEAD OF
RIM IS OPTIONAL
.920-.020
(23.37-0.51)
1.280(32.51) MAX
SMITH & WESSON LONG
1.235(31.37) MIN
1.210(30.73) MIN
COLT NEW POLICE

⊗ .056(1.42) MIN
.070(1.78) MAX
.325(8.26) B
.3395(8.623)△
.3396(8.626)
.3412(8.666)
.3140(7.976)△
.3140(7.976)
.303(7.70)
BORE DIA
.312(7.92)
GROOVE DIA
BREECH FACE
CYLINDER FACE
.379+.012
(9.63+0.30)
.3415△
(8.674)
12°30'B
.200 B
(5.08)
.700(17.78) B
.9410(23.901)△
.9737(24.732)
.9985(25.362)△
BARREL FACE
△ 5 GROOVES
△ .095+.002(2.41+0.05) WIDE
TWIST 18.75(476.3) LH-
OPTIONAL
MIN BORE & GROOVE AREA
.0743 SQ IN. (47.935 mm2)

NOT ALL MANUFACTURERS
USE A RECESS IN THE
CYLINDER

NOTE
B = BASIC
(XX.XX) = MILLIMETERS
⊗ = HEADSPACE DIMENSION
△ = REFERENCE DIMENSION
* DIMENSIONS ARE TO INTERSECTION OF LINES
ALL CALCULATIONS APPLY AT MAXIMUM MATERIAL CONDITION (MMC)

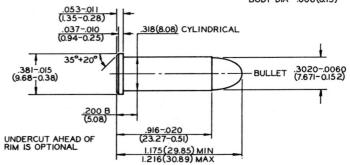

.053-.011
(1.35-0.28)
.037-.010
(0.94-0.25)
.318(8.08) CYLINDRICAL
35°+20°
.381-.015
(9.68-0.38)
BULLET
.3020-.0060
(7.671-0.152)
.200 B
(5.08)
UNDERCUT AHEAD OF
RIM IS OPTIONAL
.916-.020
(23.27-0.51)
1.175(29.85) MIN
1.216(30.89) MAX

.32 LONG COLT

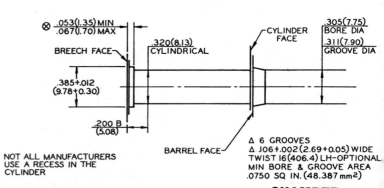

⊗ .053(1.35) MIN
.067(1.70) MAX
.320(8.13)
CYLINDRICAL
CYLINDER FACE
.305(7.75)
BORE DIA
.311(7.90)
GROOVE DIA
BREECH FACE
.385+.012
(9.78+0.30)
.200 B
(5.08)
BARREL FACE
△ 6 GROOVES
△ .106+.002(2.69+0.05) WIDE
TWIST 16(406.4) LH-OPTIONAL
MIN BORE & GROOVE AREA
.0750 SQ IN. (48.387 mm2)

NOT ALL MANUFACTURERS
USE A RECESS IN THE
CYLINDER

NOTE
B = BASIC
(XX.XX) = MILLIMETERS
⊗ = HEADSPACE DIMENSION
△ = REFERENCE DIMENSION
* DIMENSIONS ARE TO INTERSECTION OF LINES
ALL CALCULATIONS APPLY AT MAXIMUM MATERIAL CONDITION (MMC)

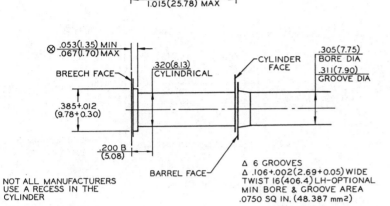

CARTRIDGE
UNLESS OTHERWISE NOTED
BODY DIA -.006 (0.15)

.053-.011
(1.35-0.28)
.037-.010
(0.94-0.25)
.318(8.08)
CYLINDRICAL
35°+20°
.375-.012
(9.53-0.30)
BULLET
.3140-.0060
(7.976-0.152)
.200 B
(5.08)
UNDERCUT AHEAD OF
RIM IS OPTIONAL
.650-.020
(16.51-0.51)
.985(25.02) MIN
1.015(25.78) MAX

⊗ .053(1.35) MIN
.067(1.70) MAX
BREECH FACE
.320(8.13)
CYLINDRICAL
CYLINDER
FACE
.305(7.75)
BORE DIA
.311(7.90)
GROOVE DIA
.385+.012
(9.78+0.30)
.200 B
(5.08)
BARREL FACE
NOT ALL MANUFACTURERS
USE A RECESS IN THE
CYLINDER

Δ 6 GROOVES
Δ .106+.002(2.69+0.05) WIDE
TWIST 16(406.4) LH-OPTIONAL
MIN BORE & GROOVE AREA
.0750 SQ IN. (48.387 mm2)

CHAMBER
UNLESS OTHERWISE NOTED
ALL DIA +.004 (0.10)
LENGTH TOL +.015 (0.38)

.32 SHORT COLT

NOTE
B=BASIC
(XX.XX)=MILLIMETERS
⊗ = HEADSPACE DIMENSION
Δ = REFERENCE DIMENSION
* DIMENSIONS ARE TO INTERSECTION OF LINES
ALL CALCULATIONS APPLY AT MAXIMUM MATERIAL CONDITION (MMC)

CARTRIDGE
UNLESS OTHERWISE NOTED
BODY DIA -.006 (0.15)

.054-.010
(1.37-0.25)
.039-.010
(0.99-0.25)
.339(8.61) CYLINDRICAL
35°+20°
.378-.012
(9.60-0.30)
BULLET
.3150-.0060
(8.001-0.152)
.200 B
(5.08)
UNDERCUT AHEAD OF RIM
IS OPTIONAL
.605-.020
(15.37-0.51)
.890(22.61) MIN
.930(23.62) MAX

.325(8.26)B
.3395(8.623)Δ
.3140(7.976)Δ
⊗ .055(1.40) MIN
.069(1.75) MAX
.3396
(8.626)
.3140(7.976)
BREECH FACE
.3400
(8.636)
CYLINDER
FACE
.303(7.70)
BORE DIA
.312(7.92)
GROOVE DIA
12°30'
B
.382+.012
(9.70+0.30)
.3402 Δ
(8.641)
.200 B
(5.08)
.350 B
(8.89)Δ
.6089(15.466)Δ
.6417(16.299)
.6665(16.929)Δ
BARREL FACE
NOT ALL MANUFACTURERS
USE A RECESS IN THE CYL-
INDER

Δ 5 GROOVES
Δ .095+.002(2.41+0.05) WIDE
TWIST 18.75(476.3) RH-
OPTIONAL
MIN BORE & GROOVE AREA
.0743 SQ IN. (47.935 mm2)

CHAMBER
UNLESS OTHERWISE NOTED
ALL DIA +.002(0.05)
LENGTH TOL +.015(0.38)

.32 SMITH
& WESSON

NOTE
B=BASIC
(XX.XX)=MILLIMETERS
⊗ = HEADSPACE DIMENSION
Δ = REFERENCE DIMENSION
* DIMENSIONS ARE TO INTERSECTION OF LINES
ALL CALCULATIONS APPLY AT MAXIMUM MATERIAL CONDITION (MMC)

.357 MAGNUM

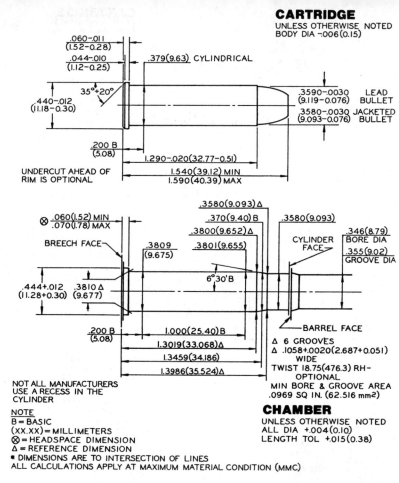

.060−.011
(1.52−0.28)
.044−.010
(1.12−0.25)

.379 (9.63) CYLINDRICAL

35°+20°

.440−.012
(11.18−0.30)

.3590−.0030 LEAD
(9.119−0.076) BULLET
.3580−.0030 JACKETED
(9.093−0.076) BULLET

.200 B
(5.08)

1.290−.020 (32.77−0.51)
1.540 (39.12) MIN
1.590 (40.39) MAX

UNDERCUT AHEAD OF
RIM IS OPTIONAL

⊗ .060 (1.52) MIN
.070 (1.78) MAX

.3580 (9.093) Δ
.370 (9.40) B
.3800 (9.652) Δ
.3801 (9.655)
.3580 (9.093)

BREECH FACE

.3809
(9.675)

CYLINDER
FACE

.346 (8.79)
BORE DIA
.355 (9.02)
GROOVE DIA

6°30'B

.444+.012
(11.28+0.30)

.3810 Δ
(9.677)

BARREL FACE

.200 B
(5.08)

1.000 (25.40) B
1.3019 (33.068) Δ
1.3459 (34.186)
1.3986 (35.524) Δ

NOT ALL MANUFACTURERS
USE A RECESS IN THE
CYLINDER

Δ 6 GROOVES
Δ .1058+.0020 (2.687+0.051)
   WIDE
TWIST 18.75 (476.3) RH−
OPTIONAL
MIN BORE & GROOVE AREA
.0969 SQ IN. (62.516 mm2)

CHAMBER
UNLESS OTHERWISE NOTED
ALL DIA +.004 (0.10)
LENGTH TOL +.015 (0.38)

NOTE
B = BASIC
(XX.XX) = MILLIMETERS
⊗ = HEADSPACE DIMENSION
Δ = REFERENCE DIMENSION
* DIMENSIONS ARE TO INTERSECTION OF LINES
ALL CALCULATIONS APPLY AT MAXIMUM MATERIAL CONDITION (MMC)

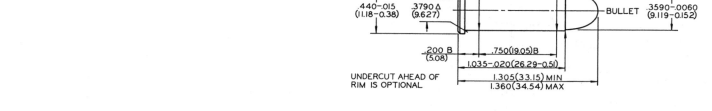

.38 LONG COLT

.060−.011
(1.52−0.28)
.044−.010
(1.12−0.25)

.3781 (9.604)
.3789 (9.624)
.3780 (9.601) Δ

35°+20°

.440−.015
(11.18−0.38)

.3790 Δ
(9.627)

BULLET

.3590−.0060
(9.119−0.152)

.200 B
(5.08)

.750 (19.05) B
1.035−.020 (26.29−0.51)
1.305 (33.15) MIN
1.360 (34.54) MAX

UNDERCUT AHEAD OF
RIM IS OPTIONAL

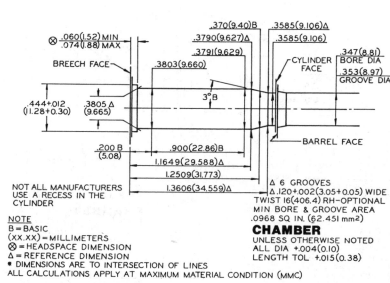

⊗ .060 (1.52) MIN
.074 (1.88) MAX

.370 (9.40) B
.3790 (9.627) Δ
.3791 (9.629)
.3803 (9.660)

.3585 (9.106) Δ
.3585 (9.106)

BREECH FACE

CYLINDER
FACE

.347 (8.81)
BORE DIA
.353 (8.97)
GROOVE DIA

3°B

.444+.012
(11.28+0.30)

.3805 Δ
(9.665)

BARREL FACE

.200 B
(5.08)

.900 (22.86) B
1.1649 (29.588) Δ
1.2509 (31.773)
1.3606 (34.559) Δ

NOT ALL MANUFACTURERS
USE A RECESS IN THE
CYLINDER

Δ 6 GROOVES
Δ .120+.002 (3.05+0.05) WIDE
TWIST 16 (406.4) RH−OPTIONAL
MIN BORE & GROOVE AREA
.0968 SQ IN. (62.451 mm2)

CHAMBER
UNLESS OTHERWISE NOTED
ALL DIA +.004 (0.10)
LENGTH TOL +.015 (0.38)

NOTE
B = BASIC
(XX.XX) = MILLIMETERS
⊗ = HEADSPACE DIMENSION
Δ = REFERENCE DIMENSION
* DIMENSIONS ARE TO INTERSECTION OF LINES
ALL CALCULATIONS APPLY AT MAXIMUM MATERIAL CONDITION (MMC)

.38 SHORT COLT

CARTRIDGE
UNLESS OTHERWISE NOTED
BODY DIA -.006 (0.15)

.060-.011
(1.52-0.28)
.044-.010
(1.12-0.25)
.379(9.63) CYLINDRICAL
35°+20°
.440-.012
(11.18-0.30)
BULLET
.3750-.0060
(9.525-0.152)
.200 B
(5.08)
.765-.020
(19.43-0.51)
UNDERCUT AHEAD OF
RIM IS OPTIONAL
1.085(27.56) MIN
1.200(30.48) MAX

⊗ .060(1.52) MIN
.074(1.88) MAX
BREECH FACE
.370(9.40)B
.3790(9.627)Δ
.3791(9.629)
.3803(9.660)
.3585(9.106)Δ
.3585(9.106)
CYLINDER FACE
.347(8.81) BORE DIA
.353(8.97) GROOVE DIA
.444+.012
(11.28+0.30)
.3805 Δ
(9.665)
3°B
BARREL FACE
.200 B
(5.08)
.900(22.86)B
1.1649(29.588)Δ
1.2509(31.773)
1.3606(34.559)Δ

NOT ALL MANUFACTURERS
USE A RECESS IN THE
CYLINDER

Δ 6 GROOVES
Δ .120+.002(3.05+0.05) WIDE
TWIST 16(406.4)RH-OPTIONAL
MIN BORE & GROOVE AREA
.0968 SQ IN. (62.451 mm2)

CHAMBER
UNLESS OTHERWISE NOTED
ALL DIA +.004(0.10)
LENGTH TOL +.015(0.38)

NOTE
B = BASIC
(XX.XX) = MILLIMETERS
⊗ = HEADSPACE DIMENSION
Δ = REFERENCE DIMENSION
✱ DIMENSIONS ARE TO INTERSECTION OF LINES
ALL CALCULATIONS APPLY AT MAXIMUM MATERIAL CONDITION (MMC)

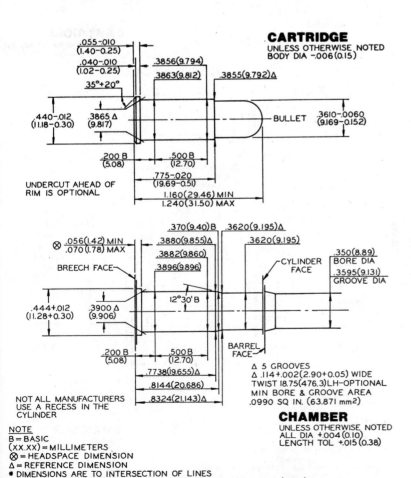

CARTRIDGE
UNLESS OTHERWISE NOTED
BODY DIA -.006 (0.15)

.055-.010
(1.40-0.25)
.040-.010
(1.02-0.25)
.3856(9.794)
.3863(9.812)
.3855(9.792)Δ
35°+20°
.440-.012
(11.18-0.30)
.3865 Δ
(9.817)
BULLET
.3610-.0060
(9.169-0.152)
.200 B
(5.08)
.500 B
(12.70)
.775-.020
(19.69-0.51)
UNDERCUT AHEAD OF
RIM IS OPTIONAL
1.160(29.46) MIN
1.240(31.50) MAX

⊗ .056(1.42) MIN
.070(1.78) MAX
BREECH FACE
.370(9.40)B
.3880(9.855)Δ
.3882(9.860)
.3896(9.896)
.3620(9.195)Δ
.3620(9.195)
CYLINDER FACE
.350(8.89) BORE DIA
.3595(9.131) GROOVE DIA
.444+.012
(11.28+0.30)
12°30'B
.3900 Δ
(9.906)
BARREL FACE
.200 B
(5.08)
.500 B
(12.70)
.7738(19.655)Δ
.8144(20.686)
.8324(21.143)Δ

NOT ALL MANUFACTURERS
USE A RECESS IN THE
CYLINDER

Δ 5 GROOVES
Δ .114+.002(2.90+0.05) WIDE
TWIST 18.75(476.3)LH-OPTIONAL
MIN BORE & GROOVE AREA
.0990 SQ IN. (63.871 mm2)

CHAMBER
UNLESS OTHERWISE NOTED
ALL DIA +.004(0.10)
LENGTH TOL +.015(0.38)

.38 SMITH & WESSON (.38 COLT NEW POLICE)

NOTE
B = BASIC
(XX.XX) = MILLIMETERS
⊗ = HEADSPACE DIMENSION
Δ = REFERENCE DIMENSION
✱ DIMENSIONS ARE TO INTERSECTION OF LINES
ALL CALCULATIONS APPLY AT MAXIMUM MATERIAL CONDITION (MMC)

.38 SPECIAL

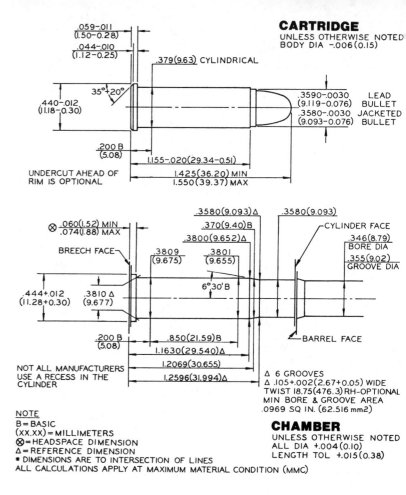

CARTRIDGE
UNLESS OTHERWISE NOTED
BODY DIA -.006(0.15)

.059-.011
(1.50-0.28)

.044-.010
(1.12-0.25)

.379(9.63) CYLINDRICAL

35°+20°

.440-.012
(11.18-0.30)

.3590-.0030
(9.119-0.076) LEAD BULLET
.3580-.0030
(9.093-0.076) JACKETED BULLET

.200 B
(5.08)

1.155-.020(29.34-0.51)
1.425(36.20) MIN
1.550(39.37) MAX

UNDERCUT AHEAD OF
RIM IS OPTIONAL

⊗ .060(1.52) MIN
.074(1.88) MAX

BREECH FACE

.3580(9.093)Δ
.370(9.40)B
.3800(9.652)Δ
.3580(9.093)

CYLINDER FACE

.3809
(9.675)

.3801
(9.655)

6°30'B

.346(8.79)
BORE DIA
.355(9.02)
GROOVE DIA

.444+.012
(11.28+0.30)

.3810 Δ
(9.677)

BARREL FACE

.200 B
(5.08)

.850(21.59)B

1.1630(29.540)Δ
1.2069(30.655)
1.2596(31.994)Δ

NOT ALL MANUFACTURERS
USE A RECESS IN THE
CYLINDER

Δ 6 GROOVES
Δ .105+.002(2.67+0.05) WIDE
TWIST 18.75(476.3) RH-OPTIONAL
MIN BORE & GROOVE AREA
.0969 SQ IN. (62.516 mm2)

NOTE
B = BASIC
(XX.XX) = MILLIMETERS
⊗ = HEADSPACE DIMENSION
Δ = REFERENCE DIMENSION
* DIMENSIONS ARE TO INTERSECTION OF LINES
ALL CALCULATIONS APPLY AT MAXIMUM MATERIAL CONDITION (MMC)

CHAMBER
UNLESS OTHERWISE NOTED
ALL DIA +.004(0.10)
LENGTH TOL +.015(0.38)

.38 SPECIAL MATCH (REVOLVER)

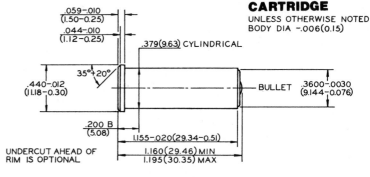

CARTRIDGE
UNLESS OTHERWISE NOTED
BODY DIA -.006(0.15)

.059-.010
(1.50-0.25)

.044-.010
(1.12-0.25)

.379(9.63) CYLINDRICAL

35°+20°

.440-.012
(11.18-0.30)

BULLET
.3600-.0030
(9.144-0.076)

.200 B
(5.08)

1.155-.020(29.34-0.51)
1.160(29.46) MIN
1.195(30.35) MAX

UNDERCUT AHEAD OF
RIM IS OPTIONAL

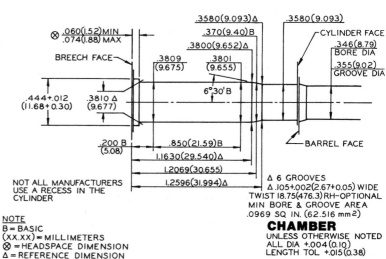

⊗ .060(1.52) MIN
.074(1.88) MAX

BREECH FACE

.3580(9.093)Δ
.370(9.40)B
.3800(9.652)Δ
.3580(9.093)

CYLINDER FACE

.3809
(9.675)

.3801
(9.655)

6°30'B

.346(8.79)
BORE DIA
.355(9.02)
GROOVE DIA

.444+.012
(11.68+0.30)

.3810 Δ
(9.677)

BARREL FACE

.200 B
(5.08)

.850(21.59)B

1.1630(29.540)Δ
1.2069(30.655)
1.2596(31.994)Δ

NOT ALL MANUFACTURERS
USE A RECESS IN THE
CYLINDER

Δ 6 GROOVES
Δ .105+.002(2.67+0.05) WIDE
TWIST 18.75(476.3) RH-OPTIONAL
MIN BORE & GROOVE AREA
.0969 SQ IN. (62.516 mm2)

NOTE
B = BASIC
(XX.XX) = MILLIMETERS
⊗ = HEADSPACE DIMENSION
Δ = REFERENCE DIMENSION
* DIMENSIONS ARE TO INTERSECTION OF LINES
ALL CALCULATIONS APPLY AT MAXIMUM MATERIAL CONDITION (MMC)

CHAMBER
UNLESS OTHERWISE NOTED
ALL DIA +.004(0.10)
LENGTH TOL +.015(0.38)

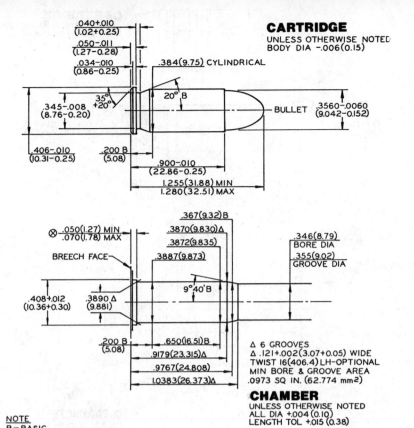

CARTRIDGE
UNLESS OTHERWISE NOTED
BODY DIA -.006(0.15)

.040+.010
(1.02+0.25)
.050-.011
(1.27-0.28)
.034-.010
(0.86-0.25)
.384(9.75) CYLINDRICAL
20° B
35°
+20°
.345-.008
(8.76-0.20)
BULLET
.3560-.0060
(9.042-0.152)
.406-.010
(10.31-0.25)
.200 B
(5.08)
.900-.010
(22.86-0.25)
1.255(31.88) MIN
1.280(32.51) MAX

.050(1.27) MIN
.070(1.78) MAX
⊗
.367(9.32)B
.3870(9.830)Δ
.3872(9.835)
.3887(9.873)
BREECH FACE
9°40'B
.346(8.79)
BORE DIA
.355(9.02)
GROOVE DIA
.408+.012
(10.36+0.30)
.3890 Δ
(9.881)
.200 B
(5.08)
.650(16.51)B
.9179(23.315)Δ
.9767(24.808)
1.0383(26.373)Δ

Δ 6 GROOVES
Δ .121+.002(3.07+0.05) WIDE
TWIST 16(406.4) LH-OPTIONAL
MIN BORE & GROOVE AREA
.0973 SQ IN. (62.774 mm2)

CHAMBER
UNLESS OTHERWISE NOTED
ALL DIA +.004 (0.10)
LENGTH TOL +.015 (0.38)

NOTE
B=BASIC
(XX.XX)=MILLIMETERS
⊗ = HEADSPACE DIMENSION
Δ = REFERENCE DIMENSION
* DIMENSIONS ARE TO INTERSECTION OF LINES
ALL CALCULATIONS APPLY AT MAXIMUM MATERIAL CONDITION (MMC)

.38 SUPER AUTOMATIC +P AND .38 AUTOMATIC

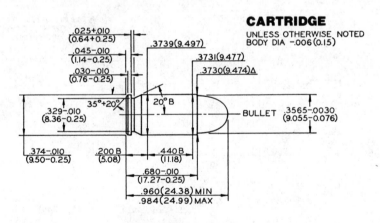

CARTRIDGE
UNLESS OTHERWISE NOTED
BODY DIA -.006(0.15)

.025+.010
(0.64+0.25)
.045-.010
(1.14-0.25)
.030-.010
(0.76-0.25)
.3739(9.497)
.3731(9.477)
.3730(9.474)Δ
35°+20°
20° B
.329-.010
(8.36-0.25)
BULLET
.3565-.0030
(9.055-0.076)
.374-.010
(9.50-0.25)
.200 B
(5.08)
.440B
(11.18)
.680-.010
(17.27-0.25)
.960(24.38)MIN
.984(24.99)MAX

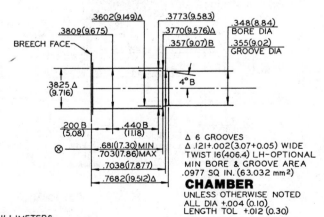

.3602(9.149)Δ
.3809(9.675)
.3773(9.583)
.3770(9.576)Δ
.357(9.07)B
.348(8.84)
BORE DIA
.355(9.02)
GROOVE DIA
BREECH FACE
.3825 Δ
(9.716)
4° B
.200 B
(5.08)
.440B
(11.18)
⊗
.681(17.30)MIN
.703(17.86)MAX
.7038(17.877)
.7682(19.512)Δ

Δ 6 GROOVES
Δ .121+.002(3.07+0.05) WIDE
TWIST 16(406.4) LH-OPTIONAL
MIN BORE & GROOVE AREA
.0977 SQ IN. (63.032 mm2)

CHAMBER
UNLESS OTHERWISE NOTED
ALL DIA +.004 (0.10)
LENGTH TOL +.012 (0.30)

NOTE
B=BASIC
(XX.XX)=MILLIMETERS
⊗ = HEADSPACE DIMENSION
Δ = REFERENCE DIMENSION
* DIMENSIONS ARE TO INTERSECTION OF LINES
ALL CALCULATIONS APPLY AT MAXIMUM MATERIAL CONDITION (MMC)

.380 AUTOMATIC

.41 REMINGTON MAGNUM

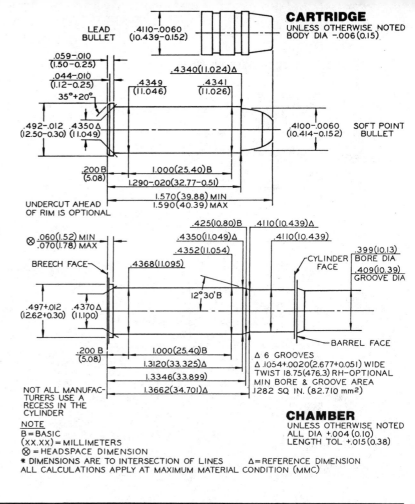

CARTRIDGE
UNLESS OTHERWISE NOTED
BODY DIA -.006 (0.15)

LEAD BULLET

.4110-.0060
(10.439-0.152)

.059-.010
(1.50-0.25)

.044-.010
(1.12-0.25)

35°+20°

.4340(11.024)△

.4349
(11.046)

.4341
(11.026)

.492-.012   .4350△
(12.50-0.30) (11.049)

.4100-.0060
(10.414-0.152)

SOFT POINT
BULLET

.200 B
(5.08)

1.000(25.40)B

1.290-.020(32.77-0.51)

1.570(39.88) MIN
1.590(40.39) MAX

UNDERCUT AHEAD
OF RIM IS OPTIONAL

⊗ .060(1.52) MIN
.070(1.78) MAX

.425(10.80)B   .4110(10.439)△

.4350(11.049)△   .4110(10.439)

.4352(11.054)

BREECH FACE

.4368(11.095)

CYLINDER FACE

.399(10.13) BORE DIA
.409(10.39) GROOVE DIA

12°30'B

.497+.012   .4370△
(12.62+0.30) (11.100)

BARREL FACE

.200 B
(5.08)

1.000(25.40)B

1.3120(33.325)△

1.3346(33.899)

1.3662(34.701)△

△ 6 GROOVES
△ .1054+.0020(2.677+0.051) WIDE
TWIST 18.75(476.3) RH-OPTIONAL
MIN BORE & GROOVE AREA
.1282 SQ IN. (82.710 mm2)

NOT ALL MANUFAC-
TURERS USE A
RECESS IN THE
CYLINDER

NOTE
B = BASIC
(XX.XX) = MILLIMETERS
⊗ = HEADSPACE DIMENSION
* DIMENSIONS ARE TO INTERSECTION OF LINES   △ = REFERENCE DIMENSION
ALL CALCULATIONS APPLY AT MAXIMUM MATERIAL CONDITION (MMC)

CHAMBER
UNLESS OTHERWISE NOTED
ALL DIA +.004 (0.10)
LENGTH TOL +.015 (0.38)

.44 REMINGTON MAGNUM

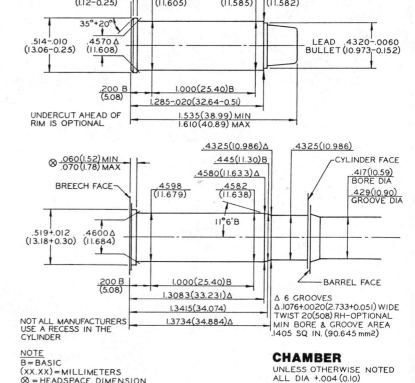

CARTRIDGE
UNLESS OTHERWISE NOTED
BODY DIA -.006 (0.15)

.060-.011
(1.52-0.28)

.044-.010
(1.12-0.25)

35°+20°

.4569
(11.605)

.4561
(11.585)

.4560△
(11.582)

.514-.010   .4570△
(13.06-0.25) (11.608)

LEAD .4320-.0060
BULLET (10.973-0.152)

.200 B
(5.08)

1.000(25.40)B

1.285-.020(32.64-0.51)

1.535(38.99) MIN
1.610(40.89) MAX

UNDERCUT AHEAD OF
RIM IS OPTIONAL

⊗ .060(1.52) MIN
.070(1.78) MAX

.4325(10.986)△   .4325(10.986)

.445(11.30)B

.4580(11.633)△

CYLINDER FACE

.417(10.59) BORE DIA
.429(10.90) GROOVE DIA

BREECH FACE

.4598
(11.679)

.4582
(11.638)

11°6'B

.519+.012   .4600△
(13.18+0.30) (11.684)

BARREL FACE

.200 B
(5.08)

1.000(25.40)B

1.3083(33.231)△

1.3415(34.074)

1.3734(34.884)△

△ 6 GROOVES
△ .1076+.0020(2.733+0.051) WIDE
TWIST 20(508) RH-OPTIONAL
MIN BORE & GROOVE AREA
.1405 SQ IN. (90.645 mm2)

NOT ALL MANUFACTURERS
USE A RECESS IN THE
CYLINDER

NOTE
B = BASIC
(XX.XX) = MILLIMETERS
⊗ = HEADSPACE DIMENSION
△ = REFERENCE DIMENSION
* DIMENSIONS ARE TO INTERSECTION OF LINES
ALL CALCULATIONS APPLY AT MAXIMUM MATERIAL CONDITION (MMC)

CHAMBER
UNLESS OTHERWISE NOTED
ALL DIA +.004 (0.10)
LENGTH TOL +.015 (0.38)

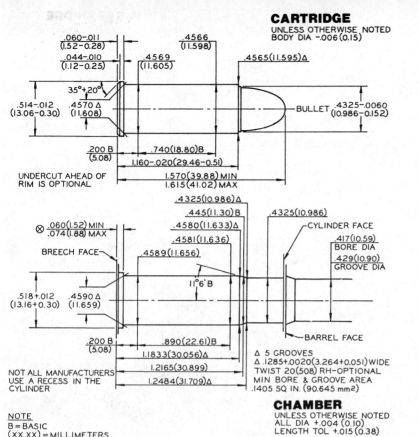

CARTRIDGE
UNLESS OTHERWISE NOTED
BODY DIA -.006 (0.15)

.060-.011
(1.52-0.28)

.044-.010
(1.12-0.25)

.4569
(11.605)

.4566
(11.598)

.4565(11.595)△

35°±20°

.514-.012
(13.06-0.30)

.4570 △
(11.608)

BULLET .4325-.0060
(10.986-0.152)

.200 B
(5.08)

.740(18.80)B

1.160-.020(29.46-0.51)

1.570(39.88) MIN
1.615(41.02) MAX

UNDERCUT AHEAD OF
RIM IS OPTIONAL

.060(1.52) MIN
.074(1.88) MAX

BREECH FACE

.4325(10.986)△

.445(11.30)B

.4580(11.633)△

.4581(11.636)

.4589(11.656)

.4325(10.986)

CYLINDER FACE

.417(10.59)
BORE DIA

.429(10.90)
GROOVE DIA

11°6'B

.518+.012
(13.16+0.30)

.4590 △
(11.659)

.200 B
(5.08)

.890(22.61)B

BARREL FACE

1.1833(30.056)△

1.2165(30.899)

1.2484(31.709)△

NOT ALL MANUFACTURERS
USE A RECESS IN THE
CYLINDER

△ 5 GROOVES
△ .1285+.0020(3.264+.051) WIDE
TWIST 20(508) RH-OPTIONAL
MIN BORE & GROOVE AREA
.1405 SQ IN. (90.645 mm2)

CHAMBER
UNLESS OTHERWISE NOTED
ALL DIA +.004 (0.10)
LENGTH TOL +.015 (0.38)

NOTE
B = BASIC
(XX.XX) = MILLIMETERS
⊗ = HEADSPACE DIMENSION
△ = REFERENCE DIMENSION
* DIMENSIONS ARE TO INTERSECTION OF LINES
ALL CALCULATIONS APPLY AT MAXIMUM MATERIAL CONDITION (MMC)

.44 SMITH & WESSON SPECIAL

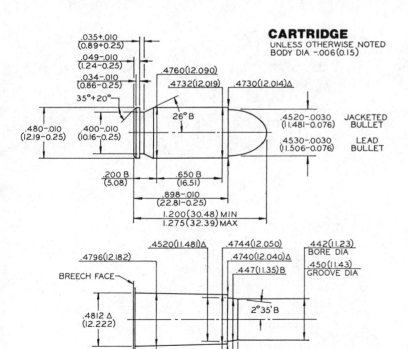

CARTRIDGE
UNLESS OTHERWISE NOTED
BODY DIA -.006(0.15)

.035+.010
(0.89+0.25)

.049-.010
(1.24-0.25)

.034-.010
(0.86-0.25)

.4760(12.090)

.4732(12.019)

.4730(12.014)△

35°±20°

26°B

.480-.010
(12.19-0.25)

.400-.010
(10.16-0.25)

.4520-.0030
(11.481-0.076)
JACKETED
BULLET

.4530-.0030
(11.506-0.076)
LEAD
BULLET

.200 B
(5.08)

.650 B
(16.51)

.898-.010
(22.81-0.25)

1.200(30.48) MIN
1.275(32.39) MAX

.4796(12.182)

.4520(11.481)△

.4744(12.050)

.4740(12.040)△

.442(11.23)
BORE DIA

.450(11.43)
GROOVE DIA

.447(11.35)B

BREECH FACE

2°35'B

.4812 △
(12.222)

.200 B
(5.08)

.650 B
(16.51)

⊗

.898(22.81) MIN
.920(23.37) MAX

.9534(24.216)

1.0088(25.624)△

△ 6 GROOVES
△ .147+.002(3.73+0.05) WIDE
TWIST 16(406.4) LH-OPTIONAL
MIN BORE & GROOVE AREA
.1570 SQ IN. (101.290 mm2)

CHAMBER
UNLESS OTHERWISE NOTED
ALL DIA +.004 (0.10)
LENGTH TOL +.012 (0.30)

NOTE
B = BASIC
(XX.XX) = MILLIMETERS
⊗ = HEADSPACE DIMENSION
△ = REFERENCE DIMENSION
* DIMENSIONS ARE TO INTERSECTION OF LINES
ALL CALCULATIONS APPLY AT MAXIMUM MATERIAL CONDITION (MMC)

.45 AUTOMATIC

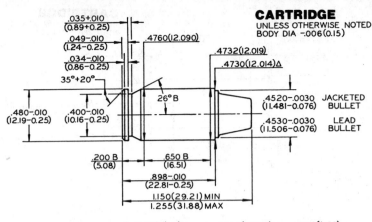

.45 AUTOMATIC MATCH

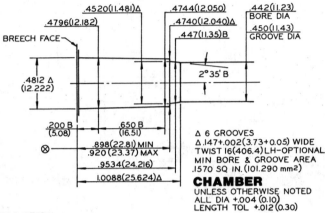

CARTRIDGE
UNLESS OTHERWISE NOTED
BODY DIA -.006 (0.15)

.4760 (12.090)
.4732 (12.019)
.4730 (12.014) Δ
.035 +.010 (0.89 +0.25)
.049 -.010 (1.24 -0.25)
.034 -.010 (0.86 -0.25)
35° +20°
26° B
.480 -.010 (12.19 -0.25)
.400 -.010 (10.16 -0.25)
.4520 -.0030 (11.481 -0.076) JACKETED BULLET
.4530 -.0030 (11.506 -0.076) LEAD BULLET
.200 B (5.08)
.650 B (16.51)
.898 -.010 (22.81 -0.25)
1.150 (29.21) MIN
1.255 (31.88) MAX

.4520 (11.481) Δ
.4796 (12.182)
BREECH FACE
.4744 (12.050)
.4740 (12.040) Δ
.447 (11.35) B
.442 (11.23) BORE DIA
.450 (11.43) GROOVE DIA
.4812 Δ (12.222)
2° 35' B
.200 B (5.08)
.650 B (16.51)
.898 (22.81) MIN
.920 (23.37) MAX
.9534 (24.216)
1.0088 (25.624) Δ

Δ 6 GROOVES
Δ .147 +.002 (3.73 +0.05) WIDE
TWIST 16 (406.4) LH-OPTIONAL
MIN BORE & GROOVE AREA
.1570 SQ IN. (101.290 mm2)

CHAMBER
UNLESS OTHERWISE NOTED
ALL DIA +.004 (0.10)
LENGTH TOL +.012 (0.30)

NOTE
B = BASIC
(XX.XX) = MILLIMETERS
⊗ = HEADSPACE DIMENSION
Δ = REFERENCE DIMENSION
* DIMENSIONS ARE TO INTERSECTION OF LINES
ALL CALCULATIONS APPLY AT MAXIMUM MATERIAL CONDITION (MMC)

.45 AUTO RIM

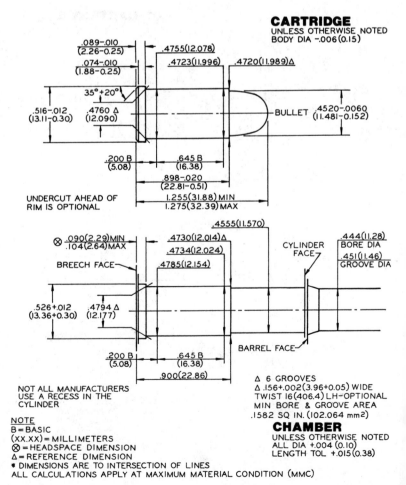

CARTRIDGE
UNLESS OTHERWISE NOTED
BODY DIA -.006 (0.15)

.089 -.010 (2.26 -0.25)
.074 -.010 (1.88 -0.25)
.4755 (12.078)
.4723 (11.996)
.4720 (11.989) Δ
35° +20°
.516 -.012 (13.11 -0.30)
.4760 Δ (12.090)
BULLET
.4520 -.0060 (11.481 -0.152)
.200 B (5.08)
.645 B (16.38)
.898 -.020 (22.81 -0.51)
UNDERCUT AHEAD OF RIM IS OPTIONAL
1.255 (31.88) MIN
1.275 (32.39) MAX

⊗ .090 (2.29) MIN
.104 (2.64) MAX
.4555 (11.570)
.4730 (12.014) Δ
.4734 (12.024)
.4785 (12.154)
BREECH FACE
CYLINDER FACE
.444 (11.28) BORE DIA
.451 (11.46) GROOVE DIA
.526 +.012 (13.36 +0.30)
.4794 Δ (12.177)
BARREL FACE
.200 B (5.08)
.645 B (16.38)
.900 (22.86)

NOT ALL MANUFACTURERS
USE A RECESS IN THE
CYLINDER

Δ 6 GROOVES
Δ .156 +.002 (3.96 +0.05) WIDE
TWIST 16 (406.4) LH-OPTIONAL
MIN BORE & GROOVE AREA
.1582 SQ IN. (102.064 mm2)

CHAMBER
UNLESS OTHERWISE NOTED
ALL DIA +.004 (0.10)
LENGTH TOL +.015 (0.38)

NOTE
B = BASIC
(XX.XX) = MILLIMETERS
⊗ = HEADSPACE DIMENSION
Δ = REFERENCE DIMENSION
* DIMENSIONS ARE TO INTERSECTION OF LINES
ALL CALCULATIONS APPLY AT MAXIMUM MATERIAL CONDITION (MMC)

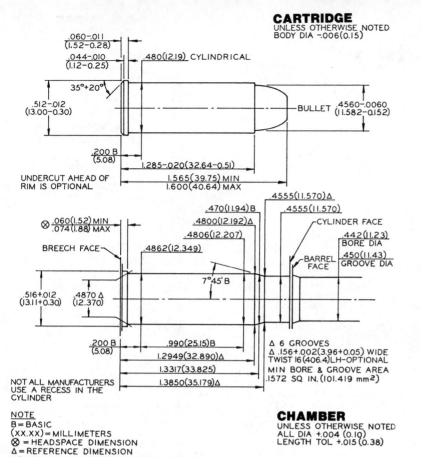

CARTRIDGE
UNLESS OTHERWISE NOTED
BODY DIA −.006(0.15)

.060−.011
(1.52−0.28)
.044−.010
(1.12−0.25)
.480(12.19) CYLINDRICAL
35°+20°
.512−012
(13.00−0.30)
BULLET
.4560−.0060
(11.582−0.152)
.200 B
(5.08)
UNDERCUT AHEAD OF
RIM IS OPTIONAL
1.285−.020(32.64−0.51)
1.565(39.75) MIN
1.600(40.64) MAX

⊗ .060(1.52) MIN
.074(1.88) MAX
BREECH FACE
.470(11.94)B
.4800(12.192)△
.4806(12.207)
.4862(12.349)
.4555(11.570)△
.4555(11.570)
CYLINDER FACE
.442(11.23)
BORE DIA
.450(11.43)
GROOVE DIA
BARREL
FACE
7°45'B
.516+012
(13.11+0.30)
.4870 △
(12.370)
.200 B
(5.08)
NOT ALL MANUFACTURERS
USE A RECESS IN THE
CYLINDER
.990(25.15)B
1.2949(32.890)△
1.3317(33.825)
1.3850(35.179)△

△ 6 GROOVES
△ .156+.002(3.96+0.05) WIDE
TWIST 16(406.4)LH−OPTIONAL
MIN BORE & GROOVE AREA
.1572 SQ IN.(101.419 mm²)

CHAMBER
UNLESS OTHERWISE NOTED
ALL DIA +.004 (0.10)
LENGTH TOL +.015 (0.38)

NOTE
B = BASIC
(XX.XX) = MILLIMETERS
⊗ = HEADSPACE DIMENSION
△ = REFERENCE DIMENSION
✱ DIMENSIONS ARE TO INTERSECTION OF LINES
ALL CALCULATIONS APPLY AT MAXIMUM MATERIAL CONDITION (MMC)

.45 COLT

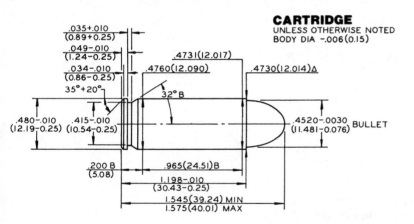

CARTRIDGE
UNLESS OTHERWISE NOTED
BODY DIA −.006(0.15)

.035+.010
(0.89+0.25)
.049−.010
(1.24−0.25)
.034−.010
(0.86−0.25)
35°+20°
.4731(12.017)
.4760(12.090)
.4730(12.014)△
32°B
.480−.010
(12.19−0.25)
.415−.010
(10.54−0.25)
.4520−.0030
(11.481−0.076) BULLET
.200 B
(5.08)
.965(24.51)B
1.198−.010
(30.43−0.25)
1.545(39.24) MIN
1.575(40.01) MAX

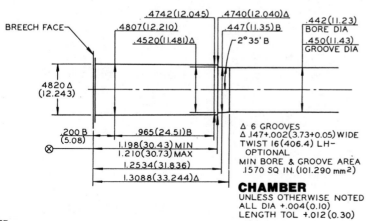

BREECH FACE
.4742(12.045)
.4807(12.210)
.4520(11.481)△
.4740(12.040)△
.447(11.35)B
2°35'B
.442(11.23)
BORE DIA
.450(11.43)
GROOVE DIA
.4820 △
(12.243)
.200 B
(5.08)
⊗
.965(24.51)B
1.198(30.43) MIN
1.210(30.73) MAX
1.2534(31.836)
1.3088(33.244)△

△ 6 GROOVES
△ .147+.002(3.73+0.05) WIDE
TWIST 16(406.4) LH−
OPTIONAL
MIN BORE & GROOVE AREA
.1570 SQ IN. (101.290 mm²)

CHAMBER
UNLESS OTHERWISE NOTED
ALL DIA +.004(0.10)
LENGTH TOL +.012 (0.30)

.45 WINCHESTER MAGNUM

NOTE
B = BASIC   (XX.XX) = MILLIMETERS   ⊗ = HEADSPACE DIMENSION
✱ DIMENSIONS ARE TO INTERSECTION OF LINES   △ = REFERENCE DIMENSION
ALL CALCULATIONS APPLY AT MAXIMUM MATERIAL CONDITION (MMC)

Weatherby Cartridge and Chamber Dimensions

By Permission of Weatherby
South Gate California

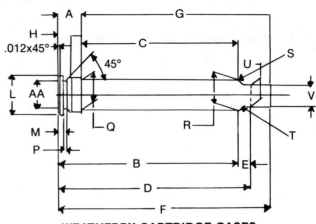

**WEATHERBY CARTRIDGE CASES
MAXIMUM EXTERIOR DIMENSIONS**

CALIBER	A	B	C	D	E	F	G	H	L	M	P	Q	R	S	T	U	V	AA
.224	.1980	1.486	1.288	1.671	.185	1.923	1.725	.125	.430	.050	.045	.415	.395	.130	.151	.250	.250	.369
.240	.219	1.992	1.773	2.190	.200	2.500	2.281	.130	.473	.050	.040	.453	.432	.125	.156	.2715	.2715	.409
.257	.219	2.012	1.793	2.230	.217	2.549	2.330	.138	.531	.051	.049	.512	.492	.130	.151	.283	.283	.457
.270	.219	2.012	1.793	2.221	.209	2.549	2.330	.138	.531	.051	.049	.512	.492	.130	.151	.303	.303	.457
7mm	.219	2.012	1.793	2.218	.206	2.549	2.330	.138	.531	.051	.049	.512	.492	.130	.151	.310	.310	.457
.300	.219	2.298	2.079	2.504	.206	2.825	2.606	.138	.531	.051	.049	.512	.492	.130	.182	.335	.335	.457
.340	.219	2.298	2.079	2.485	.187	2.825	2.606	.138	.531	.051	.049	.512	.492	.130	.182	.364	.364	.457
.375	.219	2.396	2.177	2.556	.160	2.860	2.641	.138	.531	.051	.049	.512	.492	.130	.182	.400	.400	.457
.378	.252	2.345	2.093	2.540	.195	2.913	2.661	.167	.604	.063	.049	.585	.561	.130	.151	.400	.400	.495
.460	.252	2.345	2.093	2.493	.150	2.913	2.661	.167	.604	.063	.049	.585	.561	.130	.186	.486	.486	.495

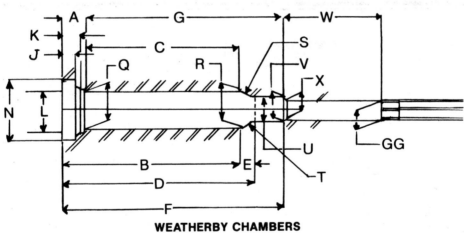

**WEATHERBY CHAMBERS
MINIMUM DIMENSIONS**

CALIBER	A	B	C	D	E	F	G	J	K	L	N	Q	R	S	T	U	V	W	X	GG
.224	.1999	1.490	1.290	1.675	.185	1.935	1.735	.126	.150	.432	.596	.417	.398	.120	.151	.256	.254	.162	.224	.224
.240	.220	1.995	1.775	2.195	.200	2.510	2.293	.134	.165	.476	.731	.454	.433	.120	.151	.277	.275	.168	.2435	.2435
.257	.220	2.015	1.795	2.232	.217	2.560	2.340	.134	.165	.534	.731	.514	.496	.120	.151	.290	.288	.377	.2574	.2574
.270	.220	2.015	1.795	2.224	.209	2.560	2.340	.134	.165	.534	.731	.514	.496	.120	.151	.310	.308	.377	.2774	.2774
7mm	.220	2.015	1.795	2.221	.206	2.560	2.340	.134	.165	.534	.731	.514	.496	.120	.151	.317	.315	.377	.2844	.2844
.300	.220	2.301	2.081	2.507	.206	2.840	2.620	.134	.165	.534	.731	.514	.496	.120	.182	.340	.339	.361	.3084	.3084
.340	.220	2.301	2.081	2.488	.187	2.840	2.620	.134	.165	.534	.731	.514	.496	.120	.182	.371	.369	.372	.338	.3384
.375	.220	2.399	2.179	2.559	.160	2.867	2.647	.134	.165	.534	.731	.514	.496	.120	.182	.407	.405	.755	.3754	.375
.378	.254	2.349	2.095	2.544	.195	2.934	2.680	.134	.165	.606	.731	.585	.565	.120	.151	.407	.405	.755	.3754	.3754
.460	.254	2.349	2.095	2.499	.150	2.934	2.680	.134	.165	.606	.731	.585	.565	.120	.186	.493	.491	.755	.4584	.4584

Norma Cartridge Dimensions

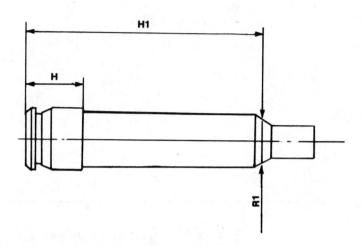

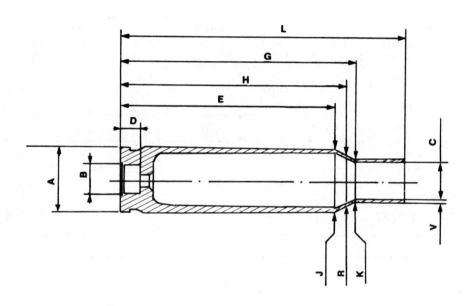

CARTRIDGE	UNITS	A	B	C	D	E	G	H	H1	J	K	R	R1	V	L
6.5x54mm M. Sch.	mm	11.5	5.33	6.65	3.30	41.82	45.73	43.33		10.87	7.39	9.525		0.37	53.65
	inch	.453	.210	.262	.130	1.646	1.800	1.706		.428	.291	.375		.015	2.112
6.5mm Japanese	mm	11.95	5.33	6.65	3.30	38.49	43.29	40.22		10.47	7.35	9.525		0.35	50.40
	inch	.470	.210	.262	.130	1.515	1.704	1.583		.412	.289	.375		.014	1.984
6.5mm Carcano	mm	11.45	5.33	6.65	3.30	41.28	45.13	42.83		10.94	7.83	9.525		0.39	52.55
	inch	.451	.210	.262	.130	1.625	1.777	1.686		.431	.308	.375		.015	2.069
6.5x55mm	mm	12.20	5.33	6.65	3.30	43.45	47.13	46.46		11.04	7.56	8.150		0.40	55.00
	inch	.480	.210	.262	.130	1.71	1.856	1.829		.435	.298	.321		.016	2.165
7x61 mm Super	mm	13.50	5.33	7.15	3.30	45.20	47.30	5.60	51.80	11.90	7.99		10.05	0.40	61.00
	inch	.531	.210	.281	.130	1.780	1.862	.220	2.039	.469	.315		.396	.016	2.402
7.65mm Argentina	mm	12.10	5.33	7.86	3.30	44.60	47.18	46.18		10.90	8.66	9.525		0.40	53.50
	inch	.476	.210	.309	.130	1.756	1.857	1.818		.429	.341	.375		.016	2.106
7.7mm Japanese	mm	12.00	5.33	7.86	3.30	47.55	50.07	48.65		10.85	8.45	9.80		0.30	57.75
	inch	.472	.210	.309	.130	1.872	1.971	1.915		.427	.333	.386		.012	2.274
.308 Norma Mag.	mm	13.50	5.33	7.77	3.30	52.94	57.03	5.56	54.88	12.45	8.55		10.60	0.39	65.00
	inch	.531	.210	.306	.130	2.084	2.245	.218	2.160	.490	.337		.417	.015	2.559
.358 Norma Mag.	mm	13.50	5.33	9.04	3.30	52.94	55.78	5.56	54.88	12.45	9.74		10.60	0.35	64.00
	inch	.531	.210	.356	.130	2.084	2.196	.218	2.160	.490	.383		.417	.014	2.520
7.5mm Swiss	mm	12.65	5.33	7.77	3.30	44.50	47.47	45.87		11.60	8.47	10.16		0.35	55.60
	inch	.498	.210	.306	.130	1.751	1.869	1.806		.457	.333	.400		.014	2.189

U.S. Boxer Primer Chart

	Large Rifle	Large Rifle Magnum	Small Rifle	Small Rifle Magnum	Large Pistol	Large Pistol Magnum	Small Pistol	Small Pistol Magnum
Alcan	Large Rifle Max-Fire		Small Rifle Max-Fire		Large Pistol Max-Fire		Small Pistol Max-Fire	
CCI	200	250	400	450	300	350	500	550
Federal	210	215	200		150		100	
Remington	9½	9½M	6½	7½	2½		1½	5½
Winchester Western	8½-120		6½-116		7-111		1½-108	1½M-108

FACTORY BALLISTICS TABLES

Automatic Pistol Ballistics (Approximate)

Federal Load No.	Caliber	Bullet Style	Bullet Weight in Grains	Velocity in Feet Per Second Muzzle	50 yds.	Energy in Foot/Lbs. Muzzle	50 yds.	Mid-range Trajectory 50 yds.	Test Barrel Length
25AP	25 Auto Pistol (6.35mm)	Metal Case	50	810	775	73	63	1.8″	2″
32AP	32 Auto Pistol (7.65mm)	Metal Case	71	905	855	129	115	1.4″	4″
380AP	380 Auto Pistol	Metal Case	95	955	865	190	160	1.4″	3¾″
380BP	380 Auto Pistol	Jacketed Hollow Point	90	1000	890	200	160	1.4″	3¾″
9AP	9mm Luger Auto Pistol	Metal Case	123	1120	1030	345	290	1.0″	4″
9BP	9mm Luger Auto Pistol	Jacketed Hollow Point	115	1160	1060	345	285	0.9″	4″
45A	45 Automatic (Match)	Metal Case	230	850	810	370	335	1.6″	5″
45B	45 Automatic (Match)	Metal Case, S.W.C.	185	775	695	247	200	2.0″	5″
45C	45 Automatic	Jacketed Hollow Point	185	950	900	370	335	1.3″	5″

Rifle Cartridge Ballistics

Federal Load No.	Caliber	Bullet Weight in Grains	Bullet Style	Factory Primer	Velocity In Feet Per Second Muzzle	100 yds	200 yds	300 yds	400 yds	500 yds	Energy In Foot Pounds Muzzle	100 yds	200 yds	300 yds	400 yds	500 yds
222A	222 Remington	50	Soft Point	205	3140	2600	2120	1700	1350	1110	1090	750	500	320	200	135
22250A	22-250 Remington	55	Soft Point	210	3730	3180	2700	2260	1860	1520	1700	1240	885	620	425	280
223A	223 Remington	55	Soft Point	205	3240	2750	2300	1910	1550	1270	1280	920	650	445	295	195
223B	223 Remington	55	Full Metal Case Boat Tail	205	3240	2880	2540	2230	1940	1680	1280	1010	790	610	460	340
6A	6mm Remington	80	Soft Point	210	3470	3060	2690	2350	2040	1750	2140	1670	1290	980	740	540
6B		100	Hi-Shok S.P.	210	3130	2860	2600	2360	2130	1910	2180	1810	1500	1230	1000	810
243A	243 Winchester	80	Soft Point	210	3420	3020	2650	2310	2000	1720	2080	1620	1250	950	710	520
243B		100	Hi-Shok S.P.	210	2960	2700	2450	2220	1990	1790	1950	1620	1330	1090	880	710
2506A	25-'06 Remington	90	Hollow Point	210	3440	3040	2680	2340	2030	1750	2360	1850	1440	1100	825	610
2506B		117	Hi-Shok S.P.	210	3060	2790	2530	2280	2050	1840	2430	2020	1660	1360	1100	875
270A	270 Winchester	130	Hi-Shok S.P.	210	3110	2850	2600	2370	2150	1940	2790	2340	1960	1620	1330	1090
270B		150	Hi-Shok S.P.	210	2900	2550	2230	1930	1650	1420	2800	2170	1650	1240	910	665
7A	7mm Mauser	175	Hi-Shok S.P.	210	2470	2170	1880	1630	1400	1220	2370	1820	1380	1030	765	575
▲7B		139	Hi-Shok S.P.	210	2660	2400	2150	1910	1690	1500	2180	1770	1420	1130	885	690
7RA	7mm Remington Magnum	150	Hi-Shok S.P.	215	3110	2830	2570	2320	2090	1870	3220	2670	2200	1790	1450	1160
7RB		175	Hi-Shok S.P.	215	2860	2650	2440	2240	2060	1880	3180	2720	2310	1960	1640	1370
*†30CA	30 Carbine	110	Soft Point	200	1990	1570	1240	1040	920	840	965	600	375	260	210	175
*†30CB	30 Carbine	110	Full Metal Case	200	1990	1600	1280	1070	950	870	970	620	400	280	220	190
3030A	30-30 Winchester	150	Hi-Shok S.P.	210	2390	2020	1680	1400	1180	1040	1900	1360	945	650	460	355
3030B		170	Hi-Shok S.P.	210	2200	1900	1620	1380	1190	1060	1830	1360	990	720	535	425
3030C		125	Hollow Point	210	2570	2090	1660	1320	1080	960	1830	1210	770	480	320	260
3006A	30-'06 Springfield	150	Hi-Shok S.P.	210	2910	2620	2340	2080	1840	1620	2820	2280	1830	1450	1130	875
3006B		180	Hi-Shok S.P.	210	2700	2470	2250	2040	1850	1660	2910	2440	2020	1670	1360	1110
3006C		125	Soft Point	210	3140	2780	2450	2140	1850	1600	2740	2150	1660	1270	955	705
3006D		165	Boat Tail S.P.	210	2800	2610	2420	2240	2070	1910	2870	2490	2150	1840	1580	1340
3006E		200	Boat Tail S.P.	210	2550	2400	2260	2120	1990	1860	2890	2560	2270	2000	1760	1540
300WB	300 Winchester Magnum	180	Hi-Shok S.P.	215	3000	2780	2580	2380	2190	2010	3600	3100	2650	2260	1920	1640
300A	300 Savage	150	Hi-Shok S.P.	210	2630	2350	2100	1850	1630	1430	2300	1850	1460	1140	885	685
300B		180	Hi-Shok S.P.	210	2350	2140	1940	1750	1570	1410	2210	1830	1500	1220	985	800
308A	308 Winchester	150	Hi-Shok S.P.	210	2820	2530	2260	2010	1770	1560	2650	2140	1710	1340	1050	810
308B		180	Hi-Shok S.P.	210	2620	2390	2180	1970	1780	1600	2740	2290	1900	1560	1270	1030
**8A	8mm Mauser	170	Hi-Shok S.P.	210	2510	2110	1740	1430	1190	1040	2380	1670	1140	770	530	400
32A	32 Winchester Special	170	Hi-Shok S.P.	210	2250	1920	1630	1370	1170	1040	1910	1390	1000	710	520	410
35A	35 Remington	200	Hi-Shok S.P.	210	2080	1700	1380	1140	1000	910	1920	1280	840	575	445	370
*††44A	44 Remington Magnum	240	Hollow S.P.	150	1760	1380	1090	950	860	790	1650	1015	640	485	395	330
*4570A	45-'70 Government	300	Hollow S.P.	210	1810	1410	1120	970	875	NA	2180	1320	840	630	510	NA

Unless otherwise noted, ballistic specifications were derived from test barrels 24 inches in length.
†Test Barrel Length 18 Inches.   ††Test Barrel Length 20 Inches.   *Without Cartridge Carrier.
**Only for use in barrels intended for .323 inch diameter bullets. Do not use in 8mm Commission Rifles (M1888) or sporting arms of similar bore diameter.
▲Discontinued; orders subject to stock on hand.

Revolver Ballistics—Vented Barrel* (Approximate)

Federal Load No.	Caliber	Bullet Style	Bullet Weight in Grains	Velocity in Feet Per Second Muzzle	50 yds.	Energy in ft./lbs. Muzzle	50 yds.	Mid-range Trajectory 50 yds.	Test Barrel Length
38A	38 Special (Match)	Lead Wadcutter	148	710	634	166	132	2.4"	4"
38 ALL	38 Special (Match) NEW	Jacketed Wadcutter	148	710	634	166	132	2.4"	4"
38B	38 Special	Lead Round Nose	158	755	723	200	183	2.0"	4"
38C	38 Special	Lead Semi-Wadcutter	158	755	723	200	183	2.0"	4"
▲ 38D	38 Special (High Velocity + P)	Lead Round Nose	158	915	878	294	270	1.4"	4"
▲ 38E	38 Special (High Velocity + P)	Jacketed Hollow Point	125	945	898	248	224	1.3"	4"
▲ 38F	38 Special (High Velocity + P)	Jacketed Hollow Point	110	1020	945	254	218	1.1"	4"
▲ 38G	38 Special (High Velocity + P)	Lead, Semi-Wadcutter Hollow Point	158	915	878	294	270	1.4"	4"
▲ 38H	38 Special (High Velocity + P)	Lead Semi-Wadcutter	158	915	878	294	270	1.4"	4"
38J	38 Special (High Velocity + P)	Jacketed Soft Point	125	945	898	248	224	1.3"	4"
357A	357 Magnum	Jacketed Soft Point	158	1235	1104	535	428	0.8"	4"
357B	357 Magnum	Jacketed Hollow Point	125	1450	1240	583	427	0.6"	4"
357C	357 Magnum	Lead Semi-Wadcutter	158	1235	1104	535	428	0.8"	4"
357D	357 Magnum	Jacketed Hollow Point	110	1295	1094	410	292	0.8"	4"
357E	357 Magnum	Jacketed Hollow Point	158	1235	1104	535	428	0.8"	4"
44A	44 Rem. Magnum	Jacketed Hollow Point	240	1180	1081	741	623	0.9"	4"
44B	44 Rem. Magnum	Jacketed Hollow Point	180	1610	1365	1045	750	0.5"	4"
45LCA	45 Colt	Semi-Wadcutter Hollow Point	225	900†	860	405	369	1.6"	5½"

*To simulate service conditions, these figures were obtained from a 4" length vented test barrel with a .008" cylinder gap and with the powder positioned horizontally inside the cartridge case.
†Estimated Ballistics

▲This ammunition is loaded to a higher pressure, as indicated by the "+P" marking on the case

---

Bullet Drop In Inches From Bore Line — Drift In Inches In 10 mph Crosswind — Height of Trajectory

Inches above line of sight if sighted in at ⊕ yards. For sights .9" above bore.
Trajectory figures show the height of bullet impact above or below the line of sight at the indicated yardages. Aim low indicated amount for + figures and high for − figures. Zero ranges indicated by circled crosses.

Columns: Bullet Drop (100, 200, 300, 400, 500 yds) | Drift (100, 200, 300, 400, 500 yds) | Height of Trajectory group 1 (50, 100, 150, 200, 250, 300 yds) | Height of Trajectory group 2 (100, 150, 200, 250, 300, 400, 500 yds)

100	200	300	400	500	100	200	300	400	500	50	100	150	200	250	300	100	150	200	250	300	400	500
2.0	9.2	24.3	51.6	98.2	1.7	7.3	18.3	36.4	63.1	+0.5	+0.9	⊕	−2.5	−6.9	−13.7	+2.2	+1.9	⊕	−3.8	−10.0	−32.3	−73.8
1.4	6.2	16.0	32.6	59.4	1.2	5.1	12.3	23.9	41.2	+0.2	+0.5	⊕	−1.5	−4.3	−8.4	+2.2	+2.6	+1.9	⊕	−3.3	−15.4	−37.7
1.8	8.4	21.5	44.4	81.8	1.4	6.1	15.0	29.4	50.8	+0.4	+0.8	⊕	−2.2	−6.0	−11.8	+1.9	+1.6	⊕	−3.3	−8.5	−26.7	−59.6
1.8	7.8	19.2	37.7	65.4	1.0	4.2	10.1	19.2	32.1	+0.4	+0.7	⊕	−1.9	−5.1	−9.9	+1.7	+1.4	⊕	−2.8	−7.1	−21.2	−44.6
1.6	6.9	17.0	33.4	58.3	1.0	4.1	9.9	18.8	31.6	+0.3	+0.6	⊕	−1.6	−4.5	−8.7	+2.4	+2.7	+1.9	⊕	−3.3	−14.9	−35.0
1.9	8.0	19.4	37.0	62.3	0.8	3.3	7.8	14.5	23.8	+0.4	+0.7	⊕	−1.9	−5.1	−9.7	+1.7	+1.4	⊕	−2.7	−6.8	−20.0	−40.8
1.6	7.1	17.5	34.5	60.2	1.0	4.2	10.1	19.2	32.3	+0.3	+0.6	⊕	−1.7	−4.6	−9.0	+2.5	+2.8	+2.0	⊕	−3.4	−15.4	−36.2
2.1	9.0	21.7	41.6	70.2	0.9	3.6	8.4	15.7	25.8	+0.5	+0.9	⊕	−2.2	−5.8	−11.0	+1.9	+1.6	⊕	−3.1	−7.8	−22.6	−46.3
1.6	7.0	17.2	33.8	58.9	1.0	4.1	9.8	18.7	31.3	+0.3	+0.6	⊕	−1.7	−4.5	−8.8	+2.4	+2.7	+2.0	⊕	−3.4	−15.0	−35.2
2.0	8.4	20.4	39.0	65.9	0.8	3.5	8.2	15.3	25.2	+0.5	+0.8	⊕	−2.0	−5.4	−10.3	+1.8	+1.5	⊕	−2.9	−7.3	−21.2	−43.4
1.9	8.1	19.4	37.0	62.1	0.8	3.2	7.4	13.9	22.7	+0.4	+0.7	⊕	−1.9	−5.1	−9.7	+1.7	+1.4	⊕	−2.7	−6.8	−19.9	−40.5
2.2	9.9	24.6	48.8	85.4	1.2	5.2	12.5	23.9	40.2	+0.6	+1.0	⊕	−2.5	−6.8	−13.1	+2.2	+1.9	⊕	−3.6	−9.3	−28.1	−59.7
3.1	13.7	34.1	67.8	119.3	1.5	6.2	15.0	28.7	47.8	+0.4	⊕	−2.2	−6.6	−13.4	−23.0	+1.5	⊕	−3.6	−9.7	−18.6	−46.8	−92.8
2.6	11.4	27.7	53.5	91.6	1.1	4.5	10.7	20.2	33.6	+0.2	⊕	−1.7	−5.2	−10.5	−18.0	+2.6	+2.1	⊕	−4.0	−10.2	−29.9	−61.8
1.9	8.2	19.7	37.6	63.9	0.8	3.4	8.1	15.1	24.9	+0.4	+0.8	⊕	−1.9	−5.2	−9.9	+1.7	+1.5	⊕	−2.8	−7.0	−20.5	−42.1
2.2	9.5	22.5	42.5	70.8	0.7	3.1	7.2	13.3	21.7	+0.6	+0.9	⊕	−2.3	−6.0	−11.3	+2.0	+1.7	⊕	−3.2	−7.9	−22.7	−45.8
5.2	24.8	67.2	142.0	257.6	3.4	15.0	35.5	63.2	96.7	+0.9	⊕	−4.5	−13.5	−28.3	−49.9	⊕	−4.5	−13.5	−28.3	−49.9	−118.6	−228.1
5.1	24.1	64.5	135.1	244.1	3.1	13.7	32.6	58.7	90.3	+0.9	⊕	−4.3	−13.0	−26.9	−47.4	+2.9	⊕	−7.2	−19.7	−38.7	−100.4	−200.5
3.4	15.4	39.9	82.3	149.8	2.0	8.5	20.9	40.1	66.1	+0.5	⊕	−2.6	−7.7	−16.0	−27.9	+1.7	⊕	−4.3	−11.6	−22.7	−59.1	−120.5
4.0	17.7	44.8	90.3	160.2	1.9	8.0	19.4	36.7	59.8	+0.6	⊕	−3.0	−8.9	−18.0	−31.1	+2.0	⊕	−4.8	−13.0	−25.1	−63.6	−126.7
3.0	14.2	38.0	81.0	148.7	2.2	10.1	25.4	49.4	81.6	+0.1	⊕	−2.0	−7.3	−15.8	−28.1	+3.2	+2.4	⊕	−5.5	−15.8	−51.7	−112.3
2.2	9.5	23.2	44.9	76.9	1.0	4.2	9.9	18.7	31.2	+0.6	+0.9	⊕	−2.3	−6.3	−12.0	+2.1	+1.8	⊕	−3.3	−8.5	−25.0	−51.8
2.5	10.8	25.9	49.4	83.2	0.9	3.7	8.8	16.5	27.1	+0.2	⊕	−1.6	−4.8	−9.7	−16.5	+2.4	+2.0	⊕	−3.7	−9.3	−27.0	−54.9
1.9	8.3	20.6	40.6	70.7	1.1	4.5	10.8	20.5	34.4	+0.4	+0.8	⊕	−2.1	−5.6	−10.7	+1.8	+1.5	⊕	−3.0	−7.7	−23.0	−48.5
2.2	9.5	22.7	42.7	71.0	0.7	2.8	6.6	12.3	19.9	+0.5	⊕	−1.1	−4.2	−8.8	−14.3	+2.1	+1.8	⊕	−3.0	−8.0	−22.9	−45.9
2.6	11.2	26.6	59.7	81.6	0.6	2.6	6.0	11.0	17.7	+0.6	⊕	−2.7	−6.0	−12.4	−18.8	+2.3	+1.8	⊕	−4.1	−9.0	−25.8	−51.3
2.6	11.0	26.4	50.3	84.8	0.7	2.8	6.5	12.0	19.6	+0.5	+0.8	⊕	−2.0	−5.3	−10.1	+1.8	+1.5	⊕	−2.8	−7.0	−20.2	−40.7
2.7	11.7	28.7	55.8	96.1	1.1	4.8	11.6	21.9	36.3	+0.3	⊕	−1.8	−5.4	−11.0	−18.8	+2.7	+2.2	⊕	−4.2	−10.7	−31.5	−65.5
3.4	14.3	34.7	66.4	112.3	1.1	4.6	10.9	20.3	33.3	+0.4	⊕	−2.3	−6.7	−13.5	−22.8	+1.5	⊕	−3.6	−9.6	−18.2	−44.1	−84.2
2.3	10.1	24.8	48.0	82.4	1.0	4.4	10.4	19.7	32.7	+0.2	⊕	−1.5	−4.5	−9.3	−15.9	+2.3	+1.9	⊕	−3.6	−9.1	−26.9	−55.7
2.7	11.5	27.6	52.7	88.8	0.9	3.9	9.2	17.2	28.3	+0.2	⊕	−1.8	−5.2	−10.4	−17.7	+2.6	+2.1	⊕	−4.0	−9.9	−28.9	−58.8
3.1	14.2	36.8	76.7	141.2	1.9	8.5	21.0	40.6	67.5	+0.4	⊕	−2.3	−7.0	−14.6	−25.7	+1.6	⊕	−3.9	−10.7	−21.0	−55.4	−114.3
3.8	17.1	43.7	88.9	159.3	1.9	8.4	20.3	38.6	63.0	+0.6	⊕	−2.9	−8.6	−17.6	−30.5	+1.9	⊕	−4.7	−12.7	−24.7	−63.2	−126.9
4.6	21.5	56.9	118.9	215.6	2.7	12.0	29.0	53.3	83.3	+0.8	⊕	−3.8	−11.3	−23.5	−41.2	+2.5	⊕	−6.3	−17.1	−33.6	−87.7	−176.3
6.7	32.4	87.0	179.8	319.6	4.2	17.8	39.8	68.3	102.5	⊕	−2.7	−10.2	−23.6	−44.2	−73.3	⊕	−6.1	−18.1	−37.4	−65.1	−150.3	−282.5
6.2	30.3	81.9	170.0	NA	4.0	17.2	38.9	67.2	NA	⊕	−2.5	−9.5	−22.0	−41.5	−69.0	⊕	−5.7	−17.0	−35.2	−61.4	−142.5	NA

NOTE: These trajectory tables were calculated by computer and are given here unaltered. The computer used a standard modern scientific technique to predict trajectories from the best available data for each round. Each trajectory is expected to be reasonably representative of the behavior of the ammunition at sea level conditions, but the shooter is cautioned that trajectories differ because of variations in ammunition, rifles, and atmospheric conditions.

WINCHESTER Western

CALIBER	BULLET WT. GRS.	BULLET TYPE	SYMBOL	PRIMER
25 Automatic (6.35mm)	50	FMC	X25AP	1½-108
256 Winchester Magnum Super-X	60	OPE(HP)	X2561P	6½-116
30 Luger (7.65mm)	93	FMC	X30LP	1½-108
32 Automatic	71	FMC	X32AP	1½-108
32 Automatic	60	STHP	X32ASHP	1½-108
32 Smith & Wesson (inside lubricated)	85	Lead	X32SWP	1½-108
32 Smith & Wesson Long (inside lubricated)	98	Lead	X32SWLP	1½-108
32 Short Colt (greased)	80	Lead	X32SCP	1½-108
32 Long Colt (inside lubricated)	82	Lead	X32LCP	1½-108
357 Magnum Jacketed Hollow Point Super-X	110	JHP	X3573P	1½-108
357 Magnum Jacketed Hollow Point Super-X	125	JHP	X3576P	1½-108
357 Magnun Super-X (inside lubricated)	158	Lead	X3571P	1½-108
357 Magnum Jacketed Hollow Point Super-X	158	JHP	X3574P	1½-108
357 Magnum Jacketed Soft Point Super-X	158	JSP	X3575P	1½-108
357 Magnum Metal Piercing Super-X (inside lubricated, lead bearing)	158	Met. Pierc.	X3572P	1½-108
9 mm Luger (Parabellum)	95	JSP	X9MMJSP	1½-108
9 mm Luger (Parabellum)	100	JHP	X9MMJHP	1½-108
9 mm Luger (Parabellum)	115	FMC	X9LP	1½-108
9 mm Luger (Parabellum)	115	STHP	X9MMSHP	1½-108
9 mm Winchester Magnum Super-X	115	FMC	X9MMWM	1½-108
38 Smith & Wesson (inside lubricated)	145	Lead	X38SWP	1½-108
38 Special (inside lubricated)	158	Lead	X38S1P	1½-108
38 Special Metal Point (inside lubricated, lead bearing)	158	Met. Pt.	X38S2P	1½-108
38 Special Super Police (inside lubricated)	200	Lead	X38S3P	1½-108
38 Special Super-X Jacketed Hollow Point +P	110	JHP	X38S6PH	1½-108
38 Special Super-X Jacketed Hollow Point +P	125	JHP	X38S7PH	1½-108
38 Special Super-X +P	95	STHP	X38SSHP	1½-108
38 Special Super-X (inside lubricated) +P	150	Lead	X38S4P	1½-108
38 Special Metal Piercing Super-X (inside lubricated, lead bearing) +P	150	Met. Pierc.	X38S5P	1½-108
38 Special Super-X (inside lubricated) +P	158	Lead-HP	X38SPD	1½-108
38 Special Super-X Semi-Wad Cutter (inside lubricated) +P	158	Lead-SWC	X38WCP	1½-108
38 Special Super-Match and Match Mid-Range Clean Cutting (inside lubricated)	148	Lead-WC	X38SMRP	1½-108
38 Special Super Match (inside lubricated)	158	Lead	X38SMP	1½-108
38 Short Colt (greased)	130	Lead	X38SCP	1½-108
38 Long Colt (inside lubricated)	150	Lead	X38LCP	1½-108
38 Automatic Super-X (For use only in 38 Colt Super and Colt Commander Automatic Pistols)	125	JHP	X38A3P	1½-108
38 Automatic Super-X +P (For use only in 38 Colt Super and Colt Commander Automatic Pistols)	130	FMC	X38A1P	1½-108
38 Automatic (For all 38 Colt Automatic Pistols)	130	FMC	X38A2P	1½-108
380 Automatic	95	FMC	X380AP	1½-108
380 Automatic	85	STHP	X380ASHP	1½-108
41 Remington Magnum Super-X (inside lubricated)	210	Lead	X41MP	7-111F
41 Remington Magnum Super-X Jacketed Soft Point	210	JSP	X41MJSP	7-111F
44 Smith & Wesson Special (inside lubricated)	246	Lead	X44SP	7-111
44 Remington Magnum Super-X (Gas Check) (inside lubricated)	240	Lead	X44MP	7-111F
45 Colt (inside lubricated)	255	Lead	X45CP	7-111
45 Automatic	185	STHP	X45ASHP	7-111
45 Automatic	230	FMC	X45A1P	7-111
45 Automatic Super-Match Clean Cutting	185	FMC-WC	X45AWCP	7-111
45 Winchester Magnum Super-X	230	FMC	X45WM	7-111

Met. Pierc.-Metal Piercing FMC-Full Metal Case SP-Soft Point JHP-Jacketed Hollow Point JSP-Jacketed Soft Point Met. Pt.-Metal Point
OPE-Open Point Expanding HP-Hollow Point PP-Power Point WC-Wad Cutter SWC-Semi Wad Cutter STHP-Silvertip Hollow Point
Specifications are nominal. Test barrels are used to determine ballistics figures. Individual firearms may differ from these test barrel statistics.

25 Auto.   256 Win.   30 Luger   32 Auto.   32 S&W   32 S&W Long   32 Short Colt   32 Long Colt   32-20 Win.   357 Mag.   9mm Luger   38 S&W   38 Special   38 Special S.M.

CENTERFIRE PISTOL and REVOLVER CARTRIDGES

VELOCITY-FPS			ENERGY FT-LBS.			MID RANGE TRAJECTORY INCHES		BARREL LENGTH INCHES
MUZZLE	50 YDS.	100 YDS.	MUZZLE	50 YDS.	100 YDS.	50 YDS.	100 YDS.	
810	755	700	73	63	54	1.8	7.7	2
2350	2030	1760	735	550	415	0.3	1.1	8½
1220	1110	1040	305	255	225	0.9	3.5	4½
905	855	810	129	115	97	1.4	5.8	4
970	895	835	125	107	93	1.3	5.4	4
680	645	610	90	81	73	2.5	10.5	3
705	670	635	115	98	88	2.3	10.5	4
745	665	590	100	79	62	2.2	9.9	4
755	715	675	100	93	83	2.0	8.7	4
1295	1094	975	410	292	232	0.8	3.5	4V
1450	1240	1090	583	427	330	0.6	2.8	4V
1235	1104	1015	535	428	361	0.8	3.5	4V
1235	1104	1015	535	428	361	0.8	3.5	4V
1235	1104	1015	535	428	361	0.8	3.5	4V
1235	1104	1015	535	428	361	0.8	3.5	4V
1355	1140	1008	387	274	214	0.7	3.3	4
1320	1114	991	387	275	218	0.7	3.4	4
1155	1047	971	341	280	241	0.9	3.9	4
1225	1095	1007	383	306	259	0.8	3.6	4
1475	1264	1109	556	408	314	0.6	2.7	5
685	650	620	150	135	125	2.4	10.0	4
755	723	693	200	183	168	2.0	8.3	4V
755	723	693	200	183	168	2.0	8.3	4V
635	614	594	179	168	157	2.8	11.5	4V
1020	945	887	254	218	192	1.1	4.8	4V
945	898	858	248	224	204	1.3	5.4	4V
1100	1002	932	255	212	183	1.0	4.3	4V
910	870	835	276	252	232	1.4	5.7	4V
910	870	835	276	252	232	1.4	5.7	4V
915	878	844	294	270	250	1.4	5.6	4V
915	878	844	294	270	250	1.4	5.6	4V
710	634	566	166	132	105	2.4	10.8	4V
755	723	693	200	183	168	2.0	8.3	4V
730	685	645	150	130	115	2.2	9.4	6
730	700	670	175	165	150	2.1	8.8	6
1245	1105	1010	430	340	285	0.8	3.6	5
1280	1140	1050	475	375	320	0.8	3.4	5
1040	980	925	310	275	245	1.0	4.7	4½
955	865	785	190	160	130	1.4	5.9	3¾
1000	921	860	189	160	140	1.2	5.1	3¾
965	898	842	434	376	331	1.3	5.4	4V
1300	1162	1062	788	630	526	0.7	3.2	4V
755	725	695	310	285	265	2.0	8.3	6½
1350	1186	1069	971	749	608	0.7	3.1	4V
860	820	780	420	380	345	1.5	6.1	5½
1000	938	888	411	362	324	1.2	4.9	5
810	776	745	335	308	284	1.7	7.2	5
770	707	650	244	205	174	2.0	8.7	5
1400	1232	1107	1001	775	636	0.6	2.8	5

+P Ammunition with (+P) on the case head stamp is loaded to higher pressure. Use only in firearms designated for this cartridge and so recommended by the gun manufacturer.

V-Data is based on velocity obtained from 4" vented barrels for revolver cartridges (38 Special, 357 Magnum, 41 Rem. Mag. and 44 Rem. Mag.) and unvented (solid) test barrels of the length specified for 9mm and 45 auto pistols.

38 Short Colt — 38 Long Colt — 38 Auto. — 380 Auto. — 38-40 Win. — 41 Rem. Mag. — 44 S&W Special — 44 Rem Mag. — 44-40 Win. — 45 Colt — 45 Auto. — 45 Auto S.T.H.P.

CARTRIDGE	GAME SELECTOR GUIDE	BULLET WT. GRS.	TYPE	SYMBOL	PRIMER	BARREL LENGTH INCHES	MUZZLE	100	200	300 YARDS	400	500
218 Bee Super-X	S	46	OPE(HP)	X218B	6½-116	24	2760	2102	1550	1155	961	850
22 Hornet Super-X	S	45	SP	X22H1	6½-116	24	2690	2042	1502	1128	948	840
22 Hornet Super-X	S	46	OPE(HP)	X22H2	6½-116	24	2690	2042	1502	1128	948	841
22-250 Remington Super-X	S	55	PSP	X222501	8½-120	24	3730	3180	2695	2257	1863	1519
222 Remington Super-X	S	50	PSP	X222R	6½-116	24	3140	2602	2123	1700	1350	1107
222 Remington Super-X	S	55	FMC	X222R1	6½-116	24	3020	2675	2355	2057	1783	1537
223 Remington Super-X	S	55	PSP	X223R	6½-116	24	3240	2747	2304	1905	1554	1270
223 Remington Super-X	S	55	FMC	X223R1	6½-116	24	3240	2877	2543	2232	1943	1679
225 Winchester Super-X	S	55	PSP	X2251	8½-120	24	3570	3066	2616	2208	1838	1514
243 Winchester Super-X	S	80	PSP	X2431	8½-120	24	3350	2955	2593	2259	1951	1670
243 Winchester Super-X	D,O/P	100	PP(SP)	X2432	8½-120	24	2960	2697	2449	2215	1993	1786
6 MM Remington Super-X	S	80	PSP	X6MMR1	8½-120	24	3470	3064	2694	2352	2036	1747
6 MM Remington Super-X	D,O/P	100	PP(SP)	X6MMR2	8½-120	24	3130	2857	2600	2357	2127	1911
25-06 Remington Super-X	S	90	PEP	X25061	8½-120	24	3440	3043	2680	2344	2034	1749
25-06 Remington Super-X	D,O/P	120	PEP	X25062	8½-120	24	3010	2749	2502	2269	2048	1840
25-20 Winchester		86	SP	X25202	6½-116	24	1460	1194	1030	931	858	798
25-20 Winchester		86	Lead	X25201	6½-116	24	1460	1194	1030	931	858	798
25-35 Winchester Super-X		117	SP	X2535	8½-120	24	2230	1866	1545	1282	1097	984
250 Savage Super-X	S	87	PSP	X2501	8½-120	24	3030	2673	2342	2036	1755	1504
250 Savage Super-X	D,O/P	100	ST	X2503	8½-120	24	2820	2467	2140	1839	1569	1339
256 Winchester Mag. Super-X	S	60	OPE(HP)	X2561P	6½-116	24	2760	2097	1542	1149	957	846
257 Roberts Super-X	S	87	PSP	X2571	8½-120	24	3170	2802	2462	2147	1857	1594
257 Roberts Super-X	D,O/P	100	ST	X2572	8½-120	24	2900	2541	2210	1904	1627	1387
257 Roberts Super-X	D,O/P	117	PP(SP)	X2573	8½-120	24	2650	2291	1961	1663	1404	1199
264 Winchester Mag. Super-X	S	100	PSP	X2641	8½-120	24	3320	2926	2565	2231	1923	1644
264 Winchester Mag. Super-X	D,O/P	140	PP(SP)	X2642	8½-120	24	3030	2782	2548	2326	2114	1914
270 Winchester Super-X	S	100	PSP	X2701	8½-120	24	3480	3067	2690	2343	2023	1730
270 Winchester Super-X	D,O/P	130	PP(SP)	X2705	8½-120	24	3110	2849	2604	2371	2150	1941
270 Winchester Super-X	D,O/P	130	ST	X2703	8½-120	24	3110	2823	2554	2300	2061	1837
270 Winchester Super-X	D,L	150	PP(SP)	X2704	8½-120	24	2900	2632	2380	2142	1918	1709
284 Winchester Super-X	D,O/P	125	PP(SP)	X2841	8½-120	24	3140	2829	2538	2265	2010	1772
284 Winchester Super-X	D,O/P,L	150	PP(SP)	X2842	8½-120	24	2860	2595	2344	2108	1886	1680
7 MM Mauser (7 x 57) Super-X	D	175	SP	X7MM	8½-120	24	2440	2137	1857	1603	1382	1204
7 MM Remington Mag. Super-X	D,O/P	125	PP(SP)	X7MMR3	8½-120	24	3310	2976	2666	2376	2105	1852
7 MM Remington Mag. Super-X	D,O/P	150	PP(SP)	X7MMR1	8½-120	24	3110	2830	2568	2320	2085	1866
7 MM Remington Mag. Super-X	D,O/P,L	175	PP(SP)	X7MMR2	8½-120	24	2860	2645	2440	2244	2057	1879
30 Carbine		110	HSP	X30M1	6½-116	20	1990	1567	1236	1035	923	842
30 Carbine		110	FMC	X30M2	6½-116	20	1990	1596	1278	1070	952	870
30-30 Winchester Super-X	D	150	OPE	X30301	8½-120	24	2390	2018	1684	1398	1177	1036
30-30 Winchester Super-X	D	150	PP(SP)	X30306	8½-120	24	2390	2018	1684	1398	1177	1036
30-30 Winchester Super-X	D	150	ST	X30302	8½-120	24	2390	2018	1684	1398	1177	1036
30-30 Winchester Super-X	D	170	PP(SP)	X30303	8½-120	24	2200	1895	1619	1381	1191	1061
30-30 Winchester Super-X	D	170	ST	X30304	8½-120	24	2200	1895	1619	1381	1191	1061
30 Remington Super-X	D	170	ST	X30R2	8½-120	24	2120	1822	1555	1328	1153	1036
30-06 Springfield Super-X	S	110	PSP	X30060	8½-120	24	3380	2843	2365	1936	1561	1261
30-06 Springfield Super-X	S	125	PSP	X30062	8½-120	24	3140	2780	2447	2138	1853	1595
30-06 Springfield Super-X	D,O/P	150	PP(SP)	X30061	8½-120	24	2920	2580	2265	1972	1704	1466
30-06 Springfield Super-X	D,O/P	150	ST	X30063	8½-120	24	2910	2617	2342	2083	1843	1622
30-06 Springfield Super-X	D,O/P,L	180	PP(SP)	X30064	8½-120	24	2700	2348	2023	1727	1466	1251
30-06 Springfield Super-X	D,O/P,L	180	ST	X30066	8½-120	24	2700	2469	2250	2042	1846	1663
30-06 Springfield Super-X	L	220	PP(SP)	X30068	8½-120	24	2410	2130	1870	1632	1422	1246
30-06 Springfield Super-X	L	220	ST	X30069	8½-120	24	2410	2192	1985	1791	1611	1448

GAME SELECTOR CODE

S = Small game   O/P = Open or Plains shooting   XL = Extra Large game
D = Deer   (i.e. Antelope, Deer)   (i.e. Kodiak bear)
        L = Large game (i.e. Moose, Elk)

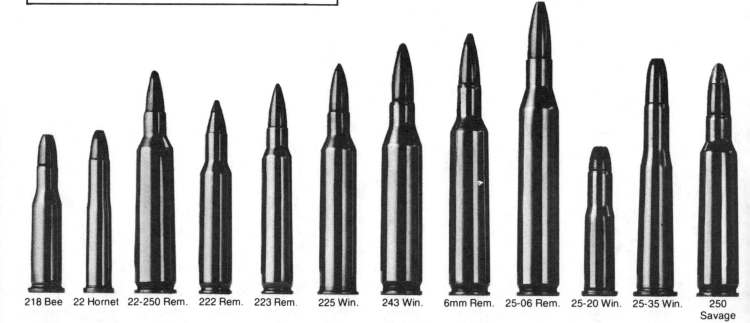

218 Bee   22 Hornet   22-250 Rem.   222 Rem.   223 Rem.   225 Win.   243 Win.   6mm Rem.   25-06 Rem.   25-20 Win.   25-35 Win.   250 Savage

ARTRIDGES

TRAJECTORY Inches above (+) or below(-) line of sight 0 = Indicates yardage at which rifle is sighted in.

| ENERGY IN FOOT POUNDS (YARDS) ||||||| SHORT RANGE (YARDS) |||||| LONG RANGE (YARDS) |||||||
MUZZLE	100	200	300	400	500	50	100	150	200	250	300	100	150	200	250	300	400	500
778	451	245	136	94	74	0.3	0	-2.3	-7.2	-15.8	-29.4	1.5	0	-4.2	-12.0	-24.8	-71.4	-155.6
723	417	225	127	90	70	0.3	0	-2.4	-7.7	-16.9	-31.3	1.6	0	-4.5	-12.8	-26.4	-75.6	-163.4
739	426	230	130	92	72	0.3	0	-2.4	-7.7	-16.9	-31.3	1.6	0	-4.5	-12.8	-26.4	-75.5	-163.3
1699	1235	887	622	424	282	0.2	0.5	0	-1.5	-4.3	-8.4	2.2	2.6	1.9	0	-3.3	-15.4	-37.7
1094	752	500	321	202	136	0.5	0.9	0	-2.5	-6.9	-13.7	2.2	1.9	0	-3.8	-10.0	-32.3	-73.8
1114	874	677	517	388	288	0.5	0.9	0	-2.2	-6.1	-11.7	2.0	1.7	0	-3.3	-8.3	-24.9	-52.5
1282	921	648	443	295	197	0.4	0.8	0	-2.2	-6.0	-11.8	1.9	1.6	0	-3.3	-8.5	-26.7	-59.6
1282	1011	790	608	461	344	0.4	0.7	0	-1.9	-5.1	-9.9	1.7	1.4	0	-2.8	-7.1	-21.2	-44.6
1556	1148	836	595	412	280	0.2	0.6	0	-1.7	-4.6	-9.0	2.4	2.8	2.0	0	-3.5	-16.3	-39.5
1993	1551	1194	906	676	495	0.3	0.7	0	-1.8	-4.9	-9.4	2.6	2.9	2.1	0	-3.6	-16.2	-37.9
1945	1615	1332	1089	882	708	0.5	0.9	0	-2.2	-5.8	-11.0	1.9	1.6	0	-3.1	-7.8	-22.6	-46.3
2139	1667	1289	982	736	542	0.3	0.6	0	-1.6	-4.5	-8.7	2.4	2.7	1.9	0	-3.3	-14.9	-35.0
2175	1812	1501	1233	1004	811	0.4	0.7	0	-1.9	-5.1	-9.7	1.7	1.4	0	-2.7	-6.8	-20.0	-40.8
2364	1850	1435	1098	827	611	0.3	0.6	0	-1.7	-4.5	-8.8	2.4	2.7	2.0	0	-3.4	-15.0	-35.2
2414	2013	1668	1372	1117	902	0.5	0.8	0	-2.1	-5.5	-10.5	1.9	1.6	0	-2.9	-7.4	-21.6	-44.2
407	272	203	165	141	122	0	-4.1	-14.4	-31.8	-57.3	-92.0	0	-8.2	-23.5	-47.0	-79.6	-175.9	-319.4
407	272	203	165	141	122	0	-4.1	-14.4	-31.8	-57.3	-92.0	0	-8.2	-23.5	-47.0	-79.6	-175.9	-319.4
1292	904	620	427	313	252	0.6	0	-3.1	-9.2	-19.0	-33.1	2.1	0	-5.1	-13.8	-27.0	-70.1	-142.0
1773	1380	1059	801	595	437	0.5	0.9	0	-2.3	-6.1	-11.8	2.0	1.7	0	-3.3	-8.4	-25.2	-53.4
1765	1351	1017	751	547	398	0.2	0	-1.6	-4.9	-10.0	-17.4	2.4	2.0	0	-3.9	-10.1	-30.5	-65.2
1015	586	317	176	122	95	0.3	0	-2.3	-7.3	-15.9	-29.6	1.5	0	-4.2	-12.1	-25.0	-72.1	-157.2
1941	1516	1171	890	666	491	0.4	0.8	0	-2.0	-5.5	-10.6	1.8	1.5	0	-3.0	-7.5	-22.7	-48.0
1867	1433	1084	805	588	427	0.6	1.0	0	-2.5	-6.9	-13.2	2.3	1.9	0	-3.7	-9.4	-28.6	-60.9
1824	1363	999	718	512	373	0.3	0	-1.9	-5.8	-11.9	-20.7	2.9	2.4	0	-4.7	-12.0	-36.7	-79.2
2447	1901	1461	1105	821	600	0.3	0.7	0	-1.8	-5.0	-9.7	2.7	3.0	2.2	0	-3.7	-16.6	-38.9
2854	2406	2018	1682	1389	1139	0.5	0.8	0	-2.0	-5.4	-10.2	1.8	1.5	0	-2.9	-7.2	-20.8	-42.2
2689	2088	1606	1219	909	664	0.3	0.6	0	-1.6	-4.5	-8.7	2.4	2.7	1.9	0	-3.3	-15.0	-35.2
2791	2343	1957	1622	1334	1087	0.4	0.7	0	-1.9	-5.1	-9.7	1.7	1.4	0	-2.7	-6.8	-19.9	-40.5
2791	2300	1883	1527	1226	974	0.4	0.8	0	-2.0	-5.3	-10.0	1.7	1.5	0	-2.8	-7.1	-20.8	-42.7
2801	2307	1886	1528	1225	973	0.6	0.9	0	-2.3	-6.1	-11.7	2.1	1.7	0	-3.3	-8.2	-24.1	-49.4
2736	2221	1788	1424	1121	871	0.4	0.8	0	-2.0	-5.3	-10.1	1.7	1.5	0	-2.8	-7.2	-21.1	-43.7
2724	2243	1830	1480	1185	940	0.6	1.0	0	-2.4	-6.3	-12.1	2.1	1.8	0	-3.4	-8.5	-24.8	-51.0
2313	1774	1340	998	742	563	0.4	0	-2.3	-6.8	-13.8	-23.7	1.5	0	-3.7	-10.0	-19.1	-48.1	-95.4
3040	2458	1972	1567	1230	952	0.3	0.6	0	-1.7	-4.7	-9.1	2.5	2.8	2.0	0	-3.4	-15.0	-34.5
3221	2667	2196	1792	1448	1160	0.4	0.8	0	-1.9	-5.2	-9.9	1.7	1.5	0	-2.8	-7.0	-20.5	-42.1
3178	2718	2313	1956	1644	1372	0.6	0.9	0	-2.3	-6.0	-11.3	2.0	1.7	0	-3.2	-7.9	-22.7	-45.8
967	600	373	262	208	173	0.9	0	-4.5	-13.5	-28.3	-49.9	0	-4.5	-13.5	-28.3	-49.9	-118.6	-228.2
967	622	399	280	221	185	0.9	0	-4.3	-13.0	-26.9	-47.4	2.9	0	-7.2	-19.7	-38.7	-100.4	-200.5
1902	1356	944	651	461	357	0.5	0	-2.6	-7.7	-16.0	-27.9	1.7	0	-4.3	-11.6	-22.7	-59.1	-120.5
1902	1356	944	651	461	357	0.5	0	-2.6	-7.7	-16.0	-27.9	1.7	0	-4.3	-11.6	-22.7	-59.1	-120.5
1902	1356	944	651	461	357	0.5	0	-2.6	-7.7	-16.0	-27.9	1.7	0	-4.3	-11.6	-22.7	-59.1	-120.5
1827	1355	989	720	535	425	0.6	0	-3.0	-8.9	-18.0	-31.1	2.0	0	-4.8	-13.0	-25.1	-63.6	-126.7
1827	1355	989	720	535	425	0.6	0	-3.0	-8.9	-18.0	-31.1	2.0	0	-4.8	-13.0	-25.1	-63.6	-126.7
1696	1253	913	666	502	405	0.7	0	-3.3	-9.7	-19.6	-33.8	2.2	0	-5.3	-14.1	-27.2	-69.0	-136.9
2790	1974	1366	915	595	388	0.4	0.7	0	-2.0	-5.6	-11.1	1.7	1.5	0	-3.1	-8.0	-25.5	-57.4
2736	2145	1662	1269	953	706	0.4	0.8	0	-2.1	-5.6	-10.7	1.8	1.5	0	-3.0	-7.7	-23.0	-48.5
2839	2217	1708	1295	967	716	0.6	1.0	0	-2.4	-6.6	-12.7	2.2	1.8	0	-3.5	-9.0	-27.0	-57.1
2820	2281	1827	1445	1131	876	0.6	0.9	0	-2.3	-6.3	-12.0	2.1	1.8	0	-3.3	-8.5	-25.0	-51.8
2913	2203	1635	1192	859	625	0.2	0	-1.8	-5.5	-11.2	-19.5	2.7	2.3	0	-4.4	-11.3	-34.4	-73.7
2913	2436	2023	1666	1362	1105	0.2	0	-1.6	-4.8	-9.7	-16.5	2.4	2.0	0	-3.7	-9.3	-27.0	-54.9
2837	2216	1708	1301	988	758	0.4	0	-2.3	-6.8	-13.8	-23.6	1.5	0	-3.7	-9.9	-19.0	-47.4	-93.1
2837	2347	1924	1567	1268	1024	0.4	0	-2.2	-6.4	-12.7	-21.6	1.5	0	-3.5	-9.1	-17.2	-41.8	-79.9

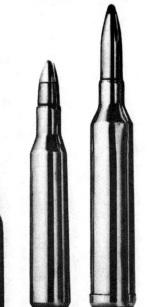

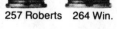

256 Win. Mag.

257 Roberts

264 Win.

270 Win.

284 Win.

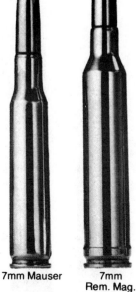

7mm Mauser

7mm Rem. Mag.

30 Carbine   30-30 Win.

30 Rem.

30-06 Springfield

CARTRIDGE	GAME SELECTOR GUIDE	BULLET WT. GRS.	BULLET TYPE	SYMBOL	PRIMER	BARREL LENGTH INCHES	MUZZLE	100	200	300 YARDS	400	500
30-40 Krag Super-X	D	180	PP(SP)	X30401	8½-120	24	2430	2099	1795	1525	1298	1128
30-40 Krag Super-X	D	180	ST	X30403	8½-120	24	2430	2213	2007	1813	1632	1468
30-40 Krag Super-X	L	220	ST	X30404	8½-120	24	2160	1956	1765	1587	1427	1287
300 Winchester Mag. Super-X	D,O/P	150	PP(SP)	X30WM1	8½-120	24	3290	2951	2636	2342	2068	1813
300 Winchester Mag. Super-X	O/P,L	180	PP(SP)	X30WM2	8½-120	24	2960	2745	2540	2344	2157	1979
300 Winchester Mag. Super-X	L,XL	220	ST	X30WM3	8½-120	24	2680	2448	2228	2020	1823	1640
300 H.&H. Magnum Super-X	O/P	150	ST	X300H1	8½-120	24	3130	2822	2534	2264	2011	1776
300 H.&H. Magnum Super-X	O/P,L	180	ST	X300H2	8½-120	24	2880	2640	2412	2196	1991	1798
300 H.&H. Magnum Super-X	L,XL	220	ST	X300H3	8½-120	24	2580	2341	2114	1901	1702	1520
300 Savage Super-X	D,O/P	150	PP(SP)	X3001	8½-120	24	2630	2311	2015	1743	1500	1295
300 Savage Super-X	D,O/P	150	ST	X3003	8½-120	24	2630	2354	2095	1853	1631	1434
300 Savage Super-X	D	180	PP(SP)	X3004	8½-120	24	2350	2025	1728	1467	1252	1098
300 Savage Super-X	D	180	ST	X3005	8½-120	24	2350	2137	1935	1745	1570	1413
303 Savage Super-X	D	190	ST	X3032	8½-120	24	1940	1657	1410	1211	1073	982
303 British Super-X	D	180	PP(SP)	X303B1	8½-120	24	2460	2233	2018	1816	1629	1459
308 Winchester Super-X	S	110	PSP	X3081	8½-120	24	3180	2666	2206	1795	1444	1178
308 Winchester Super-X	S	125	PSP	X3087	8½-120	24	3050	2697	2370	2067	1788	1537
308 Winchester Super-X	D,O/P	150	PP(SP)	X3085	8½-120	24	2820	2488	2179	1893	1633	1405
308 Winchester Super-X	D,O/P	150	ST	X3082	8½-120	24	2820	2533	2263	2009	1774	1560
308 Winchester Super-X	D,O/P,L	180	PP(SP)	X3086	8½-120	24	2620	2274	1955	1666	1414	1212
308 Winchester Super-X	D,O/P,L	180	ST	X3083	8½-120	24	2620	2393	2178	1974	1782	1604
308 Winchester Super-X	L	200	ST	X3084	8½-120	24	2450	2208	1980	1767	1572	1397
32 Win. Special Super-X	D	170	PP(SP)	X32WS2	8½-120	24	2250	1870	1537	1267	1082	971
32 Win. Special Super-X	D	170	ST	X32WS3	8½-120	24	2250	1870	1537	1267	1082	971
32 Remington Super-X	D	170	ST	X32R2	8½-120	24	2140	1785	1475	1228	1064	963
32-20 Winchester		100	SP	X32202	6½-116	24	1210	1021	913	834	769	712
32-20 Winchester		100	Lead	X32201	6½-116	24	1210	1021	913	834	769	712
8mm Mauser (8x57) Super-X	D	170	PP(SP)	X8MM	8½-120	24	2360	1969	1622	1333	1123	997
338 Winchester Mag. Super-X	D,O/P	200	PP(SP)	X3381	8½-120	24	2960	2658	2375	2110	1862	1635
338 Winchester Mag. Super-X	L,XL	225	SP	X3383	8½-120	24	2780	2572	2374	2184	2003	1832
338 Winchester Mag. Super-X	L,XL	250	ST	X3382	8½-120	24	2660	2395	2145	1910	1693	1497
348 Winchester Super-X	D,L	200	ST	X3482	8½-120	24	2520	2215	1931	1672	1443	1253
35 Remington Super-X	D	200	PP(SP)	X35R1	8½-120	24	2020	1646	1335	1114	985	901
35 Remington Super-X	D	200	ST	X35R3	8½-120	24	2020	1646	1335	1114	985	901
351 Winchester S.L.	D	180	SP	X351SL2	6½-116	20	1850	1556	1310	1128	1012	933
358 Winchester Super-X	D,L	200	ST	X3581	8½-120	24	2490	2171	1876	1610	1379	1194
358 Winchester Super-X	L	250	ST	X3582	8½-120	24	2230	1988	1762	1557	1375	1224
375 Winchester	D,L	200	PP(SP)	X375W	8½-120	24	2200	1841	1526	1268	1089	980
375 Winchester	D,L	250	PP(SP)	X375W1	8½-120	24	1900	1647	1424	1239	1103	1011
375 H.&H. Magnum Super-X	L,XL	270	PP(SP)	X375H1	8½-120	24	2690	2420	2166	1928	1707	1507
375 H.&H. Magnum Super-X	L,XL	300	ST	X375H2	8½-120	24	2530	2268	2022	1793	1583	1397
375 H.&H. Magnum Super-X	L,XL	300	FMC	X375H3	8½-120	24	2530	2171	1843	1551	1307	1126
38-40 Winchester		180	SP	X3840	7-111	24	1160	999	901	827	764	710
38-55 Winchester	D	255	SP	X3855	8½-120	24	1320	1190	1091	1018	963	917
44 Remington Magnum Super-X	D	240	HSP	X44MHSP	7M-111F	20	1760	1362	1094	953	861	789
44-40 Winchester		200	SP	X4440	7-111	24	1190	1006	900	822	756	699
45-70 Government		405	SP	X4570	8½-120	24	1330	1168	1055	977	918	869
458 Winchester Mag. Super-X	XL	500	FMC	X4580	8½-120	24	2040	1823	1623	1442	1287	1161
458 Winchester Mag. Super-X	L,XL	510	SP	X4581	8½-120	24	2040	1770	1527	1319	1157	1046

GAME SELECTOR CODE

S = Small game
D = Deer
O/P = Open or Plains shooting (i.e. Antelope, Deer)
L = Large game (i.e. Moose, Elk)
XL = Extra Large game (i.e. Kodiak bear)

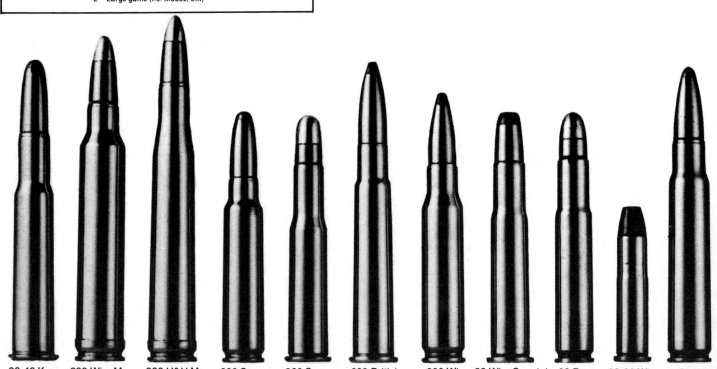

30-40 Krag | 300 Win. Mag. | 300 H&H Mag. | 300 Savage | 303 Savage | 303 British | 308 Win. | 32 Win. Special | 32 Rem. | 32-20 Win. | 8mm Mauser

	ENERGY IN FOOT POUNDS (YARDS)					TRAJECTORY — Inches above (+) or below (-) line of sight. 0 = Indicates yardage at which rifle is sighted in.												
						SHORT RANGE (YARDS)						LONG RANGE (YARDS)						
MUZZLE	100	200	300	400	500	50	100	150	200	250	300	100	150	200	250	300	400	500
2360	1761	1288	929	673	508	0.4	0	-2.4	-7.1	-14.5	-25.0	1.6	0	-3.9	-10.5	-20.3	-51.7	-103.9
2360	1957	1610	1314	1064	861	0.4	0	-2.1	-6.2	-12.5	-21.1	1.4	0	-3.4	-8.9	-16.8	-40.9	-78.1
2279	1869	1522	1230	995	809	0.6	0	-2.9	-8.2	-16.4	-27.6	1.9	0	-4.4	-11.6	-21.9	-53.3	-101.8
3605	2900	2314	1827	1424	1095	0.3	0.7	0	-1.8	-4.8	-9.3	2.6	2.9	2.1	0	-3.5	-15.4	-35.5
3501	3011	2578	2196	1859	1565	0.5	0.8	0	-2.2	-5.5	-10.4	1.9	1.6	0	-2.9	-7.3	-20.9	-41.9
3508	2927	2424	1993	1623	1314	0.2	0	-1.7	-4.9	-9.9	-16.9	2.5	2.0	0	-3.8	-9.5	-27.5	-56.1
3262	2652	2138	1707	1347	1050	0.4	0.8	0	-2.0	-5.3	-10.1	1.7	1.5	0	-2.8	-7.2	-21.2	-43.8
3315	2785	2325	1927	1584	1292	0.6	0.9	0	-2.3	-6.0	-11.5	2.1	1.7	0	-3.2	-8.0	-23.3	-47.4
3251	2677	2183	1765	1415	1128	0.3	0	-1.9	-5.5	-11.0	-18.7	2.7	2.2	0	-4.2	-10.5	-30.7	-63.0
2303	1779	1352	1012	749	558	0.3	0	-1.9	-5.7	-11.6	-19.9	2.8	2.3	0	-4.5	-11.5	-34.4	-73.0
2303	1845	1462	1143	886	685	0.3	0	-1.8	-5.4	-11.0	-18.8	2.7	2.2	0	-4.2	-10.7	-31.5	-65.5
2207	1639	1193	860	626	482	0.5	0	-2.6	-7.7	-15.6	-27.1	1.7	0	-4.2	-11.3	-21.9	-55.8	-112.0
2207	1825	1496	1217	985	798	0.4	0	-2.3	-6.7	-13.5	-22.8	1.5	0	-3.6	-9.6	-18.2	-44.1	-84.2
1588	1158	839	619	486	407	0.9	0	-4.1	-11.9	-24.1	-41.4	2.7	0	-6.4	-17.3	-33.2	-83.7	-164.4
2418	1993	1627	1318	1060	851	0.3	0	-2.1	-6.1	-12.2	-20.8	1.4	0	-3.3	-8.8	-16.6	-40.4	-77.4
2470	1736	1188	787	509	339	0.5	0.9	0	-2.3	-6.5	-12.8	2.0	1.8	0	-3.5	-9.3	-29.5	-66.7
2582	2019	1559	1186	887	656	0.5	0.8	0	-2.2	-6.0	-11.5	2.0	1.7	0	-3.2	-8.2	-24.6	-51.9
2648	2061	1581	1193	888	657	0.2	0	-1.6	-4.8	-9.8	-16.9	2.4	2.0	0	-3.8	-9.8	-29.3	-62.0
2648	2137	1705	1344	1048	810	0.2	0	-1.5	-4.5	-9.3	-15.9	2.3	1.9	0	-3.6	-9.1	-26.9	-55.7
2743	2066	1527	1109	799	587	0.3	0	-2.0	-5.9	-12.1	-20.9	2.6	2.4	0	-4.7	-12.1	-36.9	-79.1
2743	2288	1896	1557	1269	1028	0.2	0	-1.8	-5.2	-10.4	-17.7	2.6	2.1	0	-4.0	-9.9	-28.9	-58.9
2665	2165	1741	1386	1097	867	-0.4	0	-2.1	-6.3	-12.6	-21.4	1.4	0	-3.4	-9.0	-17.2	-42.1	-81.1
1911	1320	892	606	442	356	0.6	0	-3.1	-9.2	-19.0	-33.2	2.0	0	-5.1	-13.8	-27.1	-70.9	-144.3
1911	1320	892	606	442	356	0.6	0	-3.1	-9.2	-19.0	-33.2	2.0	0	-5.1	-13.8	-27.1	-70.9	-144.3
1728	1203	821	569	427	350	0.7	0	-3.4	-10.2	-20.9	-36.5	2.3	0	-5.6	-15.2	-29.6	-76.7	-154.5
325	231	185	154	131	113	0	-6.3	-20.9	-44.9	-79.3	-125.1	0	-11.5	-32.3	-63.6	-106.3	-230.3	-413.3
325	231	185	154	131	113	0	-6.3	-20.9	-44.9	-79.3	-125.1	0	-11.5	-32.3	-63.6	-106.3	-230.3	-413.3
2102	1463	993	671	476	375	0.5	0	-2.7	-8.2	-17.1	-29.8	1.8	0	-4.5	-12.4	-24.3	-63.8	-130.7
3890	3137	2505	1977	1539	1187	0.5	0.9	0	-2.3	-6.1	-11.6	2.0	1.7	0	-3.2	-8.2	-24.3	-50.4
3862	3306	2816	2384	2005	1677	1.2	1.3	0	-2.7	-7.1	-12.9	2.7	2.1	0	-3.6	-9.4	-25.0	-49.9
3927	3184	2554	2025	1591	1244	0.2	0	-1.7	-5.2	-10.5	-18.0	2.6	2.1	0	-4.0	-10.2	-30.0	-61.9
2820	2178	1656	1241	925	697	0.3	0	-2.1	-6.2	-12.7	-21.9	1.4	0	-3.4	-9.2	-17.7	-44.4	-87.9
1812	1203	791	551	431	360	0.9	0	-4.1	-12.1	-25.1	-43.9	2.7	0	-6.7	-18.3	-35.8	-92.8	-185.5
1812	1203	791	551	431	360	0.9	0	-4.1	-12.1	-25.1	-43.9	2.7	0	-6.7	-18.3	-35.8	-92.8	-185.5
1368	968	686	508	409	348	0	-2.1	-7.8	-17.8	-32.9	-53.9	0	-4.7	-13.6	-27.6	-47.5	-108.8	-203.9
2753	2093	1563	1151	844	633	0.4	0	-2.2	-6.5	-13.3	-23.0	1.5	0	-3.6	-9.7	-18.6	-47.2	-94.1
2760	2194	1723	1346	1049	832	0.5	0	-2.7	-7.9	-16.0	-27.1	1.8	0	-4.3	-11.4	-21.7	-53.5	-103.7
2150	1506	1034	714	527	427	0.6	0	-3.0	-9.5	-19.5	-33.8	2.1	0	-5.2	-14.1	-27.4	-70.1	-138.1
2005	1506	1126	852	676	568	0.9	0	-4.1	-12.0	-24.0	-40.9	2.7	0	-6.5	-17.2	-32.7	-80.6	-154.1
4337	3510	2812	2228	1747	1361	0.2	0	-1.7	-5.1	-10.3	-17.6	2.5	2.1	0	-3.9	-10.0	-29.4	-60.7
4263	3426	2723	2141	1669	1300	0.3	0	-2.0	-5.9	-11.9	-20.3	2.9	2.4	0	-4.5	-11.5	-33.8	-70.1
4263	3139	2262	1602	1138	844	0.3	0	-2.2	-6.5	-13.5	-23.4	1.5	0	-3.6	-9.8	-19.1	-49.1	-99.5
538	399	324	273	233	201	0	-6.7	-22.2	-47.3	-83.2	-130.8	0	-12.1	-33.9	-66.4	-110.6	-238.3	-425.6
987	802	674	587	525	476	0	-4.7	-15.4	-32.7	-57.2	-89.3	0	-8.4	-23.4	-45.6	-75.2	-158.8	-277.4
1650	988	638	484	395	232	0	-2.7	-10.2	-23.6	-44.2	-73.3	0	-6.1	-18.1	-37.4	-65.1	-150.3	-282.5
629	449	360	300	254	217	0	-6.5	-21.6	-46.3	-81.8	-129.1	0	-11.8	-33.3	-65.5	-109.5	-237.4	-426.2
1590	1227	1001	858	758	679	0	-4.7	-15.8	-34.0	-60.0	-94.5	0	-8.7	-24.6	-48.2	-80.3	-172.4	-305.9
4620	3689	2924	2308	1839	1496	0.7	0	-3.3	-9.6	-19.2	-32.5	2.2	0	-5.2	-13.6	-25.8	-63.2	-121.7
4712	3547	2640	1970	1516	1239	0.8	0	-3.5	-10.3	-20.8	-35.6	2.4	0	-5.6	-14.9	-28.5	-71.5	-140.4

Met. Pierc. - Metal Piercing   FMC - Full Metal Case   SP - Soft Point   JHP - Jacketed Hollow Point   JSP - Jacketed Soft Point   Met. Pt. - Metal Point
OPE - Open Point Expanding   HP - Hollow Point   PP - Power Point   WC - Wad Cutter   SWC - Semi Wad Cutter   STHP - Silvertip Hollow Point
Specifications are nominal. Test barrels are used to determine ballistics figures. Individual firearms may differ from these test barrel statistics.

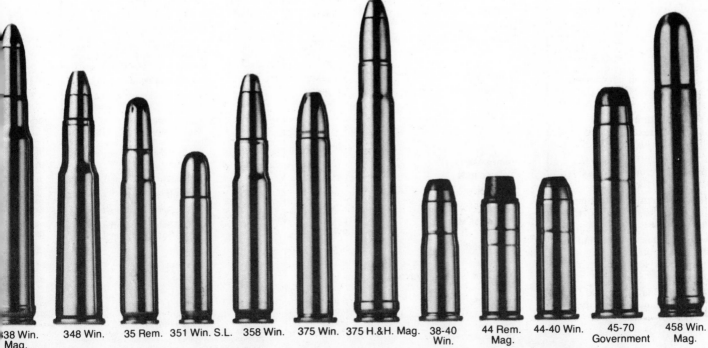

38 Win. Mag.   348 Win.   35 Rem.   351 Win. S.L.   358 Win.   375 Win.   375 H.&H. Mag.   38-40 Win.   44 Rem. Mag.   44-40 Win.   45-70 Government   458 Win. Mag.

REMINGTON CENTER FIRE RIFLE CARTRIDGES.

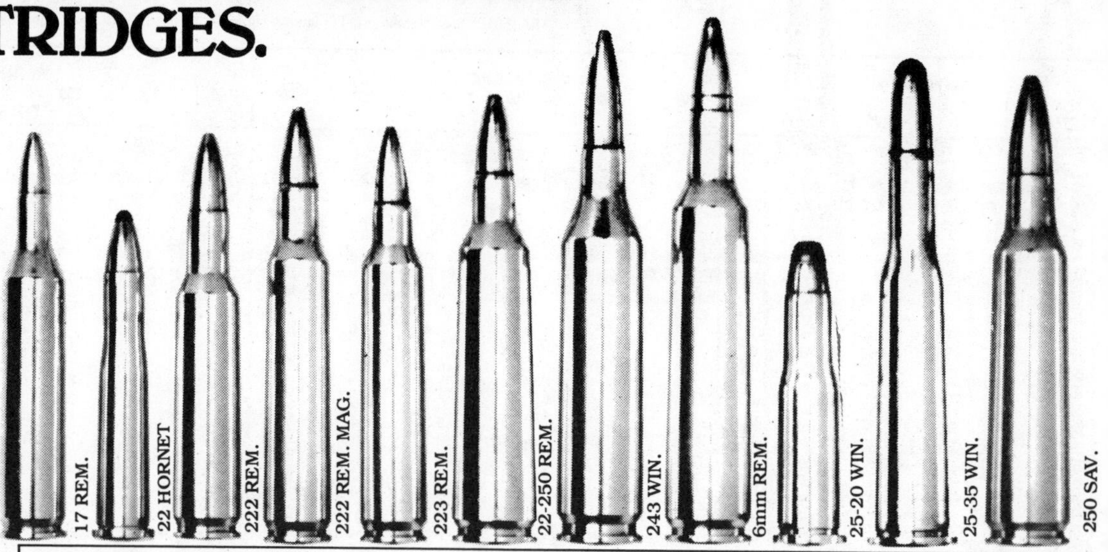

These tables were calculated by computer. A standard scientific technique was used to predict trajectories from the best available data for each round. Each trajectory is expected to be representative of the ammunition's performance at sea level, but you should be cautioned that trajectories may vary due to atmospheric conditions, equipment, and the ammunition itself.

You may note that these tables differ in many respects from those of other years. There is no reason for concern; different computation techniques, revised barrel lengths, and revised muzzle velocity levels contribute to the changes.

All velocity and energy figures in these charts have been derived by using test barrels of established lengths.

Ballistics shown are for 24" barrels, except those for 30 carbine, 350 Rem. Mag., and 44 Rem. Mag., which are for 20" barrels. These barrel lengths were chosen as representative, as it would be difficult to show performance figures for every barrel length currently available.

By using the chart below, you can determine reasonable approximations of velocity for various barrel lengths.

CENTER FIRE RIFLE VELOCITY VS. BARREL LENGTH

Muzzle Velocity Range (fps)	Approx. Change in Muzzle Velocity per 1" Change in Barrel Length
2000-2500	10
2500-3000	20
3000-3500	30
3500-4000	40

1. Determine how much shorter, or longer, your barrel is than the test barrel.

2. In the left column of the above table, select the muzzle-velocity class of your cartridge.

3. To the right of that class read the approximate change in velocity per inch of barrel length.

4. Multiply this number by the difference in length of your barrel from that of the test barrel.

5. If your barrel is shorter than the test barrel, subtract this figure from the muzzle velocity shown for your cartridge.

6. If your barrel is longer, add this figure to the muzzle velocity shown.

Cartridge illustrations: 17 REM., 22 HORNET, 222 REM., 222 REM. MAG., 223 REM., 22-250 REM., 243 WIN., 6mm REM., 25-20 WIN., 25-35 WIN., 250 SAV.

Remington Ballistics

★ NEW

CALIBERS	REMINGTON Order No.	BULLET Wt.-Grs.	BULLET Style	Primer No.
17 REM.	R17REM	25*	Hollow Point Power-Lokt®	7½
22 HORNET	R22HN1	45*	Pointed Soft Point	6½
	R22HN2	45	Hollow Point	6½
222 REM.	R222R1	50	Pointed Soft Point	7½
	R222R2	50	Metal Case	7½
	R222R3	50*	Hollow Point Power-Lokt	7½
222 REM. MAG.	R222M1	55*	Pointed Soft Point	7½
	R222M2	55	Hollow Point Power-Lokt	7½
223 REM.	R223R1	55	Pointed Soft Point	7½
	R223R2	55*	Hollow Point Power-Lokt	7½
★	R223R3	55	Metal Case	7½
22-250 REM.	R22501	55*	Pointed Soft Point	9½
	R22502	55	Hollow Point Power-Lokt	9½
243 WIN.	R243W1	80	Pointed Soft Point	9½
	R243W2	80*	Hollow Point Power-Lokt	9½
	R243W3	100	Pointed Soft Point Core-Lokt®	9½
6mm REM.	R6MM1	80**	Pointed Soft Point	9½
	R6MM2	80**	Hollow Point Power-Lokt	9½
	R6MM3	90**	Pointed Soft Point Core-Lokt®	9½
	R6MM4	100*	Pointed Soft Point Core-Lokt	9½
25-20 WIN.	R25202	86*	Soft Point	6½
25-35 WIN.	R2535W	117*‡	Soft Point Core-Lokt	9½
250 SAV.	R250SV	100*	Pointed Soft Point	9½
257 ROBERTS	R257	117*	Soft Point Core-Lokt	9½
25-06 REM.	R25061	87	Hollow Point Power-Lokt	9½
	R25062	100*	Pointed Soft Point Core-Lokt	9½
	R25063	120	Pointed Soft Point Core-Lokt	9½
6.5mm REM. MAG.	R65MM2	120*	Pointed Soft Point Core-Lokt	9½M
264 WIN. MAG.	R264W1	100‡	Pointed Soft Point Core-Lokt	9½M
	R264W2	140*	Pointed Soft Point Core-Lokt	9½M
270 WIN.	R270W1	100	Pointed Soft Point	9½
	R270W2	130*	Pointed Soft Point Core-Lokt	9½
	R270W3	130	Bronze Point	9½
	R270W4	150	Soft Point Core-Lokt	9½
7mm MAUSER	R7MSR	175*	Soft Point	9½
7mm-08 REM.	★ R7M081	140*	Pointed Soft Point Core-Lokt	9½
280 REM.††	R280R2	165*	Soft Point Core-Lokt	9½
7mm EXPRESS REM.	R7M061	150*	Pointed Soft Point Core-Lokt	9½
7mm REM. MAG.	R7MM2	150*	Pointed Soft Point Core-Lokt	9½M
	R7MM3	175	Pointed Soft Point Core-Lokt	9½M
30 CARBINE	R30CAR	110*	Soft Point	6½
30 REM.	R30REM	170*	Soft Point Core-Lokt	9½
30-30 WIN. "ACCELERATOR"	R3030A "Accelerator"	55*	Soft Point	9½
30-30 WIN.	R30301	150*	Soft Point Core-Lokt	9½
	R30302	170	Soft Point Core-Lokt	9½
	R30303	170	Hollow Point Core-Lokt	9½

Cartridge illustrations not actual size.

††280 Rem. and 7mm Express Rem. are interchangeable.
*Illustrated   **Interchangeable in 244 Rem.   ‡Subject to stock on han[d]

Cartridges shown left to right: 25-06 REM., 6.5mm REM. MAG., 264 WIN. MAG., 270 WIN., 7mm MAUSER, 7mm-08 REM., 280 REM., 7mm EXPRESS REM., 7mm REM. MAG., 30 CARBINE, 30 REM., 30-30 WIN. "ACCELERATOR", 30-30 WIN.

TRAJECTORY† 0.0 Indicates yardage at which rifle was sighted in.

| VELOCITY FEET PER SECOND | | | | | | ENERGY FOOT-POUNDS | | | | | | SHORT RANGE — Bullet does not rise more than one inch above line of sight from muzzle to sighting-in range. | | | | | | LONG RANGE — Bullet does not rise more than three inches above line of sight from muzzle to sighting-in range. | | | | | | | BARREL LENGTH |
Muzzle	100 Yds.	200 Yds.	300 Yds.	400 Yds.	500 Yds.	Muzzle	100 Yds.	200 Yds.	300 Yds.	400 Yds.	500 Yds.	50 Yds.	100 Yds.	150 Yds.	200 Yds.	250 Yds.	300 Yds.	100 Yds.	150 Yds.	200 Yds.	250 Yds.	300 Yds.	400 Yds.	500 Yds.	
4040	3284	2644	2086	1606	1235	906	599	388	242	143	85	0.1	0.5	0.0	-1.5	-4.2	-8.5	2.1	2.5	1.9	0.0	-3.4	-17.0	-44.3	24"
2690	2042	1502	1128	948	840	723	417	225	127	90	70	0.3	0.0	-2.4	-7.7	-16.9	-31.3	1.6	0.0	-4.5	-12.8	-26.4	-75.6	-163.4	
2690	2042	1502	1128	948	840	723	417	225	127	90	70	0.3	0.0	-2.4	-7.7	-16.9	-31.3	1.6	0.0	-4.5	-12.8	-26.4	-75.6	-163.4	24"
3140	2602	2123	1700	1350	1107	1094	752	500	321	202	136	0.5	0.9	0.0	-2.5	-6.9	-13.7	2.2	1.9	0.0	-3.8	-10.0	-32.3	-73.8	
3140	2602	2123	1700	1350	1107	1094	752	500	321	202	136	0.5	0.9	0.0	-2.5	-6.9	-13.7	2.2	1.9	0.0	-3.8	-10.0	-32.3	-73.8	24"
3140	2635	2182	1777	1432	1172	1094	771	529	351	228	152	0.5	0.9	0.0	-2.4	-6.6	-13.1	2.1	1.8	0.0	-3.6	-9.5	-30.2	-68.1	
3240	2748	2305	1906	1556	1272	1282	922	649	444	296	198	0.4	0.8	0.0	-2.2	-6.0	-11.8	1.9	1.6	0.0	-3.3	-8.5	-26.7	-59.5	24"
3240	2773	2352	1969	1627	1341	1282	939	675	473	323	220	0.4	0.8	0.0	-2.1	-5.8	-11.4	1.8	1.6	0.0	-3.2	-8.2	-25.5	-56.0	
3240	2747	2304	1905	1554	1270	1282	921	648	443	295	197	0.4	0.8	0.0	-2.2	-6.0	-11.8	1.9	1.6	0.2	-3.3	-8.5	-26.7	-59.6	24"
3240	2773	2352	1969	1627	1341	1282	939	675	473	323	220	0.4	0.8	0.0	-2.1	-5.8	-11.4	1.8	1.6	0.0	-3.2	-8.2	-25.5	-56.0	
3240	2759	2326	1933	1587	1301	1282	929	660	456	307	207	0.4	0.8	0.0	-2.1	-5.9	-11.6	1.9	1.6	0.0	-3.2	-8.4	-26.2	-57.9	
3730	3180	2695	2257	1863	1519	1699	1235	887	622	424	282	0.2	0.5	0.0	-1.5	-4.3	-8.4	2.2	2.6	1.9	0.0	-3.3	-15.4	-37.7	24"
3730	3253	2826	2436	2079	1755	1699	1292	975	725	528	376	0.2	0.5	0.0	-1.4	-4.0	-7.7	2.1	2.4	1.7	0.0	-3.0	-13.6	-32.4	
3350	2955	2593	2259	1951	1670	1993	1551	1194	906	676	495	0.3	0.7	0.0	-1.8	-4.9	-9.4	2.6	2.9	2.1	0.0	-3.6	-16.2	-37.9	24"
3350	2955	2593	2259	1951	1670	1993	1551	1194	906	676	495	0.3	0.7	0.0	-1.8	-4.9	-9.4	2.6	2.9	2.1	0.0	-3.6	-16.2	-37.9	
2960	2697	2449	2215	1993	1786	1945	1615	1332	1089	882	708	0.5	0.9	0.0	-2.2	-5.8	-11.0	1.9	1.6	0.0	-3.1	-7.8	-22.6	-46.3	
3470	3064	2694	2352	2036	1747	2139	1667	1289	982	736	542	0.3	0.6	0.0	-1.6	-4.5	-8.7	2.4	2.7	1.9	0.0	-3.3	-14.9	-35.0	24"
3470	3064	2694	2352	2036	1747	2139	1667	1289	982	736	542	0.3	0.6	0.0	-1.6	-4.5	-8.7	2.4	2.7	1.9	0.0	-3.3	-14.9	-35.0	
3190	2863	2558	2273	2007	1760	2033	1638	1307	1032	805	619	0.4	0.7	0.0	-1.9	-5.2	-9.9	1.7	1.4	0.0	-2.8	-7.0	-20.8	-43.3	
3130	2857	2600	2357	2127	1911	2175	1812	1501	1233	1004	811	0.4	0.7	0.0	-1.9	-5.1	-9.7	1.7	1.4	0.0	-2.7	-6.8	-20.0	-40.8	
1460	1194	1030	931	858	797	407	272	203	165	141	121	0.0	-4.1	-14.4	-31.8	-57.3	-92.0	0.0	-8.2	-23.5	-47.0	-79.6	-175.9	-319.4	24"
2230	1905	1613	1363	1169	1041	1249	943	676	483	355	281	0.6	0.0	-3.0	-8.8	-17.9	-31.0	2.0	0.0	-4.8	-13.0	-25.1	-64.2	-128.7	24"
2820	2504	2210	1936	1684	1461	1765	1392	1084	832	630	474	0.2	0.0	-1.6	-4.7	-9.6	-16.5	2.3	2.0	0.0	-3.7	-9.5	-28.3	-59.5	24"
2650	2291	1961	1663	1404	1199	1824	1363	999	718	512	373	0.3	0.0	-1.9	-5.8	-11.9	-20.7	2.9	2.4	0.0	-4.7	-12.0	-36.7	-79.2	24"
3440	2995	2591	2222	1884	1583	2286	1733	1297	954	686	484	0.3	0.6	0.0	-1.7	-4.8	-9.3	2.5	2.9	2.1	0.0	-3.6	-16.4	-39.1	24"
3230	2893	2580	2287	2014	1762	2316	1858	1478	1161	901	689	0.4	0.7	0.0	-1.9	-5.0	-9.7	1.6	1.4	0.0	-2.7	-6.9	-20.5	-42.7	
3010	2749	2502	2269	2048	1840	2414	2013	1668	1372	1117	902	-0.5	0.8	0.0	-2.1	-5.5	-10.5	1.9	1.6	0.0	-2.9	-7.4	-21.6	-44.2	
3210	2905	2621	2353	2102	1867	2745	2248	1830	1475	1177	929	0.4	0.7	0.0	-1.8	-4.9	-9.5	2.7	3.0	2.1	0.0	-3.5	-15.5	-35.3	24"
3320	2926	2565	2231	1923	1644	2447	1901	1461	1105	821	600	0.3	0.7	0.0	-1.8	-5.0	-9.7	2.7	3.0	2.2	0.0	-3.3	-16.6	-38.9	
3030	2782	2548	2326	2114	1914	2854	2406	2018	1682	1389	1139	0.5	0.8	0.0	-2.0	-5.4	-10.2	1.8	1.5	0.0	-2.9	-7.2	-20.8	-42.2	
3480	3067	2690	2343	2023	1730	2689	2088	1606	1219	909	664	0.3	0.6	0.0	-1.6	-4.5	-8.7	2.4	2.7	1.9	0.0	-3.3	-15.0	-35.2	24"
3110	2823	2554	2300	2061	1837	2791	2300	1883	1527	1226	974	0.4	0.8	0.0	-2.0	-5.3	-10.0	1.7	1.5	0.0	-2.8	-7.1	-20.8	-42.7	
3110	2849	2604	2371	2150	1941	2791	2343	1957	1622	1334	1087	0.4	0.7	0.0	-1.9	-5.1	-9.7	1.7	1.4	0.0	-2.7	-6.8	-19.9	-40.5	
2900	2550	2225	1926	1653	1415	2801	2165	1649	1235	910	667	0.6	1.0	0.0	-2.5	-6.8	-13.1	2.2	1.9	0.0	-3.6	-9.3	-28.1	-59.7	
2440	2137	1857	1603	1382	1204	2313	1774	1430	998	742	563	0.4	0.0	-2.3	-6.8	-13.8	-23.7	1.5	0.0	-3.7	-10.0	-19.1	-48.1	-95.4	24"
2860	2625	2402	2189	1988	1778	2542	2142	1793	1490	1228	1005	0.6	0.9	0.0	-2.3	-6.1	-11.6	2.1	1.7	0.0	-3.2	-8.1	-23.5	-47.7	24"
2820	2510	2220	1950	1701	1479	2913	2308	1805	1393	1060	801	0.2	0.0	-1.5	-4.6	-9.5	-16.4	2.3	1.9	0.0	-3.7	-9.4	-28.1	-58.8	24"
2970	2699	2444	2203	1975	1763	2937	2426	1989	1616	1299	1035	0.5	0.9	0.0	-2.2	-5.8	-11.0	1.9	1.6	0.0	-3.1	-7.8	-22.8	-46.7	
3110	2830	2568	2320	2085	1866	3221	2667	2196	1792	1448	1160	0.4	0.8	0.0	-1.9	-5.2	-9.9	1.7	1.5	0.0	-2.8	-7.0	-20.5	-42.1	
2860	2645	2440	2244	2057	1879	3178	2718	2313	1956	1644	1372	0.6	0.9	0.0	-2.3	-6.0	-11.3	2.0	1.7	0.0	-3.2	-7.9	-22.7	-45.8	24"
1990	1567	1236	1035	923	842	967	600	373	262	208	173	0.9	0.0	-4.5	-13.5	-28.3	-49.9	0.0	-4.5	-13.5	-28.3	-49.9	-118.6	-228.2	20"
2120	1822	1555	1328	1153	1036	1696	1253	913	666	502	405	0.7	0.0	-3.3	-9.7	-19.6	-33.8	2.2	0.0	-5.3	-14.1	-27.2	-69.0	-136.9	24"
3400	2693	2085	1570	1187	986	1412	886	521	301	172	119	0.4	0.8	0.0	-2.4	-6.7	-13.8	2.0	1.8	0.0	-3.8	-10.2	-35.0	-84.4	24"
2390	1973	1605	1303	1095	974	1902	1296	858	565	399	316	0.5	0.0	-2.7	-8.2	-17.0	-30.0	1.8	0.0	-4.6	-12.5	-24.6	-65.3	-134.9	
2200	1895	1619	1381	1191	1061	1827	1355	989	720	535	425	0.6	0.0	-3.0	-8.9	-18.0	-31.1	2.0	0.0	-4.8	-13.0	-25.1	-63.6	-126.7	24"
2200	1895	1619	1381	1191	1061	1827	1355	989	720	535	425	0.6	0.0	-3.0	-8.9	-18.0	-31.1	2.0	0.0	-4.8	-13.0	-25.1	-63.6	-126.7	

† Inches above or below line of sight. Hold low for positive numbers, high for negative numbers. Specifications are nominal.
Ballistics figures established in test barrels. Individual rifles may vary from test-barrel specifications.

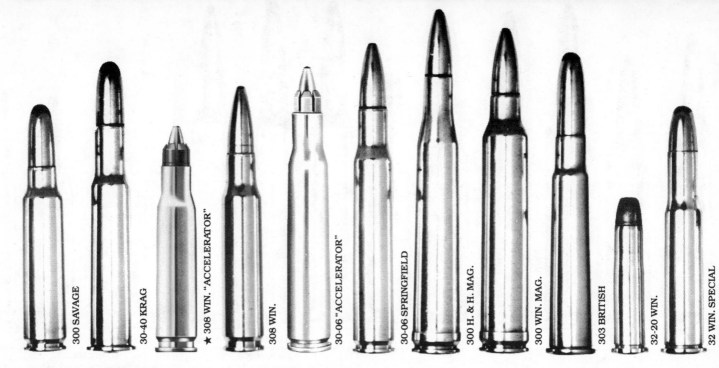

300 SAVAGE | 30-40 KRAG | 308 WIN. "ACCELERATOR" | 308 WIN. | 30-06 "ACCELERATOR" | 30-06 SPRINGFIELD | 300 H. & H. MAG. | 300 WIN. MAG. | 303 BRITISH | 32-20 WIN. | 32 WIN. SPECIAL

Remington Ballistics

★ NEW

CALIBERS	REMINGTON Order No.	BULLET			Primer No.	VELOCITY FEET PER SECOND					
		Wt.-Grs.	Style			Muzzle	100 Yds.	200 Yds.	300 Yds.	400 Yds.	500 Yds.
300 SAVAGE	R30SV1	150	Soft Point Core-Lokt		9½	2630	2247	1897	1585	1324	1131
	R30SV2	150*	Pointed Soft Point Core-Lokt		9½	2630	2354	2095	1853	1631	1433
	R30SV3	180	Soft Point Core-Lokt		9½	2350	2025	1728	1467	1252	1098
	R30SV4	180	Pointed Soft Point Core-Lokt		9½	2350	2137	1935	1745	1570	1413
30-40 KRAG	R30401	180	Soft Point Core-Lokt		9½	2430	2098	1795	1525	1298	1128
	R30402	180*	Pointed Soft Point Core-Lokt		9½	2430	2213	2007	1813	1632	1468
308 WIN "ACCELERATOR"	★ R308W5 "Accelerator"	55*	Pointed Soft Point		9½	3770	3215	2726	2286	1888	1541
308 WIN.	R308W1	150*	Pointed Soft Point Core-Lokt		9½	2820	2533	2263	2009	1774	1560
	R308W2	180	Soft Point Core-Lokt		9½	2620	2274	1955	1666	1414	1212
	R308W3	180	Pointed Soft Point Core-Lokt		9½	2620	2393	2178	1974	1782	1604
30-06 "ACCELERATOR"	R30069 "Accelerator"	55*	Pointed Soft Point		9½	4080	3485	2965	2502	2083	1709
30-06 SPRINGFIELD	R30061	125	Pointed Soft Point		9½	3140	2780	2447	2138	1853	1595
	R30062	150	Pointed Soft Point Core-Lokt		9½	2910	2617	2342	2083	1843	1622
	R30063	150	Bronze Point		9½	2910	2656	2416	2189	1974	1773
	R3006B	165*	Pointed Soft Point Core-Lokt		9½	2800	2534	2283	2047	1825	1621
	R30064	180	Soft Point Core-Lokt		9½	2700	2348	2023	1727	1466	1251
	R30065	180	Pointed Soft Point Core-Lokt		9½	2700	2469	2250	2042	1846	1663
	R30066	180	Bronze Point		9½	2700	2485	2280	2084	1899	1725
	R30067	220	Soft Point Core-Lokt		9½	2410	2130	1870	1632	1422	1246
300 H. & H. MAG.	R300HH	180*	Pointed Soft Point Core-Lokt		9½M	2880	2640	2412	2196	1990	1798
300 WIN. MAG.	R300W1	150	Pointed Soft Point Core-Lokt		9½M	3290	2951	2636	2342	2068	1813
	R300W2	180*	Pointed Soft Point Core-Lokt		9½M	2960	2745	2540	2344	2157	1979
303 BRITISH	R303B1	180*	Soft Point Core-Lokt		9½	2460	2124	1817	1542	1311	1137
32-20 WIN.	R32201	100	Lead		6½	1210	1021	913	834	769	712
	R32202	100*	Soft Point		6½	1210	1021	913	834	769	712
32 WIN. SPECIAL	R32WS2	170*	Soft Point Core-Lokt		9½	2250	1921	1626	1372	1175	1044
8mm MAUSER	R8MSR	170*	Soft Point Core-Lokt		9½	2360	1969	1622	1333	1123	997
8mm REM. MAG.	R8MM1	185*	Pointed Soft Point Core-Lokt		9½M	3080	2761	2464	2186	1927	1688
	R8MM2	220	Pointed Soft Point Core-Lokt		9½M	2830	2581	2346	2123	1913	1716
35 REM.	R35R1	150	Pointed Soft Point Core-Lokt		9½	2300	1874	1506	1218	1039	434
	R35R2	200*	Soft Point Core-Lokt		9½	2020	1646	1335	1114	985	901
350 REM. MAG.	R350M1	200*	Pointed Soft Point Core-Lokt		9½M	2710	2410	2130	1870	1631	1421
375 H. & H. MAG.	R375M1	270*	Soft Point		9½M	2690	2420	2166	1928	1707	1507
	R375M2	300	Metal Case		9½M	2530	2171	1843	1551	1307	1126
38-40 WIN.	R3840W	180*‡	Soft Point		2½	1160	999	901	827	764	710
44-40 WIN.	R4440W	200	Soft Point		2½	1190	1006	900	822	756	699
44 REM. MAG.	R44MG2	240	Soft Point		2½	1760	1380	1114	970	878	806
	R44MG3	240	Semi-Jacketed Hollow Point		2½	1760	1380	1114	970	878	806
444 MAR.	R444M	240	Soft Point		9½	2350	1815	1377	1087	941	846
	★ R444M2	265*	Soft Point		9½	2120	1733	1405	1160	1012	920
45-70 GOVERNMENT	R4570G	405*	Soft Point		9½	1330	1168	1055	977	918	869
458 WIN. MAG.	R458W1	500	Metal Case		9½M	2040	1823	1623	1442	1237	1161
	R458W2	510*	Soft Point		9½M	2040	1770	1527	1319	1157	1046

‡Subject to stock on hand.
*Illustrated

8mm REM. MAG. · 35 REM. · 350 REM. MAG. · 375 H. & H. MAG. · 38-40 WIN. · 44-40 WIN. · ★ 444 MAR. · 45-70 GOVERNMENT · 458 WIN. MAG.

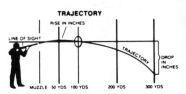

TRAJECTORY
RISE IN INCHES
LINE OF SIGHT
TRAJECTORY
DROP IN INCHES
MUZZLE · 50 YDS · 100 YDS · 200 YDS · 300 YDS

The trajectory figures shown in these ballistic tables are the rise or drop, in inches, of the bullet from a direct line of sight at selected yardages. Sighting-in distances have been set at 100 to 250 yards. (See the drawing above.)

The line of sight used in the computations is 0.9″ above the axis of the bore. This height is common to iron sights and low-mounted scopes.

The trajectory tables may be used as well for rifles with high-mounted scopes, that is, 1½″ above the axis of the bore. The difference in drops at even the extreme 500-yard range is not significant enough to negate the figures for low-mounted scopes.

Since the rise or drop figures shown at the stated yardages are points of impact, you must hold low for positive figures, high for negative figures.

If you use the same cartridge very often, it's a good idea to commit the rise or drop figures for that cartridge to memory, or tape them to your rifle stock. That way you'll know instantly the right "hold" as soon as you estimate your target's range.

Vented Test-Barrel Ballistics. This Remington-patented, industry-accepted method provides data that more precisely reflects actual use of revolver ammunition. It considers cylinder gap, barrel length, powder position, production tolerances, even wear and tear. Plus reams of data accumulated industry-wide. Although final values differ from conventional figures, the ammunition is unchanged.

Key elements of our patented procedure include: (a) horizontal powder orientation; (b) cylinder gap: .008″; (c) barrel length: 4″. Since each of these factors affects velocity, our method permits shooters to predict bullet performance in barrels of any length.

ENERGY FOOT-POUNDS						TRAJECTORY† 0.0 Indicates yardage at which rifle was sighted in.													BARREL LENGTH
						SHORT RANGE Bullet does not rise more than one inch above line of sight from muzzle to sighting-in range.						LONG RANGE Bullet does not rise more than three inches above line of sight from muzzle to sighting-in range.							
Muzzle	100 Yds.	200 Yds.	300 Yds.	400 Yds.	500 Yds.	50 Yds.	100 Yds.	150 Yds.	200 Yds.	250 Yds.	300 Yds.	100 Yds.	150 Yds.	200 Yds.	250 Yds.	300 Yds.	400 Yds.	500 Yds.	
2303	1681	1198	837	584	426	0.3	0.0	-2.0	-6.1	-12.5	-21.9	1.3	0.0	-3.4	-9.2	-17.9	-46.3	-94.8	
2303	1845	1462	1143	886	685	0.3	0.0	-1.8	-5.4	-11.0	-18.8	2.7	2.2	0.0	-4.2	-10.7	-31.5	-65.5	24″
2207	1639	1193	860	626	482	0.5	0.0	-2.6	-7.7	-15.6	-27.1	1.7	0.0	-4.2	-11.3	-21.9	-55.8	-112.0	
2207	1825	1496	1217	985	798	0.4	0.0	-2.3	-6.7	-13.5	-22.8	1.5	0.0	-3.6	-9.6	-18.2	-44.1	-84.2	24″
2360	1761	1288	929	673	508	0.4	0.0	-2.4	-7.1	-14.5	-25.0	1.6	0.0	-3.9	-10.5	-20.3	-51.7	-103.0	
2360	1957	1610	1314	1064	861	0.4	0.0	-2.1	-6.2	-12.5	-21.1	1.4	0.0	-3.4	-8.9	-16.8	-40.9	-78.1	24″
1735	1262	907	638	435	290	0.2	0.5	0.0	-1.5	-4.2	-8.2	2.2	2.5	1.8	0.0	-3.2	-15.0	-36.7	24″
2648	2137	1705	1344	1048	810	0.2	0.0	-1.5	-4.5	-9.3	-15.9	2.3	1.9	0.0	-3.6	-9.1	-26.9	-55.7	
2743	2066	1527	1109	799	587	0.3	0.0	-2.0	-5.9	-12.1	-20.9	2.9	2.4	0.0	-4.7	-12.1	-36.9	-79.1	24″
2743	2288	1896	1557	1269	1028	0.2	0.0	-1.8	-5.2	-10.4	-17.7	2.6	2.1	0.0	-4.0	-9.9	-28.9	-58.8	
2033	1483	1074	764	530	356	0.4	1.0	0.9	0.0	-1.9	-5.0	1.8	2.1	1.5	0.0	-2.7	-12.5	-30.5	24″
2736	2145	1662	1269	953	706	0.4	0.8	0.0	-2.1	-5.6	-10.7	1.8	1.5	0.0	-3.0	-7.7	-23.0	-48.5	
2820	2281	1827	1445	1131	876	0.6	0.9	0.0	-2.3	-6.3	-12.0	2.1	1.8	0.0	-3.3	-8.5	-25.0	-51.8	
2820	2349	1944	1596	1298	1047	0.6	0.9	0.0	-2.2	-6.0	-11.4	2.0	1.7	0.0	-3.2	-8.0	-23.3	-47.5	
2872	2352	1909	1534	1220	963	0.7	1.0	0.0	-2.5	-6.7	-12.7	2.3	1.9	0.0	-3.6	-9.0	-26.3	-54.1	
2913	2203	1635	1192	859	625	0.2	0.0	-1.8	-5.5	-11.2	-19.5	2.7	2.3	0.0	-4.4	-11.3	-34.4	-73.7	
2913	2436	2023	1666	1362	1105	0.2	0.0	-1.6	-4.8	-9.7	-16.5	2.4	2.0	0.0	-3.7	-9.3	-27.0	-54.9	
2913	2468	2077	1736	1441	1189	0.2	0.0	-1.6	-4.7	-9.6	-16.2	2.4	2.0	0.0	-3.6	-9.1	-26.2	-53.0	
2837	2216	1708	1301	988	758	0.4	0.0	-2.3	-6.8	-13.8	-23.6	1.5	0.0	-3.7	-9.9	-19.0	-47.4	-93.1	24″
3315	2785	2325	1927	1583	1292	0.6	0.9	0.0	-2.3	-6.0	-11.5	2.1	1.7	0.0	-3.2	-8.0	-23.3	-47.4	24″
3605	2900	2314	1827	1424	1095	0.3	0.7	0.0	-1.8	-4.8	-9.3	2.6	2.9	2.1	0.0	-3.5	-15.4	-35.5	24″
3501	3011	2578	2196	1859	1565	0.5	0.8	0.0	-2.1	-5.5	-10.4	1.9	1.6	0.0	-2.9	-7.3	-20.9	-41.9	24″
2418	1803	1319	950	687	517	0.4	0.0	-2.3	-6.9	-14.1	-24.4	1.5	0.0	-3.8	-10.2	-19.8	-50.5	-101.5	24″
325	231	185	154	131	113	0.0	-6.3	-20.9	-44.9	-79.3	-125.1	0.0	-11.5	-32.3	-63.8	-106.3	-230.3	-413.3	24″
325	231	185	154	131	113	0.0	-6.3	-20.9	-44.9	-79.3	-125.1	0.0	-11.5	-32.3	-63.6	-106.3	-230.3	-413.3	24″
1911	1393	998	710	521	411	0.6	0.0	-2.9	-8.6	-17.6	-30.5	1.9	0.0	-4.7	-12.7	-24.7	-63.2	-126.9	24″
2102	1463	993	671	476	375	0.5	0.0	-2.7	-8.2	-17.0	-29.8	1.8	0.0	-4.5	-12.4	-24.3	-63.8	-130.7	24″
3896	3131	2494	1963	1525	1170	0.5	0.8	0.0	-2.1	-5.6	-10.7	1.8	1.6	0.0	-3.0	-7.6	-22.5	-46.8	24″
3912	3254	2688	2201	1787	1438	0.6	1.0	0.0	-2.4	-6.4	-12.1	2.2	1.8	0.0	-3.4	-8.5	-24.7	-50.5	
1762	1169	755	494	359	291	0.6	0.0	-3.0	-9.2	-19.1	-33.9	2.0	0.0	-5.1	-14.1	-27.8	-74.0	-152.3	24″
1812	1203	791	551	431	360	0.9	0.0	-4.1	-12.1	-25.1	-43.9	2.7	0.0	-6.7	-18.3	-35.8	-92.8	-185.5	
3261	2579	2014	1553	1181	897	0.2	0.0	-1.7	-5.1	-10.4	-17.9	2.6	2.1	0.0	-4.0	-10.3	-30.5	-64.0	20″
4337	3510	2812	2228	1747	1361	0.2	0.0	-1.7	-5.1	-10.3	-17.6	2.5	2.1	0.0	-3.9	-10.0	-29.4	-60.7	
4263	3139	2262	1602	1138	844	0.3	0.0	-2.2	-6.5	-13.5	-23.4	1.5	0.0	-3.6	-9.8	-19.1	-49.1	-99.5	24″
538	399	324	273	233	201	0.0	-6.7	-22.2	-47.3	-83.2	-130.8	0.0	-12.1	-33.9	-66.4	-110.6	-238.5	-425.6	24″
629	449	360	300	254	217	0.0	-6.5	-21.6	-46.3	-81.8	-129.1	0.0	-11.8	-33.3	-65.5	-109.5	-237.4	-426.2	24″
1650	1015	661	501	411	346	0.0	-2.7	-10.0	-23.0	-43.0	-71.2	0.0	-5.9	-17.6	-36.3	-63.1	-145.5	-273.0	20″
1650	1015	661	501	411	346	0.0	-2.7	-10.0	-23.0	-43.0	-71.2	0.0	-5.9	-17.6	-36.3	-63.1	-145.5	-273.0	
2942	1755	1010	630	472	381	0.6	0.0	-3.2	-9.9	-21.3	-38.5	2.1	0.0	-5.6	-15.9	-32.1	-87.8	-182.7	24″
2644	1768	1162	791	603	498	0.7	0.0	-3.6	-10.8	-22.5	-39.5	2.4	0.0	-6.0	-16.4	-32.2	-84.3	-170.2	
1590	1227	1001	858	758	679	0.0	-4.7	-15.8	-34.0	-60.0	-94.5	0.0	-8.7	-24.6	-48.2	-80.3	-172.4	-305.9	24″
4620	3689	2924	2308	1839	1469	0.7	0.0	-3.3	-9.6	-19.2	-32.5	2.2	0.0	-5.2	-13.6	-25.8	-63.2	-121.7	24″
4712	3547	2640	1970	1516	1239	0.8	0.0	-3.5	-10.3	-20.8	-35.6	2.4	0.0	-5.6	-14.9	-28.5	-71.5	-140.4	24″

†Inches above or below line of sight. Hold low for positive numbers, high for negative numbers. Specifications are nominal.
Ballistics figures established in test barrels. Individual rifles may vary from test-barrel specifications.

Remington Centerfire Pistol and Revolver Cartridges

Semi-Jacketed Hollow Point for maximum expansion.

Metal Case ensures positive functioning in autoloaders.

Wadcutter, solid lead for precision target shooting.

Metal Point, jacketed for best penetration.

Lead Gas-Check, minimizes lead fouling in higher-velocity loads.

Lead, our general-purpose bullet.

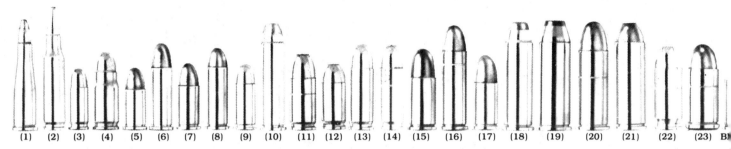

(1) (2) (3) (4) (5) (6) (7) (8) (9) (10) (11) (12) (13) (14) (15) (16) (17) (18) (19) (20) (21) (22) (23) B

Remington Ballistics

★ NEW

CALIBER	REMINGTON Order No.	Primer No.	Wt.-Grs.	Style (BULLET)	Muzzle (VELOCITY)	50 Yds.	100 Yds.	Muzzle (ENERGY)	50 Yds.	100 Yds.	50 Yds. (MID-RANGE TRAJECTORY)	100 Yds.	LENGTH
(1) 22 REM. "JET" MAG.	R22JET	6½	40*	Soft Point	2100	1790	1510	390	285	200	0.3"	1.4"	8³
(2) 221 REM. "FIRE BALL"	R221F	7½	50*	Pointed Soft Point	2650	2380	2130	780	630	505	0.2"	0.8"	10¹
(3) 25 (6.35mm) AUTO. PISTOL	R25AP	1½	50*	Metal Case	810	755	700	73	63	54	1.8"	7.7"	2"
(4) 30 (7.65mm) LUGER AUTO. PISTOL	R30LUG	1½	93*‡	Metal Case	1220	1110	1040	305	255	225	0.9"	3.5"	4¹
(5) 32 S. & W.	R32SW	5½	88*	Lead	680	645	610	90	81	73	2.5"	10.5"	3"
(6) 32 S. & W. LONG	R32SWL	1½	98*	Lead	705	670	635	115	98	88	2.3"	10.5"	4"
(7) 32 SHORT COLT	R32SC	1½	82*	Lead	745	665	590	100	79	62	2.2"	9.9"	4"
(8) 32 LONG COLT	R32LC	1½	82*	Lead	755	715	675	100	93	83	2.0"	8.7"	4"
(9) 32 (7.65mm) AUTO. PISTOL	R32AP	1½	71*	Metal Case	905	855	810	129	115	97	1.4"	5.8"	4"
(10) 357 MAG. Vented Barrel	R357M7	5½	110	Semi-Jacketed H.P.	1295	1094	975	410	292	232	0.8"	3.5"	4"
	R357M1	5½	125	Semi-Jacketed H.P.	1450	1240	1090	583	427	330	0.6"	2.8"	4"
	R357M2	5½	158	Semi-Jacketed H.P.	1235	1104	1015	535	428	361	0.8"	3.5"	4"
	R357M3	5½	158	Soft Point	1235	1104	1015	535	428	361	0.8"	3.5"	4"
	R357M4	5½	158	Metal Point	1235	1104	1015	535	428	361	0.8"	3.5"	4"
	R357M5	5½	158*	Semi-Jacketed H.P.	1235	1104	1015	535	428	361	0.8"	3.5"	4"
	R357M6	5½	158	Lead (Brass case)	1235	1104	1015	535	428	361	0.8"	3.5"	4"
(11) 9mm LUGER AUTO. PISTOL	R9MM1	1½	115*	Jacketed H.P.	1110	1030	971	339	292	259	1.0"	4.1"	4"
	R9MM2	1½	124	Metal Case	1115	1047	971	341	280	241	0.9"	3.9"	4"
(12) 380 AUTO. PISTOL	R380AP	1½	95	Metal Case	955	865	785	190	160	130	1.4"	5.9"	4"
	R380A1	1½	88*	Jacketed H.P.	990	920	868	191	165	146	1.2"	5.1"	4"
(13) 38 AUTO. COLT PISTOL	R38ACP	1½	130*	Metal Case	1040	980	925	310	275	245	1.0"	4.7"	4"
(14) 38 SUPER AUTO. COLT PISTOL	R38SU1	1½	115*	Jacketed H.P. (+P)†	1300	1147	1041	431	336	277	0.7"	3.3"	5"
	R38SUP	1½	130	Metal Case (+P)†	1280	1140	1050	475	375	320	0.8"	3.4"	5"
(15) 38 S. & W.	R38SW	1½	146*	Lead	685	650	620	150	135	125	2.4"	10.0"	4"
	R38S1	1½	95	Semi-Jacketed H.P. (+P)†	1175	1044	959	291	230	194	0.9"	3.9"	4"
	R38S10	1½	110	Semi-Jacketed H.P. (+P)†	1020	945	887	254	218	192	1.1"	4.9"	4"
	R38S2	1½	125	Semi-Jacketed H.P. (+P)†	945	898	858	248	224	204	1.3"	5.4"	4"
	R38S3	1½	148	"Targetmaster" Lead W.C.	710	634	566	166	132	105	2.4"	10.8"	4"
(16) 38 SPECIAL Vented Barrel	R38S4	1½	158	"Targetmaster" Lead Round Nose	755	723	692	200	183	168	2.0"	8.3"	4"
	R38S5	1½	158*	Lead	755	723	692	200	183	168	2.0"	8.3"	4"
	R38S6	1½	158	Semi-Wadcutter	755	723	692	200	183	168	2.0"	8.3"	4"
	R38S7	1½	158	Metal Point	755	723	692	200	183	168	2.0"	8.3"	4"
	R38S8	1½	158	Lead (+P)†	915	878	844	294	270	250	1.4"	5.6"	4"
	R38S12	1½	158	Lead H.P. (+P)†	915	878	844	294	270	250	1.4"	5.6"	4"
	R38S9	1½	200	Lead	635	614	594	179	168	157	2.8"	11.5"	4"
(17) 38 SHORT COLT	R38SC	1½	125*	Lead	730	685	645	150	130	115	2.2"	9.4"	6"
(18) 41 REM. MAG. Vented Barrel	R41MG1	2½	210*	Soft Point	1300	1162	1062	788	630	526	0.7"	3.2"	4"
	R41MG2	2½	210	Lead	965	898	842	434	376	331	1.3"	5.4"	4"
(19) 44 REM. MAG. Vented Barrel	★ R44MG5	2½	180*	Semi-Jacketed H.P.	1610	1365	1175	1036	745	551	0.5"	2.3"	4"
	R44MG1	2½	240	Lead Gas Check	1350	1186	1069	971	749	608	0.7"	3.1"	4"
	R44MG2	2½	240	Soft Point	1180	1081	1010	741	623	543	0.9"	3.7"	4"
	R44MG3	2½	240	Semi-Jacketed H.P.	1180	1081	1010	741	623	543	0.9"	3.7"	4"
Conventional Barrel	R44MG4	2½	240	Lead (Med. Vel.)	1000	947	902	533	477	433	1.1"	4.8"	6¹
(20) 44 S. & W. SPECIAL	R44SW	2½	246*	Lead	755	725	695	310	285	265	2.0"	8.3"	6¹
(21) 45 COLT	R45C	2½	250*	Lead	860	820	780	410	375	340	1.6"	6.6"	5¹
	R45AP1	2½	185	Metal Case Wadcutter	770	707	650	244	205	174	2.0"	8.7"	5"
	R45AP2	2½	185*	Jacketed H.P.	940	890	846	363	325	294	1.3"	5.5"	5"
(22) 45 AUTO.	R45AP3	2½	230	Metal Case, "Targetmaster"	810	776	745	335	308	284	1.7"	7.2"	5"
	R45AP4	2½	230	Metal Case	810	776	745	335	308	284	1.7"	7.2"	5"
(23) 45 AUTO. RIM	R45AR	2½	230*	Lead	810	770	730	335	305	270	1.8"	7.4"	5¹
Blank — 38 S. & W.	R38SWBL	1½	—*	Blank	—	—	—	—	—	—	—	—	
Blank — 32 S. & W.	R32BLNK	5½	—	Blank	—	—	—	—	—	—	—	—	
Blank — 38 SPECIAL	R38BLNK	1½	—	Blank	—	—	—	—	—	—	—	—	

† Ammunition with (+P) on the case headstamp is loaded to higher pressure. Use only in firearms designated for this cartridge and so recommended by the gun manufacturer.

‡ Subject to stock on hand. *Illustrated. Illustrations not actual size.

APPENDIX

Addresses of Reloading Suppliers

Cartridge, Cases—Custom

Bill Ballard, Box 656, Billings, Mont. 59103 (obsolete)
Brass Extrusion Laboratories Ltd., 800 W. Maple La., Bensenville, Ill. 60106 (Obsolete brass)
L. M. Burney Inc., P.O. Box 398, Lamesa, Texas 79331 (.41 Long Colt, others)
Dixie Gun Works, Union City, Tenn. 38261 (.50 Basic Brass)
Kenneth O. Gray, P.O. Box 333, Port Huenne, Calif. 93041 (Obsolete brass & English Ammunition)
Moody's Reloading Service, 2108 Broadway, Helena, Mont. 59601
The Powder Horn, 1032½ Linwood Blvd., Columbus, Ga. 31901
RCBS, P.O. Box 1919, Oroville, Calif. 95965 (.45-3″ Basic Brass)
R. F. Sailer, Box L, Owen, Wisc. 54460
3-D., Inc., Box 142, Doniphan, Neb. 68832
Whitney Cartridge Co., P.O. Box 608, Cortez, Col. 81321

Bullets

Bahler Die Shop, Box 386, Florence, Ore. 97439 (.17 Cal.)
Lee Baker, 10314 Langmuir Ave., Sunland, Calif. 91040 (.17 Cal. bullets)
Bitterroot Bullet Co., P.O. Box 412, Lewiston, Idaho 83501
Bullet Boys, The, Box 367, Jaffrey, N.H. 03452 (Cast Bullets)
CCI-Speer Operations, P.O. Box 856, Lewiston, Idaho 83501 (Speer)
Clerke Recreation Products, Inc., 2219 Main Street, Santa Monica, Calif. 90405 (Lapua)
Colorado Custom Bullets, Box 215, American Fork, Utah 84003 (Barnes)
Curry Bullet Co., 4504 E. Washington Blvd., Los Angeles, Calif. 90022
Elk Mountain Shooters Supply, 1719 Marie, Pasco, Wash. 99301
G. J. Godwin, 455 Fox Lane, Orange Park, Fla. 32073
Green Bay Bullets, 233 N. Ashland, Green Bay, Wisconsin 54303 (cast bullets)
Hornady Mfg. Co., Box 1848, Grand Island, Nebr. 68801
Meyer Bros., Wabasha, Minn. 55981 (shotgun slugs)
Michael's Antiques, Box 233, Copiague, L.I., N.Y. 11726 (shotgun slugs)
Miller Trading Co., 20 So. Front St., Wilmington, N.C. 28401 (cast bullets)
Norma-Precision, 1404 Van Ness Ave., Lansing, N.Y. 14882
Nosler Bullets, Inc., P.O. Box 688, Beaverton, Oregon 97005
Remco Corp., 1404 Whiteboro St., Utica, N.Y. 13502 (shot capsules)
Remington Arms Co., Inc., 939 Barnum Ave., Bridgeport, Conn. 06602
Sierra Bullets, 10532 So. Painter Ave., Santa Fe Springs, Calif. 90670
Sisk Bullet Co., Box 874, Iowa Park, Texas 76367
Speedy Bullets, P.O. Box 1262 Lincoln, Nebr. 68501
Taylor Bullets, 327 E. Hutchins Pl., P.O. Box 21254, San Antonio, Texas 78221
Western Draw Products, 2116 N. 10th Ave., Tucson, Ariz., 85705 (Centrix bullets)
Winchester-Western, 275 Winchester Ave., New Haven, Conn. 06504
Zero Bullet Co., P.O. Box 1012, Cullman, Ala. 35055

Lubricants—Bullet & Case Sizing

Alox Corporation, P.O. Box 556, Niagara Falls, N.Y. 14302
Birchwood-Casey Co., Inc., 7900 Fuller Rd., Eden Prairie, Minn. 55343
Bonanza Sports, Inc., Faribault, Minn. 55021 (case lubricant)
John Cain, Box 227, Kensington, Md. 20795 (Alox-beeswax lubricant)
Chopie Mfg. Co., 531 Copeland, La Crosse, Wisc. 54601 (Black-Solve)
Cooper-Woodward, Box 972W, Riverside, Calif. 92502 (Perfect-Lube)
Hodgdon Powder Co., Shawnee Mission, Kansas 66202
IPCO, Box 14, Bedford, Mass. 01730 (graphite lubricant)
Javelina Rifle Supply, Box 337, San Bernardino, Calif. 92402 (Alox-beeswax lubricant)
Lyman Products for Shooters, Rt. 147, Middlefield, Conn. 06455
Micro Shooters Supply, Box 213, Las Cruces, New Mexico 88001 (Micro-Lube)
RCBS, Inc., Box 1919, Oroville, Calif. 95965 (case lubricant)
SAECO, Inc., P.O. Box 778, Carpinteria, Calif. 93013

Primers & Propellants

Dixie Gun Works, Union City, Tenn. 38261 (Percussion Caps)
E.I. duPont de Nemours, Explosives Dept., Wilmington, Del. 19898
Eastern Sports Int'l., Savage Rd., Milford, N.H. 03055 (Berdan Primers)
Federal Cartridge Corp., 2700 Foshay Tower, Minneapolis, Minn. 55402
Hercules Inc., 910 Market St., Wilmington, Del. 19899
Hodgdon Powder Co., 7710 W. 50 Hwy., Shawnee Mission, Kans. 66202
Norma-Precision, 1404 Van Ness Ave., Lansing, N.Y. 14882
Old West Gun Room, 3509 Carlson Blvd., El Cerrito, Calif. 94530 (RWS-Berdan Primers)
Omark-CCI Inc., Box 856, Lewiston, Idaho 83501
Remington Arms Co., Inc., 939 Barnum Ave., Bridgeport, Conn. 06602
Service Armament Co., 689 Bergen Blvd., Ridgefield, N.J. 07657 (Berdan Primers, Percussion Caps)
Smith & Wesson, 2100 Roosevelt Ave., Springfield, Mass. 01101
Stoeger Industries, 55 Ruta Court, South Hackensack, N.J. 07606
Winchester-Western, 275 Winchester Ave., New Haven, Conn. 06504

Reloading Tools & Equipment

Bear Reloaders, 57 Glendale Ave., Akron, Ohio 44308
Belding and Mull, 102 N. Fourth St., Philipsburg, Pa. 16866
Bonanza Sports Mfg. Co., 412 Western Ave., Faribault, Minn. 55021
Brown Precision Co., 5869 Indian Ave., San Jose, Calif. 95123 (Little Wiggler)
B-Square Co., Box 11281, Ft. Worth, Texas 76109
C-H Tool & Die Corp., Box L, Owen, Wisc. 54460
Camdex, Inc., 23880 Hoover Rd., Warren, Mich. 48089
Carbide Die & Manufacturing Co., Box 226, Covina, Calif. 91722
Central Products for Shooters, 435 Rt. 18, E. Brunswick, N.J. 08816

Corbin Mfg. & Supply, Inc., P.O. Box 44, North Bend, Or 97459 (bullet swaging)
Eagle Products Co., 1520 Adelia Ave., South El Mont Calif 91733
Effemes Enterprises, P.O. Box 122M, Bay Shore, N. 11706 (Berdan De Capper)
W. H. English, 4411 S.W. 100th, Seattle, Wash. 98166 (Pa Tool)
Forster-Appelt Mfg. Co., 82 E. Lanark Ave., Lanark, 61046
H-S Precision, P.O. Box 512, Prescott, Az. 86301
Robert W. Hart & Son, Inc., 401 Montgomery Nescopeck, Pa. 18635
Hensley & Gibbs, Box 10, Murphy, Oreg. 97533 (bull molds)
Herter's, Inc., R. R. #1, Waseca, Minn. 56093
Hulme Firearm Service, Box 83, Millbrae, Calif. 940. (Automatic case feeder)
Neil A. Jones, 686 Baldwin St., Meadville, Pa. 16335
Lee Prescision Manufacturing, Highway U, Hartford, Wis 53027 (bullet molds, lead melters, shotshell loader)
LLF Die Shop, 1281 Highway 99 North, Eugene, Ore 97402
Lyman Products for Shooters, Rt. 147, Middlefield, Con 06455
Marquart Precision Co., Box 1740, Prescott, Az. 86301
McKillen & Heyer, 3871 Kirtland, Willoughby, Ohio 4409 (Case Gauge)
Michigan Ammo Co., 4680 High Street, Ecorse, Mic 48229 (Bullet Puller)
Pacific Tool Company, P.O. Box 2048, Grand Island, Neb 68801
Perfection Die Co., 1614 S. Choctaw, El Reno, Okla. 730.
Plum City Ballistics Range, Rt. 1, Box 29A, Plum City, W 54761 (case gauge)
Ponsness-Warren Inc., P.O. Box 1818, Eugene, Oreg. 974(
Potter Engineering Co., 1410 Santa Anna Drive, Dunedi Fla. 33528
Quinetics Corp., P.O. Box 13237, San Antonio, Tex. 782.
RCBS, Inc., P.O. Box 1919, Oroville, Calif. 95965
Redding-Hunter, Inc., 114 Starr Rd., Cortland, N.Y. 130-
SAECO, Inc., Box 778, Carpinteria, Calif. 93013
Jerry Simmons, 713 Middlebury St., Goshen, In. 46526
Star Machine Works, 418 10th Ave., San Diego, Cali 92101
Tecto Sporting Goods, 8575 Central Ave., N.E., Blain Minn. 55434
Vickerman Mfg. Co., 505 W. 3rd Ave., Ellensburg, Was 98926
Walker Manufacturing Co., 8296 South Channel, Harse Island, Mich. 48026
Weatherby, Inc., 2781 Firestone Blvd., Southgate, Cali 90280
Webster Scale Mfg. Co., Box 188, Sebring, Fla. 33870
Whitney Sales, Inc., Box 875, Reseda, Calif. 913. (Hollywood Tools)
L. E. Wilson, Box 324, Cashmere, Wash. 98815
Whitney Sales, Inc., P.O. Box 875, Reseda, Calif. 91335

Boxes, Cartridge

Fitz, P.O. Box 49697, Los Angeles, Ca. 90049
Flambeau Plastics Corp., Baraboo, Wis. 53913
Hodgdon Powder Co., 7710 W. 50 Hwy., Shawnee Missio Ks. 66202
MTM Molded Products Co., P.O. Box 14902, Dayton, O 45414
Shooters Supplies, 8724 E. Research Ctr. Rd., Minneapol Mn. 55428